MAX LERNER

AMERICA as a CIVILIZATION

Volume One

THE BASIC FRAME

A TOUCHSTONE BOOK
PUBLISHED BY SIMON AND SCHUSTER

A TOUCHSTONE BOOK
PUBLISHED BY SIMON AND SCHUSTER
A DIVISION OF GULF & WESTERN CORPORATION
SIMON & SCHUSTER BUILDING
ROCKEFELLER CENTER
1230 AVENUE OF THE AMERICAS
NEW YORK, NEW YORK 10020

12 13 14 15 16 17

ISBN 0-671-20161-1

"On an Invitation to the United States," by Thomas Hardy, from *Collected Poems of Thomas Hardy,* © 1926 by The Macmillan Company; used with the publisher's permission.

Translation of poem by Goethe, from *The American Spirit* by Charles and Mary Beard, © by The Macmillan Company; used with the publisher's permission.

"Frescoes for Mr. Rockefeller's City," by Archibald MacLeish, published by Houghton Mifflin Company.

"America Remembers," from *American Song* by Paul Engle, © 1933 by Doubleday & Company, Inc.

LIBRARY OF CONGRESS CATALOG CARD NUMBER: 57-10979
MANUFACTURED IN THE UNITED STATES OF AMERICA

FOR

MICHAEL

AND HIS GENERATION

CONTENTS

Foreword

AMERICANS are beginning to turn a searchlight on themselves and their civilization, and interpret both to the world. The present study is intended as a trial essay in this direction.

I start with what the book is not—neither a history of American civilization nor a description of life today in the American regions, states, and cities. Both have been done well by a number of scholars and journalists. Nor have I written here an indictment or apologia, either a celebration of "the American way" or a lament about it. Finally, this is not a "whither, whither" book embodying the prophecy of disaster. In short, those who are looking for the historical, the descriptive, the polemic, or the apocalyptic must look elsewhere.

What I have tried, rather, is to grasp—however awkwardly—the pattern and inner meaning of contemporary American civilization and its relation to the world of today.

A personal word may not be out of place. You write a book not for the elaborate reasons you spell out but mainly because you can't help it. Whatever I have written, thought, felt in the past has converged on the grand theme of the nature and meaning of the American experience. Whenever I have tried to chip off a fragment—on American government, on liberalism, on foreign policy, on morals—I found that it lost some of its meaning when torn from the rest. Yet to attempt the subject as a whole seemed a formidable, even arrogant, task. In 1945 I finally overrode my hesitation and started the book on its present scale. It has been more than a decade in the writing.

No American, perhaps no one alive today, can pretend to view American civilization with an anthropological detachment. The "anthropological attitude" (Kroeber) and the "sense of cultural shock" (Benedict) come from seeing values in a culture almost wholly disparate from your own. No American can achieve detachment in studying America, and I doubt whether even a European or Asian can. Paraphrasing Lord Acton, one might say that the only detached student of American civilization would be a dead one, since he would no longer care. The best you can do to achieve perspective is to keep a certain emotional distance from your subject. When the subject is your own people and civilization it is hard to keep the distance. Your hopes and fears for America manage to break through and color the analysis.

Obviously any book about America published at a time of international discord and seething world revolution is bound to be interpreted within this frame of planetary turmoil, and the question will inevitably be asked whether this book is "for" or "against" America, whether it is a rosy and euphoric picture seen in a haze of promise or an unsparing indictment.

I have tried to avoid both these sins—for an American the sin of complacency and the sin of self-hatred. I love my country and my culture, but it is no service to them, nor to the creed of democracy, to gloss over the rough facts of American life. Similarly, much have I traveled in the realms of Europe and Asia—and even in the realms of Marx and Veblen —and if there is a single count in the anti-American indictment I have not at some point confronted, it has not been through lack of diligence or realism. But it would be no service to the most committed critics of America to give them a distorted picture of American civilization only in order to nourish their distaste. Let the great world debate about America go on as it will and must: the task I set for myself is intended to have no strategic relation to it.

America is by any standard a towering technology and culture, with economic, military, and political power, the only rival power-mass being Russia. Wherever you find so much vitality packed tightly in a segment of human society, it is evidence of a striking convergence of history, environment, biological stock, psychological traits, institutional patterns, collective will and drive. When such a combination catches fire in the world's imagination and polarizes the emotional energies of men—whether for love or hate—you have a memorable civilization.

In dealing with something so provocative it is easy to be waylaid by the transient and miss the enduring. I have tried to remember that political struggles and economic programs wither and grow stale, the controversies which fill the pages of today's press become jangled images tomorrow, and party leaders end up as dimly remembered steel-plate engravings in the history books. America is not only changes and chances. It is also permanence.

That is why the questions I ask about Americans are those one would have to ask about the people of any great civilization. What are their traditions, biological stock, environments? How do they make a living, govern themselves, handle the inevitable problems of power and freedom? How are they divided into ethnic and class groupings? What are they like in their deep and enduring strains? What is their life history like, in its characteristic phases from birth to death? How do they court, marry, bring up and educate children? How do they work, play, and express their creativeness in art and literature? What are the connective and organizing principles that hold their civilization together? What gods do they worship, what beliefs hold them in thrall or give them strength, what attitudes do they own up to, what convictions animate them, what culture patterns do they move in, what dreams are they moved by, what myths run through their being, what incentives propel them, what fears restrain them, what forms of power invest their striving, what tensions and divisions tear them apart, what sense of society cements them?

What, in short, is it that makes America not "a congeries of possessors and pursuers," of individual wills and greeds and collective power, but a civilization?

M. L.

CHAPTER I

Heritage

1. The Sense of the Past

2. The Sources of the Heritage

3. The Slaying of the European Father

4. Why Was America a Success?

5. American History As Extended Genesis

6. Tradition and the Frame of Power

7. American Dynamism

IN WHICH we start by examining American history as folk memory and evoking the American spirit in a succession of images from the past ("The Sense of the Past"). We trace the emergence of the American heritage out of the conquest of the continent, the slavery experience, and the great migrations ("The Sources of the Heritage"), and assess the emotional impact of these migrations on the American mind ("The Slaying of the European Father"). We consider the ways in which American history has been written and the theories advanced for the greatness and power America has reached ("Why Was America a Success?"), and reconsider the Turner theory of the frontier ("American History As Extended Genesis"). Reflecting on the cult of the American tradition and the emergence of a "new conservatism" ("Tradition and the Frame of Power"), we end by focusing on some crucial elements which run through what is usually called the "American spirit" ("American Dynamism"). The chapter as a whole is an effort to evoke the American spirit by evoking its past, and to interpret the American tradition as a living heritage with changing meanings.

CHAPTER I

Heritage

1. The Sense of the Past

LIKE a person, a civilization is more than the sum of its parts. Describe a man's features, give his life history, tell where he lives and how, place him in his class or group, define his ethics and politics—and still you will not have the man himself. What slips through is his total style, quick and dead: whatever it is that makes him himself, and different from other men. Thus St. Francis had a style, and Samuel Johnson, Martin Luther, Voltaire, and Dean Swift, Alexander and Asoka, Napoleon and Goethe, Lincoln and Carnegie and Justice Holmes. History remembers this about the great men, but the rest of us remember it also about the nameless people we have known: remember the way they moved, their tricks of speech and habit, their taut or relaxed quality, the superfluous things they did and with what grace or clumsiness, what cavalry pounded through their brain, what inner battles they fought.

So it is with a civilization. When you have described its people, armies, technology, economics, politics, arts, regions and cities, class and caste, mores and morals, there is something elusive left—an inner civilization style.

In Lytton Strachey's biography, *Queen Victoria,* there is a climactic (if unhistoric) scene, with the queen lying on her deathbed as the memorable events of her life pass through her mind. A people too has its sense of the past—the remembered record of what happened, the force of the collective experience. The individual American may know little of history and is probably inarticulate about what he does know. But if (using Carl Becker's phrase) everyman is his own historian, it is because he is in some measure a sifter and selecter of his nation's past—of the quickening ideas, the hardships and heroisms, the degradation and injustices, the boisterous fables. "Everyman" will have a very different picture of the American past from that of the cultivated scholars, yet there will be something in common between them. I venture to pass some of the heritage quickly in kaleidoscopic review as it has unrolled—half myth, half fact—in the minds of many Americans from high-school age to maturity.

. . . The voyage of adventure and discovery across the far seas, *mundus novus,* the English sea dogs and the Spanish conquistadores, Cortes being worshiped as a god by the Indians of the Mexicos, De Soto's body tied up in a sack and dropped into the Mississippi which he had discovered. The quest of gold and new lands for the glory of God and the enrichment of divine-right monarchs and proprietary landlords. The odyssey of the first settlers amidst scurvy, dysentery and filth in the holds of ships—an odyssey to be re-enacted by the shiploads of indentured servants, the slave ships from Africa, and in the steerage of the later immigration. The rigors of the early settlements, caught between the sea and the woods, winter and the savages. The dream of a new Jerusalem on a rock-bound coast. The dark forest, the thrust into the unknown; the wild birds flying, the huge turkeys, the ospreys and eagles, the deer, the fields red with strawberries; the Indian corn and the tobacco crops; the furs of beaver, otter, muskrat, racoon.

The coming of explorer, conqueror, trader, missionary, colonizer. The painted dignity of savage chieftains on the red man's continent; the land bought of them for a few gimcracks, the twists and cunning of English land law, the despoiling of a people; the struggle of European empires for a hold on a new continent. The stockade settlements, the lonely vigils, the descent of terror out of the darkness, the scalpings and massacres, the long captivities. The Pilgrims and Puritans, little theocratic communities encroaching on the wilderness; the metaphysical passion which had crossed the oceans expressing itself in a belief in demonology and possession. The satanic apparitions, the constant living within the frame of an invisible malignant world. The idea of faith and salvation, prosperity and Heaven, filling the whole ambit of life; the interminable sermons, the droning hymns, the impassioned harangues of the revivalists.

The colonist as a Southern gentleman riding among his tobacco fields. The building and sailing of ships; the rise of manufactures, of cities, wharves and warehouses. The transplanting from England of the idea of compact; schools springing up in the unlikely wilderness—William and Mary, Harvard, Boston Latin. Lawyers marshaling their arguments not only for their clients but for the colonies, editors setting in type thunderbolts against governors and judges. Rebellious voices raised against patrician landlords and rich merchants as well as against foreign tyrannies. James Otis, in barrister's gown, arguing before the Massachusetts judges against the "writs of assistance"; young American politicians searching in the classics for "natural rights" and the fundamentals of governmental theory. The town meetings, the Burgesses, the new phenomenon of a society of planters and merchants who meant to rule themselves, and joined with artisans and farmers for that purpose. The spate of hot, angry pamphlets; "taxation without representation"; the Sons of Liberty and the committees of correspondence; the splitting of the tea chests in the solemn painted mummery at Griffin's Wharf in the quiet Boston night; the voice of a Plutarchian hero from Virginia—"Is life so dear or peace so sweet as to be purchased at the price of chains and slavery?"; the drilling of young men on the village commons, the first blood spilled by the early-morning gunfire at Lexington. Paine's words: "The blood of the slain, the weeping voice of Nature cries, ' 'Tis time to part.' " The clear, firm Declaration: "We hold these truths to be self-evident"; the huddled little "rabble in arms" shivering in winter quarters, without food or pay or hope in an unending war; "You might have tracked the army by the blood of their feet"; spies and betrayals, "the summer soldier and the sunshine patriot." The dignity and the moral strength of Washington, the bootless British victories, the guerrilla warfare in the hills from the Green Mountains to the Catawba and the Santee, the freeing of the Northwest, American diplomats asking help at European courts, the surrender at Yorktown. The new free republic on this continent.

With freedom won, the Revolutionary soldiers coming home to feeble and vulnerable times; Daniel Shays and his debt-ridden farmers; the Founding Fathers assembled at Independence Hall, the swirling debates and compromises among the men of substance; the signing of the Constitution; Franklin saying gracefully, "It is the rising, not the setting sun." Three men putting down in *The Federalist* the fundamentals of power and stability in human society. The Bill of Rights forced through at the insistence of Jefferson and his followers. Washington being rowed across New York Harbor on an Inaugural barge and riding under triumphal arches to become the first President of the United States of America. The new statesmen and the first great State Papers; a tall soldier leaving his farewell admonitions to his people; the straggling village on the Potomac that became the new Capital; Abigail Adams, as First Lady, hanging her washing to dry in the unfinished Audience Room at the White House. The struggle between aristocracy and democracy, between property and Populism; the leaders fearful of parties but powerless to prevent their rise; the fight against the Sedition Acts and the conviction of ten editors and printers; the rising tide of democratic belief, the Republic moving toward a Democracy. The "Jeffersonian Revolution"; "we are all Republicans, we are all Federalists"; the vast new accession of American earth in the Louisiana Purchase; the embargo, the young War Hawks, and "Mr. Madison's War"; the burning of Washington ("this harbor of Yankee democracy") by Admiral Cockburn; the heroism of the little American frigates in battle, "We have met the enemy, and they are ours." The young eagle nation spreading its wings in the judicial nationalism of John Marshall's decisions and the political nationalism of Monroe's challenge to the European Powers.

The triple forward movement of the frontier, the machine, and the democratic surge.

The pushing onward of the frontier lines, sporadically but with a persistent thrust toward expansion; the traders and hunters, scouts, missionaries and settlers—a nation of backwoodsmen; Lewis and Clark as the explorers of a nation's destiny; Calhoun saying in 1817, "We are greatly and rapidly—I was about to say fearfully—growing"; the armada of prairie schooners, with their human freight, crossing the mountains and plains; "a rifle, an axe, and a bag of corn." The ways of the pioneers, the rough working and drinking and playing, the cornhusking frolics, the brawling and wrestling and eye-gouging, the Yankee and backwoodsman as folk characters; "the gamecock of the wilderness," the Mike Fink and Davy Crockett legends, the tall stories, the comic boasting: "Sired by a hurricane, dam'd by an earthquake, half-brother to the cholera . . . Whoo-oop! I'm the bloodiest son of a wildcat that lives." The circuit-riding lawyers and doctors and preachers, the "old-time religion." The constant danger and constant beauty of life; the great plains, the canals, the torrential, muddy rivers, the rafts and flatboats and keelboats, and then the river steamers. The Mississippi as the grand highway of a new continent. "Remember the Alamo," "Manifest Destiny," Frémont crossing the mountains into Sacramento Valley, the gold at Sutter's Mill, the race of the clipper ships to San Francisco. The mushrooming mining camps and cowtowns, the long drive north of the Texas longhorns to the railheads, the open range turned into barbed-wire enclosures, a continent rounded out.

The new frontiers of the brain's cunning; American tinkering, the spate of inventions, the heyday of the Yankee toolmakers, the march of the machine across the American spirit; factories jostling the wharves, jutting out into the prairies; the mill girls at Lowell, child workers in mines. Cotton spreading along the Gulf plain, and Negro hands to pick the snowy harvest. The rich earth caught up in the disk plow and automatic reaper, the span of far distances shrunk by railroad ties and the telegraphic spark. Wealth untold spilling out of the land and machines and human hands.

The rise of democracy. The assertive common man, with muddy boots, stomping into the White House at Jackson's Inaugural. Old Hickory's struggle against Biddle and the Bank. Free homesteads, free schools, the whittling away of suffrage restrictions, the battle cry of States' Rights. The fall of King Caucus, the hysteria of the party convention, the rise of the political managers, the clan spirit of the Irish countryman transposed to make the ward machine run. Thoreau in Concord jail asking Emerson what he was doing outside; Melville's pursuit of Moby Dick through the whale waters; the ferment of social revolt; Dorr's Rebellion in Rhode Island; the dream of perfectibility at Brook Farm and the phalansteries; Walt Whitman on the Brooklyn Ferry glimpsing his democratic vistas.

The division of a nation into two economies and two ways of life, the tyranny of King Cotton over the mind of the Old South, the Confederate dream of a Greek republic founded on slavery on the shores of the Gulf, the shadow of slaves' chains falling across the American soul. The slave revolts and the massacres on both sides, the underground railroad, the knock in the rainy night; the heroism of Frederick Douglass and Harriet Tubman, John Brown at the arsenal at Harpers Ferry. The days of the great Senate debates, a gangling boy growing up in Illinois, "a house divided against itself cannot stand," the Presidential car transferred from one station to another at Baltimore in the quiet of the early hours. The freeing of the slaves, the draft riots, Lincoln passing long lines of hospital cots with rough jokes to hide the heart's sorrow; the scene at Gettysburg, "the world will little note nor long remember"; the burning bales of cotton in Southern ports, brothers killing brothers in the Battle of the Wilderness, Sherman's march to the sea; two soldiers at Appomattox. "With malice toward none," the fateful course of Booth's bullet, the tragic mask of death, "when lilacs last in the dooryard bloom'd." The grim, stony faces of the whites in Southern legislatures, the carpetbaggers, the bewildered freedmen, terror-riders in the Southern darkness, the tragic heritage of civil conflict.

The corruptions of the "Gilded Age," the buying and selling of the American promise. The rise of the business giant: "industrial statesman" or "robber baron"? The new empires of finance, the gushing streams of profit from oil, steel, railroads, lumber; the strenuous ascent to fortune; power sitting on top of a heap of money. The cult of size and magnificence, the gleaming confidence of the self-made man, the brownstone fronts on Fifth Avenue, "society" at Newport. The alternation of boom and bust; the Populist upsurge, the Anarchist bomb and the ordeal of Altgeld, young Billy Bryan from the River Platte, the obsession of Henry George with the single tax, Bellamy's dream of a socialist utopia, the scientific politics of Mark Hanna. The swarming of immigrants to the promised land, "your tired, your poor, your huddled masses, yearning to breathe free." Sam Gompers reading to a shopful of cigar-makers; the flare-ups of violence, the sputtering of dynamite across the land. The victorious imperialists coming back from "Mr. Hearst's war" to be annihilated by Mr. Dooley and Mark Twain. The rising energies of the quest for social justice; the Roughrider jousting both at the "muckrakers" and at the "malefactors of great wealth," Holmes on the Supreme Court impaling a dogma on a phrase, Brandeis as "the People's Attorney," Thorstein Veblen's corroding polysyllables, T.R.'s "New Nationalism," Woodrow Wilson's "New Freedom."

America taking its place as a world power. The long shadow of Sarajevo; parades, embarkations, high hopes; American blood and wealth flowing into Europe, turning the tide of war; a former Princeton professor landing on European shores, cheered by European throngs, to sit in the mirrored halls of Versailles as the innocent arbiter of world order. A spent President, stricken on his train in the West; the killing of the League of Nations—a masque of death. Sacco and Vanzetti and the radical hunts; the illusion of "normalcy" in a world without landmarks; the closing of the "golden door" against the immigrant; the greed and slackness of Teapot Dome; "Silent Cal" Coolidge saying that "the business of America is business." The Babylonianism of American life in the twenties; the movie cathedrals, black-veiled women swooning over Valentino's grave, greed and violence spilling over into rackets and hijacking, the alchemy of getting something for nothing, the tumbling walls of a stock-market Jericho. The "battle of Anacostia Flats," the trek across the Dust Bowl, the "Grapes of Wrath," the shutting of the banks, the bread lines and unemployment. A paralyzed President lighting again the fires of the American will; "the only thing we have to fear is fear itself"; the Blue Eagle and the other symbols of a collective effort; the battle over the New Deal; "we have only just begun to fight"; the achievement of the TVA, the soil of democracy still rich at the grass roots.

The new monster shapes across the world, America too stricken with its own maladies to care, then rising like a Gulliver lumberingly to its full height. The shattered hulks at Pearl Harbor: "a day that will live in infamy." The fighting and death on foreign soil; the memories of great battlefields of the world wars—the village of Saint-Mihiel, the sun-beaten rock of Corregidor, the volcanic sand of Iwo Jima, the desert at Kasserine Pass, the rubble at Monte Cassino, the shattered fir trees of Hurtgen Forest, the landings at Omaha Beach and Tarawa, the crossing of Remagen Bridge, the rains and the mud at Guadalcanal. The American soldier, wandering like Odysseus over the far places of the world, always turning by a sure instinct back to the home of his remembrance. A haggard man in a blue cloak posing for pictures at Yalta. The news from Warm Springs, the people mourning in the streets. A huddle of scientists waiting for a blast in a trench at Los Alamos, the fateful plane over Hiroshima. The precarious infancy of the UN, the soldier in the White House struggling with problems of peace. The power and the challenge and the anxiety forever and ever. . . .

The troubled reader will say, "But this is not history; it is imagism." He will be right. It is a history of the American *imago,* a memorandum on American history couched not in terms of forces, causes, or events but of images picked from the national tradition. What it recalls is not "eras" and "factors" but dramatic moments, crisis situations, sometimes only stereotyped episodes and hackneyed slogans. It rests on the premise that memories help to shape the style of a people as they do of a person.

Yet the charge has often been made that Americans, unlike the history-saturated European or Asiatic peoples, are a people without a history. To be historyless is presumably to lack tradition and texture, complex motivation, nuances of the spirit. It is to be, not an old gnarled tree with its roots deep in the rich soil of the past, but a row of young saplings planted in haste and standing surface-deep against a lorn sky. Much of this charge is compressed in Thomas Hardy's answer when he was invited to visit America:

I shrink to seek a modern coast
Whose riper times have yet to be;
Where the new regions claim them free
From that long drip of human tears
Which people old in tragedy
Have left upon the centuried years.

Hardy, who was sensitive to the style of his own European civilization, proved himself insensitive to the very different style of the American. Goethe, writing a century earlier in 1827 on the eve of the Jacksonian era, felt a greater sympathy for the republic whose memories had scarcely begun to accumulate. As he suggests, the American experience is happily free from the Old World sense of the past, which clusters around great landed families, Junkerism, aristocracy, and what Spengler later called *"Blut und Boden."** And Hegel joined with him when he said that

* Amerika, du hast es besser
Als unser Kontinent, der alte,
Du hast keine verfallenen Schlosser
Und keine Basalte.

Dich stort nicht im Innern
Zu lebendiger Zeit
Unnutzes Errinern
Und vergeblicher Streit.

Benutzt die Gegenwart mit Gluck!
Und wenn nun eure Kinder dichten,
Bewahre sie ein gut' Geschick
Vor Ritter-, Rauber-und Gespenstergeschichten.

I take this from Charles and Mary Beard's *The American Spirit* (1942), pp. 147-8 Freely translated, it might read:

America, thou farest better
Than our own continent, the old one,
Thou hast no crumbling castles,
No basalt wreckage.

Thou art not shaken in this hour of life
By useless memories and futile strife.

Take the Present with joy,
And when thy children write their songs
May good luck guard them well
From tales of knights, robbers, and ghosts.

"America is the land of the future where, in the ages that lie before us, the burden of the world's history shall reveal itself."*

America has not, of course, achieved the mellowness of long continuities, nor has it been inbred long enough to fashion many ethnic uniformities. But it has been a crossroads for the sweep of cultural battles in the Western world, just as surely as the tablelands of the Eurasian plateau were a geographical crossroads for the sweep of invasion and conquest. The nomadism that made the rovers of the Asiatic grasslands "land sailors" (in the picturesque phrase of Sir John Maynard) was transmuted, in the American instance, into the social wayfaring that we call American mobility. The American tradition has grown by movement, not by sitting.

There was a period in American life when Americans—perhaps ashamed of their raw, booming growth, and convinced they were historyless—tried to atone for it by reverence for Old World sites. But that phase is over, as evidenced by Archibald MacLeish's answer to such an unhappy Miniver Cheevy:

The Cinquecento is nothing at all like Nome
Or Natchez or Wounded Knee or the Shenandoah;

Your vulgarity Tennessee; your violence Texas
The rocks under your fields Ohio Connecticut;

Your clay Missouri your clay; you have driven him out;
You have shadowed his life Appalachians purple mountains

There is much too much of your flowing Mississippi;
He prefers a tidier stream with a terrace for trippers and

Cypresses mentioned in Horace or Henry James:
He prefers a country where everything carries the name of

Countess or real king or an actual palace . . .

(From "Frescoes for Mr. Rockefeller's City")

The American sense of the past is not a fumbling for ancestors or a nostalgia for ruins. But the fact that Americans have an assurance about their future does not exclude a pride about their past—a past whose roots (as we shall see) reach deep and spread widely.

* From the *Philosophy of History,* first given as lectures in 1822, published after his death.

2. *The Sources of the Heritage*

America was born out of the first stages of the breakup of Europe, and helped the process of breakup. As a colonizing and imperial continent, Europe gave largely of its strength and heritage to the civilization which was destined to replace it in power and vitality. The richest resource of a civilization is the people themselves, and the most important fact about a people is the life force carried along from its cultural origins and crossed, blended, and transmuted with others in a developing civilization.

Generalizations about the "American tradition" are difficult because there are as many subtraditions as there were national and ethnic groups that came to America, and each has left a heritage. Usually the writers on American immigration have in mind only the white immigrants, largely the European whites. Actually there were four great separable migration families that moved to the American continent. The first was probably from Asia—that of the men who formed the strain of the American Indians. The second was from the British Isles and western Europe. The third was from Africa—the Negro strain. The fourth was from Mediterranean, central, and eastern Europe, from Asia, from Latin America and everywhere else—the polyglot ethnic strain.

In a long section of De Tocqueville,* there is a remarkable study in the contact and clash of three of these ethnic cultures in the America of his own day—the Indian, the Negro, and the European. De Tocqueville describes the extermination of the first by the predacity of the conquerors, the degradation of the second by slavery, and the effects of both in turn on the third, who were the possessors and pursuers.

How long ago the men who were to become the American Indians first came over from Asia, probably across the Bering Strait, is still in dispute. Estimates vary from two or three thousand years to twenty-five thousand. Nor is it clear whether there was a single migration or as many as five or six. Today most of the Indians both of North and South America live in such squalor that it is hard to see them as the heirs of the cultural splendor of the past. Yet there is little question that in their crops, hunts, wars, and celebrations, their language and dance, myths, rituals, magic and gods, their kinship systems, social organization, law and government, symbolism, art and decoration, the Indian cultures were not simply those of "painted savages." Whether it was the highly polished Mayan and Aztec cultures of Mexico and Guatemala, or the Inca culture of Peru, or

* *Democracy in America*, "On the Present and Probable Future Condition of the Three Races That Inherit the Territory of the United States," Bradley ed. (Anchor Books), Vol. 1, Ch. XVIII, pp. 343-452.

that of the Plains Indians in North America, they made up an impressive network of civilizations.

Impressive, that is, except in their power of defense against the men of the West. Their first response to the conquistadores and in the Caribbean area was gentle and even receptive. For a breathless moment the Indian may have felt that the white man was Quetzalcoatl, the liberating hero whose return he was expecting; but the illusion vanished and he saw the Spaniards for what they were: treasure-hunters, conquerors, enslavers. They took the land without compunction, seized the wealth of the temples and palaces, shackled the Indians throughout New Spain with a form of land tenure—the encomienda—that was in effect a system of forced labor. There followed bloody resistance and insurrection, bloodily put down. The barbarism of the conquest aroused a barbarism of the conquered, which proved true as well for the Plains Indians of North America, where the English and French joined the Spanish as conquerors.

But for all their fierceness when aroused, the Indians were like spindrift before the great tides of European immigration and settlement and the powerful movement northward and westward. They were helpless against such weapons of civilization as gunfire and alcohol, European land systems and speculators, traders and treaty-makers, force and fraud, tuberculosis and measles. They became the victims of a cruel cold war whose story no American historian has been able to relate with pride. It is a story of implacable pressure on one side and of bitterly resentful yielding on the other. In the U.S. they were finally assigned to reservations, their culture all but wiped out. There is a biting irony in De Tocqueville's closing paragraph:

> The Spaniards were unable to exterminate the Indian race by those unparalleled atrocities which brand them with indelible shame, nor did even succeed in wholly depriving it of its rights; but the Americans of the United States have accomplished this twofold purpose with singular felicity; tranquilly, legally, philanthropically, without shedding blood, and without violating a single great principle of morality in the eyes of the world. It is impossible to destroy men with more respect for humanity.

It would be hard to imagine two cultures more cross-grained and less likely to mix than the Indian and European. On the one hand there was the culture of the western European conquerors, which already showed signs of what was to become a technical, rationalist, highly mobile and acquisitive society. On the other there was the symbolic, nonrational, ritualist, passive culture of the Indians. One was dynamic, and had either to conquer or be conquered. The other could not achieve the first or suffer the second.

The methods of settlement revealed something of the outlook and inner conflicts of the colonizing Powers. The Spanish, their own economic life weakened by their religious policies, needed the New World's wealth and tried to get it too quickly. Their leaders were often brave and sometimes brilliant men, but they made implacable enemies of the Indians, using up their labor power ruthlessly but shaping no institutions to fit the needs of the New World. Otherwise they left a strong heritage behind, of language and blood and religion, and if they had been able to consolidate their foothold on the American Continent and keep the later British settlements out, the whole political and social history of America would have been different.

The British came to America carrying with them high principles of morality, religious freedom, and the rule of law. Unable to give scope to their expansive thrust (as the Spaniards did) in the name of religion, they suppressed it, and the dammed-up aggressions found another outlet. They came to identify God, freedom, and acquisitiveness with the image of the continent they were seeking to possess. If there had been room for the Indian in such a scheme, they would have included him. The Indian might have made an effort to absorb the culture of the Europeans, might have adopted wholly the settled ways of agriculture and industry, learned new techniques as well as a new language and a new religion, accepted work as a means both to earthly accumulation and Divine Grace, and stripped himself of the values which linked him with the inner social structure of family, village-community, and tribe. But even when some of the tribes made the effort, as with the Cherokees in Georgia, it didn't work. On one side there was a burning resentment at being thrust out of land and hunting grounds, on the other a haste at staking out and possessing a continent. The whole policy of Indian removal and reservations in the Southern territory was aimed at opening the Cotton Kingdom for the Southern slaveholder. Take the Puritan assurance of an inner rightness of purpose, plus the 100 per-centism of the Yankee spirit of "go" and "get," plus the land hunger of the pioneer and the profit hunger of the land speculator, plus the dynamism of the "westward course of empire" and the doctrine of America's "Manifest Destiny"—add these and you get the fateful formula of the doom of the Indian culture.

When the Indians held out against selling their land for almost nothing the whites solemnly made treaties with them and gaily broke them. When the Indians learned to combine for a stand, as with Pontiac and Osceola, the whites used their superior technology and overwhelmed them. Leaders like Washington and Marshall felt a sense of shame. But Washington's attack on the land speculators was ignored, and when Chief Justice Marshall rendered his decision in *Worcester v. Georgia* (1832) confirming the right of the Cherokees as "a distinct community, occupying its own territory . . . in which the laws of Georgia can have no force," and reserving Indian treaty relations to the Federal government, Jackson's reported answer, "John Marshall has made his decision—now let him enforce it," showed (even if the remark itself was legendary) the ruthless purpose inherent in the New Order that was arising. This New Order disposed of the hope of Indian survival as an autonomous subculture within the larger culture.

Yet the Indians left their mark on the conquerors. It reaches beyond the crops they gave America, beyond the wonderful place names and the heritage of woodlore and woodcraft, much of which became part of the growing-up years of American boys. The real mark was the image the Indian left of himself.

The early Americans, not as deeply impressed by the "noble savage" image as the French Romantic writers, could not idealize the Indian when he was an ever-present enemy. Every people needs a symbol of hostility and even savagery to round out the picture of the hardships of its beginnings and to bolster the boastings of its heroism and virility. The tales of sudden descent of Indians on white villages became part of American memory—the burnings and pillagings, the swing of the tomahawk, the transporting of victims into captivity, the babies with their skulls bashed against the trees, the burning at the stake, the burial alive to the most grisly accompaniments of torture. It is now clear that much of this savagery was real, but much also was legendary, born of the overwrought imagination of contemporaries. For the Puritans and their descendants the image of the Indian filled a psychic need as a graphic representation of the hard pilgrimage in this world and the terror in the next—a sort of native background for an American *Pilgrim's Progress.*

Just when the Indian himself was at the point of being destroyed, a new image of him was forming in the mind of the white. Fenimore Cooper's generation found his portrayal of the Indian not only romantically appealing but psychologically valid. While he idealized the young Indian braves, he drew "bad" as well as "good" Indians. What he said was that heroes and villains were to be found among them pretty much as among the whites. If Cooper relied mainly on printed sources, George Catlin spent years traveling among the Indians and painted them from life—Red Jacket, the great orator of the Senecas, and the Seminole Chief, Osceola, in his imprisonment in the Carolinas. We laugh at his depicting them as Greek heroes, but recent scholarly studies show the Indian chieftains to have had inner serenity and a kind of statesmanship as well as courage. "My God," Daniel Webster exclaimed when he saw Catlin's paintings, "I was blind to all this red majesty and beauty and mystery that we are trampling down." Francis Parkman, in his original journals of the trip on which *The Oregon Trail* was based, also saw integrity and sawdust in Indians and whites alike. Parkman described himself as the historian of "the American forest and the American Indian at the period when both received their final doom." By the time he got to them the Indians had become badly disintegrated and lived "not much better than brutes," but the whites on the frontier were also "a race of boors, about as uncouth, mean, and stupid as the hogs they seem chiefly to delight in." The post-Parkman generations belatedly tried to do justice, and perhaps more, to the personality and culture of the Indian. In the regional literature of the West and Southwest his figure has loomed larger than the historical reality, invoking a culture that became a heroic symbol after its death.

In "The Redskin and the Paleface," D. H. Lawrence saw an America "haunted by the Indian." If he was right, then the sense of guilt that overtook some Americans brought a new romanticism of the Indian which went deeper than that of Montaigne or Chateaubriand, Cooper or Catlin or Parkman. John Collier and other champions of the Indians pointed out that, harried and decimated as they were, their "grouphoods, languages, religions, culture systems, symbolisms and emotional attitudes toward the self and the world continued to live on." He finds a central secret of this continuity in the "passion and reverence for human personality and for the web of life and the earth which the American Indians have tended as a central, sacred fire since before the Stone Age." There is a measure of truth in this, despite the pathos of applying it to the straggling, impoverished remnants of a people, living in isolation, with tribal councils that no longer function. There has been a recent tendency to return to the sources of Indian feeling and the Indian outlook as to a road not taken but missed somehow in the scramble to make America a success.

Failing to tame the race they found peopling the continent and unable to keep white indentured labor in subjection or make it pay, the European colonizers brought in from another continent a race more easily managed because "they came in chains." The Spanish first brought them from Africa to their West Indies colony to replace the dwindling supply of Indian labor when the encomienda system began to break down. In defeating the Spanish sea power the Elizabethan adventurers enabled Britain eventually to take over the lucrative slave trade as a source of the prosperity of its ports and as one of the foundations of its expanding capitalist power. Later the Americans organized the slave trade on a large scale, and much of American prosperity rested on the crops and industries which depended on Negro labor.

The Negroes who came to America as a commodity had been captured by other Negroes in raids on the West African coast or traded to an expanding white market by warring tribal chieftains. They were chained and crowded into the hulls of the ships, both for economy and to break their spirits, and set to work on the plantations of the New World. The plantation system, which extended from the Southern United States through the whole Caribbean and Latin-American area, was linked with slave labor because large-scale agriculture could better afford the high initial cost of slaves and supply the necessary supervision. When the first census was taken in 1790, there were 757,000 Negroes, nine out of ten of them slaves. The African slave trade became illegal in 1808, and slaves were the more valued as property because they could no longer be imported.

In a sense, slavery was a way of life for both races. For the small elite of white planters in the South it made possible a life passed in the tall-columned "Great Houses" built in the classic Greek style, with feudal paternalism at its core. But it was also a life of intermittent fear of slave rebellion, and of efforts to rationalize the obvious evil of the "peculiar institution" of slavery. For the Negroes it was not always (as some Southern historians have rediscovered) a life of bloodhounds and Simon Legrees. There were, of course, the terrible burdens of slave life, as one reads about them in Solomon Northrop's account of a slave's workday or Frederick Douglass's description of the bleak succession of intolerable days in the field, dawn to dark, in every weather. All labor was hard in rural and early industrial America, and sometimes the Northern white worker said he was worse off than the Southern slave. But the Abolitionists who saw slavery in the image of its worst examples had hold of a deep truth: the cancer of slavery, as Avery Craven has put it, was in the idea of slavery itself—of one man owning another—and in the fact that there was nothing to keep the worst type of white from owning and exploiting those who were better men than himself. The slave died young. His women were often taken sexually by the overseer and the master's sons, whether out of passion or for sport, as the record of racial mixture abundantly shows. Yet since slaves were valuable property they were usually treated with some care, and a rough affection often developed on both sides. Discipline was maintained; if the slave protested he was whipped; if he sought to escape he was tracked down. He lived in ignorance but in a bare kind of comfort. While most of the churches admitted him to membership and the Quakers championed his cause, too many Christian churchgoers considered him outside the scope of their charity, compassion, and militancy.

Slavery as a human institution had many faces: it differed depending on the state, the crop, the plantation, the master. Yet its common pattern was intolerable. There were periodic slave-labor strikes and local uprisings in which the Negroes fought against hopeless odds. The one known as Nat Turner's Rebellion in 1831, was led by a Virginia slave locally known as "the Preacher" who had visions like Joan of Arc and saw himself destined to bring it to pass that "the first shall be last and the last shall be first." His venture led to perhaps a hundred deaths on both sides, but it showed how little life mattered in a feudal domain when weighed against freedom and despair.

Eventually the slaves were freed, at the expense of a Civil War. The heritage of slavery lay heavily on the whites in their fratricidal struggle and afterward in their abiding sense of guilt. The Negro also carried a heritage of embitterment. He had to pay a painful price for his freedom, grasping at it with unrealistic eagerness only to find that liberation could not liberate so long as the former oppressors kept their power. So he was hurtled from his first dream of freedom back into the terror of Reconstruction days. He found he had to achieve everything again from scratch—to fight disfranchisement and his own ignorance, and poverty, disease, economic and sexual exploitation, the bleakness of segregation and the atmosphere of terror. At first some of the better-educated whites were ready to join with the Negro in the venture of forming a tolerable working community of both races. And the Populist movement, under leaders like Tom Watson, took the first steps to unite Negroes and whites on an equal basis in a common struggle against the economic and political exploitation of both races. For a brief interval, between the late 1870s and the 1890s, there was a flash of hope that the two races could live side by side without segregation. But it was not sustained. C. Vann Woodward, in his books on the post-Civil War South, has brilliantly traced the history both of the hope and of this failure and of the new alliance that came into being under the banner of the former Populist leaders, between the lower-class whites who wanted someone still lower to look down upon and the master group for whom every gain in Negro status was a reminder of the humiliation of Civil War defeat and who were bent on irredentist revenge. The result was the erratic course of segregation—the "strange career of Jim Crow."

Through every possible means—through direct and indirect segregation, through a racist theory of Negro inferiority and the social power of white supremacy, through propaganda and terror—pressures were exerted on the Negro to accept his traditional position. For a time his leaders acquiesced, but in the end a new and more militant leadership arose which demanded equal rights for the Negro. Confronted by a people whose docility had bounds, who—even though they came from a more primitive culture—learned quickly, the Southern whites felt that their whole way of life was endangered and came close to building a kind of garrison society.

The Negro showed himself to be a good borrower and facile adapter to a form of life that had for centuries grown in a different direction from his own. He took over much of the class and prestige hierarchy of the whites, and the respectability and middle-class qualities. Nevertheless he also showed a good deal of cultural resistance and tenacity. He proved buoyant in the face of every hardship. Even in the South he steadily asserted and won a measure of civil rights, wrested a better education, gained a foothold in politics. Throughout the nation he made an irresistible bid for equality. He was helped by two world wars, the march of industrialism, the higher living standards of the Negroes, their massed purchasing power, and the supremacy of Federal law on matters of civil rights, even in such local concerns as schooling and transportation.

Out of the sharpness of the change from African tribalism to American slavery, and out of the suffering and sorrow of the Negro, came a characteristic blend of elements in his outlook. It was an amalgam of ecstatic supernaturalism, submission to fate, a belief in luck, a humorous acceptance of the contradictions of life, a buoyant gaiety mingled with sadness, and—from the sense of alienation—a dark strain of violence.

The religion of the Negro came close to the primitivism of the early Christian church, when religion was the creed of the slave and the persecuted. With a literalism born of plantation experience rather than of the inner torments of conscience, Hell became an arena of fire and torture and damnation, with the Devil as Simon Legree. Jordan and Canaan and the Promised Land took on concreteness. Heaven became a refuge from oppression and a surcease from sorrow, as well as a reward for faith. Jesus became a force to be invoked by a propitiatory magic—a Man of Sorrows who was understood with a peculiar intimacy by those who had experienced so many of their own. God the Father became the head of a tribal patriarchate whose serenity was untouched by the turmoil of the world below. These religious attitudes, born of Negro life in the ante-bellum South, persisted among Negroes throughout the nation long after the end of the Civil War. In America a force which reinvigorated the lagging religious consciousness was bound to ramify beyond religion itself to the culture as a whole. Thus the religion of the Negroes took its place, along with New England Calvinism and frontier revivalism, as one of the crucial influences on the American religious consciousness—not in the sense of influencing Christian ritual or theology but in investing again with a naïve wonder the early strivings of Christian faith.

The beat of Negro life found its way not only into the religious "Spirituals," in which the Negro sometimes adapted old Baptist and Methodist revival songs, but also into the work songs of the plantation and logging camp and railroad, the "blues," and the more violent dance rhythms of American jazz. For all the somberness of the Negro's slave life he maintained an irrepressible gaiety that broke the mold of New England dourness and the high-flown gallantry of Southern feudal society. In the training of the Southern "belle" and "beau," the Negro "mammy" became a symbol of maternal warmth which persisted long beyond the slave society. The American Negro expressed in his rhythms, in his belief in magic, and in his relaxed, noncompetitive sense some of the irrationals of living that were later to form a sharp contrast to the rigidities of science and the machine. Unlike the European heritage (except for the case of the European peasant), the Negro heritage was prescientific, preindustrial, outside the whole scope of Western culture. In the contact of European and African cultures in America something striking was bound to happen to the new amalgam. The quality of American music, dance. literature, theater, religion, today is evidence that it did.*

The migration that is usually called prescriptively "American" is that of the explorers, conquerors, and settlers from western Europe, especially from the British Isles. Statistically the British influence has not been decisive. Out of a total immigration of some thirty-five million, not more than five million Englishmen came to America. But they came early so that the portion of the population with a strain of British blood now, in addition to the British cultural inheritance, is much greater than the 10 per cent or 15 per cent that the British contributed to the immigration itself. Even more important, the impact came in the formative years of colonial growth and the history of the Republic, and it did much to shape the basic American attitudes and institutions.

It might have turned out differently. In the years of discovery and exploration, Spain and France rather than Britain were the Great Powers of Europe. Had either or both of them held on to their colonies, the United States might have become another Latin America or French Canada. But the Spanish hold was weak, largely because of Indian hostility and Spain's inner weakness and its defeats in Europe. In the crucial and protracted struggle (described so well by Parkman) between the French and British for the control of North America, the French too had to yield. Their imperial energies were distracted in the Caribbean, in India, and in Europe; internally they were split by religious and civil wars. The Spanish and French empires were on the downward sweep of their arc of power, the British with their rising commercial and industrial strength were on the upward sweep. Whenever the Spanish and French had colonized in the New World they left behind, in Parkman's phrasing, a people "bereft of civil liberty" and burdened by "a weight

* For a further treatment of the place of the Negro in American life, see Ch. VII, Sec. 6, "The Negro in America"; also Ch. X, Sec. 1, "God and the Churches," and Ch. XI, Sec. 7, "Jazz As American Idiom."

of ecclesiastical tutelage." For America the stakes of conflict lay in the question of whether the United States would become primarily feudal, Catholic, hierarchic, and authoritarian, or industrial, Protestant, capitalistic, and libertarian. It is in the choice of these great historical alternatives that the British triumph was decisive and the British influence beyond any statistical calculus.

The core of the language is English, although the native elements added to it have given it an "American" character. American law grew out of, and is still largely rooted in, the English common law. American political institutions and ideas—including representative government, the limited state, the right of revolt, the stress on individualism, the tradition of civil liberties—came largely from the British. They were an organic part of the American mind because they grew out of the political struggles in England during the Tudor-Stuart period, when America was still part of the British Empire. The American Revolution itself made the Americans more British, since they were fighting for the "true British" order and heritage that were (they felt) being lost in the mother country. American technology took its methods and ideas from the British Industrial Revolution until the Americans outstripped their teachers. The American belief in the sanctity of property and contract was derived from the British. The pluralism of the American Protestant religious sects, the emphasis on individual Bible reading and on freedom of worship, are largely British in inspiration. So also are the small-town pattern, the complexity of local government, the private ("public" in England) schools, the colleges, the charities and philanthropies, the whole network of voluntary associations, the corporations and trade-unions. The literary heritage is mainly British. So is the press, reaching back to Defoe and Cobbett. Until the end of the nineteenth century, when the German influence became strong, the contacts of American scientists and scholars were, with some important exceptions, British. In painting, sculpture, architecture, the British influence was strong until the French strains made themselves felt toward the turn of the twentieth century.

One special phase of this heritage was Puritanism. Although there is a temptation to believe it was a native American product, actually (as Perry Miller pointed out) nine tenths of what we associate with Puritanism was British. The Puritan qualities were intense, inverted, crotchety, rather than judicious or humanist. There was a tautness about the Puritans that came from their sense of living under tension and of applying pressure all down the line in order to take by storm God's grace and strength. The wilderness itself along with the Indian dangers made the "good fight" more real, and the New World with its ever-present strangeness kept the wonder-working Providence ever busy. As children of the whole Judaeo-Christian culture the Puritans considered human nature vile and kept an eye on the next world, but the other eye was kept lustily on the enterprises of this world. Their heritage accounts for much in the American combination of the visionary and the pragmatic, the righteous and the profitable. Not only New England but the Old South as well took its fashions, its education, its books and ideas, its values, even its snobbisms, from Great Britain. The two great aristocracies America has had—the intellectual aristocracy of New England and the planter aristocracy of the South—derive from the two phases of British society at the time of American colonial growth which the Americans came to think of (in somewhat mythical terms) as those of the Puritans and the Cavaliers.

I have put the case for the British heritage so strongly because it has been played down recently by the "cultural pluralists," in recoil from the "Anglo-Saxon" cult of the turn of the century and the still earlier colonialism of American thought which played up everything British. But Britain's role in the shaping of the American tradition was that of a carrier for European thought and life as a whole. If the leaders of American life in the early days of the Republic were "true-born Englishmen" they were also good Europeans, anxious to weave into the pattern of their new venture every strand of European striving. The intellectual generation that framed the Declaration and Constitution, and wrote and read *The Federalist,* was heir to the culture of the Greek and Italian Renaissance, the Reformation, the *philosophes,* and later of the French Revolution itself. The new republicans of America looked to the political history of Greece and Rome for their models of republican virtue. Early American architecture derived from the pure classicism of the French as well as from Palladio's Renaissance style, American educational ideals came from the progressive teaching of Rousseau and Pestalozzi, and American theological controversies—especially in the era of the Transcendentalists—were carried on in the murky atmosphere of Göttingen and other centers of German romanticism.*

The last of the shaping sources of the American tradition was so diversified that it can only be called the polyglot heritage. In addition to the British, the Scotch-Irish, the French Huguenots, the early German settlers from the Palatine and the later Germans who left behind the abortive German revolutions of 1848, many other strains came to America. There were Irish Catholics, driven by famine and an inner restlessness; there were Norwegians, Swedes and Danes, Hungarians, Austrians, Bohemians and Moravians, Spaniards and Portuguese; there

* For a further discussion, especially of the impact of Puritanism, see Ch. X, Sec. 1, "God and the Churches," and Sec. 2, "American Thought: the Angle of Vision." For the influence of English law and politics, see Ch. VI, especially Sec. 8, "Law and Justice." For the English language, see Ch. XI, Sec. 3, "Heroes, Legends, and Speech."

were Swiss, Italians, Serbs, Greeks, and Armenians; there were Russian and Polish peasants, Lithuanians and Finns; there were Jews, hoping that America would be the last stop in their history of wandering; there were Mexicans and Canadians, crossing not a sea but only a border; there were Latin Americans; there were Chinese, Japanese, Filipinos.

The speech of America became a medley of tongues from every language family, each helping to give form to the emerging American language. The dance of America took its shape not only from the African jungle but also from the folk rhythms of the Central Europeans and the Slavs and from the pampas of Latin America. The choral societies and *Männerverbände* of Central Europe were transplanted to Midwestern cities; the cookery of the French, the Italians, the Hungarians, the Swedes, entered as ingredients in the American menu. The vendettas of Sicily and the tong warfare of China were re-enacted on American streets. The political heterodoxies of German *émigré* Marxists and the religious heterodoxies of innumerable sects and prophets of true believers found room for community testing on the Midwestern plains; the political skills of the Irish found expression in new American cities, while the intellectual and business skills of the Jews reasserted themselves in the new favoring climate.

Thus it became part of the American tradition to be an amalgam of many traditions, even while there were pressures to select one of them (the British–West European) as *the* "American" one. The shaping forces of American society, and of its outlook and thought, grew unimaginably. To the heritage of the Indian and Negro cultural strains, of British institutional life, of the Greco-Roman and Judaeo-Christian world, of French revolutionary doctrine and artistic life, of German romanticism and the political and religious consciousness of the 1848 immigration, there were added the whole Mediterranean world, the Slavic, the Celtic-Catholic, the Hispanic-American, the Arab-Moslem, the Oriental. Each immigrant group contributed whatever elements of its tradition were absorbable by the American heritage, while in turn it absorbed the elements it found.*

In Augustan Rome the Emperor asked the poet Virgil to write an epic that would expound and consolidate the Roman tradition. But an American Virgil, commanded similarly to celebrate the American tradition, would find the task overpowering. For it would mean tracing the course of numberless rivers of thought and influence as they flowed into the central ocean of an American tradition which is still in the making.

* On the polyglot tradition, see Ch. III, Sec. 1, "Is There an American Stock?" and Sec. 2, "The Immigrant Experience"; also Ch. VII, Sec. 5, "The Minority Situation."

3. The Slaying of the European Father

THE PEOPLE WHO CAME to the American shores felt intensely about the American experience because for each of them America was the wall broken down, door broken open. Some, like the Negroes, came against their will and in chains. But as for the rest, whether they came for land or economic opportunity or freedom, they came because of the past denials in their lives. It was their pre-American experience that gave point to their life in America. The earlier memories were, of course, not wholly negative. The new setting gave the bitter memories of deprivation a chance to mellow, and it often brought to the fore a gentle nostalgia for the old culture which fused with the patriotic feeling for the new.

Thus the bundles of Old World memories, jostling each other in the New World, have enriched the American tradition. America was the place where the old memories found a new meaning. Every item of experience in the New World was packed with a heightened tension, every event was projected into a past more contrasting and into a future more exacting than in any other culture, thus forming the American image in the immigrant mind.

Although many of the later immigrants were doubtless passive, coming to America mainly because of the unsettlement of Europe, the notion of the "American promise"—of America as a cornucopia of well-being and freedom—was to some degree imbedded in their mind from the first settlers to the latest. The earliest image of the American promise was widely spread by documents like Columbus's Letter of 1493 and the *mundus novus* attributed to Amerigo Vespucci, with its picture of sensuality as well as danger. The more authentic early writings depicted an America of rich soil, where a man had room to move. In the age of capitalism the image of America became one of a land of business opportunity where an able man could start at the bottom and reach the top. Throughout, from the Spanish quest of El Dorado to the twentieth-century folklore of Sicilian and Slavic villages, the myth persisted of America as the land of untold riches where everyone dressed in finery and the paving blocks were of gold.

Whatever the reality, these myths were among the powerful forces that stirred the European mind. The dominant literary themes of Europe have often reached outside Europe: the imaginary voyage, the noble savage, the Byronic hero eating his heart out in some mountain fastness, the splendor of the exotic Orient or Africa. But in the European folk mind the myth of golden America has far outshone all these literary themes of the elite. The popular mind made the transition from Utopia to an actual democracy and from aiming at the moon to aiming at America. There is no other civilization in whose life history promise has played so great a part, nor one whose promise has meant so much to the older civilizations.

But being built on a promise, American civilization was open to questions about the degree of its fulfillment. National self-criticism had been strong from Thoreau and Theodore Parker to Whitman, but it mounted after the Civil War with the ending of the frontier, the dominance of the money mentality, the awakening of labor protest, and the havoc of recurrent economic breakdown. "America was promises," wrote Archibald MacLeish in the 1930s, and his choice of tense summed up the temper of American self-criticism. Yet what interests a student of American civilization is less the lack of fullness in the fulfillment than the persistence of the promise. The theme of promise has been America's great "social myth," using the term in the sense of an imaginative idea which—whatever its truth—induces men to feel and act. Santayana once spoke of the "metaphysical passion" which moved men to cross the seas to America to set up a new civilization. He was right. For all the scorn of metaphysics that you will find in American writing, the metaphysic of promise has been as crucial an element in the American civilization as the metaphysic of Christianity in the civilization of Europe from St. Augustine to Thomas Aquinas.

The medieval metaphysic was one of renunciation and otherworldliness. It dominated European thought until the new science, discoveries, and wealth undercut it. With the Commercial Revolution and the unsettling effects of the Renaissance and Reformation, a new temper was shaped. Men sought the Golden Age not in a primitive past or murky future but here on earth and now. In fact, the quest for America was the quest at once for gold and the Golden Age. Thus was the foundation laid for the metaphysic of secular promise. Even in its imperial phase of the struggle of great power systems it had its roots in the Protestant ethic and in the humanist and secular energies loosed by the Renaissance. The promise of American life had its way prepared by the humanism of Europe, and the energies of American life had their origin in the awakened energies of Europe.

This has been largely obscured in the literature of American revolt, in which Europe was something broken away from and left behind. You get this theme in De Crèvecoeur, with his talk of the wholly "new" American; in Jefferson, with his recoil from the dynastic blood-feuds of the European despotisms; and you get it in Emerson's speech at Manchester in the midst of the 1847 depression, with which he closes his *English Traits:*

> If the courage of England goes with the chances of a commercial crisis, I will go back to the capes of Massachusetts and my own Indian stream, and say to my countrymen, the old race are all gone, and the elasticity and hope of mankind must henceforth remain on the Allegheny ranges, or nowhere.

But while Americans rejected Europe, the act of rejection was also one of carry-over, and the act of revolt was itself an expression of the European consciousness. Thus Jefferson avowed that in drawing up the Declaration of Independence he had aimed at no originality but had sought only "to place before mankind the common sense of the subject"; after tracing the varied sources of European thought from which Jefferson had drawn, Julian Boyd remarks that "for a people who were to embrace many races and many creeds, nothing could have been more appropriate than that the act of renouncing the ties of consanguinity should have drawn its philosophical justification from traditions common to all." Without taking over the European heritage the Americans could not have revolted against Europe. The ships that crossed the Atlantic to America carried with them not only the European economy but also European aspirations and the European system of thought. The revolutionary elements in that system of thought had begun to show themselves before the settlement of America. In fact, the rise of American civilization was the product both of revolution and dissolution in Europe.

In America the vigorous European elements were brought into play as against the exhausted ones. It was free enterprise arrayed against mercantilism, *laissez faire* against cameralism, individualism against hierarchy, natural rights against monarchy, popular nationalism against the dynastic regimes, social mobility against caste, the pioneering spirit against the status quo. For before the American dream there was the European dream. Sometimes internal conflicts are resolved by revolution within, sometimes by the bursting out into colonization and revolution without. If the settlement of America helped drain off Europe's revolutionary energies, the revolution in America gave expression to those energies. The new world of which Europe had so long dreamed came to fruition under American skies. The European dream made America possible: and the American experience gave the European dream concreteness.

This was the America-Europe nexus. Why then the rejection of Europe so chronic in the American tradition? An answer is suggested by the theme which runs through Frazer's *The Golden Bough*—the tribal killing of the sacrificial king, or (as we may generalize it) the symbolic slaying of the father. The motive for slaying, one may hazard, was to ward off evil by establishing the separateness of the tribe from the king, much as an adolescent has to disown a parent to assert himself as a person in his own right. Taking the suggestion of the Swiss-Italian theorist Roberto Michels that every nation has two dominant myths—the myth of origin and the myth of mission—America's rejection of Europe and the rebellion against the father may be seen as part of its mythology.

Was the strength of the rejection due partly to the feelings of inferiority in a culture which for almost two centuries was colonial?—plus the bitterness of a revolutionary war?—plus the cockiness of success and the rapid strides toward power on the part of a once derided people?—plus a metaphysic of promise which demanded that the sources of the promise be as home-grown as its prospects were glorious? Yet there remains the paradox that the Americans who led in the rejection of Europe were themselves intellectuals deeply indebted to European books and ideas.

There is the example of Jefferson, whose passion for freedom was rooted in the classical and English philosophers and whose feeling for the independent American farmer had been foreshadowed by the emphasis of the Physiocrats. As for his opponents, John Adams's doctrine of mixed government went back to the English constitutional tradition, and Alexander Hamilton expressed better than the European thinkers themselves the fears of the possessors about the naked will of the people. Inveighing against European monarchies and social despotism, Jefferson made political capital for the Republicans by fixing the stigma of a monarchist Europe on the Federalists. Hamilton, on his side, by inveighing against European revolutionary terrorists, lumped with them the author of the *Letter to Mazzei*. Each used Europe as a weapon in his political battles.

The use of these symbols was strengthened by the continued inpouring of immigration. The big anti-immigrant movements of American history—the Native Americans and Know-Nothings of the 1840s and 1850s, the Sand-Lot party in California in the 1870s which set off the Exclusion bills, the American Protective Association in the Midwest, and the revived Ku Klux Klan after World War I—were related to the raw energies of a new capitalist democracy and the personal and social tensions of living in a fiercely competitive society. In a nation made up of successive layers of immigrants there was a marginal prestige in having left Europe earlier and a marginal stigma in having left it later. Each new batch, feeling its "Americanism" challenged, found itself blatantly claiming to be more American than the others. This led to a mounting xenophobia, an overrapid drive toward "assimilation," and an effort to equate "radical" and "alien" and use them almost interchangeably.*

This psychic necessity for rejecting Europe has affected the whole spectrum of American social thinking. It is true that there is an underlying self-confidence in American thought. Yet for his self-respect the young American intellectual of today is led to reject ideas for social change far less radical than the radical democracy of Channing and Wendell Phillips, of Henry Demarest Lloyd and Edward Bellamy and Lincoln Steffens, on the ground that they are "European" and "Marxian." In his spiritual isolation the middle-class American seems to suffer from a sense of encirclement and to identify with a "European" or "foreign" source whatever ills he feels he is subject to. Some of the major *grands peurs* to which American men of property have been subject have been dramatized in these terms, and the more easily dramatized because the rejection of Europe preceded even the Socialist scares created by the European revolutions of the 1840s or the Paris Commune of 1870. Finally, because a sense of encirclement fortifies a policy of isolationism, the considerations of national interest which until recently led to such a foreign policy found psychological bolstering here.

To be sure, the best American thinkers suffered from the sense that they were missing something by their separation from Europe. Emerson preached self-reliance to Americans, yet he was mature enough to know that self-reliance excluded fear of Europe as well as abasement before it; his relations with Carlyle and the other British men of letters were relations between men who had something to say to each other. But other American writers have veered between an overassertive nativism and a votive dependence. From Henry James in the old London houses that drew him so, to the literary proconsuls of the 1940s and 1950s in Paris and Rome, American writers went to Europe seeking some quality—aesthetic sensitivity, a freer expressiveness in living, old traditions, a sense of community, dedication to artistic discipline—which the cruder energies of the American civilization had not provided.

The sharp change in the American attitude toward Europe came with the world wars. Once it became clear that Europe was no longer the father demanding obedience and exerting his authority but an endangered civilization needing help, America's response changed. It broke through the isolationist sheath to aid western Europe in two great wars, and afterward it helped to rebuild Europe's economic strength. Yet even here Americans had to dress up their aid in the ideological garment of a struggle against tyranny and authoritarianism. You ended by helping

* For a further discussion, see Ch. III, Sec. 2, "The Immigrant Experience," and Ch. VII, Sec. 5, "The Minority Situation."

the father you had rebelled against, but you did it by continuing to slay another potential authority-image.

Thus did Americans compensate for the sacrificial slaying of the father; and thus did they continue, in the act of compensation, to maintain their connection with their image of themselves as free and rebellious spirits.*

4. Why Was America a Success?

THE VERSIONS A CULTURE has of its own strength and success are as important parts of its tradition as the versions it has of its origins or mission. Some of the early historians believed they saw the hand of God operating exclusively in American history and did not trouble to inquire why He should have shown so special a solicitude for this particular breed of His children. Not counting the inevitable drivel about the superior virtues of Anglo-Saxonism, there were also a few accepted historians (Bancroft, Fiske, Mahan come to mind) who wrote of Americans as a Chosen People in the Biblical sense of one through whose history some Higher Power works out an inscrutable design for the whole human race. There was also a tendency to guard the unblemished reputation of the revolutionary heroes and give more than life-size stature to the Founding Fathers. But the recent studies of Franklin, Washington, Jefferson, Hamilton, Adams, and Madison view them with their frailties as well as their basic greatness.

Stronger than the impulse to see America as a Chosen People is the impulse to see it as a unique historic experience. The idea of American "exceptionalism" is valid if you take it in the sense that America has its own civilization pattern, which does not follow the pattern of others and is not linked by any inevitable destiny to their doom. This does not cut America off from the universal experience of other civilizations, nor does it make America immune to the age-old forces that have seen other civilizations rise and flourish, decay and die. It does, however, stress the ways in which America has been favored by geography and historical circumstance. One view of the geographical theory underscores the expanse of continent, another the expanse of oceans. The continental version points out that America has been blessed with a richness of resources—soil, forest, water power, coal, minerals—as few other nations. The oceanic version points to the stretch of the Atlantic and the Pacific which enabled America to develop, especially in its formative pe-

* For a further discussion of American metaphysical assumptions, see Ch. X, Sec. 2, "American Thought: the Angle of Vision." For the ideas and emotions underlying American foreign policy, see Ch. XII.

riod, far from the wars and dynastic struggles of other nations. Thus one may say that the tutelary divinities of land and water watched over America's destinies.

Another variant of the theory of exceptionalism is the argument from pluralism—that American greatness derives from its special blend of ethnic, religious, and linguistic strains. This is the view that America was a success because it was not a nation but (in Walt Whitman's phrase) "a nation of nations." As DeWitt Clinton, the New York politician, put it as early as 1814: "Perhaps our mingled descent from various nations may have a benign influence upon genius. . . . The extraordinary characters which the United States have produced may be, in some measure, ascribed to the mixed blood of so many nations flowing in our veins." A later writer spoke of the processes of Nature as always tending "to enrich the whole by this electrical and enlivening relation between the parts." Randolph Bourne, who reflected the intellectual currents of the period before World War I, also spoke of the "trans-national" character of the culture. Here again, by the denial of a narrow ethnic view, America expressed its sense of its own uniqueness: for the crossing of so many strains presumably produced a richer and stronger new strain, the American as the New Man. Or if he was not new, there was at least in him the densest distillation of universal humanity, and in that sense too America was unique.

Even when American thinkers seemed to use other explanations of American success, the notion of exceptionalism often showed through the slits of the mask. This was true of those who saw American history as illustrating "the principle of freedom" (in George Bancroft's phrase), or the later radical democrats who made a cult of the common man and saw him shaping a unique civilization under unique conditions of freedom. For them, as for many other commentators on America, the theme of American uniqueness has been (in Rush Welter's words) "a fact transcending any particular explanation, yet evidenced by their proliferation."*

Of the American institutions singled out for the riddle of American success, the three that have received most attention are the Constitution, individualist capitalism, and the frontier.

For a century and a half the worship of the Constitution has been part of American traditional thought and emotion. It may have taken root as a way of giving Americans the sense of their place in the sun, after the struggle for freedom. It continued in the latter part of the nineteenth century as a way of fighting radical legislation and the "im-

* For a further discussion of the problem of the uniqueness of America, see Ch. II, Sec. 4, "American Exceptionalism."

ported European philosophies." Today it counts most as a symbol of the nontotalitarian organization of human living—especially important, as Clinton Rossiter has noted, for a people who lack a large store of inherited symbols of a mystical nature. Even among those skeptical of spread-eagle patriotism, there is a sober sense that the American political genius has here added something of its own to the tradition of government.

To be sure, the creative elements of the American political contribution are to be found outside as well as inside the Constitution. The party system, judicial review of legislation, the flexibility of Presidential power, the government of atomic energy, the whole administrative arm of the government—none of these are explicit in the Constitution but have grown up outside it. Yet in the popular mind they are lumped together under the Constitutional symbol. What was perhaps least to be expected was the record of the Supreme Court, in the last two decades, in refusing to make the symbol too rigid. The healthy conflict of opinion between the Justices is a sign that all of them, conservatives and liberals alike, regard the Constitution not as a sacred text but as an instrument of government, however much they may differ on how it is to be used wisely.

There is still, of course, the temptation to pay homage to a sacred document, unchanging amidst the tides and storms of the world. The document is thereby assigned an efficacy in itself which it can have only when it is seen as a living Constitution, interpreted flexibly and with a generosity of social purpose by men who are human beings and have biographies and political creeds. As an object of cult worship the Constitution becomes all too easy an explanation of American greatness and has thereby at times become an obstacle to the dynamism of the American experience.*

One of the least noted changes in the undercurrent of American attitudes has been the merging of the Constitution with the idea-of-progress strain in American thought. As the technical achievement of America became clearer in the 1870s and 1880s, the idea of progress was linked with the unfolding of the productive power of the machine and the human energies released by it. These in turn were seen to depend on capitalism, which by still another remove rested on the initiative of individual enterprise and the Constitutional guarantees of individual freedom. Thus the answer increasingly given to the riddle of American success was one linked with the institution of individualist capitalism.

The European theorist on whom the American champions of individualist capitalism most relied was Herbert Spencer. It was to turn his

* For a further discussion of the Constitution and constitutionalism, see Ch. VI, Sec. 9. "Keepers of the Covenant."

theory topsy-turvy that Thorstein Veblen wrote his *Theory of the Leisure Class;* and a quarter century later Veblen rounded out his thinking in *Absentee Ownership and Business Enterprise: The Case of America* (1923), which was an indictment of the whole capitalist thesis. Ironically, one of Veblen's teachers at Carleton College was John Bates Clark, one of his Yale teachers was William Graham Sumner, and his teacher and friend both at Cornell and Chicago was J. Laurence Laughlin. These three were the militant defenders of capitalist individualism at the turn of the century. Sumner's defense of the moral aspects of individualism and *laissez faire* paved the way for the economic individualism of the dominant school of American economic theory. The fruits of their view may be found in the speeches made at any convention of the N.A.M., in the institutional advertising of any corporation, and in the columns and editorials of almost any American newspaper.

This view is attractive as an explanation of American dynamism, since it runs in terms of the role of freedom in the release of men's energies. It offers the individual an unlimited field for careerism and enrichment and yet ties these up with the social interest, giving the twentieth-century American the feeling, at once complacent and revolutionary, of the eighteenth-century European when Adam Smith told him that each man, by pursuing his self-interest, helps the common good. It has on its side the massive facts of American material wealth and high living standards and is linked with the emphasis on the limited state and the contempt for bureaucrats.

But the champions of individualist capitalism have not gone unchallenged. Foreign observers like Harold Laski and Americans like Robert S. Lynd and C. Wright Mills have assigned it a corrosive role in American development, stressing the impact of its acquisitiveness, planlessness, and moral blindness on democratic institutions. The anticapitalist emphasis was in a sense foreshadowed by the agrarian antiprivilege thinking of John Taylor of Carolina, one of Jefferson's lieutenants, and by the similar protest of the Populist and reformist thinkers not so much against capitalism itself as against corrupt wealth and the inequalities of American life. The anticapitalist thinkers of the first half of our century have pointed to the concentration of economic power, the increasing pressures on small business, the recurring boom-bust cycles of inflation and unemployment, the waste, the jungle of competitive greeds, the desert stretches of frustration and relative poverty alongside the high living standards. The doubt they raise is whether big-scale capitalism was responsible for the prosperity of America or was itself a by-product of the margin of waste afforded by America's immense resources and geographic position. They point to the capitalist experience of other countries, with its frustrated energies and increasingly bitter social struggles, as an indication that the creative phase of American capitalism is past and the future will be that of an Iron Age.

Like other forms of determinism in America, this one has had rough going. "The theory of economic determinism," wrote the youthful and cocky Charles Beard in 1913, "has not been tried out in American history, and until it is tried out it cannot be found wanting." He later retreated from this position and denied that he had ever quite meant to try it out, yet the boldness of *An Economic Interpretation of the Constitution* left its mark on the teaching and writing of American history. His major work, with Mary Beard, on *The Rise of American Civilization* continued to stress the economic factor as the revolutionary shaping force in American development. Somewhat before Beard, but almost contemporary with him, Thorstein Veblen worked out more systematically an interpretation of society and opinion in America that (while not an economic determinism) stressed the conflict of the technological and pecuniary factors—"the making of goods and the making of money"—rather than the intangibles of the national character and destiny. And Brooks Adams, Henry's brother, starting from very different premises, developed an even more vigorous economic interpretation of his own—partly geographical (the determinism of changing trade routes), partly that of economic and administrative concentration (the "law of civilization and decay").

Thus there was a historical moment in America—somewhere between the rise of Populism and the New Deal—when the twin doctrines of capitalist apologetic and anticapitalist indictment fought it out, although under a bewildering variety of verbal disguises. Veblen insisted on an impersonal explanation, using his theory of the impersonality of the machine process and bringing within its incidence the whole structure of social thought as well. Beard was influenced not only by Veblen and Brooks Adams but also by James Madison, and was fond of quoting the famous Number Ten of *The Federalist,* where Madison analyzed the growth of party factions in terms of universal conflicts of class interest. But whether Madisonian or Marxian, Veblenian, Adamsian or Beardian, this emphasis has been attacked as too impersonal and too determinist—sometimes by the very same people who accept the impersonal market determinism of the "immutable" laws of neoclassical economics.

In its most effective form the anticapitalist indictment in America charges that capitalism turned its back on earlier American experience. Certainly the *laissez-faire* emphasis of capitalism was a latter-day one: state economic action was common and unchallenged before the Civil War. It was the continental resources and the favoring historical conditions of America (so this theory goes) that gave capitalism its start, but once started it ran berserk, so that the changes it brought over American life have betrayed the original meaning of the American Revolution. This was the favorite thesis of the intellectuals in the Populist and social-reform era. It was J. Allen Smith's thesis, and that of Smith's more famous disciple, Vernon L. Parrington. It was the thesis of Henry Demarest Lloyd and of Lincoln Steffens, of Edward Bellamy and of William Dean Howells. And in a different form it underlies the attack on capitalism by the Southern Agrarians of the 1920s and 1930s.

Answering these charges, a more sophisticated form of capitalist thinking has emerged which recognizes that *laissez-faire* capitalism no longer exists and that the giant corporation has made capitalist individualism archaic. In *U.S.A.: The Permanent Revolution,* Russell Davenport argued for the double thesis of American uniqueness and universalism. He saw American capitalism as the unique and history-chosen guardian of the universal values of freedom and abundance, holding it to be America's peculiar mission to guard these values for the rest of the world. He felt that the recent changes in capitalism—which have spread the ownership of corporate wealth and made ordinary people the participants in capitalism—have made it a "popular" or "welfare" capitalism, still holding the secret to American dynamism: in fact, so continuously revolutionary in its consequences that the American experience alone deserves the phrase Trotsky sought to apply to Communist dynamism—the "permanent revolution." Something of the same view may be found stated, with greater learning and more qualifications, in Adolf Berle's *American Capitalist Revolution.*

I shall be returning to an examination of these ideas in my chapter on the American economy.* Here I want only to say that American capitalism has been both overpraised and overindicted; that it is neither the Plumed Knight nor the monstrous Robber Barony it has been depicted; that it is responsible neither for all the blessings nor all the ills of American society; and that it cannot be brandished as the single key either to American greatness or American infamy. On no other phase of the American tradition has discussion shown the quality of excess it has shown on the nature of the American economy and its leadership. If Beard, Parrington, and Matthew Josephson in the 1920s and 1930s oversimplified the relation between economic power and stratification and the state of American civilization, the razzle-dazzle chromium-plated laudators of American capitalism in the 1950s were even more at fault in assuming that they had solved the secret of perpetual motion for American wealth and prosperity, that economic mergers, corporate cannibalism, stock dispersion, and the automatic factory would nail

* Ch. V, "Capitalist Economy and Business Civilization."

down the gifts of the gods on the American land, and that the power and the glory would go on forever and ever.

One of the most interesting efforts to explain American success was the Turner theory of the moving frontier. While Frederick J. Turner put his theory in terms of frontier democracy as well as frontier individualism, it has been used subtly to bolster the argument from individualism—and therefore from *laissez-faire* capitalism—as the source of America's greatness. Charles Beard asked acidly why Sumner's theory of individualism in economics was quickly challenged and destroyed by the progressive economists while Turner's similar theory of individualism in history got no such response from the historians. Turner has since been challenged, yet the query was a valid one. One answer is that while Sumner's argument was couched in universal terms—and Clark and Laughlin after him froze it into the eternal laws of economics—Turner's theory focused on the uniqueness of the American experience even while he gave it the force of historic law.

Turner's theory—that the characteristic American institutions were born out of the American forest and were shaped by America's characteristic frontier experience—was in one sense a pessimistic formulation, since Turner knew that the frontier was closing even while he wrote, and the closed frontier presumably meant the decline of opportunity and of democratic vigor. Yet its strong impact was positive and derived from confirming Americans in the feeling of their uniqueness, the sense of being not part of a universal equation but a fresh experiment in history. Henry Nash Smith has pointed out that Turner was in effect a poet dealing with the stuff of legend—the myth of America as the "garden of the world." What he wrote was thus part of the metaphysic of American promise and shed some light for Americans on how it happened that a people endowed as others of God's children were endowed could nevertheless create so special and successful a culture. It weakened the potential hold either of a Marxist theory of the iron laws of capitalist development and doom, or a theory of a racial elite which other peoples had found consolatory. Instead it gave Americans a theory of the shaping of their institutions and character which ran in naturalistic terms of the frontier as a process yet made them almost as elect as if they had been born of the Sun God or been given some special Aryan dispensation.

With its nostalgic evocation of a frontier America and its code of agrarian-democratic values, the Turner theory gave to highly urbanized twentieth-century Americans the flavor of the soil. Turner had broken with his teacher, Herbert Baxter Adams, who had traced American democracy from the barbarian tribes in the German forests: yet Turner, in a sense, transplanted the Teutonic forest to the American scene. "American democracy," he wrote, "was born of no theorist's dream. . . . It came out of the American forest, and it gained strength each time it touched a new frontier." This philosophy enabled the dwellers of the city to equate themselves with the dying yet romantic figure of the cabin farmer. They were able to live in a very unfrontierlike way and still regard themselves as frontiersmen, to develop massive corporate organizations while speaking of the individual entrepreneur, and to build up a Big Government with a far-flung imperium while still cherishing in politics the cult of the log cabin and the whistle-stop, back-platform campaign speech.

Most of all, Turner's appeal lay in the fact that while he talked in terms of individualism (what John Dewey called the *"old* individualism") the traits in America whose psychological sources he was seeking were the traits of democracy. This is what made him attractive to New Dealers and conservatives alike. Where Sumner and his followers had tried to show why the inequalities of an unequal society were inevitable, Turner tried to explain how Americans, despite their actual social inequalities, continued to believe in the idea of equality. To have a theory like this, which combined the pride of individualism *and* the cult of democracy, was a satisfying experience because it resolved the nation's inner split and made it whole.

Yet with all these blandishments, it could not have had its impact without a core of validity. Turner had a deep insight into the conditions under which the crucial American institutions were shaped. To this insight we now turn.

5. American History As Extended Genesis

America as a dream of riches has become so familiar a world image that we almost forget how hard the American environment was at its start. From the first attempted settlement of the "lost colony" at Roanoke and the privations at Jamestown and Massachusetts Bay, through the opening of the last strip of frontier, the "challenge of hard ground" has come up afresh across the larger span of America's history.

Almost every civilization has its genesis under hard conditions, and it is during this formative period when new things are happening that a people's institutions and national character take shape. Sometimes catastrophe overtakes them early, and then comes either the darkness of the end or else the catastrophe serves to bring a rebirth of creativeness. Sometimes a process of social revolution may renew the lagging energies or break the log jam of the dammed-up ones. But in most instances, after the springtime of great creativeness, a civilization settles down to live on the accumulated capital of its achievement, loses its sense of newness and power, grows rigid. It becomes the hulk of what men once dreamed it and hugs its past instead of fashioning its future. It becomes, in Eliot's phrase, an "old man in a dry season."

Although America is still a relatively young civilization, the sense of beginnings in it has been a protracted one. Viewing the life history of American civilization as a whole, it is clear that never in history has a civilization risen to world power in so short a span (even the rise of Rome took longer, and Russia goes back for its origins to the Middle Ages) and never has the larger portion of that span been so permeated by a sense of new beginnings. Even before the thin strip of Atlantic colonies had achieved their freedom and a degree of unity, American settlement had already begun to move inland and make inroads on the continental interior. Every new gain in national consciousness and in wealth and power on the part of the settled regions was paralleled by a deeper penetration into the unsettled ones and the opening of new reaches for the national imagination. From the Jamestown settlement to the present, the span of American history has been some 350 years. The conventional date for the end of the frontier as a continuous line of settlement is in the 1890s, although much land continued to be homesteaded for some time after. Thus about 300 of the 350 were years of continued genesis. During those three centuries there was never a time when somewhere in America settlements of men and women were not starting anew, wrestling with their natural environment and hewing out of the wilderness a new community, a new feeling of achievement, new profits, prosperity, and power.

This brings us back to Turner and the role of the moving frontier in keeping alive American individualism and democracy. Translate the history of the moving frontier into terms of the civilization process and it becomes the history of an extended genesis. When we think in terms of the comparative life histories of civilizations, questions come up which Turner's theory, limited as it was to the American experience (Walter Prescott Webb has extended it admirably in his *Great Frontier*), did not even raise. Toynbee, for example, propounds as a "law" of history that "geographical expansion produces social retardation." This runs headlong into the American experience. Yet one may say instead that in and of itself there is no social magic in the expansion of frontier settlement, as the history of other cultures has shown. Even Turner saw that the first result of the frontier was reduction to a more primitive condition: by diluting the intensity of the cultural experience it may actually have the retarding effect Toynbee describes.

America has not been the only civilization which retained a large, thinly settled frontier area over a long time span. It has also been true, to pick random examples, of Russia, Australia, Canada, Argentina, Brazil. It is true of any big continental stretch which has unsettled land in an expanse stretching beyond the settled population centers. Yet in none of these cases, despite some similarities that Turner noted, were the social results of frontier settlement comparable to the American. Why? What was crucially lacking in their experience and present in the American that may account for the difference?

Here Turner's analysis must be stretched. With his agrarian emphasis he tended to focus on the periphery of new settlement. Despite some later indications of his broader view after the famous first essay on the significance of the frontier, he took little account of the pattern as a whole which included the center and the lines of influence between center and periphery. Along with the ferment of a moving frontier there was the ferment of democratization and industrial development in the area of early settlement. What Russia, Australia, and the other instances of frontier settlement lacked, and the American instance had, was a major industrial and capitalist revolution taking place at the same time as the frontier settlement and linked with it, and an extension of the democratic idea linked with both.

This triple line of new development, or extended genesis, meant that American life was being transformed vertically in the original centers of settlement at the same time that it was being extended horizontally in the new areas. Thus there was a double process of dynamism in operation, the vertical and horizontal. In other words, while the march of geographical settlement was necessary to the extended genesis, it would not in itself have been adequate. To move into the wilderness with the intent of creating fresh settlements means that you refresh and keep alive whatever it is you take with you. But you must have something to take. The sense of renewal of the frontiersmen came not only from facing a natural environment with directness but from never losing contact with the sources of mechanical and governmental transformation that gave Americans their commanding control over the environment as a whole.

If the Jacksonian period is seen as a great watershed of American development, when the ferment of new energies was most evident both to Americans and to foreign observers, the triple source of the new strength is fairly clear. There was, first, the moving frontier itself. Jackson was a man of the frontier, representing its quickness of perception, freshness of experience, habit of decisive action. Second, there was the movement of the American economy, which (to parallel the moving frontier) we may call the "moving technology." The inventiveness and self-reliance that were necessary qualities on the frontier were also necessary in the Eastern towns and cities among the new "mechanics," the toolmakers, the mill and foundry managers, the businessmen.

In the third area—that of government and political ideas—the freshness of thinking and sturdiness of assertion that had shown themselves since the Founding Fathers were strengthened in the Jacksonian era. That period saw the emergence of a coalition of frontier farmers, urban workingmen, businessmen, and intellectuals who expressed the common outlook of both groups and who gave direction to their energies. George Bancroft and Orestes Brownson were New Englanders, as were Emerson, Thoreau, Alcott, and the whole Concord group, who stood aside from the Jacksonian movement and were basically Whigs. Jacksonians like Leggett, Bryant, Godwin, Greeley, Vethake, were New Yorkers and Pennsylvanians. Both groups were Easterners and formed part of the "American Renaissance" which furnished the intellectual setting for the frontier movement.

Every idea tends to move toward its limits, by cumulative force and by the extension of its inner logic. That happened to the democratic idea which moved ahead as if by some inner propulsion. Groups sprang up to work for abolitionism, prison reform, and equality for women, for trade-unionism, utopian community schemes, popular control of banking and financial power. Few of these were wholly native, and few but had their origins or parallels in Europe. Yet they serve to illustrate that along with the "moving frontier" and the "moving technology" there was something like a "moving democratic idea."

America had, in short, a major industrial and capitalist revolution and a major political and intellectual revolution alongside the revolution of frontier settlement and linked with it. American life was being transformed vertically at the same time that it was being extended horizontally, and the dynamism of each fed and was fed by the dynamism of the other. On one level Americans continued to wrestle directly with the natural environment, while on another level they contrived machines that gave them (despite the complaints of workers and intellectuals) the exhilaration of a commanding mechanical mastery over Nature. They were at once Prometheus and Dr. Faustus, and each role nourished their feeling of creativeness and their conviction of mission.

Thus, while the adherents of the Turner thesis are right to stress the fresher democratic energies of the West, there was a truer sense in which both West and East drew from the same source. For the Eastern businessman, however conservative, long retained the unquenchable *élan* of discovery; while the Western frontiersman, however progressive, never lost the Lockean sense that by mixing with his labor the domain he was hewing out of the forest he was creating a new property for himself. Somewhere the noble savage met the Alchemist. Somewhere Davy Crockett became Andrew Carnegie. And somewhere both elements were tempered by the passion of a Jackson and a Taney in subduing the power of the Bank of the United States. Where these three strains met and fused, at that point America was made, and the traits which make up its national character were roughly determined.

Under other conditions the expansion of the frontier could have taken on something like the Australian pattern—a permanent metropolis plus a permanent hinterland. But the constant growth of trade and manufacturing, the opening of new markets at home as well as abroad, the advancing state of the industrial arts, the continuing alertness both of American management and American labor—all these made certain that the hinterland was steadily absorbed by the moving industrialism, and the moving democracy went (although against great resistance and at a lagging pace) along with both.

With this clue we can understand two principal facets of the American character. Self-reliance, courage, alertness, obstinate endurance, friendliness, a democratic informality, are traits that emerged from the continuous cycles of land settlement. A sharp and shrewd aggressiveness, a willingness to take chances, an organizing capacity, a genius with machines, a sense of bigness and of power, an assumption of destiny, are traits that emerged from industrialism and the capital markets of the metropolis. The two sets of traits were fused in the national character because the two strands of development were interwoven in the crucial phases of American history. David Potter has put it well by saying that the moving frontier was one phase of the larger situation of opportunity and abundance which has marked the Americans as a "people of plenty."

6. *Tradition and the Frame of Power*

The newness of the American tradition is one of the facts that gives it unity. America is the only great nation of modern times whose history is also the history of the three shaping forces of the modern Western world—*industrialism* as a technology, *capitalism* as a way of organizing it, and *democracy* as a way of running both. The American tradition, woven from these elements, took on their dynamism.

The first English, French, and Dutch settlers brought with them the knowledge of crafts and manufactures which had come out of the early phase of the Industrial Revolution. The year in which American independence was declared—1776—was also the year of the invention of the steam engine and the publication of the most important manifesto of the spirit of capitalist enterprise, Adam Smith's *Wealth of Nations*—a fact which may stand as a symbol of the relation of all three shaping forces. The matrix of the American democratic idea lay in the span between the Cromwellian Revolution and the French Revolution, and while it suffered a sea change when it came over to American shores, it was recognizably democratic by the time the new Republic was formed. There was only a brief span in the American national life that could be termed predemocratic, preindustrial, or precapitalist. As Louis Hartz has pointed out, the American tradition included no dominating feudal regime needing to be overthrown.

One must contrast this with the history of peoples whose origins reach much further back—the English, the French, the Mediterranean, the pre-Soviet Russian. Their traditions were already well established by the time the trinity of industrialism, capitalism, and democracy came to the world stage. They had to absorb them and play down whatever elements in the trinity did not fit into their tradition. These were the conservative cultures. There is another kind of contrast between the case of America and the Communist cultures of present-day Russia, eastern Europe, China, and southeast Asia. They had to rediscover their national traditions and absorb them into their new ideologies, playing down whatever in the tradition did not jibe with the new structure of power and the new system of class relations.

America, on the other hand, has not had to play down drastically either the new forces because of its tradition or its tradition because of the new forces. As a result there has been a continuity between the elements that make up the contemporary industrial-capitalist-democratic culture. It is a continuity between the remembered national past and the living present—one that has been so organic as to be perilously deceptive, and lulls the unwary observer into the illusion that the heritage does not even exist and that America is "traditionless" as well as "historyless." The exception, of course, is the case of the South, where slavery and the tragic Civil War defeat broke the continuity of history much as feudalism and revolution did in Europe. This may explain why the South has had so tragic a sense of destructiveness and has been so conscious of its history.

But for the nation as a whole the continuity of history and tradition is one reason for the activism of Americans. They do not think of themselves—to use John Dollard's phrase—as "the passive porters of a cultural tradition." They have made their tradition as well as their culture in the same act.

One important fact must be added. America, one of the youngest

of the great civilizations of the world, is one of the oldest and most continuous of the social systems. Three and a half centuries is a short time as the span of a civilization goes, but it is a long time as the span of uninterrupted social power goes.

Of the important peoples today the French had their Revolution shortly after the Americans, but a series of catastrophes in three successive wars wiped out much of the staying power of the ruling class and brought a chronic instability of regimes. The Germans had a frustrated social revolution in 1918 and a Fascist one in 1933 for which they had to pay heavily in social chaos. After several abortive attempts, the Russians had their Communist revolution in 1917, changing the base of class power; and their subsequent leadership of the world Communist movement has made them underline the newness of their social system. The modern Chinese had one revolution in 1911 and, after a protracted civil war, a successful Communist revolution in 1948-49. India, after winning its freedom by a revolution of passive resistance, launched a mixed economy with Socialist elements; the same is true to differing degrees of Burma, Israel, Indonesia. Of the Latin-American nations, Brazil and Argentina are typical in having broken away from European rule by revolution, which in turn was followed by a series of internal revolts and military coups. Even in Britain, where the system of capitalist power has lasted longer than anywhere except America, the pressures toward a Socialist economy and society have been stronger than anything in the American experience.

Not only has there been in America an unbroken succession of national administrations without violence, but all of them—whether Federalist or Jeffersonian, Whig or Jacksonian, conservative Republican or New Deal—have stayed within roughly the same broad frame of capitalist power. In this sense one may say (perhaps with too much flipness) that the system of class power has remained unchanged from the days of Cotton Mather to those of the Cotton Exchange, from General Washington to General Eisenhower and General Motors, from Hamilton and Biddle to Alcoa and Du Pont. The revolution against England was accompanied, to be sure, by a social revolution in the sense that the feudal residues which had not been left behind in transit from Europe were wiped out. But when we speak of the American Revolution as a "social revolution," we must not forget that while it was antimercantilist and (in the sense above) antifeudal, it was not anticapitalist. It did not aim at ousting one class from power and replacing it with another. Its language carried a far-reaching revolutionary potential in the social sense too. But while it embodied the emerging social thought of its day, it was followed by a Constitution which limited the potential revolutionary majority, and which protected funded property, landed property, slave property, and business property. The frame of capitalist power was built within that scheme of thought and protection.

American history has, of course, had its major party battles, in the era of Jefferson, Jackson, Cleveland, Wilson, and Franklin Roosevelt—party battles which were notable because they also marked conflicts of class interest and shifts of class power. Yet it remains true that these battles were staged within roughly the same frame of power. Whatever the differences between Federalists and Jeffersonians, Whigs and Jacksonians, Republicans and Populists, Old Guard and New Deal, they were differences within a common frame of social structure and capitalist assumptions. Only in the Civil War was there a struggle between two economic and social systems, and the victory of one over the other. But Louis Hartz quite rightly observes that even the "great conservative reaction" of George Fitzhugh "died without impact on the mind of a nation." The liberal capitalist system of action, thought, and power remained in possession of the field.*

What is the nature of this frame of power and the sources of its tenacity? A system of individualist small enterprise has been replaced largely by corporate capitalism, the individual's freedom has been limited by Big Government and the "private governments" of Big Business and Big Labor, and a system of economic incentives and controls once useful in expanding the frontiers and exploiting the resources of a continent has had to adapt itself to meet the pace of a changing technology. Yet the hope for the career open to talents is still active in the American heart, and social mobility remains a reality in the vast middle reaches of the American class pyramid, even if at the top and bottom it continues relatively rigid.

With a civilization as with a person, the wealth and power it possesses count for less than the animating idea that possesses it. The American social system, when it was young, was filled with a great hope and an animating dream. But youth is never recapturable, and it is often indecent to protract it. A time comes when it is less important to be young than to be whole. No civilization can too long tolerate a cleavage between the professing rhetoric of its tradition and the possessive force of its frame of power.

The anthropologists point out that cultures are both fulfilling and frustrating. A functional view of any society will show that its priesthood, its system of magic, its family institution, its ways of ownership and of leadership, operate as they do because they fulfill some strong drive in those who make up the society. If you take the view of a cultural

* For a further discussion of the American social system as a system of capitalist assumptions, see Ch. V and Ch. VII.

anthropologist, you will see the other side of the functional shield: how repressive the major institutions are to the individuals in the society, damming their energies, stifling their creativeness, splitting their purposes. The fact is that cultures are bundles of conflicting and even contradictory tendencies. A living culture, however much it may strive to resolve its contradictions, retains the clashes of purpose, the overlappings, and the sense of paradox of any living and growing organism.

Nowhere is this truer than in a culture like the American. The conservatives emphasize how stable the American tradition has been, and they are right. It has been open to change through the methods of majority will checked by minority right and power. It has achieved a variety of fulfillments for the dreams and ambitions of a variety of people. It has thus channeled off the energies which, in less flexible and more impoverished systems, have led to the European type of class struggles and to radical shifts of class power.

But the spokesmen of the possessing groups forget that the American tradition was shaped as part of a revolutionary quest for the good life. Some of them want to use it now as a sedative against the fretful, sleepless night of the modern world. They are like children who use any tool or plaything as a way of expressing their anxieties, a weapon with which to subdue the recalcitrant object before them. That is why the symbols of the heritage which the conservatives stress are the due-process concept, the weak state, the checks and divisions within the governmental powers, the system of federalism which divides power between the central government and the states and thus offers loopholes for escape from controls, the fear of bureaucracy, the belittling of "politics," the boast of classlessness, the stress on "Americanism" as opposed to "foreign" influences. And that is why the values they stress are those of order, inequality, and the authority of the past, as against change, the guarantee of social minima, and the claims of the future. That is also, finally, why the figures they invoke in the American tradition are those of John Adams, Daniel Webster, and John Calhoun.

Usually this version of the tradition avoids the symbols of revolution, as though the conservative spokesmen felt that the fact of change in the world around them could be exorcised by silence about their own revolutionary past. Latterly there has been an effort to make the "free-enterprise system" the center and sum of the American tradition. This obviously seeks to capitalize on the emotional value of the symbols of freedom when invoked in the cause of power, but it forgets that free enterprise was itself the product of a revolutionary movement, and that in the era of Jackson it was one of the slogans of the liberals. What happened later in history was that "free enterprise" became the slogan of big enterprise, and the "free-enterprise economy" came to link the civil liberties tradition with the economic power of a class. Behind the symbol of these freedoms is that of the Constitution itself, which guarantees them. Thus the equation becomes "Constitution equals Freedoms equals Free-Enterprise System," and by easy stages a system of economic power becomes invested with the sanctity of the Constitution itself. In this sense the trappings of the tradition have become the shrewd ceremonial of the insecure spirit of the possessing classes.

Unlike the Europeans, Americans have never turned traditionalism into a major political and social philosophy and a party movement. In Great Britain the Tory thinkers and politicians built a great Conservative movement. But the history of the Continent has been disfigured by a peculiar amalgam of literary interpretation, religious passion, and reactionary mysticism such as one finds in clerical writers like Bonald and De Maistre, in the "integral nationalism" school of Maurras, or in the "Prussian Socialism" of Spengler, not to speak of the racist writers. These European theories sought to convert traditionalism into an intellectual system which could serve as the base for a popular political movement. Since they had to work in a milieu of sharp class consciousness they sometimes directed their appeal to the declassed intellectuals, sometimes to the insecure middle class that wanted to identify with the faded feudal values of the past, sometimes even (as with the racists) to the formless mass of the lower classes.

There have been no similar roots for a traditionalist movement in America. The closest approach to a philosophy of traditionalism in America has been in the romantic cult of the section-as-nation in Calhoun's thought and George Fitzhugh's, in the glorifying of a "natural aristocracy" and the parading of democratic disasters by antimajoritarian writers like Irving Babbitt and Paul Elmer More, and in the jealous guardianship of the property tradition in the interests of business by a series of champions from Daniel Webster through Robert A. Taft. More recently Russell Kirk and a few other writers tried to evoke a "new conservatism" from a nostalgic hankering for the values of tradition, loyalty, power, and order. Their passion fluttered the academic dovecots for a passing moment, as the Southern agrarians had done in the 1920s. In a more moderate vein, writers like Clinton Rossiter, August Heckscher, and Peter Viereck tried to chart out a very different kind of "New Conservative" traditionalism: they had made their peace with the New-Deal-as-history and with modern American society, but they put more store by the centuries of past experience than by the urgencies of the present. Yet no political movements and no theorist and political leader of the stature of Calhoun emerged to convert these varied fumblings into something meaningful and powerful.

It is worth noting that when American traditionalists seek an intellectual authority on which to build, many of them turn to Burke, Disraeli, and Winston Churchill, attracted by the tradition of an aristocracy which had cohesion and perspective and kept itself free of contact with the parvenu mercantile class. A few are now willing to invoke as patron saints the spokesmen of American business and property—John Adams and Marshall, Hamilton and Webster, Grant and Choate and Mark Hanna, William Graham Sumner and Andrew Carnegie, J. P. Morgan, John D. Rockefeller, and Elihu Root. In the British case there were at least two ordered elites—the Lords Spiritual who were invested with spiritual sanctions in a state-supported Church, and the Lords Temporal who were a landed aristocracy with inherited status—neither of which the American case possesses. Nor does America possess the aristocratic arbiters of the Continent who dictated conduct and morals for the rest of the population. Thus in the anxious quest for some cementing force for a Good Society, the American traditionalists find themselves tempted to go outside the American tradition.

Another trouble with the chronic invokers of the conservative American tradition is that there is a deep split between the intellectuals of the group who shape the conservative philosophies and the political leaders who shape the conservative policies. With leaders like Theodore Roosevelt and Wendell Willkie the conservative intellectuals found common ground, as they did with judges like Charles Evans Hughes and administrators like Frederick Stimson. But the kind of teamplay the liberal intellectuals achieved with the politicians under Roosevelt's New Deal and Truman's Fair Deal, or the sympathy the "eggheads" found with Adlai Stevenson and with the large number of liberal Democratic Senators, is one for which the conservative intellectuals hanker fruitlessly. Disdaining the optimism, the cult of progress, the reliance on man's rationality, and the easy clichés of many of the liberals, and recoiling from the primitivism of the new radical Right (a more powerful movement than that of the "new conservatives") they find themselves rootless and homeless.

They feel thus also because they have no major tradition in American history to fall back upon. The doctrine of elites chosen by Divine Right to rule others, the pessimist doctrines of human sin and depravity, the fear of rapid change, the image of a hierarchical society in which each man knows and holds to the privileges and duties that attach to his place—these represent a minor, not a major, strain in the American tradition. The main current of the tradition, including even some of the Federalist and Whig figures as well as Jeffersonian, Jacksonian, and New Deal, is Lockean, optimist, libertarian, antihierarchical, fluid, dynamic.

There can be no better proof of this than a hard look at the strongest oligarchy America has had—that of the business and managerial group. I call it an oligarchy rather than an aristocracy, as De Tocqueville did, because birth and inheritance play less of a role in it than energy and resourcefulness. "Fame and success," said Samuel E. Morison, "await one who will make a fresh distillation of our entire history with the conservative tradition acting as a leaven." He was calling, in short, for someone who would take the Beards' *Rise of American Civilization* and turn it upside down, or who would follow up on the cry of Henry Cabot Lodge and Albert Beveridge that "the Democrats are always wrong."

Someday some young conservative historian will perhaps do it. Or, even better, he may follow the suggestion of Elisha Douglas that the Puritan tradition led to a "secularized Puritanism" which found expression in the tradition of stewardship by an elite of wisdom, virtue, and education. If he emphasizes the later business conservatism—that of acquisition rather than values—he will find that the tradition of American business is drastically different from the aristocracies and oligarchies of Europe: that it is based on Locke's conception both of property and of civil government, that it is buoyantly optimistic, that it out-liberals the liberals in its belief in progress, that its passion is not for order but for production and profit records, that it cares less for hierarchy than for power, that it is always in revolution because it is always being churned up in its goals and methods by technological changes which in large measure it begets, that its morality rarely rises above the moral standards of the rest of the society, that its creed is not integrity but acquisitiveness, not moderation but go-gettism and dynamism.

In any event it would be healthy for American conservatives to reappraise the elements in the American tradition that attract them most, including a fresh look at the leadership qualities and administrative ability of George Washington, the brilliance of John Adams and John Randolph, the nation-building genius of Hamilton and Marshall, the innate moderation of Lincoln, and even (as Richard Hofstadter points out) the conservative core in men like Theodore Roosevelt and Woodrow Wilson. It would be productive for them to follow the lead of historians like Nevins and Hacker and make an effort to refurbish the reputations of the "Robber Barons"* and to see the big business corporation as one of the organic units of American history. They would find that there are an endless number of points at which the major liberal and minor conservative strands in the American tradition converge and are interwoven, that the American welfare corporation offers them a

* For a discussion of the Nevins thesis on business history, see Ch. V, Sec. 2, "The Rise and Decline of the Titan."

better base to build on than the European aristocracies, that the best products of the American aristocracy from Jefferson to Franklin Roosevelt to Adlai Stevenson and Averell Harriman have found their self-expression in leading mass progressive movements, and that the ideas of dynamism and of welfare (the welfare corporation, welfare trade-union, welfare state) are common elements that run through American history, whether viewed by conservatives or liberals.*

Americans will not respond to a stick-in-the-mud creed of traditionalism that cherishes the past as a way of shutting out the facts and tasks of the present. The American spirit is inclusive rather than exclusive, optimistic rather than fear-ridden, dynamic rather than obsessed with order and hierarchy.

7. *American Dynamism*

THUS THE BROADEST and most inclusive approach to the American tradition would put the emphasis on its dynamism. This makes the tradition something other than a thin apologia for a "democratic totalitarianism" that would break with history, or an effort to cover oligarchical power with the trappings of the American past. American dynamism has been gradualist, continuous, persistent. It has always transcended the past in the process of incorporating it. As Nietzsche put it: "The verdict of the past is always an oracle: only as architects of the future, as knowers of the present, will you understand it." American history vindicates this insight into the nature of a dynamic civilization.

This dynamism cannot be chastely selective, with its elements chosen or rejected on the basis of class outlook and political belief. Some seek the dynamism of America only in the history of the democratic idea, others only in the history of American property and capitalism. Some seek it only on the farm or frontier, or only in the factory, only at the grass roots or only in the city, only in the quest for profits or only in the crusade against the profit system, only in American world leadership or only in the struggles on the domestic front. Some seek it only in literature and art and the works of the American elite mind, and others only in popular culture.

The fact is that the American experience has operated in every area. There has been the dynamism of the pioneer and the mechanic, the independent farmer and the trade-union worker; of the toolmaker, the inventor, the financier. There has been the dynamism of the "company men"—the managers, the factory organizers, the salesmen who have

* See also the treatment of conservatism, radicalism. and liberalism in Ch. X, Sec. 2, "American Thought: the Angle of Vision."

made the irrepressible practical imagination of Americans world-famous. There has been the dynamism of the engineering mind, whether in technology or in the "social engineering" of law or public health, social work or social legislation. There has been the dynamism of the pamphleteer, the political leader, the intellectual who saw with clarity and wrote with courage, the government administrator who worked on blueprints for river-valley development and the charting of new patterns for community life. There has been the dynamism of the men of business power whose resourcefulness and single-mindedness gave them economic mastery in a political democracy; and there has been also the dynamism of the insurgent movements of mass democracy, the successive and irresistible pulsations of a democratic will that has challenged the oligarchs and set limits to their power.

There is an often quoted passage in the letter Walt Whitman sent to Emerson with *Leaves of Grass:* "Master, I am a man who has perfect faith. Master, we have not come through centuries, caste, heroisms, fables, to halt in this land today." One could not find a better summary of American dynamism.

What crucial elements in the American experience gave it this quality? There was the fact of a fresh start, with rich resources, by men who carried with them a passion for freedom and an aversion to authoritarianism. There was the vast expanse of a continent, lending a largeness of outlook to those who lived on it. There was the richness of racial and ethnic mixture which is part of a larger pluralism in American life—a pluralism not only of stock but of regional environments, of Federal political units, of economic forms, and of religious sects. There was a system of opportunity that gave scope to the energies of its young people and managed tolerably to give work its opportunity, aspiration its outlet, talent its stimulus, and ability its reward. There was an optimistic view of American prospects and a tough concreteness of outlook that judged ideas and values by their results. There was, finally, the idea of equality which, in spite of economic obstructions, educational discriminations, and the distorting hatreds of racism, was kept alive as the ruling passion of American life.

These—the expanse of space, the mixture of race, the pluralism of region and religion, the fresh start, the release of energies, the access to opportunity, the optimism and pragmatism of a society in motion, the passion for equality—were the crucial shaping forces of the American heritage.

Throughout American history new forces have been at work transforming the specific shapes the heritage has taken. One can trace four periods which were the seedbeds of what is most viable in the American tradition.

The first was the period of revolution and consolidation, from the 1770s through 1800, when the American people went beyond discontent to revolution and beyond revolution to national unity. The second was the period of the 1830s and 1840s, when a frontier exuberance combined with a developing industrialism, an emerging workers' movement, a full consciousness of nationality, a radical democratic impulse, and a literary Renaissance to produce the classic ("Jacksonian") phase of a democracy's early strength. The third was the period roughly from 1890 to 1910, when capitalist industrialism reached its high point before it became a corporate bureaucracy, when the great waves of immigration brought new energies to American shores, when rural ways of thought were merged with new urban ways of life to produce the characteristic American middle-class amalgam, when the sweep of Populism set new sights for Americans and the cry for "reform" and "social justice" renewed the equalitarian impulse.

The fourth is the contemporary period of the "Big Change" in American society which concerns us in this study, starting with the New Deal in 1933 and continuing through the turbulent years of the war and the postwar period. This was a quarter century during which Americans transformed their family structure, population growth, suburbs, energy resources, mechanization, corporations, trade-unions, class structure, and mass media almost beyond recognition. It was the period of sprouting babies and autos, of atomic energy for war and peace, of the automatic factory, of the new middle classes, of crowded universities, of TV elections, of stock-market boom and high taxes and skyrocketing incomes which everyone lived beyond. It was also a period when Americans discovered that they could surmount the sharpest economic crises and build a viable economy regardless of the labels of "socialist" or "capitalist," and that their democratic destiny could be fulfilled only in a world framework.

This does not mean that the elements of the earlier tradition were wholly left behind. Perhaps because of their English heritage, perhaps because Americans learned through everyday experience the meaning of St. Paul's injunction, "Prove all things and hold fast to that which is good," their dynamism has been a gradualist one. Individualism—the most vaunted and celebrated of American attitudes—no longer exists in its classic economic form, but the individual's welfare remains for most the test of social striving: Americans understand that while the social means must be collective the end product must be the fulfillment of the individual life. The same sort of change, to take another example has taken place in traditional antistatism: the idea of a weak state was necessarily replaced by one that can govern in a turbulent world, but Americans retain their suspicion of concentrated power, whether in government, corporation, or trade-union. Though they know power must be there to be exercised, they insist on administering it wherever possible within a frame of safeguards and within an autonomous unit.

When I make dynamism so central in American tradition I am aware that it is a concept which carries its dangers. Walter P. Webb has traced the origins of modern Western dynamism to the boom effects of the opening of the New World frontiers upon the "metropolis" of the settled areas. The eighteenth and nineteenth centuries were the centuries of the Great Hope in the Western world, when progress was taken for granted, anything was possible, and nothing was excluded from human goals. In the end this *élan* led in Europe and Asia to the totalitarian view that nothing was excluded from human means either. History became, in Hitler's terms, "the art of the impossible"—a phrase which turned out to include the techniques of genocide. Recoiling from these prospects, American thought has recently tended toward the pessimist view of human nature expressed by Reinhold Niebuhr. As sensitive a political thinker as Walter Lippmann, who had once flirted with Socialism and called for "mastery" rather than "drift," now took over the Oriental conception of society as governed by a set of moral imperatives which were the "mandate of Heaven."

However persuasive these anxieties, they did not express the energies of the American spirit, which remained generally dynamic. True, there have been stretches, especially during depressions or in periods of danger for internal freedom, when large numbers of Americans were assailed by doubts about the reality of the America they had believed in. Yet even in crisis or stagnation most Americans persisted in their image of America as an unfinished country in which history was the art of the possible, but in which the possible, by experience, seemed to stretch farther than anywhere else. That is why they have continued —rightly or wrongly—to see their own country as a model which other peoples are bound in the end to follow.

Since the beginning there have been two crucial images in the American mind. One is that of the self-reliant craftsman, whether pioneer, farmer, or mechanic—the man who could make something of the American resources, apply his strength and skill to Nature's abundance, fashion new tools and machines, imagine and carry through new constructions. Without taking himself overseriously, the American has generally regarded the great engineering, business, and governmental tasks as jobs to be done, agenda for the craftsman.

The second has been an image from the American environment: that of a vast continent to be discovered, explored, cleared, built up, populated, energized; which has not excluded the image of a continent to be rifled, despoiled, much of it wasted, for there has been an enormous margin of waste. Scott Fitzgerald has called this continental image "the last and greatest of all human dreams; for a transitory enchanted moment man must have held his breath in the presence of this continent, compelled into an aesthetic contemplation he neither understood nor desired, face to face for the last time in history with something commensurate to his capacity for wonder."

But not, I think, for the last time. Part of the American heritage is the spirit that hates a cribbed confinement. In a world whose dimensions have shrunk so that the urgencies of possible breakdown and world suicide have come closing in like the walls in "The Pit and the Pendulum," the American will not tolerate the fate of being boxed in, like a trapped rat. He will somehow break free, even if the new independence he must win is an independence from vested power groups within and the threat of world anarchy without, even if the new federalism he must help construct is that of an expanse of diverse social systems held within the frame of an open world society.*

* For the further development of this theme, see Ch. XII, Sec. 3, "National Interest and an Open World."

CHAPTER II

The Idea of American Civilization

IN WHICH, after having looked at the meaning of American history, we take a look at the central idea of the book—the idea that America is best seen as a total civilization pattern—and grapple with some of the difficulties involved in it. In the process the reader is taken on some excursions to explore the terrain of cultural anthropology, the newer psychologies, and the philosophy of history, seeking clues to the "Figure in the Carpet." We pay our respects to the condescensions of Spengler and Toynbee, among others ("Is America a Civilization?") and try to draw a portrait—the portrait of the American as the "Archetypal Man of the West" who has focused the characteristic energies of the modern world. We review what the leading foreign and American commentators have done in trying to isolate what gives America whatever distinctiveness it has ("American Exceptionalism"), and end by pointing out that there is no single key to the "American spirit" or the "American character," but a pattern of polar and often conflicting impulses ("Single Key—or Polar Pattern?").

The reader is warned that the going is hard here and the ground treacherous. He may want to move rapidly and lightly over it and perhaps return to it after he has read Chapter IX, "Character and Society," or at the end of the book.

CHAPTER II

The Idea of American Civilization

1. Figure in the Carpet

SOME of my readers, reflecting on the title I have given this book, may ask why I choose to call America a civilization, and whether Americans or any other highly technological people are in reality "civilized." This may be prompted by the prevailing view that in a world which may run amuck with nuclear weapons man has himself become a prehistoric monster scuttling across the floor of primitive seas, and his civilization a grim kind of joke.

The trouble with the term *civilization* is that it has been badly mauled and its meaning twisted. Sometimes it is used to mean that a particular society is urbane and mature, relatively free of the irrational Serpent in the rational Garden of Eden. In that sense there has never been a truly civilized people except in the literature of the imaginary voyages and the Utopian romances. There is a second sense in which politicians and editorial writers use the term as a "we or they" bludgeon against the enemy, whether in war or cold war. We have so often heard that "civilization is at stake" in the outcome of some struggle, martial or diplomatic, that we may well wish the wretched term disposed of forever. This is how Mark Twain felt about Western civilization at the time of the Boer War, when he said, "My idea of our civilization is that it is a shabby poor thing and full of cruelties, vanities, arrogancies, meannesses, and hypocrisies. As for the word, I hate the sound of it, for it conveys a lie; and as for the thing itself, I wish it was in Hell, where it belongs." But he hastens to add: *"Provided* we could get something better in the place of it. . . . Poor as it is it is better than real savagery." These inner tortures of Mark Twain, so much like the splits in intellectuals today, are further evidence that *civilization* as a concept must be extricated from emotional distortions and used objectively.

America as a democracy has had its impact on the world, and from Alexis de Tocqueville to Harold Laski most of the foreign observers have written about it from that angle. But while democracy is still America's most important idea and ideal, it is no longer—as it was in De Tocqueville's time or even in Bryce's—a novelty to be explained to the world or an experiment whose implications need to be spelled out. We must shift the focus of study from the master idea of democracy to a more inclusive and meaningful one. Anyone using democracy as the be-all and end-all of America, as the final test of everything in the culture, is bound to emerge (as Laski did in *The American Democracy*) with an irretrievable fault line between the rhetoric of democracy and the actualities of American life. We tend to forget that, by the world at large, America is being assessed not just as a democracy but in its total impact as a civilization.

Thus one can begin to shift the focus of American analysis from democracy only, from capitalism only, from a standardized and materialist machine civilization only, from popular culture only, or from foreign policy only, to the total American civilization pattern.

Fortunately the social sciences have reached the stage where such a shift of focus has become possible. We have moved beyond both political man and economic man, and beyond both the political and economic segments of the culture. Just as the new approaches to psychology and philosophy are helping us study the total person, so anthropology and social theory in its broadest sense are helping us understand the total culture, and the studies "on the growing edge" of the social sciences are focusing on the relation of culture and personality. Much of the meaningful recent work has been done on this "edge"—on the borders between the established disciplines, or by people using the techniques of several of them who have contributed major insights to make the study of the whole American civilization pattern possible.

The first is the culture concept, largely derived from the anthropologists who discovered that every people, no matter how primitive, had an organic culture. What they found was that a primitive people had its literature, even if only a body of folklore; had its science, even if only a system of magic; had its religion, even if only the worship and propitiation of idols; had its moral and legal system, even if only a set of tribal customs and sanctions. By observing the results of the contact of "higher" and "lower" cultures, our generation has learned what happens when a primitive people is "helped" or "uplifted" by one of the imperial peoples. The effect of such culture contacts on the American Indians or on the South Sea peoples is well known in Western literature. But its full meaning was not clear until the French sociologist Durkheim developed the concept of "anomie"—the collapse of traditional norms and values in a culture or a segment of it; and until anthropologists like Malinowski and Radcliffe-Brown developed a "functional" approach to the traits of primitive cultures. What emerged from their work, and especially from that of Ruth Benedict and

Margaret Mead, was the key idea that cultures are organic patterns to be treated as living wholes. This does not mean that such practices as child sacrifice or the disfigurement of women are justified by any function they may perform after they have been pushed beyond the point of value to the culture. But it does mean that institutions cannot be lifted out and displaced or replaced without jolting the rest, and must be set in the perspective of the whole culture before their meaning can be understood.

It only needed a reverse twist to turn this idea of the organic primitive culture back again to the contemporary nonprimitive ones. The insights that the anthropologists gained in studying the Eskimos, Bantu, or Melanesians illumined American and European societies too. The "anthropology of modern life" involved a fresh look at contemporary cultures as organic patterns, each with unique and characteristic features, yet each using certain social methods and fulfilling certain life purposes common to all human societies. The recent "cross-cultural" studies have sought to find common denominators between cultures, but the deeper truth is the wholeness of each culture in itself, primitive and modern alike.

Inevitably modern psychiatry got into the picture, to furnish the second major insight, and theorists argued hotly about the relative merits of the "psychological" and the "cultural" approaches. But the search for the roots of personality disturbances was bound to lead beyond the individual life history to the culture as a whole. Students and practitioners alike found that they could not understand the total person without setting him in the total culture and seeing the relation of his needs and burdens to the common drives and purposes within the culture. This search for the conditions of individual mental health led logically to a quest for the roots of cultural unhealth and dislocation. In the area of child-raising and the dislocations of family life, in the persistent outcroppings of juvenile delinquency, in the study of sexual behavior, of religion, and of economic competition, we have not only learned things about the social conditioning of the individual's inner life but indirectly about the culture as a whole.

The historians too—especially those who are philosophers of history—have provided the third major insight through their study of whole civilizations and of their rhythms of growth and decline. Arnold Toynbee studied "societies" or "civilizations" with certain tidal uniformities of rise and decay. His predecessor, Oswald Spengler, had seen the Egyptian, classical, Chinese, and Western societies in semibiological terms, tracing their rise and fall as one might trace the life history of plants. Both of them had at least one truth by the tail: the cultures men live in are not filing cases or collections of bits and pieces but organic wholes to be studied as such in the fluctuations of their energies and fortunes, in their actions and passions, their norms, institutions, striving, failure and achievement. The enduring work of these philosophers of history may prove to lie less in their discovery of any "laws" of history than in their dogged assumption that civilizations like western Europe, Russia, Islam, India, China, America, had a life to live and a death to endure, each with a heart and will and personality of its own. The philosophers of history may thus be seen as poets trying to find ways to present through symbols the inner-civilization style of historical peoples.

But no civilization pattern can be grasped as a whole unless the figure-in-the-carpet is somehow traced. The philosopher tries to do it by uncovering basic symbolic ways of life. Nietzsche, for example, used his studies in the origins of Greek tragedy to develop the idea of the Dionysian and Apollonian civilization styles. Spengler, who learned as much from Nietzsche as he did from Goethe, took the Faustus symbol as the key to modern Western man. Toynbee, who learned from both as also from Jung and the theologians, saw the figure-in-the-carpet as embodying the racial and cultural unconscious and therefore the whole buried history of social and emotional experience. Less concerned than Spengler with assigning a principle and name to each of the great civilizations, Toynbee looked for recurring patterns of behavior in all of them which would uncover the persistent riddle of rise and fall—and he emerged mainly with a bundle of poetic and religious insights.

2. *Is America a Civilization?*

WHERE DOES AMERICA fit into this picture? Almost without exception the great theories of history find no room for any concept of America as a civilization in its own right.

Since Spengler's purpose was to show the West on the downward arc of the life-history curve, he placed the West of his own day at a point on the arc parallel to where the Roman world was in the days of the shattering Imperial wars. In both cases (as Spengler saw it) the springtime creativeness of the folk-mind had dried up, the roots and traditions of the land had been replaced by the rootlessness of "megalopolis," the early class system of aristocracy, clergy, and peasants had been pushed aside first by a middle class with its money materialism and then by a proletariat, and the world struggle had set the stage for the emergence of a world empire under a succession of Caesars.

Given this scheme, one might expect Spengler to have been struck by its terrifying relevance to the case of America, yet he himself hesitated to make it explicit. His American disciples (see E. F. Dakin, *Today and History*) went the whole way, seeing America as the only possible Rome of today, fated to produce its Caesars and to thrust at a world imperium. But in Spengler's thinking the role of Rome was to be played by the Germans. Writing between World Wars I and II, he was still unable to see America as much more than a truncated morphological specimen that didn't quite fit into his theory of the rhythms of culture and civilization. America for Spengler was a derivative civilization—only an offshoot, perhaps an excrescence, of the West.

Toynbee too made summary shrift of America as a civilization. In his bold image of the "cliff-hangers," to describe man's painful pilgrimage through six thousand years of human history, he lists only five civilizations (out of nineteen or twenty-one) as still active—the Western, orthodox Christian, Islamic, Hindu, and Far Eastern civilizations. Since his units were broadly delimited by religion, geography, technology, he included in Western civilization the world shaped at once by Roman and Protestant Christianity and by the techniques of modern industrialism. His discussions of America are of a nation-state on the margin of this civilization, an arid late-comer in the history of Western Christian industrial society—affected with all the latter-day scars and curses of that society without many discernible graces to offset them.

In taking issue with Spengler and Toynbee, I am not arguing for a chauvinist view of America as the source and center of Western civilization. But it is worth asking whether we must deal with America always as a fragment of a larger civilization unit whose creative center is assigned elsewhere. It is unfair even to Europe to make something called the "West" the great isolable unit: for as the initiative in technology and in economic and military power shifts steadily across the Atlantic, there is danger of Europe's being dismissed as only a tributary of American civilization. Malraux rightly argues for the concept of "European man," although he recognizes the ties of Europe with America; similarly, recognizing the ties of America with Europe, one can argue for America as a civilization.

For good or ill, America is what it is—a culture in its own right, with many characteristic lines of power and meaning of its own, ranking with Greece and Rome as one of the great distinctive civilizations of history.

Actually the American historians have been working in practice on a premise which the social thinkers were unwilling to admit in theory. Charles and Mary Beard, in their classic history *The Rise of American Civilization,* used the term "civilization" quite deliberately for the whole emerging pattern of thought, action, and aspiration. As they wrote later, "No idea, such as democracy, liberty, or the American way of life, expresses the American spirit so coherently, comprehensively, or systematically as does the idea of civilization."

I must pause here for a note on the meaning of several crucial terms as I shall be using them. I use the idea of American civilization as the master theme of this book instead of "democracy" (De Tocqueville, Laski) or "commonwealth" (Bryce), which are too narrowly political; or "character" (Gorer, Riesman), which refers too directly to personality structure. There remain the broad terms, "culture" and "society," which have a body of common meaning with "civilization." Spengler called the earlier seasonal phases of germination and bloom "culture," and the season of dry winter-hardening "civilization"; but that was his own peculiar scheme. Some American social thinkers use "civilization" for the total institutional *means* whereby a people seeks to achieve the *ends* which are implied in "culture." This is suggestive, yet means and ends, institutions and values, frame and content, are always connected in a two-way relation: it is difficult to say that the courthouse in which a marriage is licensed or a criminal tried is part of American civilization, but that the marriage beliefs or the legal system belong to American culture.

America is at once *culture* and *civilization,* and *society* as well. The terms refer to different aspects of the same whole rather than to different segments of it. "Culture" has been used by anthropologists since E. B. Tylor's famous definition of it: "that complex whole which includes knowledge, belief, art, morals, law, custom, and any other capabilities and habits acquired by man as a member of society." More recently, in the sense defined by Kluckhohn and Kelly as "a historically derived system of explicit and implicit designs for living which tend to be shared by all or specially designated members of a group," it has become the key term of the social sciences. I use it to mean the *matrix* of American living, the stuff of life that is transmitted, learned, and relearned, with the stress on the "designs for living"—the norms and beliefs and all the curious and twisted shapes they take. I use "society" to put the emphasis elsewhere: on the common structure of American living, on the group units within which it clusters (family, club, gang, neighborhood, town, suburb, army, school, church), and on the relations between them. Thus "society" refers to the total group and institutional framework, and the processes of living together and being knit together within it as *socii* or members of the same commonalty.

I use "civilization" as my broadest concept. When a culture—which is the set of blueprints for a society—has grown highly complex and has cut a wide swath in history and in the minds of men, one looks for a term more highly charged with the overtones of these meanings

"Civilization" is such a term. One thinks of the civilizations of Greece and Rome, of China and Britain, of the Aztec-Mayan civilization, of India, of Renaissance Italy, of Spain and France, of Russia and America. They differ from the archaic cultures of, let us say, the Bushmen or Pygmies or the Andaman Islanders because each of them at some phase of its history has been a great going concern leaving a deep imprint on the human consciousness, a scar on men's minds. They had a way of life and a world view that have become deeply part of human experience.

I believe this to be true of America. It is likely that historians will look back on American life and see it—with its truths and errors, its callownesses and obsessions and insights, its childishness and its power—as one of the memorable civilizations of history. Whoever wants to convey this sense of the total pattern and total impact in canvassing the actions and strivings and passions of America may well fall back on the idea of American civilization.

3. *Archetypal Man of the West*

COMMENTATORS ON AMERICAN TRAITS delight in quoting De Crèvecoeur's classic remark that "the American is a new man who acts on new principles." One should add that while the American was a *novus homo* when De Crèvecoeur wrote his *Letters from an American Farmer* toward the end of the eighteenth century, he is no longer so in the mid-twentieth. He is no longer an experiment: he has been proved a success, by every standard of wealth, glitter, prestige, freedom, and power. Wherever history pours fresh molten metal, in industrial achievement, living standards, and political freedom, inevitably it makes him at least in part the mold. The American has become the "New World man"—the archetypal man of the West.

For an American to write thus may seem too boastful, yet I try to write it as if I were not American but a detached observer noting a new phenomenon. Americans are not loved in the world today, although they deeply desire affection. In the countries of color there is a good deal of suspicion of them, and even some hatred. In the older civilizations of Europe there is a kind of patronizing contempt which passes for anti-Americanism. Throughout the world there is a fear of the current American stress on arms and money. Yet it remains true that the principal imperialism the American exercises is the imperialism of attraction. If he is not admired, he is envied; and even his enemies and rivals pay him the homage of imitation. People throughout the world turn almost as by a tropism to the American image. To be American is no longer to be only a nationality. It has become, along with Communism and in rivalry with it, a key pattern of action and values.

So summary a conquest of the world's imagination, never before achieved without arms and colonization, is proof of an inner harmony between America and the modern spirit. It is because of this harmony that America has acted as a suction force, drawing from everywhere people attuned to its basic modes of life. The migration to America, from the start, of capital and of human labor and talent, was followed by the migration from America of capital, talent, economic and military strength. Both migrations, to and from America, have multiplied its influence. Having absorbed the world's strength to form its own, America has been fusing its own strength with the world's.

There has been from the start a marriage of true minds between the American and the type-man of the modern era, the New World man. To the question, wonderfully put in 1782 by De Crèvecoeur in his *American Farmer,* "What then is the American, this new man?" De Tocqueville sought an answer on his visit in the 1830s. The greatness of his book lay at least partly in its portrayal of a young civilization in which incipient European forces could reach their climactic form. In America the main trends of tendency that were dammed up in Europe itself were to find expression. As Robert Payne has put it, "America is Europe with all the walls down." Although I have insisted that America is a definable civilization in itself, it first emerged as an offshoot from the larger entity of the West which was seeking a New World form. The American is thus the concentrated embodiment of Western man, more sharply delineated, developed under more urgent conditions, but with most of the essential traits present.

Consider some of these traits. I am trying here to describe, not the American alone, but a type which has cropped up all over Europe as well since the Reformation and the rise of science.*

He is mobile, restless. He has largely broken with status and moves more freely than Old World man moved up and down the ladder of wealth and class rank, as he moved over large areas, conquering space. He rifles the sciences as he opens up the continents, quenchless in his thirst for experience. He is this-worldly and not otherworldly, with a

* I have in mind, although I have not strictly followed, some of the delineations of modern Western man by Mumford, Huizinga, Toynbee, Ortega y Gasset, Alfonso Reyes. The best recent treatment is in Lewis Mumford, *The Transformations of Man* (1956), appearing after this book was finished. It gives remarkable portraits of Old World Man, New World Man, and the monstrous "Post-Historic Man" which is a projection of tendencies present in both American and Russian civilization. I deal with these tendencies, and with both the portent and promise of the future in Ch. XII, "America As a World Power," especially Sec. 7, "The Destiny of a Civilization."

sharp sense of time and its uses: the objects of his ambition are secular rather than sacred. Accustomed to thinking in terms of the attainable, he is optimistic, with a belief in progress and a respect for technical skills and material success. He is *homo faber,* stamping his imprint on products and on machines that make products and on machines that run machines, and increasingly in the same spirit on art and ideas. He believes in whatever can be touched, grasped, measured. He is a technical man, whose absorption is not with *to what good* but with *how.* He is non-ascetic, with a taste for comfort and a belief that the means, if not the goal, of life are found in a higher living standard.

He is *l'homme moyen sensuel,* not too finicky in his sexual life about caste or class lines or about rigid standards of virtue. Hungering for a sense of personal worth, he is torn between the materialisms he can achieve and the feeling of wholeness which eludes him. He has a disquieting sense that the old gods too have eluded him and wonders when the new ones will arrive. Yet, unlike men of previous ages, it is not salvation he is after, nor virtue, nor saintliness, nor beauty, nor status. He is an amoral man of energy, mastery, and power. Above all else, he is a man for whom the walls have been broken down. He is the double figure in Marlowe, of Tamerlane and Dr. Faustus, the one sweeping like a footloose barbarian across the plains to overleap the barriers of earlier civilizations, the other breaking the taboos against knowledge and experience, even at the cost of his soul.

For this modern man the world has not yet become one world, and as the contemporary tensions attest, some time will elapse before it does. Yet what is likely to count in this direction is less the outlook of the diplomats than of the new geographers who complete the work of the cartographers of the Renaissance. Being technical men, they turn the globe around every possible way, but basically theirs is the airman's view for whom political boundaries are minor, and the heavens arch over them to be pierced and the earth stretches out to be engirded by flight. For the airman, racial boundaries do not exist either: what he sees from the air is not the color of men but how well the fields are laid out and irrigated and cultivated, what has been done in uncovering and using Nature's resources, what chimneys and spires are the witnesses of industry and culture, what clusters of community life there are in villages, cities, metropolitan areas. This was the glimpse that Wendell Willkie had—that despite divergences of economic systems, of race and color and language and social structure, the world is compassable, interdependent, organic.

Thus the great themes of the Renaissance and Reformation are fulfilled in the American as the archetypal modern man—the discovery of new areas, the charting of the skies, the lure of power, the realization of self in works, the magic of science, the consciousness of the individual, the sense of the unity of history. These are the themes that have left their mark on modern man. Perceiving this, Wyndham Lewis said of America that "the logic of the geographical position and history of the U.S. leads . . . to the ultimate formation of a society that will not be as other societies, but an epitome of all societies." He had in mind specifically the ethnic pluralism and democratic inclusiveness of America which hold the world in microcosm. It is this trans-national character of American society which, despite the surviving American tribalisms, makes it congruous with the strivings of other peoples. The same applies to the structure of the American personality, which is mobile, ethnically diverse, energy-charged, amoral, optimistic, genial, technic-minded, power-oriented. The question is not whether these traits are admirable or lovable but whether they polarized the energies of much of the world—as they do.

4. American Exceptionalism

THE PORTRAIT OF American—and New World—man I have just drawn is not meant to be an idealized one. It has shadows as well as lights. And it poses a riddle of both logic and history: logically, how we can speak of the American as the "archetypal" man of the modern world and at the same time assert that American civilization is a pattern within itself, whole and unique; historically, how America has developed out of the common conditions of the modern world, yet developed with such an acceleration of energy and power; and whether the future arc of its development is likely to recapitulate the course of experience of European and Asiatic civilizations.

I do not underestimate the difficulties of this riddle. That is why I am little inclined to see America within any of the rather grandiose schemes of historical determinism, whose real value is to suggest lines of study and not to close them. The seduction of historical parallels should not lure us away from studying America as a civilization pattern in itself—its tensions, its lines of development, its weaknesses and strengths. The learning of Vico and Hegel, of Marx, of Spengler and Toynbee, of Sorokin, would still leave unexplained the unlikely genesis of America, its rapid rise to power, the contrast of its outer image and its inner qualities, its materialism and idealism, its isolationism and leadership role. Whether such a civilization will survive or is doomed will depend less on grand historical "laws" than upon how Americans grapple with their problems and use their characteristic resources and energies.

If I do not subscribe to the cry of "America is doomed," neither am I pleading for the distorted version of "American exceptionalism" which has been the pious theme of spread-eagle theorists seeking to depict America as immune from the forces of history and the laws of life. This version of exceptionalism is easily used as an idea weapon in the anti-democratic struggle, as Schlesinger shows in citing the attack on the efforts to organize trade-unions in the Jacksonian period. Ever since then the cry that "America is different" has been an unfailing answer to any challenge that might disturb the structure of existing power, and the carriers of the challenge have been regarded as "un-American," "alien," and therefore "subversive."

But these distortions should not blind us to the valid elements in the theory of exceptionalism. The fact is that while American civilization is not immune to the surging beat of world forces, it has developed its own characteristic institutions, traits, and social conditions within the larger frame. America represents, as I have stressed above, the naked embodiment of the most dynamic elements of modern Western history. What this implies is that exceptionalism *includes* an acceptance of the European ties and does not reject them. The idea of American exceptionalism and the idea of American integration into the broader Western pattern are not mutually exclusive but are polar facets of the same field of energy. When you speak of American uniqueness, you must speak also in the same framework about the European diversity. It is in this sense of what is *characteristically American* that I use the idea of exceptionalism.

A rapid listing of some of the outstanding books on America will show that almost every commentator has fixed on some unique elements in it. De Tocqueville saw the whole of American life as a new form of society which he called *democracy*. Charles Dickens had never seen anything to equal American money-mad materialism. Bryce was impressed with the uniqueness of the Federal system and the party system. Whitman, castigating American corruption, nevertheless glimpsed democratic vistas beyond them more stirring than ever before in history. Henry and Brooks Adams saw the degradation of the democratic dogma stretched further in America than anywhere else in the democratic world. Thorstein Veblen, who felt that American capitalism had been carried to a unique degree of power, concentration, and finesse, did a series of studies in absentee ownership showing how business enterprise in modern times had taken characteristic forms in the case of America—developing such home-grown products as the country town, the independent farmer, the captain of industry, the technology of physics and chemistry.

Herbert Croly found a peculiar "promise" in American life he found nowhere else. Waldo Frank, in his "rediscovery" of America, found equally a characteristically excessive power and excessive childishness in the American mind. D. H. Lawrence found in "classical" American literature a mixture of the primitive and the bourgeois, in the clash of which he located the characteristic split in the American soul. H. L. Mencken, studying the one feature of American life which might have been expected to follow the pattern of its English parent—its speech—found elements of originality in it so marked as to make it a separate American language. André Siegfried, explaining America in the 1920s and again in the 1950s, saw its peculiar problems in the clash between the "Anglo-Saxon tradition" and the later immigrant strains; but he also asserted that America was a new civilization that had left the European far behind. Robert and Helen Lynd, in their two *Middletown* studies, wryly found the distillation of American thinking in the "Middletown spirit"—a body of folk-belief that set Americans off from any other culture. Margaret Mead saw the core of the American character in the distinctive effects of the authority-and-freedom pattern on the interaction of the sexes and the growing-up process within the family. D. W. Brogan saw an interrelation between the paradoxes within the American political system and within the national character. Geoffrey Gorer, arguing that the child in America is conditioned to seek love and success above all else, deduced from it a different but still characteristic American personality pattern. Wyndham Lewis saw in the ethnic mixtures of the American stock, and their ways of living together, the seeds of "cosmic man."

David Riesman explored the American character in terms of its increasing submission to the tyranny of opinion and the failure of the individual to heal his loneliness in the crowd. David M. Potter saw the Americans as a "people of plenty" and the crucial traits of the American character as arising from situations of abundance and opportunity. Daniel Boorstin saw the genius of American politics in the American's habit of taking his own premises and values for granted as "givens," not to be thought about. Louis Hartz saw the specific character of an institution as shaped by the fact that Americans never had an old feudal order to destroy by revolutionary overturn, as the Europeans did.

I do not mean to imply that each of these writers was an adherent of the theory of American exceptionalism. I do say that these important studies of the whole or some segment of American life use, as a practical matter, the working hypothesis of an American character and culture which are set off distinctively from others in history and in the contemporary world.

5. *National Character and the Civilization Pattern*

THE CONVENIENT WAY to deal with the problem of national character is to list a people's traits, presenting them as "American traits," the "American mind," or the "American spirit."* Some of the commentators enumerate the traits mechanically, as if it were a question of a grocery list or a warehouse inventory of odds-and-ends items. One trouble with this method of delineating character by enumeration is that the lists tend to cancel each other out. Lee Coleman, culling the lists of American traits from the available commentaries on America, found he could spot the exact opposite in some other list. Thus Americans are generous and niggardly, sympathetic and unfeeling, idealistic and cynical, visionary and practical—which leaves us with the conclusion, true but not novel, that Americans are bewilderingly human. Another difficulty is that the traits change over the generations. Compare the Garden of Eden picture of American traits in De Crèvecoeur at the end of the eighteenth century with De Tocqueville's for the late 1830s and 1840s, Bryce's contemporary picture for the 1880s and 1890s, or (retrospectively) Commager's *The American Mind* for the same period.

There are, however, certain salient traits which commentators attribute to the American in every period: Coleman finds that these are the

* Among the listings in recent books, I may cite Hacker, *The Shaping of the American Tradition* (religious freedom, enterprise freedom, the weak state, equality of opportunity, a strong middle class, responsibility under the law, the separation of powers, grass roots decentralization, and pressure-group politics); Davis, Bredemeier, and Levy, *Modern American Society,* in a final listing by the editors of the "American Value System" (ethical equality, equal opportunity, free competition, separation and balance of interests, public education, freedom of expression, tolerance, and individualism); Laski, *The American Democracy,* in the opening chapter on the "American Spirit" (future-looking, dynamism, worship of bigness, sense of destiny, fluidity of classes, pioneer spirit, individualism, antistatism, versatility, empiricism and the priority of the practical, zeal for careers and wealth, self-help and self-interest, gospel of hard work, sense of property). Robin M. Williams, Jr., *American Society,* lists fifteen "major value orientations": stress on achievement and success; stress on activity and work; a tendency to see the world in moral terms; humanitarianism; stress on efficiency and practicality; belief in progress; valuing of material comfort; avowal and (to an extent) practice of equality; ditto for freedom; emphasis on external conformity; belief in science and in secular rationality; stress on nationalism and patriotism; stress on democracy; cult of the individual personality, and its value and dignity; belief in racism and group superiority. Commager's *American Mind* gives an interesting list of traits characterizing the American mind in the 1890s. The enumeration of elements of the "American Creed" in Myrdal's *The American Dilemma* has become classic.

For collections of trait descriptions of America by travelers, see Commager, *America in Perspective;* Nevins, *America Through British Eyes;* and Handlin, *This Was America.*

tendency to club together or "join" in associations, the belief in democracy, the belief in equality, individual freedom, "direct action" in disregard of law, stress on local government, practicality, prosperity and material well-being, Puritanism, the influence of religion, uniformity and conformity.

It is hard to define the American national character by listing traits or even "value clusters," mainly because there are difficulties inherent in the idea of national character itself. Many writers are wary of it because it has been used cynically in war and power struggles to blacken the enemy symbol or sustain the conceit of a God-given or history-given national superiority. Caught between the Fascist theorists who have used it to bolster their doctrine of racist purity and pollution, and the Marxist theorists who reject it for placing too little stress on class interest and class militancy, the idea of national character has become a thorny and controversial one.

While it is risky to attribute a national character to any people, as if its qualities and destiny could be ripped out of the living body of history, it is also true that nations are realities, that their cultures develop along different paths, and that the world inside the heads of their people is a characteristic world. Much of the chauvinist and racist treachery of the term can be avoided if it is remembered that national character is a doctrine not of blood but of culture. It consists of a body of values, social habits, attitudes, traits held in common by most members of the culture. Thus the psychological field of action, thought, and emotion into which an American is born differs not only from the Russian or Chinese but even from that of an Englishman.

Traditionally, national character has been used as a semi-literary rule-of-thumb to differentiate one nationality type from another or give impressionistic force to generalization about a whole people. One of the classics here is Emerson's *English Traits,* which is witness that literary insight may be worth more than all the paraphernalia of recent social science. Yet the new anthropological and psychiatric techniques did mark a turning point in the approach to national character. First they were applied to the study of primitive personality structure, and then to psychological warfare in World War II. The psychiatrists knew from their experience that diagnosis and therapy vary with individuals of differing character types, and that these character types apply not only to neurotics and psychotics but to presumably normal persons. At the same time the anthropologists, studying contemporary primitive groups, found that each culture has its own pattern, within which there are also several different variants of character and personality. In World War II, before the military strategists could lay their plans for an assault on the enemy mind, they had to know what the enemy mind was like—hence the American studies of the Germans and Japanese, in which the theory of national character was tested in the crucible of life-and-death action. Thus the war studies converged with the work of the psychiatrists and anthropologists to form a new strain, one whose by-product has been an effort to apply the same techniques to contemporary America.

This strain of inquiry now makes possible a new way of getting at what has usually been called the "American character" or the "American spirit." It is not a disembodied presence in the sky or some mystical force inherent in race or history. Neither is it the body of folk-belief that Americans derive from their mass media and their whole cultural environment. It is best sought at the point where cultural norms in America shape personality and character, and where in turn the human material and the energies of Americans leave their impact on the fabric of the culture.

I may cite as an example of this process the way children are brought up in America, how their personalities are shaped by the emotional atmosphere of the family and the structure of authority and freedom within it, how the whole tone of growing up is set by the inordinate concentration on the child, the pervasive influence of the new big-audience media, the seeping in of the cultural values of success, prestige, and security, and the clash between permissive and restrictive codes as it is reflected in the child's mind. One can find similar examples in what is happening to the American character and spirit today as a result of suburban living, or the conditions of work and incentive within the new corporate structures, or the wave of "do-it-yourself" amateurism which has come as a recoil from the trend toward complete mechanization, or the sense of encirclement that leads to a stress on "loyalty" and "security," or the virtual ending of immigration, or the emergence of new elites and a complex, far-reaching middle class. These are only a few instances of how the energies of the individual American are channeled by characteristic cultural conditions of training and living, shaping certain common character traits for whole groups of individuals and weaving them into the fabric of the civilization.

This does not mean that, by some necromantic determinism, every little American who is born alive comes out stamped with exactly the same traits or propensities. There are in-groups, out-groups, and marginal groups; there are regional, class, and ethnic variations; there is a bewildering variety of individual personality patterns and traits. Yet the central stream of tendency remains, and with it the shaping interrelations of American personality and culture.

What are some of the ways of uncovering this interrelation? One way is a study of mental disorders, asking, as the psychiatrists do, what are the characteristic sources of personality breakdown—what it is that makes Americans crack up when and as they do? To answer this means to get some insight into the strains under which men live in America, the expectations the culture sets up in them as against the satisfactions it places within their reach, the norms of conduct and thought it seeks to enforce, the fault lines and frustrations that develop within them. Another way is to ask what personality types can be most clearly discerned among Americans, and what modes of life and striving within the culture account for the impulse toward those personality types. A third is to ask what life goals the Americans set up for themselves and what they make a cult of and are obsessed with, making sure to distinguish between the conscious and irrational levels of their striving.

One can dig deeper, perhaps, and seek some hidden dimension of the American character which symbolizes the basic American life view. Thus F. S. C. Northrop (*The Meeting of East and West*) takes the deepest thing about any civilization to be its metaphysic—its assumptions and beliefs about the constitution of the unseen universe, and he suggests that it was the reception by America of the atomistic metaphysics of Locke and Hume which has influenced the individualism and fragmentation of American life. Thus also Charles W. Morris (*Six Ways of Life*) attempts an approach through symbolic value systems. He lists the crucial systems in history as the Dionysian (surrender to the instinctual life), the Buddhist (annihilation of self for serenity), the Christian (purifying of self for spiritual values), the Mohammedan (merging of self in a holy war against the enemies of the true way), the Apollonian (conserving of traditional values), and the Promethean (conquest and organization of the environment by science and technology). He sees American civilization as primarily Promethean, but with elements of the Christian and the Apollonian, pointing out that the Promethean strain puts the emphasis on the instrumental, that the Apollonian has hardened into a Toryism of the spirit which could mean a static civilization, and that the Christian strain has had to be subordinated when it has conflicted with the more dominant elements of the civilization. I cite this suggestive scheme to illustrate how the study of the great world myths can shed light on what Americans are like and what they live by.

Since most of this is speculative, American observers have tried to approach their own civilization by the very different and more modest road of community surveys and cross-section area studies—of "Middletown," "Jonesville," "Yankeetown," "Elmtown," "Southern Town," "Plainville." What these studies offer is a degree of verification for certain theoretical leads, or of doubt cast upon others; they can show the extent to which the members of the American culture verbalize the articles in the American creed, and how they see themselves (and others) in the class system and the success-and-rating system of their time. But the community studies can never be broader or deeper than the issues they pose, nor more imaginative than the questions they raise.

Discussions of national character sometimes remind you of one of Cagliostro's magical spells or the incantatory hokum of a side-show barker telling the virtues of some nostrum. There is no talismanic quality in any of the newer approaches to national character. The hard work of giving contour to the mass of known material on American civilization cannot be dispensed with. The insights of the psychiatrists and anthropologists are all to the good, if they do not overstress some single symbolic key to the national character. The method of Gorer, for example, as used in the Gorer-Rickman study, *The People of Great Russia,* has been sharply satirized as the "swaddling theory" because it takes the infantile experience of the Russian peasant child, who was closely swaddled in the early months of his life, as a pre-verbal emotional conditioning to the rage, guilt, and violent alternations of emotion in the Russian as an adult. In *The American People,* Gorer put stress on the cult of the mother, the rejection of the father, the child's craving for affection, and the fear of loneliness, and again saw them as clue—if not cause—to the national character. A good deal depends on how hard the thesis is pushed. If we take it not as a verified truth but as impressionistic lead for further research and analysis, it is all to the good. The course of wisdom is to recognize the limits of any study of personality traits and to see the whole of the national character as one phase of the total civilization pattern.

6. *Single Key—or Polar Pattern?*

THE QUESTION THEN arises whether there is some single organizing principle in this civilization pattern, some key that unlocks all the doors. For generations Western thinkers have been haunted by the dream of finding the single factor that shapes all else in its image. It might be Hegel or Spencer, Marx or Sorel, Spengler, Freud or Jung, Veblen, Henry George, Brooks Adams or Henry Adams, but it was always a form of cabala. I can offer the reader no single talisman to the secret of American civilization.

The temptation is great to seek it. Following the lead of Marx or Veblen, one might stress the march of technology and the system of business power, and build all the rest on that. After Laski's *American Democracy,* which applied that method unsparingly to the analysis of contemporary America, such an approach would yield sharply decreasing returns.

While Laski's theme is democracy, as with De Tocqueville and Bryce, it is the subject of the book only as a corpse is the subject of a murder mystery. The real theme is the system of capitalist power and its business civilization: between these and democracy Laski depicts a bitter feud. Democracy in Laski's study is a little like the hero of Clifford Odets's early play, *Waiting for Lefty:* the stage is set for the hero, everyone measures his life and aspirations by him, but he never shows up because he has fallen victim to the forces of greed and reaction. Obviously economic power and class structure are important themes in the American civilization pattern, and I shall dwell a good deal on them. But an analysis which makes them the sole key distorts a good deal and misses many of the most dramatic recent changes in American life.

Laski's approach, like Veblen's, marked a recoil from the school of political idealism, which seemed to make political institutions and ideas the end and beginning and everything in the middle. In one sense De Tocqueville belonged to that tradition, since he started with the idea of democracy and traced its ramifications through phase after phase of American life. But De Tocqueville set an example of breadth of view which could not be matched by the later students of America, even someone with the insight of Bryce, whose approach was more narrowly through the political institutions of *The American Commonwealth,* while De Tocqueville's traced out imaginatively the political and moral ramifications of the democratic idea. Bryce, moreover, had lost much of the sense of wonder and excitement one finds in De Tocqueville about the revolutionary implications of democracy and was more interested in how the political actuality had worked out. In both cases, however, the organizing principle is political.

Another approach lays the key stress on psychological and moral values. It gives primacy to beliefs and attitudes, and the creative force of religion and ideas, and derives the technology and economic achievement of America from them rather than the other way round. The unacknowledged assumption is that the way to understand America is to start with the human psyche in its American form and with its whole intellectual and moral world. One finds this approach, with mystical overtones, in Waldo Frank's *Rediscovery of America;* one finds it, with religious overtones in Toynbee and Niebuhr; one finds it, in its more direct psychological form, in the writing of the young American scholars today who are exploring the relation of culture and personality.

My own view is that both economic man and psychological man—the materialist emphasis and the individualist emphasis—are each stripped of meaning without the other. The problem of social analysis is only partially illumined by the search for causes. In much of our thinking, causation is giving way to relation and interaction. "America is this," says one observer of American life. "America is that," says another. It is likely that America is both, because America is a highly polarized field of meaning, but that neither can be fully understood except in relation to the other and to the whole intricate civilization pattern. The study of American civilization becomes thus the study of the polar pattern itself, not a search for some single key that will unlock causation. It is largely a question of what you focus upon, and against what background. The problem of American interpretation is best seen in a figure-ground perspective: but what will be figure and what will be ground will vary with the purpose at hand.

Thus my concern will be neither with the material world alone nor with the moral-psychological world alone, but with the interplay between them. If there is a figure-ground relation in American civilization it must be sought in the relation between power and ideas, science and conscience, the revolutionary machine and the conservative crust of tradition, mass production and social creativeness, individualist values and collective action, capitalist economics and democratic freedom, class structure and the image of prestige and success in the American mind, elite power and the popular arts, the growth of military power and the persistence of civilian control, the fact of an American imperium and the image of an open constitutional world.

One may see in these polar impulses the proof that American life is deeply split. One may prefer to see them as contradictory parts of a bewildering puzzle. Or one may see them as signs of an effort, on a grander scale than ever in history, to resolve the conflicting impulses that are to be found in every civilization but each of which occurs here with a strength and tenacity scarcely witnessed elsewhere.

CHAPTER III

People and Place

IN WHICH we take a preliminary look at the two basic ingredients of American civilization, the continent itself and the people who live on it—that is to say, the natural resources and the human resources of America. We broach first the dangerous question ("Is There an American Stock?") of biology and ethnic types, with the emphasis on the plasticity of the human material in America. We then explore how this myriad of stocks, drawn from every corner of the earth ("The Immigrant Experience"), living under conditions of extreme mobility ("People in Motion") in a myriad of natural environments, having at their disposal the richest possible resources ("The American Earth"), use and exploit those resources. We trace the elusive pattern of how fast they are born, how long they live, and how much vitality there is in the graphs of their population growth ("Population Profile"); how healthy they are, what their characteristic food habits are and their dwellings, how well they take care of their human material ("The Sinews of Welfare"). Taking another look at them from a different angle of vision we ask what basic ways of life they have molded out of the fusion of people and place—the life of the farmer, the life of the small town (both of them waning), and the life of the city and the suburb (both of them marking the line of current and future growth). Finally, we try still another angle of vision and see how the fusion of people and place has worked out to produce the regional ways of life and thought in New England and on the East Coast, in the Midwest, in the South and Southwest, in the Rocky Mountain region and on the Pacific Coast.

The reader is warned that this will be a long chapter because it deals with the rich diversities of the American people and their continent. Without getting a picture of these diversities the general analysis in the chapters that follow will be oversimplified and distorted.

CHAPTER III

People and Place

1. Is There an American Stock?

EVERY traveler in the tropics comes away with an unforgettable sense of the pervasive jungle enclosing him. America's jungle is its ethnic environment of a myriad of peoples. In such a tropical luxuriance every ethnic type is present, everything grows fast and intertwines with everything else, anything is ethnically possible.

The best vantage points for observing the variety of American ethnic strains are on a subway in New York or a San Francisco street or at an Army induction center. Each is a broad channel through which the human material of America streams. Every people in Europe, most of the varied stocks of European and Asian Russia; peoples from Israel and the Arabs of the Middle East; peoples from China and Southeast Asia, from the Philippines, Hawaii, Australia, from the farthest reaches of India, from Liberia and Nigeria, from the Gold Coast and the Ivory Coast, from Kaffirland and the Witwatersrand, from every country in South and Central America, from every Caribbean island, from British and French Canada, from Greenland and Iceland—there is scarcely a stock on the ethnic map of the world that is not represented in America.

Let me make my use of terms clear. I use "stock" rather than "race," and "ethnic" rather than "racial," because in both cases I mean something in which race is only one ingredient. I have in mind a compound of influences from race, nationality, language, religion, region or subregion—any recognizable strain which not only by its common descent but by its length of living on the same soil, under the same sky, and in the same community has formed a relatively stable biopsychological and cultural type.

Is any one of these ethnic stocks more "American" than the others? To say of someone that "he is of American stock" has come to mean that he is white, probably Protestant and of Anglo-Saxon descent, and that his forebears emigrated to America some generations back. But there is little of solace here for the distinction-hunters. In most civilizations the conquering stock has tried to set itself off on the one hand from the conquered natives, on the other from the newcomers who may want to get in on the power and the glory. In America this has been difficult on several scores: the natives were too few and were so ruthlessly stripped of land, home, and livelihood that the deed trailed little glory behind it. If "American stock" is to mean descent from those who were most immediately in on the kill, the leaders of the Great Predation, it would carry a guilt of which many would be gladly rid. The real conquest of America was not a military conquest, to deck out a boast that the strength of killers flows in one's blood: it was a conquest of forest and plain, of mountain and valley and river, of new technologies and new social forms; and in it every wave of immigrants took part. Although the largest single group came from the British Isles, there was no one stock that pre-empted the glory of settling America: even in the early decades of the Republic, there was a variety of stocks shaping the amalgam of "this new man, the American." Finally, the leveling force of the democratic idea has resulted in a crossbreeding and mingling of stocks which have made the task of the racial purist a hopeless one.

This effort to pre-empt the term "American" for a single strain out of many, and exclude from it all the others, is a familiar device in the technique of prescriptive prestige. Whatever meaning it may have in the case of a more inbred and homogeneous people, in America it is meaningless. Yet there are some who recoil from racism but regard the length of settlement as a crucial distinguishing mark. "Wouldn't European stocks which have been here longer," a friend writes me, "be more 'American' than the recent ones? Isn't a Lowell or a Roosevelt, for example, likely to be more 'American' than my Chinese laundryman's son?" By the test of time the most "American" stocks would be the American Indians, the descendants of the Pilgrims, and the descendants of the early Negro slaves—which is not exactly what was meant. The idea that European stocks are more "American" not by the fact of long settlement but by the fact of being European (West European, not Mediterranean or Slavic), is an idea easy to succumb to. Its strength derives from the fact that the English, Scottish, French Huguenot, and Dutch influences are interwoven with early American history. It is easier and more natural to think of a Lowell or Roosevelt as American than of a recent Chinese immigrant or a descendant of an early Indian or Negro family, but this is because the West Europeans have run the show in America since early times and have therefore made the rules and set the admission price. They feel more at home and have made others feel less at home.

Our thinking will be clearer if we say that there are three levels of meaning attached to "American": the links of family and stock with American history over time; the equal or unequal claims to rights and privileges under the law; the sense of commitment to American life. Only on the first level does the question of stock enter, however irrationally. On the second level there can be no discrimination between a Lowell or Roosevelt and the Chinese laundryman's son. On the third level the problem is one of individuals, not of stock: Americans belonging to the newer stocks may be as committed to the obligations and meanings of the American experience as the older ones, and many have enriched it greatly.

Yet in the world's most notable ethnic democracy there remains a hierarchy of prestige depending partly on stock—black, yellow, brown, and red at the bottom, white Protestant, West European on top, with the lines between the rest drawn partly in terms of closeness to Colonial descent, partly of geographic closeness to the British center of origin of the early settlements. A roughly chronological chart of the sequence of waves of immigration—English, Dutch, German, Scotch-Irish, French, Scandinavian, Irish, Mediterranean, Jewish, Balkan, Slavic, Mexican and Latin American, Filipino, Middle Eastern, Oriental—would correspond roughly to the descending scale of prestige in the ethnic hierarchy. The big divergences are that the Indians, who came first, are not at the top but toward the bottom of the pyramid; and the Negroes, who were brought over early, are not near the top but at the very bottom. On the prestige chart of the ethnic hierarchy, one could superimpose a residence map showing which stocks are distributed in slum areas, in tolerable living quarters, in middle-class districts, in residential areas. Over that one could draw an occupational chart of the functions to which the ethnic groups have been more or less specialized.

This is fluid, but the correspondences are roughly there. Making allowance for the constant breaking of the mold and the emergence of many Negroes as doctors, lawyers, teachers, ministers, businessmen, it remains true that in the South the Negroes have done and still do the heavy labor in the fields, and everywhere the dirty jobs in the factories and on the roads and wharves, in digging ditches and laying tracks and building tunnels, while their women are domestics. The Chinese, Filipinos, and Puerto Ricans are also still specialized to do domestic and routine jobs. The Mexicans (or "Spanish-speaking Americans") work at sweated labor in the factories of the Southwest and as migratory workers on the farms of the Southwest and California. The Poles, Czechs, Magyars, and Slovaks are in the coal mines of Pennsylvania, West Virginia, and Illinois, in the steel mills and at the open-hearth furnaces of Gary and Pittsburgh and Buffalo. The Scandinavians are farmers in the Midwest and loggers in the lumber camps. The Irish of the later immigration are policemen, saloonkeepers, and bartenders in New York and Boston, but also day laborers and building-trades workers, transport workers, longshoremen. The Italians and the Jews work in the garment trades of New York and the other Eastern centers; the Italians are also barbers and shoeshine boys and musicians, and they work the truck gardens in New Jersey and the vineyards of California, as do the Japanese; while the Jews move from the sweatshops into the small trades and the middlemen functions, and into medicine, law, dentistry, teaching, and the entertainment world.

But in the fluid life of America, the specialization does not stick. Cutting across the ethnic occupation map is the fact that it is the new arrivals of most stocks who do the menial and dirty work and drift to the peripheral occupations, while the earlier and resourceful ones break out of their cultural molds, buy farms and houses, get university training, attain skills, and move up to become members of the middle class. The epithets do often stick—"Wop," "Dago," "Sheeny," "Kike," "Nigger," "Norske," "Mick," "Spick," "Polack," "Hunkie," "Bohunk," "Chink," "Jap," "wetback," "greaser"—betraying a class and xenophobe animus as well as a racist one.

Sometimes, in overcompensation for this prevalent animus, one is tempted to ask whether we can in fact distinguish stock from stock, or whether there are not simply *individuals* in a rich and bewildering variety?

It is true that the differences between the stocks are not clear-cut, that one could find within one of them—say the Jews—wider differences of physiognomy, height, bone structure, skull structure, temperament, than between particular Jews on the one hand and particular Italians or Irish or Portuguese or Syrians on the other. It is also true that ethnic differences do not carry with them the differences of superiority or inferiority that the racists ascribe to them. Although there are no supermen in America, there are Americans who hunger for a cult of the blond Anglo-Saxon gods; although there are no sub-men in America, there are whites who cling to their color out of a panic sense of emptiness and who pant to assign Negroes or Puerto Ricans or Mexicans or Chinese to the category of inferior men. There are no Americans who belong to radically different branches of the human family, in the sense that their blood is of a different genus, or that some are closer to apes and others closer to gods, some born to work and others to lord it over them. There is not even an ethnically pure group in America (unless we speak of ethnic sub-pockets like the Hutterites from Russia who settled in South Dakota and have been almost completely endogamous) for at this point in history the chromosomes of any group contain also some genes from most of the others.

Yet it would be foolish to deny the reality of ethnic stocks in America and the differences between them. Those who came to America came from relatively stable ethnic groups. They brought with them obvious physical hereditary differences and habits of life that set them off from the others, and the social hostility they encountered often made them huddle together in more or less isolated ethnic communities. Many of them thus retained and even froze their sense of separateness, while others kept themselves open to every influence from other groups, including interbreeding. If we recognize that there is no stigma to membership in any one of the ethnic stocks of America the whole question of stock can be taken with realism and without passion.

The fact is that America is more than an agglomerate of individuals jumbled in hopeless confusion. America is a myriad of stocks, each with some identity maintained from the earliest to the latest migration. What gives America its biological richness is that it is a mingling of ethnic strains. What gives America its cultural richness is that it is a mingling of traditions and temperaments. Unless the stocks had brought an identity of their own, it would be meaningless to talk of their mingling. Unless those identities were changed and dissolved in the process, shaped and reshaped, caught up in the ever-flowing stream of the life of all of them together, it would be meaningless to talk of America.

Does the unlimited crossbreeding of ethnic stocks hurt or help the quality of American life? True, there are some valid objections to be raised against unlimited crossbreeding. In the process of mixture, the groups with the higher birth rate will predominate, biologically and culturally, and while a high birth rate may be one of the indices of vitality, the crucial question is that of the quality of the individuals and cultures which are crossed. There is, however, a double and contradictory line of reasoning in the "pure America" argument. One is that the more recent immigrants are clannish, refuse to intermarry, and should therefore be kept out. The other is that they will flood into the country and overwhelm and corrupt the "native" stock by the weight of numbers and birth rate and by interbreeding. One argument rests on the theory that they do not mix, the other on the theory that they mix all too much. I suspect that logic is less important here than emotion—the emotions of invidiousness, guilt, pride, and fear that dominate the thinking of the "pure America" group.

On biological grounds alone, if these emotions can be ruled out, the central argument for an exclusive concept of American stock is the argument that unlimited crossbreeding will mean the mongrelization of America. Even reputable writers seem to have been made panicky by the possible biological and cultural corruption of pure Anglo-Saxonism by the Negroes, Asians, Slavs, Jews, and Mediterranean peoples. If mongrelization has any meaning, it assumes a "pure" (but nonexistent) stock thinned out and corrupted by unlimited crossbreeding. The fear of mongrelization is the fear of strange blood and ways on the part of groups that believe their economic and social supremacy threatened by outsiders, and fix upon the racial invaders as the enemy.

This fear reaches nightmare proportions in the Southern states, where the governing group has sought to protect its "white supremacy" by a set of state miscegenation laws. States like Mississippi and Georgia, in a triumph of paranoia, enacted laws making any marriage felonious and void if it involves a white person and one with an "ascertainable trace" of African, West Indian, Asian Indian, or Mongolian blood. One of the wider aspects of the miscegenation laws, if they are regarded in terms of any rational threat of mongrelization, is that they are found in the North as well as the South, and that in eight of the states covered by them the Negroes against whom they are directed form less than 1 per cent of the population.

This is not to deny the reality of crossbreeding in America. But there can be no question of mongrelization because there is no norm of purity. Each ethnic strain, in the process of crossbreeding, "corrupts" the other; each dilutes and enriches the other. The fact is that crossbreeding is in itself neither good nor bad. Its chief effect is to increase variations at both ends of the curve of inherited traits: in other words, we may dilute the quality of what is transmitted as a result of the vast interchange of genes, but we may also get more geniuses on the top level. The range of potentials is widened in both directions. Everything depends, as I have said, on the individuals and cultures entering into the mixture. The characteristic ethnic quality of America is the outcome of the mingling of stocks and traditions on a scale unparalleled in history. Although some cultural historians maintain that the dilution of native stock is followed by cultural decadence, the example of the Italian city-states, Spain, Holland, Britain, and now Russia and India as well as America indicates that the most vigorous phase may come at the height of the mingling of many stocks. The greater danger lies in closing the gates.

No stock, once it has come to America, remains what it was. Each breeds away from type, both by the influence of the new physical environment and by the fact of intermingling. Every stock, by its migration, breaks with its past environment and enters a new one. Continued migration from one American region to another and mobility from one class and therefore one set of living standards to another continue the process of environmental reconditioning. How substantial the changes may be was shown in 1912 in the classic study by Franz Boas, *Changes in Bodily Form of Descendants of Immigrants*. Despite the prevailing view that skull measurements are an unchanging racial characteristic, Boas showed that the skull indices of the children of Jewish and Italian immigrants differed appreciably from those of the parents. This is environmental change away from ethnic type, whether due to diet, living standards, climate, or other factors in the natural and cultural environment. Boas was dealing with the physical factor that one would expect to be most resistant to change. What applied to skull changes would apply more easily to psychic and cultural changes; and what applied under the influence of environmental and standard-of-living change would apply more easily as the result of biological mixture.

I find a surprising misreading of Boas's meaning in Arnold Toynbee's *Study of History* (Vol. I, 220-1), which argues that Boas is, like his opponents, an adherent of race thinking. Boas writes that his study is suggestive "because it shows that not even those characteristics of a race which have proved to be most permanent in their old home remain the same under the new surroundings; and we are compelled to conclude that when these features of the body change, the whole bodily and mental make-up of the immigrants may change." Toynbee gathers from this "what is the fundamental postulate of all race theories: that is, the postulate that physical and psychical characteristics are correlated." But this is to miss the meaning of the phrase "*may* change," which carries with it an emphasis on the plasticity of *both* the cultural-psychic and the physical traits under environmental pressure. The whole point of racist thinking is that there is no such plasticity but that a given set of inherent physical traits of a superior or inferior caste carries with it a rigid set of psychic traits of a similarly superior or inferior caste. Boas proved the plasticity (although he felt it was a limited one) and rejected the moral hierarchy. The racists assert the moral hierarchy and reject the plasticity.

The process of plasticity has been described in Paul Engle's *America Remembers.*

The ancient features of the type were changed
Under a different sun, in a clearer air
That entered the lungs like wine, the swarthy face
Paled, cheekbones lifted and narrowed, hair
Straightened and faded, and the body moved
With a lighter step, the toes springy, the eyes
Eager as a bird's, and every man
Had a coiled spring in his nerves that drove him
In a restless fury of life.

The bloods mingled
Madly . . . . (Who knows
What strange multi-fathered child will come
Out of the nervous travail of these bloods
To fashion in a new world continent
A newer breed of men?)

Given conditions making for rapid change, the question thus put is the question of how far the plasticity of the American stock is likely to lead. Clearly, every ethnic stock in America, unless it is caught and isolated in some eddy of the American stream, is breeding away from type. But is it breeding toward a new form of its own type, where it will be more or less stabilized? Or is the process of change a continuing and cumulative one resulting in the emergence of an inclusive new ethnic type, like a loose sort of tent to cover the existing types which will survive yet be transformed?

The probabilities point to something less defined than either of these. We do not yet know what ethnic future lies ahead for America, since genetics is changing its insights and outlook so rapidly. Earnest Hooton, a physical anthropologist who liked to make bold forays into the future, predicted that "the stubby, bone-and-muscle Mr. Americas of today" are doomed to disappear or to be "reduced to the ranks of the institutionalized malefactors." They will be replaced (said Hooton) by a more "attenuated" body build, "taller and more gangling than ever, with big feet, horse faces, and deformed dental arches"; the women "less busty and buttocky than those of our generation." There are other guesses of the future stock, some of them less unattractive. But their common premise is that a new ethnic entity is forming which will carry with it the multiform freightage of all past generations, but in which there will also be some central cast of temperament, physique, and lineament that crops up more and more frequently.

This does not mean that the old stocks will disappear or that America will become ethnically uniform. The processes of heredity and their interplay with the physical and cultural environment are too complex to allow for uniformity. The gene variants of so heterogeneous a population as the American are fantastically large in number, and the potential directions of American stock are great. This is the first great instance in history where ethnic abundance has combined with so great a freedom in marriage, to produce an unimaginable ethnic future.

If then we ask again, "Is there an American stock?" the answer must be that there are many stocks in America—more than have ever been gathered together before within a national unit; that none of them, whatever its claims and arrogance, is more American than the others, and none, whatever its sense of inferiority, less American; that each is different from what it was in its area of ethnic origin—each touched and changed by the alchemy of the American environment, by the fact of living and mingling with all the others on the American continent. America has become a great biological and psychological laboratory, whose experiments may issue in undreamed-of results. In all the stocks there has been, whether obviously or subtly, a breeding away from type; there has also been, subtly rather than obviously, slowly, ever so slowly, and yet unmistakably, a breeding *toward* new types that have not yet emerged.

When they emerge they will be the creature of America, not America *their* creature. Yet as we watch the yeast working in the ever-re-created human material of America, can we doubt that the determiners of a not unimaginable American future are at work here? "There is but one victory that I know is sure," wrote Saint-Exupéry, "and that is the victory that is lodged in the energy of the seed." Given what we know about American stock, we must take this to mean the victory not of the seed's rigidity but of its plasticity.

2. *The Immigrant Experience*

For centuries the strength and richness of America have been swelled by the great tides of immigration from Europe, with the sources moving roughly from the British Isles to western Europe and the Scandinavian countries, to the Mediterranean countries, to the Slavic countries. In 1790 America had fewer than four million people, of whom three quarters of a million were Negroes: 82 per cent of the total white population was English. For the next forty years, until 1830, immigrants were slow in coming. In the 1830s the "Atlantic Migration" quickened, first with Irish countrymen, then with German farmers and artisans, and then with land-hungry Scandinavians. In the early 1880s came a greater wave of the "new" immigration—"new" in the double sense that they were no longer from western and northern Europe but from eastern and southern Europe, and that they were more likely to settle in the big cities and work in the mines and mills and factories than on the land.

A few figures tell a dramatic story. From 1800 to 1914 some fifty million people left Europe, of whom almost thirty-five million came to the United States. In the century and a half from 1800 to 1950 some forty million newcomers moved to the United States, 85 per cent of them from Europe, 11 per cent from other countries in the American hemisphere, 3 per cent from Asian countries, and 2 per cent from the rest of the world. In the single peak decade of 1904-1914, ten million came, and in the peak year of 1907 more than a million and a quarter.

As the convulsions of tyranny, war, and famine shook the world, and as the "opportunity line" thinned out in the Old World and grew bolder in the New, millions of people came spilling down the sluiceways to America, and an almost manic quality seemed to infect immigration. It was fed by the steamship companies, who sent out agents to recruit immigrants and depict the glories and grandeurs of the new star of the West; and it was aided by the increasing cheapness of transportation. But even without these stimulants the migration would have taken place. America-as-magnet exercised a hypnotic force strong enough to draw millions to the shores of promise.

It was, in the main, the peasants who came, from Ireland, from Germany, from the Scandinavian countries, from Italy, from Russia and Poland, from the Balkans. There were many others who came from the cities too—artisans without jobs, ruined shopkeepers, political *émigrés,* intellectuals who had failed to make their way and who were to establish "Latin farms" (as they were called with gentle derision) in America. But mostly the families who came had lived on the land, and the land had been unable to sustain them. The plots were too small and the village community ways were too traditionally set to yield to the new agricultural techniques. Debt was a humiliating master to serve, and poverty a bleak companion. When famine began to nibble on the margins of your life, and your little plot of land was foreclosed and you found yourself dispossessed, you began to feel the narrowing confines of your village intolerable. Ridden by the weight of feudal and clerical tradition, with no hope left for yourself and no promise to hold out to your children, what was more natural than to surrender to the image of a country where land could still be had and a man could keep moving until he had found a challenge to his strength and boundless possibilities for his young? "The rich stay in Europe," De Crèvecoeur had written much earlier, "it is only the middling and the poor that emigrate."

There was always a bitter spell of waiting and enduring between dislocation from the old home and settlement in the new. There were the weary vigils at lodging houses along the wharves in the seaport cities of Europe until passage was arranged with some broker and the ship finally sailed. The steerage quarters, oversold through greed, were often cold, crowded, dirty, disease-ridden, rat-infested. In the darkness the long nights and days differed little from each other. Scanty provisions and bad water made scurvy, dysentery, and "ship's fever" lethal adversaries. When the ship arrived the immigrant found himself, dazed and bewildered, in a world with which his traditional peasant qualities could not cope. He had to get work immediately—work of any kind, at any pay, with whatever hours and conditions—in order to sustain life; he became thus a ready prey for exploiting employers, swindling fellow countrymen, greedy moneylenders. Sometimes he settled in the first big city he came to, huddling in a ghetto with his countrymen; sometimes he was able to push on into the interior and take up a piece of land or serve his apprenticeship as a "hired man"—again, usually, near others of his own ethnic stock. In both cases he needed first to convert his work and skill into capital: for years after his arrival, thus, he had to save and scrimp, living on almost nothing, so that he could get a real start in a store or restaurant or on a farm or as a small entrepreneur.

For years, perhaps for the rest of their lives, many of these immigrants were to remain (as Oscar Handlin has so movingly described in *The Uprooted*) alienated men—alienated from the culture they had left and from the one that had not yet wholly welcomed them and that they did not understand, and alienated finally from themselves. The old patterned ways of the village community, however galling, formed a path of stability, where a man knew what was expected of him. The new ways of the buzzing big American cities and the quickly growing farm villages were bewildering. The immigrant became an object, caught within forces over which he had no mastery, having to convert his strength on the market into dollars with which he could get what he needed for life.

The tight family of the peasant community or of the Jewish tradition was subjected to the strains and dislocations of the new society; often it was fatally split, although those that survived found that the ties of cohesiveness were strengthened by the fact of their members having to face together an alien world. Most tragic of all, the immigrants often found that their own children—adapting more easily to the new ways, caught up in the new rhythms, accepting the new life goals, and eager to merge themselves with the new environment—drifted away and became alienated from their parents. Perhaps in order to wipe out the cleavage between themselves and their new fellows, they saw their father and mother through the eyes of the "Americans" and came to think of them as outsiders and strangers—in short, as objects. The circle of alienation was completed.

The immigrant experience was thus somber and tragic. Yet it would be a mistake to see it thus without adding that it was also one of excitement and ferment. Millions of the immigrants, after giving their strength to the new country, died with a sense of failure and frustration. But many more millions survived their ordeal, became men of influence in their communities, and lived to see the fulfillment of the American promise in their own lives doubly fulfilled in the lives of their children. "Everything tended to regenerate them," De Crèvecoeur wrote of his fellow immigrants, "new laws, a new mode of living, a new social system; here they are become men: in Europe they were so many useless plants, wanting vegetable mold, and refreshing showers. They withered and were mowed down by want, hunger, and war; but now by the power of transplantation, like all other plants, they have taken root and flourished!" One doubts whether this lyric description, written at the end of the eighteenth century, would have been accepted as a faithful one a century later; yet it described a process which would have meaning for many through the whole course of the immigrant experience and even more meaning for the second and third generations, who reaped the harvest of the transplanting of their fathers without having had to suffer the ordeal.

Yet there was also something in the ordeal that enriched the immigrant and his new country. He may have deemed himself a failure in the old village and helpless on the crossing, and he may have begun to doubt his manliness after every defeat. But one thing that could never be stripped from him was the immediacy of his experience: whatever he had achieved had been due to himself and his own efforts. The experience of the immigrants recapitulated the early American pioneer hardships, in many ways on harder terms, since the difficulties they encountered were those of a jungle society rather than a jungle wilderness. It added a dimension of tragic depth which American life needed: even in its most tragic phases it furnished a ferment of vitality which re-created the American experience in every decade. There was much in the American mind that tended to become fixed and conformist. The immigrant experience hurled itself against this with insistent eagerness, kindling a warmth that thawed out much of the glacial rigidity. In recent years, with the gates almost closed, there have been fewer new immigrants to keep the regenerative process going.

The immigrants eventually found their place in the American economy, each new layer that came from below pushing up the earlier arrivals to the next stratum. But the economy also felt the impact of the immigration which provided a labor force for a rapidly expanding industrialism. Whatever one may say of the importance of American natural resources, the richest resource was man power: without the immigrants America could not have found quickly enough the man power to build the railroads, mine the coal, man the open-hearth steel furnaces, and run the machines. Moreover, while most of the immigrants were pushed into the unskilled, backbreaking jobs, enough of them were skilled—carrying over techniques from a European industrialism which had made an earlier start—so that the Great Migration was not only one of people but of talents, skills, and cultural traditions. The increase of immigration also meant more consumers as well as more producers. The new machines cut production costs and prices, yet the steadily mounting millions of consumers kept big profits flowing back into industry. And since the immigrants started on so little, their living standards kept steadily improving, and the home market grew not by arithmetical but by geometrical progression.

The immigrant's obsession with rising living standards was something he gave to American life as well as something he took from it. He was a man in a hurry, not only to make money but to show he had made it, not only to sow the crop of his labor and ingenuity but to reap the harvest of his success. The stories of the "self-made man" that caught the American imagination were in many cases the Horatio Alger rags-to-riches stories of immigrant boys who rose to the top of the heap. Their business methods were little different from the methods of the earlier Americans, but since they were so avid for results the legend grew that they were distinctively unscrupulous, and there was often a cleft between the world of "respectable" (i.e., "nativist") business and "immigrant" business. Certainly there was a febrile intensity about the immigrant that was part of his world of wonder: he was the small boy with his nose pressed against the shopwindow whose sweets were out of his reach unless he could come in with a fistful of coins. He was full of wonder at the miracles of science and mechanical inventions, at the headlong course of progress, at the dizzying peaks of wealth and power. He was full of a sense of promise and possibility which renewed the pioneer spark.

When the promise faltered and the possibility ran into the sands, he could express his bitterness through labor or radical movements which started as the protest of some ethnic stock and broadened out into a dissident splinter group or even a third-party movement. But the political impact of the immigrant was felt as much in the machine politics of the big city as in the dissenting politics of the Middle West. The boss politics of Boston, Philadelphia, New York, Chicago, St. Louis, was an interchange of the loyalties of the lonely immigrants, who needed a very personal kind of help in their encounters with jobs and the law, for the protection of the men who had become sophisticated and knew the power of the massed immigrant vote.

The first-generation immigrant, whether he was on a farm or in a big city, was likely to live out his life on the margin of the new society, and from there he sent coursing through much of the culture the current of his hope, his loneliness, his individuality. It was his son, the second-generation immigrant, who was lampooned by the novelists as one driven either to imitate or to outdo the "native Americans" at their own game. He was the Sammy of Budd Schulberg's *What Makes Sammy Run?* and the Harry Bogen of Jerome Weidman's *I Can Get It for You Wholesale.* He acted as if some "equalizer" had been built into him, driving him to excesses of energy or (as in cases less noted by the novelists) to excesses of protective coloration.

The third-generation immigrant was caught in a paradox. On the one hand the continuing pressures from the world of those whose ancestors were accepted as the nation's ancestors turned him toward stability and conformism, and thus further away from his links with the immigrant experience. On the other hand Marcus Hansen pointed out in a notable essay that "what the son wishes to forget the grandson wishes to remember," and that the third-generation immigrant, no longer ashamed of his cultural ancestry, has had the courage to embrace it. Both tendencies may be found in the grandchildren and great-grandchildren of the immigrant, struggling for mastery; but I am convinced that what Hansen noted will prove the stronger.

A great change came over American attitudes toward immigration after World War I and led to the racist discrimination of the quota legislation of 1921 and 1924. Actually the movement for restrictive legislation started before the turn of the century, almost with the start of the Great Wave of the new immigration. Every people is "ethnocentric," which is a way of saying it is the sun around which the earth and moon and stars revolve; and this is particularly true of the way the dominant group feels. The Americans of English descent—whether New England Yankees or transplanted Yankees in the Middle West—felt that their old dominance had been undercut by the hordes of strange new arrivals; nurtured in the democratic dogma, some of the best of them were deeply troubled and split in their emotions. The Southern whites, trying to keep the South "a white man's country" and therefore fearful of the Negroes who surrounded them, turned their fears into a more general suspicion of "foreigners." The reserve army of labor, which meant so much to the businessman because it gave him the human material for industrial expansion, seemed a threat to many labor leaders who feared the competition of cheap labor. Some of the intellectuals of the Progressive Era, anxious about the continuity of the native tradition, turned strongly anti-immigrant. Others were influenced by European theories of racial superiority and inferiority and found "scientific" buttressing for their purist fears about what Madison Grant called "the passing of the great race."

An alliance of Yankees, Southerners, trade-unionists, Progressive intellectuals, racist theorists, population purists, and professional xenophobes made headway in convincing the descendants of the earlier immigrants that the later immigation was dangerous and should be severely restricted. They scared them with images of criminality, radicalism, and Oriental cunning, with examples drawn from the Mafia and the Black Hand, from the Haymarket anarchists and the Jewish peddlers who became international bankers. They succeeded in frightening fearful Americans who thought the country of their fathers would be made unfit for their children by newcomers who sold themselves cheap, pulled down wage standards, read dangerous books, lived like pigs, and bred like rabbits.

Certainly there was a shift in the meaning of the whole immigrant experience, on the part of both the hosts and the newcomers. Writing in the 1880s, James Bryce noted that "the intellectual and moral atmosphere into which the settlers from Europe come has more power to assimilate them than their race qualities have to change it." He thus paid tribute to the transforming power of the American environment and defended the immigrant against the charge of being a corrupting serpent in an American Eden. Yet even as he wrote, a change was coming over the American scene. To be an immigrant in the earlier years was to be part of an experience in the making. You didn't feel unwanted or a misfit, nor did you have to feel ashamed of your cultural origin. But after the Civil War, with the triumph of industrialism, America became the country where miracles were in full swing and where entrance was an admission to the miracle-making. As an immigrant coming to something no longer experimental but already tested and created, you were suspect of trying to cash in on a good thing. As a combined entrance fee and expiation, you were crowded into slums, forced to do the dirty and poorly paid jobs, made to feel an outsider.

The "natives" began to ask how these gate-crashers dared be so different from them. "If a few million members of the Alpine, Mediterranean, and Semitic races are poured among us," wrote the novelist Kenneth Roberts, "the result must inevitably be a hybrid race of people as worthless and futile as the good-for-nothing mongrels of Central America and southeastern Europe." There were so many "mongrels" pouring in; they looked strange, swarmed everywhere, were too loud; they came from a Europe thick with revolutionary conspiracy to an America where the possessors were becoming insecure. Besides, there was always in the background the monstrous (and fascinating) sexual threat that the purity of America's blood would be polluted by miscegenation with the swarthy foreigners.

Thus the later phase of immigration corroded the generous energies of the earlier America. The Israel Zangwill vision of America as a "melting pot"—a crucible into which poured metals from every country while "the great alchemist melts and fuses them with his purging flame"—was greeted with enthusiasm, but it was a dangerous metaphor since it implied that all the immigrant strains must be purified by being assimilated with something more "American." In World War I the fear cropped up of the "hyphenated American" who was not being melted, fused, and purged rapidly enough. The "Red scare" that followed the war was directed against the foreign-born and, like the even more intense furor after World War II, it reinforced the whole agonizing doubt about the nature of American identity. Some Americans found in it a sadistic outlet for their aggression; many others fell prey to intellectual and emotional confusion. The quota formula embodied in the 1921 Immigration Act was thought up by a well-intentioned China missionary who saw in the quota system a way of merging the restrictions upon Oriental immigration with more general ones and thus in effect denying their existence. In the 1924 law the base year on which the quota for each country was fixed (the "national origins provision") was pushed back in order to minimize the number of Mediterranean and East European entries. It was hard for Europeans to fathom a democratic philosophy which admitted only 3,000 French and 5,000 Italians a year, as against roughly 25,000 Germans and 65,000 British.

Immigration restriction thus became deliberately discriminatory and racist, remaining thus through the McCarran-Walter Law of 1952 to the present day. The "Golden Door" of Emma Lazarus was swung all but shut. Where, in 1900, 13 per cent of Americans were foreign-born, in 1950 only 7 per cent, in 1960 the percentage will be negligible. The irony of the exclusionist policy was that since it could not be applied to Puerto Rico (which was part of territorial America) the exclusionists had to tolerate the influx of Puerto Ricans, who were very different from their ideal type. If the purpose of immigration policy was to ensure a stable admittance of, say, 250,000 immigrants a year, this could have been achieved more rationally by setting that figure and admitting them either in the order of their application acceptance or in terms of whether they possessed the needed skills. The fight to relax the harshness of the immigration laws and their administration is still carried on but halfheartedly, as if no one believed any longer that the trend could be reversed, since (whatever the intellectuals may think) the anti-alien component in Congress and the constituencies is still strong.

Even before the door was closed the impact of the narrowing attitudes had made itself felt in the minds of the immigrants themselves. Having caught the fever of the rush to America, they were overeager and overtense. Everything in them was heightened: the love of freedom, the urge to "make good," the vulnerability to scorn, the anxiety to belong. The structure of the immigrant family was corroded, and the pride of belief in the traditions which had been brought across the seas was shaken.

The immigrant found himself caught between two ghettos. One was the outer ghetto of economic and social discrimination imposed upon him. The other was the inner ghetto which came from his feverish efforts to meet this assault either by wearing the badges and aping the ways of the new culture, thus rejecting his own family and ethnic tradition, or by an equal overemphasis on retreat within the shell of the old culture, taking the form of an ethnic chauvinism. There was thus a double process of overcompensation at work—that of an anxious assimilationism and that of a belligerent ethnic orthodoxy. In both cases it was a response to hostility and an expression of alienation. The success stories of individual immigrants do not belie this but rather confirm it. Most of the immigrant-boy-to-tycoon success stories are about men who found the transition from one culture to another too precipitous to be bridged without a single-minded effort that left its effects on the personality.

The "melting pot" phase of American thinking about the immigrants was happily short-lived. Today there are few serious writers and thinkers who do not see through the fallacy of viewing American culture as a kind of manufacturing process which stamps out cultural diversities and turns complex human material into a monolithic Great Stone Face. To be sure, the flow of new immigrants has become the merest trickle (since 1940 it has averaged not much over 100,000 a year), and the issue is therefore how the second and third and later generations are to guide their lives. Among the newer immigrant groups the current of thinking that has triumphed is the one set in motion by Randolph Bourne and Horace Kallen—the idea of a "cultural pluralism" in which the ethnic groups cherish their own traditions while refusing to isolate themselves from the larger culture.

The problem for the recent newcomers and their children, as indeed for all Americans, is to hold several cultures in organic suspension, weaving each in with the other in a process without which American society as we know it could not have been formed. The question is not whether the older traditions are to change; for change, with a measure of absorption, is inevitable. The real problem is to make certain that the pace of change is not destructively rapid and that it does not involve a flight from the rootedness of one's fathers which leaves the sons and grandsons with no base on which to make the transition. The difference is one of mood and value as well as tempo. It is the difference between *assimilation,* which is a one-way drive that attaches no value to what is left behind and marked for extinction, and *integration,* which is a two-way circuit, where the new national consciousness adds a new dimension to the older ethnic tradition, and the older tradition adds emotional depth and rootedness to the new cultural product.*

3. People in Motion

AMERICANS HAVE ALWAYS been voyagers. After crossing the ocean to find the America of their dreams, the settlers paddled, steamed, and carried freight down its network of great rivers and built canals to connect them. They proved to be good land sailors across the "sea of grass" on their prairie schooners. They built graceful clipper ships that sailed the world's seas, making America a great trading nation. They sped on iron wheels along the railway roadbeds and then on rubber wheels along the macadam automobile highways. Finally they became air voyagers: a successor to the sea and the land, the air now became the element in which they expressed their will to conquer.

"Americans are always moving on" was the opening line of Stephen Benét's unfinished heroic poem of the westward migrations. Much of American literature has been dominated by this theme of restless movement on land or river or sea. Of the historical writings, there is Turner's work on the frontier and Parkman's on the *Oregon Trail,* along with such minor classics as Morison's *Maritime History of Massachusetts,* Webb's *The Great Plains,* and De Voto's *Across the Wide Missouri.* Melville's *Moby Dick,* like his South Seas romances, would have been impossible except in a maritime as well as a Puritan civilization, where the moral quest for the principle of good and evil could naturally be presented in the story of a pursuit over the high seas. Mark Twain's *Life on the Mississippi* is an American novel of the apprentice years, expressive of the turbulence and power of the greatest of America's rivers. The majestic highway of Western life in Mark Twain's time, it was a virile world of swarming passengers, profane ship captains, tobacco-spitting, gambling, steamer races, bursting boilers, salty language, and tall stories—the perfect school of experience for a young man with a feeling for America and the knack of literary portraiture. Mark Twain's greatest novel, *Huckleberry Finn,* was also borne along, now drowsily, now tumultuously, on the current of the Mississippi. A series of books on the "Rivers of America," crowded with historic incident, has shown how interwoven America's waterways were with the whole course of its history; yet in each case the rivers have in recent years lost most of their importance.

* For a further discussion, see Ch. I, Sec. 3, "The Slaying of the European Father," and Ch. VII, Sec. 5, "The Minority Situation," where I stress not the issues of demography (as here) but the social situation of minority groups in America.

In our own time, except for Faulkner's novels and a few others like Steinbeck's *Grapes of Wrath,* the immediate natural environment has ceased to carry the symbolic themes of the writers. The violence of American life is now expressed not in the impact of the physical environment but in the jungle warfare of human living; not in the voyage across the ocean or down a river, nor in Ahab's quest for the White Whale, but in the detective hunt for the murderer whose victim is unreal and crime fantastic, and for the solution which leaves all of life's problems unsolved.

The idea of Nature, as it has been expressed in American commentary, has two aspects—that of restless mobility, as emphasized by Turner and his followers, and that of attachment to place, as emphasized by the regionalists and traditionalists. To understand America one must see them as facets of each other—a double beat of migration and the sense of place. The wanderings of Americans are due less to an innate restlessness or to the poverty of the land, as with nomadic peoples, than to a quest for opportunity. When the beat of migration has fulfilled itself, it may be expected that the same intensity which informed it will be transformed into attachment to place.

There have been three types of American migration—the transoceanic migrations, the migration to new frontiers, and those internal crisscrossings which may be called reshuffling migrations and which are basically migrations to the city and the suburbs.

The classical migration to the Western frontiers was not a planned migration in the sense in which the great dislocations of peoples on today's map are the result of the deliberate acts and policies of government. It was perhaps the last spontaneous great migration in history. Yet, looking back, one can trace a systematic progress, zone by zone, as if a campaign had been mapped out in advance; and a regular succession, wave after wave, of explorers followed by fur traders, followed by mountain men, ranchers, and miners, followed finally by farmers equipped with seed, cattle, and implements. The later stages of this classical westward movement, which crossed the Great Plains and the mountain fastnesses of the Rockies and occupied the rich areas of the Pacific Northwest and California, were filled with violence and greed as well as heroism. The hardships along the Oregon Trail, the struggle to capture the fur trade, and finally the Gold Rush to California present, in heightened form, the Faustian spirit of the classical Great Migration. Not more than one out of twenty of those who took part in the Gold Rush found anything like success, yet we have forgotten the failures and remember only the big prizes. Whole states and a whole region yielded quantities of their best young people in the "Yankee exodus" out of New England. Even after free land was no longer available, the internal reshuffling of population went on, and one may speak of a Great Trail of the past century which in its own way has been as profound in its effects as that of the classical westward movement, if less systematic in its progress.

Each road that led toward the dimly known target was a highway of hope. The contemporary hopes and the nostalgia of our own day have combined to shed a glow of idealization over the rough paths, the bumpy roads and turnpikes of an earlier day, and over stagecoach and "freighter," pony express and even the highwayman. With the railroads came a transportation revolution which left its own deposit of mythology, clustering around the gangs that laid the tracks and the engineers who drove the fast trains that seemed like fiery monsters and even the railroad barons such as Vanderbilt, Fiske, and Hill.

One of the recent phases of the transport revolution, based on the motorcar, has made America a civilization on wheels. By 1956 there were an estimated seventy-five million cars and trucks in America, owned by seventy million people, at least one for every family, including the poorer families; and the auto industry was geared to turn out eight million new cars a year, to take their place on almost four million miles of toll expressways, freeways, rural feeder roads, and city streets. One out of every seven Americans had a job in some phase of auto construction and service, and highway transport. By 1965 there should be close to a hundred million cars crowding the roads and streets, choking every artery.

America's motor technology, while it has not produced the feverish internal mobility, has made it possible. Long before he is old enough to get a driver's license the American boy, particularly in the small town and the suburb, has been holding the wheel and become conscious of himself as a potential driver. The American girl measures a male partly, at least, in terms of the kind of car he drives. Wage-earner families who live in slums—especially Negro workers—often own cars that are better than their living quarters, and a glance at the bumper-to-bumper congestion on auto roads on week ends will show that many Americans spend almost as much time in their cars as in their homes. Autos are no longer a luxury for an American elite; they have become a living-standard compulsive for the American masses. They fill a psychic need more important even than adequate housing or education or health, and form the crucial test of whether your living standards make you an accepted member of the community. The car is a house on wheels, used for daily chores, family outings and week ends, shopping, visits, business, and (by the youngsters) for "petting."

This house on wheels has developed in the past half century from a fussy, crotchety, unreliable contraption to a miracle of engineering which starts easily, shifts automatically, drives smoothly at high rates of speed, develops enormous power (although it is often driven by women and even elderly people), and comes in various shades and combinations of color to suit every taste and sometimes even to match the clothes of the owner's wife or daughter. It can be paid for on the installment plan, but it becomes quickly obsolete and is "turned in" and replaced frequently by a new one or by a better "secondhand" one. A congeries of revolutions were needed—in manufacture, quick-drying paint, macadam roads, engine power, car design, mass production, and the assembly line—to produce the end product of the American car. It congests the cities and the roads, and in the hands of the amateurs, the "hot rod" enthusiasts, and the neurotics it becomes a lethal instrument of grisly death and decimates the population. It has made the filling station, the parkway, the four-lane highway, the quick-service roadside hot-dog stand or restaurant, the "motel," the used-car lot, the trailer camp, the giant freight truck, the motor bus, the parking lot, the shopping center, the Friday-to-Sunday traffic jam, and the urban parking maze the most obtrusive features of the American landscape. It has made necessary a continual renewing of road construction, which has laid across the country a labyrinthine network of auto and truck roads, some of them toll turnpike roads financed by private bondowners, the rest financed by Federal and state funds, all of them as essential to the poor as to the rich. It has brought about a counter-railroad revolution, making freight traffic and daily travel independent of the railroad station and the commuter train, shifting factory sites and farm values, and spawning new suburbs where the family disperses every morning and reassembles every evening via the automobile. And it has made the seaside or mountain holiday and the fishing and camping vacation the routine adventure of the middle classes and even of workers' families.

The new Air Age, whose impact is just beginning to be felt, has further heightened the mobility of Americans. The sprawling airports, with the gleaming giant birds swooping in and out of them, are a portent of a time when distances will lose all meaning. Already the congestion of the airways is creating a traffic problem in the American skies much like the congestion of auto traffic. Yet the private family plane is unlikely to replace the family car, even though it may make the use of the car less obsessive. What the Air Age has done has been to make the faraway vacation possible for the boss's secretary as well as for the boss.

In the mid-1950s at least sixty million Americans left their homes for some kind of annual vacation, many of them going halfway across the Continent, some of them halfway across the world. Some go to the mountain streams of the Northeast or Northwest or to Canada for fishing, some to Florida or California for the sun, some to the resorts or the beach shacks or trailer colonies, some to Mexico or South America for its atmosphere, many to Europe for its traditions and glamour, and some simply hit the highways to get a look at the country. Tourism has become one of America's big industries, involving expenditures of close to twenty billion a year. Almost every wage-earner gets an annual vacation with pay and gets away from job and home by air, train, boat, car, or bus. The trend is toward longer vacations and therefore longer trips. However, the recent changes in life span and the quest for personal fulfillment have filled the world's capitals with middle-class and middle-aged Americans whose children have grown up and who are spending their years of leisure or "retirement" wandering over the world, armed with dictionaries, tourist guides, traveler's checks, and an insatiable hunger to see, hear, and feel. It is as if the impact of a machine civilization on the nerve centers of Americans had produced a constant mobility, whether out of boredom, curiosity, or an expressive sense of freedom, which makes the great migrations of American history seem fragmentary by comparison.

More embracing than this mobility of tourism is the restless movement from job to job and from home to home. Inside the same city there are constant residence changes with changing jobs and social status. Inside the same state there is a growing movement from farm and small town to the city, and from the core city to the suburban fringes of the larger metropolitan or cluster city. A government study of migrant families in 1937 showed that in an industrial center like Detroit, drawing constantly on new labor sources, four out of five people had not lived in the same dwelling for five years. This was an extreme case, yet it is estimated that in the decade from the mid-1940s to the mid-1950s one out of five Americans changed homes in any one year, and in the big cities the proportions might run higher.

The crucial phase of this phenomenon of Americans on the move is the movement from state to state. During wars and periods of intense arms rivalry there is a flow of workers to the defense industry areas. This has been accompanied by a steady migration of Negroes, during and after the world wars, from the Southern states to the big cities of the Northeast and the Middle West, like Philadelphia, New York, Pittsburgh, Detroit, Chicago, St. Louis, and Kansas City. In addition there has been an over-all shift of American population, along with the movement of industry, to the South, the Southwest, and the Pacific Coast, especially to Florida, Texas, California, Oregon, and Washington. In the single decade from 1940 to 1950 the population of California increased by 50 per cent, that of Oregon by 40 per cent, that of Washington by 37 per cent.

The center of American population, where presumably the whole American plane balances in an equilibrium, moved steadily westward and slightly southward until in 1950 it was in southeast Illinois. The great boom industries of automobiles, shipyards, and aviation also moved West and South. The result was a rapid increase in the proportion of native Americans living outside the state of their birth, the current figure being around 25 per cent. In the West Coast states, where the rate of population increase has been highest, the proportion is highest: in California, at mid-century, more than two out of three were born in another state.*

What gives impetus to these waves of internal migration? Industrial workers followed the shifting currents that have determined the location of industries, moving wherever new industries opened up or where their skills could command the highest wages. Farm workers with no land of their own, or small farmers whose land had been wiped out by erosion, moved with the seasonal crops—rarely settling down, creating a permanent underlying population of migratory workers. Whole industries were uprooted, either because some boom played itself out or else to get closer to better markets or a cheaper labor force. One of the results was those "ghost towns" that are especially melancholy on the American landscape because they seem like skeletons at a rich man's feast.

But in the main the internal migrations are opportunity-and-advancement migrations. They are made not out of land hunger or the quest of freedom, as was true of the original migrations from abroad, but out of the pursuit of better chances for business and profits, for work and wages, for climate, schools, living conditions. Impalpable though it may seem as a motive, one reason for America's physical mobility is its social mobility: the lack of stable class lines and of a massive traditional past makes men's feet wander. As De Tocqueville saw clearly in his classic chapter, "Why Americans Are So Restless in the Midst of Their Prosperity," the American remains restless until he has done his best to look for the place, the job, the environing physical setting and social climate in which he wants to live out his life.

Through this search for place and vocation he comes as close to finding himself as he is ever likely to come. This is the experimental part of his life. These ventures in fortune and in change of locale are, in a sense, more truly the American educational system than the schools themselves. One of the truisms about American college graduates, for example, is that their best life training comes in the decade after college

* For a further discussion of migration shifts in terms of trends in population distribution, see Sec. 5, "Human Resources: Population Profile."

when the sequence of the jobs they pick up as they roam the nation reads like an eighteenth-century picaresque novel. The 1950 census showed that, from 1947 to 1950, 28 per cent of the 18-34 age group changed homes in any one year, but only 10 per cent of the age group after 45. The most mobile groups were the professional and semiprofessional ones—young couples and single men among the doctors, engineers, and technicians—who also took the biggest jumps across the continent. Increasingly also, regardless of search or choice, the big corporations have sent their young minor executives and technicians to take up jobs and homes in branch plants and offices across the country, moving them periodically for experience or promotion and creating a new category of American transients.

It does not follow that the migrating Americans find what they are looking for. In any deep sense many of them perhaps don't. But to move is one way of breaking the fear of being caught. The feeling an American dreads most is that of being "stuck"—held fast in the mud of an environment where everything seems stagnant. In many areas of Europe and the Far East this has been men's destiny for centuries, but to an American it seems a violation of everything he has felt about life. The sensation of being trapped is the ultimate indignity. So he moves. And his moving keeps alive his sense of social possibility, the belief that something can happen; and as long as something can happen all is not lost.

This hope and the accompanying mood of adventure are a clue to the impact the internal migrations have had on the American character. They serve to explain why each new frontier, and especially the Far Western one, has been romanticized in the folk imagination. Buffalo Bill, Kit Carson and the other Indian Scouts, General Custer, the "silver kings" of the Comstock lode, and even "badmen" like Billy the Kid have become type figures of a tradition which has run itself out in the "Westerns," the movies, and the pulp fiction. Yet they are part of an idealizing strain which has a deep beat of impulse and of which the Turner thesis itself was a kind of expression.

How crucial a need the internal migrations serve for Americans was shown after the end of World War II, when a great surge of population resettlement carried millions of Americans westward in an unplanned and uncontrolled movement that seemed almost tropismatic. Through the shifting of established industries and the opening of new war industries, the war was the spur to the reshuffling of the population. Its effect was especially great on the young veterans, many of whom found themselves training on the West Coast or shifting from there to the Pacific combat area. They saw places they had never seen, with a different physical and social landscape, and they liked what they saw. At the war's end they took their young wives and found work there. In a single decade Oregon's population increased by almost 40 per cent and California's by more than 50 per cent. Many of the migrants came from the prairie states, where the land had been ravaged by erosion and overgrazing and where opportunity seemed at an end. Many were young Negro veterans who swelled the Negro population of San Francisco, Seattle, and Portland. They brought new ways of thinking to normally conservative areas and changed the political landscape of the states that became their new homes.

Yet the continuing strain of rebirth in all these migrations is evident enough. The function served in the days of the classical migration, by 160 acres of open land available for the taking (to be sure, after the railroads and speculators had carved out their share), is now served by the shift in industrial location. The young veterans went west not because it was the West but because they found opportunities in new industries located near new sources of power and new markets. One of the consequences of the idealization of the agrarian society of the frontier was to make it harder for American social thought to deal with industrial reality. The fact is that for most Americans the movement of social opportunity has to keep pace with the movement of industries and the building of power plants to harness hydroelectric energy. To explain why Americans move around as they do today, one would need a theory which took account of the relation between job opportunities, industrial location, the determination not to get stuck, the cultural images of the areas of growth, and the yearning for a home in which one can settle down and get a sense of place.

It is not easy to achieve a sense of place in a culture that is always tearing everything up by the roots, but it is none the less important. In a big country you run the risk of feeling lost, in a new country you run the risk of being anonymous, and the sense of place is a way of riveting yourself down. For those who cannot achieve distinction by amassing money or power or prestige, the attachment to place becomes one way of salvaging the individual identity.

The sense of place is one form of the sense of belonging. Sometimes the attachment to the soil, linked with a clear position in the social hierarchy, is the most positive value a society can offer. This was true in Europe in the Middle Ages, and in the pre-Civil War South in America. But the breakup of European feudal society showed that men may want a sense of belonging more satisfying than the sense of place when it carries nothing else with it. The settlement of America came from the uprooting of the rooted precapitalist European society which led to the long voyages across the seas. Out of this uprooting came a desire to strike new roots. But the new roots could not be just any piece of land or any job in any locality. They had to satisfy what men were coming to demand of life in the new social climate of opportunity. In the case of America every value gets attached to this quest for fulfillment. Thus, paradoxically, even the American sense of place is a dynamic one.

Much of it is also nostalgic. When two Americans discover that they come from the same place, a spark is lit between them. And when an American finds that you have not heard of the place his family came from there is a sense of loss and almost of shock. It is not only that Plainville is thereby denied as if it had never existed but that the whole rich private experience that clusters about it is also denied. Thus the American feels doubly isolated. To be insensitive to these local associations of his is to strip him of a portion of his personality. The dangers of a dynamic society are that they lead to a whittling down of those accretions which the sense of place gives to the personality. When you move from the place where you were known to one where you must make your way, you cling all the more to the memories of place. Thus in the wake of the Yankee migration, "New England societies" were scattered through New York and the Middle West, as far as California. In the bewilderment that comes with the change of scale, pace, and tension, and the supplanting of face-to-face relations by impersonal ones, the place names and place memories that recall the simpler past have a powerful appeal. This was why Thomas Wolfe, moving from Asheville to New York, wove a sense of place into the web of time and memory with his haunting evocation in *Look Homeward, Angel*—"a stone, a leaf, an unfound door"—to express both his longing and his feeling of being lost.

This sense of the past as a sense of place is not restricted to the rural memories. During the great period of city-building, from the 1870s to the 1890s, the town or city took over some of the affection associated with the frontier farmstead and village. It took on a personality pattern that stuck in the memory: the layout of the main streets, the residential section, Shantytown where the Negroes and the foreign slum-folk lived; the schools, dance places, movie houses, night amusement spots; the fancy districts which had about them the tang of the forbidden. In a novel like Booth Tarkington's *The Magnificent Ambersons* one gets something of this retrospective affection. Among these scenes one lived, with these one grew up, these one remembered long afterward, setting down the memories in stories and novels or in those sentimentalized autobiographies or parental biographies in which Americans delight.

The retrospective loyalties, however, form only one of the main strands in the fiber of the American sense of place. The other is the contemporary pride of belonging to a vivid, growing entity—the pride of boosterism, if you will. There is something fiercely assertive about coming from Brooklyn or St. Paul, Kansas City or San Francisco, Maine or Oregon. A novel of manners or a Broadway comedy about Americans would scarcely run true to form if it did not have a character called "Tex" who holds forth with a genial persistence on the glories of the Lone Star State. There is an almost pathetic eagerness to find identification with the characteristic grandeurs and delights of your place, whatever it be, and to draw from the stature you give it at least a cubit to add to your own stature and security.

4. Natural Resources: the American Earth

THE LOVE OF PLACE was the earliest loyalty brought to the American shores. The settlers came from countries of their own where they had loved the familiar land and skies and hills. The American landscape was strange, untidy, uncompassable; the continent was wild, of grand proportions, with a luxuriance of plant and animal life that struck all the early explorers who brought with them "the eye of discovery."

There was the stretch of the Great Forest sweeping from the Atlantic dunes with few breaks to the deep interior, and then the stretch of the Great Plains and the long-grass prairie lands across the Ohio and Mississippi and Missouri to the foothills of the Rockies, and then the short-grass grazing lands and the mountains and deserts to the fertile valleys of the Pacific Coast, with another expanse of Great Forest northward along the coast. It was a land riven by mountain chains, from the Appalachian range in the East to the Sierra in the West, scarred by canyons, watered by broad and tumultuous rivers, with a climate that spanned all the intervals, from the frost of the North Country in the Great Lakes region and the Far Northwest of the fur trappers to the mesas and tablelands of the Southwest, the bayous of Louisiana, and the tropical everglades and swamps of Florida. It was filled, when the settlers first found it, with a fecund vegetation and wildlife: buffalo herds, deer, elk and bears, wild pigeons and geese, alligators and catfish, cod, sturgeon and salmon; with dense canebrake and coarse slough grass and needle grass and bluegrass and stands of prairie dropseed and tall-growing saw-tooth sunflower. And there were the trees: fir and spruce, maple and birch and elm, chestnut, hickory, and the always incredible sequoias, and that aristocrat of all American trees—the great white pine.

For the settlers who had come from the tidy landscapes of Europe, it was not a wholly comfortable sight and it had a touch of the frightening. But it was the right kind of stage-set for the theme and proportions of the mighty drama to be enacted on it, perhaps contrived for that purpose by a Providential scenic designer with an eye for symbolism. It was as if this myriad of landscapes swept up into one was ordained to harbor a myriad of stocks which were in time to be welded into a single nation. Thus the later expansionist cry of "Manifest Destiny," which was to rise from millions of throats as the nation pushed westward, was not only a shibboleth of jingoism but almost a tropism of the American earth, part of the inner logic of a landscape too big to be limited by the historical accidents of settlement and sovereignty. The wild and lush landscape seemed to offer to the eighteenth-century mind, which personified Nature with a capital N, a charter to build on the far-stretched continent a new social system swept clean of privilege, caste, and inequity, to be governed by "the laws of Nature and of Nature's God." This charter proved, for generations of Americans, a pathway to the unchecked exploiting of untapped resources and undreamed-of wealth and power.

It is in this indirect sense, rather than that of direct conditioning, that the American landscape has helped shape the American national character. I use the term "landscape," of course, not only in the decorative and aesthetic sense but as the total physical environment in its relation to human living. It is roughly true that habitat tends to shape habit, although we don't know just how or how much. Some recent students have tried to show how the "mighty Russian plain," with its vast stretches, its extremes of protracted winter cold and intense summer heat, has carved the Russian people into a profile of intense extremes of revolutionary violence and docile endurance. Valid or not, such an approach would be unfruitful for the Americans, who are comparative newcomers and on whom the influence of earth, sky, and climate has not operated over centuries. That is why (although I am well aware of its dangers) I prefer to stress the indirect role of the American landscape as a bold setting for a venture in social construction. This had a subtle but no less powerful influence on American ideas. The environmental silhouette of the landscape bears some relation to the cultural silhouette of American attitudes. On a continent of great richness of regional variation it has been happily difficult to break down political recalcitrance and achieve complete centralization. Where Nature shows such extremes, it is not surprising that the image of an equilibrium should have come from Newtonian thought in Europe with great force into the American Constitution and political system. And where the environment offered a hard challenge to settlement, the Darwinian idea of the survival of the fittest found a fertile social soil and helped shape a competitive social system.

But the great theme of the American earth is the theme of its rich resources and how the Americans have used and abused them—not what the land has done to the people but what the people have done to the land. In a money culture it is difficult to keep clear the distinction between symbolic wealth and the real wealth of the nation. America has been fortunate in the abundance, diversity, quality, and distribution of its real wealth—not only the soil, climate, water, and wildlife but the minerals stored under the earth, the fossil-fuel energy of coal and oil, the natural gas, the hydroelectric energy, the rare minerals entering into atomic energy.

In any calculus of the world's resources—immediate, reserve, and potential—America leads the procession of the nations, with even the Soviet Union following at a distance. America was estimated (1950) to have 30 per cent of the world's harnessed water power and to produce 42 per cent of the world's total electrical power from all sources—about 430 billion kilowatt hours (western Europe produced 25 per cent, the Soviet Union 8 per cent). It used 60 per cent of the world's total petroleum production and 25 per cent of its total coal production; its per-capita use of electrical energy from all sources increased from 455 kilowatt-hours in 1924 to 3,000 kilowatt-hours in 1954, and its per-capita use of total mechanical energy was roughly like that derived from burning eight tons of coal for every person. This was six times the per-capita average for the rest of the world, 160 times the per-capita use of energy in Asia (not including Japan), eight times what Japan used, and more than triple what Europe used.

The picture of American fossil fuel reserves and future supplies and uses of industrial energy is a complex one. A 1938 survey showed America as having an estimated 3,200 billion tons of coal of all grades in reserve, out of 7,300 billion tons for the world. America had more than half the bituminous reserves of the world but a small portion of the anthracite. Some have talked much too optimistically of a 2,000- to 3,000-year supply of coal for America, but this overlooks the fact that probably only a tenth of the reserves may be economically minable, and it assumes present levels of energy consumption, which is an untenable assumption. As population and living standards go up, as the quantity and quality of fossil fuels go down, there will be greater demands on a lessened supply, and greater energy will be required to get at the available further energy. America produces almost two billion barrels of oil a year and uses seven billion; its estimated oil reserves are some fifty-five billion barrels, a ninth of the world's oil reserves. Unless the new geophysicists spot still undiscovered oil domes, the American reserves will not last beyond 1980, but new processes of converting coal, natural gas, and shale oil into liquid fuel are likely to become feasible. America in 1950 had a proved reserve of 180 trillion cubic feet of natural gas, which was about fifty times its rate of use, but by 1960 the annual volume siphoned off into pipelines and distributed over the country was likely to double, and, increasingly, chemicals as well as liquid fuels were being manufactured from natural gas close to the site of the reserves. America also had zinc, lead, bauxite, tin, tungsten, and molybdenum, although the reserves of all of these were precarious. It had limestone and aluminum clays and brown lead ores from which new processes will be able to extract new uses.

The great event that lies ahead in the use of American mineral and energy resources is the shift to new sources of supply, new kinds of energy, new modes of conversion. Harrison Brown, writing about American mineral consumption, points out that there is an annual per-capita flow of 1,260 pounds of steel through production lines, with eight tons of steel in per-capita use, and both amounts steadily rising. There are sharply diminishing reserves of iron, aluminum, copper, sulphur, and the ore seams have to be followed deep underground. The prospects are that these ores will have to be extracted from ordinary rock, and the energy for extracting them will be atomic energy. The supplies of the great energy sources—coal, petroleum, natural gas—are finite and exhaustible, and their place is likely to be taken by atomic and solar power. The uranium and thorium needed for atomic energy can, if necessary, be extracted from the plentiful granite. As Brown puts it, "the basic raw materials for the industries of the future will be sea water, air, ordinary rock, sedimentary deposits of limestone and phosphate rock, and sunlight." Thus, while in a sense America is becoming a "have-not" nation, increasingly dependent on foreign imports for crucial minerals, its resources, under the conditions of an expanding technology, may prove enough to fill its reasonable needs.

As for the soil and what grows on it, the American endowment is great. Of its 1.9 billion acres of land, nearly a fifth (400 million) is used for crops, about a half (900 million) for pasture and grazing, and less than a third (600 million) is farm woodland and forest. Despite the denuding of the Great Forest, there are still big timber stands on the Pacific Coast, in California, Washington, and especially Oregon. There are nine-feet-high cornfields in Iowa and a vast stretch of wheatland on the Great Plains from Texas through Minnesota. There are the cotton and tobacco fields of the South and the lush valleys of the Pacific slope. America has all but conquered the problem of mass hunger that plagued men through history. There were many areas in the world where the soil was better cared for than in America, and where intensive cultivation made the yield higher. But with their skills of science and machinery the Americans applied (in the Keynesian phrase) a different kind of "multiplier"—other than sheer human toil—to the fertility of the soil itself. Thus the United States became the granary and breadbasket for many areas of the world where feudal land tenure, ignorance of soil techniques, and lack of capital equipment allowed the good arable land to go wretchedly unused.

For more than a century after the founding of the Republic there was a complacent assumption that Nature's plenty need not be guarded and would resist forever the withering hand of time and man. Americans have had a self-confidence and self-admiration on the score of their resources that few other peoples could match. The record of civilization runs against the hope that Americans will learn where others have not. In Asia, Africa, and the Mediterranean areas there is the story of the using up and disintegration of the environment as a productive system. One thinks of the "classical deserts" of North Africa and the Middle East, where (as Ritchie Calder puts it) "some fifteen civilizations, cultures, or empires foundered in the dust of their own creation." Overdramatically, one may speak of the protracted large-scale plundering of the American earth and ask who were the plunderers.

The answer may be found in a combination of land hunger, greed, haste, and planlessness. Many of the settlers came from areas in Europe where land was cramped, holdings small, and the laws of succession rigid. The yield of the American grasslands and forestland when first tamed by the plow was richer than human dream. The early settlers felled the big trees, cutting over and burning over the forest, "deadening" the ever-larger clearings. Leaving badly damaged soil behind, they kept moving westward to virgin soil. On much of this American farmers have kept the yield high by crop rotation and the skillful replacement of the soil's properties. But there are also millions of acres where the methods used were those of ruthless "soil-mining," as if the soil were a repository of fossil fuels to be extracted from it and then good-by. The single-crop system of wheat, corn, and cotton impoverished the land, the complex bundle of organic processes that held the plains together was broken, and the denuded earth was left exposed to dust storms that blew it away and floods that washed the richness of the topsoil down into the rivers and seas. It has been estimated that three of the nine inches of topsoil that the American Continent possessed in Colonial times have been destroyed, most of it since the Civil War.

What happened to the wheat and corn lands happened also to the cattle lands. The opening of the great grazing plains caught the world's imagination, and to many in Europe the American cowboy with his horse and lasso and six-shooter became the type figure symbolizing the derring-do of the American. But deterioration set in with the great livestock boom that followed the Civil War. The Western lands were overstocked and overgrazed by cattle and sheep, until now their grazing capacity is less than half of what it was; erosion by wind and water set in;

dust storms came, and droughts, and "deserts on the march." The valley bottoms of the Southwest were gutted by erosion, with thousands of arroyos cut into them. The result is that the grazing areas of the West are today the slowest areas of population growth, and the young people are abandoning them.

Perhaps the most tragic phase was the devastation of the forests. America lost nine tenths of its timber to insects, forest fires, and—most of all—ruthless cutting. A good chunk of the mythology of America, and some of the folk heroes like Paul Bunyan, came out of the lumber camps and logging. But after the romance had tarnished there remained only the pathos of the predaceous. The lumber barons stripped the land of its trees with a fervor that made huge timber fortunes and then moved on to virgin timber. With the forests gone and the hills cut away, the land was despoiled of its strength, floods and drought followed, and the small farmer had to move on with the moving deserts. Paul Bunyan was succeeded by the "Okies" and by Steinbeck's Joads. In 1918 Americans were cutting almost six trees for every one that was replanted, and the denuding reached right up to the last frontier of the Oregon timber stand. The more responsible companies are now treating trees like crops, to be farmed and replaced, but there are still "gyppo" outfits that "cut out and run," never replanting what they have destroyed. To make it worse, the cattlemen are moving up on the trees, seeking to take over for "private enterprise" the grazing lands of the national forests, situated on the high-country watersheds.

Thus the hunger for land and profits and the blind application of *laissez faire* in an area where it makes no sense have left little room either for a reverence toward the American earth or a wisdom about its long-range use. Some daemonic force seemed to be driving Americans on to despoil the land and its resources. Mark Twain's *Gilded Age* depicted caustically the interweaving of public lands, legislative bribery, and real-estate promotion in the post-Civil War days. The dramatic "land-rush" episodes of the *Cimmaron* novels and the technicolor movies have blotted out the uncomfortable fact that the lion's share of the public lands went in handouts and bounties to the railroad companies and were otherwise caught up in speculation. The speculative spirit, applied to the wheat crops, was the theme of Frank Norris's highly dramatic novels, *The Pit* and *The Octopus,* which were not too far from the truth in describing the soil's product and the fate of growers and consumers alike as the playthings of the commodity exchanges and the railroads.

In the case of the oil lands, which furnish the power for America's motor civilization, the history of the industry has also been one of get-and-grab-and-squeeze-dry. The "rule of capture," carried over by analogy from a legal system adapted to a hunting economy, gave the oil to whatever producer pumped it first out of the ground. Each oilman thus had to run his well at maximum to drain off as much as possible from the common underground reservoir, and to meet this piracy of oil-stripping his neighbors had to build offset wells. The result was a ghastly waste, as well as competitive overproduction, with only a 10 per cent recovery of oil in the early years. Eventually a "proration" system was worked out between groups of owners under government regulation, but not before the oil supplies had spouted much of their richness into the sky.

An ironic later phase in the natural history of the American land expressed the hunger for "real estate" to be "developed" and "turned over" at a quick profit. The extreme symbol of this was the Florida land boom of the 1920s, when the drive to use the land not for its products but for quick speculative riches reached manic and even comic proportions. At the end of the boom all involved found themselves stripped of the paper empires they had dreamed up, with their grandiose real-estate developments memorialized only by a few street signs and billboards still standing in the surrounding emptiness, promising urban glories to come. Incidentally, many of them did come in time, in the more moderate and sustained boom of the 1940s and 1950s.

The story of the gold lands is similarly symbolic. When California gold was discovered the "gold rush" was a dramatic sign of the whole feverish effort to scoop riches out of the earth. The gold flowed into circulation and served as base for a pyramid of credit and capital such as no economy has ever built. American investments and the favorable American trade balance, like a lodestone, drew most of the remaining gold from the rest of the world to be stored again, by a fateful cycle of return, in the American earth.

The profile of the use of American resources is actually much more of a mixed picture than this suggests. To the theme of past plunder and exploitation must be added the theme of the present efforts at conservation and the accelerated discovery of new energy sources. Americans are adept at using up very fast the resources that cannot be restored and at developing new ones. It was not until the turn of the twentieth century, with Theodore Roosevelt and Gifford Pinchot, and later with George W. Norris and Franklin Roosevelt, that the conservationists tried to make Americans aware of the effects of years of haste, waste, and ruthlessness. Recently the conservation movement has entered a new phase: not only to prevent the abuse of resources but to realize their full potential. The problems of conserving the soil are being grappled with, especially through contour farming, terracing, strip cropping, irrigation, crop rotation, and the planting of tree shelter belts. Beyond that is the larger planning of conservation by approaching an entire watershed as a unit.

But the canker of heedlessness and greed has not been rooted out. One of the prime facts about natural resources in America, unlike the case in most other cultures, is that they are for the most part privately owned and exploited. The America of the mid-1950s seems largely to have forgotten the experience of the post-Civil War years and to be undoing much of the work of the New Deal years. Caught up in a complacent confidence that America had found the secret to the best use of its resources, and that private owners deserved the rich prizes because they made the best use of them for the public benefit, Congress and the state legislatures gave generously out of the national largess. The formula usually involved the transfer of resources from Federal to state control or to private associations of producers. Thus the rich offshore oil deposits, especially off the coast of Louisiana, Texas, and California, and much of the grazing land in the public domain were transferred to the states, which in turn made them available to private exploitation. The transfer of the oil deposits was not achieved without a bitter political fight and a Congressional act that overrode the Supreme Court decisions, but huge sums were at stake and big interests involved, and the outcome could not be doubted. The control of the grazing lands came into the hands of cattlemen's associations that were in effect private "guilds"—para-political organizations which were able to outmaneuver the political bureaucrats when they could not win them over. In the case of hydroelectric power there was a rollback of the New Deal effort to build giant dams under public auspices, to furnish power to private and municipal consumers, and under the impact of the Hoover Commission reports even the great achievement of the TVA was not regarded as wholly immune to this rollback.

Water has done more than any other element to force on the American a unitary approach to his environment and its resources. If Jean Brunhes was right, that "every human enterprise is a mixture of a little bit of humanity, a little bit of soil, and a little bit of water," it is the water that has proved most difficult. It forms—with droughts, erosion, and floods—an indivisible water complex. The rains, with no trees or vegetation to hold them in the earth, grow into floods. The eroded soil, washed away by torrents, flows down in millions of tons along the rivers, becoming silt, clogging up the river channels, creating new floods. But the flood-control programs have to compete for Federal funds with programs for irrigation and reclamation. To top it off, there is the problem of water scarcity. With the falling water tables and mounting industrial water demands, areas like Southern California, the Texas Panhandle, the Southwestern states, Illinois, New Jersey, and New York have been threatened by periodic water famines. The legal problem of who gets how much of what water is available has led to a water imperialism, with protracted wars between communities and sometimes whole states for the control of the watersheds of the great rivers, and with attempted water grabs by those who have been called the "Water-Seekers."

It has become clear that the best answer to this bundle of water problems is to approach it as a unit. It is to consider the whole river-valley area enclosed and interlaced by the waters as an entity demanding social and engineering solutions which involve the land and the people, agriculture and hydroelectric power and industry, as parts of the indivisible water complex. Not that every American river and river basin is like every other. Their individual forms are unique and each must be studied for its uniqueness, as the Water Resources Policy Commission did in its study of ten American river basins. But the pattern of interrelations is inescapable. It applies to the Columbia Basin, to the Missouri and the Tennessee, to the Central Valley of California, to the Rio Grande and the Colorado, to the Connecticut and the Potomac, to the Alabama-Coosa and the Ohio Basin.

The interrelations are those between an exacting, if also a munificent, natural environment and the conditions of an industrial civilization in an Age of Power. Put in another way, they are the relations between the natural and social landscapes of the American continent. Americans have put the concept into practice in the functioning of the TVA, an American invention which is being adapted to river-basin regions in India and the Middle East. A central feature of the TVA is the multiple-purpose dam—for flood control, irrigation, land reclamation, and the generating of hydroelectric power. Not surprisingly, the extension of the TVA idea to the other American river-basin areas was bitterly fought by the power companies and their legislative champions. Eventually the multiple-purpose dam and the single-river-basin approach carry a force which will be hard to resist, since the irrepressible logic of the Power Age will prove stronger even than the power empires. The new industries that mark out the line of industrial growth—aviation, chemicals, light metals, alloys, electronics, atomic energy—are insatiable consumers of power. To meet their demands, and at the same time to meet the problems of the whole river basin and its needs, is one of the new imperatives of American life, going beyond party politics and the ideology of either private or government enterprise. Whether it is the Norris Dam that is involved, or Shasta or Grand Coulee or Hell's

Canyon, they are not likely to be wished away or cramped into crippling economic forms.

To do so would be like a man-made forging of Nature's authentic signature. Nor would it make political sense to the most conservative groups in American life—the farmer and the small businessman, who are among the new customers for the power generated by the multi-purpose dam. For rural families in the TVA area or the Pacific Northwest, cheaply available electricity means the farm revolution, the kitchen revolution, and the communications revolution—that is to say, a generator, a deep-freeze, and a TV set. For the small businessman, as has been shown in the Tennessee Valley, it means community purchasing power for his products. The TVA has given new meaning to the idea of a region and of regional planning by keeping alive the interrelatedness of the region's needs, sinews, and potential growth.

I stress the exploring of future potentials here rather than the conserving of past resources. What we count as resources changes with the changing industrial arts. Americans have been of a twofold mind on the question of their natural resources. They neglected and wasted them, perhaps with the comforting conviction that "the ravens will provide"; and when they discovered the extent of their waste they grew panicky and gave themselves to an intense conservation movement. At the same time they are basically future-minded, dwelling not so much on the Great Estate they have inherited as on continuing inventories and forecasts of "needs and resources." Along with being future-minded and potential-minded, Americans are abundance-minded, as befitting (in Potter's phrase) a "people of plenty." Despite acute periodic attacks of guilt and panic, they have never taken seriously either the doctrine of closed space or the doctrine of exhausted resources. Even their haste and their predations against Nature were part of their basic optimism: men who are continually in motion and hope to transform themselves and their fortunes are unlikely to balk at defacing and transforming their environment.

A half century ago Henry Adams saw the coming of "the new American—the child of incalculable coal power, chemical power, electric power, and radiating energy, as well as of new forces yet undetermined," and predicted that he would be "a sort of God compared with any former creature of nature." For all his pessimism and his pose as an archaism in a new society, Adams and his "law of acceleration" in history expressed as well as foretold the crescendo of energy development. In 150 years America has increased perhaps fifty or sixty times its per-capita energy production from fossil fuels and water power, as compared with the America of 1800, which was mainly a consumer of wood fuel

—and the process continues. The Paley Commission of 1952 reported that since World War I the U.S. had swallowed up larger quantities of mineral fuels and of most metals than had been used in the whole span of world history. But the expanding skills of scientists also enabled them to discover synthetics, plastics, and electronics, and to open up a new dimension in the peaceful potentials of atomic energy. There was, of course, still one area of great vulnerability in the armor of resources within which America was encased. It was its dependence on foreign sources of supply for many of its strategic raw materials, such as tin and arsenic, manganese, zinc, bauxite, titanium. But this was a weakness only in the event of another world war—which in itself would destroy the whole fragile frame of technology, transport, and industry which gives American resources their meaning. The other area of vulnerability—the danger that population growth will outrun resources —was real enough, but it applied less to America than to the crowded and underdeveloped areas of the world.

America has the resources for its present and future needs, if it has the will to use them fully and the social imagination to use them equitably. What it is in danger of forgetting is that, whether in an industrial or agrarian society, in an age of giant power or of forest clearings, the web between man and his environment is broken only at his peril. The final issue goes beyond the waste or conservation of resources. It is the issue of basic attitude. Whether through land hunger or riches hunger the frontiersman rifled and used up as he went, was always in a hurry, dreamed of empires. The speculators, city-builders and empire-builders followed in his track, and the scientist kept pace with them, promising to think up new synthetic products when the old resources were used up. Despite the influence of the natural environment on the American mind, what was lacking in every case was a reverence for Nature.

Naturalists speak of the "hydrologic cycle" by which rain is imprisoned in the soil, drained into the rivers and oceans, returned to the atmosphere, and once more released for human use. They speak also of the "biotic cycle," the similar web and sequence of the growth of plant life and its use by man, and the return of its waste products and chemical properties to the soil to become once more parts of the cycle of organic growth. But encompassing both there is the balance of nature and man, by which man is sustained by the environment but only on condition that he should not murderously waste his Great Estate but "dress it and keep it." When the American loses the reverence for the American earth to which he is bound he loses more than his resources. He loses his meaning and his capacity to sustain a great civilization with its curious and ephemeral network of ways.

5. Human Resources: Population Profile

OBSERVERS WHO TRAVELED across the American Continent in the mid-1950s were usually impressed by two quantitative things they saw—the number of automobiles and TV sets, and the number of babies. The notable fact here is that a materialist America, which might have been expected to choose higher living standards rather than larger families, defied the diagnosticians and chose both. Characteristically the Americans themselves spoke of their "baby boom" as if it were little different from a housing boom or a boom in uranium stocks. Yet beneath the flipness of the phrase the "baby boom" half revealed and half concealed a dramatic revolution that overturned many accepted ideas and expectations about American population trends.

To students of civilization there are certain indices of its vitality. Borrowing and broadening an early English phrase that was restricted to a census, we may speak of these as a Domesday inventory of a people in its crucial demographic phases: its numbers, its birth rate, its death rate, its population growth, its average life span, its family size, its age distribution, its occupational and educational composition, its physical and psychic health, and the food, housing, and welfare of its people. Of these the crucial ones are the birth rate, the death rate, and population growth. The bugbear of the historians of civilization has long been the static society, or "stationary state."

Not surprisingly, most Americans share this view and get uneasy when there are signs of the slowing up of their population growth. Like some other Western peoples, they feel that a decrease in the rate of growth is somhow bad and an increase somehow good. Partly this may be an expression of the cult of numbers. But it is also a recognition that civilizations are organic and that when their inner sources of population strength dry up there will be a drying up of their national energies. History furnishes instances of peoples that failed to reproduce themselves, either because their birth rate was too low or their death rate too high. Hence the anxiety evoked by scholars in the 1930s and 1940s who talked about a "population cycle" in the history of every civilization and made projections for America showing the arc of population growth flattening out between 1950 and 1975. When the 1950 and 1955 figures stubbornly refused to follow the projections and took a sharp upturn, there was a general sense of relief, rightly or wrongly, among those who felt it to be a vindication of America's inner strength and an affirmation of the future. Instead of the population cycle determining the arc of the American life force, it turned out that the life force had something to do with shaping the population cycle.

Some of the earlier commentators on America had proved sounder prophets. Writing as "Poor Richard" in the 1780s, Benjamin Franklin addressed a prospectus to immigrants in the form of "Information to Those Who Would Remove to America": "From the salubrity of the air," he wrote, "the healthiness of the climate, and plenty of good provisions, and the encouragement to early marriages and by the certainty of subsistence in cultivating the earth, the increase of inhabitants by natural generation is very rapid in America, and becomes still more so by the accession of strangers." Franklin was justified by history: the upward curve of population came not only from immigration but also because marriages were early, the opening of new land put a premium on large families to supply labor, the economy of plenty made them possible, and the new immigration was largely of men and women in the childbearing age group.

Writing in the late 1830s, a half century later, Alexis de Tocqueville made a bold prediction of American population growth. "The time will come," he wrote at the end of the first volume of *Democracy in America,* "when 150 millions of men will be living in North America, equal in condition, the progeny of one race, owing their origin to the same cause, and preserving the same civilization, the same language, the same religion, the same habits, the same manners, imbued with the same opinions, propagated under the same forms. The rest is uncertain, but this is certain: and it is a fact new to the world—a fact fraught with such portentous consequences as to baffle the efforts even of the imagination." The 1950 census figures showed De Tocqueville's prophecy amply fulfilled. By 1957 the figures reached 170 million and were growing.

At one point there was strong evidence of a slackening of pace, when the fertility rate showed a marked decline between 1920 and 1940. The twenties and thirties were crucial years for America. Economic collapse, coming abruptly after top-pitch prosperity, produced a crisis of faith in the American experience. There was increased knowledge and use of contraception, and the size of the family unit dwindled. A study by Dennis Wrong showed that the "differential fertility" between the educated upper-income groups and the lower-income groups had been narrowing since 1910, and narrowed sharply during the Depression of the thirties. Thus the rationalistic approach to childbearing was reaching even the lower-income groups. In the "competition between consumers goods and children," as one writer put it, the children seemed to be losing out. From 1925 to 1945 there was considerable agreement that a long-range trend was in process and that the curve of growth would continue to flatten out: the Census estimate as late as 1946 was that a peak of 165 million would be reached in 1990. All the signs pointed to what some of the demographers called an "incipient decline" of the growth potential of American population.

Surprisingly, the fertility rates increased sharply after 1940, and by 1945 the increase was clear enough to cause a shift in the estimates. After reaching a low of 16.6 per thousand in 1933—the depth of the Great Depression—the birth rate moved to 17.9 in 1940 and reached a high of 25.8 in 1947. From 2.3 million births in 1933, the number rose to 3.9 million in 1947 and exceeded 4 million in 1954 and 1955. The population, which had been 130 million in 1940, grew by 35 million in fifteen years without much help from immigration.

I emphasize this episode because it is a commentary on the danger of approaching a living civilization mechanically. The scientists figured, quite understandably, that the decrease in the American death rate had pretty much reached its limits, that the doors of immigration were closed, and that the declining trajectory of the birth rate was clearly demarked. But while one can confidently study things, it is harder to mark out a path for the aberrant and incalculable ways of people. The scientists were right in saying that as people move from rural areas into the city their birth rate falls; that as women get jobs and careers and find something other to do than bearing and rearing children, it falls further; that as living standards rise they crowd out babies. But the sequel proved them wrong, because they had failed to look at an important factor. Commenting in 1954 on a paper by Joseph S. Davis (who had seen the new trend earlier than most), Frank W. Notestein looked back at the miscalculations of his fellow craftsmen: "Too much attention was paid to more than a century of experience with declining birth rates. . . . Too little consideration was given to the possibility that the processes of family formation, which had hitherto shown remarkable stability, might change with unexpected speed."

What this comes to is that American life purposes and attitudes are still in flux, as restless as the migrant movements of the people themselves. Population growth depends on the relation between fertility and mortality rates. America had made great strides in decreasing infant mortality, but for a while it seemed to run into a declining birth rate. There is a plausible explanation for the reversal of this decline in the war years, since girls preferred to marry and start their babies before their men went off to battle. The deferment of fathers helped, and so did the chance of young married veterans to go to college on the G.I. Bill of Rights at government expense. Yet the trend continued even after the end of the war. And while it is true that American family formation changed in the late 1930s and the 1940s, behind this change was a more fundamental change in values and in the images of self which American men and women had.

I have said that the stark contrast between the prosperity of the twenties and the economic collapse of the thirties produced a crisis of faith in young Americans. This crisis was somehow met and mastered in the New Deal years and those of the defense boom and full employment that followed, with results that started to show themselves in 1940. The decrease in mortality rates was a matter of science, but the increase in birth rates, at a time when birth control was readily available to most, was a matter of faith in living. Having babies is always a form of risk in giving hostages to fortune, and in modern "rational" societies it is not undertaken without a faith in the future to which the hostages are committed. With the restoration of employment and income, and the emergence of more leisure in a setting of suburban living, young Americans took an attitude toward babies baffling to everyone but themselves. They grew old-fashioned about babies and family size just when everyone was expecting them to be very modern and very cynical. As for the young wife, she belongs to a generation of women who have decided to have their children first and to think of using their talents in a career on the side or after the children are grown. The danger of a declining birth rate was a strategic one in the upper-middle and professional classes, and among the artistic and intellectual groups, since their standards and attitudes tended in time to permeate the other classes. Since 1940 there has been a marked increase in fertility rates in these crucial groups.

I have spoken of the changing image of the self as a clue to the riddle of why Americans breed as fast or as slow as they do. This is a solemn way of saying what young Americans mean when they say "it's fun" to marry young, to have babies instead of going childless (the demand for children for adoption is evidence of a feeling of pang about the childless family), to have two children instead of one or three instead of two, to buy a house in a suburb and get a car and raise a family, to put down roots, to be a "man in a gray flannel suit" who faces his responsibilities, to be the woman who meets his train in a station wagon with the children. "It's fun" even for the higher educational and living-standard groups, perhaps especially for them, since they live on a sharper edge of the search for happiness in life. To guess how these images of self—which are formed by converging lines of tendency from every part of the culture—will turn out a generation hence is to guess about the future climate of hope or despair, and what atomic energy and the automatic factory and office will do to employment, and what the ever-expanding scope of leisure and the rising living standards will do to the fertility rate.

The story of the American mortality rate is as important in population growth and composition as that of the birth rate, although it has offered less difficulty for analysis and projection. In the century from 1850 to 1950 the American population increased more than sixfold, partly because of the high immigration factor through the 1920s but mainly because of a decreasing death rate, especially since 1900, that responded to better medical care and advances in diet, clothing, housing, living standards, and public health. In America, as elsewhere in the world picture in recent centuries, the mortality rate was a more dynamic factor in population growth than was the birth rate. An American mortality rate that was 17.2 per thousand in 1900 decreased to 12 in 1920 and to 9.6 per thousand in 1950. The reduction of infant mortality changed drastically what had been for centuries the "natural" profile of age composition, increasing the number of those who reached the reproducing age, thus providing an unprecedented growth potential. The mortality reductions have been dramatic for women in childbirth (6.47 per 1,000 live births in 1927 to 0.76 in 1951), for babies in the year after birth (from a death rate of 65 out of every 1,000 in 1927 to 29 in 1951), and in general for all Americans (less so for Negroes) below forty-five. There have also been decreases in the mortality rates for those above sixty. If there are to be further reductions, they will have to come chiefly in the middle years, between forty-five and sixty, through an attack on the tension diseases which hit Americans in those years.

There remains to draw a profile of the recent changes in the make-up and distribution of the American population. In increasing the life span, the new medical techniques and the declining death rate have swelled America's population profile at both ends of the age-group distribution. A child at birth now has a far better chance of growing up (95 per cent reach at least the age of fifteen); a man or woman reaching sixty-five has a better chance of hanging on tenaciously. In the single decade from 1940 to 1950, the number of children under ten increased by almost 40 per cent, as compared with a total population increase of less than 15 per cent. In 1950 there were twenty-six million Americans over fifty-five—an increase of 30 per cent in a decade. The number over sixty-five grew from three million in 1900 (4 per cent of the population) to thirteen million in 1952 (over 8 per cent), and the likelihood is that it will reach 10 per cent in a generation. In the past half century, while the population doubled, the number over sixty-five increased fourfold.

These two trends—the conserving of children and the prolonging of life—have had effects on America that go beyond the crowding of maternity hospitals and school facilities, the craze for Hopalong Cassidy, space cadets, and Davy Crockett, and the development of geriatrics as a major branch of medicine. They have given America the paradoxical aspect of being a nation at once of the young and the elderly. And they have changed much of American thinking by changing the life expectancy. In the half century after 1900 the expectancy of an American male increased by twenty-one years; in the fourteen years from 1937 to 1951 it went up from sixty to sixty-eight and a half years. Imperceptibly the shift is producing changed attitudes toward older people and toward the pace of life: since a longer life is accessible to more people, there is a slowing down of pace in order to woo it and achieve it. There are even a number of American thinkers who are saying boldly that the problem of death can be conquered.

There are, of course, laments over America's becoming a country for the old. The median age rose by almost ten years in seventy-five years, from 20.9 in 1880 to a little over thirty in the early 1950s; since then it has declined a bit because of the continuing flood of births. But one wonders why a relatively high median age is thought undesirable, and what there is so special about a low one. The youthfulness of a population may be purchased by early death as well as by birth: it has meant historically in any culture that life was brief and pathetic, with little technological or medical development. In Asia, a newly born child is less likely to reach the age of fifteen than he would be in America to reach sixty-five. The extension of life expectancy gives the individual a chance to fulfill his promise; it gives the culture a large proportion of people who can spend their productive years in work. As for the Americans no longer being a "young" people, the answer is that words are culturally conditioned, and the population changes have also changed the meaning of "young" and "old." The span of youth in America has been stretched into the late forties, and the span of middle age into the late sixties, where the margin of old age now begins. Only in industry is it still hard for a man or woman over forty-five to get a job, but even there the old ways of thinking are beginning to yield.*

I have spoken† of the recent population shifts between states and regions, and between rural and urban areas. In these shifts the movements of migration are generally more important than birth rates. The seven fastest-growing states in the decade of the forties—California, Arizona, Florida, Nevada, Oregon, Washington, and Maryland—had greater increases from migration than from births. The four states that lost population—Mississippi, Arkansas, North Dakota, Oklahoma—had high birth rates but suffered the greatest migration loss. In general, if it were only a matter of birth and death figures, the Southern states would be the fastest-growing ones: the birth rate of the Negroes and of the "poor whites" is high. But except for states like Florida, many of

* For a further discussion of the older age groups in America, and the problems of aging, see Ch. VIII, Sec. 7, "The Middle and End of the Journey."

† See Sec. 3, "People in Motion."

the young people—white as well as Negro—are leaving the South, and the movement West continues. The freedom of internal migration makes it possible for population to adjust itself flexibly between the areas of high birth rate and low economic opportunity and those of low birth rate and high economic opportunity.

There is an important population shift away from the farms and small towns to the cities, and a shift in turn from the big cities to the suburbs on their periphery. The net result for the big-city cores, except in the areas of population boom, showed only minor gains. But on the margins of the big cities, where mass-produced houses could be bought with all the equipment of the "kitchen revolution," where autos brought people to their city jobs and recreation, and TV sets filled their leisure time at home, the population grew lushly. There was a double recoil against the stagnation of the farm and small town and against the rootless and frenetic quality of big-city living. Americans launched not a back-to-the-farm movement, as in the days of the Roman Principate, but a movement forward to the conditions under which they could have the best of both worlds.*

There has been a steady decline in the proportion of the foreign-born in the American population. By 1955 it included not much over 6 per cent of the people: the time is close when only a small fraction of Americans will have been born on foreign soil, and when the percentage of foreign-born in the South in 1955 (about 1½ per cent) will apply throughout the nation.

Before 1950 there were more men than women in America, mainly because immigration was weighted toward males and because of the high mortality of mothers in childbirth. Since 1950 the sex ratio has shifted, not only with immigration changes and the cutting of maternal mortality, but also because American women now outlive men by a bigger margin then ever. After forty-five the tension diseases hit men harder, and their wives survive to inherit the earth. As one waspish comment has it, the U.S. is becoming a "gerontomatriarchy," a society ruled by aging females.

The large American labor force—that is, the large numbers in the age groups available for running and managing the machines—has made possible the fact that with only 6 per cent of the world's population America is responsible for almost one half of the world's output of goods. The Americans "gainfully employed" in 1956 reached over seventy million, and the estimate for 1975 ran to between eighty-five and ninety-five million. The proportion of women in the work force, especially married women, is growing. The work week was reduced an average of 5 per cent every decade since 1870, and in the mid-1950s it

* For a further discussion, see Sec. 10, "The Suburban Revolution."

was about forty hours, with estimates that by 1975, under the impact of the almost automatic factory and the electronically controlled clerical offices, it would be thirty hours or even twenty-five. The striking fact is that the decreased work week has been possible without a drop in productivity: better health, less fatigue, and better chances for education have thus far made up for the reductions.

If these sentences read like a patriotic paean to American growth I don't intend them thus. The real wealth of a nation in human resources is less one of the quantity than of the quality of the population —and I propose to deal with that aspect in the next section. But the rate of American population growth has thus far not outrun either the energy resources or the productive capacity of industry and agriculture, or the available living space. The dangers of population growth as rapid as the American are that it will outrun the capacity of the agricultural and industrial plant to sustain it, especially since America now for the first time consumes more raw materials than it produces, and also because the per-capita demands on raw materials have kept increasing.

Hence there were a number of American students of resources and population in the mid-1950s who regarded the "baby boom" with horror, convinced that America might breed itself out of its potential wealth and strength and living standards through a failure to plan and a devotion to the cult of numbers. They admitted that the density of American population was still relatively small, and that it was possible in principle to support on the American continent a population of even a billion. But they argued that in such an America the living standard would fall, diet would have to be standardized in synthetic form, the complexities and hazards of daily living would be multiplied, and the trend toward totalitarianism would grow almost irresistible. Added to the Malthusian arguments there was also the aesthetic plea —the sense of distaste at the prospect of the empty spaces swarming with people, and the huge cities spilling even more cancerously over the countryside. There are a growing number of demands from scholars for the formulation of an American "population policy."

I am not arguing here against "family planning," which has the merit of leaving the question of population control where it belongs —with the joint common decision of the parents. But I find it hard to drum up much enthusiasm for an over-all "national population policy," which assumes that there is an "ideal" population size for America, and that this should be reached by a deliberate population policy. To give the decision to the government implies that we know or can know what an "optimum" population is and how to enforce it on the private decisions of people. Of that I am skeptical. The American immigration laws since 1921 have assumed such a knowledge, but it would be hard to claim that they have added to either the richness or quality of American life. If I am asked whether I see an American population growing steadily for the calculable future, I answer "Why not?" Much of the dynamic quality of American life is derived from this central dynamism of continued population growth, which in turn means new housing, new schools, new living sites, new roads and transport, a bigger home market, a larger labor force, higher productivity.

When nations have had population policies in the past, it has been either to encourage births because of a fear of stagnation (the Roman Empire, France) or a desire for war strength (prewar Japan, prewar Italy, the Soviet Union), or to discourage overrapid population growth because of crowding, famines, and diseases (India, present-day Japan, Ceylon, Puerto Rico). Sweden has adopted the most thoroughgoing population policy of all, with the goal of increasing the birth rate in order to avert a threatened national decline because of loss of numbers. But the United States no longer needs to fear either a declining population and cultural suicide or a runaway population that it will be unable to support adequately. Thus far its economy has grown stronger with increasing numbers instead of being strained by them. Thus far also the most tribalist forces of the community have been directed against continued large-scale immigration, and their hostility to "alien" ethnic groups has been—at least outwardly—based on the fear of their high birth rate. The healthier American forces have not worried overmuch about eugenic considerations or about overcrowding of the continent, because they have felt confidence in the capacity of the nation to absorb future growth as it has absorbed past growth. The fear of totalitarianism is a genuine one, and there is point to the argument that population pressure increases the danger. Yet this is only a minor factor: if totalitarianism comes to America, it will be for other and more cogent reasons than the pressure of numbers.

It is most unlikely, however, that America will have to cope with the problems of overpopulation in the near future. While there has been a recent increase in birth rates, and the death rates continue to fall, the increased knowledge of birth control is likely to keep the population in check, and the rising curve is bound to lose its momentum in time. Despite the fears of both population suicide and population runaway, the trends are likely to continue to be healthy ones, and the decisions on population policy will be made by individual families in the light of their life purposes and life expectations within the frame of increasing knowledge.

6. *The Sinews of Welfare: Health, Food, Dwelling, Security*

THE CULT OF NUMBERS is meaningless when applied to a population, unless linked with a concern for the life quality of the people. I talk of the quality of their life rather than of innate capacity because it is idle to argue whether Americans have degenerated in innate capacity: even if one could prove they had, any eugenics program imposed by an external authority to breed them better would be unthinkable. The best we can ask about the people in a culture is this: given its human beings there, do they have what is necessary for decent human living? Does the culture make available to them the sinews of welfare?

I use "sinews of welfare" here to mean the degree of well-being in terms of basic life needs that the culture enables the American people to achieve—on health and medical services, on food, clothing, shelter, on education and security. I include only the broad areas of need for both the person and the personality, on the assumption that there are minimum standards in each area (however elusive and hard to formulate) which the culture is required to provide for its people, at the peril of being judged a failure in human terms.

The American pursuit of health, plenty, leisure, security, and happiness is so well known and there is such an overspill of goods and resources that it may seem futile to inquire about the sinews of welfare. If it were only the question of minimum standards—in the sense, say, in which the term is used by students of nutrition to mean the bare margin for maintaining health—the American record would be unquestioned not only in food but in every phase of welfare. But if we go beyond minimum nutrition and talk of optimum nutrition—beyond which no diet additions would do much for health, whatever they might do for the palate and the sense of luxury—then the American sinews of welfare need revaluing on that plane. The American national product and living standards form a blade whose temper cuts away sharply all the old conceptions of subsistence living. Yet once such a standard is set, the inadequacies are shown up all the more clearly. When Franklin Roosevelt made his famous speech about "one third of a nation" being "ill-housed, ill-clad, ill-nourished," he was saying how intolerable it was that this should be true in a land of plenty.

This paradox shows up clearly in the area of health. Judged by the number and skill of their doctors, the organization of hospitals, the thoroughness of medical research, the quality of diagnosis and therapy, the array of modern machines, appliances, and available drugs, and the conquest of diseases that for centuries had scourged mankind, the Americans do well in this area. "To have lived through a revolution," wrote Sir William Osler in 1913, "to have seen a new birth of science, a new dispensation of health, reorganized medical schools, remodeled hospitals, a new outlook for humanity, is not given to every generation." And Laurence J. Henderson referred to the same revolution when he said that somewhere around 1911 the progress of medicine in America made it possible to say that "a random patient with a random disease consulting a physician at random stood better than a 50-50 chance of benefiting from the encounter."

Americans have for a half century been living in an age and land of medical miracles. They have stood in awe of these miracles, have at times resented and resisted them, but have ended by laying claim to their full benefit for all. The experience of World War II, when the whole matchless armory of American medicine, surgery, and dentistry were put at the disposal of the humblest private from Mississippi or Oklahoma, proved decisive in bringing these claims to the surface. Access to medical care came to be considered a kind of Constitutional right for all Americans, a new imperative of our time. What had once been deemed the province of the rich became a necessity for all classes, and economists soon took to surveying America's health "needs" on the assumption that their fulfillment was a prescriptive right. This assumption—even more than the medical miracles—capped the revolution in health.

Yet the dismal fact is that all this fabulous armory of skills and contrivances, which vanquished many of the dread infectious diseases, transformed childbirth, and made the human body a terrain for brilliant research, has not produced a healthy population. For one thing there is the differential health picture in South Carolina as compared with Connecticut, or in rural as against urban areas, or in the slum and low-income groups as compared with the middle classes. For another, there is the mental health picture, with ten million Americans (one out of sixteen) counted mentally ill, with a million and a half of them psychotics, with as many filled beds in mental hospitals as in all others combined.

Finally there is the dramatic evidence of the draft rejection figures—evidence from an unintended mammoth inventory of the health of young Americans, mainly from eighteen through their twenties. Of the first two million men drafted for the armed services in 1940-41, 50 per cent were rejected for either physical or mental disturbances; at the end of World War II the figure had fallen to 33 per cent, but mainly because the standards were lowered; in the period 1948-52 the rejections were 45 per cent; at the start of the Korean War they rose to 58 per cent, but at the end they dropped again to 33 per cent. The figures ought not to be used uncritically: it is true that a man may be rejected by the Army for bad eyesight or hearing or other physical disabilities, or as a "psychoneurotic," and still function well at his job or even live a long life. It is also true that when the figures for volunteers were included, the percentage of rejections fell. It might be argued finally that the American armed services held to higher standards of physical fitness because—given the large pool of man power in the military age groups—they could afford to. Yet the figures are at best bad enough in a nation and era of great medical progress. What makes them worse is the estimate that a large proportion were correctable, which means that they fell in classes where medical care was economically out of reach, or in backward communities where doctors were too few and hospital facilities inadequate. The figures on chronic diseases heighten the shadows in the American health picture. One of six Americans suffers from some chronic illness, and from six to seven million of them suffer seriously, including the victims of arthritis, hypertension, arteriosclerosis, cerebral palsy, and muscular dystrophy.

These figures have spurred the efforts at multiple screening, early diagnosis and preventive treatment of sickness, at campaigns for public-health education, and at the painstaking task of rehabilitation. They have also brought up the constant question of the scarcity of doctors. In 1955 there were 225,000 doctors in the U.S., or one for every 720 people. The problem was not one of attracting too few young men but of discouraging many of them for the wrong reasons (for example, religious and racist bias) and of not having enough schools with enough funds to meet the need for doctors. Federal grants for scholarship aid were rejected on the ground that they might put the schools in a strait jacket, although the similar potential corruption of Federal research funds was cheerfully risked. While Federal funds were refused, industry subvention—regarded as safe—was not forthcoming.

The greater difficulty thus far, however, has been the high cost of medical care, especially for the lower middle classes who fall between the free public facilities and the expensive private ones. A five-dollar office call, a ten-dollar house call, a fancy surgery fee, a sky-high fee for specialized consultants, additional fees for X rays, and the cost of expensive medicines exhaust a modest family income. Only rarely was this the fault of the doctors, most of whom were hard-working and devoted men. In a lush and byzantine economy it was idle to expect them to practice ascetic renunciation. The efforts to provide a system of compulsory health insurance, largely with Federal funds, were fought bitterly by the American Medical Association as "socialized medicine."

The A.M.A. hierarchy, while it complained of being too frequently a target for abuse, was not wholly innocent in heart; it was skillful in marshaling political pressures against the provision of medical security and forgot that while the medical profession is a sector of private enterprise, it is more deeply affected with a public interest than any profession except warfare and teaching.

Willy-nilly the achievement of medical security is on its way: through a system of voluntary group insurance for hospitalization and (to some extent) for doctor's fees, which provides at least partial coverage for more than half the people; through agreement with working teams of doctors, whether on a prepaid plan covering all ailments or on a fee-for-service basis; and through employer-union agreements providing for sickness benefits and medical care. In New York State the employer-financed health and welfare plans cover three quarters of those covered by state unemployment insurance. Yet with all these mushrooming plans there are still some Americans left out: a million families, for example, spent half their income on medical bills in "catastrophic" cases. America has lagged behind Great Britain and the Scandinavian countries in the social organization of medical facilities. The tragic episode, in 1955, of the initial bungling in preparing the Salk anti-polio vaccine while the Canadian government carried through successfully in the same circumstances, is an instance of how the cult of private enterprise in medicine hobbles American public-health measures.

But the statement by the Committee on the Cost of Medical Care in 1932—that "human life in the U.S. is being wasted as recklessly, as surely, in times of peace as in times of war"—is far less true now. In a generation the gridiron intermeshing of voluntary group plans, doctor's medical groups, industry health and welfare plans, Federal care of veterans, and Federal and state support of medical services in other forms, is bound to be all but complete.

This still leaves the question of how diseases fare in America. Here the striking fact has been the shifting pattern of national diseases, which sheds an intense light on the nature of the culture. Since 1900, deaths from pneumonia, TB, diarrhea, bronchitis, influenza, appendicitis, rheumatic fever, and syphilis have been steeply cut. In their place, since men remain mortal, have come other great killers—heart disease, the high-tension circulatory diseases including cerebral hemorrhage and arteriosclerosis, cancer, and death by violence. The heart and circulation diseases in 1953 accounted for 54 per cent of the deaths, and cancer an additional 15 per cent—together almost 70 per cent, or seven out of ten deaths. Other diseases that came to the forefront in American statistics as cripplers and disablers were mental illnesses (nine million cases in 1953), arthritis and rheumatic diseases (cerebral palsy, epilepsy, multiple sclerosis, Parkinson's Disease). One must add, as special categories of mental illness, at least 60,000 narcotics addicts, and almost 4,000,000 "problem drinkers," of whom close to a million are chronic alcoholics. One should also add that six or seven of every ten Americans suffer from headaches, and that 40 per cent of the cases of draft rejection or medical discharge after induction in World War II were cases of psychopathic personality, mental deficiency, drug addiction, or homosexuality.

One could counter this by arguing that "health" must be defined not just anatomically but functionally, that many Americans manage to live with their chronic illnesses, and that the sharp recent decreases in the death rate and increases in the life span carry with them inevitably the fact of the diseases of aging. But the paradoxical fact remains that Americans are suffering from the diseases accompanying the very dynamism which has done so much to vanquish disease. It would be too pat to say that the leading diseases in America are characteristic of the current tension of living, and that deaths in auto and industrial accidents, coronaries, hardened arteries, cerebral hemorrhages, and stomach ulcers—if not cancer—bear the hallmark "Made in America." Yet there would be a core of truth in it. Someone called the 1920s and 1930s the "aspirin age": if so, the 1940s and 1950s should be called the "sleeping-pill age," the "coronary age," the "tranquilizer age," or the "age of the fifty-minute hour." Pointing out that Americans have met and mastered the killer infections, have lengthened the life span, and must now cope with the chronic and degenerative diseases, Alan Gregg writes that "we have traded mortality for morbidity." Americans have tracked down the spoor of germs and bacilli only to confess themselves thus far powerless before the runaway cell, the strained and lesioned heart, the out-of-kilter ganglia of the nervous system, the disarranged sexual impulses, and the disturbed psyche that casts a pall of anxiety over worried days and sleepless nights—when it does not go berserk with frustrations and fears.

The character of the diseases of American middle age was dramatically illustrated by President Eisenhower's two attacks in 1955-56—one coronary, the other gastrointestinal. The fact that for months the whole American people focused its attention on charts and diagrams of the President's internal organs and the details of his bodily functioning was the result of more than political interest: it was an index of the concern of Americans with their own health. Every middle-aged and aging male saw himself reflected in the President. In making public some data on the functioning of the President's bowels Dr. Paul Dudley White explained that Americans had become "bowel-conscious." When his doctors made their optimistic announcements about the President's life chances, they were echoing the title one American writer used for a book, *Thank God for My Heart Attack,* which was a commentary on the American belief that the real killer is thoughtless drive and tension, and that to "take it easy" is the road to health.

By an interesting irony the doctors, medical administrators, and researchers responsible for the achievements of American health are often themselves the victims of the pace of American life, and die early of tension diseases. There is a restless quality about the attitudes of Americans toward health and disease. They are oversold on medical advances and expect to read about new medical miracles in every issue of *Time* and *Reader's Digest.* They are overeager about the "wonder drug" antibiotics and rely so much on the efficacy of penicillin (in the decade 1945-55 they consumed 3,000 tons, or 3,000 trillion units), the various mycins, cortisone, and ACTH, that bodily resistances against them have developed. They respond quickly to new drugs and pills—to barbiturates for sleeping, and other pills for staying awake, and "tranquilizers," drugs for calming down. Similarly the staffs in mental hospitals overuse electrical and insulin shock therapy: everywhere there is an eagerness to handle mass diseases on a mass basis and find a short cut to a cure.

In the public-health field American medical organizers have developed the institution of the "drive"—against heart disease, against cancer, against cerebral palsy—partly to raise funds for research, partly to make the people conscious of the "dread killers," with all the statistics about the casualties, the man hours lost, and how much the dead would have added to the national income had they lived. As a result, the people battered now by one "drive," now by another, become not only conscious of but anxious about disease. While the medical advances have led to a lengthening of the life span, they have also produced a nation of medical worriers about the ills of the flesh and the mind who follow every diet fad, take reducing pills or tranquilizer drugs, count their pulse beats and cherish their blood-pressure charts, vex themselves about not being able to stop smoking, meditate Narcissuslike on their kidneys and colon, and fill the bathroom medicine cabinet with an assortment of prescription bottles and "packaged remedies" (patent medicines) which keep huge industries solvent.

Foreign observers have noted that all American doctors want to "do research," and that the American medical schools—perhaps the best in the world—spend less time on transmitting what is known about medicine than in pointing out what is still unknown. This is an aspect of the theme of dynamism I have stressed in the American tradition. While there has been some swingback to the general practitioner and a considerable nostalgia for the old-fashioned "country doctor," the long-range trend is in two directions: toward further specialization, which will mean that no doctor looks at the whole patient and that doctors will increasingly become members of "teams"; and toward new institutional forms of medical care. Since, with rising medical costs and despite voluntary group insurance, good medical care is still out of the reach of many workers and especially the ethnic minorities, the trend toward corporate health plans and trade-union projects will increase. American medicine will have escaped the government but not the twin giants of the corporation and trade-union, which will become the new employers of medical and research talent. All of which is understandable, since the genius of American medicine has all along been an organizing genius.*

Next to his health the American is most concerned about his security —including even the people who are sternly set against the "creeping Socialism" of a "welfare state." Several generations behind the European and Commonwealth experience in these matters, because the individualist momentum carried them further before they could make a start on social-security plans, the Americans are tardily taking the same steps—but in their own way. The idea of a complete system of governmental security frightened some substantial citizens because they thought (probably wrongly) that it would play havoc with the powerful institution of the private insurance company, whose interests ramify into every area of industry, banking, and investment. Thus the private-enterprise core of the American security system has been left intact, and to it has been added a system of Federal old-age and survivors insurance, and state unemployment insurance, with contributions levied on both worker and employer. There is also a system of Federal grants-in-aid to the states for the blind and disabled, for old-age assistance, and for child care.

At the start all this was held revolutionary: now it is accepted almost as a commonplace, even when Republicans rule the White House and Congress. The recent extensions of the original system of old-age and survivors insurance have included domestics and white-collar workers but still exclude the migratory workers. Unemployment insurance is still inadequate: it must ultimately be extended to include every gainfully employed person, including the self-employed, so that no one becomes a casualty of the pathos of dependence. Another important development has been the assumption of responsibility for one segment of security by the corporation and the trade-union, through welfare funds, fringe benefits, and (most recently) the movement for the guaranteed annual wage. It is these growths that are rounding out the American security system.

* For further discussion of mental health, see Ch. IX, Sec. 8, "Life Goals and the Pursuit of Happiness."

Since the area of security necessarily involved the emergence of a welfare state to carry part of the burden and responsibility, storms and turbulences have raged around it ever since the turn of the twentieth century. It has been the arena of the great reform movements of America, and administrative efforts of Democratic and liberal Republican administrations alike have had to meet resistance of interest groups. The period between 1900 and World War I saw the founding of a myriad of organizations aimed at attacking national problems of welfare on a national scale—child labor, mental hygiene, public health, the protection of children, labor legislation. The New Deal period consolidated what the earlier period had begun and launched new programs that resulted in the great Social Security Act of 1935, which was extended a number of times in the next two decades. Yet the fault lines in the system were at mid-century still glaring. There is no system of compulsory health insurance, nor any provisions that give everyone access to medical care without a means test. There is little that applies the principles of social insurance to the risks of disability and illness as well as of old-age dependence. There is no protection for the families of those who become disabled by factors unrelated to their jobs.

The individualist strain in American thinking raised resistance to this trend from the early days when the New England humanitarian movements provoked Emerson into his classic outburst: "I tell thee, thou foolish philanthropist, that I grudge the dollar, the dime, the cent I give to such men as do not belong to me and to whom I do not belong," and led him to speak contemptuously of "alms for sots." Yet it was not the philanthropic impulse alone but the spur of need and emergency that led to the growth of the welfare network. The catastrophe of the Great Depression was a psychic shock, dramatizing the erratic course of Fortune's wheel which might claim as victim even the patently secure and leaving the fear of insecurity as a continuing residue in the American mind. This led to the corollary that people with troubles are the concern of all—the common concern of the commonwealth. With World War II and the Korean War there came the understanding that the ill and incapacitated, the mentally unfit and the badly educated, the products of slum housing and submarginal incomes, were a drain on the available national man power; and measures were admitted through the back door of war needs that would have been kept waiting at the front door of human fellow feeling. Yet despite Emerson's words and the derisive contemporary epithets applied to "do-gooders" and "bleeding hearts," the fellow feeling is there and is as abundantly part of the American human and cultural cast as of any other in history. Every era of free-swinging heady advance in technical and economic achievement brings with it the paradoxical double attitude of a ruthless scorn for the misfits and failures and a sense of men's interdependence with men.

Just as there is a seamless web in American welfare needs, so there is one in the response to them—although not in the sense that Americans respond to them as a whole. They have responded piecemeal and in irregular fashion to the need for workmen's compensation, unemployment benefits, old-age insurance, subsidized low-cost housing, health insurance, corporate-sponsored welfare funds, the annual wage. Their relatedness is rarely grasped except by the professional students of the problem. The American response has been consistent in a different sense: what has emerged in each area of welfare is the acceptance of the principle of responsibility but with the least challenge to private enterprise, the least burden on the tax structure, and the greatest reliance on the voluntary principle. The broad formula has been for the government to set a floor below which security and welfare cannot fall, to use government funds for the more clamant forms of social insurance but to let the others go, to give the states the widest possible discretion, to steer away from centralized authority and administration, to rely wherever possible on forms of group insurance, to work through private companies (as in workmen's compensation) even when the state provides the funds, to underwrite the private risks (as in housing), to make ampler provision for soldiers and veterans than for civilians, to put the burden of expanding the programs upon continued popular pressures.

The chances are strong, given American dynamism, that these pressures will continue. The coverage of welfare protection is still incomplete and in some cases pathetically so; the insurance benefits are still low, allowing for only a portion of the normal income deriving from the job, thus incurring the danger that inadequacies of food, housing, education, and psychic security in the lives of the children will be handed on for several generations. The financing of security is either left to the individual's means in private insurance, savings, stock holdings, or the group plans, or rests on a payroll tax which is regressive because proportionately it bears more heavily on the lower incomes.

These point to the remaining agenda of welfare: yet despite what remains to be done, America has grappled with the problem of security, sometimes with an inventiveness that has added to the European experience instead of merely imitating it. And in doing so it has passed through a revolution in action, thought, and feeling which makes its welfare structure wholly different from the America of the 1920s which most European commentators still take as their prevailing image.

What about the habitations of the American inhabitants? In anthropological terms a tribe needs shelter, in social terms a community needs housing, in psychological terms a family needs a home. The statisticians speak of the number of dwelling units that Americans have, whether they be flats, apartments, "row houses," or estates. The test of welfare here is not only whether people have somewhere to lay their head but whether the place is clean or disease-ridden, spacious or congested, beautiful or dreary and ugly. American abundance is such that the minimal needs of "adequate" shelter no longer express the true criteria of what the society does with the means at its disposal.

It is no longer true of mid-century America that one third of it is "ill-housed." There has been a flattening out of the curve of housing at both extremes of the income scale: the purple imperial mansions of the Vanderbilts and other multimillionaires of the turn of the century are no longer considered good taste, and even the top crust lives more simply on its estates; and the slums, while still scarring the face of the country, are slowly—all too slowly—being razed and used as sites for low-cost housing projects. The big housing bulge comes at the middle of the income scale, where millions of housing units have been built in our time.

America has been the scene of a housing "revolution" similar to the medical and social-security "revolutions," but coming at a different time. During the reform decades before World War I, when so many associations were cropping up to deal with the inadequacies of American society, there was also a movement for tenement reform, to get rid of the firetraps and clean up the pesthouses, and frame and enforce the "multiple dwelling" laws. But the New Deal in the mid-thirties raised the sights of the whole housing movement, with federally subsidized large-scale housing projects that started the clearing of the city slums and revived the lagging housing industry. Adequate shelter had become a pressing welfare need for millions of Americans, and the method the New Deal used was to appropriate money to local housing authorities, to work through private construction firms, and to build tall apartment houses and row-house projects. Generally they increased the density of the population in the same area but were "decent, safe, and sanitary" (in the phrase of the U.S. Housing Act), with some green space around them. The life-insurance companies took their cue from the Federal government and built Stuyvesant Towns of their own. The Resettlement Administration built a few Greenbelt Towns—garden cities for government and white-collar workers. During World War II the process continued in the war-industry centers, because it had been learned that people wouldn't pick up and move, or work productively, without minimum housing of some sort. After the war there was a splurge of too hastily and shoddily built housing for young veterans and their families. And then the housing boom began in earnest: in a decade, during the Truman and Eisenhower regimes, ten million dwelling units went up, rehousing from thirty-five to forty million people at an average cost of $10,000 and a total one of 100 billion, and housing became the biggest industry in the nation.

Drawing the profile of contemporary housing, one would start with the derelict areas such as those in Chicago's South Side or the Puerto Rican ghetto in New York—the 9 per cent of decrepit American dwelling units that are rated as "dilapidated" dwellings and tell the deterioration story of the big city cores, the small-city "shanty towns," and the small-town houses "on the other side of the tracks"—littered, tattered bedlams which are cold in winter and unbearable in summer, with few bathrooms, rat-infested, sheltering mainly unskilled workers or the people who live on relief or part-time jobs or old-age pensions. One would go on to the more tolerable tenements and to the "row houses" like those of Baltimore and Philadelphia, where skilled workers and white-collar families live wall to wall in constricted and standardized monotony; then to the towering monolithic canyons of low- and middle-income urban building projects I have described—some still segregated, others having made the first breaks in the segregation taboo; then to the myriad crowded beehive individual houses that blanket the suburban areas, where you get five or six rooms plus a garage and can pick one of five standardized colors and styles, and have a back yard that juts into your neighbor's, and be near a shopping center; then to the more spacious "homes" in the "residential sections" of the richer suburbs or the more expensive "developments," Tudor or Spanish Moorish or California ranch house, set in synthetic "villages"; then finally to the "house on the hill" and the lavish estates of the parvenu millionaires and the quieter ones of those who have wealth-over-time.

There is no common denominator for all these forms. But of the newer ones it can be said that they embody a feeble attempt at individuality within a cellular framework of standardization. In the years immediately following World War II it was thought that prefabricated houses might break the housing bottleneck, but they struck several snags, including the jungle of building restrictions and trade-union hostility in the building trades. Then came the idea, associated with the Levitts, that instead of bringing housing to the factory, the solution was to apply factory methods to the building lot, using a small number of basic designs with minor variations and getting mass-production savings by large-scale purchasing of materials and by a basic plumbing and kitchen core, with TV sets and access to community pools and playgrounds thrown in as added lures.

Following this pattern, the splurge of "community developments" on the outskirts of cities has become the dominant feature of the American landscape. The costs, while reduced by large-scale building and the cheapness of land outside the cities, are still high. Because of archaic building codes and union practices, a committee of architects and builders has estimated that too much cement, lumber, steel, and piping are used; the housing "revolution" is still not a technological one. Yet standardization is the price paid for what has been achieved. More and more middle-class Americans were coming to live in houses as constricted in standardized forms as the Fords, Plymouths, and Buicks that were parked outside their doors. Like the cars also, the houses were bought on credit; to do this their owners plunged, not without some misgivings, into mortgaged debt: the stigma that had once attached to the family mortgage no longer applied. Americans unashamedly were out to purchase "gracious living" on the installment plan, and a continuously rising housing market wiped out most of the mistakes.

The new houses were not only standardized: they were also mechanized. The oil burner, the deep-freeze, the dishwasher, and the laundry equipment operated on the principle of the automatic feedback; there were toasters, mixers, pressure cookers, electric stoves, and garbage disposers to take much of the burden from kitchen work; there was a TV set and an automatic record turner. All this mechanized complexity went along with both the high cost of building and the scarcity of domestics in the labor market, so that income groups which once ran their households with several servants now were servantless, except for an occasional baby-sitter. To accomplish this it was necessary to simplify the layout of the house. The parlor, living room, and dining room were compressed into a single all-purpose room; in some cases, even the kitchen became a subdivision of the room. This was the extreme point reached by the trend toward the small house. The opposite trend was toward privacy. Compared with the European house the American had space enough to enable parents and children to sleep in separate rooms; given the small size of the American family, this often meant in middle-class families that each child had a room of his own. This was the principle of cellular housing—of individual cells for individual units—carried to its logical extreme.

As with the social-security system, the Americans have tried to carry through the housing revolution with a minimum of socialization and a maximum of private enterprise and profit. Yet the impressive fact was the degree of Federal intervention in housing that was taken for granted by Democrats and Republicans alike. The housing business was not only a large-scale operation but also a thoroughly "mixed" enterprise. The Federal government subsidized public housing, slum clearance, redevelopment and renewal of slum areas: it also took over most of the risk for "private" housing. More than four million of the ten million houses of the 1945-55 decade were financed with mortgages guaranteed by either the Federal Housing Administration (FHA) or the Veterans Administration (VA). In some metropolitan areas the proportion was as high as 75 per cent. The kind of suburban subdivision I have mentioned above

—which formed the core of the suburban revolution—was essentially the creature of the FHA mortgage-insurance system, which began in 1934 as an emergency measure and then grew to be a more permanently established feature on the housing scene than public housing itself. The fact that between half and two thirds of American homes were occupied by their owners was largely due to this kind of Federal intervention-through-underwriting. Despite its involving Federal action it was palatable to the banks, insurance companies, and private builders (and was extended under the Eisenhower Administration) because it guaranteed them against losses and spurred their business and profits.

Thus the "housing Socialism" (even Senator Robert A. Taft was accused of being a Socialist because he backed this program) amounted actually to a socializing of business losses and an underwriting of business profits. As such it has met with scorn from European Socialists—yet for America it seemed to work. Actually there were very few losses for the government to assume, although another Depression might tell a different story. More important was the fact that as mortgage underwriters the Federal government had to establish the basic standards and conditions that controlled private construction. At one point the FHA forced builders applying for mortgage funds in certain areas of mixed ethnic groups to write restrictive covenants into their deeds. Yet the Federal power can be turned in a quite different direction, and a committee of housing officials headed by Catherine Bauer has recommended an affirmative program for eliminating racist bias in housing. Following the Supreme Court decision in the school segregation cases, the Court was likely sooner or later to rule against discrimination in housing built with Federal aid. When this happens there will be a good deal of turmoil in the politics of housing. But in the long run the impossible situation of what Charles Abrams has called "forbidden neighbors" in housing is bound to be eliminated.*

The most elementary ingredient of welfare—food—is one that most Americans take most for granted, although next to shelter, food takes the largest cut (thirty-one cents) out of the consumer's dollar. The impulse of countries with traditions of famine is to save every crumb because someday the food may not be there. In America the food is almost always there in abundance. Even for the immigrant the question was not whether there would be food but how to buy it; later the question became *what kind* of food to choose from abundance. There have been times, especially in war, when a combination of war needs and maldis-

* For further analyses of American dwelling, see Sec. 9, "City Lights and Shadows," and Sec. 10, "The Suburban Revolution," in this chapter. See also Ch. VIII, Sec. 2, "The Family As Going Concern," for the American home. And for building and architecture, see Ch. XI, Sec. 8, "Building, Design, and the Arts."

tribution undercut the sense of plenty. In 1941, for example, a poll showed that one of every two Americans wanted more to eat than he could get. But the surveys by the Food and Agriculture Organization of the UN show the diet of the United States since World War II to be at the extreme of the world food scale, averaging 3,200 calories a day per person, with 1,800 pounds of food intake a year and a high protein diet, while an Asian area like Java is at the other extreme (2,000 calories, largely rice, with 800 pounds food intake and a low protein diet). The diet differences are so great that a fifteen-year-old boy of Asian immigrant parents in the United States, living on an American diet, is likely to be four inches taller than a boy of the same age in Asia living on the lesser diet.

In the past quarter century, especially since World War II, American food habits changed drastically. The change was best signalized by two ideas—that of the "balanced diet" and that of prepared ready-to-eat foods that defy time and space, being both freezable and compressible.

The idea of a balanced diet came from the nutrition studies, which started with the chemical elements the body needs and translated them into terms of available foods. But the food-education program would not have come home to the mass of people without the Army experience of World War II which introduced millions of young men to new food emphases. Soldiers from mountain and farm areas who had grown up on corn pone, fried pork, hot biscuit, and potatoes learned the uses of leafy vegetables, orange juice, and milk. The heavy reliance on grains and breads shifted to meats and fish for large sections of the population who had eaten little of either; the reliance on fats and carbohydrates also shifted; the protein content of the diet increased; the words "proteins," "calories," and "vitamins" came into everyday use. The measure of the change was shown by the fact that vigorous American males—at college and in Army camps—were not ashamed to drink milk: while some called this a sign of the American male's dependence on his mother, the less tortured conclusion is simply that Americans became nutrition-conscious. The seamier side of this impulse was in the health-food faddism, the anxious counting of calories, the compulsive weighing, the multiplication of trick diets, and the obsession of Americans—especially women—with "reducing" as a standard both of beauty and will power, the outward sign of an inner grace.

Americans overeat badly, as one might expect in a country where immigrant origins and memories linger among people who are "upward mobile"; they overdrink badly, as one might expect where there is so much stress on happiness and so much frustration in its pursuit. There is no country in the world where obesity is so much of a problem (many rank it as the most serious of American diseases) yet where people are so constantly aware of the danger. It was largely this fear, plus the fear of dental decay, that caused a drop of three pounds in the per-capita candy consumption in the decade from 1945 to 1955. The American child is fattened like some heifer meant for sacrifice; the American female starts to "reduce" as a young matron or even sooner as an adolescent, and the American male at middle age. The life cycle is traced in the taking on and sloughing off of poundage.

But this nutrition-consciousness was less true of America in the 1950s than it was in the 1930s and 1940s. It had become embodied and absorbed in institutional food planning—in the school, church, university, factory, hospital, Army—where so many meals were served. The newer trend was toward new experimentalism about food as taste. The ethnic pluralism of America proved on this score both a problem and a treasure house. It was a problem because of the large number of food backgrounds that were brought to mingle in an American city. The cafeteria, for example, developed largely as a way of breaking a menu down into individual units which could be reassembled by each person according to his own traditions and taste. It was thus an ingenious device for individualism in food habits and is rapidly spreading over the world. But the myriad of ethnic traditions also added a culinary richness to American life which merged with the myriad of regional cooking traditions.

The Puritans had seen food as part of a life measured out in duty, effort, and reward, and the later immigrant, in a similar spirit, had taught his children to finish whatever was on the plate. But there was another American strain too, rooted in Virginia, the Carolinas, and Louisiana, which went with Southern plantation largess and the arts of Negro cooking. Having little truck with health, nutrition, calories, vitamins, or a balanced diet, it saw eating as pleasure rather than duty, and it gave scope not only for individual taste in eating but for individual expressiveness in cooking and preparing meals. The American soldiers and travelers abroad, who had discovered how much love could be squandered by Parisians, Florentines, and Viennese upon wines, sauces, salads, and condiments, came back to rediscover the glories of their own ethnic and regional cooking traditions.

For such people the old delicatessen store and the new supermarket, with their array of treasures, furnished more provocation to stir the patriot blood than all the loyalty hunts of the 1940s and 1950s. Cooking became an art for millions of dedicated amateurs, men as well as women. They were further prodded into doing their own cooking by the virtual disappearance of domestic servants, and they were encouraged by one of the great events of contemporary America—the rise of "convenience foods" (frozen, processed, packaged, "prepared mixes") and the perfection of the home "deep-freezes." To some extent these were a phase of

America-in-a-hurry, and often the prepared foods were too synthetic and the refined foods (as in the case of bread) had important materials refined out of them.

In general, American cooking still leaves much to be desired, and not only for the gourmets. The average American cooking tastes are perhaps best evidenced by the luncheon menus at a Childs restaurant or a Howard Johnson road stand. It has been observed that even when its income increases an American family's food habits are the last to feel the effects of the change. But for a growing number of Americans the new technology of food restored taste as an adventure, added a ceremonial element to it, brought in informal cookbooks and conversation about food, and rounded out the "eating revolution" which had begun with the shift of diets.

It is not yet clear whether this changed approach will have much impact on the emotional meanings with which Americans ordinarily invest food. Since the formation of eating habits forms part of the "socializing" of the child, food has come to be the center of a pattern of emotional tensions between parent and child, involving a system of rewards and punishments and the granting and withholding of love. Mostly these tensions operate between mother and child, although latterly the father is likely also to take part in the wrangles over feeding: the mother, however, is the marketer, the selecter of diets, the judge of what is "good" or "bad" for the child, the arbiter of table manners and habits. It is she who uses cajolery, scolding, punishment, in her unflagging effort to build a strong and healthy child.

The result is too often that the process of eating becomes invested with anxiety or hostility, with the child's submission to authority or the adolescent's assertion of independence. Certain foods take on excessive symbolic value within the family context, leading sometimes to neurotic disorders and psychosomatic diseases. It is just possible that the newer tendency of the adults to enjoy food in a relaxed way may also over the generations serve to relax the parent-child tensions: where the basic attitude is hedonist rather than Puritan, the obsession with food-as-duty for both mother and child is likely to lessen.

There are more genial food obsessions, coming less directly from the family and more generally from the culture, that will probably endure. Certain foods, by nostalgic memories of childhood and the home place, have become evocatively American—wheatcakes and sirup, baked beans, fried chicken, sirloin steak, the Thanksgiving and Christmas turkey dinner, baked potato, blueberry pie or peach cobbler. To these should be added the almost compulsive American drinks—hot steaming coffee, Bourbon whisky, ice-cream soda, and the various "cola" drinks. I single these out as the contemporary symbols, but George Stewart is right in emphasizing that there are two drinks rarely mentioned but more characteristically American than any of them—milk (somehow regarded and highly publicized as healthful) and ice water for drinking, neither of which has as much vogue in other cultures. Human beings cherish the symbolic, and Americans traveling abroad or returning from a war are likely to be haunted by these short cuts to a sense of longing and belonging. Yet these stereotypes tend to obscure the bigger fact of the myriad richness of American dishes and cooking.

7. *The Way of the Farmer*

WITH ALL THE MARVELS of science in increasing energy sources and food abundance it is easy to forget that the final source of food is the land, and that the way of life on the land is the way of the farmer. This is not because of any deficiency of sentiment. Ever since Jefferson's dream of a society of free farmers, Americans have idealized the rural way of life, even while it was being displaced by the urban—perhaps exactly *because* it was being displaced. Many of the men in *Who's Who* come from farm backgrounds. It is not only the disproportionate political strength of the rural areas that gives farm-aid and crop-support programs an easy passage through Congress but also the folk-belief that the farmers form the nation's backbone and that there is somehow a healing grace and an elixir of sturdiness and integrity in contact with the soil which are not to be derived from contact with city pavements.

The way of the farmer, enthroned in American sentiment, has fared erratically in American reality. Until seventy-five years ago America was predominantly an agricultural economy, an agrarian polity, and a rural society. It is no longer any of the three. Fewer than twenty-two million, or only 13½ per cent of the population, lived on and from the land in 1955, as contrasted with 25 per cent in 1930. Even while frontier lands were still accessible the proportion of farmers to the total working force kept dropping. Around 1825 three fourths of the gainfully employed Americans were on the farm; around 1875 the proportion was one half; in 1955 the farmers and farm workers comprised fewer than seven million out of sixty-five million Americans with gainful jobs, or less than 11 per cent. Of these seven million, three million are farm workers, either hired men on small- and medium-sized farms, sharecroppers, or migratory workers on the large corporation farms of the West and Southwest. This leaves only some four million in the category of the independent farmer on the family-size farm. One should further subtract from this figure the "one-mule" cotton farmer and those still clinging to impoverished and eroded land and earning only the meagerest of submarginal livings from it. It was estimated in 1955 that between 800,000 and 1,750,000 farm families were unable to earn a decent living on the land and would be better off if they were shifted to industry.

All this has been part of what Gilbert Burck, writing in *Fortune*, has called the "magnificent decline" of American agriculture. The quantitative decline is clear enough. In a quarter century, from 1930 to 1955, the number of farms shrank from 6,300,000 to 5,200,000, with the likelihood that they would continue to shrink as the submarginal farms were pushed out. It was estimated that in another quarter century, by 1980, the 13½ per cent of the American people living on farms in 1955 would have become 8 per cent, and extended far enough the curve would end in a small, professionalized group of firms running a highly mechanized and productive farm industry much as any other industry is run in America.

The "magnificent" element in the decline of American agriculture is to be found in the productivity gains. The break-through came late in the 1930s, largely because of the basic research on plant genetics, hybridization, and crossbreeding which has been done for years under the schools of agriculture and came to fruition under the New Deal; it was given impetus by World War II, and it reached its pitch in the decade from 1945 to 1955. In the latter year 37 per cent less farm man power produced 54 per cent more than in 1930, and farm productivity had increased 110 per cent in only a quarter century. The acreage remained relatively stable, and the man hours decreased. What then made the difference? The answer lies in science and industrialization—in new forms of fertilizer, new hybrid breeds of corn, new ways of feeding hogs, new insecticides and pest controls, new methods of irrigation, new machinery, new capital investment, new techniques of business (cost accounting) management.

What has happened is that the sweep of the business spirit and of the machine has caught up the whole enterprise of farming and transformed it in the image of industrial enterprise. Far from being an overnight growth, mechanization has been a fact of American agriculture from the start. American farmers carried their initial crops and livestock over from Europe and made brilliant adaptations of them to the conditions of their own climate and soil. Scientific farming started in Europe and its techniques were used in England long before they were used in America. But the farm machinery, as embodied in the work of Whitney, McCormick, and Case, was America's own invention. The motorizing of the farm through the reaper, the threshing machine, the combine harvester, the multi-row cultivator, and the cotton picker was largely the product of necessity, since there was plenty of land in a new country but a scarcity of labor. In Europe, where land was scarce and population crowded, the standard of progress was productivity per acre: it is still true that the intensive European agriculture gets an extremely high per-acre yield—but with a large expenditure of man power. In America the standard of progress has been productivity per man hour.

In recent years, however, the conquests of American farm machinery have been unparalleled. In 1935, American farms had a million tractors; in 1955 they had 4,500,000, along with 2,500,000 trucks, almost a million combines, and three quarters of a million milking machines. The "motor revolution" was followed by an electrical revolution: in 1955 at least nine out of ten farms had electric power, as a result of the far-sighted thinking of the founders of the Rural Electrification Administration—Morris L. Cooke and John Carmody, and the creative work of the electric co-operatives. Corn pickers in Iowa, haystackers in Montana, combines in the wheat country of Washington, potato harvesters on Long Island, citrus sprayers in Florida, cotton pickers in the South—these were the typical expressions of an investment of close to twenty billion dollars in farm machinery. On a California corporate farm the "big-time growers" level the soil with bulldozers, spray it from airplanes, irrigate it with deep-well pumps, and get a yield of cotton per man hour undreamed of in agricultural history. In the same spirit the hogs are fed by a nutrition calculus on a production-line basis, and the beef cattle are fattened with female sex hormones.

This has been called the coming of "automation" to the farm, which is inaccurate since human labor is still the indispensable factor in farming. Yet the march of mechanization on the farm is clear. A complex cotton-picking machine in 1955 did the work formerly done by sixty or seventy men. The small farmer, who cannot afford to operate on a scale to encompass it, is becoming an archaism. The average size of the American farm in 1955 was 215 acres, and if the submarginal farms were not counted it was much higher. About two million American farms, grossing $2,500 a year, formed the heart of the farm operations. The bigger farmer, able to invest in machinery, has shaken his spear across the land. Were Thomas Jefferson to come back, with his dream of a small-scale agrarian America, he would turn in dismay from what would seem to him a monster of technocracy—man-hour productivity, chemical and hormone science, production-line efficiency, high capital investment, and motor and electrical mechanization.

Thus the machine and its camp followers have gone far to transform the way of the farmer. His relation to science, industrialism, and business power has changed. The lines of energy now flow from the center, once represented by the small independent farmer, toward the big farmer and the corporate farm, with its massive, impersonal organization: yet one cannot ignore the less characteristic submarginal farmer, the sharecropper on tired soil, the migratory hired field worker.

The independent farmer as the "masterless man" has dwindled in importance. He may still be found growing corn in Kansas and steers and hogs in Iowa, potatoes in Maine or on Long Island, or grazing cattle in Wyoming. His wife is peerless at baking pies and putting up preserves, which she now does in an electrically equipped kitchen; his children belong to the 4-H clubs (Head, Heart, Hands, Health), raise blue-ribbon fair winners of their own, play basketball at high school, attend land-grant universities, drive cars and tractors, and study science; he is usually a Republican (except in periods of steeply falling prices), a churchgoer, a moviegoer, a TV set owner, a book-club subscriber, reader of *Life, Time, Newsweek, Look,* and the *Reader's Digest,* a member of the Farm Bureau or the Grange, a political power in his community. Yet he is not, as he was in Jefferson's or Jackson's time or even Bryan's, the bulwark of the American community.

In looking at the splendid efficiency of the best American farming, it is easy to forget how much of it rides on the backs of humble, anonymous men. In California, for example, there were over a half million farm workers; through the whole Southwest (although their number was recently reduced) there were still swarms of Mexican-American "wetbacks," or illegals, who swam the Rio Grande at night, turning the border into a sieve, and had to be rounded up periodically and deported by airlift; and there were many contract workers, some of whom settled down as American citizens, while some came and returned each year. In California's San Joaquin and Imperial valleys the corporate farms, which were once described by Carey McWilliams as "factories in the field," have improved considerably in their condition; yet their workers are not included in Federal security and social legislation, are still paid submarginal wages, and buy their food from company commissaries.

In the South also it would be hard to talk of the "independent farmer." The South suffered in the past from being a one-crop region, where Cotton was King until very recently, when agriculture became more diversified. With other countries now growing cotton, America's share of the world market decreased sharply, and the pressures were toward efficiency. In the Mississippi Delta, in Texas, in some areas of Alabama, cotton growing was mechanized on a large scale, feasible only for the "plantation farms" or for those with capital to invest or for co-operatives banding together to buy farm machinery. The small cotton grower of the South, a victim of high labor cost on the unmechanized one-mule farm, and of the boll weevil and debt, is on the way out. On the eroded soil only the wretched living standards of the submarginal croppers and subsistence farmers and on the good soil only the mechanized and large-scale farms are now possible.

I do not mean to give the impression of backwardness on the American soil. Compare the American farmer with the Malayan or Indonesian peasant—impoverished, sick, undernourished, badly housed and clothed, a prey to the usurer, without incentive, tilling land he does not own—and the contrast is dramatic. Take the family-size farm in the mixed-farming areas of Ohio, Wisconsin, Minnesota, Illinois, and in the corn-wheat-hog and prime-beef areas of Kansas, Iowa, Nebraska, and the Dakotas, and compare it with the European peasantry that exasperated Karl Marx into talking of "rural idiocy" and of the farmer as a primitive "troglodyte": again the contrast is dramatic.

Yet every system of agriculture pays its own kind of social price for the methods it uses. In the late nineteenth century much of American farming was a kind of soil mining which stripped the land while it made production cheap. (Incidentally, by undercutting the more highly priced British agriculture of the time and selling their food cheaply in England, the Americans almost killed British farming.) At present the highly organized and rationalized nature of American farming carries with it a different kind of social price. The acreage under cultivation has remained steady while the number of farms and farmers has decreased. The traditional "hired man," who was close to the farmer's family, is disappearing and is being displaced by migrants and machine tenders in the fields and in the dairy. Landlessness has become a reality: there are the landless croppers and tenants, the landless Negroes, the landless seasonal workers. The reach of landlessness grows in direct proportion to the reach of mechanization. California, for example, where agriculture developed late and as part of the machine era, shows the clearest cleavage between the controllers of the mechanized corporate farms and the landless casual laborers whose situation is worse than that of the machine tenders in the factories because they have no unions, are not protected by social legislation, and lack access to the leisure activities and the popular culture of urban life.

One may grow unduly sentimental about the disappearance of the Jeffersonian image of the farmer on his soil, and of the old family-size farm that was not part of the machine technology. "The truth is," wrote Louis Bromfield, "that farming as a way of life is infinitely more pleasurable and satisfactory when it is planned, scientific, specialized, mechanized, and stripped of the long hours and the drudgery of the old-fashioned, obsolete pattern of the frontier or general farm." This has always been the case for agricultural rationalization. Yet it cannot obscure the fact that the old love of the soil has been replaced by a fetishism of output, efficiency, and cost accounting. This is already evident in the arguments of the efficiency-minded agricultural experts who say that the small, "inadequate" farmer will simply have to get off the land. What applies now to the small farmer is bound in time to apply to the middle-sized farmer. The logic of this latter-day advance of capitalism upon the land is as unyielding as in the case of the historical enclosure movements. The fact that the victims of the large-scale expulsion from the land are being absorbed in industry does not make it any less an expulsion.

There is a striking paradox at the heart of the relation between farming and the American capitalist economy. On the one hand farming has become thoroughly mechanized and industrialized and has thus become part of the larger wide-flung economy: the farmer, purchasing chemicals and machinery on a large scale and applying them to the land, has become largely a processor. On the other hand, farming is the only large sector of the economy—apart from national defense—that is subsidized and thus stands apart from the rest of the economy.

There are two basic reasons for this dependent state. One is the limited expansionism of the demand for farm products. Even with the "eating revolution" and the new habits of the American worker in consuming meats and dairy products, the rise in living standards does not mean a proportionate rise in food consumption. What is true of the home market for industry—that lower production cost has led to larger demand, the rise of new industries, and the indefinite expansion of old ones—is thus not true of farming. The second factor is that farm prices are fluctuating prices, and historically the fluctuations have been violent and the farmer has been at their mercy. In high-price periods, especially war periods, the American farmer historically gave way to his land hunger, and in an expansionist spree he mortgaged himself to buy up more land and nourish his pride of ownership. In low-price periods he was wiped out.

That is one reason why the "farm problem" was finally stabilized by making the farmer in a sense the ward of the state—by price support, parity payments, crop restriction, acreage control, "soil bank," and government purchase and storing of the farmer's surplus so that he would not again be the victim of the price fluctuations of the free-enterprise system. Another reason was the failure of farm income to keep pace either with the advance of the national income as a whole or with industrial prices. In 1929 the farmer's share of the national income was 7 per cent; in 1954 it had fallen to 4 per cent. Roughly it doubled in that period, but the national income increased fourfold. The position of the marginal farmer made the situation worse. By the 1950 census figures, over a million and a half farm families had a cash income of less than $1,000 a year, mostly on eroded or poor soil, or on sandy soil on the coastal plain, or on tiny tracts in the South. Even the national average farm income was less than $4,000 per farm—which was low when compared with nonfarm income in America, although very high when compared with farmers in other countries.

The farmer used his massive political strength—far disproportionate to his numbers—to get government price supports which would balance these inequities and give his income some stability. Although the original policies of price support developed out of the New Deal, no Republican administration has dared abandon them. In 1955 there was a seven-billion-dollar surplus of farm products under government price support. The granaries and storage space were full to bursting. The efforts to ease the problem by finding foreign markets were necessarily limited by the adverse effect of dumping policies on American foreign relations. The efforts at acreage reduction were also futile, since they were easily evaded, and the productivity was rising higher than the acreage decrease.

There has been a good deal of discussion of the American "rural mind," but it is hard to talk of it as if it were a single entity. The "mind" of the Arena Imperial Company is different from that of an Iowa corn farmer, which in turn is different from that of a Maine potato farmer, or an Alabama "red-neck" or Georgia "cracker" or "wool hat," and all in turn are different from the mind of an Arkansas Negro cropper, a Rio Grande Valley wetback, or a Jamaican or Puerto Rican contract laborer on the Eastern truck garden or tobacco farms. The mind of a corn-belt farmer is different from that of a cotton-belt farmer, a wheat-belt farmer, a Wisconsin or Pennsylvania or New York dairy farmer, a Rocky Mountain range cattle grazer or sheep grazer, a Florida or California citrus grower. Economic, sectional, ethnic, and class variations, not to speak of individual differences, cut across the conditionings of the farm life itself.

Are there common elements forming what may still be called the farmer's outlook? Veblen thought it was precapitalist and "animistic," due to the farmer's having been by-passed by the technology—and therefore by the psychology—of the machine; that the farmer was conservative because he dealt with a physical environment he could neither calculate nor control, and that he was therefore more inclined to a belief in the magical aspects of social institutions than the industrial worker whose animism had been rubbed away by habituation to the machine.

The trouble with this view—aside from its ignoring of the later machine revolution on the farm—is that it turns the facts of American history on their head. It was the farmers who were associated with the historical American movements of political protest and dissent. From Shays' Rebellion to the twenty-four-hour violence of the farm-holiday movement of the Great Depression, earlier American radicalism was largely agrarian. This radicalism may have been an assertive opposition to the business power the farmers saw challenging them, and their Populism from Bryan's time to La Follette's may have been a last stand against the monopolists who had taken over both the economy and the government. Agrarian radicalism always had in it a strong sense of property and traditionalism: the Populists wanted more to recapture an imaginary agricultural independence than to create new conditions. It was also a radicalism which found room for a heavy component of isolationism and anti-Semitism, as the currents of thought showed in the late 1930s. But it would be hard in any event to maintain Veblen's thesis of the farmer's conservatism in American history.

What was the source of this radicalism and why did it all but disappear? The core of the farmer's attitude has been a fierce individualism. As individualism became more and more linked with the anti-interventionist antibureaucratic doctrines of Republican conservatism, the farmers became the great conservative force of America. The Granger Revolt, the Farmers' Alliance, the Farmer-Labor parties, the Non-Partisan leagues, the Populist and Progressive groups whose center was in the agricultural states of the Middle West, were largely ironed out of the American political picture. The "sons of the wild jackass" who used to come to Congress from the Midwestern states are no more. This does not mean the Republicans can always count on the "farm vote." The elections for a twenty-year period, from 1932 through 1952, showed that the farmer shops around for price supports. But his basic conservatism of outlook survived the New Deal and Fair Deal. Strikingly, this change from agrarian radicalism to agrarian conservatism became more pronounced with the mechanization of agriculture. In the case of the farmers, Veblen's "discipline of the machine" has worked in an inverse way. It would be more to the point to say that the farmer grew more conservative as his living standard rose.

The farmer's individualism had its roots in the fact that, except for the corporate farms and the co-ops, the farmer has to wrestle with soil and climate, bugs and boll weevils, chemistry and hormones, largely by himself. It is not that he deals (in Veblen's terms) with "magic" but that whatever he deals with he has to deal with as an individual enterpriser: the directness of effort and reward, the Lockean sense of property as whatever a man has acquired by mixing his sweat with the soil, are as nakedly manifested in the family farm as in small-scale business enterprise. This has made both of them areas of individualism.

In one respect the American farmer differs from farmers all over the world. He is not a village-dweller. In India, for example, three quarters of the population lives in the traditional farm village. The European village-community might conceivably have been transferred to America and for a time in New England—while the dangers from the Indians were still felt—the farmers huddled together. But except for the Mormon settlements in Utah and the village culture of the Spanish-speaking groups in the Southwest, the way of the American farmer is to live on his farm homestead and leave the village and town to the traders, farm-implement dealers, grain and feed dealers, storekeepers, mill-workers, and service groups. The decisive historical moment here came in the settlement of the Middle West. The Homestead Acts required residence on the land to support the title: the typical homestead was a "quarter section" of 160 acres, which meant that the farmers lived scattered over the land, separated by far distances, with a one-room schoolhouse for their children and a small church set in the open country for their worship. The difficulties of transport kept the farm community within the distance of the "team haul." The result was a fierce localism which laid its stress on local autonomy, a fear of statism, an isolated way of life that led to isolationism in outlook. The farmer's relation to the town was one of hostility: it was the relation of a producer to the middleman who bought his products cheap, and the storekeepers who sold him other products dear; it was the relation of the debtor to the banker, the creditor, the mortgage-holder. This increased his individualism, his isolationism, his burning sense of grievance.

Life has changed for the independent farmer, whether in the Midwest or elsewhere. He has come into a new relation to the standardizing forces of American culture and has become part of the communications revolution. The automobile, the radio, movies, and TV have brought him out of his isolation; he does his shopping and trading less in the farm village and more in the larger industrial center where he can get spare parts for his machinery and the newest fashions for his wife and daughters. His one-room schoolhouse has become a consolidated school located in the trade center to which his children ride daily on a school bus; his land is no longer heavily mortgaged; his crops are price-supported by the Federal government, and in raising them he gets the help of government technicians. The work of a farmer is still hard, heavy work, and the risks of weather and market fluctuations are still real risks. But as farming has become a subsidized sector of the economy, and the security of the farmer one of the tasks of the welfare state, his antistatism is shown up as an anachronism. Nevertheless as a traditional "agin-er," it is still as logical for him to be "agin" the state which subsidized him as it was for him to be "agin" the system of business power which organized the home-market and world-market demand for his products.

In most areas of the world the rural population is custom-bound. In the United States custom has largely loosened its hold, and the farmer is battered by all the dislocating forces of contemporary life. What used to be called the "rural community" has been churned up and is to be found across the country in various stages of disorganization. There has been a steady movement away from the land. The farmer's daughter who has been to the university moves to the towns and cities for marriage or a career; the farmer's son who has gone to an agricultural college sometimes stays to manage the farm, sometimes is drawn away by the more powerful suction force of city life. The slack is taken up by bigger farm units and by corporate management.

The pull of the farm has not vanished: every year there are young Americans who would like to take up farming as a way of life, but the only available government land is the small tracts of Western public lands newly reclaimed by irrigation, and the waiting list for each is a long one. A more important trend is that of the man with a career in the city who likes to farm as a supplementary way of life (much like the English gentleman of the eighteenth and nineteenth centuries) and can afford the investment it requires—and in many cases writes the loss off against his high-bracket income tax. He is another example of how the farmer's way has been swept up into the powerful sway of the pecuniary culture of America.

8. The Decline of the Small Town

THE AMERICAN PLACE started with small population units, rapidly grew to big ones, and has ever since been under the double tension of moving from the small unit to the big one and at the same time moving from the center of the bigger unit outward toward the rim. Traditionally the small town has been held to embody the American spirit better than the larger frame. De Tocqueville affirmed that the township as a unit both of government and of living had preceded the state and nation in America and was more important than either. In New England the township has lasted over three hundred years, and while it has been battered by heavy pressures from state, nation, and economy, it still retains traces of the two goods that Americans have always seen in it—

the friendliness of face-to-face relations and the concern about the town's affairs felt by all its citizens.

De Tocqueville had a reason of his own for his tub-thumping about the New England township—his hatred for French centralization, which made a person "a kind of settler, indifferent to the fate of the spot which he inhabits. The greatest changes are effected there without his concurrence. . . . The condition of his village, the police of his street, the repairs of the church or parsonage, do not concern him; for he looks upon all these things as unconnected with himself and as the property of a powerful stranger whom he calls the government." He saw American town government as the ideal contrast to this lugubrious picture. For all his bias he was nonetheless right about the "provincial independence" of the American small town and the fierce identification of even its poorest citizens with the disputes and rivalries that raged about its affairs. This intensity still prevails in many New England towns, governed by three "Selectmen," who draw up annual budgets that are examined, item for item, by the entire citizenry sitting in the primary democracy of the town meeting. In the early days of the Republic the small town was the tap spring of the revolutionary spirit and of cultural strength. There were few Presidents from Lincoln and Grant to Truman and Eisenhower who were not the products of small-town culture. During most of American history, until the turn of the twentieth century, it was the basic community form for most Americans.

But the growing point of American life is scarcely to be found in the small town today. Latterly the important lines of growth have been elsewhere. It is partly that all the small units in American life are having to wage a losing fight—not only the small town but the small farm, the small business firm, the small college, even the neighborhood within the big city. Somewhere between the turn of the century and the New Deal the small town felt the withering touch of the Great Artifact that we call American society, and in the quarter century between 1930 and 1955 the decisive turn was made, away from small-town life. The currents of American energy moved around and beyond the small towns, leaving them isolated, demoralized, with their young people leaving them behind like abandoned ghost towns.

What happened was that the small town lost its economic and cultural base. Partly this happened in the areas most badly scarred by soil erosion, where the destruction of the rural hinterland stripped away the substance of small-town existence. But actually this was a marginal force. Everywhere, even in the most prosperous areas, the small town was undercut by the big changes in American life—the auto and super-highway, the supermarket and the market center, the mail-order house.

the radio and TV, the growth of national advertising, the mechanization of farming—so that it turned its face directly to the centers of technology. It was the city and the suburb—the cluster-city complex—that became the focus of working and living, consuming and leisure. "None of the kids ever come back here to live after they've gone away to school," said an older man from Shannon Center, Iowa, which had lost almost half its population in the 1940s. The young people go on to find jobs in factories or businesses far from where they grew up, or they go away to college or technical school and get the kind of training for which the small town, with its limited opportunities, simply cannot offer a demand.

I have been talking here of an entity hard to define, especially in drawing a line between the small town and the city. The Census Bureau calls any community of over 2,500 people "urban," and for 1950 showed some 3,000 communities in America with a population between 1,000 and 2,500; more than 3,000 with a population from 2,500 to 10,000; and 3,800 with a population between 2,500 and 25,000. One might put the dividing line at around 10,000 or 15,000 people, but it would be an arbitrary line.

The test is at what point the town grows too big to make life compassable. The value of small-town living lies in the face-to-face relations that it makes possible throughout the community. One might say that a small town ceases to be one as soon as someone who has lived in it a number of years finds unfamiliar faces as he walks down the street and is not moved to discover who they are and how they got there. For in a small town it is the unfamiliar that is remarkable, just as in a big city the memorable experience is to meet in a random walk through the streets someone you know. It has occurred to more than one observer that if a big-city inhabitant were to respond to all the people he meets to the same degree as a small-town inhabitant, he would end as a raving lunatic.

One notes that most of the communities in the spate of recent surveys (the Newburyport of Lloyd Warner's *Yankee City,* the Morris of his *Democracy in Jonesville,* the Natchez of John Dollard's *Caste and Class in a Southern Town,* the Grafton of Granville Hicks's *Small Town*) were about towns of less than 25,000. Muncie of the *Middletown* studies by Robert and Helen Lynd (38,000 at the time of the first study, 48,000 at the second) was somewhat larger. Each study was an effort to catch the distillation of American life through a microscopic analysis of a cross section of it. Clearly, the small town lends itself most easily to this kind of inductive study because it is small enough to grasp. But I doubt the symbolic value it is intended to have for America as a whole.

What the studies are discovering is the America of an earlier generation. The changes operative in the growth centers of American life are reflected in distorted form in the small town, like the shadows in Plato's cave.

The idea that the small town is the seed ground of what is characteristically American has not been restricted to its glorifiers or to the survey-makers. It may be found in so hostile a critic as Thorstein Veblen, in his classic essay on "The Country Town" (*Absentee Ownership in America*). He wrote as an agrarian radical of the Scandinavian Midwest, resenting the Yankee merchants and bankers who had come from New England to take over the Great Plains. He saw in the country town the roots of the capitalist attitude—the "predatory" and "prehensile" spirit of American business enterprise, middleman rather than producer, quick to discern a profit, greedy to grasp it, tenacious in holding on to it. It was ruthless evaluation yet not without its insight. A history of American industry will show how many of the men who came to the top of the heap spent their formative years in the small town and in many instances got their business start there. But even when Veblen wrote in the mid-1920s the small town was ceasing to be the focus of the capitalist spirit.

The fact that the small town is dwindling in importance makes Americans idealize it all the more. The phrase "small town" has come itself to carry a double layer of meaning, at once sentimental and condescending. There is still a belief that democracy is more idyllic at the "grass roots," that the business spirit is purer, that the middle class is more intensely middling. There is also a feeling that by the fact of being small the small town somehow escapes the corruptions of life in the city and the dominant contagions that infest the more glittering places. History, geography, and economics gave each American town some distinctive traits of style that are imbedded in the mind, and the memory of this style is all the more marked because of the nostalgia felt, in a largely urban America, for what seems the lost serenity of small-town childhoods.

This was probably part of the basis for the "Renaissance" of the small town at mid-century, just when its decay and the movement of population from it were most marked. There was a return to it emotionally, if not intellectually, as a repository of the older and more traditional values. A number of writers, advertising men, newspapermen, and artists dreamed of forsaking the competitive tensions of New York, Chicago, or Hollywood to settle down in a small town and find the abandoned "heart of America." In the university centers some of the professors made heroic efforts to revive the energies of the small town and recapture its control for the people, much as the Russian *Narodniki* at the turn of the century dreamed of "going to the people" and finding among them new strength with which to grapple with the tasks of social revolution and reconstruction.

The question few of them faced was why the small town had declined and been rejected by the younger people. One might have expected the face-to-face quality of its living and the strong personal ties it afforded to have served as an attraction to young families settling down to a tranquil and satisfying way of life. But this reckons without the counterforce of recoil from the torpor and tyranny of the small town. The best clue to this counterforce showed up in the literature of the 1910s and 1920s—in the portrait of Spoon River in Edgar Lee Masters' poems, in the Gopher Prairie of Sinclair Lewis's *Main Street,* in the bitter narratives of Sherwood Anderson and Theodore Dreiser. As early as 1882 Ed Howe had laid bare the meanness and sterility of small-town life in *The Story of a Country Town.* All these writers depicted mercilessly the provincialism of small-town life, the stifling constraints, the sense of stagnation that came from living in a closed room. It is unlikely that the forces of American conformism were more cruelly displayed anywhere than in the heavy hand that the small town habitually laid on the man or woman who too rashly broke the moral code. Just as heavy was the hand one laid on one's own rebel impulses. The record at once of the outer social tyranny and the inner repression may be read in the stony faces of Grant Wood's provincials.

Even the efforts at "reform" were part of the mood of disillusionment. Carol Kennicott, who tried to bring culture to Gopher Prairie, was in the line of succession of the women who had founded the Minerva Clubs, the Ladies' History Clubs, and the Ladies' Library Associations of Sioux Falls, S.D., and Weeping Waters, Neb., and Sleepy Eye, Minn., seeking to bring culture to the moving frontier. Yet while Carol was not new, she expressed a change of mood. Sinclair Lewis, like Masters, Dreiser, and Anderson, drew for much of his creativeness upon his smoldering rebellion against the "lassitude and futility" of Gopher Prairie. Its Main Street, he wrote, "is the continuation of Main Streets everywhere." And he added, with his heavy satiric underscoring, "Main Street is the climax of civilization"—although it is worth adding that in his later novels Lewis reversed his position and took back his satire. His fellow townsmen were meanwhile content with Main Street. "Somehow Harry Lewis didn't like it here," was the way one of his boyhood friends from Sauk Center put it many years later. But this was no crotchet of Lewis's: it was true of other writers and artists. The city revolution had brought with it a widening of horizons and a dislocation of social ties. The sensitive ones who were left behind felt cheated of life.

A number of critics, including T. S. Eliot, have linked creative achievement with the face-to-face relations possible in a small community. This may be so, but in the United States the poets and novelists of the period wrote as they did not because they had ties with the small town but because they were breaking their ties. The creatively releasing force for them was the sense of breaking through the encrusted mold of custom. The very smallness of the small town gave them compassable symbols of grievance and hatred, and it dramatized both the clash between the small town and the Great Society and also the sense of breakthrough. Even in the 1950s many young men writing their first novels chose the macrocosm of some small town to depict, as in *Sironia, Texas*. But in a sense the 1920s saw "the last of the provincials," as Maxwell Geismar put it, and the great writing moved away from the small town and its life to the city and its suburbs and the outside world.

What happened to the small town was not only that the big social changes undercut it and swirled around it, leaving it isolated, but they also drained it of its store of power. The power of America today is to be found largely with the business and community leaders of the city, who initiate policies for corporate empires, trade-unions, national pressure groups, and big-audience media. Knowing this, we tend to forget that in an earlier America the decisions that expressed the American will were largely made by small-town lawyers, bankers, merchants, editors. As merchandizing, transport, and recreation shifted, the locus of power shifted. The town could no longer perform most of its functions alone—roadbuilding, relief, education, taxation, public works—and it came to depend on subsidies from the Federal and state governments. As the power diminished, however, the intensity of the feuds and rivalries did not always subside, and the small town sometimes offered the unreal spectacle of an intensified struggle over dwindling stakes of power.

To the outward eye, the town of the 1950s, with its church spires, its Town Hall, its Main Street stores, its bank, its weekly newspaper, seemed what it always was. But its decay was unmistakable, taking the form of a displacement of its power and a disorganization of its traditional ways of life. Charles Francis Adams had seen it generations earlier, in his poetic description (in *Three Episodes of Massachusetts History*) of the disappearance of the New England village. Even the close controls which the code-makers of the town once exerted on its moral standards had to be relaxed in the face of the general moral confusion.

George Homans pointed out, in commenting on a study of the social disorganization of "Hilltown"—a Massachusetts farming town of about 1,000 people—that a town clerk who absconded with community funds was no longer dealt with draconically as in similar cases in the past, that girls being dated were expected to "come across" sexually, and that virginity before marriage was no longer stressed or counted upon. Few would argue today that the condition of mental health in the small town is better than in the city, or that there is less alcoholism or a better family situation. Nor can one any longer underplay the seamier sides of American localism—the heartbreaking inertia, the presence of corruption and greed even at the grass roots. Human meanness and human generosity are widely distributed in a culture, and the pursuit of the cultural life goals goes on with little reference to the unit of living. There may be greater tranquillity in the small town but no more happiness; there are face-to-face relations but no deeper understanding of the human situation; there is a more compassable universe to grasp, physically and socially, but in reality it is no less bewildering.

If I have been unsparing here in dealing with the legend of small-town superiority, I do not mean to belittle the enduring although lesser place the small town is likely to have in American life. The growth of a highly urban and mechanized Great Society has by-passed not only the town itself but also some of the values with which it was historically linked. Emerson's Concord, Lincoln's Springfield, William Allen White's Emporia, Truman's Independence, and Eisenhower's Abilene must have borne along on their current a way of life strong enough to shape the men they produced. Some of America's towns, especially in New England and in the prosperous areas of the Middle West, are still conscious of being the carriers of a tradition and a philosophy. When Harry Truman, commenting on the problem of juvenile delinquency, wrote that "our children need fewer gadgets and more chores," he was expressing a recognizable small-town philosophy—the direct, no-nonsense, keep-life-simple philosophy of small-town mores. Truman's own personality—informal, downright, salty, with its strong sense of task, its stress on personal loyalties and obligations, its rejection of cant, its shrewd assessment of men and issues, and its built-in moral code—is the distillation of what is healthiest and most pungent in the surviving values of small-town culture. Although most small-town politicians (and much of American politics still derives from the small town) would shy away from Truman's identification with majority aspirations and minority causes, with labor interests and civil liberties and Negro civil rights, enough of them are enough like Truman to make a fusion of urban and small-town values conceivable. If the small town is wholly sacrificed there will be sacrificed along with it some continuity of face-to-face relations, an awareness of identity, a striving to be part of a compassable whole, a sense of counting for something and being recognized as a person and not a cipher.

A number of recent American writings indicate that the nostalgia for the small town need not be construed as directed toward the town itself: it is rather a "quest for community" (as Robert Nisbet puts it)—a nostalgia for a compassable and integral living unit. The critical question is not whether the small town can be rehabilitated in the image of its earlier strength and growth—for clearly it cannot—but whether American life will be able to evolve any other integral community to replace it. This is what I call the problem of place in America, and unless it is somehow resolved, American life will become more jangled and fragmented than it is, and American personality will continue to be unquiet and unfulfilled.

If the small town survives at all in a future America, it will have to survive within this frame and on a new economic base—not as the minor metropolis of a farming area, or as a mill town or mining town, but as a fusion of farming and industrial life along with the residential spill-over from the city and the suburb. I shall deal with both these forms in what follows, but it is worth saying here that neither the mammoth city nor the dormitory suburb is as it stands an adequate solution of the problem of place in America. Neither is the small town as it stands. But it can diversify its economic base, especially with the trend toward decentralizing industry. With the new modes of transport it can reach even the distant big city easily—for work or recreation, school, medical facilities, or friends. And it can build a way of life which forms a continuity with the small town of the past but without its cluttering accompaniments of provincialism and torpor.

9. *City Lights and Shadows*

America was formed in its present mold in the process of city building, and it is still true—even in the era of the suburban revolution—that wherever American places are being shaped anew the new forms irrepressibly move toward becoming cities. While making goods and making money, the American has become in the process a city maker as well.

Lewis Mumford, in his *Culture of Cities,* has traced with learning and passion the historical rise of the city as shelter, fortress, industrial center, mechanical way of life—the stages toward "Megalopolis." In every civilization the rise of the big city has been a by-product of technical and industrial development. This has been true not only in

Europe, whose cities grew big earlier than America's and whose population density is higher, but also in Asia, where the recent upsurge of population and the ferment of new forces have raised the size of the big cities staggeringly high. It is truer of the American city, however, that the rise of megalopolis has meant the accumulation not only of masses of people but of masses of power. The growth of the American city has gone along with—and been the product of—revolutions in production, motive power, transport, communications. Every transformation in the economy, including the rise of new industries and the changes from roads to canals to railroads to autos and aviation, and from steam to gasoline to electric and atomic power, has further complicated the web of city life. Yet the changes move inexorably, and as they occur they keep transforming the outer sky line and the inner structure and life of the city. Every new step in technology tends to destroy the inner forms of the cities on which they rest and which have made them possible, and on their ruins new forms arise.

The statistical growth line is by now familiar enough. In 1790 when the American nation first emerged it had no cities, large or small, that could compare with the glory of European cities. There were a few small "cities in the wilderness"—three between 10,000 and 25,000, two over 25,000, none as large as 50,000. Not until 1820 did New York have 100,000 and not until 1880 did it have a million people. By 1955 it had over eight million, five other cities were over a million, and twenty ranged from New York's vast mass to the roughly half million of Cincinnati, Seattle, and Kansas City. There were 106 cities of over 100,000. Putting the figures differently, the urban population by Census Bureau definition (those living in places of over 2,500) increased between 1940 and 1950 from around seventy-five million to around eighty-nine million, the latter figure representing almost two thirds (64 per cent) of the total population; in the Northeast the proportion was some 80 per cent, in the West 70 per cent, in the South 50 per cent. Add to this the fact that much of the nonfarming rural population is really urban, in the sense that it lives on the outskirts of metropolitan areas, with city jobs and values, and the urban percentage then goes as high as 80 to 82 per cent for the whole nation. Taking a still different approach, and using 25,000 to 100,000 as the range for a small- and middle-sized city, there were seventeen million Americans living in 378 such cities in 1950, while there were forty-four million living in cities of over 100,000—some sixty-one million in all living in cities of over 25,000.

Each of these cities has a character and style of its own. New York and Boston are proud of their role as intellectual centers, but Chicago, "hog-butcher of the world," was the scene of a literary Renaissance in the early decades of the century and later became an educational center. A number of cities—San Francisco, New Orleans, Charleston—have a sure sense of their style and picturesqueness as carriers of a history-laden or exotic tradition, but Boston, Philadelphia, and Baltimore would make rival claims on that score. Some cities in turn are proud of their recent growth as boom towns—Los Angeles, Detroit, Houston, Dallas, Seattle, Portland; and in America the claim to boom is more swaggering than the claim to tradition. Most American cities owe their growth to industry and transport, yet Washington is what it is because it is the nation's capital; Los Angeles, the movie center of America, is also in an area of oil production and owed its original boom to the silver mining of the Sierras.

Emphasizing this, there is a danger of forgetting the strength of the agricultural hinterland out of which many of the American cities grew. They got their start as marketing centers for the products of the surrounding areas: Chicago and Kansas City became shipping centers for the steers of Texas and the Far West. But Pittsburgh and Cleveland owe most of their growth to iron and steel, and Detroit is the automobile center of America. Miami is the center of the vacationing and leisure industries, although recently it has been developing light industries less seasonal and precarious. In the East, cities like Boston, New York, Philadelphia, Charleston, and Atlanta got their start as strategic ports and others rose because they were at the convergence of the great trails and rivers or dominated high ground as forts. There are instances where a city of promising growth remained small while another grew into a metropolis, mainly because in laying out transcontinental railroads the line by-passed one and went through another. Thus many of the Western cities without natural location on rivers are mainly the result of the accident of transportation history, often aided by political pressure, land speculation, and outright bribery.

At some point in its history every American city has been a "boom" city, meaning the sudden spurt of growth when a particular city exerts a suction force upon people looking for opportunity, jobs, profits. Often this spurt of growth takes on a motive force of its own and threatens to run away with the city, outstripping its productive base. The great example of a synthetic boom was that of Florida in the 1920s when blueprint cities were staked out, with water systems, lighting systems, and even community centers. Some later boomed again, and successfully; others remained as derelict reminders that a city cannot be wholly the creation of hope, hysteria, and paper profits. Even in the Paradise of real-estate values a city responds to organic laws of growth. When that growth has a valid base the initial boom will be succeeded by others in mounting succession. The original Chicago boom was that of a stockyard and railroad center; its later phases were those of farm-machinery manufacture, grain and commodity exchanges and speculation, and then war research and production. In Los Angeles a silver-mining boom was succeeded by an oil boom, a movie boom, and a war boom. In Houston and Dallas the booms were chiefly those of oil, real estate, and war industries. A smaller city like Norfolk grew originally as a port and then achieved a shipbuilding boom during World War II.

But the story of city growth is not summed up in the strategy of industrial location. Once the cities were established they exerted a suction force on many diverse groups. Until World War I the city magnet drew immigrants from Europe and boys and girls from farms and small towns. In the forties and fifties it drew Negroes from the South and (in the case of New York) Puerto Rican immigrants. In most cases the trinity of motifs was comfort, opportunity, glamour.

The comfort motif was the answer a later generation gave to the harshness of frontier life that earlier generations had encountered. It was especially important for American women, who had found the frontier settlements bleak and welcomed the restoration of European comfort to the American situation. The middle class carried this motif further, and the calculated comfort of American heating, the American bathroom, and the garishness of the American hotel became symbols of "materialism" which the rest of the world first ridiculed, then envied and imitated.

Related to it is the glamour of city life. In the 1880s the magazine illustrations called it the "lure of the city." They depicted a country lad lying on a hillock, gazing longingly into the distance toward the towers and spires of the city. The mass city—Chicago, Detroit, Minneapolis, Cleveland, Pittsburgh, Boston, New York—was what the young men yearned for. It was their City of God. As for the young women, they turned toward the freedom and blandishments of the city and its romantic possibilities. It was in the cities that the young people hoped to find the excitement and fulfillment which the dynamism of their culture made them ask of life. Where people clustered together there was a greater choice of people, a chance to show one's beauty and wit to advantage, a chance for dress and gaiety, sexual adventure, love and marriage. The glamour of city life was part of the impulse back of the great migration from country to city in the past seventy-five years.

The greatest of the trinity of motifs was the idea of limitless opportunities for the young, strong, and able. Often the mass city proved to be a jungle in which many were destroyed and the survivors brutalized. But those who build a temple to the idols of success do not inquire too closely about the burdens of the sacrifices.

As a result of city living, Americans are becoming a people whose earliest memories are less apt to be of the farm or village or the main street of a small town than of pavements and movies, and swimming at the docks, and running in gangs, and "going downtown." They have had to get accustomed to the jangle of city sounds striking on the nerve centers, to new ways of dodging city traffic or of waiting it out patiently, to the complexity and pavements of the "asphalt jungle."

Why do they stand it? The answer is that many don't, hence the Great Exodus to the suburbs. For those who do, the city has become more than a convenience: it is a necessity. This is true for workers who must be near factories, railroad yards, and offices; for businessmen who must be near their markets and customers; for writers and artists, advertisers, workers in the big media, who must be near the centers of the nation's life.

The city is no longer a mode of comfort, as it was in its earlier phases. In some ways it has become the acme of discomfort—congested, traffic-stalled, smog-filled, shut out from sunlight, with scarcely space for breathing and no feel of soil beneath one's feet and no sense of the rhythm of the seasons. Any subway rider during the rush hours in New York can testify that city life has rigors challenging the frontier. This *ascesis* is made endurable (at least for the eggheads) because of the excitement of theaters, concerts, night clubs, restaurants, sports events, universities, art schools, which only the city can furnish and for which even the big media and the modern arts of mass reproduction are no substitutes. Beyond these amenities the core attraction of the city as a way of life is tension, movement, opportunity, and a swarming kind of warmth. A recent survey of Detroit, into which waves of workers have swept from farms and small towns, shows that most of them do not share the fashionable despair about city living. They like living in Detroit. It is as if there were an unlocalized yearning for what is big in size, dense in numbers, varied in type and stock of people, mobile, responsive. The cities are fed by this restlessness and grow through it.

Thus the American city as a way of life is the product not only of technical and economic factors but also of loneliness. It is here that the byzantine aspect of American city culture becomes important. What is involved is not only the quest for liquor and night clubs, late hours, sexual excitement and sexual opportunity. These are the more obvious garments of a Faustian hunger and an almost pathetic fear of being left out of things. The city is at once the product and symbol of human alienation and the longed-for antidote against it. It is the sum of all the signatures that a restless spirit has left on a people sensitive to experience. "This city," as E. B. White put it in a prose hymn to New York which is the distillation of the urban mood, "this mischievous and marvelous monument which not to look upon would be like death."

So dedicated an attachment does not exclude a sense of the realities of city life. White has said that there are three New Yorks—that of the natives, which gives continuity to the life of the city; that of the commuters, who use the city for business during the day and for evening forays but live in the suburbs; that of the migrants—the polyglot invaders from Europe, Africa and Asia, and from Puerto Rico nearer to home, and the youngsters coming from the Midwest to make a career and discover a universe. To some extent other cities are streaked with the same strata. The big cities offer a greater variation of ethnic stock and a heavier emphasis on the professional and intellectual classes. But otherwise any American city contains, in replica, much the same pyramid of class and mass, of wealth and poverty, of conspicuous consumption and heartbreaking scrimping that American life as a whole contains. The difference is that in a city the contrasts are heightened because there are greater extremes at both ends and because the whole is brought within the compass of a single area.

At one end of the scale the big cities furnish the frame of American wealth and power. They provide the banking and financial mechanisms for the rest of the country, the centers of communication, the starting points of advertising, publications, and salesmanship. This does not mean that they are unproductive, since every big city owed its rise to some crucial relation to the American productive economy. But what the city adds as its own is the pecuniary frame of American society. This is where the money is, this is where the credit structure rests, and with the money and credit go the power and the glory.

Big cities are centers of absentee power, often holding the small ones in fief. In a medium city like Elmira, N.Y., for example, only a few of the big plants on which income and employment depend are locally owned. The others are subsidiaries of corporations with home offices in New York, Pittsburgh, Detroit. In Elmira even labor has an absentee structure of authority, because the national labor contracts on which the Elmira contracts are modeled are signed elsewhere, after negotiations that are carried on at conferences elsewhere. This absenteeism of ownership and control is especially true of the South and Far West, which are linked with control centers in the East and Midwest. A big city like Atlanta and a small city like Decatur, Ala. (pop. 25,000), bid anxiously against other cities for plants which will be the subsidiaries of absentee corporations. The chief function of chambers of commerce is to sell the city as a potential location for new industry. Newspapers, banks, mayors, and city administrations join forces to lure industry to the city. A corporation looking for a Southern plant close to cheap power will get bids from perhaps a score of cities offering hydroelectric power, cheap labor power, low taxes, and political favors. Once the city has the plant, it is dependent on a massive impersonal corporation that makes its decisions within the frame not of local conditions but of its whole empire. Face-to-face relations in the everyday area of job life become impossible. And when the corporation abandons the plant for a cheaper or more favorable spot, the effect on workers and merchants is devastating.

Although the gods whom it must propitiate for its destiny are not local deities but the gods of "business conditions," each city has its sense of welfare and catastrophe. The usual "community feeling" is a hopped-up, synthetic semihysteria called "boosterism." To be a "booster" is to sing your city's praises, push its wares, and defend its good name against defamers. It is an item in a spurious mythology of city promotion, tending to cancel out against the synthetic mythologies of the other cities. But at a time of general joblessness, the false front falls away and people feel caught in a common plight. The plants close down, the pay envelopes shrink, you buy on credit and face the threat of eviction notices. In such crises, or in the event of hurricane or flood disaster, the city discovers itself not just as a chance collection of atoms but as a whole whose parts are members of each other.

Despite the fond conviction abroad that all American cities look alike, each has its own characteristic architecture, its own sky line, its own style of building and of living, its own mood. Each has also its natural history, passing through a series of phases at each of which its characteristic style changed. Philadelphia and Boston, once the great political and cultural capitals of America, are now a mixture of the provincial and the ethnically pluralist. Several cities that started in a somewhat lurid fashion as centers of promiscuous frontier gambling and scarlet sex—such as San Francisco, Cincinnati, New Orleans—are now almost as respectable as their sister cities. From some cities, like Indianapolis, the stamp of rural provincialism is hard to efface. But others—Chicago, Cleveland, Cincinnati, Minneapolis, Kansas City, Louisville, Houston, Dallas—to which lecturers and theater troupes and concert companies used to come only as an act of condescension or uplift have become centers of regional culture.

Compared with the slow growth of the great cities of Europe, the American cities seemed to shoot up overnight. There were several turning points at which the efforts made to plan their growth might have taken hold and become a permanent part of the American scheme. For a time in the colonial America of Charleston, Annapolis, and Williamsburg some ideas of spacious planning were set in motion, but the Revolution interrupted them. After the emergence of the nation there were city plans in the air on a grand scale—not only for the Washington of Major L'Enfant but also for Boston and Philadelphia, and for the new frontier cities of Buffalo, Cleveland, and Detroit. But except in Washington and Savannah they came to little, largely because most cities were growing too fast to allow for the luxury of planned squares and open spaces at the city core, or for broad avenues fanning out on a radial pattern with houses well set back and with space between them. A New York study, which rejected such planning in favor of a cheaper and quicker gridiron pattern divided into uniform rectangles and subdivided with building lots, was later described by Edith Wharton as the expression of "a society of prosperous businessmen who have no desire to row against the current."

Once again, at the turn of the twentieth century, there was a Renaissance of city planning, sparked by the apprenticeship of American architects in Paris and by the Chicago Exposition of 1893. But while it yielded an influential Chicago plan and an attempt to put a beautiful façade on cities from coast to coast, under men like Daniel Burnham, Frederick Olmstead, and Charles McKim, the inertia of haphazard city growth was too great to arrest. What was called the City Beautiful movement caught the imagination and pride of American architects. It was a movement that dealt with state capitols, civic centers, universities, churches, and even railroad stations; eventually, inspired by the garden-city movement of England, it also left its impact on the layout of suburbs. Yet essentially its weakness was that it focused on boulevards and parks for the rich and did little about wider sidewalks and better quarters for the poor. "It had a lot of democratic phrases," writes William Wheaton, "but little democratic action."

A hundred years had elapsed between the city-planning movement at the turn of the nineteenth century and the one at the turn of the twentieth. Not only had vested interests become encrusted but so had habits of building, thinking, living. They were held fast by a century of custom and by greed and speed and the mistaken *laissez faire* that carried over from the realm of moneymaking into the realm of beauty, utility, and orderly growth. Still to follow were remarkable feats of city engineering and the building of skyscrapers, auto parkways, and thruways. But as for city planning, the movement was renewed so heartbreakingly late that it was no match for the strength of real-estate groups and the down-to-earth sense of the "practical" men. The American cities had already established their basic pattern of growth. By the time the Depression had stripped away the burnished surface of the cities and revealed the blight beneath, and governmental housing projects were started under the New Deal and new city planning commissions established, they could do little except operate within the accomplished fact of city history.

The core of that accomplished fact was planlessness. Most American cities had risen helter-skelter, wherever some convenience of location might place them or some rapacity push them. They grew up thus—grim and unlovely; often wrongly situated for health, huddling against tracks and wharves, clustered around railroad stations, stockyards, chemical factories, and power plants, with the scars of congested slums on them; swept by fires, vulnerable to epidemics, cradled often in low-lying areas periodically ravaged by floods; their air poisoned with smoke and polluted from the slag of the furnaces: sprawling and crowded aggregates that grew by haphazard and piled-up wealth and excitement but offered large segments of their people a mode of living which was neither spacious nor gracious, with neither plan nor meaning.

To say the cities were without plan does not mean that their growth lacked any discernible principle. A group of thoughtful students of city development have tried ingeniously to uncover a theory by which planless growth unfolded in various cities according to somewhat similar patterns. It became clear, for example, that many cities had a central core—the downtown business and shopping district, with hotels, banks, theaters, movie houses, office buildings, and the City Hall; and that around this core the other areas were to be found—the warehouses, railroad yards, factories; the wholesale and light-manufacturing districts; the blighted area with slums, rooming houses, and tenements (some of them once residences but later abandoned); the better low-cost houses of the skilled workers living near their work and the middle-class homes and apartment houses; the heavy manufacturing district; sometimes an outlying business district; the "residential" area of bigger houses, set off from the street with trees and space around them; finally the suburban ring of commuters, including residential and industrial suburbs and comprising high and low incomes alike.

At first it was thought that the districts grouped themselves around the core in widening concentric zones, with the expansive energy pushing from the center outward. Then with the coming of modern transport, a radial sector theory depicted the city as growing outward from the center along the lines of automobile and bus transportation, always away from low-lying, blighted, and dead-end areas toward higher and open country. Finally, to take account of the complex and bewildering growth of metropolitan cities, the theorists developed the idea of the multiple-nuclei city which grows around a number of cores.

Obviously all this was theorizing after the fact, and the naked fact was that the growth of the American city followed profitability and transport. The real arbiters of city growth were the railroad (which often pre-empted some of the best open space), auto traffic, and the real-estate promoter. It is these forces that dictated the shape of city growth far more than any city plan. To some this may seem evidence that American cities have grown organically rather than by some synthetic design, but haphazard growth is not organic. It is possible to provide for informal as well as formal features of growth, for variety as well as regularity, but the essential thing is to allow scope for both by taking thought.

In its layout the city tends to reflect the life history of its movements of immigration. The history of Brooklyn, for example, was that of successive migrations of Dutch, British, New Englanders, Irish, Jews, Italians, Negroes, Scandinavians, East Europeans, Syrians, Puerto Ricans, and even a colony of Mohawk Indians. They form a polyglot gridiron across the face of the city, with enough distinctness so that each section has its ethnic core and gives each neighborhood a sense of ethnic identity. This is why it has been said that in New York every street becomes a village, every area of ten or a dozen blocks becomes a neighborhood.

One of the results of the failure to take thought is the American city slum. Every big city has its slum area. Tolstoy's famous sentence—that all happy families are alike but every unhappy family is unhappy in its own way—applies inversely to cities: their gleaming and burnished streets belong uniquely to the city itself, but there is a deadly sameness about most slum areas. It is the universal quality of the scabrous areas where poverty and disease, delinquency and prostitution, walk together. The pattern of ethnic ghettos and race violence that has scarred some cities with blood and hate—among them Chicago, St. Louis, Detroit—comes out of elements that have a haunting similarity. The Negro slums in Atlanta do not differ much from those of Memphis, Birmingham, or Jacksonville. The Polish slums in Detroit, Buffalo, and Chicago are similar. The Mexican-American slums in San Antonio are worse than in Denver, but it is a difference of degree rather than of kind, and it is paralleled by the Barrio in New York City where the newly arrived Puerto Rican immigrants cluster.

William Bolitho once called the slums of Glasgow the "cancer of Empire," a phrase even better for the American slums, which are the blight on the gaudy flowers of American prosperity and power. The first buildings meant to house workers and immigrant families in the big Eastern cities were put up in the 1830s. They were followed by a dreary line of successors, each uglier and more macabre than what it replaced, with a greater population density and a blanker separation from the living needs of the time. They usually provided a higher profit return than the better housing units and were a continuing temptation to the exploiting of human helplessness. "I rent to the people no one else will take," said a Philadelphia "firetrap" landlord in 1956. Some of the slum houses were multiple dwellings encased in the old "balloon frame"; others were "three-decker" wooden tenements or rotting brownstones; still others were railroad flats stretching out endlessly in the "dumb-bell tenements," with windows looking out into narrow side courts; or they were five- and six-story walk-up tenements.

The 1940 Census revealed that in fact one third of American dwellings were substandard. As late as 1948 the head of the St. Louis Chamber of Commerce said that 30 per cent of the quarter million dwelling units in the city lacked bath and toilet; in 1950 it was possible for Alfred Roth, a Swiss architect teaching in St. Louis, to say of its slums: "I've been many times in the slums of London. I've seen the damaged areas of western Europe. But never in my life have I seen anything like this." Families everywhere lived doubled up and looked often into sunless shafts. Periodically the newspapers of Chicago or St. Louis or New York sent reporters out to survey the slums. They found a jungle of garbage cans spilling over, people living in dark basements, back yards, and vacant lots, with kids playing among tin cans and broken bottles, decaying dock areas and trash-laden river fronts, children growing up to delinquency. Along with the neighborliness that the poor never lose, they would also find hustlers and jackals, and amidst the overcrowding they might (if they were acute enough) find a dimension of loneliness and terror that no tenement law could isolate or prohibit. This is the aspect of city life that Nelson Algren's novels depicted, even in the 1950s.

No account of the mass city can exclude the pathos of life for the millions who don't get the prizes, the mean and scrubby struggle for a few scraps from the table of plenty, the wreckage of derelicts cast up by the unyielding tides of city struggle, the manic perversions and crimes, the organized preying on women, the conscription of children into vice. An American city shows to the defeated a different face from the one it shows the conquerors. With the slums come the vice areas, acknowledged and unacknowledged—those of brothels, "boarding houses," cheap hotels, saloons; those of narcotics addicts, whores, and pimps. It is for them that the Biblical words run true: "So shall thy poverty come as a robber, and thy want as an armed man."

What makes the slums ominous is that they represent a blight which, to a lesser degree, infects larger areas of the city as the restless movement of population shifts from one to another neighborhood. Land values in any particular segment of a big city are either moving up or down; neighborhoods are either gaining in prestige or getting "run down." Once they start to deteriorate the process moves with cumulative swiftness: the ethnic "undesirables" begin to make inroads, panic sets in, and soon the whole character of the area has shifted. As the new transition zones are swept by the crosswinds of ethnic struggle, the schools express some of the tension, and street fights break out. The exodus may be to other neighborhoods or it may be wholly out of the city to the suburbs. The vitality of neighborhood and city is drained.

Decay and blight have occurred, of course, in every phase of the city's cycle of growth. In the past they have been followed by renewal, where the old was continually displaced by the new. But the city today is asked to find the energies for renewal exactly when it is faced with pyramiding costs of government, throttling traffic, mounting crime, and a drain on its more prosperous and educated population (it is largely the lower income groups who remain because they have nowhere else to go). As its people join the Great Exodus to live in the suburbs, they remain as users of the city's services and facilities, but they are no longer taxed for them, getting a "free ride": thus far the efforts to combine the city and its suburbs into a single tax-and-governmental unit, to share the costs, burdens, and services of government in the metropolitan community, have failed. The suburbanite swells the throng who seek entrance to the city by car every morning and exit at night, clogging bridges, tunnels, and thruways, congesting the streets, snarling the traffic. Ironically those who live in the city all week join the monster auto rally on week ends, eager to get away for a day or two, and spending hours in traffic jams on the way out of the city and back.

Thus the mass city, which came into its present stature as a by-product of the revolutions in transport, finds itself being choked by the millions of artifacts the auto industry has created. The city seems to have become mainly a temporary stopover place for men and families in motion—which may explain why so many of the efforts at city replanning are geared to its traffic problems and its auto arteries. It is true that the network of roads leading, let us say, out of New York and Newark to the New Jersey Turnpike, was not only an engineering achievement but (seen from the air) of breathtaking beauty of design. But to rebuild cities mainly around road design and traffic clearance was to make man an adjunct of his creature, the automobile, and to lose sight of him as a human being needing roots in a living community. It meant undoing thousands of years of human evolution since the discovery of the wheel and making man the servant of the wheel, incomplete without it.

The American city is being replanned and rebuilt, but in what form, and with how much forethought, and with what image in mind of man and his needs? As the city core decays one would think it would not be too hard to buy up the deteriorated property and start afresh, with living quarters embodying what we know about the kind of work life and leisure life that will be within reach of the American family in the latter half of the century. But this is to reckon without the tenacity of vested institutions and habits of thought. The New Deal set in motion a sequence of housing projects that did more for slum clearance in a decade than had been done in a century. But the houses thus built had at least the same population density as the razed slums they displaced; and often they were built without adequate provision for neighborhood schools, churches, or markets or for pooled facilities for supervised play —which led Lewis Mumford to quote a sentence Patrick Geddes wrote in 1915: "Slum, semi-slum, and super-slum: to this has come the evolution of our cities."

The bleak, efficient, multi-story, barracklike apartment houses that are likely more and more to dominate the sky line of the big American cities are the expressions of the industrial organism, and their parallels will in time be found in the Communist societies of Moscow and Peiping as well as in capitalist New York. This is the skeletal frame within which industrial man is encasing himself, and here again the American has not so much created a distinctive pattern of man but foreshadowed the direction that industrial man is taking.

The new urban personality which is emerging in America is the product of the machine—but also of a good deal more. The machine aspects of city living are obvious enough. Who can forget the swift tunneling of the machine-as-subway in the earth, the scurrying of the machine-as-automobile over its surface, the exacting regularity of the machine-as-traffic-light, the droning of the machine-as-television, the stream of print emerging from the machine-as-press, the silent power and precision of the machine-as-dynamo? Who can escape the tempo of the mass city—hurrying to work, to appointments, to crises, to pleasure, to tragedy?

Yet what gives the city its character as living is not the tempo or discipline of the machine but the effort to reach for values beyond it. The youngster becomes a member of the city gang, partly at least because the gang gives him a chance for a sense of belonging and feudal allegiance. Similarly with mechanized sports and amusements in the big city. Prize fighters pummel each other like gladiators before thousands; baseball contests are commercial events staged on schedule, with team standings calculated down to the fourth decimal point; movies and TV project the same *imago* on thousands of screens to the accompaniment of millions of fluttering pulses; choruses of dancing girls tap out their rhythms in night clubs with machinelike precision. Yet the big fact about all of them is not that they are mechanical, which is true enough, but that they furnish channels for mass emotion which relieve the tension of machine living.

Within this frame the city has developed a type of American character different from the type that De Crèvecoeur, De Tocqueville, or even Bryce depicted. It is less conditioned to the soil and the seasons, less religious, more skeptical about motives and chary of being "played for a sucker," less illusioned in the sense in which illusions—about friendship, work, sex, love, and God—provide an internal sustaining force for the personality. It has been psychologically hardened by innumerable brief encounters—in public schools, on subways and busses, in restaurants, in the course of shopping—which would become intolerable if one did not sheathe oneself against them with a constricted response. It is precocious about money matters and sex, since so many city people grow up in crowded quarters where few things are concealed from them. It is stoical in the face of hardship and the man-made catastrophes of economic life. It is not "urbane" except in the small groups in which one can afford to be generous, but it is much more likely to strip the jungle life of the city down to the nakedness of the human animal. It economizes time with an almost manic earnestness during the hours of business, only to waste it with equally manic intensity during the hours of pleasure and recreation. It lays stress (within limits) on individual traits of personality, on uniqueness in dress and sophistication in taste, on awareness, on the dramatic impact that the individual makes in his brief meetings with others. It has replaced fear by anxiety, and the concern about danger from elemental forces with a vague concern about security, safety, and the opinions of others.

What this means is that city living has carried men and women ever further away from their instinctual endowment. The city is not the root of the planlessness, the tensions, and the conformism of American life, but it is the envelope that encloses them. Or, to change the figure, the city is the battleground of the values of the culture.

In addition to its slums every city has its vice area and its crime problem. Whenever some vice inquiry has caught national attention or a newspaper puts on pressure or a city reform administration gets to power, the police force develops a spurt of energy. At such times there are "roundups" of petty criminals, prostitutes, or even the usual lodging-house population, and sometimes the more scabrous criminals also are kept moving and forced to seek other hunting grounds. But reform administrations are short-lived, and the ties between vice and politics, and between "rackets" and the respectable business elements of the city, are too close to be easily broken. In many cities the dynasty of political bosses started with the saloonkeeper who knew the weaknesses and tragedies of the slum people and built his political empire on the exchange of loyalty for favors. At a later stage in the dynasty, the boss may have become a contractor, dealing by a Providential coincidence with the very materials the city needed for its public works. There is scarcely a big American city whose administration is not at least marginally involved in this trinity of crime, political corruption, and business favors.

The city "machine" got its name because it operated with an impersonal efficiency to retain in power a group of political professionals who claim to know how to "deliver the vote." City crime is also mechanized, and the gangs, rackets, and shakedown outfits operate on a nation-wide plane. Yet in the case of both politics and crime the machine aspects can be overplayed. The political machine was usually run by a highly personal "boss" who gave a dramatic color to big-city corruption, as in the old days of Boss Croker in New York or more recently Boss Crump in Memphis or Boss Curley in Boston (it is Curley who is the protagonist of Edwin O'Connor's novel, *The Last Hurrah*). The function of the machine was to keep a firm hold on blocs of cohesive ethnic voters and thus capitalize on the inertia of the rest of the public. The relation of the political professionals to the ethnic blocs was mainly an emotional one of exchange of loyalties. The outward mechanism of the political machine conceals this inner structure of almost feudal allegiance—a structure of hierarchy, fealty to the overlords, and subinfeudation. Similarly the criminal machine reaches on the one side to the feudal gangsters, who are held together by greed and loyalty, and on the other side to the business community. The racket kings, levying their toll on the victims, are lawless versions of the "barons of the bags" who levy their toll on competitors and consumers.

But the problems of city government have now reached beyond crime and corruption. The big city generated administrative tasks which were never foreseen in the earlier years of American political thinking. Since the country was rural for most of its history, its political institutions were intended for small governmental units. The Founding Fathers could not have dreamed of a metropolitan unit like New York City, or of the web that it would spread from Westchester to Jersey City. The budget of New York City is higher than that of most state governments, and its administrative task is second only to that of the Federal government. It must run a huge police system, a school system that has to deal with Irish and Jewish children, Negroes and Puerto Ricans; it must run its subways through a Transit Authority, direct its bridge traffic through a Tri-Boro Bridge Authority, solve its harbor, truck, and air-line terminal problems through a Port Authority; it must run a network of public hospitals and clinics, a penal and prison system; it must deal with juvenile delinquency, run a set of magistrate's courts, and take care of the indigent who are "on welfare."

At best this involves an array of administrative services that can be only loosely held together. American cities have groped at once for the kind of technical civil service to be found in the Federal government, and for the kind of political leadership for which the American Presidency is the symbol. The city-manager movement, combined with the focusing of political leadership on the mayor, may convert city government into something a good deal better than what James Bryce lamented in his *American Commonwealth.*

The big fact about the mass city is that it has become so massive as to burst its bounds. It has become a "runaway city." New York, Cleveland, and Chicago each now contains a set of "satellite cities," which have developed their own civic pride and striven to become autonomous units within the larger metropolis. Yet the more difficult development has been that of the suburban communities which are functionally part of the metropolitan city but do not share its financial or administrative burdens. Like the single metropolitan area from Westchester to Jersey City, there are similar stretches through the industrial centers of Connecticut and Massachusetts, and around Buffalo, Pittsburgh, Chicago, and Los Angeles, where workers in chemical, automobile, and airplane factories cluster in a central city and in suburban communities that stretch for hundreds of miles in a continuous stream. These aggregates are not so much cities in the old sense but provinces in a larger industrial empire.

A number of American architects and planners have had a vision of how these monstrous masses can be kept within limits, the central cities renewed and replanned, the fringe growths contained, the whole turned into a set of decentralized communities each with an integrated pattern of work, residence, and recreation inside the far-flung larger frame. It is a moving vision, yet it would be surprising if Americans who had tolerated a planless past of the cities were to be converted—even under the spur of need—to a drawing-board-planned future.

In one area there are signs of concerted action—that of urban renewal. By 1955 there were 250 cities involved somehow in this effort, some to a minor degree, a number in a major way. They were starting to tear down the deteriorated parts of the central areas and rebuild them; they were taking steps to rehabilitate the indifferent areas; they were growing alert to the need for conserving the healthy ones. Except in cases like Pittsburgh and St. Louis, it was still being done without imaginative boldness, on a scale of cost suitable to the past and not to the staggering resources of the present. Yet the big fact was the emergence of the conviction that governments have a responsibility for city redevelopment.

Under the New Deal there was for the first time a clear recognition that the big metropolitan cities could not survive without Federal subsidies for crucial tasks, like housing, health, and unemployment relief, which affect the national interest. The countertendency was to follow the doctrine of states' rights and to give both the burden and the power to state governments. Since these state governments tend to be dominated by the rural members of their legislatures, the big cities fought this trend, feeling that their relationship should be directly with the Federal government.

The fact is* that the growth of the metropolitan city has destroyed the base of the earlier version of federalism. A new equilibrium must be achieved between not just the center and the rim but between a whole new set of nuclear centers in the form of metropolitan cities as well as in Washington, and their rim in the rurally-oriented state capitals. Hence a new alliance is emerging between city needs and Federal aid, to break the old dependence on the states. While Republican administrations are more reluctant than Democratic ones to push this alliance, they have recognized and continued Federal aid to private housing construction, to public housing, to slum clearance and the relocation of slum families, to community facilities like water and sewage. This aid, in turn, has spurred more comprehensive city replanning, and to feed the hope that in a generation or two the older city areas will be recast, the problems of the new runaway city will be grappled with, and both will become fitter places in which to live, work, and play.

I have talked entirely here of the city in peacetime. But after 1945 the atomic shadow darkened a good deal of city planning. The American mass city and the industrial stretch of the greater metropolitan city form an unparalleled target for atomic and radiation destruction. One answer has been that of the dispersal of the industrial concentration in the cities, so that the target would be more scattered. Actually, some kind of dispersal and decentralization has been taking place. Industries have tended to move out of the city itself to be nearer their source of labor supply in the suburbs. Department stores have established suburban branches. Retail stores have grouped themselves into shopping centers in suburban neighborhoods. But what this dispersal has done, desirable as it has been, has been to form a more or less solid line of industrial and popu-

* See Ch. VI, Sec. 5, "Power and Equilibrium."

lation growth. It has burst the boundaries of the mass city, but it has not solved the problem of its survival in atomic war. The vulnerable areas still exist, but they have been stretched thinner. The "city panic" has not been wholly removed from the minds of millions of city and suburban dwellers, and it may be revived.

The firmest answer has been given by those who say that dispersal and burrowing in the ground may save lives but that they will not save civilization; that the city grew out of the expansive energies of America and that if the city does not survive a suicidal war the civilization itself may perish. The destinies of the two are intertwined, and the best way to save both is by the kind of affirmation from which the cities originally drew their strength.*

10. The Suburban Revolution

An air view of America in the mid-1950s compared with one a decade earlier would show a wholly different picture of people and place. Where once there had been open spaces between the farms, towns, and big cities, one would now find an almost continuous line of settlement and population. This line stretched from Massachusetts to North Carolina, from Chicago to Detroit and Buffalo and then to Pittsburgh, and from San Francisco to the Mexican border. The formerly open spaces were being rapidly filled in; the movement of population was out of the small towns and the cities into the unsettled areas between them; it was not only a decentralizing movement but also an interstitial one. Its product was the suburb and the greater cluster city.

The emergence of the suburb as the characteristic form of American place, supplanting as well as supplementing the city, has been so rapid, with consequences so far-reaching, as to be revolutionary. The drift out of the cities had started in the 1920s, when discussion of the "metropolitan community" began; it was seen then as a city of wards and boroughs with a *hinterland* of small towns to which the rich had been retreating since the late nineteenth century. But at the turn of the century the railroad commuter appeared, shuttling between job and home, and in the 1920s, in the era of the automobile, he was joined by the car commuter. In the Depression years of the 1930s the movement marked time. After World War II it began again at an intense pace, with the building of ranch-house "developments" and apartment courts in the "dormitory" or "bedroom" suburbs. In the 1950s it speeded up still more, with whole new communities growing up where once there had been meadow and

* For a further discussion of city, from the standpoint of building, architecture, and planning, see Ch. XI, Sec. 8, "Building, Design, and the Arts."

scrub brush and potato fields, and with department-store branches and shopping centers breaking the downtown city's marketing monopoly.

The suburbs ceased to be either a hinterland for the city or its dormitories: each suburb became a center of a community life of its own but connected with the city by complex strands. Something had come into American life that was not there before. It was a new kind of relation between people and place—not just an overgrown or runaway city but a living-complex that resulted when the city reached out to form the suburbs and the suburbs reached back to transform the city and at the same time create a hinterland of their own; and all three—city and suburban nuclei and hinterland—became entangled with other forms like them in a sprawling, complex pattern that I call the cluster city.

By using one kind of definition of the suburbanite (one who works in the city, lives where there is more space, and can afford to commute between the two), it was estimated that in 1953 there were thirty million suburbanites in America, and that the great increase (from twenty-one to thirty million) came since 1947. Of these, eleven million lived in the older suburbs within the limits of the metropolitan city, and nineteen million in politically independent newer ones outside. Using another definition that would include the ring of settlement on the fringe of the suburbs, usually more distant from the city ("semi-suburban" or "exurban"), the figure was forty-two million.

By the 1950s suburban living was no longer confined mainly to the Northeast, Great Lakes, and Far Western regions but had come to include the Southeast, Southwest, and Plains regions as well; in every area except parts of the Deep South (it was to be found in Florida) it was the form of American living that was coming into the ascendant. In two decades, between 1934 and 1954, the suburbs grew by 75 per cent while the total population grew by 25 per cent. Between 1940 and 1954 people living in 168 "standard metropolitan" central cities increased by 14 per cent, those in the suburban rings around the cities increased by 35 per cent, and those living in the semi-suburban rural rings around the suburbs increased by 41 per cent. Thus the drift was a double one—from the city (and small towns) to the suburbs, and from the suburb-cities to the sparser settled areas around their rim and fringes. The prospects were that the trend would continue until the suburbs had generated suburbs of their own, and most Americans lived in a continuous semi-urban and semisuburban line of cluster cities.

The meaning of what was happening was that America was resettling itself, wherever it could, looking for open spaces and "grass for the children to walk on," and better schools, and a garage for the car, and a closer-knit community. As the automobile was brought within the reach of most, and TV carried urban culture into every home, the suburbs could afford to stretch further away from the metropolitan center. The "garden city" or "satellite town" which Ebenezer Howard first envisaged in England took a very different form in the American suburb, not so clearly planned or laid out, nor so definitely separated from the central city by open spaces. Nor was this the rationalized metropolis of Le Corbusier. Americans were too much in a hurry to wait for a plan or for rationality, and too bent on profit to waste any open spaces. Even in getting away from the cities they made use of the city principle of maximizing ground rent.

The whole process was a kind of development by sprawl. Young married people preferred moving to where they could bring up children and tinker around the house. If they didn't have enough money to buy a house in the suburbs, they could get a low-down-payment, long-amortization loan under the FHA and later the VA provisions, from private funds but insured by the Federal government. High building costs led them naturally to the real-estate "developments" that bought up cheap land outside the cities, built houses on a mass scale, and sold them on easy terms. The rapid mobility of their jobs in corporate organizations (as in the armed services, the younger men were moved about freely from corporate branch to branch) required them to find ready-made communities where they could strike roots easily and leave them without too much pang, and could quickly resell the houses they had bought. Thus the suburb as an institution moved into the vacuum of the American home place left by the decline of the small town, the unlivability and decay of the city, the sheer statistical pressure of population, and the fluidity of the corporate managers, junior executives, and technicians who came to the suburb to live.

I have spoken of the suburbs as growing by sprawl. Despite all the publicity clatter about "planned communities," they did not (except for a few instances) grow by plan. One must understand here the nature of the real-estate "development" which was the carrier of suburban growth. To "develop" a community meant to buy a tract of open ground, clear it of brush and trees, level its hills and straighten its curves, install utilities, build roads, subdivide the space into building lots, set up a number of basic "model" houses to serve as choices for prospective buyers, apply factory-on-the-site methods of construction, and come away with a good profit. In a few cases (the "Levittowns" on Long Island and in Pennsylvania, of which William J. Levitt was the moving figure, or Drexelbrook near Philadelphia, or Parkmerced near San Francisco, or Park Forest outside Chicago whose mover and shaper was Philip Klutznick) the planning went further. Community recreation and activity centers were built. Land was provided for schools and churches, which the homeowners had somehow to build and subsidize; and in a few instances a village government was set in motion.

But mostly the planning never went beyond the real-estate necessities. The bulldozing of the area to make construction costs easier also resulted in stripping the terrain of much of its beauty and naturalness. The sinking of hundreds of thousands of cesspools was the despair of public-health officials. Rarely was provision made for open areas in the center which could serve as the core of the communities of the future, such as the Greek and Italian cities and the New England town, but which most American cities lack. In too many instances the greed to sell every acre of land for building meant there was nothing left for parks; the expectation that everything would be park meant that no one made provision that anything should be park. As suburb spilled over into suburb, like cars bumper to bumper on the week-end treks, few open spaces were left between them to give the community a natural setting. Inside the suburb the spacious shaded avenues that gave their character to Southern cities were rarely laid out.

As the new incursions of population came in, new problems of zoning arose which had not been anticipated, and caused political wrangling. Ironically also those who had fled from the traffic congestion of the city found new traffic and parking problems springing up like dragon's teeth in the suburb. The schools could not keep pace with the increased demand for them, since the suburb rarely had industries to carry the main tax burden as they did in the city and even the rural school districts. (In Park Forest the development company provided land for the schools, with subsidies for their operation—but this was unusual.) As a real-estate development the suburb grew as a residence area, and the absence of factory smoke and grime was one of its attractions. But in time the suburban dwellers and planners were to learn that a community must embody a balance between industry and residence, as it must also have variety and surprise in its outward aspect, and a balance of age and class groups, of ethnic groups, of innovation and tradition.

Most of these the suburb lacked. It was too new, too raw, too uniform in look, too homogeneous in composition, too hurried in construction. It arose with frantic haste to meet the needs of the new middle classes and the new era of mass leisure. The fault did not lie with those who took part in the Great Exodus: they were responding to the pressures behind them and to their hopes for a way of life for their children. It lay rather with the leaders and officials who failed to provide ways of planning and control to regulate the growing suburb. This suburb recapitulated in a few decades the problems that most cities had encountered over the centuries. What it chiefly showed was that the Americans had learned little and forgotten little from their experience; that the lacks and defects which critics of American life had been at pains to point out had not cut deep into the consciousness of most Americans; and that when they were given a chance at a fresh start, this was how they did it.

The shift to the new suburbs also meant a shift in class composition. The suburbs used to be the residential areas for wealthy businessmen, bankers, and lawyers who wanted the manorial touch. But now the "rich" suburbs, like Bronxville (near New York) and Winnetka (near Chicago) or the Quogue that Fitzgerald celebrated in his *Great Gatsby* (it was set in what he called West Egg, on Long Island), have been outstripped by others. There were the rented or purchased homes in the big "developments," like the Levittowns and the Park Forests, which were filled by professional people and by technicians and junior executives of the big corporations; there were the suburbs of skilled workers, usually mushrooming around aviation plants and other defense industries that had to be built in open territory or near power sources, as in the Buffalo–Niagara Falls area; there were even trailer courts for retired middle-class couples as well as for war workers.

Geographically one could speak of the *inner* suburbs (nestling near the cities), and the *outer* suburbs (at a commuting distance). One would have to add *exurbia* (the "country") which A. C. Spectorsky explored and placed on the American map—the Eastern rural area (including Fairfield County in Connecticut, Bucks County in Pennsylvania, Rockland County in New York) of week-enders, gentlemen farmers, and either the artistic or prosperous who didn't have to go to the city regularly. But the scheme was too neat, and class composition meant more than geographic distance.

Suburban America was mainly middle-class America. It was recognized as such by the builders who laid out the houses at middle-class prices for middle-class incomes and living, and also by the department stores and chain stores which hastened to set up suburban branches. In fact, there are some who discuss the American suburbia largely as a business market which came into being as a prosperous middle-class appendage to the new marketing methods. But the truth was that the new middle class, comprising corporate and government bureaucrats, advertising and sales executives, technicians, professional people, and white-collar workers represented the growing point of the American class system. Anxious to live under better conditions than the crowded apartments in violence-ridden neighborhoods of the city, they sought "warmer" living in communities which would be within striking distance of the cultural services of the metropolis. It gave them the sense of status that was crucial to their self-respect. It enabled them to have the best of both worlds—of the big city and the small town.

Thus the suburban movement was an effort of the new middle classes to find a garment for their living that would express outwardly the changes that had already taken place inwardly in their image of themselves and in their relation to their society. They no longer wished to be identified with the "city masses," nor could they stand the anonymity of urban life where the lonely are terribly lonely and no one knows anybody else who happens to live in the same big apartment house. They were the transients, living in an era of transiency, and therefore they were all the more seized by the panic of temporariness: thus they wanted a home of their own, whose mortgage they could at least in part pay off, with whose lawn and garden they could mix their sweat, and where they could putter in a toolshed or garden and have a garage with a car of their own that could carry them away from it all. This was class in action—that is to say, a class personality assumed in the act of striking new roots for itself.

So the would-be suburbanite picked his plot and his house type and got his homeowners' loan, and made a down payment. He moved his belongings to a row of Cape Cod or "ranch-type" or "split-level" houses. His wife furnished it to look like the layouts in *House Beautiful* and she shopped in supermarkets, highway stores, and shopping centers where she could park and get everything at once. She filled the house with the latest kitchen appliances, and there was a TV set in the living room. There were rows of middle-priced sedans and hard-top convertibles lining the block which were as interchangeable and standardized as the houses, deep-freezes, TV sets, magazines, processed foods, and permanent waves that a community survey would reveal. Husband and wife wore casual clothes which gave them a sense of release from the "rat race" of competitive dressing, while giving them also a leisure-class "country" feeling. They did without domestic help, except for an occasional baby-sitter or cleaning woman; they mowed and manicured their own lawns, cooked their own meals, and with the aid of self-help manuals they did for themselves on a variety of chores where outside expert help was too costly. The husband was in the city most of the day, and an intensive father from the time he came home from work until the children went to bed. It was calculated that in a lifetime, as a commuter, he traveled a half million miles (twenty times around the world) between home and office. But the reason he endured perpetual motion was that he might occupy that secure spot in the center of his tornado—in this case, the middle-class status of suburbanite.

As a way of life it defied all the traditional claptrap about American individualism. It was largely standardized and to a surprising degree collectivized. The intensive study of suburbia included in William H. Whyte, Jr.'s *The Organization Man* depicts brilliantly the emerging way of life today which may become the dominant way of life tomorrow. The suburbanites found new roots for their lives in a new sense of neighborhood which was closer than anything in previous American experience except college dormitories or fraternities or the communal settlements of the early nineteenth century. The neighbors in the same apartment court dropped in on one another with casual intimacy, rarely bothering to knock. Not only did the doors within houses tend to disappear (for economy, and to give a sense of space) but the outside doors ceased to have much function, and picture windows took their place. Newcomers were expected to become "outgoing" and to "join the gang"; introversion was frowned upon, and the society of ex-introverts was like the society of ex-sinners. There was intensive "joining" in club work and community participation, including greatly increased church membership, and there were daily morning get-togethers of the women in *Kaffeeklatsches.* There was little chance for the contemplative life. Privacy became "clandestine," in the sense that those who sought it did so apologetically. "Keeping up with the Joneses" was considered a form of exhibitionism; instead of "conspicuous consumption" the rule became "inconspicuous consumption," so that no one would embarrass anyone else. There were car pools for shuttling children to school and back; there was almost communal use of bicycles, books, and baby toys; there was an enforced intimacy, so that everyone's life was known to everyone, and no one had to face his problems alone. In Whyte's phrase, the suburbanites were "imprisoned in brotherhood."

This kind of living has some elements of the co-operativeness-in-crisis of the American frontier, some elements of Army life, and some of Socialist collectivism. The thinkers who celebrate the mystique of the organic community as against the atomistic individual may shudder a bit when they study the American "package suburb" as the flowering of the community impulse under conditions of American standardization. What made the standardization even bleaker was the uniformity of age, income, and class outlook. In their early stages these suburbs tended to comprise mainly young married couples (there were no bachelors and few chances for unmarried girls), with an average income of between $6,000 and $7,000, with children below ten (the childless couple was an anomaly, as were old people), and with a strikingly similar class outlook that was at once tolerant, mobile, hard-working, ambitious, and hopeful for the future.

But it would be a mistake to call it an entirely one-class society, except in the sense that so much of the new America is middle class. The big suburban "development" was not nearly as selective as the earlier and smaller suburbs had been. It had to appeal to a mass market, and so it accepted Catholics and Jews as well as Protestants (while drawing the line at the Negro), clerical and technical as well as professional groups, blue collar as well as white collar—taking all of them into the same neighborhood. The common denominators were income, age, and reliability. It was a democracy of a kind, on a broader spectrum of inclusion than was true of the "residential" and "restricted" neighborhoods in the cities and the earlier suburbs. Yet its exclusion of Negroes, mainly for fear that they would cheapen real-estate values, showed how limited a democratic dream it still was, and how the same dependence on the market that released it from some of the fetters of prejudice kept it fettered in others.

Suburban society was deeply involved with the mobile elements of the American class system. As a man moved from production line to foreman to shop superintendent or from salesman to division manager to sales manager, he would also move from one type of suburb to another. As the family income went up by stages the family moved from court apartment to ranch house and learned new ways of behavior, new standards of tastes, and met new circles of friends to keep pace with its rise. To some extent even the "lower-class" family could find its suburban niche—that of the plumber or carpenter, for example, which could live in the middle-class neighborhood to which the family income admitted it, even though the occupational level was that of the worker. But these gradations were roughly inside the broad limits of the middle class, and there was little of the sense of class crossing, class transcendence or class betrayal that one found in a less homogeneous society. The extremes of income were in the central city, not in the metropolitan rings.

I don't mean that Suburbia, U.S.A., is a conformist society. Its outer aspects are standardized and its ways of life tend to be uniform; yet this is different from conformism. The social intimacy that prevails in the suburb is partly a quest for roots, partly (as I have said) a flight from the temporariness and the loneliness of American life. To some extent it is also an effort to mitigate the bleakness of spending one's life within the confines of the same corporate "organization" and in pursuit of the same technical or sales proficiency. The chance to be intimate with people of different faiths and backgrounds, to share with them the experience of building a new community, and to take part in group action is an appealing one to those who have absorbed the cultural ideals and stereotypes of America. It would not be easy to impose conformity from without upon the suburbanites: but the conformity that comes from mutual accessibility and a yearning for group "belongingness" needs no outside pressures because the impulses from within are leveling ones. There were some observers who feared that this was the kind of society which the "organization man" would ulti mately create in the image of his corporate ideal—a one-neighborhood, one-gang, one-class, one-perspective society.

There was substance to the fears. When Erich Fromm, among other writers, singled out the herd aspect of suburbia for attack he was adding a new facet to his escape-from-freedom thesis. But when, in his *Sane Society,* he added a vision of the way out which was strikingly similar to the Fourierist communities of the nineteenth century, he ignored the fact that it is precisely in the suburb where you would find a kind of new Fourierism. The defect of individualism is isolation, the defect of community living is standardization and conformism.

Meanwhile few of the suburbanites had such fears or reflections. Instead they had a stir of excitement in them because they had a widening of horizons and an accession of experience. What G. M. Trevelyan said of the English middle class in the eighteenth century might apply equally to this segment of the new American middle class in the mid-1950s: "Meanwhile the hour was theirs and it was golden."

But the golden hour was streaked with dross and was bound in time to pass. A one-class community like the new suburb was a community without a labor supply, and hence without an industrial base. The balanced community is not to be achieved without paying a price. The price is that of refusing to withdraw from the diversity and bustle of American life, but of embodying some of its noise and grime along with its energies. The parents in most American suburbs were certain they wanted only "the best" for their children in the way of schools, yet they were usually unwilling to subsidize that "best" by including taxable industries in their communities—even on the assumption that they could attract them if they tried. Often they rezoned the suburbs in order to keep out "undesirable" income groups and then wondered why their schools, thus cut off from a cross segment of an American life, proved to be aseptic and sterile. In the long run the suburb would have to turn by an inevitable tropism toward the centers of industrial life and find links with those centers.

There was also the question of the relation between the home and the job. The ideal of town planners was that a man would be able to walk to work and walk home after work. But when the reality of the suburb came, the journey to work was dependent on the automobile and became in most cases a traffic struggle every morning and evening. The newer trend involved a migration of a good deal of the commercial and industrial activities out of the central city into the suburban and metropolitan areas, so that large numbers of suburban dwellers ceased to be Central City commuters but found their jobs on the rim, closer to home. If these trends continued there was a good chance that the industrial and residential zones would be intermingled in the complex pattern, as was already true of the northern New Jersey area in the mid-1950s.

This meant a loose, sprawling cluster city, spreading out across the landscape, still depending on the automobile, but with job-home patterns now running both ways instead of only one. Unexpectedly it came closer to Frank Lloyd Wright's Broadacre City than to the comfortable and segregated "new towns" about which the English and American planners had dreamed. When I said earlier that the trend toward suburban America would continue I did not mean that the suburbs, growing in numbers and importance, would be self-contained, insulated entities. The phase of dispersal from the city was bound to be transformed into a phase of reintegration of the city and suburb in some pattern.

To take New York as an instance, it was clear that the five boroughs were reaching out across state barriers and forming—along with the suburbs in a larger industrial-residential complex—a vast cluster city. Its extent could scarcely be calculated because its boundaries spread out in an octopus pattern. In the 1950s it had reached fifteen million people, perhaps more; by 1975 it would have passed twenty million people—larger than many sovereign countries. The migration to the suburbs changed the character of the central city too, leaving it an "underdeveloped area" which needed rebuilding and renewal, and leaving it also an area of steep class contrasts, with a diminishing middle class to mediate the abrupt differences between the rich town-house families and the low-income groups, often Negro and polyglot.

But neither the city nor the suburbs could survive by themselves: I have described what the new suburban way of life meant and the functions it filled; the city continued to serve its own constellation of functions, in industry and finance, in fashions, in recreation and the arts, in intellectual stir. Together the city-suburb complex would have to discover some new form of a cluster community government, which would require creativeness if it was to hurdle all the obstacles of law, habit, and convention. Yet whatever happened to the cluster community as a whole, the suburb was destined to be a permanent part of it, not as a hinterland to the city but as an equal among equals.

All this was being accomplished by Americans at considerable social and aesthetic costs. The cluster city, filling in the interstices that had once existed between cities, was consuming open space voraciously. There was often the kind of ugliness in the landscape that made a British writer, watching the same thing happening on his own countryside, call it a "subtopia." Yet here as elsewhere the Americans were accomplishing a transformation in their way of living which, despite its improvised quality, was an exciting response to their new needs and conditions of life. They were doing it in their own way. They did not follow the British lead of the "new towns" approach, although a number of the cities that were being planned for government and industrial workers around the centers of atomic experiment and power were "new towns." Nor did they follow the earlier American architectural dream of a landscape dotted with "Greenbelts." To the extent that a balanced community was emerging—which was doubtful—it represented a balance not within the central city nor within the new suburb, but between the larger frame of the cluster city.

It looked as if Americans were achieving this only through a chance combination of pressures and changes. If there was an internal logic in the improvisation it was the logic to be found in the rest of the American pattern.*

11. *Regions: the Fusion of People and Place*

THE IMPULSE TOWARD forming living units that cut across governmental boundary lines—of which the trans-urban city is an instance—runs throughout American history. Despite the need for speaking of an "America" and thus making it seem unitary, it is clearly not a single and homogeneous entity. America has not one signature but many. It is divided formally into forty-eight states, and while their boundaries don't bound anything in particular, most of the states have over the years developed their local prides, prejudices, and personalities. Less artificial are the aggregates of states called "sections," each of which Turner described as being fashioned in "the faint image of a European nation." Sections, like states, are the counters on the political chessboard. A realistic party leader must reckon with sectional appeals in campaigns, sectional pressures inside his party, sectional blocs in Congress.

But the more meaningful divisions are the fusions of people and place, of environment, stock, economics, dialect, history, consciousness, and ways of life, which are called "regions" and "subregions." The section may be the region in its political aspect, but it has divisive overtones, while the region has cohesive ones. The region may be the unplanned outgrowth of a historic process; its unity may, as in the case of the river-valley developments, be reinforced by engineering and regional planning. But always it operates as a compassable fragment of an otherwise unwieldy American whole. For the continental expanse of America is too big to crowd into the ambit of the individual life,

* For further discussion of the impact of the suburban revolution, see Ch. VI on American politics and Ch. VIII on the American family and life cycle.

while the town or city may be too particular to satisfy the reaching for meaning. The region is somewhere "between the village and the continent." What it does—and the subregion too—is to act as a counterforce against both the standardizing and atomizing forces of American life.

By its nature the outlines of the region are elusive. The most frequent usage (no two lists will agree) is to speak of New England, the Middle-Atlantic region, the Upper South, the Deep South, the Southwest, the Midwest, the Great Lakes region, the Rocky Mountain region, the Far West, and the Pacific Northwest. These are at once geographic, economic, and cultural units. There are also agricultural groupings which cut across them: the type-farming regions such as the Cotton Belt, the Wheat Belt, the Range Livestock area, the Dairy area, the Western Specialty Crop area.

The larger regional units are in turn broken up into subregions. One type is built around the river valley or river basin as a nucleus—the Tennessee, Missouri, Arkansas, Mississippi, Columbia, Ohio, Connecticut, Shenandoah, Wabash, Santa Fe, Red, Colorado, Sacramento, Salinas. Since a number of these are the sites of flood-control and hydroelectric dams, they are sometimes called "technical regions." One could make a somewhat similar regional map for the mountain areas, including not only the Rockies and the Appalachians but also the White Mountains, the Green Mountains, the Berkshires, the Blue Ridge, the Ozarks. The titles of the volumes in the "American Folkways" series suggest the type of subregion involved: "Lakes Country," "Blue Ridge Country," "North Star Country," "Palmetto Country," "Deep Delta Country," "Ozark Country," "Mormon Country," "Short Grass Country," "Snowshoe Country," "Golden Gate Country," "Desert Country," "Piñon Country," and "Panhandle Country." The picturesque calendar of such subregions could stretch almost endlessly. For a region is a cultural unit within a frame; in some areas the frame may be mountains or river basin or lakes, delta or bayou or desert; in others it may be the type of crop grown there; in still others the decisive element may be the enforced isolation or the uniformity of stock and tradition. The components may vary, but to form a region or subregion there must be a roughly homogeneous physical environment and a roughly homogeneous economic unity which together serve as a frame for community living and a common history and consciousness.

These regional cultures are the carriers of American diversity. If the stock of America is made up of a myriad of peoples, the regions of America form a myriad of environments. This pluralism is one of the facts that gives Americans their impulse to cohesion, in pulling together the diverse strands of their universe.

Often this leads to antagonisms which must be accepted as part of the balance-sheet of regionalism. There is usually an urban-agrarian hostility, which may pit downstate Illinois against Chicago, or upstate New York against New York City. One can almost always premise a struggle of hinterland against metropolis. Sometimes the same region or even state may include several subregions whose way of thinking is different because their ethnic strains and traditional ways of living are different. The Salinas Valley area of California is sharply different from the Southern California region. The political history of Louisiana would not be what it is without the hostility between the English-Protestant culture of the hills and the French culture of the bayous. The red-soil, red-neck, red-gallus hill region of the Georgia crackers is a different South from that of industrialized Atlanta.

American thinkers of the 1930s and 1940s were wary of regional loyalties that cut across class lines, and they tended to deny reality to the "regional mind," whether of the South or Middle West, New England or the Pacific Coast. Influenced by the class emphasis in Veblen and Beard, they saw regional and subregional cultures as part of the backwash of the stream of history, a residue of pre-industrial cultural attitudes.

The result was to leave regionalism largely to the traditionalists, especially among the Southern writers. The Southern Agrarians of the 1920s sought to turn it into a conservative economic and political program and a literary principle and used it as a weapon against the pragmatic humanitarianism of the North. Another school of Southern regionalism, centering at the University of North Carolina, was more academic and liberal. It is interesting that regionalism, both as an intellectual system and as a literary movement, flourished best in the South, with an almost metaphysical intensity of passion. No doubt it was because the great issues of slavery, the Civil War, and Reconstruction drove a wedge between the South and the rest of the nation. These, along with the caste system, ruralism, evangelicism, and the low standard of living, forced Southern writers to re-evaluate their identity and to seek the connection between their art and thought and the nature of the South as a culture.

If we ask what the nature of American regionalism is, the clues to the answer must come from an examination of each of the regions.

There is no single New England mind. How should there be, since there are obvious differences between the up-north Maine Yankee, whether potato farmer or shipyard worker or fisherman, and the industrial workers of the Housatonic and Connecticut valleys; between the old aristocracy of Boston's State Street and Harvard Yard and the political leaders of the newer Irish immigration; between the Vermont and New Hampshire Yankee farmers and the owners of big mansions and big wealth in Newport or Greenwich; even between the French-Catholic immigration in the mill towns of New Hampshire and Vermont and the Irish-Catholic and Italian-Catholic immigration in Massachusetts, Connecticut, and Rhode Island? But whatever new materials have been poured into the old mold, the mold itself has not broken. There are some who doubt the survival of the Yankee in the land of his origin. Yet if New England has a regional culture style I should still call it that of the Yankee—spare, austere, shrewd, Calvinist, individualist, with a ramrod down his back, tenacious of his dissents as he is confident in his affirmations.

At its best this tradition has produced a great line of American writers and thinkers. Its early divines, including the greatest of them, Jonathan Edwards, had a fanaticism about them, but it was a complex and self-torturing one and it imposed even greater rigors on oneself than it demanded of others. The New England temperament is a little like the climate, ranging from temperate to severe but always with the tang of sharpness in it; and a little also like the soil, where a farmer can make a living if he works hard—but even in the early days he did not have the richness of the Midwest earth at his command.

Although the "Last Puritan" presumably has vanished, and George Apley only now and then is seen at the dining and supper clubs of Beacon Hill and Louisburg Square, there is still a controlled strength in the New England mind at its best, coming out of its Puritan heritage and nourished by soil, climate, and history. From the intense commitment of Calvinism came the movements of Transcendentalism and abolitionism, the radical-equalitarian rebellions of Shays and Dorr, the anarchist doctrine of Josiah Tucker. There is a continuing craggy skepticism in New England which counterbalances the Utopians and Messianists. From Thoreau to Calvin Coolidge, its philosophy has been astringent and its humor closer to Britain than to the folk tales of the Southern mountains or the tall yarns of the lumber camps of the Northwest. Emerson could write *English Traits* because there was a good deal of Old England that survived in New England, including a species of Stonehenge that may still be found in the rocky Maine setting or with the tight-lipped Vermont farmer or the State Street banker.

If Justice Holmes was a "Yankee strayed from Olympus," his combination of intellectual aloofness with the shrewdness of the common experience is central to the New England outlook. One finds it in Lowell's *Biglow Papers,* in the Yankee shipbuilders who—however exotic the seas they sailed—never lost their sense of the New England shore, in the spare adjectiveless poetry of Robert Frost. One finds it in the Adamses, who were men of property and substance at the same time that they explored statesmanship, abolitionism, diplomacy, medieval cathedrals, the history of trade routes, and the laws of energy in human history. The great New England families—Adams, Lowell, Peabody, Holmes—were as close as America ever came to an intellectual aristocracy. They kept reaffirming their right to their lineage by an energy that sought productive outlets.

Yet the specific political contributions of New England came in the realm not of oligarchy but of democracy—that of the congregation and the town meeting. Or better, it was a peculiar amalgam of oligarchy and democracy. Nowhere else do you get the Calvinist individualism on which the mercantile, textile, and financial fortunes were built, along with the radicalism that flourished in the atmosphere of dissent. It is the tradition of the dissenters that is New England's greatest tradition. "Resistance to something," Henry Adams wrote, "was the law of New England's nature. The boy looked out on the world with the instinct of resistance; for . . . generations his predecessors had viewed the world as chiefly a thing to be reformed, filled with evil forces to be abolished. . . . The New Englander, whether boy or man, in a long struggle with a stingy or hostile universe, had learned also to love the pleasure of hating; his joys were few." This self-portrait suggests the dream New England had of itself—a dream that flaunts its austerity as if it were chosen as the elect of a spare and stony universe by contrast with the materialist indulgence elsewhere. The idea of a hardy elect has at times led to a rock-ribbed Republicanism, at others to radicalism, but it is disdainful of an easy conformism.

Latterly New England found its textile industries moving South or West, its wharves idle, its former financial supremacy stripped away. Its economists, asking what had happened to the famed "Yankee ingenuity," were spurred to make regional surveys looking toward an economic Renaissance. Partly New England industry, with a lagging technology, had to pay the "penalty of taking the lead"; partly it suffered because of its stubborn resistance to Federal hydroelectric projects. The old theocracy of the Puritan divines was overcome, but a new Catholic population with a cohesive attachment to its Church made a bid for power. The sense of bewilderment which Henry Adams had expressed at the confident industrialism that was breaking up his inherited world was replaced by an almost resigned acceptance of the New Order of society.

Yet with the passing of the traditional New England mind, American thought and expression lost a source of brooding intensity. The novels of Hawthorne expressed Americans in tragic life more probingly than any others, and the somewhat prosaic satire of a Marquand did not replace them. Nor was the Day-of-Doom self-analysis of a Cotton Mather or a Jonathan Edwards adequately replaced by the statistical survey of the mind of "Yankee City." The burden of the dark strain of American literature passed to the writers of the Deep South who used it to express a different agony of conscience from that of New England —less a sense of original sin and inevitable doom than the stain of guilt.

Some of New England's traits came in for good-natured caricature, like the hub-of-the-universe illusions gathered in Cleveland Amory's *Proper Bostonians.* When one Beacon Hill lady was chided for her failure to travel she asked, "Why should I travel when I'm already there?" Another, when asked where the ladies of Boston got their hats, said simply, "Our hats? Why, we *have* our hats." The New England scientist, Agassiz, reported that "New England is the oldest spot on the earth's surface." Many Americans of other regions resented the New England pride of past—the bland assumption that Boston was "Athens, with culture," and that New England had achieved a monopoly of that commodity. In the amiable ribbing of the Brahmins and Beacon Street and the "institution men" with their eccentric habits and unruffled ways, it is good to have Perry Miller remind us that historical New England was filled with passions and conflicts, and that the stable elite society did not tell the whole story. New Englanders risked their lives for Abolitionism and in strike riots, they spread themselves all over America in the "Yankee Exodus," they dared to fight the land-grabbers and monopolists, they became the conscience of every community they settled. Their willingness to wear themselves to the bone for the glory of God and 10 per cent on their investment gives point to Van Wyck Brooks's remark that the New Englander was an amalgam of the Puritan and the freebooter. The freebooter was indeed strong in him, yet in the process he built much and felt intensely, and no other region can so securely claim to have been the matrix of the American mind.

The New England mind and social structure were in part transplanted to the Midwest. But in place of the stony, niggardly New England soil there were rich prairies, and in place of the New England village there were far-flung homesteads. As New England's Puritanism crossed the continent it became evangelistic and Fundamentalist, and the mentality of Calvinism gave way to the mentality of what Mencken joyously called the "Bible Belt." As for political attitudes, the difference between the Adams family of Massachusetts and the Taft family of Ohio is an index of the difference between New England and Midwest conservatism. The first had the flair of aristocracy in it and a devotion to dissent even while it affirmed orthodoxy. But Midwest conservatism—that of McKinley and Hanna, of Harding and the Tafts—was that of the small-town and business middle class, with a lack of imaginativeness a little suggestive of the flatness and bareness of the landscape. Midwest radicalism became largely agrarian and Populist—the radicalism of farmers in protest against absentee wealth, and of ethnic minorities like the Scandinavians and Germans against the home-grown groups. Actually there have been two Midwests: the area of Ohio, Indiana, Illinois, and Michigan which in the past proved the stronghold of conservatism, while that of Missouri, Minnesota, and Wisconsin was the area of an agrarian radicalism. Ohio played the role of "mother of Presidents" for the Republicans, while the Populist states were the cradle of reformist stirrings. In the mid-1950s Minnesota and Michigan alone continued the radical tradition of the past.

The political picture that was true in the days of Hanna and Bryan, of Altgeld and the La Follettes, is no longer true at mid-century. The intensity of Midwest radicalism has dimmed, and Midwest isolationism—which has been ethnic as well as geographical, but the single political trait most readily associated with the region—was buried at Pearl Harbor, although its ghost still stubbornly and spasmodically walks the battlements of foreign policy. The Midwest which gave birth to the Republican party is still usually Republican by a margin but never by a wholly safe one. Giant industry, the mass city and the shift of balance to ethnic groups geared to industrial pursuits, like Negroes, Poles, Czechs, and Irish, have destroyed the political picture of a predominantly agrarian region. The comment that might have been made in the 1920s and 1930s—that the industrialism of the Midwest was more primitive in its social outlook than that of the East—would not hold in the mid-1950s: the Midwest pattern of heavy industry, consumer-goods industry, processing, distribution, and finance gave scope to every business energy, so that whatever sense of economic provincialism the Midwest had cherished no longer retained a valid base. It was true that political primitives like Senator Joseph McCarthy still cropped up in the Midwest, as they did in the South, spurred by a similar deep animosity toward the East. But, at least in McCarthy's case, they proved a national rather than a regional phenomenon.

The danger of persisting regional labels, as I have suggested, is best shown in the phrase "Midwest isolationism." The fear and dislike of anything "foreign" and "radical" was to be found in the South as well as the Midwest; but while in the South it fused ruralism and the caste system with the tradition of the martial virtues, in the Midwest it fed a distrust of the dimly known, turbulent world beyond American shores and expressed itself in the impulse to have no truck with that world.

The sturdy symbol of that "isolationism" was Senator Robert A. Taft; yet before his death he had come to accept much of the Eisenhower foreign policy, as indeed he had absorbed a considerable measure of public intervention in housing and health. There had also been a more radical Midwest isolationist strain than Taft's—the Jeffersonian "continentalism" of Charles A. Beard, which held that America could work out its democratic destiny on a continental scale if it were not beset by foreign troubles and could deal with its problems in peace. Both these strains of thinking met and crossed in the interior of America. Both were made archaic by atomic weapons and the intercontinental missile.

Graham Hutton, an Englishman who in his *Midwest at Noon* laid bare the Midwest mind with more success than most other foreign visitors, thought it could be partly explained in terms of a climate of radical intensities, one which has almost no spring or fall but follows a stretch of summer heat with a stretch of winter cold. I have cited earlier Veblen's effort to explain it through the linkage between the prehensile tenacity of the mercantile and business mind with the social climate of the small town. The Lynds, in their study of Muncie, Indiana (*Middletown*), and Warner in his study of Morris, Illinois (*Democracy in Jonesville*), stressed in different ways the dominance of middle-class values in the communities they surveyed. Their premise was that while the whole of American culture is middle class, the Midwest reveals the American social structure and mentality more sharply than the other regions. It has been difficult for anyone—whether novelist, poet, traveler, or sociologist—to write about the Midwest without assuming that any light cast upon it would somehow light up the whole of the American character. It has long held a special niche in the American consciousness as being more crucially "American" than the rest of the country.

This has been the image that Midwesterners have held about themselves. They have seen the East as the seat of a stodgy plutocracy, the South as caught in the stagnant pool of a past grandeur, the Far West as a still unformed fledgling region. But they have seen their own region as at once solid and hustling, carrying the best of both the conservative and progressive worlds. This idyllic feeling which Midwesterners themselves and outside observers have had about the region is a perilous one, since the idealization is bound to wear off and give way to disillusionment. A strain of this double feeling runs through much of the Midwestern literature. As the gap between the middle-class myth and the realities of middle-class experience became clearer, the disillusioned strain in the literature grew stronger. Dreiser expressed his rebellion against the sexual Puritanism of the Midwest, daring to draw Nietzschean figures against the flatness of the conventional folk. Sherwood

Anderson's *Winesburg, Ohio* portrays the rancorous inner struggles of the spirit which portended that the Midwest dream was near its end. The *Spoon River* of Edgar Lee Masters depicted the descendants of the pioneers as having betrayed their spirit, "with so much of the old strength gone,/And the old faith gone,/And the old mastery of life gone,/And the old courage gone."

But Masters and his fellows were too quick to write the epitaph of the region. The shrewd constructiveness that built new industrial empires did not end with Henry Ford and could still be found in steel and rubber, machine tools, aviation, and electronics. The inventive genius of the Wright Brothers did not wholly disappear. The architectural daring of Louis Sullivan and Frank Lloyd Wright, which transformed the sky line and landscape of America, found successors among the architects of Chicago and Detroit. The folk quality that produced the "yarns" and tall tales carried over in Sandburg. In politics, a Missourian called Harry Truman illustrated again the Jacksonian premise that an uncommon common man can stretch his qualities to meet the demands of great political office; a Kansas soldier called Dwight Eisenhower tried fitfully to restore some of the fading energies of Republican leadership; and two lawyers called Wendell Willkie and Adlai Stevenson, one from Indiana and one from Illinois, both of them political failures, gave a new pungency to the American political tradition.

It is better to approach the Midwest without either idealizing it as the "heart of America" or overreacting to it as a Chamber of Horrors of American middle-class Babbittry. The truth is that the Midwest has been the crossroads of American experience in more than a geographic sense and has therefore absorbed both the strengths and weaknesses of that experience. There are some who feel that it never was a region in a true sense and is not one now: that it has no geographic, economic, ethnic, or cultural unity. Certainly it is today less a region than, let us say, the Deep South or the Southwest, the Far West, or even New England. Its qualities have been fused and absorbed with the generalized qualities of America as a whole.

Actually the Midwest went through a series of phases in its relation to the rest of the country. There was a phase when it was the frontier, and a wild one too; then there was a phase when it was the most quickly growing segment of American industrial and city life; but in the mid-1950s it was no longer either frontier or a laboratory of overnight growth. In fact, its very name as a region—the Midwest—no longer suited it, since to the real Westerners it seems part of the East.

It had become the American Midlands or Mid-country. It was Middle America. As such it was still a geographic and cultural crossroads, but the institutional forces that swept through it were new ones. The historian will underscore the fact that the shaping of the Midwest did much to shape the whole of America—in the nature of its small town and its city alike, in its political attitudes, in its friendliness toward people and its hostility to new ideas, in its rapid class mobility. The shaping role of the Midwestern frontier is well known. Almost equally well known is the decisive part that the Midwest played in the Civil War, which may even be viewed as a struggle between North and South to control the future development of the Midwestern area. The speed with which industrial profits were plowed back into industry by Midwestern businessmen gave the whole of American industrial growth much of its stamp of feverishness.

But the outlines of the America which was emerging in the mid-1950s were also largely identifiable with the outlines of the newly emerging Middle America. There was the renewed cult of the businessman, who had as warm a place in President Eisenhower's heart as in President Grant's. There was the same profusion of wealth and gadgetry and the same confusion about life purposes. If you looked at the most marked traits in Middle America today—the drift toward conformism, the sense of loneliness, the emphasis on middle-class habits of living and thought, new patterns of suburban living, the informal neighborliness of people, the intolerance of strange-sounding ideas, the chaos of moral standards, the influx of educational and leisure opportunities, the uses of popular culture—you would also see the most marked traits of the whole of American culture. Thus if New England was the matrix of the elite culture of America, the Midwest was the crossroads of its popular culture.

Unlike New England it never had a stable social elite, nor did it have one at mid-century. Its folk hero was the businessman, but the circulation of this elite was too rapid ever to give it stability as a shaping group. Its prime characteristic, like that of America as a whole, is that it has been always in flux, a more or less faithful barometer of the cultural climate surrounding it. Other Americans have both idealized it and condescended to it, but it has gone ahead at its own pace and toward its own goals. It has been too much in a hurry to care much about beauty, it has lacked grace, it has been a prey to some of the worst intolerances in American life, and it is today the locus of the "organization man." But for better or worse it carries with it a good deal of the meaning and future of America. If Middle America is unattractive and undigestible to anyone experiencing or studying it, then he had better conclude that this is true of America as a whole.

What is usually called the South is in reality three subregional cultures—the Deep South, the Upper South (a border strip of states), and the Southwest. The Deep South is the region where the one-crop system has lingered, where agriculture is still important, and where the Negroes either outnumber the whites (in the Black Belt counties) or are still numerous enough to sustain the Great Fear. Roughly this area includes Georgia, Alabama, Mississippi, South Carolina, Louisiana, and Florida, while the Virginias, North Carolina, Kentucky, and Tennessee are in the border strip of the Upper South, and Texas, Oklahoma, and Arkansas may be seen as part of another border strip adjoining the Southwest. For most Americans all three areas form part of a going regional unity they call "the South."

Most of the characteristic traits of the Southern mind are a heritage from the past. The old aristocracy dreamed of the South as an autonomous nation—a Greek republic rising proudly from the cotton fields and savannas, built firmly on the economic base of the plantation system and the social base of slavery. The imaginative flame of this dream burned intensely in the political theory of Calhoun and Fitzhugh, and their followers saw the South as a separate culture, conscious of its destiny. But the Civil War and the Reconstruction destroyed the old aristocracy and undercut the plantation system. The South paid a terrible price for the war, in a whole young generation that was killed off, in economic ruin, in the memory of armed occupation and corruption, in hatred.

The "new South" that Henry Grady evoked in the 1880s, and which has been three quarters of a century in coming, is still turned toward the past, with a nostalgia for its lost glamour and glory, a hatred of the Northern absentee owners whom it identifies with the conquering enemy, and a sense of guilt about slavery which is interwoven with a fear of the encircling Negro population. The South is the only region in America tied together not by its common consciousness of present growth and future potentials but by its past, not by what it can achieve or build but by what it cherishes and fears. Its sense of destiny has been carried over but has become mainly a tenacious clutching of past enmities and ideals.

I do not mean to imply that there is a single Southern mentality or a one-class system in the South. One may validly ask, when the South is discussed, "Whose South?" Is it the South of the Negro field hand or share tenant, or the South of the white textile-mill worker, or the South of the cotton farmer, or the South of the new sales and distributive middle class, or the South of the Coca-Cola or insurance-company executive, or the South of the universities at Chapel Hill, Charlottesville, Memphis, Austin, Norman, and Fayetteville, or the South of pastors or labor organizers or newspapermen who take daily risks in challenging the prevailing prejudices around them? This is only to say the South is changing so rapidly that it is almost as fragmented in its attitudes and its classes as other regions are, and that a phrase like "the South" necessarily conceals far more complexity than the unity it premises.

The class cleavage is not, however, wholly recent. There was a cleavage in the Old South between the planter-aristocrats and the democratic farmers: the former lived in the world of Sir Walter Scott, Lord Byron, and Carlyle, imitating the ways of life and thought of the British rural gentry, and were often aristocrats of only one generation; while the latter were rough and boisterous and Jacksonian. The Civil War defeat changed the picture by forcing the classes into a more cohesive mold. But as the result of Reconstruction a new class emerged —that of the educated and well-to-do "Redeemers" like Gordon, Grady, and Watterson, who aimed at moderation and adopted the cunning of the fox in place of the suicidal courage of the lion. They worked closely with Northern capitalists, and C. Vann Woodward has documented the secret deals they made with the Republicans, one of which led to the election of President Hayes as the price for a *laissez-faire* solution of the Reconstruction problem. When the whites of the lower economic groups rebelled against their power, the rebellion took the form of Southern Populism, and its leaders were men like Tom Watson and Ben Tillman.

There was a continuity between the Jacksonian Democrats of the prewar South and the Populists of Watson's day, but by an ironic twist of history the political and economic militancy of the Populists turned into the most illiberal racism. The later figure of Huey Long partook of some of the same mixture of radicalism and totalitarianism, although he was the least racist of the Southern demagogues. Both Watson and Long remain in the Southern memory as half-mythical figures around whom legendry clusters. Their Populism was mainly negative, consisting of an antagonism to the business and finance of the North. Their radicalism sprang out of resentment, and it was not too hard for events to turn it (in Watson's case) into racist demagoguery and (in Long's case) into a cynical Fascist demagoguery. Watson used a behind-the-scenes power to make and break governors of Georgia for a decade; Long held absolute power over his Louisiana empire. The careers of both, and of their successors, are part of the penalty the South has had to pay for the bitter memories of its defeat. The role once played by the Jacksonian Democrats of the South has now been taken over not by the Populists but by the Southern liberal Democrats—in the newspapers, the universities, the courts, the legislatures, and local governments, the embattled movements for a humanist approach to race and a modernist approach to economics.

Social changes are coming fast to the region which used to be called "Dixie," with connotations of Arcadian quaintness and charm. A common folk saying had it that "cotton is going West, cattle are coming East, Negroes are going North, Yankees are coming South, money is coming in." In twenty years, between 1930 and 1950, the South's population employed in agriculture went down from 5.5 million to 3.2 million. Shaken by the Depression, the New Deal, and World War II, by mechanized agriculture and the migration of Negroes, the South changed so drastically that in the mid-1950s a liberal Southerner could write an "Epitaph on Dixie."

The old agrarian South is no longer agrarian but has become substantially industrialized. Offering power sites and cheaper labor, Southern cities have bid for factories moving from the North. A new middle class has risen which has lost much of its nostalgia for the faded glories of the old aristocracy. The type-figure of the South is no longer the plantation farmer or the courthouse politician but the member of the local chamber of commerce. In the 1950 figures the South (counting Texas) had seven metropolitan cities of over a half million people—Houston, New Orleans, Atlanta, Dallas, Louisville, Birmingham, and San Antonio, with Miami and Memphis crowding them closely. Even suburban life—that expression of the modern American condition—has invaded the South. With the new middle class has come a breakup in the one-party system of the once "Solid South." The migration of industry, especially textile mills, also brought with it efforts to unionize the workers. To the extent that these efforts succeed, they change the consciousness of the "poor whites" and make them less amenable as dupes of racist demagoguery.

A movement for civil rights under Federal authority cut across the states'-rights complex which had sustained the Southern sense of autonomy, and Supreme Court decisions of a far-reaching character gave young Southern Negroes at least a fighting chance at normal education, stripped of the hypocrisy of the "separate but equal" doctrine. The long tenure of the Democrats in national power from 1932 to 1952 gave a number of Southern Senators and Congressmen experience at the helm of national affairs. In the Supreme Court decisions of Justice Hugo L. Black something new emerged from the South—a strain of radical democracy with its source in the Southern Populist tradition, crossed with New Deal conceptions, wholly dissociated from racist bigotry. Coming out of the red clay of Alabama, it had about it a hard, sunbaked quality which gave it a regional uniqueness. The era of Virginian political creativeness (Virginia had produced Jefferson, Madison, Monroe, John Taylor, and Edmund Randolph) was over, and the locus of Southern political ferment shifted to industrialized border states like Kentucky and Tennessee and to Georgia and Alabama in the Deep South.

It was in the Deep South that, for weal or woe, one of the planetary battles of the American experience was being fought out. There was an intransigent quality about this struggle, reminiscent of the "old-time religion" with which Southern culture is saturated (Calvinism was the only import from New England which the South welcomed in the period just before the Civil War). The South has an unmistakable culture style of its own which shows itself even more clearly in its periods of stress than in its moments of easy grace. Watch a jury at a Southern trial, or loiterers on the steps of a courthouse, or young people at a Southern college dance, or a crowd at a small-town Southern political meeting, or sheriffs in action at a Southern plant where a strike is taking place, or a marketing center on a Saturday night, and the traits of the Southern culture style come through. Power takes a more naked form in the South than in any other region; political passions are more primitive; all the colors are primary colors. The White Citizens' Councils that arose in the Deep South to meet the challenge of desegregated schools distilled the potential violence of the tradition that reached back beyond the early days of the Klan. Equally, the liberalism of the South was a home-grown regional liberalism, deeply steeped in religious consciousness and imbued with a sense of mission. It took more courage in the mid-1950s to be a genuine liberal in the South than in any other part of America. And it was harder to maintain a middle ground there than anywhere else.

The new South, emerging under the driving force of rapid social change, had to pay the price for the swiftness of the change. Under the double impact of industrial transformation and Negro militancy, the single-mindedness of the South was crumbling, and despite the flurry of strong feeling during the school desegregation fight it was unlikely ever again to achieve the certitude about its cause that it had in the Civil War and in Reconstruction. As it moved away from its economic colonialism and its single-party system, it had to confront responsibilities and tasks that could not be resolved by the old defensive slogans.

Some signs of maturity were not lacking. Floyd Hunter's study of "decision-making" and the local power structure in "Regional City" showed a cross section of community living that mirrored the power struggles in the country as a whole, along with the specifically Southern ones. Even the class structure of the South, which had traditionally been far more rigid than in any other region, showed signs of loosening. The five-class layers—Negroes, poor whites, middle class, residues of the old aristocracy (sometimes still powerful, more often considerably frayed), and the old aristocratic class—were more clearly stratified than in the class system elsewhere in America, but they were unmistakably in flux. There were Negroes moving into the middle class, there were poor whites in the trade-union movement, members of the old aristocracy were having to become absorbed in the middle class under threat of sinking down further, and the movement into the high-income groups was bewilderingly rapid. The rise in the general income level in the South was faster in the quarter century from 1930 to 1955 than anywhere else in the nation.

Out of this ferment came a burst of creativeness in Southern writing that placed it with the best American writing of our time. In fact, the "Southern renaissance" parallels the Midwestern literary movement of the early twentieth century and the Renaissance of the New England "Golden Day." From Ellen Glasgow through Thomas Wolfe to William Faulkner and Eudora Welty, in Robert Penn Warren and in Tennessee Williams, Southern writers reflected the deep internal stirrings produced by regional conflict and change. Something of the same sort happened in the Midwest when Dreiser, Sherwood Anderson, and Sinclair Lewis expressed the heightened awareness that came from watching their world being transformed from an agrarian and small-town world into a city world of industrialism and of revolution in moral standards. In the case of Southern writers, one feels that while they are being pushed reluctantly into the future they are forced into a similar heightened awareness of their regional past, and of the moral and psychological transformation being wrought around them. To push the parallel further, New England's literary renaissance also took place during the period when the coming of industrialism compelled New England's writers and thinkers to re-evaluate their Calvinist tradition and the nature of the human personality that was being threatened by the changes.

It is not unusual for a literary and artistic flowering to come just when the outlines of the culture are changing radically and when something that seemed eternally stable is disappearing forever. It is this pang of loss which has jolted Southern writers into an intense awareness of the Southern place and of the time dimension, so that it is not unusual for them to write on several time levels, shuttling from one to another. The tragic enactments of the Southern scene since the Civil War, juxtaposed against the turbulence of contemporary change, produced a violence of mood and interior action which fascinated foreign as well as American critics. Faulkner's novels bear somewhat the same relation to the guilt and pride of the South that Hawthorne's novels bore to the guilt and pride of Puritan New England. Faulkner's career was an agonized effort to re-create in symbolic terms the life history of the Southern consciousness and the emotional structure of the status system. But he has been more than a regional writer, because in the process he has reached to the universal values of the human condition. The same has been true of the novels of Robert Penn Warren, particularly *All the King's Men,* which dealt with the Huey Long theme. It was true in a different sense of Thomas Wolfe's turbulent lashings, like a Polyphemus among his sheep. One may guess that Wolfe's classic search for his father was a search for a principle of authority, all the more intense because of his break with the culture and values of the Old South. The South as a region has shown an almost compulsive hold upon the minds of its writers, far beyond any other American region. It seems to demand either celebration or rejection, and those who write in it must write about it.

Yet it is an interesting fact that the greatest contemporary Southern writers are not social realists like Lillian Smith, whose *Strange Fruit* indicts the system of caste and the heritage of hate for producing emotional blockages and stunting the growth process for Negroes and whites alike. It is as if the social reality of the South were a Medusa head turning those who confront it with too much directness into stone. The novelists and playwrights I have mentioned, from Faulkner and Warren, Wolfe, Eudora Welty, and Tennessee Williams, preferred to deal with it by indirection, through allegory and symbolism and an antinaturalist style. Their world was drenched with a sense of sin and the fall from grace which was at once religious and classical. To a lesser degree they reproduced the great flowering of literature in Czarist Russia at the time of Turgenev and Dostoevski, who also dealt in a non-naturalist fashion with a feudal society that was passing forever.

While the themes and moods of the Southern writers derive from the passing of the Old South, the turbulence in their writing reflects the turbulence of the contemporary South. The persisting problems of poverty and race relations have not vanished, even though they have been allayed by both economic and political advance. While the population ratio of Negroes to whites diminished with Negro migration, there were still states—Mississippi, Alabama, Georgia, South Carolina—where the whites had a sense of being encircled by Negroes. This produced a garrison mentality which often expressed itself in a hatred of "foreigners" and "radicals" as well as of Negroes and Northerners. The political uses of this hatred were all too apparent in stirring up popular passions to maintain the mold of segregation and caste. There was also a curious attraction-repulsion pattern in the relation of Southern white to Negro, which John Dollard and others explored, based on the conflict between a long-standing physical proximity and sexual attraction and the rigorous requirements of White Supremacy.

I have not meant in this regional portrait to exclude the elements of grace in Southern living which persist side by side with its violence and sadism. The reason why the cultural flowering of the South has taken the form of literary expression is because the South has traditionally had a verbal grace, which goes back beyond the Southern orators, journalists, and political thinkers to the English romantic school on which the Old South was nurtured. The military tradition—the Southern plantation owners lived almost literally on horseback—also persists, and the South from Virginia to Texas still furnishes the core of military enlistments and of the officer group in the Army and Air Force.

The memory of this distinctive way of life tempts some Southern leaders into the delusion that the South can maintain a condition of nullification of Federal law and semi-secession from the Federal Union. The South remembers the history in which it is steeped: it remembers that in the slavery crisis it stubbornly refused to retreat and preferred the havoc of war, and in the Reconstruction crisis it held its ground until the Northern radicals and the carpetbaggers were beaten. It may feel that in this third great crisis of civil rights and desegregation it can maintain autonomy with equal success. It forgets, what Vann Woodward has tried to point out, that segregation is not an ancient Southern institution, and that Jim Crow laws are relatively recent, dating in their vigor only back to the turn of the century. Thus curiously a history-obsessed culture nourishes an unhistorical delusion.

This delusion may help explain why the South, which has produced novelists and dramatists, poets, and literary critics of the first rank, has not produced a political or social thinker of note (I put Justice Black in the category of legal thinkers) since the days of Calhoun. To think greatly on a political and social level requires confronting your problems directly, which is almost impossible in the Southern atmosphere today; the social fictions which have to be maintained are creative soil for fiction and poetry but not for political thinking and the life of ideas. For some time the intellectual process in the South has been not a dialogue but a monologue: the arts of persuasion have found their ground pre-empted by the arts of rhetoric and force. The irony is that when the condition of semi-secession is resolved, and the South once more is absorbed into the social structure and the political mores of the rest of the nation, it may also lose the literary creativeness and the regional culture style that give it its distinctive stamp today.*

* For further treatment of the South and its problems, see Ch. I, Sec. 2, "The Sources of the Heritage," and Ch. VII, Sec. 6, "The Negro in America"; also the section on Civil Liberties in Ch. VI, Sec. 10. For a further discussion of the American novel, see Ch. XI, Sec. 2.

The Southwest is caught between the culture of the Southern staple crops and the culture of the Great Plains, the Great Desert, and the Great Mountains. It shades off in one direction to the single-crop system and the White Supremacy of the Deep South, in another to the wheatlands of the prairie Midwest, in still another to the cattle-grazing lands of the mountain states. Its own economic base is in the oil and cattle lands and the new industries of Texas and Oklahoma, and the tourism and irrigated farming of New Mexico, Arizona, and Southern California. From the South it gets some share of its intensity along with a leisurely grace; it owes a good deal to the Indian whose land it stripped from him but who left behind a heritage of art and spirit, and something also to the old Spanish culture and its mission architecture; from the adjacent Great Plains and mountain states, as well as from its own cattle lands and desert, it gets a sense of space and magnificence. In the blend it is achieving a regional culture of its own, not yet clearly formed but in the making.

It is today one of the fastest-growing areas of American economic expansion and therefore re-creates the "American spirit" of boom, recalling the booster optimism that the Midwest had in its years of early growth. The capitalist of Dallas, Houston, and Los Angeles is close in spirit to the capitalist of Chicago and Cleveland a quarter century ago. Some of the fabulously wealthy men of contemporary America are to be found among the Texas oil kings who rule over complicated domains of corporate wealth and whose oil fortunes—added to the real-estate and cattle fortunes—make the bonanza mentality dominant in the Southwest. Its mood is still that of the great American myth: that anything is possible and will probably happen.

Individualism in the old freebooter sense has probably found its last foothold here. It expresses itself in the intransigence with which big corporations have fought public utility and power regulations; its great victory came when Congress by-passed the Supreme Court and turned the rich tideland oil deposits over to private exploitation under state control. There are few areas in the country in which labor remains as unorganized as it does in this region, partly because of the inferior status of the Spanish-speaking migrant and wetback farm workers, partly because the role of the frontier in weakening labor militancy is being reenacted on the quasi-frontier of the Southwest.

It is the incongruous mixture of historic frontier and booming industrialism that gives the Southwest its dramatic contrasts. The graceful culture of the Navajos, the Hopi, and the Zuñi suffered from the invasion of industrialism, leaving the area a happy hunting ground for ethnological expeditions. A lusty folklore gathered around the cattle and coyotes of the great Texas plains, and a body of legend was built on the cow-boys and rustlers in badman territory. But the type-figures of the Southwestern past—the Indian, the Spanish conquistador and Jesuit, the cattle rustler, the gambler, the cowboy—have been replaced by cattle and oil kings, real-estate speculators, large-scale corporate farms, Army airfields and aviation factories, luxury hotels that serve as gambling resorts, giant conservation projects and hydroelectric dams.

As the newest frontier, the American Southwest may (in the Turner tradition) lay claim to being the seedbed of a rawer and more vigorous democracy—but it does not follow. A reversion to earlier forms of national experience is not necessarily a renewal of national vitality: it may be only a treadmill retraversing of the past or a throwback to an earlier form of social organization, under conditions not present in the original frontier experience, and may prove distintegrating.

The case of Texas presents this puzzle along with several others. Texas is the most cussed and discussed, demeaned and explained, celebrated and orated state in the Union. Much effort has been spent to rationalize why Texans are what they are—and to decide what it is exactly that they are. Its key word is scale: the magnitudes of place and capitalism have converged, so that everything in Texas is bigger than elsewhere. Texans spoke louder, more confidently, and more boisterously than most other Americans. They had the sureness of a Golden Era. Money was quick in the making and ostentatious in the spending. A close student of Texas estimated in the 1950s that there were 400 millionaires in Houston alone. Many of them had started as farm boys or cowhands; they grew rich from oil and boom, and from tax provisions that gave oilmen a generous untaxed annual "depletion allowance" for their oil wells. When wealth came many of them were unprepared to use or spend it. The garish display of Rolls Royces, diamonds, minks and vicuñas, and the lavish spending outdid the vulgarities of America in its Gilded Age and of the new super-rich in Chicago at the turn of the century. The strong streak of anti-intellectualism (even a Texas newspaperman boasted that Texas had produced no poets) may have derived from the fact that there was no elite tradition, as there was in the South and in New England, to serve as a frame for business and frontier energies. The political emotions were also raw ones; wealth and power came so quickly that the tolerances which a successful democracy requires had less chance to develop than they had in the other centers of business power. Texas grew rich before it came of age, and its years of confidence came ahead of its years of maturity.

There was also another Southwest—that of the Spanish and Indian country, where a modern industrial culture has been built on an old Spanish one, and that in turn on a still earlier Indian culture. This Southwest had a wholly different rhythm of life from the boom Southwest of Texas and Oklahoma: it had neither oil tankers nor skyscrapers; the pace of life was slower and lazier; the impassivity of the Indian, the passion of Spanish Catholicism, and the grandeur of mesa, mountain and desert, had left their mark on it. To writers as diverse as D. H. Lawrence, Mary Austin, Edmund Wilson and J. B. Priestley and Jacquetta Hawkes its appeal was prehistoric and mystical, and the same appeal has drawn colonies of artists to it.

There are equally dramatic contrasts and contradictions in the Far West, which still retains the Gold Rush psychology of its early days and has, like the Southwest, the feeling that anything is possible. It has a natural grandeur of scene which, in both the Rocky Mountain and the Pacific Coast regions, surpasses anything in America. The canyons, the high grazing lands, the deposits of ferrous and precious metals, the great stands of timber, are witness to the largess of Nature in this area.

There are, of course, marked differences of topography between the Rocky Mountain region, which is high and dry and rugged, and the Pacific Coast, where the soil is rich and the vegetation lush. There are similar contrasts in the economic mood and structure of the two regions. The Rocky Mountain region is largely still a captive economy whose great mines and other resources are under absentee ownership, so that the region is largely colonial to the corporate empires of the East and the Midwest. The story of the Anaconda Copper Company not only dominates the history of Montana but is also symbolic of the exploitation of the whole region. I have spoken earlier of the movement of population away from the eroded grazing soil of the livestock areas to industrial centers. The great hope of the region is that land reclamation will arrest this trend, that hydroelectric dams will harness the power of the region and invite new industry, and that the new requirements of an age of atomic energy will revive the prosperity of an area which depends on the metals deep under ground.

The economic mood of the Pacific Coast region is a dramatically different one. It has grown so rapidly in population, industry, and prosperity that there has been a kind of "law of combined development" operating: all the stages through which the East and Midwest had passed have been foreshortened on the Pacific Coast and quickened as in a rapid-motion movie. The rich resources of the plains, valleys, and forests were brought into the market at a time when industrial techniques were already highly developed and the power and mastery of the machine were at their summit. The result is an amalgam of frontier roughness along with capitalist power and anticapitalist attitudes of an extreme sort. The industrial prizes opened up to the American industrial system came relatively late in the social and class development of

American society, so that they became the stakes of a more bitter industrial-labor conflict than elsewhere in the nation. In this respect the social and political climate of the Pacific Coast resembles that of Texas, both areas representing the combination of frontier boom and industrial power. In both areas also there is a friendliness toward easy folkways of behavior along with an extreme intolerance of dissenting thought. One might say of both these regions that in their hurry to get rich quick they skipped some of the stages in the slower industrial and political development of the East and Midwest, and skipped also some of the discipline of democratic experience which they had painfully to endure.

One striking difference may be noted in the intellectual climate of the two boom areas: where Texas was undistinguished in literature, the written word runs through the whole course of California history. Bret Harte, Mark Twain (really a Midwesterner, but he got his start in journalism in the Western mining towns and on the California frontier), John Muir, Ambrose Bierce, Jack London, Frank Norris, Robinson Jeffers, John Steinbeck, all attest to the literary vigor which the region drew as much from its ardent society as from its natural environment.

There remains to speak of "the East," or the Middle-Atlantic region —a strip of Atlantic seaboard states caught between New England and the South, between the ocean and the Great Lakes. Beyond Pittsburgh and Buffalo you are in the Midwest, beyond Washington you are in the South, beyond Long Island you are in New England. All up and down this stretch you find an almost unbroken line of industrial plants, metropolitan cities, old and new suburbs. Here are the centers of manufacturing, trade, finance, advertising, and of much of the intellectual and political life of the nation. Having been dominant in American life since the beginning of the nation and grown accustomed to dominance, the Middle-Atlantic region is not moved by the striving for a place in the American sun, which has given the other areas much of their consciousness of regional identity. Polyglot in ethnic composition, cosmopolitan in attitude, highly urban and industrial, these states are not usually regarded as a genuine region. They have less of a consciousness of the natural environment, less feeling than the South, Midwest, and Far West have of their regional destiny in fighting against the distant centers of power—because they *are* the centers of power. Facing in one direction toward Europe, in the other toward the interior of the country, they have a sense of centrality that has kept a feeling of separate regional identity from growing, as it has also saved them from (or denied them) the smoldering grievances and resentments of the interior.

The heart of this area is, of course, New York itself. New York City and its suburbs form a "regional city" in themselves. The familiar warning that "New York is not America" is doubtless true, but neither is any other regional culture. The fact that this obvious proposition has to be asserted is more than an index of the common hostilities to New York: it shows the extent to which New York's culture has impinged on the imagination of America and the world.

New York has a double heritage—that of the old Dutch aristocracy, now supplanted by the aristocracy of finance, talent, and "café society," and the intellectual heritage of western Europe toward which it faces. It has fused, adapted, and transformed that heritage, and used it as a base for a cosmopolitan culture which is nonetheless American because it results from the enormous suction force it has exerted on the world. Its ethnically diverse population is drawn from every corner of the world and from every region and subregion of America. Latterly the currents of population in and out of New York have changed its character, making it largely Catholic, Jewish, Negro, and Puerto Rican. But this is to see it residentially. As a working entity, or as a regional city, it reaches into the surrounding counties and states and retains millions who still work in it and use it as the center of their energies although they make their homes elsewhere.

Its lodestone strength continues. The constant stream of young people who come to New York to make their careers brings with it a continual refreshing of the American image. And if New York gets its productive forces from the nation, as is so often asserted, then the finished products—art and the theater, radio and TV, newspapers, magazines, advertising, books, ideas, managerial patterns, trade-union techniques, intellectual movements—make their way all over the nation. It is because of this power and fertility that New York is suspected, feared, and not a little hated by the rest of America. The greatest bitterness comes from the South, Midwest, and Southwest, sometimes from a defensive feeling of cultural difference or newness, sometimes expressing historic conflicts or current frustrations. But one must add that part of this hostility is repayment for the attacks on Midwest "provincialism" and Southern "White Supremacy" made by the liberal intellectuals of New York and the East.

It must be clear that regionalism is not so much a "movement" as a fact—one of the massive facts about America. It embodies the pluralism of the American environments and cultures. Where there have been regional movements they have been largely afterthoughts. What the regional movements have been able to do has been to make Americans more conscious of their regional heritage, prouder of their characteristic diversities, more aware of the material they offer for literature and art, of their folklore and folkways. There is always a danger, of course, that people will go on from the self-conscious to the cultist. But the centralizing and standardizing forces of American life are so insistent that the merely cultist and archaic has no chance for survival against them. Only the tough-fibered regional energies can make the fight, and thus far they have done pretty well.

It is possible, of course, to overestimate the importance and endurance of regional differences. American change moves at two levels and by two clocks, one being the changes common to the nation, the other those peculiar to the region and locality. The regional changes are the wheel within the larger national wheel, and many are trivial and many ephemeral. But it is no superstition to see them as essential parts of the total pattern of diversity. Foreigners who have never been to America are likely to have a single image of it, like a monstrous monolith hewn out of undifferentiated rock. The hardest thing to understand about America, even for many Americans, is that it contains diversities as well as uniformities of speech, dress, consciousness, pace and ways of living, patterns of thought, modes of character. From the white pine and blue water of Maine to the big redwoods and the ocean coast line of California, from the subzero frosts of the upper Great Lakes to the King Ranch and the Galveston docks in Texas, America eludes the single formula that its praisers and damners would force upon it. This does not mean that it is a snatch-batch of unrelated local traits and vagaries, but that it is richly diversified within its unmistakable and frightening uniformities, and the abbreviated symbol of some of these diversities is the region.

The standardizing trend is stronger in America now than it has ever been. It is largely a by-product of American technology. The regional differences are obviously diminishing. Hartford, Atlanta, Wilmington, Akron, Dallas, Denver, and Seattle have more in common than they had a quarter century ago, and this is even truer of the suburbs around them and the small towns that dot them. Any research team, studying their ways of life and thought, would find them largely made up of interchangeable parts. There is a swift and striking erosion of regionalism taking place, especially in the older regions like New England and the South where the consciousness of region goes back for centuries. The regional concept persists even after the regional reality has begun to give way and the differentiations are losing their sharpness of outline.

A distinction may be useful here between what relates to society, or the social structure, and what relates to the culture or the community ways. In their structure as a society—in their business and labor trends, their machines and machine living, their class directions, in transport, in distributive systems, in their use of the big media, in advertising and salesmanship, in consumers' goods and processed foods—the regions are being fused into a national standardized pattern. It is this pattern that one sees in magazines and movies and on TV. But in whatever concerns group life, race relations and attitudes, legal customs, architecture and building, walk and talk, song and dance, the arts, the pace of living, in the use of leisure (except for the big media), in the life of the mind, in prejudices and loves and hates, in the way people grow up and die and the way they feel about the place where they live, the regions still retain or are capable of autonomous creativeness. The process of erosion goes on here too but less swiftly than in the more external social forms that are being standardized.

Take as an instance the musical idiom known as "jazz," which is regarded throughout the world as characteristically American. It was a local creation, coming out of the life of Negroes in New Orleans, out of the marching songs at their funerals and the honky-tonks of Bourbon Street. Gathering strands from the idioms of Africa and the Caribbean, it developed in New Orleans until it achieved its own form; then it was joined by similar forms that developed in St. Louis and Harlem, came into the stream of national life, and ceased to be merely a regional idiom. Something of the same may be said of the folk tales and ballads of the Ozarks, the badman legends of the Far West, the architectural style of mission and pueblo and ranch house of the Southwest, the writing of a small group of Mississippians, the cooking of the Deep South, the religious revivalism of the Midwest, the passion for dissent of New England, the openness of New York to winds of doctrine from every quarter.

Is this regional creativeness coming to an end? I have talked with New Orleans writers who tell me that the walls of regional insulation there have broken down, that Bourbon Street is a playground for visiting tired businessmen from the East and Midwest, and the Mardi Gras has become synthetic. They say that the big media and the big money have destroyed the sense of regional and folk uniqueness from which the creative impulses came, and that nothing as fresh or delightful as jazz will ever be born again, whether in New Orleans or St. Louis or anywhere else. There is a streak of truth in this, and a sad one. I should add that when one of my friends who spoke thus had a chance to leave New Orleans and get at the big media and the big money in New York, he preferred to work and write where he felt at home. There would seem to be a persisting autonomous element that is still regional.

We shall probably never know what historic combination of circumstances and talents produced New Orleans jazz or New England dissent, just as we shall never know the secret of individual creativeness. In this sense the regional culture—the fusion of place, people, and tradition—is a primary datum of American life. In the course of American history, now one region and now another has acted for a time as the principal carrier of cultural creativeness and has had a formative role in shaping the national character. Just when it has seemed that this vein of gold was running out in one region it has turned out that elsewhere another deposit has been gathering, secretly and slowly, richer than any Comstock Lode that ever brought its lucky exploiters to the heights of Nob Hill.

I do not say, as some do, that only the regional culture can keep America from being ironed out into a flat conformist country. The champions of regionalism conveniently forget that the region may harbor a rigorous cultural tyranny. The region is a force against national patterns of standardization, but there is a difference between standardization, which has to do with the outward life, and conformity or nonconformity of spirit. Since the region is a more compassable unit of living, it may also, like the small town, be a more compassable unit for enforcing conformity.

One cannot expect of the regional culture that it should save America from the anthill society. Only the autonomous impulses of the unlegislated individual, working in small groups with others like himself, conscious of the larger directions of American life and of his place in them, owning loyalties of a richly diverse kind yet remaining a person within these loyalties, can perform that difficult role. What the region can do, in its more limited way, is to serve as a buffer between the individual and the impersonal forces shaping national life. In that role the best that American regional cultures can hope for is to find a healthy balance between insulation and accessibility.

CHAPTER IV

The Culture of Science and the Machine

1. The Enormous Laboratory: Science and Power
2. Science in an Open Society
3. Big Technology and Neutral Technicians
4. Work and the Automatic Factory
5. The Wilderness of Commodities
6. The Culture of Machine Living

IN WHICH we examine how modern science and its machines have fared under the conditions of American life and what contributions Americans have made to both. We trace the relations between power as it is expressed throughout American life and power as it shows itself in the characteristic sciences (Sec. 1, "The Enormous Laboratory: Science and Power"), and we ask how much the climate of a free society in America is crucial to the growth of science and its fruits (Sec. 2, "Science in an Open Society").

Tracing the series of industrial revolutions that have given America the sense of being in a "permanent revolution," we examine the technician and pose the probably insoluble question of whether he (and the scientist too) can be "neutral" when faced with the choices of what shall be done with his science and machines (Sec. 3, "Big Technology and Neutral Technicians"). Shifting to the worker and looking at the same scene from his vantage point, we analyze the factory as a society, ask what has happened to work as a calling, what incentives spur the best kind of work, and what lies ahead for the worker in a society where his machine-tending role is diminishing. We stop for a glimpse into the future of "automation" and the almost workerless industrial plant and office (Sec. 4, "Work and the Automatic Factory").

Shifting now to the consumer, we look at the array of commodities that America creates daily, ask what life values they serve and how they can serve them best, and trace the effect of plenty upon American thinking (Sec. 5, "The Wilderness of Commodities"). Finally we tackle the moot question of the "standardization" of American life by the machine and examine how a humanist culture can best be developed not only in spite of but through the machine as instrument (Sec. 6, "The Culture of Machine Living").

CHAPTER IV

The Culture of Science and the Machine

1. The Enormous Laboratory: Science and Power

AMERICA is a civilization founded on science and rooted in its achievements. Without science the whole ribbed frame of American technology, and with it American power, would have been impossible. America itself was born at the beginning of the great age of European science. Back of the flowering modern technology were the long centuries when the seed grew silently in the earth. The same expansive forces that produced the intellectual discoveries of that *saeculum mirabile* of European science—the seventeenth century—produced the American settlements as well. Europe reached out intellectually, as it reached out physically, for new frontiers. In England, the history of the Royal Society paralleled that of the plantation companies. The whole atmosphere surrounding the settlement and peopling of America was an atmosphere of scientific beginnings. Except in a climate of innovation the American experiment would have been impossible; conversely, it was in the intensely innovating social climate of America that invention was bound to flourish.

To be sure, science as the heir of centuries of intellectual development needed something better than a wilderness to grow in. It needed universities, intellectual exchange, and the leisure for idle curiosity; it needed also a consciousness of national strength which did not come until the era of Jackson. Mitchell Wilson has pointed out that during the first half century of the nation's history American invention was sparse and imitative, and American science lagged behind that of Europe. There were hopes that invention would flourish, but by 1834 (when the present patent law was passed) there were only a little more than 1,200 patents on file. The great burst of inventiveness began in the following period. But once started on its career, American science had a few crucial things in its favor. It had the whole body of Europe's science to use as an unlimited drawing account; yet it had also the advantage of distance—the extra margin of freedom from the grooves of conventional thinking which often hemmed in the European scientists.

An amusing example may be found, even in the earlier period, in Benjamin Franklin's career as a scientist. Franklin is one of the important world names in electricity. He began to putter with it when an English friend sent him some rudimentary equipment with a few hints on how to use it. Without European science he could not have started; but once started he worked with a sense of excitement and in an atmosphere of intense popular interest. So much was he on his own that when he wrote his friends in Europe about his experiments, he didn't know whether the terms he had newly coined for what he observed were the first. With the growth of his fame as a scientist his European friends sent him the literature containing the orthodox vocabulary and the traditional ideas on electricity. "As he learned from books, rather than his own investigations," says Franklin's editor, I. Bernard Cohen, "he ceased to have a free, unfettered mind. As he became more and more familiar with the literature of electricity, he made fewer and fewer discoveries until finally he made no more." Franklin's discoveries were discussed in the Royal Society, which when asked to protect a powder magazine from the effects of lightning recommended the Franklin lightning rod, with pointed conductors. One committee member dissented, insisting on blunt conductors (or "knobs") instead of "points." He continued to attack Franklin without success—until the Revolutionary War, when George III intervened and ordered "blunt" conductors for the Royal Palace. When the head of the Royal Society refused to reverse the committee's recommendation on the Franklin rod, the King forced his resignation.

One may take this delightful story as a somewhat distorted allegory of the conditions of science in Europe and America. I do not mean to overstate the favoring conditions of American scientific work or to give an inflated impression of its achievement in its early phase. Such early scientists of note as Joseph Henry and Draper did work that stood out like mountain peaks from the general flatness of the amateur work around them, much of which repeated what had already been done in Europe with greater subtlety. The lack of contact with other working scientists, which gave a few men of genius a chance at originality, also cut many others off from the access to other working scientists without which they could get no stimulation. Yet there were important institutional hindrances from which American science was free. It could pursue the laws of Nature without troubling about the laws of monarchies; it could work in an atmosphere in which it did not have to cope with a codified body of religious taboos or with a church rooted in state power; it did not have to reckon with either priestly or aristocratic castes. It was free to follow its impulse and develop the resources of a continent. In that impulse were tied together the main threads of the American mind—its Puritan emphasis on work, its sense of newness and confidence, its technical skill, its energy, its sense of the "go" of things.

But American achievement has been less in pure than in applied science—that is, in invention and technology. When an American today thinks of science, he is likely to think of test tubes and laboratories, of such end-product inventions as atom bombs or antibiotics, guided missiles, proximity fuses, or the latest process for cracking oil. The great scientific revolution of the seventeenth and eighteenth centuries had already taken place by the time America became a going concern. A raw country could not quickly develop an intellectual tradition out of which emerges the giant figure of an Aristotle or Euclid, a Galileo, a Newton or Darwin or Mendel, a Faraday or Einstein. The names that keep cropping up in the American histories, biographies, and current scientific literature are distinguished enough: Franklin himself; Joseph Henry, a physicist who made some remarkable discoveries in electricity and magnetism; Nathaniel Bowditch, mathematician and "Practical Navigator"; Audubon, ornithologist; Simon Newcomb, astronomer; Benjamin Silliman, chemist; Asa Gray, botanist; Willard Gibbs, physicist; Holmes and Morton, who did much for childbirth and anesthesia; John W. Draper, Thomas A. Edison, and George Eastman, the trio whose connected work did much for the modern sciences of communication. The list could be lengthened with names like Millikan, Langmuir and Gilbert Lewis, with G. W. Hill and Birkhoff in mathematics, with Julian Schwinger, I. I. Rabi, and Robert Oppenheimer in physics (I omit those who developed as scientists abroad and came to America as refugees), with Urey in chemistry, T. H. Morgan and H. J. Muller in genetics, W. B. Cannon in the theory of homeostasis, and names like Hale, Boade, Hubble, and Shapley in astrophysics. To these must be added a galaxy of contemporary names linked with radio, television, electronics, automation, and atomic energy.

It is a rich and diversified list and disproves any idea that Americans do not carry their share of the burden of scientific research and thinking. Yet of the whole list, there is only one—Gibbs—who would clearly be recognized as a theoretical scientist of the highest world rank, standing apart from the productive laboratory experimenters, scientific organizers and classifiers, distinguished teachers, and brilliant inventors. Much of the enormous laboratory of modern American scientific power rests on the laws of chemical energetics that Gibbs discovered. The processes of separating metals from their ores, refining petroleum, fixing nitrogen, synthesizing rubber, and many other operations make use of

Gibbs's "phase rule" and other formulas. Yet even in Gibbs's case his great theoretical work in physics and chemistry was carried on under a blanket of indifference on the part of the universities, the industrialists, and the public. Even the European scientists failed to see the meaning of his work. When, in 1876, Clerk Maxwell gave a lengthy analysis and appreciation of it before a European audience, he got little response.

The American achievement in the atomic era may seem to disprove the scarcity of great American theoretical work. Yet the theoretical groundwork for atomic fission was laid in Europe, and the achievements at Hanford, Chicago, Los Alamos, and Oak Ridge are based on the revolution in theoretical physics begun with Einstein's 1905 paper in Germany and with the work of Heisenberg, Born, De Broglie, Schroedinger, and Dirac, which overturned the ideas about time, space, mass, and length. The theoretical discoveries were the result of world-wide knowledge, but it was America that took over the knowledge, organized it, underwrote it, and thus got out in front. The achievement of the Americans was a triumph of engineering and of hospitality in giving harbor to scientists like Einstein, Fermi, and Szilard who had fled from tyranny. The Americans achieved what they did through the division and distribution of the research, the fitting of the findings into a pattern, the construction of plants, machinery, and machine tools, the combination of economic power with wealth and inventiveness, and with an experimental and empiric cast of mind.

Heine once said that while England ruled the seas, Germany ruled the clouds, and his jibe at the vaporous metaphysical broodings of his countrymen has been echoed by others. For great theoretical work in science, Americans, boasting that their feet are always on the ground, have not been in the clouds enough. It is this feet-on-the-ground compulsion that has kept American genius largely limited to applied science and engineering. The strain of empiricism runs through the whole of the history of the American mind. Americans find their ideas in things: they understand generalizations in terms of the operations involved in using them. The segment of the European philosophic heritage they took over was in the main the British segment, which ran less in terms of absolutes than the others; and the portion of the British segment that influenced them most was the thinking of Hume and Locke, who distilled the empiricism of the British tradition. It is also characteristic of American science that its most brilliant theorist in the philosophy of science was Charles S. Peirce, the founder of the Pragmatic school, for whom the "meaning of a statement" lay in the effects which the belief in it has on human behavior. This strain of thinking helps make a civilization a technological one, using scientific theories to the hilt but not generating great new ones. The place of science in American civilization is thus closely linked with the characteristic cast of the American mind.

The question about a civilization is not whether it uses science but how it uses science, what contributions it makes to it, what sciences are closest to its temper and civilization style. While the Greeks did important work in astronomy and physics, the characteristic Greek sciences were botany, zoology, biology, and mathematics, as befitted a people absorbed with the individual, the category, and their relations. The characteristic sciences of American technology turned out to be chemistry and physics, electronics and radiation, as befits a people absorbed with energy and speed, communication and power. In both cases the sciences are a key to the crucial civilization traits. In one case they are mainly the life sciences and the sciences of order, in the other the sciences of energy and power.

Spengler had at least a half-truth by the tail when, writing in his *Decline of the West* on the Faustian and Apollonian nature conceptions, he said that "force is the mechanical Nature-picture of Western man. . . . The primary ideas of this physics stood firm long before the first physicist was born." While this notion—that the science type in any civilization exists long before the science—has an element of poetry, it cannot be ignored. Veblen brushed the same problem in the 1920s when he linked the American "technology of physics and chemistry" (radiation and electronics had not yet emerged) with "absentee ownership" by and of corporations. And if you push absentee ownership and corporate power still further back, you get the "natural rights" of property.

Here, I think, we reach a significant relationship. The American conceptions of science went hand in hand with the American conceptions of nature: the Declaration of Independence, with its theory of the natural rights of the individual, was the forerunner of the great upsurge of American energy which led to the technological triumphs of the nineteenth century. The Federalist Papers are in themselves a microcosm of the forces in the American mind that were to shape the uses of science: on the one hand an equilibrium-politics, on the other a drive on purely pragmatic grounds to establish the principle of a central authority with the power to govern essential for survival. The two may seem inconsistent to the critical student of today, and their inconsistency has been shown in the creaking of the American governmental machine: yet the important fact is that they were both part of the eighteenth-century American mind, and the sense of natural law in the equilibrium principle coexisted with the empirical power sense in the principle of central authority.

These two—the sense of natural law and a power empiricism—have been the formative forces in American science and technology, as they have been in American political science and economics. The "reception" that the Americans gave the principles of John Locke, as Walton Hamilton has analyzed it and Merle Curti has traced it, is another instance of the transforming drive in the American civilization: for the Locke that emerged from American thinking on property was very different from the Locke that came into it from the English. It is in the nature of a civilization's "genius" that whatever material it borrows from others it transforms in its own image. When John Locke came out of the American transforming machine his name was Andrew Carnegie and Henry Ford. The Declaration of Independence became the "due process" decisions of the Supreme Court; Tom Paine's flaming pamphlet on natural law became the comfortable doctrines that bolstered property interests; the American idea of Nature turned into corporate ownership, and its servant was the technology of chemistry and physics. The congruity between American science and the driving spirit of American political and economic development was the congruity of *élan* and energy. The geography and resources of America invited a physics of force, and the role of Nature in American political thinking reflected it and prepared the ground for it. Out of the sciences of force came American technology and the machine process; and they in turn cast their spell back upon science.

This capacity for transforming science into technology, which accounts for so much of the success of American power, is not one to be taken for granted. The Greeks, for example, played a greater role in the history of scientific theory than the Americans. They took the great step from myth to science, just as Europeans in the seventeeth century took the final step in separating science from religion. Centuries before the Christian era there were thinkers in Thrace and Athens, in Sicily and on the coast of Asia Minor, who did basic thinking about biology and mathematics, about the nature of the world and the constitution of matter, upon which later centuries were built. At the height of the Greek achievement a Stagirite called Aristotle was able to synthesize what the Greeks knew of Nature and its workings into a system more comprehensive than any mind before or since. Yet Greek science, although it continued its achievements as science for several centuries after Aristotle, never took the crucial step from science to technology. To be sure, the Alexandrian world in the later Greek era had an impressive number of mechanical contrivances described by Hero, like the endless chain, the compound pulley, and the crane for lifting, some of which they put to practical use. Yet it remained true that Greek technology, however you measure its achievement, never explored and applied more than a small fraction of what Greek science might have made possible. It did not run machines, relieve labor of its burdens, increase man's productive capacity greatly, build a powerful industrial civilization. Why?

The clues to the Greek failure in technology may shed some light on the American success in it. Partly they lie in what may be called the slave syndrome. There is a British school of historians, including Benjamin Farrington and V. Gordon Childe, who look to the slave system for the explanation of the arrested Greek development. They have pushed their thesis too hard in applying it to science, for it is obvious that the slave-based society of the Greek city-states was well developed by Plato's time, yet Greek science went on growing for several centuries in the work of Euclid, Archimedes, and others. But the heart of the matter is less in the failure of science to develop fully than in its failure to make the transition to technology. The thinking of the Greeks was done by free men and citizens; the work was done by foreigners and slaves. Where there is a contempt for work and trade and the sweat they entail, there is a separation from the sources of experience and Nature, and a blindness to those imperatives of practice that shape innovation. The American scientist or technician, no matter how famous and whether he works at industrial research or at a university, does not cut himself off from these sources of experience. Less a creator of world views than the ancient Greek or modern European scientist, he has been a discoverer of new ways of pushing old and new things to completion.

There have, of course, been other explanations of the failure of Greek science to develop into technology. One scholar suggests that the Greeks in the Hellenistic period were developing an experimental technique, but that the invasion of the Roman "barbarians" from the Italian peninsula cut it off before it had a chance to flower. Another scholar contends that it was because the Greek ideal of life, in its stress on the public place and its underemphasis on the home, had no interest in raising living standards, and therefore no zeal for technology. Neither of these is inconsistent with the approach that stresses slavery. Even if the Roman barbarians had never come, Greek society could never have developed a revolutionary technology. Greek science developed to no small extent out of the reflectiveness possible in a leisure-class society sustained by a moral and political individualism, with a civic ideal of life. But in the context of slavery and of the leisure-class contempt for work, it could not go much beyond science and was arrested before it carried its insights over into technology.

The atmosphere of America was less favorable for the reflective than for the dynamic aspects of science; the emphasis was not on philosophy and the shaping of new world views but on experience and the mastery of the environment. The achievements in technology thus outran the creativeness in pure science.

If the South had triumphed in the Civil War (and the reason it did not was that the North had developed a technology) and had gone on to spread its "peculiar institution"—the slave syndrome—over the whole of America, the same paralysis might have befallen American technology that befell the Greek and Hellenistic. Calhoun and Jefferson Davis dreamed of a Greek slave-based Republic, and with a Southern victory the American ruling class might have lived more gracefully but less efficiently than the business elite has done. The Civil War was thus more than a moral or Constitutional struggle: exactly because it was fought over moral and Constitutional issues it was also a crisis in technological history.

Having triumphed over the plantocracy of the South, the business class went on to the conquest of a continent and the economic empire of the world. Whatever else might be said of it after the Civil War, it was hospitable to the science underlying the technological changes that had given it power. For only technology could master the needed domain for these rulers: strip the forests, open the land, build the railroads, pick the cotton, thrash the wheat, harness the energy. In Europe the business class had to fight an unremitting struggle for centuries against the political rulers and the social aristocracy: only in England and Germany did it win; especially in Germany, where Bismarck built a technological welfare state in alliance with the army. In America the sway of the business class was undisputed. It lavished its gifts on science (although not always wisely) through research funds and big laboratories, because science in turn opened a cornucopia of profits. It whipped technology on because every discovery of new techniques and processes meant the cutting of costs, the opening of new areas of investment, the reaching of new heights of productivity. America became the Enormous Laboratory.

2. *Science in an Open Society*

OUT OF THIS laboratory have poured whole new industries: electric power, aviation, the telephone, radio and TV, movies, antibiotic drugs, aluminum and other light metals, electronics, radar, isotopes, X rays and radiation therapy. The bulk of the newer arms produced in the war-geared economy of our generation comes from processes unknown, perhaps even undreamed of, in the 1920s. The people in closest contact with them must reckon with continuous obsolescence; they live within universes that must be renewed in constantly shortening cycles. The scientific revolution out of which the new industries and techniques came is itself scarcely a half century old. The earlier work in quantum mechanics, cosmic rays, the neutron and meson, and the overturning of the classical concepts of mass and measurement led to an era of scientific changes that present a challenge to a science civilization like the American. Having become an Enormous Laboratory, America had the task of maintaining its industrial and military primacy against any rival constellation.

A great scientific civilization depends on two imperatives: the mutation outcroppings of scientific genius, and the pervasiveness of the scientific outlook. Assuming a fair share of the first, there must be a favorable climate in which the insights demanded by the modern scientific revolution can flower. The young Einstein, pondering the question of the speed of light and the errant behavior of the planet Mercury, could not have reached his solution by empiricism alone. He reached it by undercutting the assumption of classical physics, seeing the universe as a series of observations by a scientist who is himself part of the frame.

The revolution in science jolted young American physicists loose from empiricism. It also jolted American industry and the government into subsidies of scientific research so extensive that one must speak of General Electric or Du Pont Chemical or General Dynamics as the new Maecenases of young talent in science. They are ready to foot the bill for theoretical research. Yet the empirical shadow of the Enormous Workshop continues to fall on the Enormous Laboratory. It is hard for a culture to rid itself of its encrusted habits of thought, even in a universe in which God emerges as the Great Mathematician rather than as the Great Artificer. The whole organized—perhaps overorganized—material civilization of America, so different from the reflective and the metaphysical, brings America closer to the symbol of Osiris than of Isis. Amidst the research endowment, science clubs, and the new bureaucracy of the vast science enterprise of America, there is a danger of losing sight of the quality that Einstein had along with Newton and Harvey: a basic simplicity of approach that cut through the clutter of intellectual and scientific bric-a-brac. Despite some brilliant and mature teaching of science in the universities, many American students are trained less in the ways of "idle curiosity" than of the technician who sees a job to be done and sets about doing it. Benjamin Franklin, who did his best scientific work in the spirit of free curiosity, left a different kind of heritage too: for the Franklin mixture was made up of equal parts of the Puritan doctrine of work, Poor Richard's bourgeois doctrine of thrift and profit, and the tinkering with new gadgets. It was a utilitarian heritage for practical men.

The scientific discovery, we have come to understand, is likely to start with the inspired hunch and end with the culminating calculation. But in a technological culture, intellectual production is viewed very much in the image of mass production and the factory belt line. The subsidizing of inspired hunches is obviously hard: it requires both risk and faith, and in a utilitarian culture the pressures on the young scientist to prove his mettle by "delivering the goods" come from within, yet are a reflection of the pressures from the culture as a whole. Conant has defined science not (as Karl Pearson did) as a classification of facts but as a series of conceptual schemes linked with observation and experiment both before and after, and has made a plea to encourage these "conceptual schemes" by emphasizing not the belt line or the job but the person. He has asked universities and industrial concerns to subsidize not the project but the scientist.

Rarely have they done so. Industrial research produces many inventions and gadgets but few scientists of top importance, and while industry and government together in the mid-1950s spent over four and a half billion dollars a year on research and employed some 400,000 scientists and engineers at it, little of the money or energy went into fundamental research as distinguished from empirical inventions. It is true that some of the industry research men contribute first-rate papers to professional journals, and that industrial raids on university faculties are often returned in a two-way process. Yet my general statement must stand. This may seem surprising in the light of America's industrial leadership and its reputation for working miracles in the solution of technical problems. But in his study, *The Organization Man,* W. H. Whyte, Jr., examines the record of industry with the result I have given. He makes a crucial distinction between empirical research, which (let us say) sets out to develop a better automobile engine or electric bulb and does so, and fundamental research, which doesn't know what it is looking for until it stumbles upon a problem, whereupon a whole series of new questions arise. Only two American scientists from the industrial laboratories—Irving Langmuir and C. J. Davisson—have received Nobel prizes, as compared with dozens from the universities. A *Fortune* study of outstanding scientists under forty, by Francis Bello, found that all but a small percentage of the creative younger men were in the universities rather than in the research laboratories of big industry. The days of Langmuir, Steinmetz, and Wallace Carothers seem to be over, and the day of the "adjusters" who are not eccentrics or troublemakers is upon us. The emphasis of the corporate managers is upon finding people who will be "co-operative" and work as part of a "team." And the same trend is beginning in the universities as well, where "team research" is making inroads as the dominant concept, wherever military subsidies support the research. As a counterforce, however, the argument has been pressed that the work in atomic energy would never have been possible without fundamental theory—but it remains to be seen whether this truth will stick in the military mind.

It is, of course, difficult to separate the individual heroic figure in science from the whole collective of scientific scholarship, in which the man who makes the culminating calculation stands on the shoulders of so many other men. But given free communication between scientists, the concentration on the scientist himself and his inner brooding and inspired hunches is an essential one if fundamental research is to flourish. The fear of "geniuses," felt through most of the industrial structure, scares off a number of men who value independent thinking and cherish their own cast of personality. But the managerial attitude is even more corrosive for the marginal men who may decide to go into industrial research and who develop their own inhibitions against original thinking once they find themselves in an atmosphere hostile to it.

While the corporate managers feel uneasy with scientific "geniuses," the community as a whole distrusts and even fears them. A survey of New England teen-agers, reflecting probably the opinion of parents as well, described science as an occupation fit for "queer geniuses" who were cold and lacked moral standards. This is part of a current of anti-intellectualism that swept in recent years not only through America but through the whole Western world, largely as a consequence of the atomic crisis.

Actually there is a double impulse of worship and fear in the way Americans feel toward science. They address it as Shelley addressed the west wind: "Destroyer and preserver; hear, oh, hear!" For the multitude, science has been a worker of miracles which they have come to take almost for granted as part of the natural course of America's development. This has led to a popular fetishism of science, which Henry Adams grasped when he used the contrasting symbols of the "virgin and the dynamo." But he failed to make the distinction between the personal and the tribal symbols of worship. To the medieval mind the Virgin had a personal immediacy; to the Americans the dynamo—or the atom bomb, or streptomycin, or the electronic brain, or whatever the current miracle symbol may be—is connected with the nation's destiny. The American makes a cult of science as a tribal symbol, just as he makes a cult of success as a personal symbol.

That—and the fear of which I have spoken—may be the reason why the man of science has not yet left as deep a mark on American literature as, let us say, the journalist, the soldier, the business Titan. The closest approach to a glorifying of the research scientist as a saintlike, dedicated person was in Sinclair Lewis's *Arrowsmith*. In the popular biographies of great scientists the laboratory process was transmuted into something else: scientific research seemed most understandable to Americans as an ascetic endurance contest or a criminal manhunt or a success story—as anything, in fact, except the penetrating simplicity of intellectual insight. The other popular image of the scientist was a cross between the heritage of the Gothic romances and Wells's *The Island of Doctor Moreau*—the diabolical scientist of the horror movies or of supernatural fiction, the Svengali of the intellectual world, a sinister and lethally dangerous figure who in the end destroys himself or is shot by the F.B.I. Most familiarly and ludicrously the scientific process was dramatized by the movies in the ritual of surgeons donning the hygienic invincibility of rubber gloves before a delicate brain operation.

Something of a revolution has taken place recently in the popularizing of scientific research through magazines like the *Scientific American,* and a group of able science writers has arisen who have technical competence along with a dramatizing capacity. On another level a genre of popular science fiction has emerged, dealing less with scientists than with the projection of the scientific imagination in the Wellsian tradition, half fantasy, half prophecy. In the form of Buck Rogers and the space ship it also reached into the comic books and television. Some of the same writers who once did pulp magazine "Westerns" now turned to the frontiers of the Space Patrol. Even the G-Men of the F.B.I. were touched by the image of the scientific investigator who operates with a deadly detachment and laboratory efficiency, and science came thus to be invoked by Americans to preserve them from subversives within as well as from enemies without.

The sharpest dilemma that science posed was in its relation to the weapons of war. The Enormous Workshop became the Enormous Arsenal. Without war science and war technology America could not produce the radar and sonar, rockets, jets and jet interceptors, guided missiles, strategic bombers, short-range interceptors, submarines, atom bombs, biological and radiological weapons which, rightly or wrongly, were considered necessary for the survival of a great modern nation. Yet the whole bundle of attitudes—awe and terror and a clinging reliance—clustering around the science-created tools of war generated an atmosphere in which the free pursuit of science became more difficult.

Science depends upon open communications, both between cultures and between scientists within a culture. But in a spy-ridden, security-conscious world of the Great Powers the inevitable response of administrators to the demands of the armament race was the sanction of secrecy. The scientist working on a defense project was investigated and cross-investigated, tagged and watched. In the past this was partly true of scientists working for corporations engaged in intense competition. But in a war-geared society the political tests became the crucial ones, and the scientist was watched for entangling alliances and even for dangerous thoughts. Since the larger share of scientific research in the universities came under the defense services, with government subsidies and government supervision, the danger was that scientists would in effect have to put on uniforms. Only a small percentage of the university and industrial projects under government contract might be "secret," yet they infected the rest. Thus American science tended to become not only project-ridden (as I have put it above) but security-ridden.

Even sympathetic students of the Soviet Union, like Sidney and Beatrice Webb, point out the remarkable degree to which the Communists developed both the cult of science and the disease of orthodoxy. Their devotion to science is crippled by the taboos of Communist thinking and by the dogma of Party Truth: so much so that, while they can expect to nurture good technicians, they cannot hope to rival the theoretical discoveries of the world outside, on which they must continue to draw either by espionage or by keeping the communications open. Yet it must be added that a conservative orthodoxy is only a little better for science, because while less rigid than a Communist orthodoxy, it may in its own way have a repressive effect on science.

I am not arguing wishfully that science can function only in an open society and that it dries up wholly under totalitarianism. The experience of the Soviet Union, where important work has continued in mathematics, physics, chemistry, and astronomy, should make anyone wary of pushing the argument too far. The important fact is that the scientific enterprise in a closed society is taken over by the state, for state ends and under state stimulus and penalties. The task of recruiting young people from the schools and universities for scientific work is performed by the party and state, and the organization of scientific societies and the rewarding of scientific work is under the same auspices. In short, the pursuit of science gets encased inside a bureaucracy and an elite, much as with the officers of an army. As long as the party and state give this elite encouragement and scope for its work, the work will continue tolerably. Where political purposes cut across scientific freedom, as was the case in Soviet genetics during the Stalin era, the work of science becomes stultified. If the strength of the state falters, and along with it the belief in the state's purposes, the morale of the scientists is bound to disintegrate and their work to suffer. Thus the fortunes of science under totalitarianism tend to rise and fall with the fortunes of the state and the incentives it furnishes to its scientific servants.

This contrasts with the case of an open society where science continues its work independently of the state and its power, and where (in fact) the fortunes of the state itself may be affected by the course of scientific thinking. True, the eighteenth- and nineteenth-century situation where the language of science was still close to the language of the ordinary educated man no longer applies. Science today speaks in esoteric symbols, and even in democracies scientists are likely to form themselves into an even tighter elite. But it is one that must remain independent of the state if its best work is to continue. It depends for recruitment upon the interest and morale of the young people in the schools, and when they feel that the life of the scientist is an unfree one they are likely to move into business or the professions instead. It depends for its creativeness upon the *élan* of men whose commitment is not to the state but to science itself and the human purposes it serves. Although they are an elite they are reluctant to function as a military one.

Thus the operation of science in an open society is a productive one, but only if the society continues open. Scientific discoveries depend on overturning the orthodoxies of received doctrine: but it is difficult to sustain habits of scientific skepticism in a society in which political conformism comes to be expected. Only in an open society can scientists undercut the basic preconceptions of their own disciplines. One trouble with scrutinizing science for subversion is that there is an irreducible element of subversiveness in scientific method itself. The creativeness of the scientific outlook lies exactly in the fact that it is no respecter of taboos.

Its method is at once bold and rational. At its best it takes nothing for granted; finds no hypothesis too daring to assume or too sacred to test; finds no past conceptual scheme too established to discard if generalization based on a different scheme fits the observations better. It is tedious and painstaking, ingenious in posing problems, bold in hunches, unsparing in making verifications. It is planful in that it looks backward at old failures and forward to new solutions. It is optimist, holding that there is nothing which will not someday yield to inquiry; it is economical, preferring the simplest formulations, opposing waste and futility.

I have tried to describe science in the phrase that Max Weber used of it: *Wissenschaft als Beruf*—science as discipline or calling. To a great degree this describes the place of science in a civilization like the American. There are some who in their overzealousness for science succeed only in distorting it. One group makes a cult of scientific neutrality. It makes of science not a method for handling experience and organizing observations but an end in itself—a dedicated, superhuman, almost inhuman way of life: in Nietzsche's words, "the last, most subtle asceticism." It regards scientific culture as the only important culture today, forgetting in its overrationalism that much of what men do and think is unreasoned, arising from the promptings of the unconscious self. It shades off into another group, which expects science to remake society with a conscious rationality of purpose.

It is true to a degree that in American society there is some obstruction offered to the free play of science, or better of technology, when new inventions would threaten existing investment and profitable patent pools, or create obsolescence too quickly. But while this has often been stressed by critics of the American economy it is only marginal, as the history of the unbroken dynamism of American science testifies. What is more crucial is that science finds itself operating in a society forced to spend billions for the discovery and manufacture of tools of war, but chary of smaller expenditures for health and education. One of the paradoxes about science, in America as elsewhere in the world, is that with all its vaunted use it has not done enough to release the social imagination (the exceptions are river-valley development, city planning, public-health work) or fortify the social will; and that the most advanced scientific methods in the realm of technology sometimes may be found side by side with surviving taboos in the realm of social thought and action.

But this is scarcely to be set down as a failure of science peculiar to America. It is part of a more widespread wave of anti-intellectualism, and a failure of commitment to humanist values on the part of the peoples of the world. It shows itself in two ways: first, in the stubbornness with which men hold on to the habit of war-making and the use of science for killing. (As Bertrand Russell once put it, "Overeating is not a serious danger, but overfighting is.") Second, in their failure to give full scope to scientific inquiry and freedom to scientists. Of all the political creeds the one that seemed to embrace science most avidly was that of the Communists; in America they taunted the businessmen with fearing to encourage the scientific method lest it undercut business power, and they laid claim to a synthesis of "science and society." The Marxist tradition, in arguing for a "scientific socialism," had asserted the unbroken web of physical and social science and had gone so far as to apply the dialectic method to science itself. Yet, if anything, science proved to be more crippled by the disease of orthodoxy in the Communist societies of Russia, China, and eastern Europe than in America, and the institutions of those countries were more subject to the arbitrary shiftings of the irrational will than in the relatively open American society.

The fact was that America, itself the child and product of the eighteenth-century Enlightenment, was committed to the values of science, freedom, and rationality, which the Enlightenment taught. In a letter to a young student, written in the closing year of the eighteenth century, Jefferson identified the struggle for freedom with the struggle for science:

> Great fields are yet to be explored to which our faculties are equal, and that to an extent of which we cannot fix the limits. I join you therefore in branding as cowardly the idea that the human mind is incapable of further advances. . . . While the art of printing is left to us, science can never be retrograde; what is once acquired of real knowledge can never be lost. To preserve the freedom of the human mind then and freedom of the press, every spirit should be ready to devote itself to martyrdom. . . . That the enthusiasm which characterizes youth should lift its parricide hands against freedom and science would be such a monstrous phenomenon as I cannot place among possible things in this age and this country.

One might expect the successive eras of discovery in American science to have carried this spirit of the Enlightenment further, but it doesn't follow and it didn't wholly happen. The impulses of the Enlightenment spent themselves and were succeeded by the impulses of technological advance and economic power. While in Jefferson's day the fight for science and the fight for freedom were parts of the same fight, they came to be split away: both were still carried on, but not in relation to each other. Moreover, the interior world of the scientists changed. What they learned in each generation became for those of the next generation not so much a heritage to be cherished but a tool to be used: in other words, as soon as science achieved its successive goals it made the transition and became technology. There followed another consequence: since a technology is to be used, science was no longer an idle curiosity, or even a form of objective knowledge, but a mode of action. The final step in this sequence of logic—or illogic—has proved ironic enough: since science is a mode of action, and since the world of action belongs centrally to the men of affairs, in government, business, and the armed services, it seemed to follow that the scientist ought to be judged by the values of these men of action and by their view of the prevailing social ethic. Hence scientists came to be assailed for their failure to conform to the dominant mood and policy of the time, as happened in the classical case of the security hearings of Robert Oppenheimer in 1954. Science thus helped to set in motion some of the anti-intellectual feeling which in the end threatened the survival of the scientific spirit itself and the freedom of scientists to pursue their unknown goal.

I speak of it as an unknown goal because the traditional image of the world of the scientist as a tidy and rational world, with all the loose ends fitting together, is no longer a true image—if it ever was. It is a world of bewildering duality that even the scientists themselves do not understand. In atomic physics, for example, the classical description in terms of Newtonian mechanics seemed no longer adequate to the scientists. The same phenomenon can be described from one standpoint as a wave of light, from another as a particle of matter; and while the two cannot logically be reconciled, functionally they fit the needs of scientific action and come closest to portraying the image of the world with which the scientists must operate.

Within such a frame the old dream of Descartes, that the individual's reason could move and shape a universe, left out of account the deep springs of the irrational within man himself. Einsteinian physics brought the observer back into the physical universe from which Newton left him out; but (if I may stretch the parallel unduly) a social science which brings the irrational impulses of the human being once more into the picture of the social universe is unlikely to expect the method of science to yield a progressive mastery of the social environment. Physics has shown man himself to be the measure of his universe. He must be the measure of his social universe as well, but the methods by which he can achieve a mastery according to this measure are even more complex than the quantum theory and more elusive than the principle of uncertainty in physics.

Some recognition of this may have kept Americans reluctant to accept an emerging elite of scientists based on the theory that superinventions must be the product of supermen. Nor is there, despite some doleful beliefs to the contrary, an emerging religion of science in America. It is true that science has done much to eat away the old structures of belief, and it is true that the old gods no longer rule over the American cosmos. But neither have the gods of science quite taken their place. So far from being wholly materialist, the scientific outlook did not prevent Dean Edmund Sinnott from speaking of "the biology of the spirit." So far from being wholly rationalist, science has led some of its most penetrating observers to a firmer belief in an unscientific religion which embodies some of the mystery that science has been unable to penetrate. To the Americans there is a duality about science, at once benign and baleful, which makes them wary of committing themselves wholly to it. They have learned that science can destroy as well as create, and they fear as well as embrace the miracles that seem to emerge from it.

Their crucial approach to science is manipulative. Compared with the Latin word *scientia* and the German *Wissenschaft,* the popular American word *know-how* distills the whole American approach, making sure to add the "how" to the "know." That is why science in America is not only a description of how things work (as it has been since Thales) but so quickly becomes a technique for making them work. It thrusts into the background the "why" of the philosophers and fails to ask the crucial question the Greeks asked: *To what end?* Science for Americans is a means toward ends never specifically delimited but taken for granted, perhaps because it is felt they are implicit in the technique itself. Thus a means which is limited to technology runs the danger of becoming a servant of the machine process.

For some Americans the potentials of science seem far darker exactly because of this failure to master the machine. It is the Destroyer that they see in science and not the Preserver. They sense that a science which came to liberate has left man not with a cosmos he can order but a vacuum from which he recoils and a predicament he cannot resolve. In the past a gloomy group of thinkers has argued from the laws of entropy that the world's energy is running down, and more recently another group has feared the destruction of the world through cosmic rays. But this sense of the seeds of destruction within the universe is not what troubles those who fear science today. They are troubled far more by what a science-created atomic cloud can do, or science-created radiological poison. In the case of some, at least, what was once the cult of science has become an antiscience panic.

Most Americans, however, with an organic optimism largely bred out of their experience of technological gains, are not troubled by these anxieties. They see science, and especially technology, as a means in the quest for an attainable good, and they feel certain that the good need never be explicitly defined but is implicit in the scientific quest. They regard the television eye and the electronic brain as proof that science has never lost the secret of mastery. They live within the realm of science and technology much as the American farmer once lived with the soil, as something close to their mood and experience. It is a medium in which they move much as they move in the air that they breathe.

Yet the gap between the scientist and the ordinary man, as they confront each other, is still an open one. The scientist is skeptical of every certainty except that of the method which makes him skeptical; he doubts everything except what enables his doubts to be productive of new formulations. He tries to rid himself of any sacred-cow beliefs in social institutions except for the open society without which he cannot breathe as a scientist. The common man, on the other hand, does seek certainties and is fearful that the scientist may destroy them. He wants a universe which is closed and comfortable, compact and finished. The universe of the scientist is still an expanding one, discontinuous and open. To keep it thus the scientist requires the willingness of an open society to let him follow his nose and give him the right to be wrong, both as scientist and as citizen.

3. Big Technology and Neutral Technicians

THE AMERICANS DID NOT develop modern machine technology first, but they have carried it furthest and shown the most marked affinity for it. The sway of the machine is less disputed in America than that of any other institution, including the science which made it possible, the capitalism which has organized its use, and the democracy governing the distribution of the power that flows from it. Unlike the democratic idea, which is assigned to the realm of what ought to be, the empire of Big Technology is an integral part of the daily living and thinking of Americans. They pride themselves on their "production miracles," much as the English used to call their islands the "workshop of the world."

The Big Technology has been for Americans what the Cross was for the Emperor Constantine: *In hoc signo vincas*. It set the pace for an impressively swift and thorough conquest of a new environment and of world leadership. The American has been a machine-intoxicated man. The love affair (it has been nothing less) between the Americans and their Big Technology has been fateful, for it has joined the impersonal power of the machine to the dynamism of the American character. As by some tropism of the spirit the Americans have followed out the logic of technology all the way. The world has seen civilizations based on diverse principles: on beauty and an equipoise of living, on otherworldliness and the reality of the supernatural, on close personal allegiance, on military prowess, on ascetic control of the self. But in each case the principle was embodied in the life and outlook of an elite group. Never before has the motive principle of a civilization spread so pervasively through all strata of its population, changing the lives of its ordinary people.

Veblen's ironic argument on the "merits of borrowing" (in *Imperial Germany and the Industrial Revolution*) is now familiar: that England, where the Industrial Revolution was first given scope, paid the "penalty for taking the lead" by falling behind in the later industrial race, and that the borrowing countries—America, Germany, Japan, Russia—forged ahead because they started on a higher technological level, without the cluttering bric-a-brac of customs and vested interests which Britain had developed. Toynbee, an Englishman himself, ruefully approaches the same problem in terms of "hosts" and "parasites," quoting J. B. S. Haldane's "A step in evolution in any animal group is followed by an evolutionary advance on the part of their parasites." (*A Study of History,* Vol. IV, p. 430.) Yet one cannot fail to notice that aside from the Americans the other "parasites" or "borrowers," whatever they be called, do not make the same effective use of their borrowings or hosts; and that the Germans, the Japanese, even the Russians still seem technologically like bright and enterprising younger brothers of the Americans, trying hard to catch up with his skills. There is more complexity in the machine achievement of America than is dreamed of in the philosophy of Veblen and Toynbee.

What I have said above about the social climate that favored the development of the borrowed science in America applies even more to the flowering of the borrowed seeds of technology. The resources, the separating ocean which at first spurred self-sufficiency and then served as a carrier of commerce, the lack of institutional hindrances, the tinkering skill of the craftsmen and the organizing skill of the managers, the lure of profit, the growing population and markets, the Promethean sense throughout of the mastery of a continent: it was in the frame of these influences that the Big Technology came into its empire in America.

This technological flowering came early in America's industrial revolution, so that even before the Civil War the movement of America toward industrial pre-eminence was already recognized in Europe: the testimony of Adam Smith and Malthus was that the American living standard even in their day was higher than the European for the consumption levels of the comparable classes. While the financial leadership of Britain was to continue until the turn of the century there was little doubt about where the industrial pre-eminence belonged. Not the least of the factors spurring America on this path was, as Ray Ginger has pointed out, the scarcity and mobility of American labor. Since labor was scarce, wages high, and the turnover great, an industry like American textiles had to introduce labor-saving devices rapidly and avail itself of what labor it could get, including unskilled female operators for the looms. It was a case of labor necessity mothering technical invention.

More than anything else, this pace of technological change is what gives America its revolutionary character today. It is idle to talk of a second or a third Industrial Revolution in America. The changes in production and motive power, in transport and communications, on the farm and in the city, in the air and on the ground and under the ground, have been so unremitting as to merit somewhat Trotsky's phrase, the "Permanent Revolution," which by a bold twist the editors of *Fortune* applied to the American technical and social scene. While the phrase is ripped out of its context of class meaning that Trotsky had intended, the vaguer idea of a continuing dynamism with far-reaching consequences still makes sense. The technological advance, through war and peace, through prosperity and slump, has been so constant as to become an element of the surrounding American atmosphere, easily taken for granted. The American is scarcely aware of the changes in the physical conditions of his living almost day to day; he takes a longer measurement of it by the span of generations when he compares his grandfather's daily life with his own, and that in turn with the life his grandchildren will live.

There have been brilliant American inventors, from the colonial craftsmen and the Yankee toolmakers, through Eli Whitney and Samuel Morse and Charles Goodyear, Thomas Edison and the Wright Brothers, to Lee De Forest, Leo Backeland, and Vladimir Zworykin. Yet the nature of the Big Technology cannot be understood in terms of the drama of the inventions; nor even in terms of the billions of energy units which the horsepower school of American technological greatness is fond of citing. For the transformations of power are only one phase of the characteristic pattern of American technology.

Item two is the use of precision machine tools, which have made possible the mass production not only of commodities but of machines themselves. Item three: the principle of interchangeable parts which allow the machine not only to be assembled but to be repaired with standardized ease. Item four: the "assembly line" or "belt line" method of processing an operation, first applied to iron and steel in the earlier foundries and to meat slaughtering in Cincinnati and Chicago, and then made famous by Ford in automobile manufacture. This has been modernized into a system of "continuous assembly," with conveyor belts and fork trucks both to feed the parts to the assembly line itself and also to take the finished product away; and with the whole factory laid out around the central assembly line, as around the heart arteries. Item five: the related principle of "automation," as applied to the process industries, especially to America's newest and greatest industrial segment, the chemical industries, in the form of the "continuous-flow" operation in chemical plants. In 1952 an entire napalm plant in Ohio required only four operators per shift, thus "missing 100 per cent automaticity by a hair," as a recent article on "The Factory of the Future" put it. Item six: the vacuum tube principle, which carries the automatic machine to its furthest reach in the "robot machines": already developed in the electronic calculators and the magnetic tape recorders, and likely to go much further in making the assembly line automatic and in revolutionizing not only the factory but the office as well.

Obviously not all of this is American. The development of precision machine tools is largely British, the use of power sources comes from the common Western technology, and some of the elements of the continuous-flow process were contributed by the German chemical industries. The roots of the whole mass-production process go back several centuries to the beginnings of the Industrial Revolution in Europe. American technology is the logical fulfillment of them.

One element the Americans have emphasized is the over-all principle that organizes all the technical elements—what used to be called "scientific management" and is still called the "managerial function." This has led to a high degree of resourcefulness and flexibility in both process and product, and the imaginative use of a technology that was available to all. Out of it has come an emphasis that would be impossible except where the principle of industrial organization is central: the focusing on productivity per man hour. This has become for Americans the measure and common denominator of all forms of technical progress. The strides in productivity were what amazed the Europeans most in the American production record; and when under the E.C.A. the Europeans expressed a desire to know more about the methods of American technology, they were asked by Paul Hoffman to send "productivity teams" to visit American factories and study their methods. This emphasis on a rising productivity has helped give Americans the self-confident *élan* which Nietzsche saw as a possible by-product of modern technology, and which accounts for much of the optimism and bounce in their character.

But where the Americans hold their foremost position most securely is in the machine skills. Whether they be those of scientist, inventor, machine-maker, engineer, factory planner and manager, or skilled worker, it is the skills that count most in a technology. In the abstraction of the "machine" we tend to forget that machines are created by human beings, organized and run by them. American technology is the collective possession, as it is the collective creation, of the American community. Individual inventors have been responsible for specific additions to the sum total of knowledge, tinkering, and experiment, but in every case they have stood on the shoulders of all their predecessors. Giedion, in his masterly summary of Western (especially American) technology, *Mechanization Takes Command* (1948), calls his book "anonymous history"—the story of what has been created by thousands of men whose names have in many cases been lost. This includes also the additional thousands whose ingeniously contrived ideas and gadgets never found practical use and are gathering dust in the files of the Patent Office, yet left some mark on the successful ones that follow them.

Today the task of the American inventor has become harder. If he is a lone wolf he must find a laboratory to work in, the capital to make his invention "practical" and "marketable," the factory to produce it, and the sales organization to sell it. The days are over when a couple of bicycle fixers called Wilbur and Orville Wright got some pointers for the wing design of their plane by watching the flight of birds and then built a foot-square windbox for a couple of dollars to test the wings for the flight across the sand dunes of Kitty Hawk. Plane designers today need a wind tunnel costing millions, capable of testing the stresses on planes under conditions of supersonic speed. Many inventions today are therefore the product of corporate employees working in corporate laboratories with corporate research funds, seeking new processes and products that can be subjected to corporate mass-production methods and marketed under a corporate patent monopoly by corporate distributive mechanisms to a vast mass market for corporate profit, with the inventor getting sometimes only his employee pay, and sometimes a small royalty payment added.

Americans call these collective skills underlying their technology, as they call technology itself, by the expressive word *know-how*. More and more there has been a transfer of this know-how from the many workers who used to tend the machines to the many machines that now need ever fewer workers to tend them. The crucial technological skills are now located in a small elite group of engineers and technicians who design the machines and lay out the continuous-process operations, and who know what to do when the machines break down. They are in the highest demand in industry, and every year the graduates of professional engineering schools are eagerly grabbed up by the corporations. The ultimate goal of this process is, of course, the Aldous Huxley nightmare of an auto factory or chemical plant with no worker on the assembly line, directed only by other machines which direct and feed themselves and need only taping by man's hand to set them on their course. The goal of complete automation may never be reached but it is always being approached more closely.

This process has not, as expected, resulted in the much mooted "technological unemployment." There have been two other results. One is the steady shifting of workers from the unskilled (the earth-lifting machines have almost wholly done away with the pick-and-shovel man) to the semiskilled, and from the semiskilled in turn to the skilled and highly skilled, or the technicians. Since the latter group remains small, the second result has been a further shift of workers out of the industrial occupations themselves into the merchandizing, distributive, and white-collar groups of the corporations, the professions, and the government and Army bureaucracies.

Thus by an ironic twist of history the American industrial mass civilization which seemed about to conscript the whole population into machine occupations is actually becoming something very different. It is emerging as a civilization with small specialized industrial groups, with a growing population of machines and a dwindling population of machine tenders, and with an ever larger portion of the population in nonindustrial (what Veblen used to call "pecuniary") occupations. Thus the reliance of industry on the workers is growing less, and its reliance on the machines themselves is growing greater.

As a consequence the competitive strategy of corporations is also shifting. It is less important now to keep wages down than to use the new machines in increasing productivity per man hour. And it is less important to be near a supply of cheap labor power than it is to have control of a patent tool, either to keep one's competitors at a disadvantage or to control the use of the patents by them and to collect royalties for their use. The Big Technology made the strategy of patent control the crucial strategy of American business; but it did not wipe out the fact that patent tools and patent rights themselves have little meaning except as broken-off segments of the collective heritage of community know-how.

Given these changes, and the changing patterns of work in America (which I shall discuss in the next section), there is a problem which has baffled students of American society, especially those who come to it from the experience of European history. Here (they argue) is a working population cut off from the soil, severed from its tools and from the idea of work as craft and calling: why does it not become the victim of revolutionary movements and demagogues? Granted that the unique conditions of American history have played hob with the idea of a self-conscious revolutionary proletariat, why has not America retraversed the experience of the Roman Empire, whose landless, rootless, tool-less population was used by adventurist leaders? Or the similar experience of Hitler's Germany?

Behind these questions there is the running theme of alienation and its political effects, which has been emphasized in the literature of Socialism and psychiatry from Marx to Erich Fromm. Most Americans, especially the industrial and white-collar classes, have been alienated from some crucial life experiences—from the soil, from independent enterprise, from the ownership of tools, from the sense of craft and the dignity of work, from the feeling of relation to the total product. One might expect this to turn the American into the "formless" man whom Nietzsche dreaded and whose emergence in the modern machine world Ortega y Gasset has described, and thus into easy material for either revolutionary or reactionary adventurers.

The catch is in the failure to see that men uprooted from one kind of social and institutional soil can become rooted in another. The loss of some of the old life values may affect the long-range survival of the culture, but what counts for the cohesion of a culture in the generations immediately ahead is whether people have (or think they have) what their culture has taught them to value. While the American has been alienated by the machine from his old role as independent farmer-artisan-entrepreneur, his culture still has a strong hold on him. The loss of a sense of independence in the productive processes has been replaced by a feeling of well-being in consumption and living standards. The pull of property, no longer in tools or productive land but in consumers' goods; the sense of power and pleasure in the means of sight and sound and movement placed at his disposal by the communications revolution; the glorying in what makes the world of drama and entertainment accessible; the whole range of popular culture; the feeling of access to new gradients of income and experience: these form the new soil in which the American has found new roots.

The values of income, consumption, status, and popular culture are a different set of values from those of soil and craft and small-scale productive property, and in that sense the whole ground tone of American civilization has changed under the Big Technology. But the point is that in their own way they are values, not emptiness or formlessness. Even more strikingly, it is the Big Technology that has raised living standards, created leisure, carried through the communications revolution, and set the conditions for the new popular culture. That is to say, it is the machine itself that has cut American industrial, white-collar, and professional workers away from the machine and has transferred their interest and life energies from the making of goods to the making of money with which to buy and enjoy the goods.

In this sense Big Technology has been a conservative rather than a revolutionary political force. This runs counter to Veblen's classic theory that the "instinct of workmanship" has been left in the trusteeship of the industrial workers and engineers, and that the unremitting "discipline of the machine process" is bound to undercut the "price system," whose values are at variance both with technology and the instinct of workmanship. Veblen worked out his thesis with an impressive and subtle detail. He even took account of the suction force of "leisure-class" (capitalist and consumption) values on the "underlying population," while contending that it is more than counterbalanced by the daily contact with the material and tangible and the daily submission to precision techniques. He read into the machine process, however, a psychological potency for inducing political skepticism which it does not seem to possess. Russia was industrialized under a Communist regime and Japan under a militarist one, yet in neither case did the introduction of Big Technology shape minds prepared to question the bases of authoritarianism. America was industrialized under capitalism, but the minds of the machine workers have been more concerned with their place in capitalist production and their share of capitalist distribution than with questioning the power and glory of the system which carried industrialism through.

In fact, under every system of power it is not the industrial or white-collar worker—subject to precision techniques or engineering or calculating techniques—who questions the basis of power but the intellectual dealing in ideas, values, and other intangibles. The machine process tends to make the mind more conservative by limiting the sense of personal reliance and the play of the imagination. To the worker accustomed to the tangibles of the machine, the intellectual who deals with ideas seems "up in the air" and therefore dangerous. The machine tender is likely to seek only relaxation from the machine's rigors and a larger share of the enjoyment which the machine's products place within his reach.

The sense of craftsmanship that was spread widely through the whole of the earlier agrarian-artisan society has, under the Big Technology, been specialized with the group of technicians. From Saint-Simon in nineteenth-century France to Veblen and James Burnham in twentieth-century America, students have written about the technicians ("engineers," "managers") as the carriers of social transformations. There was a brief moment during the Great Depression when the technocracy movement seemed to promise or threaten a social system run by what Veblen had called a "soviet of engineers," in terms of energy (ergs) rather than prices, profits, and wages. But technocracy, with its hopes and fears, was only a spluttering brief candle. Of more long-range importance is the "managerial revolution" which has brought about in every industrialized society a reshuffling of class lines and a shift of power. In America it would be farfetched to say that the technicians have taken power, but they have come to represent a fairly well-defined group with some marks of an elite.*

The technicians feel themselves the creators and guardians of the community's productive skills. Once the men who made the products had this sense of guardianship. Now it is the men who design and make the machines and machine tools, lay out the factories, and plan the industrial and plant operations. It is this monopoly of skills and sense of guardianship rather than any special status or power that give them the character of an elite.

I speak here, in the first instance, of the industrial technicians, but for some purposes we may stretch the category of "technician" and bring in the organizers and managers from other areas as well. There are problems of definition and analysis here which have sometimes led to confusion. When Burnham talked of the "managerial revolution," he included those who deal with people as well as those who deal with things, but the two are worth separating. In industry, for example, there are the engineers who deal with machines and production, and the executives who deal with people. Both groups may be called technicians and both may be called managers. But as technicians their skills are different, since one group is technically skilled in designing or directing the actual processes of production, while the other group is technically skilled in the business aspects of the corporation; as managers, one group is skilled in manipulating Nature and co-ordinating the tangible processes that result in making goods, while the other organizes the intangibles and manipulates men and their minds.

Both groups are integral to American life today, but while one has developed in the shadow of Big Technology, the other has developed in the shadow of the corporate empires. The two differ also in power terms. An "engineer" or "technician" usually holds an intermediate place in the corporate hierarchy, while the "managers" or "executives" are on the top rungs. When C. Wright Mills speaks of the "power elite" he includes the "chief executives" but omits the engineers and technicians. This illustrates a tendency on the part of some American observers, following Veblen, to stress the manipulative and power aspects of the new managerial groups, while they underplay their technical aspects. You can, of course, squeeze a good deal of irony out of the paradox that the top men in industry actually know relatively little about the technical

* I am here primarily concerned with the technician as engineer, who deals with things and materials. For the technician as businessman or "chief executive" of a corporation, see Ch. V, especially Sec. 2, "The Rise and Decline of the Titan," and Sec. 3, "The Corporate Empires." For a further discussion of political technicians, see Ch. VI, Sec. 4, "The Party System and the Voter," and Sec. 6, "The Governmental Managers," and for the military technicians, see Ch. XII, Sec. 4, "Landscape with Soldiers."

processes of production and get paid mainly for manipulating and coordinating men. They can therefore shift almost at will from one industry to another—from autos to cigarettes to electronics—and they become thereby the truly mobile men of American society.

Yet this should serve as a clue to what I am myself stressing here—the central neutrality of the technician (whether engineer, manager, or executive), in the sense of his dissociation from passion, commitment, or value other than his own skill in execution. The very fact that an executive can shift, without a break in his career, from cracker-making to radio-making is a sign of this neutrality. Equally a sign of it is the fact that since the executives don't own the business they manage, the profits and losses and risks are not their own. To be sure, they possess power and relish it, but even their power may be called a neutral one: it is a disembodied power that can be linked now with one enterprise, now with another. Not only the engineers but the executives as well thus have a kind of neutrality, in the sense of seeing themselves as executors of interests and purposes not their own. They have not taken over the governing functions, nor is there any sign that they want to or can. They have concentrated on the fact of their skills rather than on the uses to which their skills are put. The question of the *cui bono* the technician regards as beyond his own competence. With his training in specialization and the division of labor, he is the more inclined to leave the values of politics to the politician, war to the general, beauty to the artist, and religion and morals to the preacher.

The role of the Neutral Technician thus casts its shadow over the whole present era. It becomes the Great Withdrawal, or—as Erich Kahler puts it—a kind of nihilism of values along with an exaltation of techniques. "What is the job you want done," asks the technician, "and I'll do it." Many worriers about American life have worried about commercialism in art and literature and thought, but often what seems a sell-out for money is as likely to be surrender to the technician's sense of neutrality: the feeling that the technique carries its own ethic with it and that the use of technics is not to be judged by a system of ethics outside it.

One can speak of the varieties of technical experience in America. They have obscured the fact of a unity of outlook which cuts across them, whose core is the overriding sense of technical assurance and neutrality. The engineers, corporate managers, government administrators and civil servants, scientists, Army officers, lawyers, writers for the movies and the radio, ad writers, public-relations men: however diverse they may be in other respects, they are all there to do a job whose shape and purposes are determined by others. Thus the Federal government workers are required by the Hatch Act to refrain from any political activity: America has gone much further than Britain, for example, in making political eunuchs of its civil service. A similar neutrality is coming to be expected of the growing centers of transport and communication. In the case of policemen, for example, even the right to join unions has been challenged. In the case of the military services the doctrine of neutrality is of great moment, since the swelling of military forces and of the war segment of the economy has given the officer class more power than ever in American history.

The episode of the dismissal of General MacArthur in 1951 illuminated the crisis of technical neutrality. On the one hand, the principle of civilian control of the military had been challenged by a great soldier in an important area of policy. On the other hand, much of MacArthur's popular support came from the implicit belief in the technical division of labor: since MacArthur was a general (it was reasoned) he ought to know about war and peace; therefore President Truman's effort to control him was civilian meddling. Which is to say, again, that the technic carries its own ethic.

The situation of the scientists sets them apart from the other technicians. Given their freedom to work, American scientists have paid little heed to what is done socially with their discoveries. Scientific detachment, which began as a shield against entangling alliances that might hamper the single-minded concentration on scientific work, became an isolating barrier. Objectivity became quietism and withdrawal, disinterestedness turned into uninterestedness, scientific method into social apathy. The scientists' pride of specialization buttressed the wall he had built between what was being fashioned in the realm of science and what was happening in the "unscientific" realm of human relations.

It took the atom bomb to shatter that wall and jolt American scientists into a sense of responsibility about the new world they had been so instrumental in shaping. Perhaps nothing short of the vision of atomic death—"the good news of damnation"—could have had such an effect. The American physicists became men who have known sin and cannot erase the memory. The sense of shock and guilt led some to turn their emphasis to the life sciences, led others into the cause of "world government," still others to a group vigil for civilian control of atomic energy and for the maintenance of an open society in the face of the "security" demands of the new war weapons. Almost alone among the technicians, the scientists grappled with the ethical consequences of technics.

A study by Meier of the political attitudes of scientists (in the *Bulletin of Atomic Scientists*) showed the engineers tending on the whole toward conservatism, the chemists toward the middle of the road, and the physicists toward the liberal and radical. Allowing for the vagueness of the political terms, the study is worth noting. It suggests that where science approaches most closely to the applied sciences (mainly engineering, since chemistry is borderline) the neutral role of the technician asserts itself; but with theoretical science, especially in physics, the scientist asks questions about the uses to which his work is put. For the work of theoretical science is not a reflection of the machines: it precedes them. It is work involving a high degree of imaginativeness and severe logic. Like other men of ideas, the scientists are not content, with Hamlet, "to eat the air, promise-crammed." Science and technology are revolutionary only in the sense that they have extended the realm of the socially possible to keep pace—although always at some remove—with the sense of the technically possible.

But turning back to the technicians, what makes their place in America so contradictory is that, despite the stretching of social possibility by technology itself, the technicians for the most part remain a guild of neutral artificers. They have brought a universe of living standards and popular culture within reach of a population from whose choices and dilemmas they have cut themselves off.

4. Work and the Automatic Factory

In few respects has American culture been as radically transformed as in the relation of the machine to the industrial process, and of the worker to the machine and the job. One thinks back to Emerson's "the office of America is to liberate" and wonders how the assembly line fits into this office, and whether those who tend the machines and whose work is set to their pace have been liberated.

Many of the generalizations about work, as about other aspects of life in the Old Society of Jefferson and Jackson, and even of Lincoln and Bryan, are no longer true in the New Society. The greatest change has come about in the "gospel of work." Except for the ante-bellum South there were no Greek notions in America of work as a badge of dishonor, something belonging to a lower caste while the elite cultivates the mind or the graces of living. Freshly wrested from the frontier wilderness, the American land was a living reminder of the relation between work and survival; and as America grew in wealth it was a reminder also of the relation of work to its immediate rewards.

And to ultimate rewards also, for the religious spirit of America's Protestant sects reinforced the practical reasons for work by bringing God's reasons to bear as well. The American bourgeois spirit, which existed in its purest form where economic man met religious man, regarded idleness as sinful and the way of work as the good way. "Work

. . . while it is day," said Jesus to his disciples. "For the night cometh, when no man can work." The American moralists found other ways of saying this, but the utilitarian reasons were strongly buttressed by religious sanctions. In the whole calendar of economic virtues, from Franklin's Poor Richard and Samuel Smiles and Richard Parton to Andrew Carnegie and Henry van Dyke, work was the primal source of all the others. Even the rich who did not have to work felt uneasy when they did not, and a life of complete leisure was more likely to be regarded as parasitism in the context of the Puritan tradition than anywhere else in the capitalist world. The great folk myths of America too, which expressed the proletarian spirit as Poor Richard expressed the bourgeois spirit—the stories of Paul Bunyan and Mike Fink, of Casey Jones and John Henry—are myths of mighty workers and their work prowess.

But as the myth has it, John Henry broke his heart when he tried to compete with the monstrous strength of the steam crane. I take this as an allegory of the dehumanizing of work in consequence of Big Technology.

The gospel of hard work took long to die. There has been no American chronicler of the "condition of the working classes" to equal Engels or the Hammonds for the condition of the English. But it is clear that Blake's "dark, Satanic mills" do not apply to the factory experience of America, where labor was scarce, technical innovation moved fast, and "scientific management" had an early start. The American factories in the early nineteenth century were very different from their European counterparts; the early factory owners tried to avoid the excesses of the English and the European experience, including long hours, child labor, poor pay, and scabrous working and living conditions. Eli Whitney's factories were relatively comfortable places, with decent housing provided for the workers in the vicinity. The Lowell mills were models of comfort, and the girls who came to work in them were drawn to the work in preference to the less interesting and more menial jobs of domestic work and teaching. A few years' work at Lowell provided a young girl of good family with money enough so that she could bring a respectable dowry and a dignified background to her prospective husband. The idea behind the early American factories, as Mitchell Wilson has pointed out, was that the American worker was a dignified human being entitled to decent treatment.

The panic of 1837 changed the picture, driving many millowners and manufacturers to the wall and giving them a reason for treating the workers in a more exploitative way. The new tides of immigration, by providing a large labor force whose living standards were lower, made the situation worse. Toward the end of the century there were "sweatshops" in American garment manufacture, there was child labor, and until 1923 there was a seventy-two-hour week in the steel industry. Yet despite these changes the old Protestant-bourgeois work ethic died in America for other reasons than applied to the dirty, crowded factories and the long, exhausting hours of the English Industrial Revolution.

One might say that the old work ethic died because the work became dehumanized and joyless, but this would miss the fact that joylessness in itself might strengthen the Puritan work ethic, making work an end in itself. What did happen was that, with the growth of the big corporation, work became depersonalized; and with the change in the immigrant experience and composition, hard work became associated with the foreign-born, the Negroes, the illiterates, and the underlying social strata. The atmosphere of the Big Money and the knowledge that so much of the income comes by way of what the workers consider "easy rackets," all conspired to strip work of its incentives. In the thinking both of the corporate employers and the trade-union members work came to be expressed mainly in money terms. It was cut off from a sense of creativeness and lost much of its dignity and meaning. The idea of the dignity of work died not in the "dark, Satanic mills" but in the well-lighted, ingeniously laid out, scientifically organized assembly-line plants, and in the spacious headquarters and offices of the great American corporations. What has replaced it on the employers' side is the ethic of efficiency and profit and on the workers' side the ethic of security and success.

There is a triple process of transformation that has taken place in the American work pattern. The symbol of one phase was the white-collar worker; the removal of work, for an ever-growing section of those "gainfully employed," from industrial operations themselves to the stockroom, the fileroom, the office pool, the salesroom, the promotion and advertising office. This was part of the more general bureaucratization of economic life. The functional split in the work patterns carried with it a psychological split as well, with the white-collar worker clinging to his sense of differentiated status and of superiority to the industrial worker. The second phase of the change was the assembly line, which came to dominate an ever-larger segment of what workers were still left in contact with the industrial processes themselves. The assembly line arose because of the need for connecting isolated machines and workers: this need was precisely the point at which industry became bureaucratized. The outcry against the assembly line misses the fact that a bureaucracy is the natural and necessary outgrowth of modern technology. The third, applying to those who still worked at the stationary machines and were the "machine tenders" proper, was monotony and anonymity, the carrying of the process of subdividing industrial operations so far that the worker became himself almost an interchangeable part in a factory world of interchangeable parts.

White-collar work, assembly-line work, anonymity: these were the new work patterns which transformed the American work attitudes.

The mechanical skill and curiosity of American workers have continued unabated. In a nation of tinkerers, the American youngster as he grows up delights in taking apart and putting together whatever machines and motors he can lay his hands on. The drive to understand how and why machines work is the impulse behind much of the American talent for technology. It was this impulse that furnished much of the incentive for the early toolmakers and inventors. Nor has *homo faber* died out in America, whether in the small factory, the school machine shop, or the home basement workshop. But these are residual areas in which the old sense of craftsmanship still finds scope. It is not applied as fervently to work done for impersonal corporations and invisible employers with whom the worker has no direct relation.

Life on "the job" tends to be a joyless life, squeezed dry of any zest in work. On most jobs the frame of the day is set by the time clock. On the assembly line especially, as in the auto factory, time is the master. A worker who cannot keep pace with the speed at which the line is moving disarranges the whole process and throws the work of everyone else out of gear. He is enclosed in a space out of which he can move only by invading the working space of his neighboring worker. Hour after hour he uses the same muscles in the same motions at the same operations. Armed with his power tools for setting the parts in place and tightening them, he is himself a machine using a machine for assembling another machine. The tensions on his nervous system are great, but while he must concentrate on his work he does not become absorbed with it, since neither his creative faculties nor his imagination are caught.

The crux of craftsmanship is the satisfaction of seeing the relation between the hard and monotonous detailed work and the form and quality of the finished product. This means understanding how the details are put together: even though the craftsman may work at only one segment, he must see and understand the organization and planning of the whole. The American worker gets little chance at this. Not only does he work at only a fragment, about which he cares little, of a whole he rarely sees: he also is cut off from any participation in the planning. It was therefore (as Roger Burlingame has pointed out) entirely characteristic that—except for a few top scientists—those who worked on the atom bomb project should have been unaware of its nature. This was, to a heightened degree of deliberate secrecy, the logical expression of the anonymous place the worker has in the industrial process even when no secrecy is intended. The worker, who had been torn away from the American land by Big Technology and from the ownership of his tools by large-scale capitalism, has now been torn also from his total product and denied a chance to build his personality around the processes at which he works. The idealized profile of the worker in the dithyrambic book by Ernst Jünger, *Der Arbeiter* (1932), which made so great a stir in a Germany on the brink of National Socialism, was a portrait of the modern type-figure of power who is at once planner and creator and is impelled by a mystical demiurge to the shaping of the future world. This would strike no chord in the men who work and live in Detroit or Duluth, or in the "industrial triangle" between New York, Chicago, and St. Louis.

There is little in the American industrial or white-collar worker either of Ruskin's medieval craftsman or Jünger's romantic proletarian demiurge. His life on the job is flat and two-dimensional, contained between the wage system and the price system. As a consequence of having himself been made a means rather than an end in the work relation he has in turn made his job a means rather than an end.

This has happened even while the American corporate managers have been paying considerable attention to the worker and his morale. Where England's contribution to the arts of management was the factory system itself, and Germany's was the early introduction of social legislation, America's managerial genius showed itself in "scientific management" and "human relations in industry." From Frederick W. Taylor's early time-and-motion studies to the most recent work of Elton Mayo the aim has been a double one: to keep the worker cheerful and happy (scientific managers speak of workers' "morale"—a term otherwise reserved for the wartime mood of soldiers and civilians) and at the same time to get the highest productivity per man hour out of the worker-machine combination.

The earlier scientific managers tended to think of the factory mainly as a physical arena for efficiency operations. Their layout of plants and their organization of line-and-staff functions, departmentalizing, unit size of operations, and even the fatigue factors of the job were masterpieces of forethought. But the later managers noted anxiously that workers were sullen, resisting the best-intentioned managerial layouts and reorganizations, and that—for all the ingenuity spent in keeping them happy—they had no basic interest in their work. The emphasis therefore shifted from the factory as a managerial arena to the factory as a society.

An American factory is more complex than appears on the surface. What seems a single assembly line contains a whole network of subassemblies, conveyer belts, and unloading and loading systems. And what seems a uniform group of workers is a society made up of subgroups, income and power hierarchies, status clusters. True, the job has been separated from the bar, the ball game, and the TV set, and once the worker is off the job he turns to what will recreate and recharge him. Yet almost half of his waking hours are spent on the job. The factory is thus, next to the family group, the most constant society that Americans know during the major part of their adult years. Here friendships are formed and maintained, here a man's endurance is measured against others. Here he seeks and gets his sense of prestige and status, here his rivalries are centered and his hopes or heartbreak over merit and promotion. Each man stands here in some kind of relation to an authority over him (foreman, inspector, department head, plant superintendent, owner-boss) and in many cases to subordinates or apprentices under him. The prestige divisions of the world outside the factory—between ethnic and religious groups, between native and foreign-born, between skilled and unskilled, educated and illiterate—find here their mirror and expressions.

Thus the Big Technology has gone beyond techniques and has become a principle of social order. The earlier idea, as Roethlisberger puts it, was that "all you have to do is produce, and human problems will take care of themselves." But the personnel managers and their bosses had to learn to reckon with the factory as a society. Through pamphlets and promotion material, through special courses, through social events organized for both the rank and file and the executives, they tried to link the personality of the worker with the corporation. They even reached back into the high schools, distributing literature and films to prepare the potential employee for identifying himself with the company.

How hungry some of the workers are for this kind of recognition of their human quality is shown by the work of Roethlisberger and Dickson in the Hawthorne experiments, under the guidance of Elton Mayo. In an effort to isolate the factors affecting productivity he kept shifting one factor after another, only to find a progressive increase of productivity with each shift. One conclusion has been that the workers—semi-skilled and white-collar girls—worked better because the interest shown by the investigators in their jobs and them gave them a renewed sense of the importance of both. Yet the problem was not so simple. In one of the Hawthorne studies—that of the bank wiring room—there was the same condition of the observer and his interest in the work, yet there was no increase in productivity. Mayo himself did not seem to have resolved this paradox, but Conrad Arensberg and others have suggested an explanation. The bank wiring room operated inside the ordinary channels of supervision and management; on the other hand, the girls in the test room, as part of the experimental procedure, helped make the decisions about their own working conditions.

If this key is the valid one* it has far-reaching implications. As long as the worker is treated as a physical object, as only a factor in production, the efforts to give him recognition and status will be futile. True, he reacts positively to the Hawthorne type of experiment, which deeply affected American personnel work. But eventually the feeling of being noticed peters out, and what was once special recognition becomes the expected and routine treatment. This is why wage-incentive and profit-sharing plans work only up to a certain point. Before long the incentive situation becomes the expected situation. In the end the worker must find recognition and status in his own feeling about the work he does, and if the work is trivial and he has no hand in setting it he will never feel that he has any dignity in it. That was the importance of the bank wiring study since it showed that what the worker wants is not (like a spoiled child) only some attention but the chance of a mature person to make his own decisions and set the frame of his work.

The sympathetic interest in the worker may in the end seem only synthetic to him, because the primary relation on the job is a wage-and-profit relation. Hence the "industrial-welfare offensive" always contends with the suspicion that the corporation is using its welfare plans as a dollars-and-cents device and not as a social end. A number of observers have written skeptically of the "harmony-of-interests" premise underlying the corporate "welfare offensive," whether in the form of employee representation plans or shops' councils, company unions or corporate insurance plans; and the response of many unions to the growing shift from "practical" to "sophisticated" conservatism on the part of the corporate employers has also been skeptical. Yet many unions are going along with the trend, for the simple reason that it makes sense to the workers in human terms, as well as in dollars and cents. The "welfare corporation" is emerging as a natural corollary of the "welfare state." It must be noted, however, that whether the union's attitude is sympathetic or militant, whether the premise is class harmony or class conflict, both flow from the transformation of the work relation and the alienation of the worker from his job.

Men are lined up in the closed world of the factory as items in cost accounting, along with the machine and materials, the plant, and the distributing mechanism. Rarely is the worker used to the hilt of his capacity; it is in the failure to give him scope for his full abilities that the tragic failure of Big Technology comes. Even when the corporate job gives him a chance to develop or use responsibility, the worker is

* There is still considerable doubt about this. For a brilliant study of the whole problem, see Daniel Bell, *Work and Its Discontent* (1956).

unlikely to seek it. Sensing that the crucial decisions about his work are made by others, he feels no responsibility and little creativeness in it. As for the trade-unions, even when they have fought militantly for workers' rights, they have interpreted those rights narrowly, as claims to a larger share of the income from the product. The crucial fact about a job has become the money payment, and the jobs are measured against one another almost wholly in terms of money rather than of satisfaction or craftsmanship in the work. The top-level people in the trade-unions tend to concentrate on the big economic issues, leaving the problems of human relations to be worked out on the floor of the plant by the local representatives. On that immediate level there have been, as William F. Whyte has pointed out, a number of situations in which management and the union officers have succeeded in finding substitute satisfaction for the lost sense of craftsmanship. Again this has happened mainly where the worker has been drawn into some of the decisions on the technical, economic, and social problems of the plant.

In the absence of such efforts the idea of work tends to become on both sides the idea of a job—that is to say, a dollar relation rather than a human relation. The worker knows that when his responses are not as alert or his stamina as great, he will be discarded, with pension provisions if he is lucky, but that with or without them he will feel useless. If he is a Negro there will be a limited market for his ability or training. The decline from the idea of "work" to the idea of a "job" measures the falling away from the work pattern of everything except the pecuniary factor.

The job idea is an important one for Americans. In one sense it means any technical task to be finished and disposed of: war, a political campaign, a book to be read or written, a household chore, a gangster's assignment. A good executive in any area disposes of people with dispatch and then sweeps both his desk and his mind clear of encumbrances. The periods of unemployment, when for millions there were no jobs to be had, gave an added febrile value to "the job"; but it was a value deriving not from a sense of the fitness of the work but from the fear of having none at all. The job becomes mainly an earthwork thrown up against insecurity. The primary necessity is that the job continuity should not be broken; the primary question is the amount of take-home pay. The continuity of the pay envelope is the pay-off.

While the amount of pay and the degree of security are the primary questions about the job, they are not the only ones. Elmo Roper adds from his polling experience four other elements that count for the workers: whether the job overworks them, whether merit is rewarded, whether there is a chance for advancement, and whether they find the job "interesting." It is worth noting that all except the last can be translated into terms of burden and pay, even the reward of merit and the chance for advancement. The results of Roper's polling of a cross-section of Americans on their attitudes toward their jobs show two out of three (64.7 per cent) finding them "really interesting," the rest either lukewarm or apathetic. However vague the question, it is worth noting that men were more satisfied than women, whites more than Negroes, city workers more than those in small towns and on farms, professional and executive people more than wage-earners, and the prosperous (87.2 per cent) more than the poor (48 per cent).

It is not so much that the Americans are (as Mills would have it) "cheerful robots," as that they live in a twilight world between a sense of loss and a sense of resigned acceptance. The acceptance emerges clearly from the Roper figures, provided we note that it diminishes as the job decreases in pay and status. The sense of loss is not so clear. Two out of three (62 per cent) felt that they were neither "ideally" nor "miserably" adjusted to their job and company, but felt split or apathetic about it. When asked whether, in starting their working life over again, they would choose a different trade or occupation, 57 per cent answered that they would, and only one out of three (31 per cent) that they would choose the same. Just possibly this may be an expression of dynamism, but more likely it is an indictment of the work life Americans have. Many felt their mistake had been made in not getting enough education in their youth. Many also felt certain that their sons would do better than they did—again the dual expression of dynamism and a sense of loss.

To be sure, one must be wary of taking these figures at their face value. Many workers may say they are dissatisfied with their jobs because they are *supposed* to be dissatisfied: that is the self-image they have. The fact that they don't change their jobs more often, in a relatively fluid labor market, may be the effective commentary on their supposed dissatisfaction. There are frequent complaints from management that it cannot find enough workers with skill, interest, and curiosity to fill the needed foremen's jobs. There is also the fact that many workers prefer repetitive and monotonous jobs exactly because they are undemanding and do not stretch them too much. But this lack of initiative on the part of the worker may itself be the most damning of evidence of the deterioration of the whole work relation which I have described.

"Where your treasure is, there will your heart be too." To those who complain that American workers do not have their hearts in their jobs, one may suggest that they do not feel the treasure of their creativeness to be there. It is only in wartime that the American worker is asked to devote himself and his work to a larger goal than individual gain and profit. The old question of nonpecuniary incentives is raised sharply where the psychic drives of people have been split away from their work lives. The talent for organizing that Americans have shown, the time sense and the sense of timing, the ability to break a job into small parts and reassemble them into a working whole, the feeling for effective structure shown in the distributive mechanism, add up in the end to a manipulativeness of the spirit. They are an expense of genius (for the collective managerial talent of America is nothing less) in the pursuit of ends that rarely get below the surface of the personality. With all the vaunted organization of the plant and office, what is left out is a feeling of growth and fulfillment for those involved. Whether Americans are happy and expressive, and to what extent, are moot points. But what is not moot is the fact that they pursue their happiness and get their expressiveness principally away from their jobs.

In the case of a minority there is a powerful impulse for advancement which pushes them to hard work, often to extra work beyond the call of the job: but the aim here is success, not growth and development. But for most the work on the job is so monotonous that they are incapable of generating the extra energy or imagination on the job which form part of the great American work myth. It is in this sense that a technological system so magnificent at producing and distributing commodities runs the danger of flattening out the men themselves.

How much of all this has been changed by "automation," which is the latest and perhaps the culminating phase of the American technological revolution? The essence of automation is the replacement of the worker who operates the machine by the machine that operates machinery. During the earlier phases of the continuing revolution the elements of production were broken down and assigned to machines that had to be regulated and controlled by workers. In the case of automation the productive system has developed built-in mechanisms of regulation and control. Its ultimate goal is the almost workerless factory, office, and salesroom. The characteristic of the old machine was its repetitive capacity: raw materials were fed into it while it repeated the same operation endlessly, but it had to be overseen and its products had to be assembled. What is fed into the automatic machine is not raw material but *information.* The machine then operates by the principle of *feedback,* and the results are communicated to the entire process, whether it be the generation of electric power, or the mixing of chemicals, or the making of synthetic fertilizers, soaps, and detergents, or the numberless uses of telecommunication.

Since the principle involved is similar to the mechanism of the human nervous system and even of the human brain, these machines have been spoken of as "thinking" machines, and some commentators have been moved to suggest that the machine can now replace the human brain, while the brain is little more than a machine. Such an approach misses the difference between machinery and the human spirit, between the brain itself and what the brain contrives in order to rid itself of routine burdens, and it is therefore itself a symptom of the age of automation. What concerns us here, however, is not so much the fallacy that the machine can duplicate man, but the fact that the new machinery is coming to function without the men and women who used to watch over the operation of the old machines.

The old Malthusian fear—that there would be a surplus of population over the available food supplies (and therefore jobs)—has been replaced by an anxiety about whether there will be enough jobs (and therefore food supplies) to go around when the machines have taken over the empire of industry. In the mid-1950s America was still exploring the answer to this problem. But in essence it was no different a problem from the one that had faced Americans throughout their technological revolutions. There had always been anxiety about the displacement of men by machines, and in the end the machines had always created new jobs by broadening the scope of the industrial process, by creating new income and new consumer demands, and by shifting the emphasis to distributive, social-welfare, and leisure-time services. The consequences of automation were likely to be of the same sort, but to a higher degree. Americans would need a large number of technicians to plan, make, and drive the machines. They would need fewer workers in industrial production and more in meeting the leisure needs that would flow from the reduced working day. The economy was shifting from one organized around the use of natural resources and human labor to an economy organized around the use of time and the access of more people to what the culture offered.

As another consequence of automation, Americans are looking forward to the end of drudgery-on-the-job. The trivial tasks are being turned over wholly to the machines, without the need for the strained pace-setting of the assembly line and the attention it required. What remains are what Adam Abruzzi calls the "distinguished" as against the "undistinguished" jobs—the planning for what the new machines will do, the study of the situations in which they are likely to break down, the imaginative and the contemplative challenge of thinking out the total design for work and leisure of which the machines form a part. An era was opening in which the worker might again have restored to him his skill and responsibility, and the control of his working pace.

The dogma that idleness is somehow a sin was part of an age that is passing. An age of automatic machines would put a premium on leisure in which the mind would not be idle.

This has already transformed America into a nation of amateurs. If one phase of the work revolution was summed up in "automation," another was expressed in the phrase "do-it-yourself." Nourished by the fact of the vanishing domestic servant and of skyrocketing costs, "do-it-yourself" was primarily an effort to recapture in the leisure hours the sense of the wholeness of a piece of work that had been lost in the plant and office when work was transformed into the "job." The same worker who hurried away from his plant because his job offered few psychic satisfactions was likely to spend hours tinkering with carpentry, adding an attic to his house, or painting a canvas, putting into his amateur work the emotional energy he could not express on his job. Here he could see the relation between the initial idea and the finished product; here he could follow his own pace and be his own boss. Without intending it Americans found that they were swinging back at home to the kind of work relation that had been lost somewhere in the course of building up a factory system and the job-wage nexus.

America found itself in the mid-1950s with three streams of tendency in relation to work: a factory system which was still the heart of industrialism but was losing its workers and being run by machines; a growing working population of engineers and of nonindustrial technicians, with an ever greater role for education in the further changes of the productive process; and a trend toward do-it-yourself amateurism which helped to fill the void left in work-hungry human beings by the dehumanizing of the "job."

5. *The Wilderness of Commodities*

THE WORLD of the consumer which results from American work and technology is one of profusion and variety. The consumer lives in a wilderness of commodities whose impact on the minds of Americans themselves, as on that of the world, is one of richness. American living standards are the boast of politicians and editorial writers and the target of sermons, and during the Cold War they were a main reliance in American psychological warfare against Communist systems. "No ordinary Russian," Bruce Barton told a convention of salesmen, "ever suspected such a wealth of wonderful and desirable objects exists anywhere in the world as the Sears, Roebuck catalogue presents." On a more academic level David Riesman ironically told (in "The Nylon War") how the hold of the Russian rulers was broken by a military campaign of bombarding them with millions of pairs of nylon stockings and other items from the American cornucopia. For the ordinary American the belief in the idea of progress is reinforced by the visible sign of his rising living standards. Adapting a phrase of Toynbee's, one might call this the "idolization of ephemeral enjoyments." The popular literature and culture celebrate not technology or even business and the making of money but the grandeurs and miseries of a consumer's civilization. America seems strikingly to illustrate Sorokin's category of the "sensate culture."

This has led to an indictment of Americans as "materialists," which has generally been accepted by both Americans and foreigners, by the intellectuals as well as the preachers. Recently some of the intellectuals have begun to question the indictment. "The virtue of American civilization," Mary McCarthy has ventured, "is that it is unmaterialistic. It is true that America produces and consumes more cars, more soap and bathtubs, than any other nation, but we live *among* these objects rather than *by* them."

In getting at the truth about American "materialism," we may ask what are the dominant gods in the heaven of the American as consumer?

First, there is *comfort*. Waldo Frank described it as "the violent lust for ease" on the part of the American pioneer, and it is true that after the rigors of American settlement there was an effort to cushion the rudeness of the physical environment. The pioneer had a rough life; his descendants wanted comfort—in home and travel, in hotels, cars, and planes, at the clubs, in visiting and entertainment. The Puritan made the inner *ascesis* of spirit tangible by outer denials; his descendants want neither the outer nor inner denials. Yet the persisting malaise of spirit remains, whether due to the American situation or the human condition. The more comfortless the American feels, the more he seeks to pile up physical comforts.

Next to the godliness of comfort, there is *cleanliness*. Giedion has noted how many of the American mechanical improvements have been concerned with the bathroom. The American household has a whole cleansing hierarchy, with chemical and mechanical aids to constant domestic and personal cleanliness. Every part and pore of the body has its special cleanser, disinfectant, deodorant. The most frightening surmise in the world of the fear advertisements is that you may be afflicted with the odor about which "your best friend won't tell you." Perhaps all this came from an effort to shut out the sights and smells of industrialism, perhaps from the desire to dissociate oneself from the indicia of manual labor. Some who have been struck by the constant bathing of the American—female and male alike—have even suggested that there is a relation between the obsession with cleansing and some collective and Puritanical sense of guilt. Whatever the sources, the fact is there.

Peeling away the layers of meaning in American "materialism" one comes next to *novelty:* the sheer delight in a gadget-cluttered environment, with new devices and new models constantly replacing earlier ones. The American acknowledges with a wry humor that the latest models of cars, refrigerators and bathroom fixtures, of fashions in clothes and books and ideas, do not necessarily serve the life purposes better than the previous models: yet he seems driven by a compulsion to replace them. There is, to be sure, a nostalgic affection for the days of the Stanley Steamer and other early automobile models, but with the nostalgia of yesterday there is the sense of the superiority of today.

There is, on the other hand, nothing whimsical about the American attitude toward *service.* It is the lagniappe of the bargain the American consumer makes with his machine culture, the "extra" thrown in. To get service in buying a dress, or gas for your car, or a meal in a restaurant, is to feel that your personality is recognized. To be sure, the fact is that service in crowded American restaurants or on trains and planes or at airports is often wretched: in an era of approaching automation the extra touch of concern for human sensibility may seem archaic. Yet it is exactly this function of service—as a survival of pre-machine standards in a machine age, a footnote attesting to the graces of the past—that makes it still important to the American consumer.

The comfortable, the convenient, the clean, the polished and glittering, the ingenious, the novel, the extra bit of service: these form some of the ingredients of the American "materialism." And the most marked ingredient of all, containing and encompassing all the rest, is the overwhelming measure of American consumer abundance.

It is as wide of the mark to deride this as "a Coca-Cola civilization" as it is to use the standard N.A.M. argument that this plenitude of products and gadgets is proof of America's having found the key to a good life. Actually there is a grotesque disproportion about the national values which is revealed by the direction of American spending. More is spent on cosmetics, tobacco, liquor, than on public education. The health services are relatively starved, the serious arts are sometimes neglected. And for one American family out of four or five, life is still a rat race of worry, work, and scrimping.

It remains true, however, that there are more good things available to a higher proportion of Americans than in any other society. This is not a matter of piglike, sensuous reveling in material things. The long-established image of America as a kind of golden sty is a stereotype with more envy and ignorance than truth. The vast array of available commodities has become an American way of living, but it does not follow that Americans are more likely than others to confuse living standards with life values, or mistake good things for the good life. Many Americans—like many other human beings—do live *by* things as well as *among* them. But many others know that, like the machine, the shopwindow crowded with glittering items carries no ethic with it. It does not become an end in itself except for the impoverished of spirit, who are to be found in any civilization. What is true in America is that they find it easier to disguise their impoverished spirit behind the gaudy raiments of a consumer's plenty.

A more marked element in the American situation is the drive toward competitive consumption. The "folklore of capitalism" has it that production in America is competitive and that living is co-operative. It is truer to say that competition is being crowded out of production and that its real area is now in consumption. The drive to "keep up with the Joneses"—or with the fashion magazines, the TV heroes and heroines, the movie colony, the advertising slogans—has been an undoubted spur to consumption and living standards for all classes unparalleled in history. Veblen made much of it in his satiric description of "conspicuous consumption" and "pecuniary emulation," yet he underestimated the inner drive of expanding consumption that did not depend on emulation but drew upon the pervasive hunger for commodities and material satisfactions. Erich Fromm analyzed the competitive strains in the "marketing orientation" of the personality under capitalism, but his emphasis on the "alienation" that resulted from it missed the point that Americans find a kind of wholeness in their living standard as a substitute for what they once found on the land. Riesman described the "other-directed" emphasis of the emerging American character, where less depends on what you are or even on what you enjoy than on what others think of you; but he was more interested in the impact of the popular culture than of consumption upon the national character. David Potter supplied the latter emphasis in his *People of Plenty,* where he traced the effects of consumer abundance and especially of advertising on the American personality.

On one level, competitive consumption is simply a phase of the Faustian sense of power which has shown itself throughout American history. To strive for the biggest city population, the highest office building, the largest football stadium, the most successful charity drive, the biggest national magazine circulation, the longest theater run, the most staggering book sales, is characteristic of a culture still exulting in the illusion of the illimitable. For the consumer it shows itself in the steadily enlarging dream which has brought life's necessities within the scope of most people and has made one luxury after another a necessity.

What class is the carrier of this expanding dream? Again Veblen serves as a useful measure of the distance that American living has traveled in the past half century. In his *Theory of the Leisure Class,* Veblen saw turn-of-the-century America as the climactic expression, under modern capitalist forms, of the values which were given shape by the old feudal aristocracies and which spread down to the masses. It is true that the emphasis on prowess may be found in a money culture as well as in a feudal one, and that the consumer stereotypes which Americans seek to copy were originally those of the elite. Yet this again misses at least half the point, which is that American living standards and mass-produced commodities have leveled many of the class differences. The car of the wealthy man may be a Cadillac or Chrysler, but the Oldsmobile or Plymouth or Ford of the middle and working classes may look almost as glittering and may be equally chromium-adorned. The rich woman has more dresses and more expensive ones than the suburban housewife or the secretary, but their taste is probably as good as hers. They get their styles from the same fashion magazines and often they look every bit as chic. The carrier of the consumer's dream in America is as much the middle class as the monied class or aristocracy.

The aristocracy is there—a monied aristocracy whose sons make power and whose daughters make glamour a way of life; and there is in it a luminous and magnetic force to which, as to a moon, the tides of American living standards respond. But the tides themselves are mainly middle-class tides. "Society," in the sense the term had in the days of the great mansions and the early big fortunes, no longer exists in America. The old "society" has merged with "cafe society" and the "expense-account aristocracy" and has been muted by a prevailing informality of manners, clothes, and taste. The new informality of suburban clothes is not unlike the informality of Hollywood and Palm Beach. What was not clear to Veblen and his emulators was that the new American power groups who took over the forms of past aristocracies filled them with values of their own—middle-class values; that the dog beneath the skin of the aristocratic hound was a middle-class dog; and that the copiers, however fumbling their progress in taste, were no less momentous an emergence in the history of civilization than the models had been in their day.*

The most striking fact about American consumption is that it is dominated less by a class (even the middle class) than by the tastes, fantasies,

* For a further discussion of "Society," see Ch. VII, Sec. 2, "The Seats of the Mighty," and for fashions in consumption, see Ch. IX, Sec. 3, "Manners, Taste, and Fashion."

and standards of the American woman. In American folk history the pioneer woman is the heroine of the sagas of frontier endurance; but as embodied for example in Beret, Per Hansa's wife in Rölvaag's *Giants in the Earth,* she is also the softening cultural influence in a harsh new environment, the link between the European amenities and the rough life of the frontier. In the America that emerged from its frontier phase into industrial wealth and power you could always find a female counterpart to the masculine spirit of capitalist expansion. One thinks of Undine Spragg in Edith Wharton's *Custom of the Country* who, as she listened to Elmer Moffatt tell of his business intrigues, with his

> epic recital of plot and counterplot . . . hung, a new Desdemona, on his conflict with the anthropophagi. It was of no consequence that the details and the technicalities escaped her: she knew their meaningless syllables stood for success, and what that meant was as clear as day to her. Every Wall Street term had its equivalent in the language of Fifth Avenue, and while he talked of building up railways she was building up palaces, and picturing all the multiple lives she would live in them. To have things had always seemed to her the first essential of existence, and as she listened to him the vision of the things she could have unrolled itself before her like the long triumph of the Asiatic conqueror.

Or one thinks of a later heroine, the American girl in Fitzgerald's *Tender Is the Night:*

> Nicole was the product of much ingenuity and toil. For her sake trains began their run at Chicago and traversed the round belly of the continent to California; chicle factories fumed and link belts grew link by link in factories; men mixed toothpaste in vats and drew mouthwash out of copper hogsheads; girls canned tomatoes quickly in August or worked rudely at the Five-and-Tens on Christmas Eve; half-breed Indians toiled on Brazilian coffee plantations and dreamers were muscled out of patent rights in new tractors—these were some of the people who gave a tithe to Nicole, and as the whole system swayed and thundered onward it lent a feverish bloom to such processes of hers as wholesale buying, like the flush of a fireman's face holding his own before a spreading blaze.

It is the middle-class woman and her teen-age daughter, especially in the suburbs, who are America's type consumers. To them the advertising men pay homage, for them all the blandishments of salesmanship are unrolled. It is their urge to respectability and their dreams of glamour, their psychic yearnings and fulfillments, that make the machines run. To speak of the American male dressing his wife and daughter with conspicuous extravagance is to omit woman's independent economic will and her autonomous dreams. To speak of his hiring servants to show his means and prowess is to forget that the domestic servant is a rapidly disappearing feature of the American landscape.

It would be untrue to say that the American woman's role in the culture is wholly that of the lilies of the field who toil not, yet are arrayed in glory. The middle-class woman was a household drudge before the "kitchen revolution," and the woman worker is still a factory operative or an office worker. The machine, which lightened the burdens of the one, shut the second up to work under often dreary conditions. But it also brought new levels of social experience and personal expressiveness within the reach of both, while it dangled tantalizingly before their vision still further levels that seemed always close and yet were out of reach. The American woman's creative role as consumer is a phase of her larger role as the organizer and transmitter of the culture.* It is she who decides what the house will look like, what everyone will wear (including her husband), what schools the children will attend, what books will be bought.

That is why some paths have to be cleared for her through the wilderness of commodities, and consumer reporting has become in a double sense a necessity of the American economy: on one level it guides the consumer through the maze of offerings, amidst the pitfalls of brand names, quality, durability, and value; on another level the corporation needs research on available markets and on the probable desires and responses of the buyer. Here the consumer is the target, as she is indeed the target of all the talent and ingenuity spent on merchandizing, packaging, and advertising the product. American technological skills, which have solved the problem of production by the automatic machines, are driving ever closer in the effort through advertising to make the consumer an automaton also, conditioned to give the right response to the right stimulus or slogan. Hence the cold manipulativeness of "motivational research," which seeks to lay bare the unconscious drives to which the packager and advertiser of the commodity can appeal. The cynical quality of this effort is attested by the number of novels and movies about Madison Avenue—the center of the advertising profession—and the moral recoil of bright, young advertising men from the dehumanizing task of "the hucksters."

Critics of American life have shed many tears for the powerlessness of the consumer and the formlessness of his outlook. It is true that, measured against the gigantism of corporate or trade-union power, the consumer is a puny figure. The effort to organize consumers into co-operatives has been less successful in America than in Europe. As a political pressure group the consumers are almost nonexistent, as would be clear

* For a further discussion of this, see Ch. VIII, Sec. 6, "The Ordeal of the American Woman."

from the history of any Congressional price-control measure. But viewed as a shaping force in the economy and the society as a whole, the consumer is far from negligible. It is still he—or she—who channels the productive energies and shapes much of the taste of America.

The guidance of consumer choice underscores the jungle character of the Great Market of American commodities, created by Big Technology. But the more important feature of the wilderness of commodities is not its tracklessness but its luxuriant growth and abundance, and the way in which living standards and consumer habits have been shaped in its image.

Every phase of American consumer habits is oriented to the national market. Standardized products are nationally produced, nationally distributed, and nationally advertised, and to the superficial eye they seem to play an important role in holding the national together. The American as a consumer is the target of more concentrated attention than in any other phase of his personality. There are, I have said, groups of hardworking experts in "motivational research" and "consumer depth research" whose job is to fathom "consumer psychology" so as to overcome "consumer resistance" and create "consumer demand." Americans are continually told that "the consumer is king" and that he holds the "golden key" to unlock the riddle of prosperity or depression for the entire economy. In fact, there is a school of American economic observers who go so far as to say that it is the Great Market rather than the Big Technology which is the heart of the economy, and that the "unseemly economics of opulence" (as Galbraith puts it) have provided a margin for error in economic policy and a solvent for social strains. The fiction is that consumers operate in herd fashion. Actually they represent hundreds of millions of individual decisions which comprise the Great Market, but among that multitude of decisions the experts are always on the lookout for buying trends and consumer propensities.

Certainly, once the capacity to produce a spate of commodities is given, the crucial question is whether they can be sold. From this angle of vision the consumer is central: he is more than a target; or at least he is a highly mobile and nervous one, and therefore a highly incalculable one. He tries to balance his expected income, his probable taxes, his savings (which he either has or plans for), the prices and price trends, the desirability of the available goods, and the certainty or uncertainty of the national future and his own individual one. At the end he reaches a result that could not be arrived at mechanically even by the most complex feeding of "information" into "feedback" electronic calculators. On any particular commodity or new style a shrewdly geared advertising and selling campaign may be able to win the consumer over. But in his behavior as a whole he remains incalculable—in theory the delight of the eulogists of the system, in practice their despair.

But if we look at them not in short-run but in long-run terms there are generalizations one can make about American living standards and consumption habits. It is clear that standardized products have made conspicuous consumption more difficult than in the past. It is also clear that mass production for a national market has spread to what were formerly luxury items, giving a burnished glitter to the whole realm of consumption. The spread of high-school and even college education, the war experiences of American soldiers in European countries, the new habits of tourism of the middle classes, and the extreme development and resourcefulness of the advertising arts have all contributed to narrowing the gap between the classes in their consumer habits. Marx's prediction that under capitalism the living standards of the industrial workers would fall and keep falling has been turned on its head in America. The industrial worker, as well as the middle-class self-employed person or the professional, consumes at so high a rate that he has become absorbed with the rest in the Great Market.

In a study for the National Bureau of Economic Research, Frederick C. Mills has come up with some figures which show that the national product (everything produced and sold during a year) was five times as high in the decade of the 1940s as that of the 1890s, while population doubled. Of this national product, after subtracting what was needed for customary consumer standards and for replacement of capital goods, the rest (the margin above maintenance) amounted in the decade of the 1940s to $558 billion, of which $285 billion went into increased consumption, and the rest into war goods and increased capital equipment. Thus the Americans were adding to their living standards even more than they added to their capital equipment and fed into the great maw of war. Another way of putting this is that there have been annual increases of real income in America averaging almost 2 per cent a year since 1870, and that more than half of these increases have gone into added consumption.

One might conclude, after this gleaming history of ever-higher consumption figures, that the American consumer would be approaching the satiation point. Thus far it has not happened. There is still a receding horizon for the felt needs and desires of potential purchasers. They are always seeing new things they want and thinking of new things to buy. One may say rather fliply that this is a testimony to the effects of high-pressure advertising and salesmanship: but this is to pay more homage to these highly developed arts than they can rightly claim.

Neither advertising nor salesmanship can sell what the potential purchaser is not prepared to be convinced about. The fact is that the American as a consumer of goods and services has not yet had his hunger sated, and that even when comparative satiation is approached at one end of the income scale, new classes and new income groups are brought into the Great Market from the other end of the scale.

There is little question that the American personality has had to pay a heavy toll for the advertising now lavished on material goods, not only in standardized habits of consumption but also in conformist habits of thought. When the ears and mind are continually besieged by hypnotic repetitive slogans, it is impossible that there should be no residual effect upon the responses of the whole personality to repetition and sloganeering. It is little wonder that serious students of politics have begun to speculate about the effect of Madison Avenue on the mind of the voter, and serious teachers see in it the seeds of slackness and laziness in the thinking of college students. This too is part of the price America has had to pay for the Great Technology and the Great Market.

There are, however, some signs of the approach of what George Soule has called "comparative satiety." That is to say, given their present living standards but also their hunger for the intangibles of reading, travel, and personality development, more and more Americans are now likely to choose an increase in leisure time rather than an increase in material consumer goods. American workers have already shown that they prefer the shorter working week, even when the longer hours would give them even higher wages than they get. As one observes the recent American "giveaway" shows on TV, one notes that the winners of the big cash prizes are at least as interested in "salting away" a big chunk of them for future leisure, travel, and enjoyment as they are for spending them on material goods. In short, American technology—by making ever-higher "living standards"—is now within reach of giving a new meaning to the phrase, putting the emphasis increasingly upon greater expressiveness of life rather than on material goods.

6. The Culture of Machine Living

Any principle that comes to dominate a culture can do so only by making itself part of the life processes of the people. This has happened in the case of America, and it is one of the reasons we can speak seriously, and not as a literary flourish, of the culture of machine living. Siegfried Giedion points out that the machine has mechanized such fundamentals as the soil (mechanized agriculture), bread (mechanized milling), death (assembly-line slaughtering pens and the use of by-products by the big meat packers), and the household (the kitchen revolution, the household-appliance revolution, mechanized laundering, and the mechanized bathroom). The analysis can be carried further. Mechanization has extended to transport (boats, trains, autos, busses, trucks, subways, planes), to living outside the home (hotels, motels, sleeping cars, "automats"), and to the basic phases of the communications revolution (newsprint, book publishing, magazines, telephone, telegraph, movies, radio, TV).

Aside from these arterial forms of American living there is also the interminable gadgetry. From the automatic vending machines to the automatic gas stations, from the gadgeted car to the gadgeted bed, America has taken on the aspect of a civilization cluttered with artifacts and filled with the mechanized bric-a-brac of machine living. The Big Technology of the mass-production industries is supplemented by the Little Technology of everyday living.

One could draw a gloomy picture of machine living in America and depict it as the Moloch swallowing the youth and resilience of American manhood. From Butler's *Erewhon* to Capek's *R.U.R.*, European thinkers have seized on the machine as the cancer of modern living. Some have even suggested that there is a daimon in Western man, and especially in the American, that is driving him to the monstrous destruction of his instinctual life and indeed of his whole civilization.

Part of the confusion flows from the failure to distinguish at least three phases of the machine culture. One is what I have just described: *machine living* as such, the use of machinery in work and in leisure and in the constant accompaniments of the day. The second is cultural *standardization,* aside from the machine, but a standardization that flows from machine production. The third is *conformism* in thought, attitude, and action. All three are parts of the empire of the machine but at varying removes and with different degrees of danger for the human spirit.

The danger in machine living itself is chiefly the danger of man's arrogance in exulting over the seemingly easy triumphs over Nature which he calls "progress," so that he cuts himself off increasingly from the organic processes of life itself. Thus with the soil: the erosion of the American earth is not, as some seem to believe, the result of the mechanization of agriculture; a farmer can use science and farm technology to the full, and he need not exhaust or destroy his soil but can replenish it, as has been shown in the TVA, which is itself a triumph of technology. But the machines have been accompanied by a greed for quick results and an irreverence for the soil which are responsible for destroying the balance between man and the environment. What is true of the soil is true of the household: the mechanized household appliances have not destroyed the home or undermined family life; rural electrification has made the farmer's wife less a drudge, and the mass production of suburban houses has given the white-collar family a better chance than it had for sun and living space. What threatens family life is not the "kitchen revolution" or the "housing revolution" but the restless malaise of the spirit, of which the machine is more product than creator.

Even in a society remarkable for its self-criticism the major American writers have not succumbed to the temptation of making the machine into a Devil. Most of the novelists have amply expressed the frustrations of American life, and some (Dreiser, Dos Passos, Farrell and Algren come to mind) have mirrored in their style the pulse beats of an urban mechanized civilization. But except for a few isolated works, like Elmer Rice's *Adding Machine* and Eugene O'Neill's *Dynamo,* the writers have refrained from the pathetic fallacy of ascribing the ills of the spirit to the diabolism of the machine. The greatest American work on technology and its consequences—Lewis Mumford's massive four-volume work starting with *Man and Technics* and ending with *The Conduct of Life*—makes the crucial distinction between what is due to the machine itself and what is due to the human institutions that guide it and determine its uses.

It is here, moving from machine living to cultural standardization, that the picture becomes bleaker. Henry Miller's phrase for its American form is "the air-conditioned nightmare." Someone with a satiric intent could do a withering take-off on the rituals of American standardization.

Most American babies (he might say) are born in standardized hospitals, with a standardized tag put around them to keep them from getting confused with other standardized products of the hospital. Many of them grow up either in uniform rows of tenements or of small-town or suburban houses. They are wheeled about in standard perambulators, shiny or shabby as may be, fed from standardized bottles with standardized nipples according to standardized formulas, and tied up with standardized diapers. In childhood they are fed standardized breakfast foods out of standardized boxes with pictures of standardized heroes on them. They are sent to monotonously similar schoolhouses, where almost uniformly standardized teachers ladle out to them standardized information out of standardized textbooks. They pick up the routine wisdom of the streets in standard slang and learn the routine terms which constrict the range of their language within dishearteningly narrow limits. They wear out standardized shoes playing standardized games, or as passive observers they follow through standardized newspaper accounts or standardized radio and TV programs the highly ritualized antics of grown-up professionals playing the same games. They devour in millions of uniform pulp comic books the prowess of standardized supermen.

As they grow older they dance to canned music from canned juke boxes, millions of them putting standard coins into standard slots to get standardized tunes sung by voices with standardized inflections of emotion. They date with standardized girls in standardized cars. They see automatons thrown on millions of the same movie and TV screens, watching stereotyped love scenes adapted from made-to-order stories in standardized magazines.

They spend the days of their years with monotonous regularity in factory, office, and shop, performing routinized operations at regular intervals. They take time out for standardized "coffee breaks" and later a quick standardized lunch, come home at night to eat processed or canned food, and read syndicated columns and comic strips. Dressed in standardized clothes they attend standardized club meetings, church services, and socials. They have standardized fun at standardized big-city conventions. They are drafted into standardized armies, and if they escape the death of mechanized warfare they die of highly uniform diseases, and to the accompaniment of routine platitudes they are buried in standardized graves and celebrated by standardized obituary notices.

Caricature? Yes, perhaps a crude one, but with a core of frightening validity in it. Every society has its routines and rituals, the primitive groups being sometimes more tyrannously restricted by convention than the industrial societies. The difference is that where the primitive is bound by the rituals of tradition and group life, the American is bound by the rituals of the machine, its products, and their distribution and consumption.

The role of the machine in this standardized living must be made clear. The machine mechanizes life, and since mass production is part of Big Technology, the machine also makes uniformity of life possible. But it does not compel such uniformity. The American who shaves with an electric razor and his wife who buys a standardized "home permanent" for her hair do not thereby have to wear a uniformly vacuous expression through the day. A newspaper that uses the press association wire stories and prints from a highly mechanized set of presses does not thereby have to take the same view of the world that every other paper takes. A novelist who uses a typewriter instead of a quill pen does not have to turn out machine-made historical romances.

The answer is that some do and some don't. What the machine and the mass-produced commodities have done has been to make conformism easier. To buy and use what everyone else does, and live and think as everyone else does, becomes a short cut involving no need for one's own thinking. Those Americans have been captured by conformist living who have been capturable by it.

Cultural stereotypes are an inherent part of all group living, and they become sharper with mass living. There have always been unthinking people leading formless, atomized lives. What has happened in America is that the economics of mass production has put a premium on uniformity, so that America produces more units of more commodities (although sometimes of fewer models) than other cultures. American salesmanship has sought out every potential buyer of a product, so that standardization makes its way by the force of the distributive mechanism into every life. Yet for the person who has a personality pattern and style of his own, standardization need not mean anything more than a set of conveniences which leave a larger margin of leisure and greater scope for creative living. "That we may be enamored by the negation brought by the machine," as Frank Lloyd Wright has put it, "may be inevitable for a time. But I like to imagine this novel negation to be only a platform underfoot to enable a greater splendor of life to be ours than any known to Greek or Roman, Goth or Moor. We should know a life beside which the life they knew would seem not only limited in scale and narrow in range but pale in richness of the color of imagination and integrity of spirit."

Which is to say that technology is the shell of American life, but a shell that need not hamper or stultify the modes of living and thinking. The real dangers of the American mode of life are not in the machine or even in standardization as much as they are in conformism. The dangers do not flow from the contrivances that men have fashioned to lighten their burdens, or from the material abundance which, if anything, should make a richer cultural life possible. They flow rather from the mimesis of the dominant and successful by the weak and mediocre, from the intolerance of diversity, and from the fear of being thought different from one's fellows. This is the essence of conformism.

It would be hard to make the connection between technology and conformism, unless one argues that men fashion their minds in the image of their surroundings, and that in a society of automatism, human beings themselves will become automatons. But this is simply not so. What relation there is between technology and conformism is far more subtle and less mystical. It is a double relation. On the one hand, as Jefferson foresaw, the simpler society of small-scale manufacture did not involve concentration of power in a small group, was not vulnerable to breakdown, and did not need drastic governmental controls; a society of big-scale industry has shown that it does. In that sense the big machines carry with them an imperative toward the directed society, which in turn—whether in war or peace—encourages conformism. On the second score, as De Tocqueville saw, a society in which there is no recognized elite group to serve as the arbiter of morals, thought, and style is bound to be a formless one in which the ordinary person seeks to heal his insecurity by attuning himself to the "tyranny of opinion" —to what others do and say and what they think of him. He is ruled by imitation and prestige rather than a sense of his own worth.

These are dangerous trends, but all of social living is dangerous. The notable fact is that in spite of its machines and standardization America has proved on balance less conformist than some other civilizations where the new technology has played less of a role. One thinks of the totalitarian experience of Italy, of Spain and Portugal, of Germany, of Russia and the East European countries, of Japan, of China. Some, like the Germans, the Japanese, and the Russian and Chinese Communists have been seized with an admiration for the machine; the others have had clerical and feudal traditions, and have lagged in industrial development. The totalitarian spirit can come to reside in a culture no matter what the shell of its technology is. There is no unvarying relation between machines and rigidity of living and thinking.

Americans have, it is true, an idolatry of production and consumption as they have an idolatry of success. But they have not idolized authority or submitted unquestioningly to human or supernatural oracles. They have had their cranks, eccentrics, and anarchists, and they still cling to individualism, even when it is being battered hard. It will take them some time before they can become "man in equipoise," balancing what science and the machine can do as against the demands of the life processes. But where they have failed, the failure has been less that of the machines they have wrought than of the very human fears, greeds, and competitive drives that have accompanied the building of a powerful culture.

It has been suggested that the American, like the Faustian, made a bargain with the Big Technology: a bargain to transform his ways of life and thought in the image of the machine, in return for the range of power and riches the machine would bring within his reach. It is a fine allegory. But truer than the Faustian bargain, with its connotations of the sale of one's soul to the Devil, is the image of Prometheus stealing fire from the gods in order to light a path of progress for men. The path is not yet clear, nor the meaning of progress, nor where it is leading: but the bold intent, the irreverence, and the secular daring have all become part of the American experience.

CHAPTER V

Capitalist Economy and Business Civilization

THIS CHAPTER examines the most bitterly attacked and ardently defended sector of American life—its economy, including both its business system and its labor unions, its wealth and poverty, its grandeurs and miseries, its theory and practice. The first approach is to catch an over-all view of the economy as a going concern, confronting its principal strengths and weaknesses (Sec. 1, "American Capitalism: Trial Balance"). We then look more closely at three of its aspects: what has happened to the businessman as entrepreneur and folk hero (Sec. 2, "The Rise and Decline of the Titan"); how the corporation has emerged as the type-form of American business enterprise, replacing the individual and family firm, and revolutionizing American business (Sec. 3, "The Corporate Empires"); and what the revolution has done to the old concepts of property (Sec. 4, "The Property Revolution"). Following the new forms of business enterprise into some of their ramifications, in advertising, salesmanship, the stock market, "public relations" (Sec. 5, "Business and Its Satellites"), we try to appraise what the business spirit has done to the noneconomic phases of American life (Sec. 6, "The Reach of the Business Spirit").

We then look at the other side of the shield—the role of labor and the trade-unions in the American economy and in the broader aspects of living, assessing the extent of labor power, the strategies it has adopted for its self-defense and preservation and for getting what it regards as its rightful share at the banquet of American life (Sec. 7, "Revolution in the Trade-Union"); we try to draw a portrait of the new trade-union leader and of the varied activities that the trade-union has assumed after its long history; and we note the characteristic way in which American labor operates in American political life and in the larger culture (Sec. 8, "Labor and American Society").

Finally, after examining how Americans live both at the top and at the bottom of the pyramid of income and wealth (Sec. 9, "Poverty and Wealth"), we draw a profile of the changes in the pattern of economic and governmental relations in America, which defies easy labeling as either "capitalism" or "Socialism" but is a unique amalgam of both (Sec. 10, "The Emerging Amalgam"). This gives us a chance again to take an over-all view and strike a final balance of the newer trends of the economy.

CHAPTER V

Capitalist Economy and Business Civilization

1. American Capitalism: Trial Balance

GIVEN this culture of science and the machine, how about the system of American capitalism which organizes it? The appraisal of American capitalism as a going concern must be made largely in terms of a balance sheet. Whoever embraces its achievements should not flinch from acknowledging its costs; whoever condemns the costs should be candid enough to recognize the achievement.

The record of achievement is clear enough: a continuously rising curve of man-hour productivity; a high rate of capital formation; steadily rising profits which have made a corpse of the Marxist predictions about profits under capitalism; employment levels which in the mid-1950s were at their top peacetime pitch; a wilderness of available commodities and a strong "propensity to consume," reflecting the spread of high and increasing living standards even among middle- and low-income levels; a steadily increasing growth in real wages; a continuing secular increase in the national product; a production record which has provided the military production for two world wars and the current "readiness economy" for defense, while increasing the products available for civilian consumption; a capacity to take in its stride an ever-heavier tax structure without destroying freedom of economic movement and decision within the economy; a continuing sense of economic dynamism, and finally an economy with the capacity for changing its forms under pressure so that it could in the mid-1950s lay claim to being a "people's capitalism" even while being to a high degree a corporate and monopoly capitalism.

The debit side is also clear: a haste for profits which has used up too rapidly the land and resources of the continent and built unplanned cities; an economy which made heavy productive gains (especially in World War II) through the expansion of war industries and seems still to be buttressed by a government budget for arms which runs to 15 or 20 per cent of the Gross National Product; one which has lived like a fever-chart patient by constantly taking its pulse and has not been able to control firmly the periodic swings of prosperity and depression; one in which the Big Enterprise corporations create private empires challenging the state itself; one in which the chances for a competitive start in the race for the Big Money are less open to small businessmen and depend more upon upward movement in a corporate bureaucracy; an economy in which, despite its production levels, much remains to be done in distributing the final product more fairly.

The observer is tempted to say (with Hamlet): "Look at this picture, and here at this one."

The defense of American capitalism runs largely in broad abstractions like "the American system" or "the free-enterprise economy," or in epithets like "serfdom" or "totalitarian" applied to noncapitalist systems. Underlying these catchwords are some basic arguments. One is the *argument from incentive:* that men's brains and energy work best when they have no hampering restrictions, and when they see an immediacy of relation between effort and reward. The second is the *argument from a free market:* that an economy runs best as the result of millions of individual decisions made through the operations of a free production, wage and price system; that when it goes off kilter, it can generally set itself right again by individual adjustments within a frame of government spurs and checks; and that even government regulation is best accomplished by the indirect methods of inducements and pressures on the free market, rather than the direct method of planning and control. The third is the *argument from managerial efficiency:* that the corporate managerial group is recruited from the men with the best skills, who deal with the problems of industrial production more flexibly than a governmental bureaucracy could.

The arguments, though vulnerable, are basically valid. True, the free market no longer exists in anything like its historic form, and Big Enterprise and the giant corporation, with prices largely reached by administrative decision, have in part taken its place. Yet the economy has developed its own distinctive forms of freedom, and the decisions reached in it are still freer than in a cartelized or largely government-directed economy. The system of profit and property incentives has been transformed in the giant corporation; yet new incentives have emerged that keep the corporate managers alert and drive the productive system on. The argument from corporate efficiency has much in its favor, provided we do not forget that a corporate bureaucracy has a strong inner impulse toward conformism of spirit and, like government bureaucracies, runs the danger of stagnation.

Some corollaries of these doctrines that emerge in the capitalist apologia are more open to question: the argument that the big corporations and their managers administer their power *as a trust* for the people as a whole; and the argument that there is a *harmony of interests* which ties labor and the farmers to business prosperity and therefore business decisions. While most Americans are too realistic to accept the view that Big Property is being held in trust for them, they do not resent the power of the possessing groups because they hope themselves someday to be secure enough to "take it easy." As for the harmony of interests, they may have some skepticism about it, yet they have never been caught by the European idea that class cleavages must deepen until the whole system breaks.

The real problems of capitalism, however, are not the doctrinal struggles but the operational strains—the periodic breakdowns, the sense of insecurity, the shadow of monopoly, the dependence upon war expenditures, the question of distributive justice. The American economy, because of its power and prosperity, has become the last, best hope of free economies in the world. But by the same token the issues of its capacity for survival, its social costs, and its impact on the human spirit have called in question the nature and survival value of the system of capitalism itself.

What are the elements of American capitalism as a going concern, distinguishing it from other going systems? It is customary to say that capitalism is organized as a "private-enterprise system," for private (individual or corporate) profit, with the resulting rewards protected by the state as private property. This is valid enough, except for the fact that far-reaching changes have taken place in the structure and functioning of American capitalism. The profit incentive, for example, does not operate in corporate management as it used to operate in individual enterprise, since ownership and management have split apart: it still holds, however, if it is rephrased as the drive within the manager to make the best possible profit record for the corporation. The idea of private property has also suffered a change, since industrial ownership is now widely scattered in the form of stock ownership, some of the stocks being owned by trust funds, investment trusts, other corporations, life insurance companies, and even trade-unions. The earlier picture of capitalism as a competitive system has also had to be changed. To some extent competition has been inhibited by price agreements and "oligopoly"—the control of an industry by a handful of big corporations competing only partly in price and mainly in packaging, advertising, and brand names, as in meat packing, automobiles, or cigarettes. Yet the impressive fact about the American economy is the extent to which it has effectively resisted the monopoly tendencies. The concept of bigness is not the same as the concept of monopoly, and something that can fairly be called competition is still a power regulator of the economy.

The core of capitalism then is still present. It is in essence concerned with decision-making within a profit-competitive framework. Under communism the decisions are made by a small group of political functionaries assigned to strategic industrial posts. Under democratic socialism they are made by technicians operating largely within government corporations, responsible ultimately to the people. Under American capitalism the decisions on production, pricing, advertising, and sales policies are private decisions—that is to say, they are made by individual businessmen or heads of small corporations, whether they be producers, middlemen, or retailers, and in the case of big corporations they are made by the managers to whom the power of decision is delegated by the stockholders; the decisions on wages and labor policy are generally made through collective bargaining by the managers and trade-union leaders. Obviously there are restrictions placed on these decisions by price and wage legislation, sometimes by priorities and the allocation of scarce materials in a defense economy. But within these limits the decisions are linked with ownership and management, and they are made always with a view to profit and in competition with other enterprises. At the other end of the capitalist process there are millions of decisions made by the consumer: production and investment policies are guided not by governmental decisions or by what might be considered socially necessary production but in the light of consumers' decisions about how they will spend their money and for what.

Thus at one end American capitalism is guided by decisions made by businessmen, managers, and trade-union leaders, at the other end by consumer decisions. This decision-making operates within a frame in which there are strong surviving elements of private property, private and corporate profits, and competition.

In assessing American capitalism as a going concern, one important test is the test of *productivity.* Here American capitalism shows the most impressive facet of its record. Socialists might argue that, given the resources of America and the accidents of its history, some other system of organization, ownership, and power could have attained the same productivity with a better distribution of the products. This is one of those iffy questions that will never be resolved. On the other hand it is hard to sustain the claim that the creative force in the American record of increased productivity is the capitalist entrepreneur and manager, and he alone. Science, technology, the legal and governmental framework, and the skill of the worker—all belong in the larger pattern along with the supplier of risk capital and the business organizer. Yet the American record of an increase of productivity running between 2 per cent and 3 per cent a year must be counted one of the over-all achievements of capitalism. Nor has this production record been only a matter of technology and resources. The drive toward productivity has also been due to the elements within the social structure which have invested the whole productive process with the *élan* of freedom. This is as true today as it was a century ago, as John Sawyer has shown, basing himself on the accounts of European travelers in America in the 1840s and 1850s.

All this brings us to the question of *incentive,* which is more troublesome. Those who contend that profit alone has furnished the effective incentive for industrial production must plead guilty to a lower view of human motive than applies even in an imperfect world. The fact is that the managerial function in the big corporation has been performed through incentives quite different from those of ownership profits or dividends, and more closely related to competitive performance and pride in a job well done. Through a complex mingling of profit, salary, bonus, and craftsmanship incentives, capitalism as a going concern has enlisted considerable talents in the processes of production and selling; and it has plowed back into increased production a steady portion (recently around 7 per cent) of the national product, keeping the process of capital formation an active and growing one.

It is on the test of *stability* that American capitalism is most vulnerable. American economic thought is crisscrossed by conflicts of opinion about the underlying causes of the periodic swings and breakdowns of the system, resulting in cycles of prosperity and recession, boom and depression. There are still die-hard critics of the system who believe that boom and bust are inherent in the system and will never yield to anything short of full-scale socialism. There are also True Believers of another stripe who feel, as their forerunners felt in the boom days of the 1920s, that Americans have somehow found the golden key to perpetual prosperity.

Aside from these two groups there is fairly general agreement, however, that, while the swings in the "business cycle" may not yet have been mastered, American business, labor, and government leaders have learned to detect the danger signals and put in motion some preventive measures, and have learned also—once the cycle is on its way—how to cut the length and severity of the downward swing and cushion its impact. In the mid-1950s there was an upsurge of conviction that the cycle had to a large extent been mastered and need never again operate drastically. The bitter experience after 1929 taught the nation's leaders how to use "counter-cyclical" measures in the form of tax and fiscal policies, rediscounting rates, Federal expenditures for defense and public works, state and Federal programs for building roads, schoolhouses, and hospitals. The President's Council of Economic Advisers, working with a committee of Congress, is now accepted under Republican as well as Democratic administrations. Its reports, carefully studied in business, labor, and government circles, are in effect an embryonic form of corrective and preventive planning. The government's massive role in a war-geared "readiness economy" has also given it a leverage in guiding, checking, and stimulating business activity and as such it is a form of indirect planning.

America has thus characteristically used an indirect approach to the control of the swings of business activity, aiming at stability without embracing a direct program of planning and without transferring the crucial decisions from the corporate managers and the consumers to government managers. The specter of Depression is, of course, always present. At the close of World War II there were widespread prophecies of economic catastrophe, yet the real danger proved to be not mass unemployment but inflation, not a paralysis of production but a boom induced by high demand and sustained by the armament race. This mood has lasted into the mid-1950s. Obviously there is a serious problem in the steady inflationary movement of American prices, year after year, largely due to the pressure of rising consumer demand, with its tragic effect in wiping out much of the substance and meaning of savings. Yet, while Americans are still far from solving the basic problem of boom and bust, they have at least a heightened awareness of what is involved and are willing to take decisive action. There are few economists who would accept the European notion, seemingly as widespread among scholars as among the people, that American capitalism will once again in the calculable future be as helpless as it was in the years following 1929.

On the test of *security and insecurity* American capitalism has made steady if reluctant progress. So far from interfering with prosperity, it is now accepted that effective, well-administered insurance programs make the economy more stable as well as adding to personal security. Every person must confront the tragic elements in life, but the pathetic elements can be whittled down by common action. To the degree that America has become a welfare state it is not because of effeminacy or the importation of "foreign" ideas, but of practical grappling with a deeply felt need to make the individual fate more secure.

Judged by another test—that of *income spread and distribution*—the going economy has in the past evoked strong self-criticism from American writers, if not from the economists. Especially in the decade before World War I, and in the 1920s and 1930s, they unsparingly subjected the economy to the test of equity. The extremes of wealth and poverty, the discrepancies between the Babylonian living at the top of the pyramid and the scrimping and degradation at its base, became staples of the American self-portrait. There was a time when the prospects of the future for many Americans seemed precarious. Any European or Asian who thinks that Americans need to be prodded about this should read the almost unparalleled record in which sensitive Americans have made their own indictment of their own vaunted system. But the note of self-criticism has recently grown fainter because of the overwhelming evidence of American living standards. These have improved all through the class system as productivity has increased and the trade-unions have been able to claim a share of it for their members. The problem of poverty in America is now circumscribed within the lower fourth of the population.

One could argue, of course, that the depressed groups in backward areas in other countries are far worse off than this lower fourth in America. This would be sound if American living standards were judged by productivity in other areas of the world, but they must be judged by American productivity. In every economy, as Sumner put it, "there are dinners without appetites at one end of the table, and appetites without dinners at the other." The American economy as a production miracle has evoked life claims in America not roused in the underdeveloped economies: what would be a full meal elsewhere is a skimpy one at the table of the American business system.*

The final test of a going economy is the *creativeness* it evokes and makes possible. Few systems in history have attracted so much talent and put it to use, and in no other economy have men's business abilities been so continuously tapped. The problem is not whether the economy gives scope to creativeness, but what kind of creativeness it gives scope to. The question asked is always whether a new idea or a new insight is "practical"—that is, whether it can be translated into dollar-and-cents terms. The creativeness that is not vendible is likely to be ignored and to wither. Yet within this pecuniary framework there has been broader scope for the creation of use values and life values than the critics of the money calculus have been ready to admit.

This then would be a rough trial balance of American capitalism as a going concern: that it has done brilliantly in productivity and national product; that it has done less well with the swings of the business cycle and with boom and bust, but that substantial steps have been taken to meet this; that its greatest weakness on this score lies in the dependence of the recent prosperity on the war-geared economy;† that its growth in the areas of concentrated economic power has been at

* For a fuller development of this theme, see Sec. 9, "Poverty and Wealth."

† The relation of American capitalism to war expenditures is too complex to be dealt with in this summary. For a further discussion, see Sec. 10, "The Emerging Amalgam."

the expense of small business; that in its income distribution it is a good deal better than its opponents would admit but not nearly as good as its apologists claim, good enough to retain the faith of those who are fulfilled by it but not good enough to exact the loyalty of those who feel left out; that it allows for creativeness but within a limited sense of that word; that as a whole it is an economy which has wrested from the world its envy along with a grudging respect, but not its imitation.

2. *The Rise and Decline of the Titan*

"THE TYCOON IS DEAD" was the way *Fortune,* the best spokesman for the American business mind, phrased the basic change that has come over the structure of American business. In what sense was this true?

Every civilization has its characteristic flowering in some civilization type, the *persona* of the social mask on which the ordinary man in the civilization models himself. In the Athenian civilization the *persona* was the leisure-class citizen with a turn for art and philosophy; with the Jews it was the lawgiver-prophet, in the Roman Empire the soldier-administrator, in the Middle Ages the cleric dreaming of sainthood, in the Chinese civilization the mandarin-scholar, in the Indian the ascetic, in the Italian Renaissance the patron-*condottiere,* at the height of French power the courtier, at the height of British power the merchant-adventurer and empire builder; in German and Japanese history it was the elite soldier of the *Junker* and *samurai* classes, with the Communists today it is the worker-commissar.

The *persona* of the American civilization has been the businessman—the "Titan," as Dreiser called him; the "Tycoon," as *Fortune* called him. Where other civilization types have pursued wisdom, beauty, sanctity, military glory, predacity, asceticism, the businessman pursues the magnitudes of profit with a similar single-minded drive. When confronted in business by appeals to nonpecuniary values, his comment is likely to be that he is not in business for his health. "The business of America," as Calvin Coolidge put it, "is business." The survivors in the fierce competitive struggle were those who most clearly embodied the businessman's single-mindedness of purpose. They were men like "Jupiter" Morgan, Vanderbilt, Jay Gould, Daniel Drew, John D. Rockefeller, Jay Cooke, "Bet-a-Million" Gates, Andrew Carnegie, Charles T. Yerkes, Solomon Guggenheim, Henry Ford, Irénée Du Pont. Some have been honest according to the standards of business honesty, some have not hesitated to use force, guile, and bribery. All have been unsentimental and hard in business, even when they have been pious in the church, devoted in the home, and softhearted in friendship.

The business spirit was not indigenous to America. It grew out of the history of European capitalism, and by the time of the American Revolution it had already found expression in Italy, England, and Holland. During the first half century of American national life the American business spirit lagged behind the European. While there were land speculators, a shipbuilding and commercial group, an incipient factory system, and (as John Taylor used to put it) an "aristocracy of paper and credit," the type-figure of America well into the Jacksonian era was the farmer-turned-artisan or the artisan-turned-farmer.

De Tocqueville gave only the briefest mention to the new "aristocracy of manufactures" in America, although his few pages are perceptive. He noted that "the number of large fortunes there is small, and capital is still scarce," and called America "a nation which contains, so to speak, no rich men"—compared, that is, with the great fortunes and landed families of Europe. Yet even in this early stage De Tocqueville saw that "the Americans carry their businesslike qualities and their trading passions" into all their pursuits, including farming. In other words, he saw the beginnings of that business civilization which has almost obscured every other aspect of American life. When he wrote, there was as yet no consciousness of American businessmen as a class. Yet he saw that the best talents were being attracted to business pursuits, and that the gap between employer and workers was widening.

When Charles Dickens made his second journey through America several decades later he found a hard materialist spirit everywhere. The events of the next quarter century burst the bounds of confinement which De Tocqueville had seen around the business spirit. The spread of a railway network in the 1850s, the triumph of Northern capitalism over the Southern plantation system in the 1860s, the rise of investment banking and the process of rapid capital formation in the 1870s, the trust movement of the 1880s, the harvests of money and power reaped from the Big Technology throughout this period: all these combined to make of America a Paradise for the new business fortunes and a stamping ground for the business spirit.

The result was the emergence of the Big Money and the Big Businessman. In a single decade between the election of McKinley and the Panic of 1907—the decade of the great "consolidations"—there were Harriman and Hill building railroad fortunes as well as railroads, with Harriman dreaming of a world railroad empire, like some daring Sidonia such as Disraeli had imagined; out of the steel industry were forged the fortunes of Gary, Schwab, Gates, Carnegie, Morgan; oil spouted forth a whole tribe of Rockefellers; farm machinery clattered away like the roaring of a McCormick; street railways, with their clinking nickels, built the fortunes of Widener, Whitney, Ryan, Yerkes. The armies of finance wheeled and maneuvered, attacked and retreated.

There was a time when the Titan was treated with unctuous servility. In the 1870s James Parton, a sort of American Samuel Smiles, had edited a volume of Sketches of Men of Progress, and the chapter by the Reverend Mr. McClintock on Daniel Drew had spoken of his "affording an example of industry, energy, and business talents of the highest order, combined with a sense of personal honor and unimpeachable integrity. . . . May he be long spared to enjoy the fruits of his industry, and to share in advancing the kingdom of Christ on earth, not merely by his Christian use of the large wealth of which God has made him steward, but also . . . by his living example of peaceful but active piety." Alas, Charles Francis Adams and Henry Adams, in their *Chapters of Erie,* gave a different picture of Drew, as well as of Gould and Vanderbilt, as men who cheated and tricked one another, acquired railroads and wrecked them, built paper structures of securities and unloaded them on a gullible public. By the turn of the century, after the work of the muckrakers, the mood of the press and the reading public became more realistic. By the time of the first World War the Titan had caught the imagination of the novelists as well as the populace, and for the press and magazines he became a legendary figure in a manner different from the sugar-loaf legends of the early admirers.

Americans needed no fire-breathing imperialist swaggerers to express their sense of national importance. The Titan was all the symbol they needed. Wherever he went there was a planetary turmoil and a sense of construction, and the big money poured around him. Even when the muckrakers excoriated him for corrupting legislatures, buying up city governments, and betraying the original democratic premise, they left little doubt that their target was indeed a Titan. The magazine readers glimpsed the outlines of the heroic in the subjects of the biographical exposés and felt more envy than indignation.

Some of this may be found in the novelists as well. Mark Twain, himself a businessman and absorbed in money-making schemes, wrote a blistering indictment in *The Gilded Age* of the methods by which the big fortunes were built up. William Dean Howells was torn between an admiration for honest businessmen like Silas Lapham and the anger against the men of "the Accumulation" which he set down in *A Traveler from Altruria.* Henry James recoiled from trade yet, like Scott Fitzgerald after him, he was obsessed with money and its aura. In the James tradition the Edith Wharton novels come to life, in *The House of Mirth* and *The Custom of the Country,* when she deals with her money-driven women, her female counterparts of single-minded business-men. The muckrakers themselves, as they dug around in the archives of business methods and corporate finance, were moved by a complex *odi et amo* feeling about their subjects. Even the novelists who attacked the Titan most drastically, like Frank Norris and Theodore Dreiser, were (as Kenneth Lynn has pointed out in the *Dream of Success*) covertly admirers of his greatness and sharers of his values.

Dreiser's portrait of Frank Algernon Cowperwood—which he took from Charles Tyson Yerkes, the Philadelphia and Chicago traction king—shows most clearly the combined fascination-and-recoil which, until the Great Depression, most Americans felt for the power and the ruthless drive of the business Titans. Dreiser did his studies of Cowperwood-Yerkes while he was brooding over the Darwinian doctrine that the survivors must be the fittest, and over the beyond-good-and-evil and will-to-power ideas of Nietzsche. The term he used for Cowperwood—"the Titan"—was a Lucretian image, implying that these men who operated far above the groundlings and held themselves superior to human law were not so much immoral as amoral. He wrote about Cowperwood with the sympathy of an Indiana boy out of the Midwestern climate of striving and dreaming from which so many of the business Titans came. Plebeian that he was, he was himself half in love with the symbol of the plebeian-turned-plutocrat that he portrayed. He shows Cowperwood growing up in Philadelphia like a boy with his nose pressed against a shopwindow, looking in at the wealth that spells power and is crowned by the need of beauty. The class lines in such a society had to be sharp, yet not too sharp; resistant enough to apply the spur to the hungering youthful will, yet mobile enough so that one could master them. The process of mastery involved for Cowperwood a term in a Philadelphia jail, the betrayal of his friends, the corruption of city councils and legislatures, the destruction of those closest to him Yet he lived out his willed dream, and as he did so his prowess and predacity hardened. He piled up wealth and power, crushed the men who stood in his way, combined with those he could not crush; he won a mastery over women as well—especially *their* women—the daughters of those who had been the symbols of his dream of success and the obstacles in his path. In the end he failed and got religion (in the third volume of the trilogy, *The Stoic*), but this was an afterthought of the later Dreiser.

As Dreiser and many others saw him, the Titan was half conqueror, half child. He had a daring vision and made reckless use of his resources to gain his ends; he had a quick sense for estimating and using people and an ability to see his lucky chance and grasp it. Yet with all this, there was a restless search for novelty, as with a child; a love of big things because they are big, almost as if his great projects had become only toys. There was in him a joy in the creation of means but an obtuseness about ends. Most of all, there was a quality of tenacious single-mindedness of purpose which was preindustrial in the American character, and the symbolic theme of Captain Ahab's unrelenting pursuit of the whale of *Moby Dick.*

There is one division which cuts across most of the Titans of the earlier prewar era of America—the split between the Puritan and the magnifico. J. Pierpont Morgan, the greatest of all the Titans, was a magnifico in the sense that he operated on a scale of magnificence. So also were Hill, Gates, Gould, several of the early Du Ponts, and Yerkes himself. There was a lustiness and a grandeur of scope in their private as in their business lives. They bet and gambled, lived conspicuously, gave parties, sailed yachts, were seen in the European capitals; there were legends of the stables of women they kept; they built palatial homes and crammed them with art treasures rifled from the museums and collections of Europe. There was a native optimism in them; in business as in private life they were "bullish"; their motto was Morgan's "never sell America short"; their fortunes were made on the upward arc of an expanding American economy. They saw far enough ahead to see the expansion and contributed to it their boldness and their measure of vision.

There was another strain, however, represented by Daniel Drew, the Rockefellers, Henry Ford: not the strain of magnificence but of the taut Puritan qualities. These men came out of the small towns and remained at home in small-town America. They were abstemious, churchgoing, taught Sunday-school classes. They spent little on themselves, and what they did they spent quietly. Like Rockefeller, they handed out shiny dimes; like Ford, they plowed everything back into the business. They had the eccentricities in which men can indulge when they sit on top of a pyramid of power. They were apt to be gloomy men and presented a stern visage to the world, at once unsmiling and unrelenting. Yet they were probably closer than the magnificos to the theological roots of capitalism: the demonstration of virtue through success, the doctrine of calling, the gospel of work and thrift.

Together these two strains condense the appeal of business enterprise as a way of life. To the middle-class mind the appeal is to the Puritan virtues of austerity and acquisitiveness, to the Faustian spirit of the imaginative it is that of movers and shakers and of empire builders. One stresses efficacy in the sight of God, the other power in the sight of man. One moves step by step, the other by bold leaps. One is the accumulative spirit, the other the gambling spirit. One operates best in the realm of production and managerial organization, the other in the realm of promotion and finance. Neither is complete without the other, and while in every Titan one or the other had predominated, no Titan has lacked elements of both. Their combined appeal has been powerful since even the groundlings, who could not live the life of the Titan, could identify themselves with his economic efficacy and share vicariously in his magnitudes.

As De Tocqueville noted even before the Civil War, the old European sense that there was something degrading about business quickly vanished in America, and the talented young people turned to business pursuits. The legend of the Titan attracted them almost as much as the Big Money itself. For while the formal goal of business enterprise is profit, the psychic rewards of the businessman's way of life came to consist as much in the pursuit of power as in the accumulation of money. There was a sense of risk and excitement in Big Enterprise. And while it was possible for many of the businessmen to pursue profit and power with a meanness of spirit and impoverished intellectual and emotional resources, this was not true of the outstanding figures. Unlike the worker chained to the machine, and the small businessman embittered by his struggle with his competitors and workers, the Titan often showed himself to have a spacious and creative mind.

Something happened to the Titan in the two decades after World War I. Before that time the indictment against him had stressed the enormity of his power, the charge being that he used it to betray the early ideals of the Republic. John Chamberlain has suggested that the reason for the persistent "belittling" of the Big Businessman by American novelists was their rebellion against their fathers and their search for a different kind of father symbol on the Left. Sometimes this was so, but I suspect that most of them wrote what they wrote out of the disillusionment that overcame them at the chasm between the Jeffersonian dream of a spacious and egalitarian American democracy, and the actual power of Big Business. They were protesting against the wasteland of American moral and cultural life between the time of Grant's Presidency and that of Wilson.

What happened in the Great Depression changed the image of the Titan more drastically. Big Business of the 1920s, certain that it had found the secret of perpetual prosperity, claimed the right to the policy-making decisions not only in the economy but in the government. But the economic collapse of 1929 resulted in a disillusionment with the Titan: the Big Money of the boom of the 1920s came clamoring to the

White House for extreme unction in the 1930s. Those who had seemed to be the "Lords of Creation" were stripped of a good deal of their stature and grandeur.

The businessman began to lose stature even before the Great Depression. After Dreiser's Cowperwood, Sinclair Lewis's Babbitt was a letdown. Babbitt is the biggest real-estate dealer in the minor universe of Zenith, Ohio, whose life revolves around his house, car, service clubs, lodge, and church; who mouths platitudes about business ethics but sees nothing wrong in pulling a real-estate squeeze play on a small butcher: Babbitt is no Titan, neither a great creator nor a great destroyer, but the fag end of business enterprise as a way of life. Lewis did what was in some ways a moving portrait of him, yet gave him none of the quiet dignity and sense of craftsmanship that Howells gave the painting-firm hero of *The Rise of Silas Lapham:* and the shift from the portrait of the 1890s marks the running down of a tradition.

Some of the other novelists showed an even sharper disenchantment. *U.S.A.*, the novel trilogy by John Dos Passos, applies to fiction some of the elements of Veblen's savage critique of American business enterprise. Charlie Anderson, who plays an important role in *The Big Money,* is the embodiment of constructive drives which have been corrupted by the manic passions of promotion. In a less intentional way Scott Fitzgerald's *The Great Gatsby*—the buccaneer who was part phony promoter, part racketeer, the man seemingly from nowhere whose shimmering appearance is woven out of the cloudless fabric of nothing—is also a figure of disenchantment. In Thomas Wolfe's *You Can't Go Home Again* the head of the "Company" is obsessed with finding new advertising slogans; and Wolfe portrays the squeezing of every sales executive in the lower rank by the one above him in the panicky sales hierarchy of the "Company." The emphasis was shifting from the figure of production and finance to that of promotion and sales, from the man who made the goods to the man who knew the magic of extracting something from nothing; from the major legendary figures like Morgan to the minor legends of the rising sales curve and the "hucksters" of the advertising legions. The portrait of business reached its furthest remove from the Titan in the description, in Faulkner's *The Hamlet* and *The Town,* of the locust invasion of his Mississippi county by the swarming Snopes family, which moved with mercantile ardor into all the crevices left by the crack-up of precapitalist Southern society.

But the crucial transformation of the Titan was wrought not so much by the Great Depression, nor by the invasion of the groundlings, but by the corporation. The type-figure who carved out the great industrial empires was almost submerged in the impersonality of the corporate form. In every area of life the winning of power has always required bolder and more vigorous talents than its consolidation. In the new and highly specialized technology, experts took over every phase of the corporation's activity—engineering, financing, production, promotion, advertising, salesmanship, personnel relations. In place of the heroic adventurism of the Titans came a group of "managerial skills" that required talent and judgment in the art of management but seemed earth-creeping by comparison. The increasing division of labor built up business hierarchies in which the aggressive mind of the Titan was less at home than the corporate bureaucratic mind. Once the regime of high-salaried managers was created it took on a life of its own, crowding out the life of the Titan. He ceased to be the giant in whose shadow the business institutions were shaped and became himself the shadow of the institution, taking his stature from the corporation. The corporation as instrument grew in importance while the men wielding it shrank. Those who were once considered barbarian invaders now became absorbed in the structure of the power they themselves created. The conquerors were conquered.

Does this mean that the Titan "reformed"? The big fact about the "Robber Barons" (the phrase was Matthew Josephson's) was not their personal ethics, although to a moralistic generation of reformers it may have seemed so. When Commodore Vanderbilt made his famous "public be damned" remark he was expressing a generalized sense of swaggering power. In broad perspective the ethics of the Big Businessmen were, taken as a group, no worse than the ethics of any other historical group of conquerors. Comparing how America was industrialized with the methods by which Germany, Japan, and Russia were later industrialized, the American record seems like a Sunday picnic or a huddle of innocents. Even the worst of the Robber Barons—men like Gould, Fisk, and Yerkes—were men of virtue compared with the Gauleiter and commissars who performed a similar task in their own countries. The real point is not that the Titan has "reformed," for he was never truly evil. It is rather that he has grown less colorful, less swaggering, more sophisticated; he has had to take his place in a bureaucracy in which his predecessors would have felt stifled; he has had to cope with the regulatory demands of a welfare state and the power of a labor movement; he has had to worry less about his competitors than about "business conditions," domestic and world politics, advertising, consumer demand, and the securities market. He must always feel the pulse of public opinion and be wary of alienating it. Wherever he goes he is accompanied by survey makers, "human-relations" technicians, public-opinion analysts, public-relations experts.

Once known primarily as a man of action (*furor Americanus* is what Aldous Huxley called the American cult of action), the businessman still remains that. But the areas of significant action have changed. They are no longer concerned with the crushing of competitors, the piling up of big fortunes, and the carving out of family dynastic power. The old competitive system has been replaced by a system of "imperfect competition" in which the corporations compete with one another less in prices than in brands and in "products"—that is, in alternative materials for achieving the same results. As for the big fortunes, a more drastic tax system than any continental European can envisage has made them archaic. The heads of the corporate empires no longer get their sense of fulfillment from personal accumulation, nor is their prime quality that of acquisitiveness. They are still movers and shakers, but for a different reason than before. The new Titan is still the creator and consolidator of corporate structures, the guiding mind of monopolies and cartels, the organizer of business "peak-associations." The men who run Metropolitan Life or General Motors, General Electric or U.S. Steel, Alcoa or A.T.&T., are men of power not because of their great fortunes or talents but because they have powerful instruments at their command. They have control of enormous blocks of investment and power. For income-tax purposes the new Titans allow the corporate profits to remain inside the corporation and then declare stock dividends. They create "charitable trusts" as legal fictions, and "foundations" as ways of escaping the ax of the inheritance tax. But where they once sought profit, they now seek the retention of the power over their capital investments. Their prime concern is the figure they can cut in America and the world as proconsuls administering their huge aggregates of power.

This requires and has developed a new personality profile for the Titan—that of a corporate statesman. He reads more than he used to, goes to college, makes speeches and statements (alas, too many and too platitudinous), is seen at public conferences. His suavity is more evident than his ruthlessness. He knows something of the workings of the economy and the government, and of world affairs. I am speaking, of course, not of the run-of-mill corporate vice-president, nor of the sales manager or advertising manager who may be only a contemporary Babbitt, but of the small group of sophisticated holders of business power who embody business creativeness. He has even had to take a hand in developing the idea of the welfare state itself, as Wendell Willkie did; or administering its controls over business, as Charles E. Wilson did; or in supervising the American economic aid to Europe, as Paul Hoffman did.

The Big Businessman has had to come up squarely against the problems of the survival of the economy and the organization of a transformed society. This new type of businessman—represented, for example, by the members of the Committee for Economic Development—is still not accepted by the mediocre but stubborn men who remember the old catchwords of the free-market economy and strike out blindly against any innovating doctrine. These men act sometimes like the defenders of a besieged city, a League of Frightened Men who in their panic are bent on searching out heresy in their own ranks. Once the new businessman makes clear his premise that the productivity which is the source of profits is more important than any particular profit, that an expanding economy may require the co-operative action of the welfare corporation and the welfare state, he runs the danger of being branded as a maverick and cast out of the herd.

The image of the old Titan still remains in the popular mind and colors the dreams that the young men dream. But the effective figure is a new one, in a new setting, the result of the complex and powerful transforming process of the past half century of American society.

It may be significant that no one has yet found a name for him that will stick, as "Titan" and "Tycoon" did to his predecessor. He is often called a "business statesman" by those who stand in awe of him and feel there must be some appellation of a dignity that parallels his massive business power—also sometimes his wealth. Such men as Alfred Sloan, Charles E. Wilson, and Harlow Curtice of General Motors are considered a cut above the old-fashioned, profit-seeking, money-grasping Titans. As a result they have been called on to speak as oracles not only on industrial matters but on the welfare of the nation, and sometimes have convinced themselves (often with public approval) that the country is only an enlarged image of the company and that they have the right to make decisions about what is good for both.

Perhaps the simplest name for them is what their employees tend to call them—"Mr. Big"—carrying with it a half affectionate, half scornful set of overtones. In conversation the ordinary American will say of one of these new corporate moguls that he is the "head" of such-and-such a corporate empire. These are indeed the "head men" of American life, and what gives the name some aptness is that it refers less to the stature or personality of the man himself than to his position at the head of a hierarchy of function and power. When one head man goes, another arrives to take his place. What is crucial, as in the hierarchy of the Middle Ages, is not so much the individual as the status. In fact, a number of writers have noted that these American head men are emerging as corporate seigneurs, and that their position and power have much in common with the frame of medieval society.

Yet what strikes the popular mind is their power and ruthlessness as they contend for place with the most modern of weapons—promotion schemes, mergers, corporate reorganizations. During the 1950s, a new type of novel about the businessman emerged, in which the problems of authority and ethical codes were posed. In Cameron Hawley's *Executive Suite* the tradition set up by the corporate founder, which seemed archaic to the new managerial group, finally triumphed, and with it the idea that the heart of corporate enterprise is what it can do for the workers, the community, and the values of craftsmanship. In the same author's *Cash McCall* there is a skillful delineation of the new Napoleons of corporate finance who march and wheel their chess pieces across the board without much concern for what any particular corporation is producing: here again, once the ethical problem has been posed, it is resolved (as in the case of religious conversion) by a saving insight into the productive values that transcend the merely financial ones. In a TV and movie story called *Patterns* the resolution is not so simple: the "head man" is depicted in almost Nietzschean terms as driven by an urge to stretch himself and his associates to the utmost of their powers, beyond the human. But Nietzsche never foresaw that in the American case the effort to reach to the godlike would apply to the creation not of the Superman but of Super-corporation. And the hero of this story, while seeing the evil and ruthlessness of the head man, is himself at the end half caught up in his fervor and asks only for a chance to be more ruthless himself and to make a victim of the man who has made victims of others—all in the name of the Corporation.

3. The Corporate Empires

IT IS TIME to take a closer look at the corporation as a social contrivance. A discerning anthropologist, studying characteristic American inventions such as the dating pattern, the success system, and judicial review, might seize on the corporation as the most important of all. Reaching into every area of life, it has become the instrument by which Americans organize any project demanding group effort, impersonality, continuity beyond the individual life, and limited liability. It is striking that a highly individualist people should accept a transformation of its life wrought by so impersonal a social invention.

Much ingenuity has been invested in the corporation as a mechanism. The refinements of corporate law and finance, of corporate liaisons and marriages, of corporate dissolution and reorganization, have absorbed some of the most resourceful talents of the American legal and financial elites. In the planning of corporate strategies there have been field marshals of genius and Napoleons of dazzling megalomania. Some, like Samuel Insull, came to grief; others received for their exploits the admiration of the members of the corporate fraternity. But in the main the corporate form is what it is today in America because of the patient labors of thousands of talented but largely unknown men who have been drawn to their work, by some obscure impulsion, as beavers to the construction of their dams.

The early American corporations were wards of the state, chartered only in rare cases and supervised by the state in every phase of their operation. When a group of men received a charter to build a railroad or canal, or run a toll bridge, or organize a college, the assumption was that the state was grudgingly signing away one of its inherent functions, retaining the responsibility of supervision. The corporation thus began as a state instrument, to be kept within the ambit of the state power. But such was the dynamism of American business enterprise within it that it ran away with the original intention. It helped gather vast blocs of capital by subdividing and dispersing business ownership and collecting the savings and hopes of many. By consolidating a number of enterprises and tapping the profits from their combined future growth, it anticipated these future profits and expressed them in the immediate market value of stocks. The corporate form thus suited a business spirit which sought always to capitalize the future, and in turn it created the stock market as a way of mirroring men's shifting calculations about future earnings and values.

In these ways the corporation built vast power blocs whose size and impersonality daunted the Populist thinkers of the turn of the century. Henry Demarest Lloyd felt that the "Wealth" whose concentration it made possible was destroying the "Commonwealth." Frank Norris called it the "Octopus" and portrayed in his novels how its impersonal power blasted personal lives and hopes. The generation of muckrakers called the alliance of corporation and political machine the "System," and Steffens described it by resorting to the mystical "It." William Dean Howells, writing in his Socialist phase in *A Traveler from Altruria,* called corporate power the "Accumulation," and reflected with sadness that "by a logic irresistible and inexorable, the Accumulation *was,* and we were *not.*" If American social critics today are no longer so colorful in their epithets, it is because they have come to accept the corporate form as a fact. Like Adolph Berle, they recognize it as embracing a crucial phase of "the twentieth-century capitalist revolution" and are concerned mainly with realistic ways of keeping its power within bounds, as well as being curious about the direction in which it will move and grow.

These corporate power blocs make possible the industrial concentration which was for a time the subject of repeated government investigations—the Report of the Industrial Commissions in 1904, the Pujo investigation a decade later in 1913, and the TNEC (Temporary National Economic Committee) inquiry two decades later in the 1930s. In the 1940s and 1950s there were fewer occasions and less impetus for such critical investigations—a sign not only of friendlier Administrations but, even more, of an acceptance of the dominating position of a handful of corporations in whose shadow the rest live.

A Federal Trade Commission study in 1947 showed that of some one hundred thousand corporations in America, 113 had assets of $100 million and over. Twelve of them ran into billions of dollars in their holdings. The most recent figures, at the end of the 1940s, show that 135 corporations own 45 per cent of the industrial assets of the nation, and that a few hundred men, in eight or ten loosely allied financial groups, control assets of over $100 billion. The picture in particular industries is similarly revealing. Out of twenty-six major manufacturing fields there were nineteen in which at least 60 per cent of the industry was controlled by six or fewer corporations, and thirteen in which at least 60 per cent was controlled by three or fewer. Heading the list were aluminum, tin, linoleum, copper, cigarettes, liquor, plumbing supplies, rubber tires, office equipment, automobiles, farm machinery, and meat products.

The trend toward the big corporate unit is partly explained by low production and distribution costs. The big corporations are in a real sense the children of competition. In the fierce struggle for survival and profits the pay-off is in efficiency, and those who triumph in the competitive struggle quite naturally drive their rivals to the wall, where they are willing to be bought out. This is especially true in the case of brand competition, as with automobiles, in an era where economic success depends on the psychic contagion among buyers as much as it does on the quality or utility of the product itself. It has long been known, of course, that the best producing units vary in size and are frequently a good deal smaller than the cancerous size of the giant corporation. "If God had intended us to have anything as large as the U.S. Steel Corporation," said Justice Brandeis in developing his idea of "the curse of bigness," "he would have given us the brains to run it well." But the persistent question is: "How big is too big?" American businessmen know that the steel industry, once the leader in technological advance, has fallen behind such newer industries as aviation, chemicals, and the electrical industries. Even in the relatively new industries, the size of the corporate unit extends well beyond the daily direct knowledge of any managerial officials. A corporation like General Motors has been compelled to split up its empire into more or less autonomous producing units, in order to prevent the spread of elephantiasis.

Thus one may venture that corporate bigness has as much to do with the strategic capture of power as with possible efficiencies of production. Current technology involves outlays so huge that only the big producers find them compassable: the big firms, moreover, can spend more on advertising campaigns and put a bigger and more aggressive sales force into the field. The corporate power bloc has command of raw materials often not available to its smaller competitors, especially in an armament economy, when procurement officials are hurried and harassed, and give the priority allocations as well as the contracts to the big firms. Because of its research laboratories and its ability to buy up promising inventions, it has command of patents and processes with which it can freeze others out of the market. It can attract scientists, engineers, technicians; it can set up elaborate marketing and advertising structures; it can surround itself with the artfulness of "public relations." It can control a big enough portion of the market so that its voice is heard loud and clear in the price agreements which are becoming standard practice in the corporate field. It can apply pressures to the government itself, by lobbies in the capitals and by its influence over party managers, candidates, and local machinery.

Thus the advantages of corporate bigness may come after the fact, not before. Corporations, by the very fact of their bigness, may achieve a strategic power that sometimes makes it unnecessary for them to pursue efficiencies which can cut costs. They become tired and unwilling to take risks, and in some cases grow backward in their response to technological change.

As I have noted above in speaking of the corporate head men as feudal seigneurs, the corporation which started as a legal device has ended by carving out an imperium for itself. John Dewey saw how far this had gone, and in an early essay called "The United States, Inc." he spoke of "the corporateness of society." W. J. Ghent, one of the turn-of-the-century critics of corporate capitalism, called it "the New Feudalism," which seemed an apt term for a system in which the feudal lords owed formal allegiance to the central political authorities yet retained their own domains of power.

The corporations have become, in a sense, private governments. Their decisions influence the size and distribution of the national product, the channeling of investment, the levels of employment and purchasing capacity of the workers. In effect they levy taxes on the consumer and make alliances with foreign corporations in cartel agreements. Operating basically for private purposes, with public consequences secondary, they can (as I have noted) crowd out competitors, divide the market, keep profits high, determine price levels and production volume. The picture of prices fixed in the free play of the market needs to be modified today: in a number of the mass-production industries corporate prices tend to be set "administratively," by the action of a small number of corporations, with an eye to costs, profits, volume of sales, and what the traffic will bear. This is modified somewhat by the fact that while the prices are set administratively—say by the auto companies—the retail dealer makes adjustments to a variable market through discounts and by varying the turn-in allowance for the old car. This should not, however, obscure the fact that the functions I have described affect the public interest deeply, yet they are being carried out by holders of corporate power who are not chosen by the people, responsible to them, or replaceable by them.

The defenders of corporate power sometimes make the mistake of denying its scope, picturing the American economy still in terms of the legendary capitalism of a market system of competing small enterprises. The better course is to admit the power of the corporate empires and assess its sources and uses. Adolf Berle, whose long and intimate knowledge of the corporate world demands respect, agrees that "the corporate empire wants all the commercial power it can get," but adds that "it has little instinct for going beyond that. Its political adventures are primarily to safeguard its commercial position. It has somehow got itself into a situation where it is held responsible for a great deal more than that—and is painfully trying to understand how it got there and what to do." Berle and other observers also contend that a new kind of statesmanship is developing in the corporation, with a sense of restraint and of responsibility for the public consequences of the private managerial decisions. Certainly the corporate ethos has changed since the 1920s, although innovation in business practices has not kept the same pace as innovation in technology and managerial organization. The disturbing fact is that, in the absence of strong outer controls over corporate practices, reliance must be placed on inner controls: and thus far the corporation has not developed built-in controls that restrain its behavior. It relies instead on a rising level of business education (the Harvard School of Business Administration is like nothing else in the world and has profoundly influenced the idea and performance of the managerial function) and on self-criticism within the corporate community, both of which may prove a frail line in time of acute economic stress.

The sharp question that might be put by the defenders of the corporate empires is: What was the historical alternative? Without the corporate form America could probably not have developed industrialism so rapidly or on so large a scale, nor could it have accumulated capital and plowed it back into industry as dramatically as it did. An economy of small firms was possible in Jackson's day but scarcely in ours. One alternative was national ownership with big-scale enterprise under government trusts. But this would have raised even more far-reaching issues of power than the corporate empires have done. Whatever group owns or runs the economic plant of a country has enormous power vested in it; that holds true also of the group that runs the trade-unions and even more of the group that runs the government. If the same group holds power in all three of these areas there is scarcely a crack possible in the combined monolith of power. What can be said of the American corporation as a power bloc is that, while it may sometimes control and even cow specific officials or agencies of the government, it is not in itself the government. Along with the other power institutions it presents on the American landscape a plurality of power groupings which are the better for their dispersal.

The Big Corporation, Big Unionism, and Big Government live in an uneasy ménage in America, with no one of them able to crush the others. A new constitutional structure of industry and government is emerging, with a new separation of powers that is more relevant for contemporary America than the classical separation of governmental powers. The corporation and the union have tacitly agreed roughly on the boundary lines beyond which neither interferes with the other, while there is a common area between these boundaries where they bargain collectively; and the government has agreed roughly on the limits beyond which it will not interfere with either the corporation or union, nor will they in turn seek to overthrow it. But this delimitation of provinces should not obscure the fact that the corporate system as a whole has immense weight with every American government, nor the fact that the corporate empires have revolutionized the price system, profit system, and property system, so that the actualities of American business power bear little relation to the golden legendary profile of capitalism.

There has been a recent tendency to depict the American economy as a "people's capitalism." The ownership of America's industrial plant has been diffused. In the 1950s A.T.&T., which carried stock dispersion furthest as a matter of policy, reported 1,307,000 owners (roughly one out of every fifty American families), of whom a quarter million were company employees. General Motors had 482,000 stockholders, and Westinghouse Electric had 111,000. In all, seven and a half million Americans owned stock in corporations, many of them in the companies they worked for, especially through union-employer pension funds. This has given the corporations some roots in popular acceptance. Yet most of the stockholders owned only a few shares: 60 per cent of the shares in the 200 largest industrial corporations, according to the classic Berle and Means study, *The Modern Corporation and Private Property,* were owned by 1 per cent of the stockholders. For all the companies listed on the exchanges, stockholders of over $10,000 (4 per cent of the number of stockholders) owned 60 per cent of the stocks. In the Berle-Means figures, 90 per cent of American stockholders in 1937 had incomes of less than $5,000 a year. Along with the diffusion of ownership there has also been a transformation of it. The old owner-manager no longer exists in any significant sense and has been replaced by a managerial elite that acts as deputy for the owners, whether their holdings be diffused or highly concentrated.

The striking fact here—pointed out by Veblen, developed by W. Z. Ripley, and elaborated on a major scale by Berle and Means—is that while the corporation has diffused industrial ownership, it has concentrated control and split one from the other. When an institution is as important as the corporation, its internal structure becomes of moment for the society. Berle and Means studying the 200 largest industrial corporations, found that in 88 per cent of them control was held by a small group of men: either by a management group (44 per cent) or by some legal device such as a voting trust or a holding company (21 per cent), or by a bloc of minority stockholders (23 per cent). Only in 5 per cent of them—10 of the 200 corporations—was the control in the hands of the stockholders who held a majority of the stock.

This makes a legend of the classical theory that capitalism works because private ownership is spurred to creative acts of business enterprise by the prospect of private profits. What it shows is that a new corporate managerial oligarchy has emerged which stands between ownership and the profit incentive. Ownership has had a wedge driven around it in three directions: it has been split from profit and therefore incentive, from management and therefore from direct contact with the operations of the business, and from control and therefore from the major decisions.

This three-way split has been revolutionary. It has meant that "private enterprise" and "private property" have lost much of their former meaning as effective forces. The groups that had stakes of public interest in the control of the major decisions in the economy—the owners, the workers, the consumers, the government—have been largely left out of the control. A group of "insiders" who are not the principal parties of interest have taken over the control. What seems to have happened is that the corporation, by diffusing private ownership so widely, created a vacuum of control; and by increasing the scale of business operations so greatly, it created a management bureaucracy. While everyone was looking elsewhere—at the struggles between labor and capital, between business and government, between big and small business—the corporate bureaucracy was quick to move into the vacuum of control.

But to say that the new corporate managerial group is also the controlling group is to oversimplify a complex situation. The controlling group has no sharp boundaries. The top officers of management form part of it; others in it may represent the owners of substantial but minority blocs of stock, or investment trusts that subscribe to new stock issues and thus supply risk capital, or bankers and lawyers who may have had a hand in forming or reorganizing the corporation or who hold proxies for their stockholder customers. The problem of locating control is further complicated by the bewildering network of intercorporate relations: the fact that the same men are directors in a number of corporations, that corporations hold blocs of stock in other corporations, that "holding companies" are formed to control the stock in a number of corporations. The structure of the Du Pont industrial empire may serve as one illustration of this complexity. The Du Pont Company began in munitions, expanded after World War I in automobiles, rubber, and other peacetime products. It controls both General Motors and U.S. Rubber; it ramifies into a number of satellite companies in chemicals and synthetic products. Its own stock is held by the Christiana Company, which is a holding company controlled by the Du Ponts and their friends; and at the top of the pyramid of control is the Delaware Company, an even more restricted holding company controlled by the inner circle of the Du Pont family.

Family holdings play a great role in the Du Pont empire, as they still do in the Ford empire, even after the Ford family turned the bulk of its stock over to the Ford Foundation. A number of the smaller corporations are still family-owned and also owner-managed. There are also some famous financial families, like the Rockefellers, which continue to be active in business and especially in the segment of it where their family fortune was originally made. Yet this is not typical of most of the big corporations, where the stockholding is diffused and the managerial group exercises control. The breakup of "family capitalism" in America has been far sharper than in Europe. What is left of it in the corporate form is only a fragmentary residue. In the realm of social structure this represents the counterpart of the transfer of power from the owners to the managers.

What can be clearly said of corporate control is that it is rarely wielded by the majority of stockholders, but rather by powerful overlapping oligarchies of managers and insiders. There have been a few efforts by small stockholders' committees to appear at stockholders' meetings and demand democratic procedure, but they have been ineffectual. A wistfully written sketch in *The New Yorker* by a small stockholder who took it into his head to assert his rights and attend a Du Pont meeting at Wilmington brings out satirically the lights and shadows of the grotesquely unimportant status of the ordinary "owner" of a corporation who comes to hear the report of his "employees."

It is difficult to know where to place corporate responsibility, since the corporation is an amorphous entity whose core is hard to locate. As the editors of *Fortune* put it, "The control of the typical big corporation is now in the hands of 'managers' who do not own it, and its ownership is in the hands of stockholders who do not influence its behavior. The corporation has become a disembodied, almost self-sufficient, socially 'illegitimate' force." Ironically this anonymous force achieved a number of exemptions and immunities from public regulation, both state and Federal, by claiming to be a "person" within the meaning of the due-process clause of the Fifth and Fourteenth Amendments. The story of how the Fourteenth Amendment was transformed—from a shield of the new Negro citizens against discriminatory treatment into a shield of corporate power against public regulation—is an absorbing study in American legal and intellectual history. Some of the earlier students of constitutional history treated the episode as an example of a "conspiracy" by corporate power; but the conspiracy premise proved unnecessary, the truth being that the corporate symbols exercised a hold on the legislative and judicial mind, which personalized the corporation even while the corporation was depersonalizing business enterprises.

In fact, the new corporate capitalism, which is in one sense a "popular capitalism" is in another a new and peculiarly American collectivism—a form of business syndicalism. If one were to generalize the traits of collectivism, they might run as follows: the crowding out of the "private" principle in enterprise by an authoritarian principle (not necessarily governmental); the whittling away of private property and of the profit incentive; the separation between the formal and real loci of power; the transfer of decisions from an open or "free" market to an administrative group (not necessarily governmental); the steady enlargement of the administrative units, and their pre-emption of a monopoly position; their control by a self-perpetuating bureaucratic elite, and their removal from popular responsibility.

The structure of corporate capitalism fits pretty well into this generalized pattern of collectivism. The "owners" have been relegated to the role of investors; the separation of ownership from control, along with the factor of steep taxes, has obscured the profit incentive; "private property," the "free market," and the "price system" have been changed in meaning. What remains of the profit stimulus, the sanctities of control-by-property, and the free-enterprise system must all be viewed within the framework of a corporate managerial group. The "iron law of oligarchy," which Michels saw operating in every power structure, has not left corporate capitalism exempt: the positions of power in the new elite are filled by men who wear the badges of success and can recognize them on the faces and records of the younger men coming up; the managerial elite is not a closed one, and it is highly competitive, yet there are intangibles that give a man entrance to it or can exclude him from it as surely as from the German imperial officers corps. For all its individualistic slogans, the business class in America has effectively substituted its own form of collectivism for the old individualism.

But although this collectivism has power and has shown a genius for production and marketing, it has not often shown the very quality of "statesmanship" which the champions of corporate capitalism claim for it. While the corporation has a mastery over its internal affairs, the corporate economy as a whole does not possess a self-regulating principle which can keep it going in social health and prosperity. It cannot create by itself the structure of order in which the multiple processes of far-flung enterprises are kept within a rational framework. Its failure has rested not on a lack of organizing ability, as its achievements in administrative intermeshing and legal finesse attest, but on the fact that an administrative mechanism intended for one sector of the economy cannot organize the whole, and one intended for conflict and the conquest of power is not equally useful for co-operation and order. Hence the need for a gridiron pattern of governmental, legal, and trade-union controls added to the inner controls that are being built into corporate practice. Through this pattern of voluntary decisions and institutional control a number of the problems that had plagued American capitalism—including some of the problems of the business cycle, inflation, unemployment, insecurity, and labor conflict—have been made more manageable.

Nor did a corporate General Staff emerge, as it did in other capitalist structures, as an instrument of social power. The trade-association movement proved useful in the effort at price-fixing and restriction of production, chiefly by the smaller firms, but its defect was its emphasis on freezing rather than expanding the economy. The next logical step was the formation of "peak associations" (after the German usage, *Spitzgenossenschaften*), as with the National Chamber of Commerce and notably the National Association of Manufacturers. Here too the rigidifying process set in. Alfred Cleveland's study of the N.A.M. for the period 1933-1946 showed that 125 corporations, making up less than 1 per cent of the membership, divided among them almost nine tenths of the executive committee posts and two thirds of the directors' posts of the organization; during the same period, the Cleveland study shows, the N.A.M. policies were mainly negative, being concentrated on opposing labor, taxes, and governmental restriction. The efforts of government to use the corporate form that had been so successful in business, and to develop the government corporation as entrepreneur (as with the TVA) have also been bitterly opposed by the business associations in the name of the "American way." Legislatively they have been effective as lobbies and pressure groups; politically they have operated to fight the "creeping Socialism" of the Democrats and maintain orthodoxy within Republican ranks; ideologically they have conducted "educational" campaigns in the schools, churches, and women's clubs.

But this effort has not added up either to the hopes of its organizers or the fears of some of the critics of corporation trends. The "law of centralization and decay," as formulated by Brooks Adams, has operated in corporate collectivism at least on the score of centralization, but the signs of decay are still murky. The more exacting believers in economic determinism argued in the 1930s and 1940s that the American corporate economy, with its peak associations, monopolies, and cartels, was taking the road that business power took in Italy, Germany, and Japan. Robert Brady, writing in the 1940s in *Business As a System of Power,* saw the N.A.M. as acting no differently from the Zaibatsu, the Federation of British Industries, and the German cartels, but this proved wide of the mark both as description and as prediction. Actually the experience of German business in aiding the rise of Nazism remains a scorching memory to American businessmen, who know that they would be engulfed by the totalitarian wave they invoked. Corporate collectivism has shown few signs of moving into the phase of the corporate state, although what would happen in the event of another world war cannot be foretold. It seems more inclined to digest the lessons of the boom-and-bust cycles of the past, to accept—however reluctantly—the necessary minimum of taxation and government intervention, and meanwhile to bask in the sunshine of big profits and rising prestige. American corporate capitalism shares a good measure of the pliable temper of American life as a whole. Even the corporate empires have shown little inclination either to form themselves into a monolithic common front or to raise up demagogues, supposedly to rid them of their enemies, as in a Fascist state.

How can one explain the failure of the American corporate empires to take possession of the whole society, as many observers predicted they would do, and turn the commonwealth into a corporate state? According to Marxist theory this should have happened some time back. In the first decade of the century Jack London foresaw, in *The Iron Heel,* the emergence of an oppressive power that would trample upon American society. As late as the TNEC study of *The Structure of the American Economy* there was a surviving emphasis upon the enormous power of the business corporation. At that time a number of American liberal critics, writing in the shadow of Marxism and with the heavy sense of the march of the corporate empires weighing upon them, wrote at times as if it had already in fact happened, and as if "monopoly Fascism" had already taken possession of America or was about to do so.

There are several important facts about the corporate empires to be kept in mind. One is their nonpolitical character. Even with the decline of the profit-ownership incentive, the great spur in corporate activity is still that of profit and productive achievement rather than political power. This absorption—and quite properly—is with economic aims, not primarily political. As a result, what has developed is not a corporate totalitarianism but more like a corporate syndicalism, using "syndicalism" in the sense of a concentration of power for the purposes of economic action.

Another fact is that the decisions in a corporate economy are decentralized. The classical economic theory of decisions made by small individual enterprisers, with Adam Smith's "hand of God" watching over them, is obviously no longer true—if it ever was. Yet even with the big corporations doing most of the decision-making, it is still true that each of them does it as a going economic concern, instead of its being done at the governmental centers as part of a planning process. As Galbraith puts it, "Even where the concentration of control over industry is relatively great, the final authority over production decisions is held at a comparatively large number of points." Given the high and complex living standards of the Americans, centralized decisions would be almost impossible. In a period of serious inflation they become necessary, especially on questions of price and wage ceilings, and governmental intervention moves in: even when they are necessary they make the economic process clumsy.

Finally, the corporate empires continue to struggle with one another. Using Galbraith's suggestive phrase again, the older concept of competition among a host of individual producers or sellers has now been replaced (since competition has in many senses vanished) by the concept of "countervailing power." There is a struggle inside the corporate hierarchy between the Big Corporation and Big Distribution, chiefly in the form of the chain stores and the mail-order houses; there is a struggle also between Big Agriculture, which exercises considerable political pressures, and the Big Corporation; add to that the struggle between Big Unionism and all of them; and add finally the struggle between all of them and Big Government.

In this sense there is a pull and tension within the American economy which lessens the power of monopoly capitalism itself. The drive toward centralization of power has affected not only the industrial producers but the farmers, the workers, the distributors, and the government itself. What gives the economy its freedom is no longer the "free market" in the old sense but the tug of war between power groups whose swollen strength has burst the bounds of the free market. It is the great paradox of the American economy that it escapes totalitarianism by the fact of a continuing titanic struggle of vast imperial units within itself. It follows, therefore, that the growth of monopolies and mergers, dangerous as they are because all concentrated power is dangerous, has not in itself destroyed American freedom.

It may be this kind of unconscious insight that has led Americans to allow the growth of monopolies at the same time that their logical minds have led them to put antimonopoly laws on the statute books and to make feeble efforts at enforcing them. It follows also that, given the growth of monopoly capitalism, the emergence of the powerful trade-unions has been not a menace but an element of economic and social health, as one of the great counterbalancing forces. It follows similarly that the power of the chain stores and of the agricultural bloc has operated further toward holding this balance. And, finally, the bigness of the government and its network of regulatory measures—dangerous as they are in themselves—have operated to keep the other power concentrations from destroying one another and the public welfare in the process.

Thus corporate business in America does not have anything like the political power that is sometimes ascribed to it, especially by those who are still influenced by foreign parallels. Yet in a curious way business has a good deal more power than its defenders will admit. It comes largely through default. In a mass-consumption economy of high living standards there is inevitably a de-emphasis of political struggle: the issues as between classes and interest groups grow less sharp than they were in the period before World War I or in the 1920s and 1930s. While the economy itself is maintained in something like an equilibrium by the confronting of the "Bigs," the only forces that can swing considerable power are the corporations and the trade-unions. As between the two, the corporations have more money, control the destinies of more people, and can influence the stereotypes of thinking of the whole population. They therefore tend to be the top dog, even though they may not be themselves aware of having clearly political aims and drives.

4. The Property Revolution

IN SPITE OF America's role as the chief residual defender of the system of private property in its pristine purity, the position of property in America is neither private nor pure. In a dynamic economy like the American the bundle of legal claims called "property" never remains stable: a change in technical processes, a shift in consumption habits, a new invention in technology or managerial practice, a depression or a war, may give new value to claims hitherto ignored or diminish others hitherto cherished.

Property is not a simple or single right. It has become a property-complex—a tangle of ideas, emotions, and attitudes, as well as of legal and economic practices. As such it has been drastically transformed in the era of Big Technology and the corporate empires. According to the more naïve version of the business legend, private property has always been the American "way of life" and always will be. This has lost much of its meaning. For those who possess property, in the sense of substantial stockholdings and investments, it is mainly a symbol of status for the present and security for the future. For the rest, who may have homes and automobiles but are propertyless in the sense of industrial holdings, it is something they hope to acquire for themselves or their children: this hope, along with the things in their own life that they value and enjoy, serves to link them with the holders of property and power. The forms of property have changed, but the emotions and loyalties it evokes go back deep into the American past.

The American ideas about property were deeply influenced by a trio of English thinkers—Locke, Blackstone, and Herbert Spencer—but it was the structure of American society up until the end of the nineteenth century that gave substance to their theories. The components of the property idea—that a man had a right to the things with which he had mixed his sweat, that his property was linked with his craft and job and therefore with his personality, that you could no more deprive him of his property than of his freedom and individuality, that in fact his individuality was linked with the property which made him self-sufficient and self-reliant, and that he could do what he wished with the property that was his—these elements of the property idea had force in a social setting where almost every man owned a piece of land or hoped to save enough on his job to start a small business. In the America of the farmer and the owner-enterpriser, private property was a way of organizing not only the economy but also the personality.

This was reinforced by the underlying theological premises of the

Christian idea.* The Christian allegory of death and resurrection—the sacrifice for a principle sacred to the personality—gave a militant edge to the crusade for property, which was so closely tied with the personality. The roots of individualism in the Calvinist idea of calling and election gave further strength to the secular insignia of success in vocation. The theological premises of St. Augustine's *City of God* and of Bunyan's *Grace Abounding* combined in America to give property the aura of grace. In the moral and emotional climate of the earlier America, entrance into the Heavenly City required that one be shrived of poverty and invested with property. The clinching element of the property idea was the doctrine of natural rights, by which private property came to be accepted as inalienable from the person, part of "the laws of Nature and of Nature's God" that predated human society and therefore could not be changed by human enactment. This theology of the property idea helped the possessors to hold on to their power and invested their position with the support of popular conviction. In a society that regarded property as grace, business enterprise had strong roots in the general allegiance.

But as the conditions of property changed, with Big Technology and the corporate empires, the gap between the property idea and the social reality widened, until property of the old sort—family-owned and owner-managed—became a kind of residual legend, still clung to even when it was stripped of all but a lingering historical memory. Industrial property became centralized, family ownership waned, the corporate form pushed aside the others, the size of the property unit shifted—and America, which had once been a society mainly of small property owners, became a society not only of the Big Technology and the Big Corporation but also of Big Property.

Small Property still exists in the form of small farms, small businesses, and tiny shops, but the independent farmer is a dwindling fraction of the population, the small manufacturer is being crowded by the great corporations, and the little merchant finds himself precariously caught in an economy of big department stores, chain stores, mail-order firms, and discount houses. In the division of the nation among big property, small property, and the unpropertied, big property is increasing in power, small property is increasing in numbers (there were over five million nonfarm enterprises in the mid-1950s, an increase of over a million in a quarter century) but shrinking in power, while the unpropertied are growing in numbers despite the wider diffusion of stock ownership and are as powerless as the unpropertied have always been everywhere.

Before the world wars there still seemed a chance to have the issue

* The argument given too sketchily here is discussed further as the freedom property complex, in Ch. X, Sec. 2, "American Thought: the Angle of Vision."

fought out between Big and Small Property, and the great names of the Progressive Era—Wilson and Brandeis, La Follette and Norris, J. Allen Smith and Parrington and Beard—were the men who, even in the face of the challenge from the corporate empires, clung to the Jefferson-Jackson-Lincoln conception of an America of small property. It was this issue which furnished one of the great stakes of the social struggle for several generations. The struggle was lost by Small Property, mainly because it was waged not only against the corporate empires but also against their Big Technology, which was even harder to beat. In this struggle the impersonal Big Corporation had the advantage of putting on its enemy's uniform, garbing itself in the emotion-laden insignia of the idea of individualist property that had been shaped in an era of petty trade, small handicraft, and family ownership and operation, and was being invoked to sanction the triumph of the corporation and its new managerial elite.

I do not write of Big Property here as if it were always evil and monopolist, and of Small Property as if it were always good. Neither is necessarily true. The American worship of magnitudes, even when turned upside down to become a cult of the small, still remains an obsession with numbers. The monopoly power—defined as the power to manipulate price and output by being strategically placed to do so—may apply to both big and small corporations that are thus strategically placed, although it is more likely to apply to the big ones. In the ever-greater market of a high-level, mass-production economy the increase in corporate size is bound to keep pace with the growth in the size of the market. The American economy has shown a striking capacity for maintaining its freedom of energy even while changing and seemingly rigidifying its forms.

Two examples may serve to underscore this. One is in the area of competition: to a striking degree price competition in the mass-production industries has been replaced by brand and product competition; for example, technological innovation has made glass, rubber, steel, aluminum, and plastics compete with one another in many industrial and domestic uses. The second example is in the insurance companies, the investment trusts, and the pension funds. During the 1950s it was estimated that at least 80 per cent of all the new venture capital which was supplied to the organized capital market came through these big institutional investors. In a sense it may be said that they act as trustees for the savings and holdings of the ordinary American—a new kind of trusteeship which differs from the vaunted trusteeship of the Big Corporation itself. To the extent that these institutional investors safeguard the property interests of the small man, Small Property may be said to have re-emerged in the investment market even after it had to give way in production itself.

It would be wrong to say that the corporate empires entrenched private property, but even more wrong to say that they destroyed it. A better way is to say that the modern corporation "smashed the property atom," breaking it into constituent particles and reassigning them. The bond owner now gets one kind of return; the stockholder gets another; the large-minority-bloc stockholders have a hand in corporate decisions, sharing control with the managers, while the small stockholders who may together represent the majority ownership get their dividends but have little power of control except as their interests in the profits and security of their holdings are the concern of the big institutional investors I have discussed. The worker, who once had the hope of becoming a property owner by starting a business, still makes a stab at it in many cases but with a high rate of business failures. His realistic chance of owning property rests on becoming himself a small stockholder. For a fitful moment, during the "sitdown strikes" of 1936 and 1937, there was talk of the worker's property right in his job, but this did too much violence to the whole property tradition, which was emotionally linked with owners and not workers.

What the corporate revolution did was not to strip the propertied class of its power but to extend the reach of that class and change property relations within it. Where the owner had once controlled his own industrial property and capital and received profit from his own management and risk, he still got the profits in the form of dividends, but the decisions and control on which they were based were now bureaucratized, being shifted to the managerial group.

The processes of corporate investment have also suffered a drastic change. A recent analysis of the formation of capital from 1919 to 1947 shows the following: in that period the American capital accumulation was 770 billion dollars; 34 per cent (262 billion) was undistributed profits of the corporations themselves and was plowed back; 40 per cent (310 billion) was in the form of bank credit, used for capital expansion; 26 per cent (198 billion) was individual savings—that is, the savings of the risk-taker in the classical sense. But when the last figure is broken down, one finds that most of it went into savings banks or life insurance or durable consumers' goods which count as personal capital; some of it went into corporate bonds, paying a set return. Only a little more than 3 per cent of the individual savings went into corporate stocks. In 1948, in a year when the national income was 225 billion, only a billion dollars went into new corporate stock, common and preferred.

This means that the big corporation no longer goes out into the market looking for savings. It plows back its own profits. This was foreshadowed decades ago: Charles M. Schwab, the steel industrialist, when asked in 1923 what the future of American industry would be, answered, "Why won't it be in the future as in the past, all the money you make and more put back into the business?" A few recent figures indicate that business has followed his advice. In 1929 the American corporations reinvested 20 per cent of their profits; in 1950 they reinvested 70 per cent.

There are many reasons for this high rate of corporate self-financing. With huge profits, high government taxes, and the desire of the managers to show corporate growth as an index of their own managerial skill and achievement, the corporation has become almost self-sufficient, even in terms of its capital formation. Its new bond flotations are largely taken up by savings banks and insurance companies. This has led to the suggestion that most of the corporate capital today is in a sense "conscripted capital," either plowed back by corporate administrative decision, or invested for individuals by banks and insurance companies, or taken by the government in taxes and invested in public works programs and armament industries. Even more important is the decline of the investment banker. Compare his role in the merger movement of the 1890s and 1900s with his lesser role today, and the change becomes dramatic. There has long been a conviction that whoever controls the money market controls the corporate empires, and that whoever controls credit possesses the crucial power. This conviction was the basis for the economic thinking of Louis D. Brandeis about "other peoples' money" and for a whole series of Federal investigations of the "Money Trust." It was also the core idea of the European conceptions of American "finance capitalism" from Lenin through Hilferding to the lesser Marxists of today. This is far less true now, given the new trend of corporate self-financing which keeps the economy moving. The American economy during the past half century or longer has shifted from finance capitalism to corporate capitalism.

The consequences of all this for the property idea are far-reaching. It is hard to use the individualist "natural rights" defense of corporate power and talk of the managerial elite mixing their sweat with the soil or with their tools. As for the question of profits and power as a reward for business skills, what has happened is that the profits in the form of dividends go to the stockholders who have to show few business skills except shrewdness in knowing when to buy or sell stocks, while power without profits has gone to those who show the managerial skills.

As for the idea of risk-taking, one of the stock themes of business-minded editorial writers was that risk capital was the life blood of the economy, and that the welfare state might destroy it. But the reality is that risk capital has changed its form and nature. Like the profit motive in business, it was a carry-over from the era of small business enterprise into the Era of the Sure Thing. There is still risk in corporate enterprise. In their measured and ponderous way, corporations do take risks and often very great ones. But the capital they use is not individual entrepreneur capital, and the managers do not take risks with their own money. Nevertheless they have a sense that the corporate capital that they are risking is theirs, that it might otherwise be used for dividends or for strengthening their working funds, and that their own prestige as managers depends upon risking it wisely. In addition there is the generalized risk of violent fluctuations in the economy as a whole, due to the business cycle: the Great Depression confiscated more business values, running into the tens of billions, than the New Deal could ever have done, and when President Eisenhower suffered a heart attack, the loss in corporate values by stock-market quotations was immense.

With its two main underpinnings removed—the profit incentive and the reward for risk—what remains of the original theory of private property? Not much, it must be admitted: the original theory needs drastic overhauling, yet the social reality of private property is still a force in the American economy. Private property has not been abolished, either by Big Government or the Big Corporation: it has taken new forms. It is still private in the sense that it is not statist, but it has ceased to be individualist and has become corporate, institutional, and managerial. The incentives of the owners of Big Property are no longer profit-from-skill but have become profit-from-dividends, security for life, and if possible a "killing" on the stock market.

As for the incentive of the managers, some of them get options on blocs of stock at a low price as part of their salaries and to that extent are corporate owners also. Their salary range is broad: some may get less than $25,000 a year, others more than a quarter million (the highest salaries are in tobacco, liquor, cosmetics, drugs, movies, and broadcasting), and many of them get extra "bonuses," but only a handful are in the millionaire income class. Nonetheless as a group they belong to the big-income class and consider themselves part of Big Property. They know that each quarter they must show a good profits record, along with a good production and sales-volume record and a good labor-relations record.

They are usually able men, college graduates from the Midwest or the Northeast who "get along with people," wear the right clothes, have the right friends, and possess "agreeable" personalities. They work hard, carrying their work home with them at night, are reluctant to retire, and have great pride in their craft. They may be spurred on by the pace of technical advance behind which they dare not lag, or by shifts in the market situation with which they must keep up; but their important incentives are pride, prestige, and self-expression in their work. While they may have few competitors in their own industry, the corporate rivalry is usually intense. Sometimes it is a gamelike rivalry, as with the General Motors–Ford struggle to show which of them will be Number One in the small-car market. Sometimes, as with the automobile manufacturers in the lesser companies, it is a grimmer question of whether they will be pushed out of the market altogether. The cannibalism among corporations is as great as among the tribes in the Congo jungle, although it operates with the sanction of law as well as corporate tribal practice.

One of the great spurs, for both owners and managers, is the sense of power flowing from the massive capital whose investment they organize. This includes the indirect power over legislators, government administrators, and the communications industries, which the possessors of big investments and the dispensers of big advertising can count on. The managers associate themselves with Big Property and have become its agents. A Regent has become King, but he rules in the old regal fashion, in the interests of the dynasty. The freedom to do what one will with property, which is still claimed by the corporate regents as it was once by the individualist business kings, is still the watchword of the champions of corporate "private property"; and the property fears of the managers express themselves as strongly in opposition to "dangerous" ideas at home and abroad as those of the owners ever did.

One change in attitude has, however, taken place. The managers of the big corporations are likely to have a broader vision of the economy as a whole and its place in the world than the individual small businessmen, who are close to the competitive struggle and feel embittered both by their labor difficulties and by the big chunk of their income which the government takes in taxes. No Poujadist movement has arisen among American shopkeepers and small businessmen, as it did in France in the mid-1950s, yet there is a discernible narrowness of outlook in the small sectors of the American economy as well.

There remains to speak of the property ideas of the propertyless. The path to property in the earlier America was either through small landholding, usually on the advancing frontier, or by starting a small firm and making it larger, finally building it into a great established business and even a family fortune. The path to property now is more likely to be by the carving out of a career in the managerial hierarchy. Those who are not managers may shift from one occupation to another, or from industrial worker to white collar or professional, but they remain unpropertied.

Yet it would be wrong to conclude that the property idea has no hold on them. No dogmatically Socialist appeal has ever had much success with them in America, and they have consistently refused to take on the class-conscious bitterness assigned to them by the Marxist writers. However great the gap between the corporate reality and the theory of private property, the propertyless still assign the production record of America and their own increased living standards to the regime of private property. It may be "folklore," but folklore has a way of retaining its hold on the people. They are willing to consider the masters of corporate property the trustees of the private-property system until such time as they themselves or their children (for hope has never died in their hearts) will break into the charmed circle. They are resigned to Big Property not because they believe in some "harmony of interests," or think there is no conflict between top dog and bottom dog, but because each in his heart hopes still to be a top dog and therefore tends to identify with him. Even American unionism, as Hoxie long ago pointed out, is a property-minded "business unionism."

But I do not want to emphasize too much the identification with the Big Property group. Most of the propertyless are so only when judged in terms of industrial capital or land. Their real concern is with their personal property: a "home," even if it has a mortgage; a car, even an old one; some savings, even if inflation is depleting them; clothes and fashions; a TV set and kitchen appliances; a job, which to most Americans is *theirs* and therefore has property aspects; perhaps even a few shares of stock; and the hope someday of "taking it easy" and "retiring," on a different scale from the rich corporate owner and manager, but in much the same spirit of being invested with property as grace.

5. *Business and Its Satellites*

LIKE ANY imperial force, the corporate empires have opened hitherto untapped areas of American life and added to their domain a whole array of satellite activities. Even the barest profile of the business pattern in mid-twentieth-century America shows it unlike anything De Tocqueville or Bryce dreamed of and unlike the picture of American business in even so late a study as Harold Laski's *American Democracy,* which depicted a doomed figure of business enterprise in the sickroom of capitalism. There is no doom and no sickroom. One should not underestimate the swaggering sense of power of the Big Corporation in the "New Age of Confidence" of American business. It is the confident behavior of a conqueror, not the delusional behavior of a victim.

In the galaxy of the satellites one starts with the accountants who are in charge of the anatomy of corporate enterprise and who chart the pecuniary position of tax avoidance without too openly committing evasion, and the lawyers who snarl and unsnarl the legal relations with other corporate empires or the government.

Take the long-drawn-out litigation of the antitrust suits against the nation's investment bankers or the Giannini banking chain or the Du Pont empire or the A & P chain or U.S. Steel; add intramural suits like that of Kaiser-Fraser against Cyrus Eaton of Cleveland, or the color television patent rivalry of R.C.A. and C.B.S.; add the internal battles for corporate control between rival groups of stockholders, as in the cases of Montgomery Ward, the N.Y. Central, and the Penn-Texas Co.; add new corporate creations and reorganizations; add the intricacies of calculating plant and machinery obsolescence for tax purposes, or allowances for plant expansion in the case of conversion to an armament economy; add charitable trusts, family foundations, and other devices; add transactions between the semiautonomous branches of the same corporate empire: the sum becomes a complex of activities that can be carried on only by a general staff of legal and financial trouble shooters. In Newton's universe, it has been said, God became a mathematician. In the Newtonian universe of the Big Corporation the mathematical roles of accountant, tax expert, and legal technician gave their possessors the status, if not of gods, then at least of demigods.

Then there are the statisticians, economic analysts, and survey makers. The Big Corporation is continually sensitive to the world outlook, the business outlook, the stock market, the raw material markets, the labor market, the "Washington scene," the political outlook, and the market analyses and motivational research for its own products. The alert corporate executive must either develop broad perspectives himself or get good expert advice, or both. He reads the newsletters with the "inside" of the Washington and world scene. He relies on one survey after another: in fact, this trend has even reached into the movies and the mass magazines, which can scarcely take a step without first finding out by a survey sampling of reader opinion or audience reaction what the consequences are likely to be. Thus the business executive finds his attention focused on an array of barometers.

The stock-market barometer is one of these, both for the executive and for the large massive investors. The struggle of "bulls" and "bears" has become an American form of bread-and-circuses. In the boom of the late 1920s there was a scramble for speculative profits by clerks, schoolteachers, millhands, industrial workers. Again and again they were slaughtered by "insiders," like the Meehan-Raskob-Durant-Chrysler pool in 1929 which bid up R.C.A. stock and unloaded it on the unwary outsiders for a profit of over five million. The great market crash of

1929 has become part of the folklore of America, an image of tangled ticker tape, desperate men, and ruined lives, ruefully remembered by a burned generation of amateur speculators. The Securities Exchange Commission (SEC), one of the features of reformed capitalism-on-probation, bans the cruder forms of mayhem practiced on the small-scale investor, yet for twenty years after Black Friday the sound investors stayed away from all except the bluest of blue-chip common stock and preferred bonds. The Stock Exchange finally took to advertising to persuade the public to "come back in," and some of the Exchange firms held classes to educate investors, especially the women.

More important, however, was the fact of a continuing inflationary trend after World War II, based on staggering profits and dividends, the emergence of new industries, government buying in a war-geared economy, and rising living standards. During the whole postwar decade of 1946-1956 a series of bull markets, punctuated by periodic downward bearish swoops, kept the financial and investors community in a state of almost constant buoyancy of mood, finding new devotees for the "New Era" theory of market analysis—that stock buyers should be bullish because in the New Era stock values were based on the American future itself. Some analysts asserted that an inflationary trend had become permanent in the economy; and institutional funds—savings banks, life insurance, pension funds, and private trusts—began buying common stock. In 1952 a Brookings study found 6,500,000 Americans in the stock market, holding 30,300,000 shares in stock issues traded on the organized exchanges and over the counter. In the mid-1950s the figures were even higher.

Actually the history of the market, whose daily ups and downs are read on commuters' trains and club cars like the Koran by the Moslem faithful, has shown violent fluctuations over the course of the years, resulting in what business circles know as "brokers' blood pressure" and the ulcer-diet, milk-and-cracker menus in the restaurants near the Exchange. Stock speculation—the "exchange of present money for an expectation of future money"—expresses the impatient desire of many Americans to get rick quick—at least quicker than the normal process of work and savings will allow—and thus provide security for the future and some of the luxuries which have become necessities. It also gives scope to the risk element that is being crowded out of the society, and it has a special appeal for those who lead humdrum lives on rarely fluctuating incomes. The peaks, troughs, and plateaus of the market, as shown on plotted charts, are for them the only landscape worth watching. For them the tons of market-analysis literature are produced, most of it not much better than palmistry or astrology. A study by the Cowles Commission, of the predictive success of the forecasters over the span of two generations, shows that they did no better than the guessers in a random card game. Even the famed Dow-Jones theory, of watching the monthly averages of industrial and railroad stocks and betting that a distinct trend will continue rather than change, has been described as a kind of primitive weather forecasting.

Some of the stock-market professionals, in Bernard Baruch's words, have had to study "the whole history and background of the market and all the principal companies whose stocks are on the board, as carefully as a medical student studies anatomy" and have needed "the cool nerve of a great gambler, the sixth sense of a clairvoyant, and the courage of a lion." They have made fortunes, often by selling "short" or getting out at the right time. But the mass of the people has generally shown a talent for being perversely wrong.

There is also the large, undramatic group of real investors, who are less concerned with short-range fluctuations than with long-range trends, who have a basic confidence in continued corporate prosperity and wish to share in it. Stocks enable them to become the "owners" of the majority stock of corporations, although they are like the passive spectators of mass sports and cannot control what takes place in the ring or field. They get a stake in the success and survival of the corporate system itself, which is one of the strongest psychological facts about the hold of business on the American mind. Yet even for those who do not invest, the market has continued to be a register of hopes and fears for the economy. In terms of ethnology, the fluctuating market has become the totem of the business civilization, which has moved away from the fetishism of the commodity to the fetishism of "business conditions."

A more crucial form of business magic is salesmanship. There has been a well-marked transformation of the art of the older personal seller, who either owned his own shop or had a group of customers whom he knew well, into an impersonal although synthetically "personalized" salesmanship. In an economy of the Big Technology and the Big Corporation, it is not surprising that Americans have developed Big Merchandising. One of the lessons American businessmen have learned during the last twenty years is a paradoxical one: while mass production makes mass distribution necessary, it is even truer to say that mass distribution makes mass production possible. And salesmanship is the key art of the whole structure of mass distribution.

In this sense it is the core activity of the American economy, with technology, production, and financing all subsidiary to it. A business magazine described it as "the biggest man-made force to keep the economy going. When it falters . . . recession follows." Even though competition has been drastically modified within any one mass-production industry, there is still brand and product competition and—most of all—the need to keep the machine going. The role of productivity is to set the pace: where machines are pouring out so much commodity volume, and the high profits are being plowed back into the new technology, the problem is to continue unloading the products on the consumers. As a result, the sales manager is in some way the key figure of the American corporation—more so than the engineer, the production manager, or even the financial executive. The new corporation presidents often rise to their posts because of their work as sales managers. What should have been "finance capitalism"—according to the Marxist gospel—has become a sales economy instead, and capitalism has enacted a Copernican revolution in which all the other planets are now found to be revolving around the central sun of selling.

The salesman may operate in the shop itself or "on the road"—that is, selling to shops, department-store buyers, manufacturers; he may operate on an international level, like Grover Whalen, who "sold" the World's Fair to foreign governments, or James A. Farley, who made Coca-Cola a symbol of American business enterprise all over Europe, or Paul Hoffman, who rose from Studebaker salesman to Marshall Plan Administrator. On every level American business has developed salesmanship into the "art of planned persuasion." The elements of this art are the right kind of packaging (this is notably true in cosmetics, which stress seductive and glamorous mystery, and automobiles, which stress chromium-plated razzle-dazzle); systems of installment buying and consumer financing; an effective sales "theme," sales "line," or sales "angle" (the "line" of the insurance salesman has become part of American folklore); and the stress on the personality of the salesman or salesgirl, whose "smile behind the counter is commercialized lure" and who have become part of the "personality market," where the skills are skills in selling people rather than producing things. One of the less attractive by-products of the stress on salesmanship has been the development of personality courses, charm schools, and a popular literature of self-improvement that teaches the art of manipulating people.

But this kind of manipulative face-to-face salesmanship is itself giving way to the absentee selling through advertising in national media of press, magazines, radio, and television. Like the corporation, advertising was not invented by the Americans but it has been carried furthest and is most at home within the American frame. The go-getting temper which used to be associated with the personal salesman has been transferred to advertising copy, the singing commercials on the radio. and the "selling pitch" on television. Their purpose is not so much the immediate selling of the product as the creation of a favorable climate within which either the sale becomes easy or the customer is induced to ask for the product himself.

Much of the thinking of American corporate executives is devoted to the refinements of the exact nuance to be conveyed in the advertising. A whole new industry—that of the advertising agencies, their account men, their idea men, their layout people and artists, their professional models—has arisen to extol the merits and suggest the glamour of particular commodity brands. Without such national advertising the mass-circulation magazine would have to find a different revenue base, and radio and television—at least in their present form—would wither on the vine. A literature and a cultural folklore have been built around the "hucksters"—their techniques, personality patterns, ulcers, and consciences. Where a generation ago young college men whose sole capital was their boldness and quick wits and ready charm tended to go into stockbroking, they now go into the advertising agencies. With a febrile intensity they aim at what television advertising circles call the "relaxed sell" and the "hard sell." Their craft has had a more than transient effect upon the vocabulary of the business world. "Want to mark yourself as a comer in the advertising field?" asks W. H. Whyte, Jr., in *Is Anybody Listening?* "Speak, then, of fun stories, sweet guys, the hard sell, straw men you set up to back into, and points you can hang your hat on. For each field you will find a subglossary, and, common to all of them, such universal terms as 'play it by ear,' 'the pitch,' 'the deal,' and the many expressions built on the suffix 'wise.' ('Budget-wise, Al, the pitch shapes up like this . . .')"

Advertising does more than help sell the products on which business is built: it has also provided a special kind of language for the people as a whole. Even before American children learn the language of the primer and the schoolroom they mimic the language of the commercials on TV, and of the world of comic little Disneylike men and animated packages that accompany the commercials. Even more important, as David Potter has noted, is the fact that advertising speaks in highly charged symbolic terms and surrounds Americans with a universe of images of plenty. This conditions them to the act of purchase, but it also conditions them to a view of the American economy as a cornucopia abounding in good things. Periodically there used to be attacks from the Left upon advertising as an institution: it is a proof of the efficacy of advertising that these attacks have died down. Either the critics have concluded that the whole venture is futile or they have themselves ended by being "sold" on the object of their attack.

"Public relations" is the youngest of the corporate satellites and brings with it into the corporate world a spanking brashness and an appetite for power. The theory behind public relations is that a corporation is judged not only by the products it turns out but by the total impression it leaves on public opinion. "Today's business formula," we are told, "is: make a product the public wants . . . and an impression the public likes." In a sense, it was the New Deal which created the corporate public-relations industry. When Roosevelt spoke of "driving the money-changers out of the temple," he received so impressive a popular backing that the corporations were jolted into looking around for help. They had been driven, they felt, into a gilded doghouse. They were determined to get out and never to re-enter. They have paid handsomely the "public-relations counsel," "publicity consultants," and others who would dry-clean their public wash and give them a general valet service so as always to appear in public at their best.

Some of the shrewdest and most imaginative brains of the business world have moved into the orbit of this corporate satellite. They help write the speeches of the big corporate executives, cushion the impact of bad news on the public (as with aviation accidents or disasters in the chemical industries), issue public statements for them, see that they are on the right public committees, and—most of all—try to get the right kind of stories "planted" and the wrong kind excluded from the mass-communication media which may represent life or death in the race for markets and profits. Their techniques are based on an unsentimental assessment of the hidden springs of belief, gullibility, and action in men. As an approach not only to business but to the whole of life this mentality has come to be known as the "Madison Avenue" mind, thus adding another symbolic street to Wall Street in the demonology of business. The skills of public-relations men have been taken over into politics, where they are used for the "build-up" of your own candidate and the destruction of his opponent. If anyone in America today has access to the experience which would enable him to write a new grammar of power, reclothing Machiavelli's *Prince* in more modern dress, it is the sophisticated, resourceful, amoral public-relations man.

Sitting at the center, served by these satellite activities, is the corporate executive himself. What was once a somewhat haphazard set of business offices clustering around the executive has now been transformed into a mechanized central office, with hierarchies of secretaries and sub-secretaries, with dictaphones and typist pools. In American life the industrialization of the office has been only less important than the mechanization of the kitchen. But even with new electronic machines, the sense of movement and stir which make the job of the corporate executive exciting is unlikely to be eliminated by mechanization. Sometimes he is in the top ranks of the new middle class, with strong links to the owners of big blocks of minority stock; sometimes he is himself a member of the new elite. Generally he has come up the ladder through service in the sales force or advertising, or less frequently as an engineering technician. Chester I. Barnard, himself a manager who has written searchingly on his fellow managers, lists the crucial qualities of a business executive—in a descending order—as "vitality and endurance; decisiveness; persuasiveness; responsibility; and intellectual capacity."

Much of metropolitan life has been molded by the working day and the recreations of the corporate executive: the conservative but well-tailored clothes, the long and usually liquid expense-account lunch at which "deals" are made, the institution of the cocktail hour at the end of a tense day, the gobbledygook of interoffice memoranda, the rise of a bureaucratic jargon rivaling that of a governmental bureaucracy, the athletic clubs with swimming pools, and squash courts for keeping fit, the elaborate layouts and paraphernalia for "businessmen's golf," the amenities of the club car on the commuters' trains, the heavy consumption of alcohol as a necessary stimulant, the emphasis in the theater upon musical comedies, the growth of the night club as entertainment and as industry.

This is the "executive life," as *Fortune* calls it. It has its costs, including the fifty-five- or sixty-hour week, the tension about "decision making," the agonies of promotion and firing, the characteristic executive diseases of ulcerated colitis, rheumatoid arthritis, asthma, and hypertension. It even has a characteristic "executive crack-up," which sometimes comes just after or just before success is achieved, and indicates how saturated with anxieties and conflicts the executive life can be. But it also has its triumphs and its sense of achievement. This, more than anything else, is what America has come to stand for in the deep secret images of the young Americans.

6. *The Reach of the Business Spirit*

BEYOND THESE central and satellite activities of business the reach of the commercial spirit penetrates into every area of American culture. The business principle has sometimes been confused with the machine principle. The latter is used to dispense with human labor and make possible standardized and large-scale production, while the business principle focuses on market sale for profit. It puts the making of money ahead of other craft and civilization values, gives primacy to the cultural and personal traits which lead to that end, and tends to apply money values even to the human personality.

America has often been called a business civilization, but the term is too sweeping. One cannot say that the business principle is the only one operating in American culture. In some areas—religion, education, the arts, the family—it exerts only an incipient influence. But even where it has not become decisive, there has been a creeping imperialism of business over the other domains of life.

The business principle has given a synthetic cohesion to the far-flung diversity of American life. Before the Civil War it could genuinely be said that American culture was a loose collection of principalities—those of politics, of farming and industry, of religion, of literature and art and the press—tied together mainly by a pride of pioneering and a sense of the emerging national strength, and some belief in the democratic idea. The advance of business power and values weakened the hold of the democratic idea, while translating both the pioneering sense and the nationalist pride into the boom terms of growing industrial power and profit.

In the realm of politics, the political boss has come to run his domain (the "machine") very much as an industrial boss (businessman or corporate manager) runs his. Unifying both of them is the principle of organization—the setting up of a regularly functioning structure to achieve certain ends. The difference is that where the businessman delivers commodities for profit, the politician delivers votes for power. An American may speak of belonging to an "organization" and refer to being a functionary in either a corporation or a political machine. The political "organization" has taken over much of the corporate structure. It is true that in its origins the party system in America preceded business enterprise, and its first brilliant innovator, Aaron Burr, used the Army as model. But the new model is the corporation, with the voters in the role of the owner-stockholders, the national committeemen in the role of the corporate directors, and the professional politicians in the role of the corporate managers, who are in theory the trustees and employees of the owners but in fact the decision-makers and power-wielders.

In America, as everywhere, politics has been vulnerable to bribery. Yet it is a paradox of a business civilization that there has been notably less political corruption in America than in many precapitalist societies such as in Asia, the Middle East, and South America, or even some of the Latin societies of Europe. Perhaps this is exactly because of the importance of business: for those to whom money is all-important there are in America (as in no other culture) more direct channels open to the money-making energies than through the circuitous routes of the political career and political power. Political corruption is most rampant in the cultures where for many men it is the only road to wealth and status; in America it is only one of many.

Yet the business spirit, which directly carries along in its torrential course so many of the talents and energies of men into money-making, also breaks down some of the moral barriers that had been built into the conscience for generations. The big temptation in the era of the expanding frontier was land speculation. In the era of an expanding capitalism the temptations lie less in speculation than in the sale of political influence to businessmen intent on getting some of the Big Money, by crucially placed governmental subalterns who don't see why they too should not get their cut. As in the post-Civil War days of Grant and Conkling, or the post-World War days of Harding and Daugherty, the torrents of fresh business energy which open new opportunities for big profits also carry away with them much of the terrain of social conscience. In this sense it is not the periods of business decay but the periods of business expansion and vitality which play havoc with moral principles, because they fix men's aims at the attainable goals of the Big Money.

This is true of the sins of commission within business which Edwin Sutherland analyzed as a special type of "white-collar crime." It is also true of its sins of omission. Discussing the failure of the great respectable banking firms to warn American investors against the worthless German and South American bonds in the 1920s, Herbert Pell wrote, "There is not a Morgan partner who would not give a yell to frighten ducks off a pond if he saw that they were being approached by a couple of fat hunters with pump guns. Apparently they do not extend the same protection to gulls."

There has been a growing American conviction that there is hidden gold in the Washington hills. The Wall Street legend thus merges with the Washington legend (witness Blair Bolles's *How to Get Rich in Washington*), but there is a core of truth in the legendry of both. Of the two great types of corruption in the American Federal government, it is hard to say that the efforts of small businessmen to get tax favors by gifts of mink coats or deep-freezers and to pick up arms contracts by bribery are worse than the efforts of the big corporations to get the kind of tax exemption that will save them tens of millions, or the lavish distribution of checks and the faking of pressure telegrams by corporations who want to get a tidelands-oil or a natural-gas bill through Congress. Where the impact of business has been most destructive for morality has been perhaps less in its open corruption than in the incalculable prestige that business success and power have in the eyes of city magistrates, county judges, state legislators, Congressmen, Federal administrators.

Business methods and values have also reached the national political parties, which have increasingly drawn upon the big advertising agencies for the conduct of their campaigns; public-relations firms are coming not only to advise the political managers but sometimes to replace them in the effective conduct of the campaign. The slogans that have proved successful in preparing the public mind for the sale of a deodorant, a breakfast food, or a mouthwash are also counted on to be successful in "selling" a candidate and his cause. Political campaign slogans may be tested beforehand as carefully as the advertising slogans in business sales campaigns, and the question of whether a "hard sell" or a "relaxed" one will be used may be the subject of earnest discussion among party directors who resemble a corporate board of directors.

Even crime and racketeering in America have taken over some of the organizational structure of business. Just as they have learned in some cases to assume the disguise of trade-unions, they have also a line of command and an administrative organization not crucially different from that of the corporation. To many of these criminal groups business enterprise is (in Veblen's tongue-in-cheek phrase) the "art of getting something for nothing"—which is what it seems to any greedy adventurist spirit brooding on the chance to get a "free ride" into riches. Actually, however, the racketeer imitates only the outer organization of business and has little relation to the business spirit itself. For while business flourishes by the widest publicity, what the racketeer sells is illicit; the motive for paying him is immunity from the violence to follow if the payment is not made. Racketeering is the precapitalist feudal spirit, using the techniques and structures of business enterprise and thriving because business has spread throughout America the dream of the easy-money bonanza.

Until recently, at least, the appeal of business has been as a way of making money, not as a way of life. Sensitive people have rejected the way of life but then been lured by the money; hence the split in the American attitude toward business, which has been most marked where the tradition of an educated elite has been strongest. The Adams family, for example, showed both a cultivated understanding and a cultivated fear of the new and pushing type of business activity. Writing in *The Education,* Henry Adams expressed the melancholy sense that for all the processes of civilization that had gone to make him, he was unfit to survive in the world that business values were fashioning. Brooks Adams, living as a *rentier* from corporate securities, was able to dissect pitilessly the social sources of his income, all the time ransacking history to explain the emergence of this new form of centralized power to which he owed the leisure he had for ransacking history. The third brother, Charles Francis Adams, was a railroad president who wrote with shriveling contempt for the narrowness of outlook and the niggardliness of spirit of business as a way of life. Henry James, for all his preoccupation with money and what it could buy, always pushed the question of its sources into the background and felt slightly soiled by them. He was most at home with a businessman like the hero of *The Golden Bowl,* spending in Europe the fortune he had made in America, a Maecenas who knew what he wanted and went after it with the practiced assurance that betokened the habitual conqueror. The secret that Sir Joseph Duveen discovered about American businessmen, which made his fortune as an art salesman, was that they gloried in their power over the things that money commanded but hungered for the symbols of the life values that went beyond money. Throughout the history of the business spirit, the monied men have used business first as a way of making the Big Kill, then turned to philanthropy or the life of the patron, travel, or hobbies as a way of making a life.

The business spirit, then, has not in itself been regarded as a nourishing one but as a means to bring a good life within reach. For that reason perhaps it has exerted an attraction for the young men of talent who in other civilizations might have gone into government, the Army, or the priesthood, into literature or the arts or the study of philosophy, into science or the professions. Even those in government service have, when successful, been tempted to turn their knowledge to the service of the corporation: if they have worked in the Treasury Department on taxes, or as economists in government bureaus, they can command good salaries as consultants or executives in business. If they have been good newspapermen they are eagerly recruited for public-relations jobs in the corporate world. And the corporations have learned to go directly to the colleges in recruiting young men of talent who are rarely able to resist the offer of an immediate job as against the uncertainties of a career in the arts or professions.

Even for those who stay outside business, there is a strong drive to conduct themselves in a "businesslike" way. The trade-union movement in America has been largely, as Hoxie first described it, "business-unionism," expressing the competing claims to income of the corporate employees as part of the larger structure of the business economy itself. In education the school administrator and the university president have tended to act as corporate executives. Even in the churches the temptation is to be "practical" in administering vast properties rather than unworldly in pursuing the values of the spirit. In the newspaper and magazine fields the pressure is toward building big power aggregates that can command writing talent and the reader market and get a big share of national advertising: the magazine or big newspaper is likely to make its more blatant public boasts not so much about its newsgathering or its crusading spirit as about its circulation and advertising gains. In radio and television the art forms are subsidiary to the selling of time to the business sponsors. In moviemaking, the final art product has to run the gantlet of box-office appeal, and the Hollywood values of inflated salaries and skyrocketing careers are a kind of caricature of the corporate executives. In literature the emphasis has shifted to the products that can be marketed to a mass audience, notably crime and detection thrillers.

In fact, it may turn out that the business spirit will leave its most enduring imprint on the adjoining provinces of literature and entertainment, government and opinion: for these are the areas in which capital investment counts least and personality and talent still can carve out empires. They are the last Klondikes of venture skills, which are even more important in the history of business than venture capital. The lure of the acquisitive impulse, wedded to talent and ideas, produces a powerful amalgam.

It is customary to speak of this as the "commercializing" of art and opinion. But the process is more complex. The crux of it is that the dominant activity of any civilization colors the prevailing notions of what is effective or futile in the exercise of men's talents. In a business civilization the stamp of effectiveness is placed on whatever can be exchanged in the personality market for money and success; the stamp of ineffectuality is placed on whatever talent is not vendible, whatever cannot move to a maximum degree into the channels where it is capitalized and reaches a mass market with all the accruing rewards. Thus the business spirit, itself incapable of yielding nourishing life values, has become for Americans the prime gateway to a way of life, with few questions asked about what you find when you have gone through the gates.

When one inquires what may account for the "domination effect" of the business spirit, the answer lies partly in the attractiveness of the big rewards and the big market, partly in the admiration felt for the men who have shown that they can run things best, partly in the pragmatic strain of a culture which accepts whatever is practical and successful as the valid and pays it the flattery of mimicry.

The final tribute to the domination effect of the business spirit is the extent to which the phases of the human personality are measured in its terms. In a seminal analysis of types of character structure that bear aptly on American life, Fromm has spoken of the "marketing orientation" as one that is crowding out much else in the business society. There is little question that the marketable personality is becoming the dominant one, even in areas outside business. Courtesy and charm come to be valued not for themselves but because they pay off in salesmanship; clothes must be worn well to make an impression on a prospective customer or employer; the "dreamer type" of person is dangerous because he will estrange those who seek alertness. America itself, in the impact it makes on other peoples in the struggle for world leadership, must "sell" itself and its ideas; and the clinching argument used even by liberal intellectuals against the denial of civil rights of Negroes and other minority groups is that it will interfere with such international "selling" and acceptance.

This then is what seems to have happened in the American business economy. The more strictly technical problems of production and scarcity, of income distribution, of bigness in the sense distinct from monopoly, even of the business cycle, are fairly on the way to being resolved. But the bureaucratization of life through the new managerial structures in business, the trade-union, the government, and the corrupting reach of marketing values and the money spirit are being extended through the whole culture. The real problems of the business culture are thus less the technical and strictly economic problems than the moral and psychological ones.

Yet to say, as some foreign observers and American critics have said, that only money talks in America is to vulgarize the impact of the business spirit. Other values than the acquisitive find a place in American life, and often they triumph; and other qualities than the money-making qualities blossom. But even when they do triumph, it is only after they have been measured and defended against the money values and the vendible qualities. That they survive is the final tribute to their hardihood, and when they do survive—in literature and the arts, in human relations, in religion and education and government, in the armed services, in the professions, perhaps even in business itself—they have a greater strength than in those cultures where they do not have to measure themselves so searchingly against the domination effect of the business spirit.*

* For a further discussion of the impact of markets, money, and commercialism on the American spirit, see Ch. IX, Sec. 8, "Life Goals and the Pursuit of Happiness," and Ch. XI, Sec. 9, "Artist and Audience in a Democratic Culture."

7. *Revolution in the Trade-Union*

THE "SPLITTING of the property atom" could not help carry along with it a splitting of the labor atom. There has been a far-reaching growth of labor's power and a change in its place in American society. Labor's position in the mid-1950s was diametrically different from its position at the time of the Homestead and Pullman strikes in the 1890s, or even under Harding and Hoover. This does not mean that labor dominates the economy, as implied in Sumner H. Slichter's description of America as a "laboristic economy" rather than a capitalistic one. At the heart of the economy is the network of decentralized choices by corporations, businessmen, and consumers. Yet it is also true that there is a corresponding network of labor decisions giving a massive power to the trade-unions.

Actually the corporations and trade-unions represent two galactic systems of almost sovereign power. Each has its managerial government, each its autonomous realm in which it is supreme, each is connected with its sister stars in the galaxy by loose ties of common interest and outlook. While the two systems are often locked in struggle, they are part of the same firmament in the same universe. That is why the discussion of American labor cannot be separated from a discussion of the growth of the corporation and the sweep of the business principle. American business and labor are rival empires, sometimes friendly, sometimes hostile, fighting for similar stakes, aiming at roughly similar goals, with jealously divergent power drives and interests inside the same set of cultural values.

This is why American labor did not start its mature phase until the growth of the American Federation of Labor under Gompers. The prehistory of labor before that time, with all its valorous chapters of struggle, represented a fumbling for a stable and characteristic form. In the deepest sense the trade-union arose out of the same impulse for social freedom and struggle as the American Revolution itself. From its origins there were strong influences in the American labor movement which kept it from abandoning the main stream of American experience. Labor power was scarce, land was plentiful, jobs were fewer than the men available for them, and the way was open for apprentices and mechanics, artisans and mill hands, to move on into farms or enterprises of their own. Under these conditions it was hard for any specific labor movement to take root, whether class-conscious or job-conscious. The "workingmen's associations" of the 1830s fought for free schools and other reforms and were a major element in the triumph of Jacksonian democracy. The free-workers' associations later fought also for the freedom of the Negro plantation labor of the South, formed the mass core of the abolitionist societies, and flocked into the Republican party to join with the commercial class and the New West in electing Lincoln. Thus the early phases of American labor were not the "failures" that later labor leaders have sometimes called them: they assisted in the triumph of democracy, much as European labor did in its heroic age.

When the time for growth came, and for a redefinition of labor's tasks in a democratic society, there was a double impulse: to focus on the American radical tradition in politics and society and join with men of good will in all classes to revive it; or to focus on the broad upward movement of American living standards and act in concentrated fashion by every vocational means to gain some of its benefits for labor.

Neither impulse was crotchety, each was "organic" to one of the main drives of American life. The first impulse expressed itself through the Knights of Labor, a class-wide, politically conscious movement affiliated with nonlabor reform groups, as a response to the political unrest which swept the country when the vision of a nation of small farmers and artisans was shattered by the rise of corporate power. But the Knights were too sprawling in their organization, and they made the mistake of aiming at political power before establishing a strong economic base. Under Gompers the A.F. of L. sought to rechart labor's course, devoting itself to a job-conscious, wage-and-hour unionism, restricting its political activity to lobbies and pressures, and at election time to the policy of "rewarding labor's friends and punishing labor's enemies." Thus labor had its period of conscience-searching as between the decision to challenge corporate power drastically and the decision to bargain with the corporations for a larger share of income.

It might be said that the leaders of organized labor in the 1880s made the unheroic choice by concentrating on the strategic power of the skilled workers rather than deciding to organize the unskilled. Certainly their task would have been more dangerous had they chosen to stand with the unskilled and the new immigrant workers. But they faced a difficult situation: public opinion was unsympathetic, the state legislatures and the Supreme Court were hostile, and the employers fought every form of organization. The question in such a situation was what kind of labor organization could survive and achieve stability. Where there was a high labor turnover among millions of unskilled immigrants, anxious to secure any work at any wage, it was hard to attain stability. It was among the skilled workers, who would keep an interest in their craft and who could not easily be replaced by newcomers and "scabs," that the effective organizing work could be done. This was the choice that Gompers and his young colleagues of the new labor movement made, with a devotion to the hard, pragmatic task they had cut out for themselves.

Another chance at creating industrial unionism came after World War I, when labor turnover had decreased with the disappearance of the frontier and the slowing down of immigration. But another anti-labor offensive, joined to a Red scare, headed off this chance as well. The industrial unions that had emerged suffered severe defeats in the 1920s, particularly in coal, textile, and clothing. The result was that the A.F. of L. was driven into becoming narrower than it had to be, while the "revolutionary unions" of Wobblies, bindlestiffs, and new-stock intelligentsia who sought to counterbalance it were driven into becoming more extreme and frenetic than the American occasion justified.

Once victorious, the job-conscious philosophy of Gompers and the A.F. of L. was never wholly displaced. A number of today's labor leaders were apprenticed to Socialist theory but dropped it when they came to lead a mass labor movement. The unions worked for goals set by the job, within a social framework which they sought to use and improve but not transform. Even the C.I.O. (Congress of Industrial Organizations) —which came into being when the A.F. of L. failed to expand from skilled crafts to a militant, industry-wide organization—has, in the process of breaking with the Gompers tradition, actually carried out the full logic of the Gompers philosophy by willing the necessary changes in organization and tactics for the effective protection of the job. It was Gompers who remained the great type-figure of American labor leadership.

The characteristic theory of American labor behavior—the Commons-Perlman, or "Wisconsin School," theory—aimed to show how the Gompers philosophy and tactic fitted in with the American national psychology and social system, and why it was the only plan for action under which American labor could have survived. Holding that American trade-unions are soundest when built around the protection of the job, the theory goes back (as Philip Taft points out) to the worker's "consciousness of scarcity" and of limited opportunity. Until the sense of limitation and scarcity arose, and while the frontier was still open and vital jobs had not been pre-empted, no strong trade-union movement could be formed. When workers looked forward to being farmers and capitalists they were unlikely to take their stand together as workers. It needed the end of the frontier, the inpouring waves of immigration, and a partial saturation of job opportunities before the unions could generate any propulsive force. It also needed the rise of the new corporate employers, many of whom used their power to pay low wages, locked their workers out in times of unemployment, penalized the more militant ones, and were unconcerned about what happened to their labor force when they grow sick or old or were mangled in accidents. The aim of job-conscious trade-unions was to band the workers together in order to keep them from being crushed by this new juggernaut. Neither the method nor philosophy was that of class struggle, but the intent was certainly class survival as a necessary step for the security and dignity of the individual worker.

This theory must not be taken as valid for the whole course of American labor history: it applies to only one phase of it. With the later rise of the C.I.O. in the 1930s and the reassessment of political action by the A.F. of L., the Commons-Perlman theory was also re-evaluated. There was a consensus that it illumined the period it described, but that it needed modification when applied to the present and future of American labor. Gompers saw clearly that the trade-union in America, in its phase of major growth, had to be an integral part both of the capitalist psychology and of the democratic process. The break with the European tradition of feudal rank kept the American worker from accepting the paternalism either of a tyrannical employer or of a tyrannical government. Since he saw himself as the "masterless man" he did not feel the resentments of the class struggle at whose root is a master-ridden proletariat trying to unseat its masters. Gripped by the property idea the American worker, who found he could no longer move with ease from his job to business independence, developed in its place a sense of property-in-the-job. To "have a good job" came to mean that the worker had a stake in the future worth protecting in common action with others.

Also worth fighting for. An element of violence ran like a red strand through a century of American labor experience, from the "Molly Maguires" in the Pennsylvania coal fields, through the Homestead steel strike, the Pullman railroad strike, the copper mine bloodshed, the dynamitings by West Coast "Wobblies," the violence of the Lawrence, Passaic, and Gastonia strikes in textiles, the "sitdown" strikes in the auto industry, the Herrin massacre in Illinois, and the ghastly violence of the Little Steel massacre of 1937. We may note here, incidentally, that in the past twenty years there have been no comparable incidents of bloodshed.

The hardheaded pragmatic unionism of American labor has often been decried as unheroic, perhaps because it has not talked in swaggering terms of revolutionary overthrow of state power. But it is naïve to think that the revealing Gompers trilogy of symbols—"pure and simple" unionism, "here and now" purposes, "more and more" as the stakes of conflict—excludes a heroic struggle to secure them. Along with the "pork-choppers," the swivel-chair bureaucrats, the "walking delegates," the racketeering union leaders, and the fatty degeneration in some segments of American labor life, there was a militancy in others which secured for American labor a new leadership among the world's free trade-unions. It was not only the corporate empires and their corporate managers that the unions had to meet but also a hostile Congress and state legislatures, an often hostile set of Federal and local courts, a network of "citizens' committees," a number of company policies, hired thugs, bravados, and "deputy sheriffs." Finally, they had against them the overwhelming weight of the press, the almost solid phalanx of the academies and even of the churches. Most of all, they had the hostility of farmers and lower-middle-class Americans, fearful of labor's economic power and its strike weapon. While these hostile attitudes, and also labor's fighting mood, have diminished in the contemporary generation, the tradition on both sides is still remembered.

Yet this bitter day-to-day struggle, even with the violence on both sides, has been carried on within a framework of ultimate consent. No matter how long-drawn-out the strikes, the aim after settlement has been the resumption of work; no matter how drastic the resistance to the organizing drive, the unions have in the end been recognized, not liquidated, by the force of the state.

The greatest achievement of the trade-unions in the economy as a whole has been that they have made possible the government of industry by constitutional means. If the massive corporate empires had been the sole survivors and had bargained with only the individual worker, and if collective bargaining had continued to be viewed as a conspiracy against the antitrust laws, there could have been anarchy or tyranny in American industry. Instead the weight of the big trade-union was invoked by the workers as a counterbalance for the weight of the big corporation, to achieve (as Justice Holmes put it in his dissent in *Coppage v. Kansas*) "that equality of bargaining power from which freedom of contract begins."

The classical theory of Anglo-American economics saw industrial order as the product of an equilibrium between individuals in the market, and from this individualist concept the economists evolved their elaborate justifications for antiunionism, strike breaking, and court injunctions. But with the growth of the corporate empires the conditions of the market were transformed. An equilibrium was still possible but it had to be an equilibrium between competing collectives, with the bargaining strength of the trade-union matching that of the corporation. In this sense the unions have not only raised living standards for their own workers and protected their jobs, but they have also helped give balance to the American capitalist economy.

A change of phase passed over American labor with the coming of the Great Depression of 1929 and the New Deal in the 1930s, although we are still too close to this phase to see its full outlines. The strength of the Gompers A.F. of L. tradition lay in focusing on the workers, who had group cohesiveness and bargaining power and could therefore be held together effectively even in the face of court injunctions, company police, state militia, jail sentences, and hostile middle-class opinion. Its weaknesses had become clear by the end of the 1920s. One symptom was the fact that for the first time in its history the A.F. of L. lost rather than gained members during a period of prosperity. Nor could it break through its limits of membership (somewhere around three and a half million) without organizing whole new industries, skilled and unskilled alike, which meant breaking away from the craft-union principle and experimenting with industrial unionism. The A.F. of L. did include some industrial unions, but their effectiveness had not been proved: the main issue was that the A.F. of L. leadership was itself part of the craft unions and thus conditioned by its whole life history to resist organization on an industrial basis. Moreover, with the Gompers concentration on trade-union action as against broader political action, there was no clear way for the unions to act in the national political arena to counteract the strategy of corporate power and also to organize a legislative attack upon national economic insecurity.

The process of labor's awakening to its past weaknesses and its future opportunities extended from the early days of the New Deal and its NRA (National Recovery Act) around 1934 well into the war years of the 1940s. In this decade something like a revolution took place in the trade-unions. During its early phase the leadership was assumed not by organized labor itself but by a mixed group of intellectuals, social workers, and politicians who felt that they needed a stronger labor movement to restore the balance between the corporations and their workers, and build a Big Unionism alongside the Big Corporation. The New Dealers found that they needed a strong labor movement also to give a new vitality of bargaining and purchasing power to the depressed economy. But they could not get the labor base they needed without in a sense creating a new frame for the trade-union movement. That was why the New Deal became, as the quip put it at the time, a "government in search of a labor movement."

Eventually labor responded to this stimulus by forming the C.I.O. in 1938: it symbolized, under the leadership of John L. Lewis, Philip Murray, and Sidney Hillman, better than anything else the meaning and spirit of the new phase of labor history. Labor discovered, less as a matter of dogma than as part of the harsh crucible of the Depression itself, that it could survive best in its era of trial by becoming part of the Great Coalition around the New Deal. The concepts of industrial unionism, social security, labor's stake in the total economy, the relation of corporate power and practices to the breakdowns in the economy as a whole, and the need to gain access to governmental power in order to achieve equality of bargaining: these constituted at once principles of the C.I.O. and also of the New Deal. The alliance between the two was never a formal one, nor did Roosevelt make the mistake of working politically with only one segment of the labor movement. The New Deal secured a mass following; the labor movement achieved a National Labor Relations Act which gave it a new charter of growth, and a structure of minimum-wage and social-security laws to fill out the charter. Thus was formed a working partnership between the American labor movement and the principle of welfare democracy which was to affect the history of more than one American generation.

For a time the resulting growth of the labor movement was remarkable. Membership figures for all unions moved from a low of less than three million in 1933 to over four million in 1936, over seven million in 1937, almost nine million in 1940, ten and a half million in 1941, fifteen and a half million by 1947, and seventeen million in the mid-1950s. Industries like steel and autos, which had been citadels of antiunionism, furnished the sinews of labor growth. The trade-union leaders found themselves not only sitting in the councils of the Federal Administration but they also made labor a force in the government of cities and towns where it had formerly been only tolerated. Pittsburgh and Detroit, for example, were transformed politically as well as industrially and culturally. There was in time, of course, a countermovement culminating in the Taft-Hartley Act, which chipped away labor's gains and set a pattern of restrictive action. A number of states followed, in the decade between 1945 and 1955, with harsh antiunion right-to-strike laws. Yet the counterattack could not wipe out what the original revolution had achieved.

The healthiest thing about this upheaval in labor was that it did much to heal the sense of alienation of the workers. Lacking access to governmental power and a voice in the big governmental decisions, they had necessarily felt like outsiders. But that feeling disappeared, and in its place leaders like Murray, Lewis, and Green—and later Reuther and Meany—spoke with the confidence of power. In this sense the revolution in labor deflected the potential energies of a sullen working population from more destructive revolutionary channels and became—like the New Deal—an essentially conservative force. Some revolutions shatter and destroy; others have a maturing effect even while the upheaval is in process. This one changed the character of the labor movement by bringing a change of phase, yet it did not in a broader sense break with the Gompers tradition. What it did was to develop new techniques which could achieve for its time the underlying purposes of the Gompers philosophy. For in spite of the alarms felt about labor's advances in numbers and strength, the basic idea remains of a democratic labor movement operating within a capitalist welfare economy, making possible a constitutional government of industry and trying to recapture for the worker his dignity as a human being.

Since the end of the New Deal the American labor movement has come to another change of phase, if a less drastic one. The impulses remolding American society as a whole have not left labor organization and thinking untouched. I have spoken earlier of automation and what it has done to the position of the unions, diminishing the number of workers engaged in industrial jobs, transferring many of the gainfully employed to white-collar and middle-class jobs where labor organizing has been least effective. The sustained prosperity of the 1940s and 1950s also had an impact on labor consciousness, making the unions less militant, muting the past accent on violence, and all but eliminating the resort to large-scale strikes. Within this new climate the A.F. of L. flourished—after 1945—more effectively than the C.I.O., which was riddled with internal strife, even to the extent of the expulsion of unions with close to a million members because of their Communist leadership.

The result was that the A.F. of L. and C.I.O. succeeded in 1955 in reuniting their forces within a single organization. Of its fifteen and a half million members, only four and a half million were in the C.I.O. at the time of the merger, with the other eleven million in the A.F. of L. The total figures for American trade-unions, by the U.S. Department of Labor estimate, were seventeen million, with an added million of Canadian workers affiliated with the international unions in the United States. In 1930 organized trade-unions represented only 7 per cent of the total labor force ("gainfully employed") of the nation; in 1945 they were 22 per cent; in 1955, using the base figure of over sixty-five million gainfully employed, they were more than 25 per cent. If the farm workers, the self-employed, and the professional people are excluded from the base figure, more than one third of the labor force were members of trade-unions.

Thus the current period in labor history is one of consolidation. Since American labor has no revolutionary dynamism in the class sense, it did not follow through on the revolutionary potential which the New

Deal gains gave it. Its power to strike, especially in the arterial industries and nerve centers of American economic life, might have been used to paralyze the economy, yet it was not. Seventeen million Americans, along with their families, could have shaped a labor culture if the job relation and the trade-union had been the center of their life activity. Yet they have not done so. They could build the most powerful political labor party in the democratic world. Yet they have not.

The reason is that Americans do not think of themselves as being exclusively members of any single group. A steel or automobile worker, a clerical worker, or a carpenter is not only a trade-unionist. He is also a homeowner, a stock investor, a Democrat or Republican, a Mason or Elk, a Presbyterian or Methodist or Baptist, a resident of Cleveland, Detroit, or Glendale. He may come from a farm family, and his children may be moving into the corporate managerial group or into one of the professions. He does not inherit from his father or transmit to his children a "working-class psychology." Nor is he likely to be content as a member of a labor party which seems to take him out of the main stream of American political life. In fact, he sometimes resents the efforts of his union leaders to lecture him on how and for whom to vote. His loyalties are not single but multiple. All the numberless pulls of American life operate upon him, so that—while remaining a strong trade-unionist—he is also many other things in the act of being an American. This multi-loyalty character has been partly due to his freedom from the feudal restrictions on the right of association which plagued the European worker; partly it has been due to the pluralist richness of American life and its expanding life chances. It may thus shed some light on the great question of why American society never developed in a more class-conscious direction.*

The fight for higher wages and shorter hours still goes on through American unions, especially the drive for a four-day week and a five-hour day, to cope with the impact of automation. But it has had a receding emphasis as the living standards of the workers have gone up and their life needs have moved in many directions. There has been a transfer of union interest from wage-and-hour demands to so-called "indirect wage increases," "fringe benefits," pension funds, holiday and vacation provisions, health centers, and welfare setups. There has also been a movement toward the guaranteed annual wage, already achieved in several industries and likely to be fought for in others, since the industrial worker is moving toward the status of a salaried employee instead of a wage earner. The annual wage will probably never be wholly achieved and will have especially hard going in the small-scale industries, but it

* For a further discussion of this theme, see Ch. VII, Sec. 4, "Class Profile of the Worker."

has already brought a substantial improvement in unemployment compensation.

In league with the welfare state and the welfare corporation, labor is turning to the welfare union. The constructiveness shown in the garment industries a generation ago when Hillman and Dubinsky saw that the bankruptcy of marginal employers would throw men out of work and depress labor standards, and therefore set up business clinics to revamp their managerial methods, is still operative. Studies by the National Planning Association show scores of "participating plans" scattered through industry, in which there is a creative approach on both sides to the problem of recurring grievance cases. In mining, in steel, in autos, in garments and textiles, and in dozens of other industries, both sides have worked out joint pension and welfare schemes which focus on the worker as a person. A new "industrial sociology" has grown up which recognizes tardily that the worker is a human being and the factory is a small society or subculture. While there are elements in it of what Daniel Bell has called "cow sociology," in the effort to make the workers contented in order the better to milk their productive power, there is also a wariness of making productivity the final goal, and a genuine feeling that the cultural disintegration and emptiness of the worker's life are enemies not only of productive efficiency but also of the health of the culture itself. Some conservatives may welcome this development in the hope of using it to deflect trade-union militancy. Yet the union leaders who have taken the longest steps toward a welfare unionism are exactly those who had shown the most effective record of bargaining gains for their men, and have not hesitated to use the costly weapon of the strike when there was no other recourse.

We may trace currently four main trends in the character of American unionism. One is the new interest in Administration policies in Washington, especially those that defeat wage gains through inflation, making the struggle for further wage increases a tortured spiral. The second is an interest in world affairs, to keep alive abroad the idea of free trade-unions, and to help achieve a world stability without which the American worker's struggle for a good life would be meaningless. The third was foreshadowed by the General Motors strike of 1948, when Walter Reuther demanded "a look at the books" in order to assess the truth of the corporation's contention that it could not grant the union's demand without a price increase for its products. This was summarily rejected as an invasion of managerial decision and the privacy of managerial secrets, techniques, and accounts, and it has made no headway since. Yet the growth of administrative agencies for mediation, through fact-finding and public disclosure, means inevitably a greater publicity of both corporate and union affairs. Finally, there has been a trend, still minor but increasing, toward the union as entrepreneur.

The growth of the big union empires has meant also the growth of big union funds, both from dues and from pension and welfare contributions. It is hard to estimate what disposable funds the unions have at their command, since recent guesses about union assets range from one to four billion dollars. More important than the assets is the variety of new activities in which the great trade-unions have a stake: banks, stores, consumers' co-operatives, housing, health and vacation resorts, hospitals, radio and movie projects, schools and staff-training institutes. Thus far the unions have invested their funds chiefly in government securities, but it is interesting to speculate on what will happen when they (as well as their members) invest in corporate stock issues—a logical development since such investment would be a dividend for labor's own continuing contributions to productivity.

I have not meant to suggest that all was well in the mid-1950s on the horizon of American labor. There was still widespread suspicion of its aims and methods in the population as a whole, and there were pockets of active hostility in the South, where every known method was being used to keep out union organizers. The organizing power of labor did not keep up with its barganing power: that is to say, the national unions were able to win higher wages and benefits for their members, yet they were unable to organize areas and industries that continued to resist them. Moreover, no one could tell whether a break in the expansion of American industrial life might not come to interrupt union progress or hurl it back.

But the fact remains that the American unions have become entangled in the growth, ramifications, and destiny of capitalism to a degree that would have been undreamed of not only by Terence Powderly but even by Gompers. They have not abandoned their militancy, but it operates within a framework more meaningful under American conditions than the wasteful bloodshed at Homestead or Herrin or the Memorial Day massacre at South Chicago.

8. Labor and American Society

THE REAL REVOLUTION in American labor has been the impulse to see the worker not just as a union member or a ward of the welfare state, and certainly not as a serf in the hierarchy of corporate power, but as industrial man who is part of his society.* To many Americans the organized

* This section should be read along with Ch. IV, Sec. 4, "Work and the Automatic Factory," and Ch. VII, Sec. 4, "Class Profile of the Worker."

workers in their new and massive strength have appeared like a horde of barbarians attempting to storm the gates of capitalist power. Actually, however, they have been neither barbarians coming from without, as with the Roman Empire, nor a disinherited and uprooted inner proletariat. They have emerged not from the disintegration of America but from the logic of its unfolding; nor are they a group of aliens and exiles forced by their rootlessness to create a "higher religion." They are, on the contrary, the core of American experience.

A double charge has been leveled against labor in American society. As a member of a monopoly group the worker is accused of clogging the channels of the free market and imposing his tyrannical power upon the rest of the economy. But he is also seen as a revolutionary who by the nature of his demands operates to destroy the price system.

If American trade-unions aim to become monopolies, it is only in the sense of aiming to concentrate their power beyond question. That is why they drive toward the closed shop (the union shop is a different matter) and the checkoff, and insist upon controlling the sources of the labor supply. They have learned from experience that the lack of labor unity leads to labor weakness in a showdown. Unions, moreover, sell nothing but seek to set the conditions under which their members can sell their labor advantageously. And there is point to Thurman Arnold's distinction between collective bargaining monopolies in labor and restrictive monopolies as such. Where a union, in collusion with an employer, conspires to get gravy for both at the expense of the consumer, a restrictive monopoly exists. Where "featherbedding" practices are followed, and the union seeks to fight technical advance even at the price of slowing down production, again a restrictive monopoly exists. But collective bargaining under a unified leadership need not (any more than the large-scale corporation) itself be a deadening force. This is true even when the union has a monopoly over the sources of the labor supply, forcing those who benefit from the gains of trade-unionism to take on the responsibilities of membership.

More serious is the impact of the union on the price system. It is Lindblom's thesis that American unions are revolutionary not because of any class ideology but because of the inherent upward thrust of higher wage demands on the whole price system. Since the market mechanism (the argument goes) imposes some limit on profits, the continued upward revision of wage levels can result eventually only in price inflation, or in forcing marginal producers out of the market and therefore into unemployment.

What is valid here is the fact that the unimpeded pressure of union demands would eat away profits and make business enterprise intolerable. But equally, the unimpeded pressure of business power, in the absence of a counteracting union power, would eat away wage levels, make labor a poorly paid commodity, injure consumer buying power, and thus again make business enterprise intolerable. To deny the workers their share, either in higher wages or a lighter work week, is to deny that the factors making for the increased productive capacity of labor-plus-machine are broadly social factors, such as research, invention, communication, mass distribution, rather than narrowly managerial factors in any one plant or industry. It is to treat labor as only a factor in production, calculated coldly by the managerial group, rather than as a crucial human resource in the economy and society. In this sense unions are an organic part of the capitalist economy: capitalism would destroy itself without them, and if they did not exist it would be necessary to invent them. It is true that Lindblom tries to keep ethical values out of his analysis: maybe workers should get higher wages (he says), and maybe they deserve to, but their fair gains may be subversive of the price system by inducing inflation or unemployment. The trouble with this view is that thus far the inflation in America has been induced by high demand rather than high wages, although the latter may prove true in the future. Even more, the trouble with the thesis is its static quality: it assumes profits as given and sees them whittled away gradually by wage gains, whereas the fact is in America that both profits and wages have kept rising because both come out of the dynamism of science and technology.

To those who cling to the badges of status and respectability the fear of labor persists. The crises of large-scale strikes and the constant irritation of small ones have widened the gap between the worker and the considerable middle-class group fearful of labor's power and designs. American labor is learning that strikes incur not only economic costs but also heavy opinion costs in the splitting away of "neutral" middle-class support. It has learned that antilabor legislation usually comes in the wake of a strike wave. It has also digested the lessons of European experience in which the sense of constant industrial paralysis and labor crisis was one of the effective weapons of the Fascist adventurers in lighting the fires of antilabor hatred.

The problem of the strike weapon goes beyond the relation of labor and the middle class. No society can survive if its economy can be repeatedly and successfully paralyzed. In that sense there is something of the Syndicalist philosophy of direct action inherent in every strike, however responsible, and in every trade-union, however conservative. Yet to resolve the problem by suppressing the right to strike is to make an auto-da-fé of the democratic process: a society does not grow strong by lopping off its problems but by transcending them within a larger framework of action and power. Some way of limiting the strike weapon makes sense clearly in the area of atomic energy and the munitions industries, as also in the police and public-service municipal departments. But with the increasing role of the government as employer and the banning of strikes involving government workers of every kind, the withering away of the strike weapon could mean the replacement of corporate and union monopolies by the far more dangerous monopoly of government, combining at once political and economic power.

This is not to say that the trade-union imperium is always a democratic one. Unions like those of the teamsters, carpenters, musicians, coal miners, and building trades made only a minimal attempt at internal democracy. At their best they were run by a benevolent paternalism, as with the miners and the musicians; at their worst there were unions like the teamsters of Dave Beck, which became part of the shadowy underworld of racketeering, captured by a mercenary for whatever he could shake down from workers and employers alike, the instrument for his private dream of enriching himself at their expense. Yet these dictatorial and racketeering unions, taken together, formed only the margin of labor organization. It would be curious if labor were wholly free from the scars of corruption, venality, and the easy-money, something-for-nothing creed. Most American trade-unions are guided by honest, hard-working men, trying to achieve for their followers a measure of security and continuity of work, caught between rising living costs and the dangers and costliness of the strike weapon. The greatest threat to internal union democracy would emerge in most unions with a break in the successful pattern of trade-union activity.

The big internal fact about the American labor federations is their loose and autonomous character. Labor power is scattered among about 200 international unions and some 75,000 local unions, which are covered by more than 125,000 collective bargaining agreements; nineteen of the international unions have more than 1,000 locals each. The heads of the international soon discover—as the government does—that an important local may be a little sovereignty in itself. Increasingly, power in the unions has moved from the local toward the center, yet the process cannot stretch too far without destroying the roots of consent which give a trade-union its strength. Labor autocracies still exist, and a labor baron like John L. Lewis held absolute power for a long span: yet he did so only by convincing his men that he could help them raise their living standards and better their safety and welfare. When he tried to influence their voting in Presidential elections, as in 1940 and 1944, against the clear evidence of what the New Deal had done to help them, his paternalism did not save him from failure.

The trade-union has become, like the corporation, a vast administrative organization, with a large technical staff, and with representatives sitting in on governmental commissions and international agencies. The new trade-union officials are part of the managerial elite that came into being with the growth of economic collectives. From recent studies the American union leader today emerges as younger and better educated than the earlier leaders, more likely to come from the lower middle class, more alert to national and world events. He follows the technological changes in his industry, is hardheaded and astute in his relations not only with corporate but also with the government managerial groups, and is adroit in politics. He is well paid, has a staff and an expense account, has quarters in union offices that sometimes rival in splendor those of the corporation, lives in good hotels, travels by plane; yet his rewards are not primarily financial and he finds himself fulfilled rather in terms of power and of loyalty to a group with whom he feels tied.

I do not intend this as an uncritical portrait. There are many locals and their leaders who practice Jim Crow in their own unions, although impressive progress has been made recently in this area. Men with long labor experience have documented the charge that unions tend to become monolithic and to make policy at the top. Union leaders have had to develop toughness not only in the fight against antilabor forces from the outside but also against Communist attempts to capture and hold power from within. Greater than the danger of ruthlessness is that of bureaucracy, with a tendency toward settling down to a mediocre level of officialdom. In a number of instances this has happened. Yet a group of British trade-union leaders, after a study of American unionism in 1952, reported that the American unions were more concerned than the British with raising the efficiency of submarginal plants, that they used bolder methods in publicity and educational work and were readier to accept the results of scientific management.

In the light of these strides, the question remains why American labor has not established its own party and made a bid for political power. The answer the unions give is that they have not had to, since they have been able to achieve their ends without it. They have not had to overthrow a feudal social structure and introduce the methods of political democracy. They do not think in European terms of Socialism as state ownership or government operation of industry. Gompers deliberately turned his back on the intellectuals who led the working class up to his time, insisting that union leaders—however brilliant—should come from the ranks. The tradition has continued, and Robert Ferguson may be right in suggesting that it helps explain the pragmatic bent of the American union leaders. They feel they made greater concrete strides in two decades under Roosevelt and Truman, without nationalization and without a separate labor party, than British labor made from Keir Hardie to Ramsay MacDonald.

These men may be right or wrong, but they are not *novi homines* hungering for wealth and power and admission to the ruling groups. Neither do they work from the deep resentment which Nietzsche saw operative in European revolutionary movements, with an itch for shearing the rich. Their aim is to get a welfare democracy which will estab lish adequate controls for an economy-as-a-going-concern, a juster order to increase the national income, and common action to keep life from being wretched, insecure, and pathetic for the mass of people.

To achieve this, American labor has become an active political as well as economic force. Thus far it has operated within the current two-party system, trying to hold the balance of power between the parties, or to increase the power of its voice inside the councils of the Democratic party. The unions refuse to form their own party until they are convinced that the major ones have both become hostile. Meanwhile they are an extraordinarily effective political force. They have in their favor the big fact that it is easier to organize men politically for common action when you have first organized them economically. They have also the fact that to workers pressing for social legislation and for safeguards to collective bargaining, government is not a distant and abstract affair but something quite concrete. They have finally the *élan* of common action and of knowing what they want.

But American union leaders are still considered interlopers in the political field, special pleaders for a single-interest group. Americans who have only recently come to swallow, and have not yet digested, the idea that collective bargaining is not treason are likely for some time to view labor political action as a compact with the Devil and an agreement with Hell. The legislatures and Courts will continue to block union efforts to raise campaign funds from member contributions. Although the strongest political group in the nation, labor is still a political outsider. The prevailing attitude in the major parties is that, like a mastiff, it must be kept tolerably content, but under no circumstance admitted into the house.

The final question about the American worker is the question of what kind of life he leads, how much his work means to him, and what its effect is upon his play and leisure. The "human-relations" approach has revealed the pathetic extent to which the worker responds to any show of managerial interest in him as a human being. The stress in this new approach is how to explore the worker's personality so that he will get satisfaction out of his work and do effective work, contributing to a harmony within the plant. The danger is that the worker will come to be regarded merely as an object of psychological manipulation; yet some impressive results have been achieved in this sphere, and the best unions have lost their suspicion of these efforts.

The doughtier champions of the trade-union believe it has contributed much to re-establish the dignity and pride of craftsmanship, yet one may be skeptical. Given the obsession with the protection of the job, with work rules and seniority, with absence of discrimination, with wages and hours and fringe benefits, the creativeness of the work itself has been lost sight of. Seeing in the economic world only the drive for profits and dividends, for power and efficiency, the worker finds his own drive becoming one for wages and job protection rather than an interest and joy in the work itself. The trade-union would do well to make the performance of the job in its fullest sense the core of the worker's responsibilities. But it can do so only when it feels confident and secure enough in its acceptance by the people.

However, here, as elsewhere in American society, the emphasis has shifted from the satisfactions of the producer to those of the consumer. What keeps the worker going is what the job makes possible for him, the commodities he can buy, the new social experience that has come with the communications revolution, the chances for retiring with some security while he can still enjoy the evening of his life. These are not heroic objectives, but they are part of the whole expansive movement of the American economy. Engels wrote in 1882 from England to Karl Kautsky: "There is no workers' party here, there are only Conservatives and Liberal-Radicals, and the workers merrily share the feast of England's monopoly of the world market and the Colonies." The American workers have a different kind of feast of world power to share, but they are aware of being caught up in a stream of flowing abundance, and as long as the economy continues to expand in that fashion they will be part of its pattern and its values.

9. Poverty and Wealth

EVEN AT THE PITCH of prosperity, American life does not lack its pathos of privation. This is the darker side of the crescent moon.* Americans like to call those on whom the dreary burdens of privation fall the "underprivileged groups." It is in itself a revealing periphrasis, its premise being that these are not the dispossessed or disinherited, or the ex-

* This section should be read along with sections 1 and 10 of this chapter, where the problem of poverty is placed in its setting along with other phases of the going economy; see also Ch. III, Sec. 6, "The Sinews of Welfare," and Ch. VII, Sec. 2, "The Seats of the Mighty."

ploited, or the insulted and injured, but merely some who have got less than others of the gravy of life.

Franklin Roosevelt, who was less unctuous, spoke of them in his Second Inaugural in 1937 with a classic directness. He saw them "trying to live on incomes so meager that the pall of family disaster hangs over them day by day," living "under conditions labeled indecent by a so-called polite society half a century ago . . . lacking the means to buy the products of farm and factory. . . . I see one third of a nation ill-housed, ill-clad, ill-nourished."

The situation has changed considerably since Roosevelt spoke, but the spread between what Disraeli called the "two nations" is still there. A Senate committee made a study of the 1948 income figures which showed that a fourth of the American families (9,600,000) had incomes below $2,000 a year, or about $38 a week. Many were farm families, a large number were in the charge of old people, in others a widow was wage earner or the head of the family had been disabled. In many cases the worker was too unskilled to command a decent wage and could get no education to improve his lot. Of the nonfarm families in the poverty group, one out of five were Negroes.

Given the 1948 price levels, $2,000 a year for a family was on the margin of subsistence and well below the conservative budgets for minimum decent family living. One out of every ten American families was below the $1,000-a-year mark, which means wretched poverty. Senator Sparkman's subcommittee asked some social work agencies to find out how American families managed to make ends meet on less than $2,000 a year. In a study of 100 such families it was found that they went almost entirely meatless and fruitless, ate mainly starchy foods, cut down on tobacco, could afford no milk except for babies, bought day-old bread and second-hand clothing, and lived in crowded, light-deprived slums. One need not underscore what this means in terms of disease, ignorance, crime, cultural impoverishment, and the waste of ability and life potential through the denial of opportunity.

A decade of prosperity had cut the Roosevelt "one third of a nation" to one fourth in 1948. Since that time the decrease has continued, although at a slower rate. Comparing the 1948 figures with the 1954 figures, the number of families with income of under $2,000 dropped from 9,600,000 to 8,300,000—meaning that they decreased from 25 per cent to 20 per cent, or from one fourth to one fifth of the nation. However, the price inflation made these figures less meaningful: when prices were adjusted, the drop was only from 9,600,000 to 9,400,000. This was taking place, moreover, at a time when the rise in income and living standards at the upper half of the national scale was steady and substantial.

The over-all family income figures in America portray a nation of rising prosperity. The U.S. Commerce Department figures for mid-1955 gave an average family income of $5,600 a year, with an average for nonfarm families of $6,393 a year. The Census Bureau figures were lower but applied to a somewhat earlier period; the Commerce Department figures were more descriptive of the trend of mounting prosperity and inflated prices. Even the lowest estimates gave the average family income in 1955 at $4,200 a year. But the more significant figures were those showing the increased income of Americans during the years of the postwar boom. In 1948, 21 per cent of the American families (over 8,000,000) had an income of over $5,000; in 1954 the percentage had risen to 30 per cent (12,700,000 families), with allowance for price increases. Similarly, in 1947, 5 per cent of the American families had incomes of $7,500 and over, accounting for 23 per cent of the nation's income; in 1954, 11 per cent had similar incomes, accounting for 31 per cent of the nation's income. Perhaps the most dramatic figure of all had to do with incomes between $5,000 and $10,000 a year. In 1947, 11 per cent of the American families were in this range, totaling 22 per cent of the nation's income; in 1954, 35 per cent were in the $5,000 to $10,000 range, totaling 42 per cent of the nation's income. There could be no doubt that the large middle class of Americans, as well as the elite groups, were living well in the mid-1950s.

Yet these rising living standards, along with high productivity and full employment—the three idols of liberal economic striving—proved to be compatible with a hard residuum of poverty. In a breakdown of the income changes between 1935-36 and 1948, Dewey Anderson estimated that, after making allowance for price changes, only 4 per cent of the sixty-nine-billion-dollar increase in national income went to the lowest fifth of the population, less than 20 per cent went to the lowest two fifths, while more than 36 per cent went to the top fifth. Just the increase in itself for the top fifth was almost equal to the entire income of the bottom two fifths of the population in 1948, and four times the total income of the lowest fifth. The income of the lowest fifth in the earlier period was one thirteenth that of the top fifth, and in the later period, one twelfth, indicating that the income spread was decreasing only slightly, while the living standards of all groups were going up.

The 1954 figures on the incomes of American families varied depending on the source of the figures. According to the Office of Business Economics 10 per cent of the families had incomes of less than $2,000 a year, and 20 per cent less than $3,000. The Federal Reserve figures were 15 per cent under $2,000 and 26 per cent under $3,000; the Census Bureau figures were 20 per cent under $2,000 and 32 per cent under $3,000. The OBE figures showed 50 per cent over $5,000, while the Federal Reserve showed 43 per cent and the Census Bureau 37 per cent.

Some deny that poverty in America is mainly due to a faulty distribution of America's vast national income. They argue that it is a matter of productivity. Yet a rise in general productivity is not likely to do much for sharecroppers, migratory workers, Negroes who are kept out of a living wage through discrimination in industry and in education, older men who are ousted from good jobs, disabled men waiting for a chance at rehabilitation. An increase in productivity means a greater national income and prosperity. But into what channels the prosperity flows, whether it goes mainly into salaried income or corporate dividends, whether it is diffused or concentrated, whether it is siphoned off mainly into the top income levels or is used to allay the cruder inequalities in income distribution: these are the important questions. To ignore the distributive aspect is to assume that new productivity will somehow drip down from the top to the bottom.

Thus, in terms of income, as in terms of economic power, there is still an inequality pyramid in America which the recent years of income expansion have not substantially leveled out. The standard of living for the lowest fourth of the population, difficult enough in itself because of the price inflation, was psychologically more difficult because it was measured against the backdrop of vast luxury expenditures. In a typical boom year (1949) Americans spent $37 million on horse and dog races and $233 million on pari-mutuel betting; spent $8.5 billion for alcoholic drinks, more than a half billion for taxis, and $22 billion for clothes and jewelry. The poverty at the bottom of the pyramid was the harder to bear because of the lush living not only at the top (this has been true throughout history) but even in the middle-income groups.

Thus it is that the income distribution in America is tangled up with paradoxes. Compared with the corresponding groups in Southeast Asia or the Near East, Africa or South America, Russia or China, or even Italy or Greece, the living standards of the lower fourth of America are relatively good. The distance between a maharaja and a starving Indian villager is not paralleled in America, since most of the corporate managers live unobtrusively, without the ostentation of the feudal princes, plowing their profits back or consolidating them in vast corporate holdings. There is nothing in America quite like the poverty of peasants in Haiti or the southern Mexican provinces, or the villagers of India and the fellaheen of Egypt. Americans have never become deadened to poverty, nor have they accepted disease and high infant mortality as the visitation of Providence.

The striking fact about wealth in America is that its range goes far beyond anything known in the history of the world's great fortunes. Robert Heilbroner, who has freshly surveyed the "great acquisitors of history," points out that Jacob Fugger in early modern times accumulated $75 million in his lifetime, that John D. Rockefeller left an estate of less than $900 million, but that General Motors' income before taxes in the year 1955 alone was $2.5 billion, and its income after taxes almost $1.2 billion. From 1945 to 1955 corporate business in America averaged $34 billion in profits annually before taxes, and half of that after taxes. Even more striking is the fact that in the top income brackets in 1952, with incomes of a million dollars or over, more than 45 per cent of the total incomes came from dividends, and another 45 per cent from capital gains, estates, and trusts, while only 1½ per cent came from salaries. The very rich in America, one must conclude with Heilbroner, "are not money-makers but money-receivers." The figures are only slightly different for the incomes between $½ million and $1 million. The proportion of earned to unearned income in the $100,000 to $500,000 bracket is roughly 40 to 53 per cent, and it is not until the $50,000-$100,000 bracket that they become 63 to 33 per cent. The last two brackets are roughly the corporate managers; the top two are the wealthy *rentiers* living on income from past accumulation.

The paradoxes of wealth and poverty in America stretch further than these dramatic figures. One may say that, unlike Asia and Africa, poverty is not organic to the American economic system. With all the glaring inequalities of life in India or Iran, Italy or China, the poverty of the impoverished is part of the poverty of the country as a whole. In the backward economies of Asia and Africa or even some of the once prosperous economies of western Europe, there is now not enough national income to go around. The important fact about the American economy is that there is. One would not have to cut much into the high corporate profits or into lush living at the top and the ample comfort in the middle brackets to wipe out the poverty of the lower fifth, who make less than $2,000 a year. The rich need not be much less rich for the poor to be very much less poor. The poverty of America, in fact, is almost entirely outside the economic sphere proper. An analysis of the families in the income groups below $2,000 and $3,000 shows that it is largely the poverty of anti-Negro discrimination, of exclusion from adequate education, of physical or psychological handicap. It is also, in the case of the marginal farmer or marginal petty trader, the poverty of noncapitalist enterprise. The economy of the corporate empires has little room for it. America is the first civilization in history that has at its command the means for the total abolition of poverty.

Given the nature of the hard core of poverty, the natural answer has been a welfare democracy, with its steep tax structure, its minimum-wage laws, and its growing network of social-security benefits. America has not moved so far or so fast in this direction as Britain and the

Scandinavian countries, which are far less able to carry the load. This is due mainly to the swaggering American sense that in a dynamic economy a mounting productivity will absorb all social ills; that those who fall by the way are lazy or weak; and that the concern about economic security is a debilitating trait in any culture. So ingrained has this been in the American mind that even the victims of the Great Depression used to take themselves at the valuation of the possessors and wonder whether the fault might not, after all, be their own. It is this outlook that has made "relief" so vulnerable a target for those who decried the retreat from the ancient virtues.

It is a hard thing to be a poor man in any culture, but hardest to be a poor man in a rich culture. It is equally hard to be a helpless man in a power culture that has not lost the ideals of the "masterless man." The effect of poverty on the human personality in America makes it as wasting as it is wasteful, as withering as it is needless. The people at the bottom of the pyramid spend so much of their waking hours thinking about how to make ends meet that they have little energy left for the available stir that fills American life, and none for recreation, clubs, or the cultural resources to which most Americans now have access. Worst of all, they feel alienated from the rest of the culture, with no subculture of their own (like the proletarian culture of France or Italy) to give them comfort or a sense of cohesion.

In more static societies the underlying population has learned to accept its lot as a kind of fatality; in societies with a permanent proletariat, there is a proletarian consciousness which may offer some nourishment, so that poverty has a kind of psychic balance sheet. But in a rich consumers' civilization, with abundance so pervasively present, those who are caught in scarcity feel themselves not only the despised and rejected but come to despise themselves. They are the outsiders to whom the culture gives only denials, who lose their sense of confidence, and who in many cases do not even have the consolations of a traditional, deeply felt religion.

Their only hope is that by some secular miracle what they have missed will somehow be achieved by a child who will win the big prizes and thus get into the swim of the Golden River.

10. The Emerging Amalgam

DURING THE 1930s and 1940s the Great Debate in America, aside from foreign policy, was on the relation of business and government—or, as J. S. Mill put it, "the province of government" in the economy. Much of this Great Debate moved out of the economic sphere itself and by the 1950s had become political polemics. Under both major parties the government pushed very far into what was once considered "free enterprise," and both business and labor have come to accept government's new role. As the political capital of America, Washington has become a polar center of business power to rival New York. In the war economies and "readiness economies" of the past generation, the once accepted lines of demarcation between free enterprise and government control have little meaning. Some of the biggest of the big corporations are one-customer enterprises, doing most of their work for the government and depending for their profits and existence on government contracts. On the other hand, the crucial decisions within the government on questions of priorities, allocations of scarce materials, distribution of plants, and price control are made by men identified all their lives with corporate systems. Even in the case of industries not directly involved in armaments, the scale of taxation, the control of credit and of investment, and government fiscal policies have played havoc with the old terms of "free enterprise" and "Socialism."

What is emerging in America is a new amalgam of the old elements, so welded together that they are scarcely recognizable in the final product. There are still clearly private sectors of the economy, and there are also clearly public sectors. But the trend is away from both, toward the new amalgam in which the private sector is a form of business collectivism and the public sector is a form of state capitalism.

Another way of putting the trend is to note that the old boundaries between the "private corporation" and the "welfare state" are no longer as clear as they were. The needs of continuous large-scale industrial employment, without the cost of violence and bitterness, have led many corporations to adopt welfare plans for health insurance, recreation, employee housing, retirement pensions and annuities. Thus a welfare corporation has taken its place alongside the welfare trade-union and the welfare state. Together they form a welfare democracy. There are still sharp differences about how the financial burdens shall be distributed between them, but only the dinosaur right wing of conservatism challenges the goal itself.

The main area of conflict is still the choice of techniques for organizing a stable economy. While placing stress on lower taxes, the encouragement of investment, and the minimum possible regulation by government agencies, a business group like the Committee for Economic Development shows how far the more liberal corporate managers are willing to go in accepting the amalgam itself. The emphasis of the American Keynesians is upon tax policies, credit controls, government-subsidized construction, and a periodic assessment of over-all trends and over-all needs.

In these terms the American economy is today an example neither of pure "capitalism" (as so many Europeans and Asians still seem to think) nor of "creeping Socialism" (as some of the more frightened American Tories seem to think). It is becoming a mixed economy, with large areas of freedom and varied techniques of regulation, control, and some forms of planning. Those who fear that a mixed economy is the "road to serfdom"—a halfway house toward totalitarianism—are worried about this trend. Still others wonder whether so pluralistic an economy may not lead to chaos, whether a "hybrid" economic system does not distill all the worst elements of public and private ownership without any of their merits, and whether an economic "house divided against itself" can stand.

American history since 1933 is such as to calm the doubters on at least several of these scores. The experience since the start of the New Deal has been that of dynamic economic growth. That is why the crises of European economies are not relevant to the case of America. With its immense resources and its capital accumulation, and with a national income of close to $400 billion a year, America does not have to make the cruel choice the Europeans still have to make between immediate living needs and capital equipment. The steadily rising expenditures for social services and for armaments have still left room for higher profit levels, greater capital formation, improved wage scales and living standards. This may seem to be a mathematical impossibility, but with full use of labor, resources, and machinery, the expanding national product can take much in its stride that was once considered burdensome.

The arms phase of the new amalgam raises the question of whether the continuing economic dynamism of America would be possible without arms expenditures, and whether an economy geared to war production for a generation can make the change-over to a peace economy without serious disruption. Most American economists say yes to this, pointing to the New Deal, which used a nonmilitary public-works program to considerable effect, and to the early years after World War II when the American economy prospered in a period of demobilization and against the Cassandralike forebodings of heavy unemployment. A "mature" economy, which has exhausted its capacity for rapid spontaneous growth, could not use the stimulus of war production to produce enough for the purposes of life as well as of death. But by the growth of such new industries as radio and television, antibiotics, the electrical industries, commercial aviation, and the nonarmament phases of the chemical industries, the American economy has shown that it is far from "mature" in this sense. It is capable of growth from within—from the convergence of great resources, capital formation, technology, labor skills, and consumer standards.

The only doubt about this argument is less economic than political. In the extreme emergency of economic crisis, as in 1933-36, it proved politically possible for Congress to vote a large peacetime public-works program. But afterward both the Roosevelt and Truman Administrations found it more difficult: there was always the Congressional fear that the taxes and expenditures for peacetime uses would extend "Socialism." The Eisenhower Administration left its public-works program for a new network of highways largely to state rather than Federal subsidy. Every administration finds that it is easier to get billions for defense than millions for Federal hydroelectric projects and river-valley developments. The Republicans felt that they had taken important steps under President Eisenhower to convert the economy to peacetime production and charged the Democrats with a dependence upon war expenditures for prosperity. This was an interesting reversal of the usual European situation where it is the conservatives who are under attack for relying on a war economy and the Left which takes the position that capitalism is doomed without war. But it should be remembered that the antiwar tradition in America has been mainly isolationist and Republican, and that Senator Taft opposed foreign interventionism largely on the ground of its weakening effect on the economy. The liberal Democratic economists counterattacked in the mid-1950s with the confident assertion that only a bold program of a full-employment economy could be counted upon to effect the conversion.

In economic terms the expansion through arms expenditures operates much as would any other—by a kind of investment and managerial conscription. One of the weaknesses of a "normal" capitalism is that periodically there is "oversaving," which is a way of saying that there is both underinvestment and underconsumption. In an arms economy, which is accompanied by a much higher tax rate than would otherwise be politically feasible, the high taxes cut into the savings, and the corporations—to keep expanding—have to use large blocs of their income for investment and expansion. The government does not use the taxes for investment in the private sector but as expenditures which nonetheless increase employment, thereby increasing further the capacity to consume. In this sense an arms economy keeps the economic energies flowing, but the energies must first be there: it can never be a substitute for them. It also conscripts for the purpose of the new state capitalism the managerial abilities of the best minds in the corporate bureaucracy, who would be hostile to a state capitalism under conditions that invoked their class bitterness rather than their patriotism.

With all this extension of the tax structure and government spending, the American economy continues to develop within pluralistic forms. American industry has no single pattern of operation or of power. What applies to autos or cigarettes does not apply to textiles or coal, and none of them in turn applies to magnesium or the chemical industries. A by-product of the TNEC inquiry in the mid-1930s was the evidence it gave of a kind of inventory of capitalist industrial action, showing the plurality of procedures by which the various segments of American industry operated. Even if a form of Socialism were to arise in America, it would have to reckon with such pluralistic material and be an extremely sophisticated Socialism. On the other hand, the TNEC reports also showed the similarity of the larger pattern of power under the dissimilar surfaces of industrial production, pricing, and distribution. From this at least some Americans may conclude that with the proper knowledge—and perhaps even with much of the same managerial talent—what a private corporation can do can also be done by a government corporation, such as those already existing in hydroelectric power in the Tennessee and Columbia valleys, and to some extent in atomic power. If such a new Socialism were to emerge, it would have to discard the dogma that sees nationalization as a grand and simple plan and apply the same pragmatic approach to the government corporations that is now applied to the private corporations.

For the present at least, however, the economic direction of America is not toward state Socialism, even in the form of the government corporation. It is toward the extension of the New Deal as an amalgam of state capitalism and business collectivism. This is becoming clearer in those industries which get their contracts from the government, have their supplies allocated by the government, are allowed to write off generous obsolescence at government expense for plants built at government behest, and pay heavy chunks of their profits to the government in the form of taxes, which are then plowed back into the appropriations that make the contracts possible. It is shown also within the structure of the corporation itself, where profit and private property have lost their old relations to business enterprise, and a new managerial form of business collectivism has risen to replace the old economic individualism.

Insofar as this complex economy is subject to planning, it is obviously different from the kind envisaged by Democratic Socialist theory, or practiced in such mild Socialisms as the British or Scandinavian, and it is of course drastically different from that of the Communist economies. Using the distinction between direct and indirect planning, the basic planning element in the American economy is indirect. That is to say, instead of nationalization or codes of regulation and control by government administrators, the planning is mainly by pressures, nudges, and prods. The Keynesian revolution in economic theory has largely taken over American economic policy. An excellent system of national income accounting has been developed, and an over-all survey is made periodically, presumably for the President by his Council of Economic Advisers, but actually for the whole of industry and the fraternity of economists. These and many other surveys made by corporations, foundations, and professional business analysts are studied by the whole community, and a rough consensus is always in process about what must be done to avert too-violent swings of the business cycle. The "indirect planning" controls can then be put into operation: tax policies, government bond flotation programs, Federal Reserve interest policies, armament or other public-work programs, installment selling control, credit control, price-control and wage-control policies.

These indirect methods involve a loss of speed and precision of movement, especially since many of the measures depend on Congressional action, which tends strongly to be hostile toward any efforts at economic control. Above all, it must be understood that the effectiveness of the methods depends largely on influencing corporate and trade-union policies, and must be achieved by persuasion rather than coercion. This feature of American planning, which is anathema to the dogmatic Socialists, is exactly what recommends it to the new American liberalism. For whatever may be lost in the process of this kind of planning, what is gained is a degree of spontaneous energy in the economy as a whole, a sense of freedom of movement which is the principal element in American economic dynamism. There is a clinging so far as possible to decentralized decision, a degree of devotion to economic pursuits through the spur of managerial effectiveness and private success that is hard to achieve through direct planning and impossible to achieve by coercion.

Thus America is evolving a *tertium quid* between an unmanaged capitalism and a tightly planned and managed Socialism: a loosely planned and indirectly controlled progressive capitalism, whose big prizes continue to go to the rich, but which keeps a prosperous economy going for the nation as a whole; which is sprawling, wasteful, still unjust in its distribution, Byzantine in its extravagance, precipitous in the differences between the big rewards and the mean existences; but which is nevertheless still in the process of growth, with undiminished bursting energies, already touching a $400 billion national product, and capable in time of organizing the economic life of 300 million people or more.

The long-debated question of the survival power of such an economy has been basically resolved, but not without lingering anxiety. Not an anxiety about the inherent strength and staying power of the economy and its capacity for growth, but about the ways in which it achieves stability. America is today the only great economy capable of large-scale export of capital: even the Russians cannot rival it in this respect. If we can speak of the "imperialism" of the American economy, it is in this sense of capital export: a very different type of imperalism from the classic type which sought to pump capital from the colonies into the nation instead of exporting it. But American foreign economic aid has largely aimed at helping other economies enough to keep them from moving toward communism. Its capital exports have thus had a political purpose, like its own internal arms economy. And they raise a similar question of how long they can continue without either military explosion or internal business contraction.

But this prospect is more of a logical dilemma than an actual one. By the same logic the American economy should have been doomed long ago, during the Great Depression. In this sense the turning point in the history of the American economy came with the New Deal, which tried to transform as much of the economy as was necessary to save the whole of it, along with the political, social, and moral system that went with it. While the New Deal was full of blunders and improvisations, it did hit on corrective measures which restored the vitality that had seemed wholly lost. The final pattern included a set of governmental strategies to guard against the plague of boom-and-bust cycles which had blighted the economy; to keep small business from being crowded out; to keep the bigness of the Big Corporation within controllable bounds, by holding-company legislation and anti-trust prosecutions; to set up a system of social security and deal with the more blatant forms of social misery; to equalize the bargaining power of trade-unions as against the big corporations; to lift the living standards and the purchasing power of groups whose lack of buying capacity had formerly dragged the economy down; to use fiscal controls and public-works programs as ways of preventing oversaving and of filling in the gaps left by private enterprise; to push production levels toward the full potentials of the national plant.

Thus America has moved under the prodding of necessity toward enlarged sectors of public action in the economy. In terms of dogma

Americans have looked askance at every step in the process. Some have called it "creeping Socialism" and worse. But under the spur of the Great Depression and of two world wars, and with the thrust of the traditional democratic welfare impulse, the economy has kept moving in this direction in spite of name-calling. The historic impulse of Americans has been to cling to the private sectors wherever they can and move toward the public sector only where they must.

There is no danger within the American psychology that Americans will embrace a subservience to the state out of dogmatic enthusiasm. The greater danger lies in the fact that the big power structures in America are the aggregates of corporate power; that they function very much as governments function; that more than ever they control the agencies of public opinion and influence the direction of education and belief; and that, given the necessary extensions of the public sector, they may prefer a continuing arms economy to the alternative of successive New Deals.

By way of summing up, and striking a final balance of the nature and operation of the American economy, several observations must be added.

The first is that the whole profile of what used to be called "economic problems" has changed. The strictly economic issues—those of production and productivity, of the distributive mechanisms, even to some extent the issue of the size of the economic unit and the division of the national product—have increasingly become technical problems and have been pushed into the background. What may be called the political, psychological, and moral issues of the economy have come into the foreground, and the anxiety that an observer must still feel about the economy must more and more be directed to them.

The American economy of today is not the same one that Veblen attacked at the turn of the century and John Bates Clark defended, nor is it even the same that the TNEC described and analyzed in its path-breaking survey at the end of the 1930s. There are few more remarkable stories in the history of social institutions than the way in which the American economy transformed itself and its problems in the era of the Big Technology and the Big Market.

The problem of scarcity, for example, which is so dominant a problem in other economies, has practically ceased to exist for Americans. A dramatic illustration is the decreasing number of Americans who are involved with production itself, in the sense of coming into contact with the soil or other natural resources, or even in the manufacture of basic subsistence goods. There is a style or flavor to an economy as to other segments of a culture. A vivid feature of the

American economic style is the rise of the tertiary industries, which go beyond farming and manufacture to form a distributive and service sector of the economy.

This is bound to have an impact on the psychological climate of the culture. It means the end of economic man, in the primitive sense of having to confront the eternal environment in constant struggle. It also means that the American lives and strives more derivatively than he once did, without the sense of immediacy that came from contact with the soil and from the skills of craftsmen and artisans. Perhaps a fairer way to put it is to say that the basic economic skills and arts have not vanished or become less real to the people themselves but have changed in form. The production arts—those of *homo faber*—apply to ever fewer people, and for them they are becoming highly technical and professional. For more and more Americans the economic skills have become either the engineering skills or else the middleman skills of salesmanship, advertising, distribution, and servicing.

The ordinary American has come to assume that somehow the "goods" will be there for the economy as a whole. He doesn't have to produce them or worry about them. His job and worries are either to think about the machines that will produce them and how to keep them from breaking down, or else to run around seeing people, or sit in his office or shop while they come to see him, or push pieces of typed paper around, or see that things or people get from one place to another in an orderly fashion, or think up slogans, or devise little selling tricks that will get the sales volume of one brand of car or detergent or one model of dress ahead of the others. Even the earlier economic virtues have been transformed: thrift, industriousness, tenacity, daring, have given way to efficiency, technical expertness, the ability to handle people ("human relations"), organizational adjustment and loyalty, and a high degree of mobility.

The result is a pervasive air of unreality that encompasses the economy. It is as if everyone were involved in the intermediate and satellite processes and by-products instead of in the products themselves. The American knows that he makes *his* living but has little sense of how this fits into the collective means of livelihood for others and for the society as a whole. Little wonder then that he finds it hard to identify himself with the plight of the underdeveloped economies in Asia and Africa, whose problems are so unlike those of his own economy.

The debate on the concentration and diffusion of economic power in America has largely taken the place of the older debates on centralism and federalism in government. The same dualism which runs through American attitudes in many segments of life is dramatically present in the attitude toward bigness and monopoly in economic life. As with science, the feeling about corporate bigness contains elements both of fear and attraction, of the impulse to leave it alone and the impulse toward control. In fact, this mixed attitude does not merely separate conservatives from liberals, and Hamiltonians from Jeffersonians, but it is to be found as a dual strain in every American. Lewis Galantière has put it well: "Just as every Frenchman may be said to be at one and the same time a child of monarchial authoritarianism (Richelieu, Louis XIV, Napoleon) and of Republican individualism (the Revolution of 1789), so every American contains within him the seed of Hamiltonian mercantilism and the seed of Jeffersonian agrarianism with its distrust of the merchant. Americans have encouraged unbridled business enterprise as Hamiltonians; they have been suspicious of it as Jeffersonians."

This being so, one may say that the new amalgam of economic freedom and economic control which I have described is more expressive of the American economic mind and temper than any other system could be. To put it concretely, there is a free money market but if it shows any sign of going berserk there are Federal Reserve controls to check it; there is a system of free farmers, but if their income falls too badly there are government parity payments and other subsidies to bolster it; there is free profit-making and profit-taking, but in order to perform the functions which keep them free the government takes a big bite of them in taxes; there is a free labor and talent market, but to make sure that it does not end in wretchedness there is also a governmental social-security setup; there are thousands of small firms that supply General Motors, but there is also General Motors in all its magnitude; there is wide stock dispersal of A.T.&T. and other such corporations, but there is also a tight managerial control on the conduct of their operations. If this amalgam did not already exist it would be necessary for Americans to invent it.

One of the results of the debate about business bigness has been the emergence of a "New Enlightenment" in economic thought, led notably by J. M. Clark, M. A. Adelman, Peter F. Drucker, and (in his later phase) David E. Lilienthal. Their contention, in essence, is that Americans have paid too much attention to the advantages of smallness in the business unit and free-market competition; that there are forms of business bigness which do not involve the evils of monopoly power, and that there are new forms of competition which achieve the same results as the older ones. Clark used the test of "workable competition"—not whether competition is free but whether the gains resulting from the advantages of corporate bigness, in the form of lower costs, higher wages, industrial peace, greater innovation, and more funds for research, are passed on to the consumer and the worker.

There is obviously a good deal of force to this view. Certainly there have been consumer advantages flowing from the emergence of the big automobile companies, the big food chains, and the great manufacturers of new synthetics. Nor can it be doubted that bigness must be separated from monopoly: some big corporations are not in a monopoly position but simply express the increased size of the market, while some small corporations are strategically located to exercise monopoly power. Yet it is wishful to say that because there have been social advantages from bigness, therefore the anxieties about it may be dismissed. What is happening is that the emerging amalgam has found still another form in which to express itself, that of an amalgam of competitive and monopolistic practices which defies any neat statement by the economists and adds to the pluralistic character of the American economy. It appears to be achieving some of the results that its defenders acclaim while pushing very close to some of the dangers that its critics deplore. Despite the prevailing degree of industrial oligopoly, the performance of the American economy has been a brilliant one. Yet the price that has been paid is a growing amount of vertical integration, a tendency to pass on to the consumer not only reduced costs but also the increased prices flowing from wage settlements between the Big Corporation and Big Unionism, and the power of corporate bigness to put pressure on government itself and exact conformity from its managers and technicians.

I have mentioned the doctrine of "countervailing power" which Galbraith has introduced into the economic vocabulary. This has tended to reassure a number of liberals who might otherwise have continued to fight against the trend toward bigness. The picture they get is one of "bilateral monopoly," in which the concentrated power of the corporation and the union balance each other; of inter-industry competition, where glass bottles are challenged by tin cans and they in turn by paper containers; and of an industry-government equilibrium in which the corporate power over price and output is balanced by the power of the Federal agencies to regulate and control them and by the position of the Federal government as a powerful (sometimes the only) purchaser of what the corporation is selling. But Walter Adams has shown bitingly that the corporate-union bilateral monopoly tends to end in "escalator" arrangements by which the consumer is exploited by both sides; that inter-industry competition often means only that the older monopolies enter the field of the newer product (for example, the current mergers of motion-picture chains with TV networks, or the entrance of big newspapers into the broadcasting field); and that the government agencies which are supposed to regulate the big corporations often end up by having their personnel diluted and replaced to make them more amenable to corporate pressures, while the government as the big or only purchaser of corporate products often finds the purchase contracts being written by military or civilian officials who had been connected with the industry involved.

Historically, however, the Galbraith approach has shed considerable light on some of the factors that have kept the American economy relatively stable since the Great Depression. A good part of the basis for this stability is to be found in the operation of countervailing power which has prevented any of the "Bigs" from pursuing their own interests and accumulating their own power without thought of the economic picture as a whole. There is, of course, a danger that this explanation may become a new kind of Newtonianism, with a built-in self-regulating mechanism operating between the "Bigs." Yet as a rough rule-of-thumb it is historically true that the pulls and pressures of these mastodons of business, labor, farming, distribution, and government have done much to give balance to the economy.

In themselves they could not have achieved this, but their balancing force has been aided by the fact that Americans have learned a good deal about countercyclical measures. Here again there is an emerging amalgam of measures taken at a number of levels and by a number of agencies: the periodic corporate surveys of resources, labor supply, the business market, capital expansion, and technological change; the similar surveys made on a larger scale by the Treasury, the Bureau of the Budget, and the Federal Reserve Board, and the readiness of these agencies to act through fiscal controls whenever there are danger signals; the techniques of striking a national economic trial balance periodically by the Council of Economic Advisers, which I have already discussed. All of these in turn operate inside a price system which, whatever the inroads that have been made upon it by elements of closure, is still fluid enough to adjust itself to the actions taken by these groups and agencies. It may be said that, so far as the technical and economic problems are concerned, Americans now have adequate knowledge about how to stabilize their economy: the real question is whether they have the political wisdom and the moral courage to take the necessary measures.

This leads to the most difficult question of all. If an organism is to have a healthy and stable growth, there must be a direction toward which that growth moves. One of the greatest defects of the American economic system is that, while it has undergone revolutionary changes in almost every phase and area, it lacks a sense of direction. As long as the economy was moving away from scarcity, expansion was itself a goal, and there was an internalized drive toward the "bigger and better." But Americans have learned to be skeptical of the "bigger" in and for itself. As for the "better," an acquisitive society has few ways of measuring it. For years "prosperity"—general and personal—was the aim of the American economy. America now has prosperity and is likely, unless there is a world catastrophe, to maintain it for decades at least. But where does it go from prosperity?

In wholly planned economies there are external criteria imposed by political leaders and power elites. But America has wisely kept away from fusing its economic and political leadership. As for its power elite, which is mainly in corporate enterprise, the neutrality of the technicians which I have described in the previous chapter operates to a great extent for the corporate managers as well. To be sure, there is a continuing *élan* in the economy which is largely due, as Peter Drucker points out, to the vertical mobility which corporate enterprise makes possible for very large numbers of its employees. And there is an additional *élan* in the new products, the new services, and the new leisure which the American economic achievement has made possible. Yet again it must be asked: what kinds of products, what kinds of services, and leisure for what?

The only possible answer, here as elsewhere in American life, is that in the absence of an aristocracy to answer these questions authoritatively for Americans, the answers are left to the decisions of millions of people—consumers, workers, small businessmen, farmers, corporate managers, union leaders, government policy-makers. The important fact about these decisions is, of course, a negative one: they are not imposed from without. This is why there is so much waste in American life. If Veblen had been right and if there really had been a deeply rooted leisure class in America on which to base a theory, there would have been far more direction than there is on the side of standards of consumption and living. Since there is no such direction, it is left to the millions.

Americans have a faith that four million or seven million decision-making points (the figures refer to the total number of enterprises and the number of nonfarm enterprises) are better than just a few. But they are better not because they are quantitatively greater, but only if they are free decisions and if a principle of taste and welfare informs them. One may ask how free they are when one remembers that General Motors buys six billion dollars' worth of products a year from twenty-one thousand "primary" suppliers. How much initiative and self-reliance is left to the little fish that cluster around the big fish? Similarly, there are millions of technically trained men who supply skill, ideas, and research to the economy. Yet, as I have noted, they have to do their work and make their individual decisions within a bureaucratic framework which evokes only a limited initiative and a diminishing daring and accents the less admirable qualities of manipulation and success. I speak of the limited initiative: this becomes clear when you compare even the most generous big corporation with the typical exciting story of earlier business enterprise—that of the obscure man with an idea who throws his whole life into making a product, carves out a small business until it makes its mark and becomes nationally known, and has the satisfaction of constructive achievement.

CHAPTER VI

The Political System

1. The Style and Genius of American Politics

2. The Democratic Idea

3. Presidency and Demos

4. The Party System and the Voter

5. Power and Equilibrium

6. The Governmental Managers

7. Tribunes of the People

8. Law and Justice

9. Keepers of the Covenant

10. The Struggle for Civil Liberties

IN WHICH we examine the curious but effective ways that Americans have of governing—and misgoverning—themselves. Starting with the American "political style"—the belittling of politics, the contempt for the politician, the refusal to take politics in a "grand" fashion, yet also the political daring and practical experimentalism—we ask what basic contributions Americans have made to the arts of government in a free society (Sec. 1, "The Style and Genius of American Politics"). We then take a closer look at the concept of democracy (Sec. 2, "The Democratic Idea") in its double sense of republican constitutionalism and the "leaves of grass" belief in the common man, asking how and why this idea has been frustrated so often in American history.

There follows an analysis of the most powerful office in the free world—the American Presidency—and the sources of its strength in the relation of the President to the people (Sec. 3, "Presidency and Demos"). We then examine the most difficult and elusive phase of the American political system—the operation of the parties, the conduct of American voters, the ethnic and class bases of American political behavior, and the shifting lines of party growth (Sec. 4, "The Party System and the Voter"). This leads into the problem of how the power massed within the American political system operates, how it is concentrated and dispersed, and what its consequences are: the principal themes being the question of majorities and minorities, of power at the center and power at the rim (centralism as against grass-roots localism), and the equilibrium which the American political system has succeeded in maintaining amidst its tensions and conflicts (Sec. 5, "Power and Equilibrium"). This, in turn, leads into the problem of the day-to-day operation of the American government in a managerial age, the growth of bureaucracy, and how Americans have coped with the dangers of stagnation, red tape, and arbitrary power (Sec. 6, "The Governmental Managers").

The final cluster of topics deals with American law and freedom. We examine first the Congressional lawmakers, noting how the legislative function has been limited and transformed, and how the "watchdog" or investigative function has grown (Sec. 7, "Tribunes of the People"). We then turn to the nature and operation of the legal system and the American attitude toward law (Sec. 8, "Law and Justice"). This leads into a discussion of the Constitution, and of its guardians and interpreters—the U.S. Supreme Court, along with an analysis of how the Court has performed its tasks of interpretation, including the political aspects of the legal process (Sec. 9, "Keepers of the Covenant"). Finally we examine (Sec. 10, "The Struggle for Civil Liberties") the status of civil liberties in America, the hazards to which they have been exposed and the jeopardy in which they have recently found themselves. We note the great issues over which the struggle for civil liberties has raged—segregation and desegregation, the treatment of domestic Communism, the government security programs, the impact of investigating bodies on the freedom of the individual, the tenure and loyalty of teachers, the censorship of reading matter, the use and limits of wire tapping, the place of the alien in American law, the emergence of a "radical Right" as a new fact in American popular attitudes toward civil liberties. We end by noting the ways in which America is seeking to restore the strength of its great civil-liberties tradition.

CHAPTER VI

The Political System

1. The Style and Genius of American Politics

EVERY civilization has a government of some sort, but each differs from the others in the way it organizes and conducts its political life—its mode and style of "politics." Jakob Burckhardt, writing on the *Italian Renaissance,* noted that the men of the Renaissance made even the state a "work of art." The Americans make their state, as they make their armies and corporations, a vast organizational achievement: they speak of "the business of government." To the sound middle-class American the most telling complaint against any administration is that it has been wasteful of the "taxpayer's money." On the local level, politics is often regarded as a "racket"—that is, a cushioned berth where you can make a quick and easy dollar. And viewed in terms of spectator sports in a competitive society, politics is also seen as a vast competitive contest, played for the big stakes of office and power, but nonetheless a game: "the great game of politics."

But the observer will be misled if he concludes from this that Americans view government solely through the eyes of economic man. Here is another instance of the polarity of the American character. With his ruling passion for freedom, the American is contemptuous of any government; he says, with Emerson, that "all states are corrupt." Yet since the days when Jackson had his clash with the big banking groups, the "strong" Presidents and administrations which used the power of government effectively, whatever their party or program, have received a popular accolade as well as the verdict of history. The attitude of the American toward political power is a curiously dual one. They hem in their state governors, for example, with a jungle of restrictions; they seek to balance the power of every official with another official; they maintain bicameral legislatures that are clearly archaic; they multiply agencies and offices, from the Federal to the local, instead of adding new powers to those of the old agencies. No people ever had less reason to fear the arbitrary abuse of governmental power, yet Americans have been traditionally reluctant to yield power, and they still tend to deflate it. In time of crisis, however, they view power in a practical and undogmatic way. In every great emergency of the national existence they have yielded their government and leadership the necessary power for meeting it, whether the crisis be civil war, the danger of inner economic collapse, or the tragic burdens of world war in an industrial age.

Yet while managing the problems of political power with tolerable success, they have also found it necessary to be antistate and antipolitician. The traditional American antistatism (or better, "anti-government," since Americans use "state" not as a political but as a geographic expression) has stopped just short of anarchism, although Henry Thoreau and Benjamin Tucker show that a part of the American tradition crossed that line. The American anarchist strain is not, like the Italian or Spanish, mixed with syndicalism or with a peasant hostility toward the tax-gatherers; nor is it, like the Russian, mixed with a revolutionary aim. It flows rather from the tradition of individual self-reliance. The American, especially in rural America, felt he could get along by himself, and that the mastodon power of the government threatened the conduct of his life: in urban America this antistatism has been somewhat diluted by the mingling of ethnic strains, the multiplication of new tasks for government, and the turmoil of life. Yet even in rural America and even in the South today, where antistatism remains strongest, the attitude toward government has been a split one—positive when its help is needed, resentful when it seems to interfere.

Compared with the genuine if ambivalent antistatism of the individual, the element of *laissez faire* in American thinking—the antistatism of the corporation—seems spurious. American business has not refused to accept state authority when it has taken the form of subventions, tariffs, or subsidies. *Laissez faire* has been therefore an opportunist antistatism, that of the corporation as a power form rivaling the state. It has found an echo in the American mind largely because the formative years of American political thinking were the years of revolt against British power, and back of that the period of British revolt against their own absolute monarchies; so that the corporate spokesmen had a convenient chance to clothe their cause in the intellectual garments of the struggle against Tudor and Stuart absolutism. Thus the anarchist and the rebel latent in every American have joined hands with corporate power to proclaim that "the government is best which governs least." Or, as someone put it, the American motto is "In God we trust; in government we mistrust."

The most characteristic trait of the American political style thus became the belittling of politics; and with it the professionalizing of the politician. The American is prone to suspect every government he elects. Nose-thumbing has become his traditional gesture not only of contempt for the politician but, even more, of the freedom to express contempt, to show that Americans have a corrosive skepticism about those whom they have presumably chosen to govern them. The darling of the newspaper caricaturists has for decades been the bloated, gorilla-faced, cigar-in-mouth fellow with an inevitable be-watch-chained paunch. In the political zoology of the American mind he combines the qualities of swine and fox, feeding greedily at the public trough, plotting cunningly to win and hold power. In recent years his primacy in the caricatures has been challenged only by the bureaucrat—the only word in English, as Harold Ickes put it, that can be hissed although there is not a sibilant in it.

Thus the politician and bureaucrat are fair game for every shaft, the sacrificial kings to whom the Americans grant power but whom they reserve the right to stone to death. The poorest, meanest, most misery-ridden fellow—the town drunk perhaps, the farm ne'er-do-well, or the city derelict—can say anything, no matter how scurvy, about a man in public office. Not only does he have the legal right, but it performs a therapeutic function for him: it shows who is boss, whose is the ultimate power, thus giving him an outlet for his frustrations and consoling him for the disparity in power and income between himself and his target.*

This belittling of politics is partly responsible for the abandonment of politics to the professional politician. What you despise and attack you do not engage in or give your life to. This has meant a break with the Jacksonian doctrine of rotation in office, which was based on the belief that there are no mysteries in governing, just common sense, integrity, and a devotion to the public good, and that any able citizen can therefore do it; and which was itself a way of rationalizing the spoils system, and for taking politics away from the elite of ability and education. In the rise of the big city, and its strata of new immigrants who were largely illiterate and were grateful for aid and guidance, the professional politician found his métier and gathered both money and power from it.

A vicious circle came into being: the contempt for politics as predation made the Americans shrink from the task of government; but the more they left a vacuum into which the professional politician moved, the more violently they recoiled from the result. Most of the able young people turned their talents to business and the professions,

* For a further discussion of political power, see Sec. 5, "Power and Equilibrium"; for the bureaucracy, see Sec. 6, "The Governmental Managers"; for the professional politician, see Sec. 4, "The Party System and the Voter."

where the great rewards loomed; and in many cases to the armed forces, perhaps because war represented the only nonpecuniary calling with glamour and prestige attached to it. The arts of government, which the Greeks had deemed the noblest arts within human competence, came to be considered defiling and defacing. In recent years a growing awareness of this gap between politics and creative talent has spread among the colleges and has served to counteract the tendency. This awareness was especially evident after World War II among the young veterans who came back to complete their studies under the G.I. subsidies and brought a new current of realistic intelligence into politics.

Where the professionals operate, however, is not in public office itself but behind it. The officeholders—the mayors and governors, the state legislators, the whole array of county and state administrative officials, even the Congressmen themselves—are men of varying ability and integrity who may hold office for a few years and then go back to their private business. The threads of continuity in the skein of power are furnished not by them but by the party managers, the men who make a lifetime career of manipulation and alliances and have become masters of the "deal" and the "fix." They swing the whole vast structure of patronage, political profit, and power, using apathy as their medium and the party machinery as their leverage. The fact that there is no career tradition in officeholding itself, as in England, means that there is a gap between politics and the best creative talent of the country. It is what gives the professional political managers their chance to use their own talents. As Lincoln Steffens discovered in years of interviewing them, and many other newspapermen have confirmed, they are likely to be men who combine an ancient cunning with a massive will and the freshest energies of a new country.

I have spoken of the political apathy of a large portion of the American people. But this is part of a pattern which includes also streaks of "good government" reformism and considerable emotional and political invective. The history of American political campaigns is studded with outbursts of political passion, rough-and-tumble tactics of political combat, hyperbolic professions of patriotism, and the assignment of diabolical traits and motives to one's opponents. The deflationary gap between this verbal extremism and the actual continuities of power in the hands of professionals is likely to produce a kind of despair which leads to apathy, so that American politics offers to observers the aspect of violent alternations between activity and quiescence, and between moralism and cynicism. This is true of foreign policy as well, with its alternations between isolationism and a crusading fervor.

On every showdown, however, what comes into the foreground of the pattern is the deep pragmatic strain of American political behavior: not moral doctrine and dogma, for which there is considerable scorn in the anti-intellectualism of a "practical" people, but a grappling with whatever needs to be done—and doing it. There is little doctrinal commitment in American politics. The party combats do not take place in ideological terms but rather in the assessment of personalities and what they are likely to do. The growth in the independent nonparty votes is a sign that this is increasing rather than decreasing. Unlike the Europeans, the Americans have had no "grand" political theory; they rarely talk of the "state" or even of "government," but rather of "*the* government" and "the Administration." It is almost as if there were a fear of principles because they might lead to commitments from which it would be difficult to extricate oneself. This does not, of course, prevent the rise of waves of fanatical feeling and the suppression of unpopular ideas, which have swept the nation, especially after wars. Yet America has never enthroned fanaticism in national power. It has thus far managed to avoid following an authoritarian national leader or subscribing to any party-line "truth."

One of the great political documents, which is worth study for the light it sheds on the American political style, is the series of commentaries on the Constitution which have come down as *The Federalist.* The three collaborators—Hamilton, Jay, and Madison—were of different political leanings and were to play very different roles later, yet their preferences on politics were submerged in their common assumptions about the art of government. They had read widely and deeply, had studied the new political science of their day, and were skillful in conscripting the beliefs and experience of antiquity to the purposes of the new venture in government. Yet they were not closet students but men who focused on the idea-in-action. They had a sense of the perilousness of the social fabric and at the same time of the tenacity of social habits, yet even as conservatives (which all of them were in varying degree) they had a bold capacity for political innovation. They were among the early realists who, long before Marx, saw the meaning of what we have come to call class structure and class conflict in relation to politics, yet they never lost their overriding sense of the national interest. As practical psychologists they knew about the elements of the irrational in men, which they called the "political passions"; and accordingly they sought to set limits to the power of government and were jealous of possible tyrannies in the name of the majority. Yet, though they elaborated on the checks and balances in a "mixed government" of separated powers, the state they were trying to create was an affirmative state, with more power at the center than any Republic had ever possessed, to perform the jobs of taxation, defense, and the control of the vital processes of the nation. What they sought was a government "energetic" enough, in the terms of their own day, "to preserve the Union."

In their combination of practical daring, along with conservative techniques for setting a brake on the underlying radicalism of the whole experiment, these men—like the whole group that framed the Constitution—expressed the American political genius not only of their own day but of the later centuries as well. The Americans have had to govern a vast territorial expanse, hold together diverse ethnic and sectional and economic groups, and organize a rapidly mounting mass of wealth and power. How well they have done it will long be argued, but that they have done it at all—and still survived as a tolerably free society—is no mean achievement for their system of government.

The American governmental system, in practice rather than in theory, has made some notable contributions to the arts of government. The outstanding ones are *federalism* as a working equilibrium; the clinging to the rule of law, especially through the technique of *judicial review* by both state and Federal courts; the *Constitutional convention* as a way of formulating and revising the fundamental law; the *two-party system* as a method for insuring the freedom of political opposition and for organizing power and its transfer; *Presidential government* as opposed to parliamentarianism, and Presidential leadership and responsibility as against the unstable shiftings of cabinet government; and the creation of *semi-independent administrative agencies* to carry out the burdens of democratic control of industry under conditions of modern technology.

I put these in terms of political techniques and institutions largely because the Americans themselves, with their bent for mechanism, think of them in those terms. One could argue that the rule of law (although not judicial review) and the party system were both derived from British experience, and that to a lesser extent this holds true of the administrative agencies as well. Yet the question is not only one of originality but of the final stamp. The Americans have not pushed their innovating drive nearly so far in the realm of government as in the realm of industrial technology. One may note that while they continue to imitate the Founding Fathers, the Founding Fathers imitated no one but struck out on their own. The political genius of America has not been one of doctrine but of a practical bent for political contrivances and management, and for the adjustment of old forms to new conditions. It is rarely that a nation, in the course of almost two centuries of constitutional history, is able to maintain—in the face of the changes and chances of growth and power—its essential ability to balance the conflicting drives of property and democracy, of majority power and individual freedom.

It is in this bent that the American political genius best shows itself: the combined pattern of a persisting *belief in majority rule and the democratic idea,* along with a clinging to *civil liberties and the image of a free society;* and at the same time a pragmatic approach to power and administration, showing itself in the *arts of equilibrium* between the strong pulls from every direction, and the use of Presidential leadership and other techniques in order to achieve *effective government.*

The basic instruments of the American government were shaped in an agrarian era, for the needs of a small-scale agrarian society. But it would be unwise to conclude that they are hopelessly dated in a large-scale industrial society, and that the old machinery should be scrapped and perhaps some of the old ideas as well, like democracy and civil liberties. There has been a tendency in American social thought to consider the "social lag" as a crime against progress and humanity; and many may wonder whether a bundle of institutions and practices, set in a Constitutional code long ago and changing only when change was forced upon them by haphazard event, can have greatness.

Yet, on reflection, there is nothing wrong with the "lag" of the old institutions and ideas, provided they had a valid meaning to start with. In the field of government, unlike industrial technology, basic ideas and techniques may be as old as Aristotle and still embody a permanent truth. Although the American Constitution is a written one, there has been room in it for the changes compelled by growth and time. While the Constitution is procedurally conservative, it does not operate in a substantive way to keep forever any particular economic, political, or social beliefs. It may prove as useful in protecting a liberal policy from reactionary assaults as it has been in the past in protecting the *laissez-faire* dogmas of economic conservatism. Americans have shown something of the British knack for making day-to-day changes in practice and then letting the customary practices become the acknowledged "usages" of government. That is why Americans have never taken seriously the various projects for a thorough "modernizing" of their government, to make it more logical or orderly. They have let well enough alone. It was Lord Bryce who is reported to have said that "Providence has under its special care children, idiots, and the United States of America." Which may be another way of saying that, given the industrial development and power of America, even a halting, stumbling, and outdated political system can be a success. America has had the Midas touch; everything that a rich nation touches turns to gold.

With this Midas touch there has been a sense of political brashness which has irritated foreign observers, and a lack of self-restraint that has shown itself in periodic political witch hunts, in a Congress whose utterances have sometimes made American political figures seem more stupid than they are, and in a press whose more sensational outbursts have at times reached manic levels. This has led many observers, especially Europeans, to conclude that the American political style lacks balance and is immature. In fact, the charge of immaturity is the one most frequently leveled at Americans. This is partly true and may be set down to the zest of a still growing society, although in periods of anti-Communist hysteria one is tempted to call it rather the paranoia of a declining one. But I would argue that the imbalance is largely in the outward aspects. As with much else in their life, Americans like their politics pugnacious. They operate through what Lubell calls "democracy as arena." Despite the outward violence and even childishness of word and manner there is often a balancing mechanism at work.

2. *The Democratic Idea**

"I LOVE LIBERTY," John Randolph of Roanoke once exclaimed, "and I hate equality." America is a democracy, but the inner tension that has always existed between the two poles of the democratic idea was never more passionately described than in Randolph's sentence. There are two major meanings—or better, a double aspect of meaning—of the idea of democracy. In one aspect it is free or constitutional government, a going system for assuring the safeguards within which the will of the people can express itself. In this phase—set off the more sharply because of the rise of the new totalitarianisms—the emphasis is on the natural rights of the individual and the limited powers of government, on the separation of powers, on civil liberties, on the rule of law, and the protection of freedom and property against the arbitrary encroachments of the state.

In its second aspect the democratic idea is egalitarian. In this phase it emphasizes the rule of the majority. It presents the spectacle of a demos unbound, a whole people striving however imperfectly to make social equality a premise of government. It shifts the emphasis from the narrowly political—from the ballot and the constitutional guarantees—to the economy and the class system. It stresses the conditions for putting within the reach of the ordinary man the opportunities of education and the making of a living, regardless of his confessional faith, his ethnic

* I deal with the democratic idea here as the ideological phase of American government. For its place in American thought, and an analysis of American conservatism, radicalism, and liberalism, see Ch. X, Sec. 2, "American Thought: the Angle of Vision."

group, and his social level. It carries with it that essential self-respect and refusal to truckle which formed the frontier fact of Jackson's time, that "every man is as good as any other—and a damned sight better." It is democracy defined as the institutions through which, and the social and moral context in which, the collective will can best be organized for the life purposes inherent in all human striving. It is the image that moved Whitman to his glimpses of democratic vistas, and Sandburg to set down the tall tales and the affirmations of "The People, Yes."

The recent American experiences in the context of world events have made it clear that in neither of these phases can democracy stand by itself, whether as constitutional government or popular government, "property rights" or "human rights," antistatism or welfare state. These are not different and self-sufficient "brands" of democracy, to be purchased from the shopwindows of history according to the taste, tradition, or means of a people; nor, to take the other extreme, are they merely semantic quibblings—verbal variations of the same democratic reality. They are polar ideas within the same field; or, to vary the figure, they are currents in the same stream of historic tendency. They are complementary aspects of how political communities in our time have tried to answer the central problems of power, welfare, freedom, and creativeness. They are parts of each other, each of them either barren or dangerous unless set in the context of the other. The recent experience of Europe has shown that constitutional government without popular government may end in the bread lines or in a *coup d'état,* in inner economic or political collapse—or both. It has also shown that a mass democracy (or "people's democracy") without the safeguards of freedom may end in the concentration camp or the slave labor camp.

Throughout the history of the American experience there has been a planetary struggle between the two aspects of the democratic idea. But it has not been primarily a doctrinal struggle, nor waged in academic cloisters. The battles have been waged between parties, sections, classes, pressure groups, using the opposing concepts of "aristocracy" and "people," of "republic" and "democracy," of "conservatism" and "progressivism," of "minority rights" and "majority rule" as symbolic abbreviations for their interests and outlook and aspirations.

The split reaches back into the history of European philosophy and social thought, from which the American democratic idea derived—to the struggle between the thinking of Harrington, Locke, and Montesquieu and that of the English Levelers and Rousseau, between the capitalist liberalism of the new propertied classes and the hydraulic pressure exerted by the mass aspirations still unexpressed in middle-class liberal thought, however revolutionary it was at the time. One of the difficulties in reading Parrington's *Main Currents in American*

Thought, whose first volume traces some of these conflicts in the European background as projected into the early period of the Republic, is that he writes as if it were a choice between democracy and antidemocracy. Actually it was a battle for position between two crucial, interlocked phases of the democratic idea. The correspondence, for example, between Jefferson and his circle shows how closely the early American leaders followed European thought, and how freely they drew from both the currents I have mentioned.

This was true of the authors of *The Federalist* as well, who showed a strategic skill in meeting objections to the Constitution that came from both the Right and Left, and with that skill, a knack for blending the two strains of the democratic idea. To the charge that the Constitution was a revolutionary *coup d'état,* their answer was the residual sovereignty in the people themselves to change an instrument of government inadequate for them. To those who feared a strong central government, their answer was the need for effective national power at the center in order to avert ineffectuality and chaos. By a masterful distinction they argued that the new power would be *federal* in its extent (that is, divided between two spheres and leaving an area of state power to balance the central power) but *national* in its functioning (that is, the national government would have power to act in the sphere where the states could not act effectively). To those who felt that a "mixed government," with separated powers and a system of checks and balances, was too timid an expedient in a revolutionary age, their answer was the classic one of the corruption and ambition of political leaders and the need for a rule of law to guard the people against their own worst impulses. Thus the Founding Fathers sought always not so much (as Beard felt, and J. Allen Smith before him) to guard the rights of the property owners alone, or to give unchecked rein to revolutionary impulse, but to find an equilibrium between the charged tensions of the democratic idea.

Thus, at the very beginning of American government, the two basic drives in it had already shown themselves: the government had to be strong enough to be effective and revolutionary enough to give the people the power they had been denied as colonists; but it also had to be safe against a too-rapid or far-reaching extension of the Revolution. The Hamilton group was intent on creating a going governmental concern so that property and the commercial interests could flourish in safety. The Jefferson group wanted to make certain that the people's liberties and the agrarian interest were protected by a Bill of Rights, and that the dead hand of the past did not smother a full life for even the lowliest American freeman. Each caught a glimpse of the needs of a future America, but, as in a stereoscope, both were needed to bring the picture in focus.

The question has often been raised whether the American political system should be called "democracy" or "republic," the latter being a neutral term without the equalitarian major premise of the democratic dogma. This is not merely a closet controversy carried on by scholars: it crops up in editorials and newspaper columns and in heated Congressional debates. It seems to be the whimsical notion of the "republic" school of thought that "democracy" should be dropped from the American political vocabulary. They call it a word which (despite Jefferson and the Jacksonians, De Tocqueville, Bryan and Woodrow Wilson) didn't become popular in America until Georgi Dimitrov used it at a Comintern meeting, and which is today tainted beyond redress by the "People's Democracies" of eastern Europe.

This would surrender to world Communism a concept as American as cherry cobbler. The revealing fact in the whole debate is that the stress on "republic" is on the strategy of weakening the majority will by the action of pressure groups and the corporate spokesmen in Congress and the press. Behind it is the fear that "democracy" makes too dangerous a commitment to the participation of Negroes and Jews, recent immigrants and low-income groups, in both the guarantees of civil rights and the shaping of social decisions, and the fear also (as old as the Cromwellian debates or even Aristotle) that "democracy" leads to "Socialism." There is an irony in this animus against the term, in a civilization that has become a world symbol as the most powerful carrier of the democratic idea.

A historical graph of American political development would show an alternation between the principle of constitutional democracy ("republic") and that of majority action and passion ("democracy"). Once the Constitution was a success and the new frame of government accepted by all, the emphasis was on constitutional government. Hamilton's Report on Manufactures, the Report on Credit, and the protectionist writings of the school of economists headed by Mathew Carey laid the political and intellectual basis for building an industrialized economy; and the series of brilliant decisions by John Marshall, mainly on the contract clause and the commerce power of the Federal government, served to link the rising system of capitalism with the doctrines of constitutional nationalism. But Marshall's absence of principle in the case of *Fletcher v. Peck,* when land speculation and legislative corruption were sanctioned in the zeal to establish the sacredness of contracts and the legal doctrine of vested interests, also showed the canker in the flower even while it was in bloom. John Taylor of Carolina spoke witheringly of the "aristocracy of paper and credit" that was pushing for Marshall's constitutional conceptions.

This raises the issue of what clash there is between the democratic idea and capitalist power. It was Harold Laski's major thesis that capitalism and democracy had met in the American experiment at the convergence of two lines of historical tendency, but that they were partners in an uneasy marriage of convenience rather than of true affinity. Actually, whatever clash there is between capitalism and democracy—and it is real enough—is a phase of a larger and more relevant struggle between what we may call the "dominant minority" and the "popular majority." In the correspondence of Jefferson and his friends and in the whole literature of the Jeffersonian period, this was phrased as a struggle between "aristocracy" and "democracy." Jefferson equated the aristocratic principle with that of a disbelief in man's inherent capacity for self-government. "We are told," he wrote, "that men cannot govern themselves. Can they then govern others?" His most passionate phrasing of the indictment of the principles of a dominant minority came in his classic comment that no select group of men had been born, "booted and spurred, to ride mankind."

It is true that the first group which came into American history well equipped to play the role of a dominant minority was the business class and its champions among the lawyers and political leaders. Before the rise of industry there was none equipped to take the part that a social and political aristocracy had taken in British and European life. When Fisher Ames talked of the government of "the wise, the rich, and the good" he was trying to put into American terms the principle of an elite which had no strong roots in the American soil, and which—even in the great days of Hamilton and John Adams—was too amorphous to be more than the tag end of the European tradition. To be sure, in the colonial days there was considerable frontier hostility to the commercial and business groups who were overrepresented in the legislatures and in other positions of power. But the American Revolution was not a social revolution in the European sense largely because it did not have to be one, since there was no feudal tradition and no entrenched American aristocracy to overthrow. It was the absence of such a cohesive elite which made possible the victory of Jeffersonianism in the "revolution of 1800" and the continuing power of the "Virginia dynasty" in the first quarter of the nineteenth century. By the time of the feud between the Biddle and Jackson-Taney forces over banking power, it had become clear that a new minority group was taking charge, but it had not yet found a credo.

This was the time when Ralph Waldo Emerson wrote sadly:

> Of the two great parties, which at this hour almost share the nation between them, I should say that one has the best cause, and the other contains the best men. . . . They (of the radical party) have not at heart the ends which give the name of democracy what hope and virtue are in it. The spirit of our American radicalism is destructive and aimless. . . . On the other side, the conservative party, composed of the most moderate, able, and cultivated part of the population, is timid, and merely defensive of property. It vindicates no right, it aspires to no real good, it brands no crime, it proposes no generous policy; it does not build, nor write, nor cherish the arts, nor foster religion, nor establish schools, nor encourage science, nor emancipate the slave, nor befriend the poor, or the Indian, or the immigrant. ("Politics," in *Essays: Second Series*)

If his judgment of Jacksonian democracy was (as historians see it now) too negative, Emerson was right in seeing that the conservatives had not found a fighting faith. When the Civil War came, the challenge of the plantation-owning military caste and its allies was met by a new party which—even while it kept strong continuity with the Whigs—broke with them by equating the interests of free labor and free capitalism with the interests of the nation.

But the equalitarian impulse of Lincoln, as well as of Greeley and the Abolitionists, trickled away in the Reconstruction period. The business organizers who became the new dominant minority were more swaggering and assured than any other before their time. The old Radical opposition had been disorganized by war and Reconstruction, and a new opposition had not yet come into being. The new dominant minority developed within its business organizations the habit of command: they were the "bosses" and they ran the machines in their economic empire. What more natural than that they should transfer that habit of command and operate through "bosses" and "machines" in the political empire as well, on the theory that those who own the country should run it? The far-reaching transfer of business organizing skills to politics was symbolized by Mark Hanna. How impressive was the achievement of Hanna and his class may be judged from the fact that the fusion of Populist passion with the Democratic forces under Bryan in the 1896 campaign had all the features of a sweeping and irresistible mass movement. That it was whittled away, fragmented, and finally beaten by a combination of external events and good political generalship by the Republicans underlined what capitalist power at its most efficient can do within the democratic framework.

The struggle between the capitalist power group and the popular majority has thus far been kept well within the framework of a larger national interest. It is true that business forces have not hesitated to break the fabric of political legality itself, as evidenced by the dramatic instance of the 1876 elections when a corrupt deal was worked out between the Northern Republicans (including the railroad interests) and the White Supremacists of the South, to "throw" the crucial Southern electors from Tilden to Hayes. Nevertheless the American picture has been very different from that of the European, in the sense that there has been at least a minimum consensus between the opposing forces, and the victories for the popular majority have not met with violence from the other side, but have been accepted. This was true of Woodrow Wilson's "New Freedom" as it was later true of the "New Deal" and the "Fair Deal" of the Roosevelt and Truman administrations.

There is an interweaving of these two impulses in American life beyond any hope of disentanglement. There are few members of the power groups who have not been at some point infected by the democratic idea; and even more certainly, there are few Americans who have not been touched by the property ideology. The split between capitalism and democracy is thus less a class conflict than a split within every American.

Is this likely to be a fatal split for Americans? There is no reason why it must be, unless the organization of an effective majority will become too difficult to meet the crisis of democratic life. Since effective democracy involves the organization of will, it is extremely vulnerable to the operation of minority pressures and power. The path of the democratic idea has therefore often been a *via dolorosa,* and the record of democratic action a Heartbreak House.

If a program is marked for destruction, one path open is a direct assault in the area of public attitude, where the dominant minority has a massive influence in the opinion industries. If they lose there, they can turn their energies to the prevention of a majority for the measure in either house of Congress, using to their advantage the committee system, the rules of parliamentary delay and filibuster, the high-pressure operation of lobbies, and the fact that Congressional representation is badly skewed to favor the rural conservative constituencies as against the urban liberal ones. If they lose there, they can fall back—as they did for a half century from the 1880s to the Roosevelt era—on the protection of the judicial power as interpreted by a property-minded Supreme Court. If they lose there, they can concentrate on weakening the administrative enforcement of the measure or even capturing the administrative machinery and its personnel. And always they have the chance, by their immense wealth and power, of capturing the party machinery and dictating the choice of candidates in both the major parties. In short, the battle for an affirmative democratic program is like an action in which one army, in order to win, has to take every one of a succession of fortified places, while the other army has only to win and hold one such fortified place, even though it loses all the rest.

The reader may well say that this somber view does not square with the achievement of the New Deal, the great social gains in the quarter century after 1932, and the gradual Republican acceptance of many features of a welfare democracy. I should answer that this shows another side of the democratic process—the potential of social achievement under a strong leadership like Franklin Roosevelt's. The task of the dominant minority is always hardest in the area of the Presidency, where the focusing of popular attention on a single dramatic struggle, with personal symbols to express the social forces involved, gives mass democracy a chance to organize its resources. Under the Eisenhower Administration a working alliance of Democrats and liberal Republicans was able to put through a more enlightened legislative program than in any Republican period since Theodore Roosevelt. Yet under both Truman and Eisenhower the Congressional investigating committees incited and expressed some of the popular passions corrupted by an era of military anxiety and world fear. To balance this there has been a change in the role of the judicial power. From the eighties to the New Deal constitutional crisis, the judiciary formed the last line of defense against liberal movements of opinion; but in the recent postwar period it again became, to an encouraging extent, a sword to achieve civil rights for Negroes and a shield (often, alas, too frail) against the hatreds engaged in the hunt for "dangerous thoughts."*

The political history of American democracy has thus been an alternation of social achievement and frustration or a battlefield where freedom and reaction have fought a continuing seesaw engagement. To the economically and ethnically depressed groups it may be difficult to maintain so detached a view of the democratic process. The fact is that for them the homage paid in America to the democratic idea has at times seemed an empty thing. The psychologists have found that the human personality is brilliantly resourceful in the kind of compartmental thinking in which the mind isolates contradictory ideas from each other. As the depressed groups of American life have learned to their sorrow, a culture can do the same in the separation of democratic rhetoric and practice.

Yet there is little that is surprising in the failure of American life to achieve wholly the original democratic aspiration. Democracy is a heartbreakingly difficult as well as a dangerous enterprise. The effort to combine the principle of constitutional protection along with that of

* For a further discussion of the Presidency, Congress, and the judiciary, see the relevant sections of this chapter that follow.

the organized majority will is bound to lead to strains and contradictions. The tragic results of the Rousseau-Marxist principle of "people's democracies," which has swept over half the world, have led to a reassertion of emphasis in America on constitutional democracy. The Communist regimes, whatever else they may be, are a travesty rather than a fulfillment of the democratic idea: actually they are an amalgam of apostolic religious fervor and the lust for power of a new elite group, along with some mystique of "the people" thrown in. This amalgam, which has been well called "totalitarian democracy," almost wholly excludes the rule of law and the tolerance of a political opposition. Thus it is the image of individual freedom, along with that of technological abundance, which America stresses.

With this emphasis some Americans are in danger of forgetting that the effective dynamism of the democratic idea, throughout the nineteenth century and through most of the first half of the twentieth, has been expressed by what George Santayana has called the "natural democracy" or "leaves-of-grass democracy"—the idea of equality of opportunity and of the basic fraternity of men within it. It is the image of America as a society not equal but potentially equal—an open society whose twin ideas are equal access and the dignity of the person. The equalitarian idea is, of course, subject to corruption as well, yet the corruptions in American history have been due less to flirtations with Marxist movements than to whatever racist and antilibertarian passions seemed at any time to prove useful to the dominant minority.

I have spoken of the seesaw of achievement and frustration within the framework of freedom. The frustrations have been part of the enormous difficulties of a democracy operating within a system of corporate dominance and of political machinery suited to the deadlock. The achievement, in turn, has time after time broken through the deadlock and the integuments of power, especially at times of economic crisis when the forces seeking to establish an affirmative welfare state have had a chance to move ahead. When they have done so it has been by thrusting toward the principles set forth in the Declaration of Independence: that the primary purpose of government is to protect the natural (that is, indestructible) rights of the people; that the crux of government is to discover the consent of the governed through the electoral process; and that the people, as the possessors of the ultimate power, must pass final judgment on what the men in power have done and have a right to change them. The social cost that has had to be paid for the maintenance of these natural rights in the free democratic arena has at times seemed great, yet it can never be too great, nor can it be paid and the account closed, since to maintain freedom is to maintain the machinery for social change.

To round out the meaning of American democracy, a third factor must now be added to that of individual freedom and of mass participation in the democratic process. It is the element of a moral sensitivity to the tragic human experience. America has the potential for this in the fact that one of the great sources of its democratic thinking is the Biblical tradition of Puritanism, including both the Old Testament passion for justice and the Christian allegory of love. And America which has thus far used its genius for equilibrium by balancing the demands of individual freedom and majority will may find it a harder task to balance the struggle for world power with the moral sensitivity it will need to save its democratic soul.

3. Presidency and Demos

ONE OF THE MIRACLES of American government is how it has managed, with its creaking machinery and its capacity for deadlock, to respond to emergencies. Part of the answer may be in a deceptively hidden dynamism which at the moment of crisis gathers its reserves of strength and comes crashing through. The most crucial governmental agency which shows this elasticity for change and mastery is the American Presidency. But given the net of obstructions confining an attempt to organize the national will, only the stronger and more skillful Presidents have been able successfully to break it. This is one way of defining the task of Presidential leadership.

In its present status as a great industrial and world power, Americans have learned the truth of the remark that modern democratic government is "just one damn crisis after another." That is why the center of gravity of American political life has moved from the other two branches over to the Executive power; and the system which in the early phase of the Republic was called "Congressional government," and in the *laissez-faire* decades of the late nineteenth century "government by judiciary," must now be called "Presidential government."

For a man of deep convictions, the process of getting nominated for the Presidency is itself a major feat: for to be "available" in the eyes of the political managers a man must as a rule be basically "safe" and moderate, however militant outwardly. The life of every pre-Convention candidate thus becomes a heroic wrestling match between conscience and canniness. Of those who proved "strong" Presidents, Jackson came into his first term on the wave of a mass revolt in his party, Lincoln and Franklin Roosevelt both seemed relatively mild men before election and only showed their strength later, Theodore Roosevelt became President when McKinley was assassinated, and Wilson received the nomination only after the bitterest fight in the Convention and then only with Bryan's help. Wendell Willkie was nominated in 1940 when the Republicans wanted someone not an isolationist who could run against Roosevelt; in 1944 he was passed over partly because he had been beaten but also because in the intervening years he had too clearly shown his deep liberalism and a set of internationalist convictions that made him enemies. Very often a man whom the Convention delegates support strongly, like Senator Bricker in 1940 and Senator Taft in 1952, fails of the nomination because the managers read the public-opinion polls (especially from the urban "key" states) and conclude that he could not be elected. The conditions for reaching the Presidency are so haphazard and opportunist that the way is too often open for a genial, mediocre man who means well, commands a popular following, and will not be too intractable.

But while the tradition has been against men of committed views and creative holders of the office, the most important trait of the American Presidency is that its mantle of office seems to have the magic of shrinking or expanding to the potential stature of the wearer. It has room enough for a big man to fill it out; a small man can make it seem small enough to fit him. It has been held by a Buchanan and a Lincoln, a Harding and a Roosevelt alike.

Apart from the textbook discussions of the President's constitutional powers, there is little question that the actual powers of the office have grown. There has, of course, been an ebb and flow of Presidential power depending on the aggressiveness of the incumbent. But the secular trend—despite the massive powers that Jefferson and Lincoln exercised—has been unmistakable. There are some commentators who are melancholy because they feel (wrongly, I think) that the growth of Presidential power has been largely at the expense of states' rights and the separation of powers. Others ask where in the Constitution one can find specific grants of some of the many powers the recent Presidents have assumed. The usual answer to the latter is that the Presidency operates not on a grant of specific powers but on the comprehensive executive power, which includes all the residual powers demanded by effective government and not specifically denied by the letter and spirit of the Constitution. Another answer is Theodore Roosevelt's famous "stewardship" theory, which depicts the President as holding these residual powers in stewardship for the people.

The tendency has been to take a functional rather than legalistic view of the Presidential office. There are things which none of the branches of government have explicit power to do, and which the states cannot do adequately, but which must nevertheless get done. There are conflicts to be resolved shrewdly by someone with the skill and prestige to overcome obstacles. There are crises to be met by someone who can muster the drive and find the power to meet them, and who will answer for how well or badly they are met. There are policies to be shaped by a group for whose decisions a single man will take the responsibility.

Even with this functional view of the office, the elastic doctrine of Presidential power lends itself obviously to abuse as well as use. President Franklin D. Roosevelt's threat of "packing" the Supreme Court in order to compel resignations and give him a chance for new appointments was widely attacked at the time as a dictatorial move. His "destroyers-for-bases deal" with Great Britain before America entered the war rested on a notably elastic opinion of its constitutionality from his Attorney General. President Truman, who was considered less "strong" a President than Roosevelt, also had three major encounters with the limits of Presidential power: once when he tried to break a national railroad strike by the threat of enrolling the railroad workers in the Army, again when he committed a large American Army to Europe (and later to Korea, in the U.N. "police action") without any state of war, and finally when he sought to resolve a steel industry lockout-and-strike by taking over the steel mills until a settlement should be reached, on the plea of a military emergency but without specific statutory power. He was checked on the first, was successful on the second (which illustrates that the real elasticity of Presidential power lies in foreign policy), and on the third he was sharply rebuked in a historic Supreme Court decision which held itself narrowly to the immediate issues but raised questions about the scope of the theory of implied powers.

The fact is that the whole question of Presidential power is enmeshed in a faulty idea of how the Presidency is related to the sources of its power. The Constitution, under the Court's interpretation, provides the channel through which the President's powers flow; but the power itself derives from the President's relations to the events around him and to the minds and purposes of the people whom these events affect. These are in truth the sources of the Presidential power. There are, it is usually said, two Constitutions, not one: the written document and the unwritten usages. Actually the more meaningful second Constitution is to be found not in the usages but in the outlines of economic power and interests, of religious convictions, of ethnic loyalties, of rural and urban thinking, of attitudes toward war and peace, with all of which the President must reckon as exactingly as he reckons with the written Constitution.

It might be better to say that the *authority* of a President is even more important than his *power,* because it is the authority that shapes and decides what the power shall be. I use "authority" in the sense of the President's habitual command of popular consent. The sources of the President's authority are subjective—flowing from his personality, his political style, his conduct of the office, his impact on the people—rather than being objective and forever imbedded in a constitutional document. If he has grasp, contagion, political artistry, and a mastery of his purposes and methods, then he will carry authority no matter what powers he claims or forsakes, and his authority will work magic to bolster the claims he stakes out. If, on the other hand, he is like John Adams or Herbert Hoover and fails to carry authority, then even a limited view of the Presidential power will get him into trouble, and even a clear grant of power will prove ineffectual.

The President has not only massive powers and authority; he has also massive burdens that weigh him down. The Presidency eats men. The demands on the incumbent are at once imperative and paradoxical.

Once elected,* a President must manage to unify the nation which has been temporarily split by the election ("We are all Federalists, we are all Republicans," Jefferson said in his First Inaugural), yet not abandon the program he has been elected to carry out. He must be national leader without ceasing to be party leader, and party leader without alienating the factions into which every party splits. He must frame a legislative program without seeming to deprive Congress of its exclusive control over legislation and get it through Congress without seeming to drive it. He must head up a vast and sprawling administrative system of whose workings he can know only the tiniest fraction, yet whenever anything goes wrong he must stand accountable to the people for every detail. He must select, recruit, and hold administrative talent on the basis of merit, while "playing ball" within the patronage structure. He must coordinate the workings of the thousands of interlocking cogs of the governmental machine, yet somehow find a space for creative concentration on great issues. He is by the Constitution the sole organ of foreign policy in a peacetime Great Power, and in time of war or "cold war" he is Commander in Chief of a powerful military machine and head of a vast war economy. He must express and carry through the people's wishes, yet he must function as Educator in Chief, helping them to formulate their wishes and organize their opinion. He must be a symbol of the world's greatest democracy—its vigor, its effectiveness, its potentials—and, as a symbol, remote; yet he must also have the human immediacy which gives the ordinary American the sense that he is not lost and that he has someone to speak and act for him. He must be all things to all men, yet also a bold leader hewing out a path in a single direction. In short, he must be Pooh-Bah and St. George at once.

* For a discussion of Presidential nomination, campaign, and election, see Sec. 4, "The Party System and the Voter."

Obviously only a comic-strip Superman could combine all these qualities. Actually the Presidential function is filled at any one time not by one man but by a number of men. Except at the top level, even most of the major decisions are made from day to day by a group of men each of whom serves as his alter ego in some area of policy. When a new President is elected, the commentators are as likely to turn their klieg lights on the "men around the President" as on the President himself.

No President can avoid the formation of juntas around him—insiders who are bound to have a vague conspiratorial air to the outsiders. Sometimes such a junta is actually sinister, as with the "Daugherty gang" who ran the White House under Harding; others only seem so to opposing groups within the President's own party and to the opposition party. Thus Roosevelt had his "Brain Trust," Truman his "cronies," Eisenhower his "Regency" group. Actually there are circles within circles of influence and power radiating out of the White House. To take the Eisenhower Administration as an example: there was a formal Cabinet to which the President delegated his powers over each decision-making and administrative area; there was the National Security Council, which possessed immense power and included the Secretary of State and several of the President's crucial advisers; there was an inner Cabinet group, in which the Secretaries of the Treasury, of State, and the Attorney General played the principal roles; there was an inner White House Staff group, led by Chief of Staff Sherman Adams and Press Secretary Hagerty; there was an inner Congressional group, consisting of several trusted leaders of both Houses along with the staff liaison people who served as links with Congress; and there was an inner group of the President's close friends—the "Regency" group—including leading political and business figures, who advised him from the start on crucial matters and kept a supervision over affairs on the two occasions of his serious illness.

I must add that since the President is Chief Executive, the question of what kind of executive he is is an important one. Given his military experience, Eisenhower operated in the White House also with a line-and-staff organization, leaving most matters for decision to the men in charge of the respective areas, and leaning heavily upon his Chief of Staff. His tendency was to lay down the general line of policy and then stay out of things, even relatively important things, until real trouble arose, when he came back into the picture with his power and authority to clear up the trouble. Truman, at the other extreme, arose early every day, worked intensively, had his finger on all important matters, was chary of too-inclusive delegations of power, swept his desk clean, and was ready the next morning to begin again briskly. Compared with both of them, Roosevelt was a sloppy administrator who might delegate overlapping areas of power to several of his lieutenants and could not keep his own hand and mind out of any of the areas: as he was his own Secretary of State, so he was his own Secretary of the Treasury and his own military strategy staff.

There is room for a number of types of the executive mind in the Presidency. But what is crucial in every case is that the President should avoid at one extreme the danger of so much delegation that he loses contact with the processes and temper of his administration, and at the other extreme the danger of becoming so preoccupied with details that he loses sight of his grand goals and strategies, and has no time or energy left for reflection on them.

In the end the Presidency is thus a one-man job, and that one man cannot escape either the burden of or the accounting for it. The inventory of the tasks of the Presidential office is a reminder at once of how capacious and exacting it is. Even more, it defines where the center of gravity of the office is—in the special relation of the President to the American demos.

That is why the people's instinct, in reviewing the history of the Presidency, has been not so much to ask whether Presidents have been "liberal" or "conservative," men of thought or men of action, but whether they have been "strong" or "weak" Presidents. The strength or weakness with which they have exercised their functions has been partly a matter of their own character structure and inner drive, partly of the philosophy with which they have approached their office, but to a great extent the result of the tensions which they have had to face. A man of seemingly ordinary capacities, like Harry S. Truman, showed how the Presidency stretches a man as well as eats men, and how great is its capacity to educate the man who holds it.

Even the strongest of Presidents learns that the Presidential office is the veriest Gehenna unless the people make it tolerable; that whatever powers any particular President seeks to assume, it is the ultimate power of the people that grants or checks them; and that a President is helpless except insofar as he can win the people's confidence. This relation between leader and demos is at the heart of the organization of the American political will.

Arthur M. Schlesinger, Sr., polling a number of American commentators, found that the six "great Presidents" were Lincoln, Washington, Franklin Roosevelt, Wilson, Jefferson, and Jackson, in that order. I should agree with Clinton Rossiter in adding Theodore Roosevelt to the list. Yet the notable theories of political leadership, especially the theory of "charismatic" leadership and of leadership as vocation as developed by Max Weber, apply much more to European leadership politics than to American Presidential politics. When the American thinks of his government, he thinks first of the President as its symbol. But while the President is often cursed extravagantly, he is rarely praised extravagantly. This is what Kenneth Burke has called the "debunking of the chosen symbol." Except in a rare instance like that of Eisenhower, the symbol is there to do a job under pitilessly critical examination, not to be followed blindly and adoringly. However sacred Americans may consider the Constitution itself and its judicial guardians, the bent is toward the deflation of authority in individuals.

Partly this derives from the American skepticism of all political power; partly too from the structure of authority in the American family and school system, where the emphasis is not on paternal power but on the development of individual self-reliance; partly too from a market system of *caveat emptor* in which the individual keeps himself continually on guard against being made a "sucker" from a too-unwary eagerness. Whatever the psychic sources, however, the fact is that Americans as a nation have rarely shown a sustained capacity for clinging to a political father. The only important exceptions were Washington ("the father of his country"), Lincoln (seen as "Father Abraham," although mainly in retrospect), and Franklin Roosevelt, who was a father symbol in a time of depression and world war, and then mainly for the minority groups and the underprivileged and excluded. To these must be added the figure of the soldier-as-man-of-peace, in the person of Dwight Eisenhower, whose father image was at once authoritative, kindly, and carefully kept above the party battle (although he was a shrewd politician) and who rounded out his image, as American fathers so often do, by incurring a heart attack and having an intestinal operation. But the records of the Presidential office show torrents of popular and partisan abuse of men like Adams, Jefferson, Madison, Jackson, Lincoln, Johnson, Cleveland, Theodore Roosevelt, Wilson, Franklin Roosevelt, and Truman—usually on the score that they were tyrants and dictators. A nation that has never recognized political masters needs to reassure itself continually that it is not falling under one.

The leadership qualities of Franklin Roosevelt and Dwight Eisenhower deserve special scrutiny because their common and contrasting qualities illumine the nature of "charismatic" leadership in the Presidency. James M. Burns, by calling his study of Roosevelt *The Lion and the Fox,* placed him in the tradition of Machiavellian strategy, and there is little question that Roosevelt used imaginative daring and pugnacity along with the cunning of maneuver. Both qualities led him deep into party politics, where he fought the unfaithful within (he was one of the few Presidents who tried to purge

Congressional leaders of his own party) and smote the heathen without.

Eisenhower had less both of the lion and the fox: he was not savage in attack, but usually soft-spoken; and he affected the style of staying outside political involvement and keeping above the party battles. His total political style was thus an unusual one among American Presidents. He was not an intellectual, like Wilson or Jefferson; nor a lusty exponent of the strenuous life, like Theodore Roosevelt; nor a dour Puritan, like Coolidge; nor an introvert, like Lincoln, with a flair for jokes and an undercurrent of tragedy. He was the soldier-statesman, combining the two qualities more strikingly than anyone before him since Washington. If he had some of the fuzzy outlines of another soldier-President, Ulysses Grant, who never quite learned what had happened to him when he fell among the businessmen and politicians, he was far less of an amateur in politics than he liked to seem. He knew the political uses of the genial, warming smile, of folksiness, and of the earnest moralizing little sermons with which he sprinkled his press conferences. He understood the deep American impulse toward the belittling of politics, and by seeming to avoid partisanship he could win more converts to his cause than the most partisan leader. He came at a time when Americans wanted peace desperately, after a war and a cold war, and his political style as a soldier who knew war and could therefore bring peace exactly fitted the felt psychological needs of his time. He was widely supported during his first term both within his own party and among the Democrats on issues of war and peace, particularly when he met the Russian leaders at Geneva. The genial conflict-avoiding bent of Eisenhower and his reliance on the decision-making of the men around him weakened his second term, and were of some danger to the Presidential position: increasingly Eisenhower himself became an image—and a very popular one—while the burdens of the office were more dispersed than they had been before. While the Democrats used the slogan of a "part-time Presidency" in the campaign, this dispersal of the duties and powers of the office was not wholly due to the President's illness but was integral to his personality and his political style.

Yet this is unlikely to recur often in the future. The greater probability is that the burdens of the office will increase, and that the American President will, as in the past, have to win everything the hard way. He will have to meet the problems and opposition of Congress, his Party, the judiciary, the press, the power of Big Labor and the Big Corporation, the rivalry and jealousy of sections and classes. Presidential government thus becomes an obstacle race, and the Great President the Great Hurdler.

In this context the fear that a President will abuse his powers, while real enough, is only one phase of the danger. The other phase is that all but the stoutest of heart, the firmest of will, and the most passionate of conviction will give up the struggle long before they have achieved their objective. It is only widespread popular support that will enable any President to clear his hurdles. Unless the people are with him all the way he cannot carry through his program. His last chance of having the people with him is at a time of grave social crisis and in a national emergency, and then only if he is a consummate tactician. The Presidential office is like a field headquarters, which operates best in the heat of critical battle. But the fact that it has come through well in every period of crisis is proof that in an age of disintegration, democratic government is not too fossilized and inflexible to survive.

The President combines within himself the double function of reigning and ruling. Using Walter Bagehot's idea that every government must have a "dignified" element in it, this element in America is divided between the Presidency and the Supreme Court. Of the two, the President is more subject to vituperative attack but by that token more constantly present in the minds of the people. He occupies the center of the national stage. He is a "republican king." As with the British monarch, his daily life and acts are constantly under scrutiny, and his personality style (along with that of his wife) sets a pattern which is more or less consciously imitated by millions of Americans. The fact that Woodrow Wilson read detective stories, that Franklin Roosevelt collected stamps, that Eleanor Roosevelt worked hard at welfare problems and international affairs, that Dwight Eisenhower was an ardent golf amateur, and that Mamie Eisenhower wore bangs and had a gracious manner left an impact upon the reading, stamp-collecting, and golf-playing habits of American men and on the life style of American women. A President's smile or frown or look of anxiety, when reproduced in the press, may influence the stock market and the action of foreign governments, but even more the habitual demeanor of Americans whose image is formed in the Presidential mirror.

There is also another kind of Presidential image—the composite picture that the people keep in their minds of the traits a President ought to have. For example, he ought to come from a small town rather than a big city, since the tradition of a superior virtue and strength in such origins has survived the decline of the small town itself. He is likely to be of West European family origin—English, Scottish, Dutch, Swiss, German, or some mixture of them. No American President has yet derived from Scandinavian, Latin, East European, or Slavic origins. He is likely to come from one of the big states with a heavy electoral vote which can help swing him into the Presidency. He has always been a Protestant, but since the Civil War he has never been identified with a Southern state—a serious limitation, given the political talent that the South has shown throughout its history. He is most likely to be a lawyer by profession and a politician by passion. If the Presidential aspirant is either a businessman or a labor leader, the chances are heavy against him. He must have managed to preserve an integrity of family life and (except in a few instances) avoided any public disclosure of violation of the sexual mores of his culture. Thus far no divorced man has ever been elected President, although the nomination of Adlai Stevenson in 1952 and again in 1956 despite this limitation may be a sign that the taboo is being eroded.

Like the corporation, the Presidency has been caught up in the managerial transformation of American life. In one sense it can be said that the President is himself a "manager"—in foreign relations, in war and peace, in economic affairs, in the daily functioning of the government. But it would be truer to say that the President has become a kind of Chairman of the Board, while the real managers operate the day-to-day affairs of the government and even make substantial policy decisions. When President Eisenhower had a heart attack in 1955 the national government went on functioning much as it had done before: there was an "inner group" operating under Sherman Adams, who was in effect the President of the corporate managerial nucleus, and who never burdened the Chairman of the Board with anything except crisis problems and top policy-making decisions. The effect of this is to bring the President into the decision-making picture only when and where something goes badly wrong, and only when broad new policy needs to be formed. The President thus becomes basically a conciliator between opposing factions within his administration, a resolver of crises, a god from the machine stepping out of the sky to restore order from chaos. This may help explain why the dignity and distance of the Presidential office are maintained even in the most constant struggle and bitterness of the daily political arena. Eisenhower, for example, was rarely branded with the stigma of what his underlings did. Under other Presidents as well, notably Franklin Roosevelt, the underlings who were unlucky enough to threaten the image which the administration wished to preserve in the popular mind have often had to be sacrificed.

Given this position, the President must rely on the people he picks to carry on the daily work of the government. He operates under the written Constitution as defined by the courts; but, even more, he operates under an unwritten Constitution, composed of a body of executive orders which are drawn up by the Presidential assistants and are based often only on the fact that some previous President had done something of the sort. The process of Constitution-making thus resides in the Presidency far more than in Congress and rivals the similar process in the Supreme Court. As a distributor of power, the President not only bestows his blessings on a large number of lucky individuals who come in for the political prizes and flock to Washington when their man has won: he also blesses a particular class or segment of the population. Under Roosevelt's New Deal the intellectuals got a chance at power; under both Roosevelt and Truman the labor groups were similarly cut in; under Eisenhower a large number of corporate executives, major and minor, eagerly found their place in the Washington power hierarchy.

But even with the maximum degree of delegation of Presidential duties to staff and advisers, the Presidency remains a tense and crushing office, and is likely to take its toll in the future as in the past. This has made the problem of Presidential succession, in the event of death or disabling illness, more crucial. The likelihood is that Americans will be more aware of the importance of the Vice-President in the Presidential succession, and that the Throttlebottom type of Vice-President is on his way out.

4. The Party System and the Voter

Second only to the development of Presidential government has been that of party government. The deriding of party government is a favorite American sport, and at times the disillusionment with it reaches the proportions of despair; yet few Americans would change their party system for any other. They feel about it a little as Emerson felt about some of the workaday features of his own time, including the party caucus: "Banks and tariffs, the newspaper and caucus . . . are flat and dull to dull people, but rest on the same foundations of wonder as the town of Troy and the temple of Delphos." The skeptic might say that the party system in America is indeed a "foundation of wonder," since it provides the invisible underpinning for the visible government and therefore allows the respectable show of formal decisions to be buttressed by transactions which are more effectively hidden.

Americans think of parties largely in national terms, and it is true that the national party organizations become sharply focused every four years as the Presidential elections approach. In fact, the party system has been defined as a loose aggregation of local machines that come together for the stakes of power embodied in the Presidency. Yet it is an error to view the party system primarily on the level of the national committees, and thus give too much emphasis to the Presidential stakes. The tough fabric of the party is to be found in the persistent and continuing bread-and-butter efforts to elect Senators, Congressmen, governors and other state officials, sheriffs, county attorneys, and the wide, bewildering array of administrative and judicial posts which form the jungle of American local politics. When it is remembered that there are more than a million elected officials in the United States, not to speak of the vast number of appointed ones who form the basis of the patronage system, it will be clear that the party organization which seeks to elect and appoint them constitutes the frame and musculature of American government. The relation between the local organizations and the national committees is one of mutual gain and loyalty. The party that wins can dispense patronage to the local party workers who have helped in the victory. In turn the local bosses are expected to be faithful to the national candidates at the party conventions and to "deliver" the votes in the national elections. The national organization in turn is expected to bolster the prestige of the state and local candidates and to give direction to what would otherwise be a chaos of local campaigns.

It would be too cynical to say that the only thing holding parties together is patronage and office. The party system, while resting on these, is actually a way of transmitting the broad ideas and philosophy of government from the Presidential and national leaders on top to every corner of the country, and of transmitting in turn the sentiments and impulses from every locality to the state and national capitals and to the top candidates and officials. If in terms of power it furnishes, as I have said, the frame and musculature of government, then in terms of the communication it forms the circulatory system for the ideas and convictions that animate government.

The parties have played a great functional role in American history. It is ironic that this should have been exactly the phase of the American governmental system which the framers of the Constitution were most anxious to restrain, regarding them as dangerous and fearing (as James Madison did) the rise of "factions" that would split the new society as they had once filled the Roman and Greek states with bloodshed. Yet a hundred years later it was exactly the part of the American government to which Bryce, in his *American Commonwealth,* paid most attention and for that reason got a warm review from a rising young professor of politics at Princeton called Woodrow Wilson. The vast, sprawling conglomerate of American life—with its sectional, ethnic, and religious pluralism, its welter of local governments, and its rural-urban hostilities—required some unifying thongs to hold it together. On the other hand, the stiffness of the political machinery and the diffusion of authority which always tended toward deadlock required some kind of oil to keep the creaking machinery going. The party system has helped to furnish something of both: the resiliency and the cohesion, the springs to absorb shocks and the thongs to hold the sprawling aggregate together, the oil and the cement. It has given American democracy a rough kind of politically functioning unity without the social cost that the unity of a single-party totalitarian system would have involved.

The "price of union," in Herbert Agar's phrase, has nonetheless had to be paid. That price has been the series of compromises with both political principle and doctrinal symmetry which have made American history the despair of the ideologists, and also of observers who have tried to see them in the image of the European doctrinal parties. It has also been at least a partial surrender of the heritage of the Founding Fathers to those whom Gerald Johnson has called the "Founding Uncles"—the masters and manipulators of machine politics. Although they are regarded as the black sheep of the family and are always linked with "partisan" politics, their actual role has been to temper the sharpness of conflict which, with more doctrinally committed men, could have proved intolerable. The party system has thus channeled the emotional and polemic energies that have struggled for mastery of the nation's destiny; it has—with the great exception of the Civil War—made it possible to avoid outright violence in the transfer of power from one majority to another. Viewing American history from the angle of parties, one might even say that the Civil War became inevitable when the party system broke down and when the Democratic party, which had still held the sections together loosely, was split in two.

One thing should be added about the party boss and his machine.* They too have not been immune to the changes that have swept American society. These changes—the ending of the big flow of immigration, the shift in class lines, the sustained pitch of prosperity, the emergence of the welfare state, the mobility of population, the rise of TV as the principal mode of reaching the voters—have played havoc with the textbook and newspaper cartoon figure of the boss. The old-time boss, who was gruffly illiterate, who used strong-arm methods, who recruited his stalwarts from the docks and saloons, who got his share of the gravy of city contracts, who took care of trouble in the families of his constitutents and sent them Christmas baskets, has given way to a very different kind of figure. One need only cite as examples the current or recent figures of David Lawrence of Pittsburgh, Carmine De

* For a discussion of the boss and machine in the context of urban culture, see Ch. III, Sec. 9, "City Lights and Shadows."

Sapio of New York City, James A. Finnegan of Philadelphia, and Jake Arvey and Richard Daley of Chicago, to get a flavor of the change. The new boss is likely to be highly literate; he still has a feel for tight-knit organization but has learned the methods of using surveys and polls before making any important moves; he works closely with the network of Washington agencies; he is still responsive to the needs and outlook of the minority ethnic groups which form the core of his voters, but he talks in terms of public welfare and often of national issues; on the floor of the national conventions he is interviewed on TV and delights in the image he presents as a kingmaker; rarely any longer does he reach out for some stumblebum to put into office as a front for his machine: he is far more likely to pick a liberal candidate with prestige, intellect, and glamour for the large mass of voters; while he gives this candidate a chance at office and power, the candidate in turn gives him respectability and the feeling of taking part in a meaningful political movement.

I do not mean to prettify the darker elements of the picture of political power and acquisitiveness. One can still find the alliance between the political and criminal underworlds which is part of the pathology of American life. In almost any sizable American city one can start with the gambling syndicates, the bookies, the slot machines, and the "numbers racket," and draw a line to the police and administrative officials with the reasonable expectation that somewhere along the line "protection money" will be flowing freely. On the Federal level one can start with the officials awarding public-works and defense contracts, or administering the tax laws or some phase of business regulation, and draw a line to substantial corporations and "fly-by-night" firms, and somewhere along the line one will find "kick-backs," "influence peddling," and those "conflicts of interest" which arise when a government official also has a stake in a particular business firm and its profits. Any political party long in power becomes slack in its moral standards. Any political party long out of power becomes hungry for the fleshpots. Often party lines are wholly erased, and the political machine in power "cuts in" the mercenaries of the political machine out of power.

While Americans continue to denounce corruption, they also continue to practice it. It must be obvious that such features of American life as the "fix," the "shakedown," "protection," the "pay-off," and the "racket" go deeper than the nature of local politics itself. They express a moral slackness not limited to politics but reaching into business and labor and the operative codes of what you can "get by with." The role of the local party system in this pattern is clear: by creating what Elihu Root called an "invisible government" behind the formal one, and a class of political hangers-on who live in the twilight world between the lawful and the lawless, it makes the moral breakdown easier and institutionalizes the gap between profession and behavior.

The scar left on American life by this corruption is not a negligible one. It is one of the factors that contribute to the recurring moods of political despair. The gap between the moral rhetoric of American life and the periodic revelations of what actually happens in politics and business is enough finally to desensitize the citizen and produce in him a despair of ever getting any reform accomplished. This despair leads the voter, however mistakenly, to lump the minor frailties of a "reform" candidate with the major larcenies and treacheries of the boss-dictated machine nominee. It is one of the facts of American political life that local reform administrations are rarely sustained, and that the waves of new political resolve which periodically sweep over the American conscience somehow get dissipated, leaving behind only echoes of the surge and thunder of the reformers.

A balanced picture of the local political organizations would take account of the corruption, the alternations of reform and despair, the residues of the old ethnic "machines," and the emergence of a new type of boss or "leader" who could better be described as a "manager," since he has become part of the new technical forces that organize so many sectors of American life. The drive for power is a crucial element in the motivation of these managers, but there are others as well: personal ambition, the hunger for prestige and respectability, the pull and excitement of the political "game," the eagerness for community standing on the part of members of ethnic minorities who can find such standing only in politics, the desire to be associated with the national party leaders and to appear in public with the great men on their campaign visits. This is a medley of motivations, at once petty and powerful, but one must take account of all of them or run the danger of simplifying one of the complex facts of American life.

The role of the party system is no slight achievement. What it seems is that American parties should be viewed not so much in terms of the grandeurs of statesmanship or the miseries of corrupt political machines, as of the moderating and mediating brokerage role which for better or worse both Presidents and machine bosses perform. They are brokers between the shifting desires and pressure intensities of the diverse opinion blocs that make up the "public," and the twists and turns of action by the men and agencies that make up the "government."

The brokerage function of the party system does not diminish the role of "public opinion" in America but serves to define its important place in politics. Americans are as torn in their attitude toward "public opinion" as they are toward most of their shibboleths: they both defy and despise it. They think of it mystically as a "brooding Omnipresence in the sky" which somehow decides on a shifting variety of "issues," and whose decisions are as final and as divinely inspired as the Ark of the Covenant. They are repeatedly told that "public opinion" requires this or that course of action. But it has often turned out that the "opinion" thus invoked is either a protective mantle for the interests of a small minority, or a passionate majority hatred, or an idea with which a large number of the people are obsessed. Following in the track of Graham Wallas, Walter Lippmann wrote at the beginning of the 1920s the classic American analysis of "public opinion" as a bundle of emotional stereotypes, deeply irrational and unverified, which have often been the creation of the very editors and political spokesmen who have invoked them. As a result, some Americans find themselves fitfully scorning the deity with feet of clay at whose shrine other Americans worship.

This double projection is reflected in the attitude toward the public-opinion polls, the sample tests taken of popular attitudes on political and social issues of the day. For a time Americans followed their ups and downs like anxious relatives watching the fever chart at the bedside of the patient, trusting it as a reliable and even infallible guide. But critical voices were raised to point out that this continued pulse-taking was not only treacherous but in itself symptomatic. The failure of the pollsters to predict the outcome of the 1948 Presidential election, when Dewey snatched defeat from the jaws of victory and Truman found himself elected although he was the only man who believed he would be, marked the turning point of popular disillusionment about polling. Yet even the disillusionment was focused on the wrong aspects of the polls—on the statistical percentage of error which might make them unreliable in a close election, rather than on the impossibility of reducing to count and measure in advance so complex and emotionally intricate an entity as a people's feeling about its own tangled problems and institutions.

The polls are important, however, as a sign of increasing mechanization in the process of political choice in America. This mechanization, which has transformed other areas of American life, has affected Presidential elections as well. While the local campaign oratory and the whistle-stop tours still linger and retain a real function, there is a widespread feeling that they are archaic survivals from a past that will never be retrieved. The press association wires, and more recently the radio and TV, have made political campaigning a massive, large-scale affair which is directed from the center and through which all parts of the nation are reached instantaneously. The appeals of the candidates get to the most remote areas, and the responses are checked and charted on a week-to-week graph by the "pollsters," whose fortunes rise and fall with the degree of accuracy of their predictions. This mechanizing process tends to reduce the voter to an item in a statistical calculation, and a digit in a vast radio or TV audience.

As part of the same process, elections have tended to become more and more like a business sales campaign, with the voter playing the role of a potential buyer to whom a commodity must be "sold." At this point, politics merges with the larger arts of salesmanship, packaging, and publicity. The history of American Presidential elections can be partly written as the history of slogans which expressed the felt needs of the time and jibed exactly with the mood of a particular moment. It is not that the slogans themselves, in their repetition, won or lost the elections, but that they were symbols for the interests and emotions which did. The campaign planners chart out their strategy much as they might chart a national sales campaign for their commodity. In both cases they call in the aid of the crack advertising agencies and public-relations firms. And as they test the effects of each tactic on the fever chart of the poll samplings, they shift emphasis and slogans, thus finding new wrappers in which to package the commodity they are seeking to sell to the voter.

What is most dangerous about this mechanization of politics is that it threatens to dehumanize the political process itself, which is at heart a human process. When the American corporation sells its product to a mass audience, using radio and television to capture attention, its great fear is that the program may alienate potential buyers in some ethnic, religious, or sectional group. Something of that sort happens in political campaigns. A smart candidate will evade any issue which might bring him into head-on conflict with a sizable organized group of voters. Since there are few issues that are "safe" in this sense, the trend is for the campaigner to speak in blurred generalities, except when he is appealing to a specific voting bloc or interest group and bidding for their support against his rival. The mechanization of the voter ends up in the dehydration of the candidate and of the issues.

I have described these trends toward mechanization as forcibly as possible, yet I do not believe that they will prevail and occupy the whole field, or even that they represent the larger truth about American electoral choice. It is a mistake to overemphasize the theme of mechanism in American politics. It is dangerous to assume that the American voter is a puppet, either propelled by drives of class and group interest or manipulated by professional politicians and public-relations experts. In addition to this mechanistic fallacy, as it may be called, there is a parallel tendency to depict American political parties as monstrously efficient autonomous machines, giant Tweedledums and Tweedledees which operate apart from the voters, using them cynically every four years but themselves beyond capture and control. Both these fallacies underrate the common run of American as a willing and valuing human being. They make him a passive entity, a globule who is acted upon but never acts, who is chosen but never chooses, who is led but does not shape his leadership, who is counted but does not confound his counters.

This conception of the voter is especially dear to those who find his changing behavior baffling and fear to face the fact of genuine differences between the political parties on the issues of great moment, and who therefore prefer the picture of puppets easily manipulated. One might point out that if the politicians manipulate the voters, the voters also manipulate their politicians by casting the political leader relentlessly in the role they want him to play and making a candidate a symbol of their feelings and drives regardless of how he may himself feel. In every election the leader catches the contagion of his followers just as surely as they catch his. If the voters are sometimes manipulated men, the leaders are often driven men.

But the strains of irrationalism may themselves be overstated. The fact is that, however irrational the stereotypes by which the herd does its herd thinking, politics for Americans is not only a puppet show. To some extent it is a question of whether they will have jobs or be unemployed, whether they will be able to survive as small businessmen, what they will get in their pay envelopes or for their farm products, what will happen to their unions, what will be the destiny of their kin in countries abroad, whether there will be peace or war for their sons and husbands, what measure of civil rights they will achieve and to what extent their freedoms of speech, thought, and religious worship will be protected.

Thus the image of cigar-smoking politicians sitting in a smoke-filled room, deciding the destinies of the parties and the nation, is not adequate for American politics. It is not even adequate for the party conventions that nominate the candidates. It is true that state conventions do designate the party's choice for Senators and Congressmen, and for governor and other state offices, are often (although by no means always) rubber-stamp affairs which confirm decisions already reached by the party managers. But a national convention is something very different. There are rarely any managers who can control the national party: the chairman of the National Committee is likely to be a technician, usually chosen by the titular party leader and filling a caretaker role between conventions; his value to the party is imperiled if he identifies himself too closely with any one candidate or segment of the party before the convention has made its choice. The convention itself turns into a battle between rival party "wings" and between the rival candidates for nomination, their managers, and the heads of the already committed state delegations. It is a battle whose initial skirmishes are fought in state primaries and party huddles long before the convention assembles; its techniques are usually those of making exaggerated claims of the candidate's strength, appeal, and prospects and minimizing those of his rivals; its tactics are intricate, devious, and so often carried on through commitments and "deals" behind the scenes that the TV audience (which has become an immense one in recent years) often misses the decisive elements of the battle while focusing on the overt drama of the speeches from the rostrum and the demonstrations from the floor; its final outcome may not be known for certain until a close roll call, when the delegations have already been polled but ask at the end to change their votes, either to nose out a victory at the finish line or to "get on the band wagon" when victory for one candidate seems inevitable.

There has been a movement to abandon the convention because it lends itself to manipulation by the managers and to shift the choice of candidates to state primaries which will be binding on the delegations. But I doubt whether this either will or should take place. The people would be denied the crucial thing about a national party convention: the fact that it is often genuinely an arena, although sometimes only a fake one; that it is in a sense a preliminary nation-wide election held inside the party, in which national rather than local issues can be canvassed, and the candidates can have an intense light focused on their personalities, their skill and maneuver, their candor or cunning of character, and their capacity to express the surging emotions of the time and therefore to attract votes. Manipulation does not always work. It often happens that a candidate for the party nomination will come to the convention with a number of state delegations safely sewed up, perhaps with a plurality of delegates, yet lose the nomination because the consensus of the delegates is that he cannot win the election. It also happens, as with the Republican nomination of Lincoln in 1860 and of Wendell Willkie in 1940, that several rival candidates are in deadlock and the convention decides on a third who had not been in the running ("dark horse") because the delegates hope that the qualities which give him a fresh appeal to them may appeal to the voters as well.

I do not say that politics in America is in any sense deeply ideological. It is differentiated from European politics exactly by its nonideological quality. There has always been an organic optimism in American society which Europe today lacks and which communicates itself to the party system. Equally, the lack of rigidity within the American social system is paralleled by a lack of rigidity within the party system. Just as America remains a relatively open society, so it contains a relatively open party system. The difference between Democrats and Republicans, while it is more than the difference between Tweedledum and Tweedledee, is not such as to split the society itself or invite civil conflict. The Democrats move, at most, toward a welfare state: the Republicans try to minimize some of the trends toward state power which the Democrats accept; yet the idea of welfare democracy has been so strongly established since the New Deal that it would be a reckless party or candidate who would now dare repudiate it. The choices between the two are usually substantial choices but not desperate ones. There is vituperation which runs rampant during American Presidential elections, and there is a constant stream of criticism of the Administration which may seem to most Europeans to verge on violence. Yet the violence is wholly verbal, and the vituperation is likely to be personal rather than ideological. Because there is an atmosphere of economic and social hope, the American voter still feels that he can make his choices.

These choices are not between dogmas or doctrines. They are mainly the choices between particular men, who are the symbols of a political direction more or less clearly discerned. The program itself—despite "party platforms" and "planks"—is less important than the personal symbol. That is why, especially in the back country regions of America, candidates make their appeal to the voters in a histrionic fashion. It is not unusual, in the Deep South or in Texas or in the mountain or Pacific states, for a candidate to campaign by dressing up in costume, with a familiar symbol of red suspenders or a coonskin cap or with the help of a hillbilly band. It is truer of Americans than of others that they can afford this kind of happy-go-lucky cynicism. They can afford to take politics less seriously than those peoples who live closer to the margin of survival. Yet, as I have suggested, one can easily be misled by this surface tomfoolery. American politics are a politics of ingrained attitude rather than of doctrine, yet the attitudes are based on a clear sense of interest and on social realities.

Since these social realities have been transformed by the currents of change in the past quarter century the party system has also been transformed. Utopians of the Left and Right on the margin of both major parties have long yearned either for some new and gleaming third party that would clear up all the confusions or for a realignment of elements within the two parties that would make one of them clearly "liberal" and the other clearly "conservative." Yet this has not happened nor is it likely to. Instead there have been political changes in both parties and in Congress that have left party lines as blurred as ever but, as Lubell has shown, more *nationalized* and more responsive to the deep social changes in American life and culture.

In the earlier pages I have discussed some of these changes, and in the pages to follow I shall deal with others. Among the most notable are what has happened to the city and the suburbs, to the ethnic and religious groups in America, to labor, to the middle classes, and to class mobility, to the internal population migrations, to the rural areas and the small towns, to the thinking of Americans on war and cold war and on world power and civil liberties. Party politics are the most sensitive barometer of the changes taking place in the mood and thinking of Americans. It would be surprising if American party politics had not registered these far-reaching changes by a party transformation which —while its evidences are more or less hidden—is as real as the suburban revolution or the technological one.

We must remember that the party system is more than an organization for power and spoils. It is an arena in which not only sectional and regional differences but also ethnic, religious, and class forces converge and battle it out. Traditionally the sectional divisions have thrown the "Solid South" into the Democratic column, while New England and the Middle West have been considered safely Republican. The ethnic vote generally found the Irish and (after the Smith candidacy of 1928) the Italian Catholics in the Democratic party, while the Midwestern Germans and Scandinavians and the Northern Negroes were in the Republican party. Recent events have changed the picture. With the New Deal the Negroes became more identified with the Democrats, as did the Jews (later both, especially the Negroes, began to swing back). The migration of Negroes from the South to the Northern cities opened them to the fluctuations of prosperity and depression, made them more sensitive to the struggle for civil rights, as well as placing them in a position to do something about it through their votes. In the cities they and other migrants from the farms and hills of the South and Midwest found themselves allied with second- and third-generation immigrants whose families had come from Europe before the gates were closed and settled down mainly in the big cities. The double movement of migration to the cities—from abroad and from within the nation—created the material for an ethnically conscious urban population.

It was Franklin Roosevelt's success in mustering these minority groups within the Democratic party under the big city machines, and allying them with labor, the Solid South, and to some extent the farmers, that produced the Great Coalition on which the Democrats relied for two decades. The Democratic leaders were more alert to the mood and needs of these groups and offered them greater hospitality than the Republicans. But there was a deeper reason for their success: these city groups were largely of the working class and the lower middle class, open to the ravages of unemployment, dependent upon government action to protect their interests, ready material for arguments on behalf of the welfare state. The Great Depression, by precipitating trends inherent in American politics even before Roosevelt, led to the Great Coalition.

More complex was the role of the suburbs and the new middle class in the party revolution. The movement from farm and small town to city was accompanied (as we have seen) by the movement from city to suburb. With mounting prosperity and living standards the children and grandchildren of the immigrants left the cities in search of a better life and a better social status. The new middle class, settling in the suburbs, was drawn largely from the ethnic groups that were part of the New Deal coalition. In some cases they changed their politics along with their mode of life, despite Adlai Stevenson's injunction to "vote Democrat so that you can live like Republicans." But, while the meaning of the voting shifts in the suburbs is still under study, the chances are that a number of newer suburban dwellers retained their political allegiance even with their new mode of life, so that the traditional Republican strength of the older suburbs was infiltrated by the Democratic newcomers.

The role of the middle class proved to be a very different one in the case of the South, where the course of industrialization brought a new strain of white-collar, small-business, and "organization-man" thinking into what had once been solidly sectional. For the South this middle class was an almost wholly new phenomenon, with values much more closely related to the thinking of the corporate bureaucracy and its satellites throughout the country than to the more strictly Southern concerns. Hence a new Republican strain in the South, especially in states like Florida, Texas, Virginia, and Georgia, which took the lead in industrialization. The trend toward a two-party South was unmistakable, and by the mid-1950s the Southern cities were almost on a two-party basis; yet the rural areas were still overwhelmingly Democratic, and there was still some doubt as to whether and when the South would achieve a two-party system. There could be little doubt that the once solid South would in time become a two-party South. To be sure, industrialism also brought with it a new population of industrial workers, who would normally share the Democratic preference of the trade-unions. But the drive for trade-union organization in the South lagged badly behind the new middle-class consciousness.

The role of labor and the farmer in party politics underwent changes throughout the nation. As the industrial workers grew more confident of their place in American life, and as they won most of their objectives in wages and union security, their political militancy tended to fade. While the leaders of the new labor federation were still generally part of the Democratic coalition, they knew they could not count on a solid political support from the trade-union members. The 1952 Eisenhower victory, which would have been impossible if the Republicans had not cut substantially into the labor vote, was proof that American workers do not vote wholly along class lines. But the obverse has happened in the last decade to American farmers. The farm price support program, inaugurated by the New Deal, caused normally Republican farm areas in Iowa or Minnesota to vote Democratic in several elections from 1936 through 1948. Even the traditional isolationism of the German and Scandinavian ethnic groups among the farmers (these groups usually vote on issues of war, peace, and foreign policy) could not reverse this trend. The farmer tended to vote his crops, his crop prices, and his crop parity supports as he had been doing for some time, and the vote might easily go to either party, depending on its promises and performance; but the normal tendency of the rural areas still remained Republican: they are conservative chiefly because most of the other welfare-state issues, except for the issue of farm subsidies, grow out of urban and suburban needs and outlook.

Even with a declining farm population and a lesser role for the farmer in the economy, there is no more important cleavage in American politics than the split between the rural and city forces. This is true in state even more than in national politics, as witness New York, Ohio, Wisconsin, Illinois, and Indiana, where the city-farm split reflects the division between the two major parties. Within many state governments a similar city-farm division is reflected in the tug of war between the governor and the legislature. The strength of the farm groups clearly does not lie in their numbers as voters but in their strangle hold on the legislatures, both state and national, which they retain through the failure to redraw Congressional district lines, through the seniority rule on Congressional committees, and through the "county unit" rule in a number of states where small rural population units are counted equal with heavy urban concentrations. The more than 70 per cent of Americans classified as urban pay well over 90 per cent of the taxes and elect only 20 per cent of the representatives to state legislatures. It follows that overrepresentation of the rural and small-town areas means underrepresentation of the city groups, including the racial and religious minorities and the worker and middle-class groups. It will usually be found that the divisions in Congress between the rural and the urban states or districts have more impact on the Congressional votes than the party divisions themselves.

It has been suggested, notably by Lubell, that the fluctuations of party fortunes are cyclical rather than immediate. Certainly the history of American Presidential elections would seem to bear this out, as witness the long tenure of the Republicans from Lincoln through Hoover, with the sole Democratic interruptions by Cleveland and Wilson; similarly one could trace a Democratic cycle from 1932 to 1952, broken by the Eisenhower victory. To speak of a cyclical swing is to restate the idea that party politics respond to long-range changes inside the society and the culture. But where these changes are as tangled and cross-grained as they have recently been in American life, each of the major parties is bound to be affected by them within itself. The partnership of the race-conscious South and the minority-conscious big cities is bound to be an uneasy one, although probably not an impossible one for the Democrats to maintain. Even within the ethnic minorities the political ties are often difficult to sustain: there is friction between Catholics and Jews inside the Democratic party, as indeed there is friction in a few big-city machines between the Irish and Italian political leaders. The cold war has further split the political unity of the Catholics, a number of whom have responded to Republican attacks upon the "softness" of Democratic administrations both in foreign policy and in domestic "security" and "loyalty" cases. As for the Republicans, they too have suffered serious internal splits. On the one hand there are the Eastern and big-city Republicans who feel that the best conservatism is that of consolidating the gains made by the welfare state without letting them get out of hand and become revolutionary in a destructive way. On the other hand there are the Republicans of the Midwestern power centers who are convinced that voters wanting a welfare state will vote Democratic rather than Republican, and who therefore move toward a more drastic conservative position.

Given these party shifts and internal strains, it seems academic for American political thinkers to call for stronger discipline inside the parties. This internal battle will inevitably be fought out because it is only a reflection of the deep clash of forces outside both parties, within the social system. One can speak of party discipline on some particular issue, up to the point where the issue becomes so important that it will break the party before it is itself broken. The way of politicians on such matters is to avoid both discipline and conflict and avert disaster by evading the whole issue, at least outwardly. This is a solution of a sort, but it is scarcely consistent with either ideological clarity or any meaningful party discipline. How the party strategists handle such problems as those of Southern consciousness and Negro rights, or those of Catholic and Jewish consciousness, may prove the decisive difference between party victory and defeat. Obviously any sizable minority which feels strongly enough its sectional or religious or ethnic interests becomes a balance-of-power group, staying as long as possible away from party commitments, knowing its strength and determined to exact concessions through that strength.

To add to the complexity of the picture, there has been increasing talk of the "independent" vote and a growing tendency of both parties to appeal to this vote by speaking in "moderate" language. It may have been the vote of the sizable group of voters uncommitted to either of the two major parties that threw the pollsters into confusion in 1948. Certainly it is the independent voter, once called "Mugwump," who keeps the party system from becoming rigidified and maintains the margin of free choice within it which makes it a living instrument. He prides himself on the mobility of his allegiance and on the fact that he cannot be taken for granted. It gives him the virtuous feeling of being outside the political machine, above the muck and corruption of party politics, committed to principle rather than to party. Yet it is still unclear whether the strength of this "independent" bloc will increase or diminish.

Instead of speaking of a big bloc of uncommitted voters outside the parties, it is more relevant to speak of shifting groups of voters inside the parties who are inclined to abandon them on one issue or another but will probably return when the issue is no longer a strong one. In practice the appeal to the growing number of these voters has meant at once a sharper appeal to the voting blocs cutting across the parties and an emphasis on the personality of the candidate. Eisenhower was able to win in 1952 and 1956 because he expressed the vague feelings of many voters who were caught between the parties and who responded to his earnest contention that he was a "dynamic conservative" or a "conservative progressive," a mixture of terms which meant that he preferred not to make a choice between more clear-cut sets of political principles.

This looseness has its limitations. William Allen White contended that there were four parties in America—the Liberal Republicans, the Tory Republicans, the Bryan and (later) New Deal Democrats, and the Southern Democrats. In Hoover's Administration the "sons of the wild jackass" led a Republican revolt which embarrassed the main body of conservative strength within the party. Under the Roosevelt and Truman administrations the President has had to contend with an adverse coalition of Republicans and Tory Democrats which played hob with Administration programs. Since Congress is organized on the committee system, where the shift of one member to the opposing side can make the decisive difference, this hostile coalition made the whole domestic program of the Fair Deal an ineffectual one. Hence the tendency among American political thinkers to emphasize the need for internal party discipline if the party is to maintain its identity. The problem, as throughout politics, is to find the balance between the "iron law of oligarchy" which makes all structures too rigid internally and the anarchic tendencies which make it difficult to hold any structure together for any length of time. For the present the American party system suffers more severely from anarchy than from rigidity. Yet over the decades it has managed to perform its function of canalizing without violence the energies and loyalties of Americans of diverse national origins, and of achieving a measure of political unity without imprinting on it the totalitarian stamp.

The idea of a two-party system is more crucial to keep alive now, when it is being challenged by single-party totalitarianisms, than it has ever been. Both the major parties in American politics owed their origins to movements of popular radicalism—the Democratic party having been firmly established by the Jacksonian revolution on the Jeffersonian cadre, and the Republican party having come to birth out of the anti-slavery libertarianism and free-land equalitarianism of the 1850s. The history of third party movements in America is the history of lost causes, some of whose energy, ideas, and programs were eventually absorbed by the major parties. Third parties, when they have been dangerous enough, have caused the major parties to shift their position. But to be wholly successful, a third party has had to displace the weaker of the major parties and become itself a second party. This happened when the Whigs replaced the Federalists, when the Democrats replaced the Democratic-Republicans, and when the Republicans replaced the Whigs. But in the case of the Populists, the Progressive party of La Follette, and the Socialists, the typical experience has been that of an open larceny of their platforms by the existing party system. Each of the major parties in turn is full of contradictions; but of the two, the Republicans still present a more nearly consistent adherence to business and corporate views, while the Democrats more nearly express the aspirations of the classes and minorities still struggling to find their place in the sun.

While party lines are shifting and will continue to shift, they are unlikely to add up to any drastic party realignment, least of all to the emergence of a new party like the British Labor party, with a new class base. The American parties will continue to absorb new energies and new points of view while remaining a two-party system. The line of party growth in the calculable future may possibly involve the absorption by the Republicans of a number of Democratic conservatives, and by the Democrats of Republican liberals. Yet the stronger signs point to the ever-growing strength of labor political action within the Democratic party, the fashioning of a sharper philosophy and strategy of planning and socialization, the continued absorption of a philosophy of welfare action by the Republicans, and the organization of the economically and politically lagging South. The long-term trend seems to be a consistent, if hesitant and intermittent, movement of both parties further toward the liberal direction—unless a war catastrophe changes the whole national as well as party picture.

5. *Power and Equilibrium*

I HAVE SPOKEN of the Presidency as the force that shapes the national mood and direction, and of the party as the frame that holds the polity together and keeps it functioning. But the central fact of any political system is power, and its gravest danger is that the contending power pressures will disrupt it by their intensity, or else dominate it if they become too concentrated. How has the American system met this problem? And how has it dealt with the related problem of the division of power between the central government and the states, between power at the center and power at the rim?

Power in America cannot be understood by looking only at the governmental structure. American historians and social thinkers have sometimes overvalued and sometimes undervalued the role of political power in the American story, depending on their own angle of vision and their theory of history and human nature. The conservatives, secure in their economic power, have stressed the dangers of the political. The liberals have inveighed against economic power, while counting on the political most heavily for modes of change and reform. The radicals have stressed economic power because of their class approach to history, while (as shown in the case of Veblen and Beard) they have grossly undervalued political power and its use as an instrument for change. Mostly, however, the run-of-the-mill American has shown a healthy concern for all phases of power: as a practical matter he has pursued purchasing power, admiring intensely its accumulation in the hands of the rich. While focusing his political interest on the Presidency as the core and symbol of the government, he has been wary of the Federal power and its administrative arm as too complicated for the mind to grasp. He has been suspicious of trade-union power and church power even more than of corporate power, and suspicious also of military power—at least until the period of the world wars and cold wars.

Recent American history has witnessed important changes in the distribution of power. There has been a shift from Congressional to Presidential and administrative power, a shift from formal policy-making to budget-making power which often has carried policy-making with it, a shift from local and state power to Federal power. Similarly there has been a shift of power from the churches, the universities, and the lawyers to the Big Press and the opinion industries, from the farmers and small-industry groups to the big corporate industries, from the owners to the managers of industry, from civilians to the military.

The fact about American power, as about so many other phases of

American life, is that it is plural and fluid. It is many-faceted rather than uniform; it is dispersed among a number of groups; it has shifted geographically and in its class distribution. There has been, to be sure, a steady movement toward concentration in every form of power. Yet the agencies of power have multiplied, as witness the growing distribution of economic power among the corporation, the trade-union, and the government.

Since the beginning of the nation the whole American atmosphere has been saturated with power—technological, economic, political, religious, military, financial. From the cop and the precinct boss to the foreman and trade-union leader and corporate executive, from sergeant to general, from bureau clerk to President, the sense of power has been pervasive in the American experience, and the sense of the limits of power has also been constantly present. In contrast with aristocratic or military societies, America has had no elite groups of birth or status trained to the exercise of power. There has been enough diffusion to give the nation as a whole the chance to revel in the feeling of abundant power. The Americans as a nation have been relatively parvenus in its use and have therefore distrusted its users, but what is remarkable is that this nation of parvenus has not carried the abuse of power further than it has.

The reason may perhaps be found in a distinction drawn by Santayana between *power* as a generative force and *domination* as a frustrating and destructive one. The atmosphere in which American life has developed has been one of a continued expansiveness which has kept America relatively free of the frustrations of power that more constricted cultures have incurred. This offers a clue to the fact that while there has often been corruption in American political life, there has never been a serious attempt at dictatorship. The dangers of tyranny are greatest in a society where power has never been widely diffused. As Santayana again points out, in a comment on Lord Acton's great epigram on power, only those unaccustomed to power are corrupted by it. While Santayana means it to be an argument for aristocratic societies and against popular democracies, it has actually worked differently in America, where the corruption is likely to be in the lure of the Big Money rather than of absolute political power.

This raises the question of what De Tocqueville stressed and Aristotle foresaw long before him—the dangers of a majority tyranny on the one hand and on the other the servility of the democratic mob to a demagogue-dictator. As one of the great innovations of world history, majority rule powerfully attracted De Tocqueville and other commentators to the American experiment while it raised in their minds profound doubts and fears. These doubts and fears have a real base, as shown by the popular hysterias that have swept over American opinion. Yet the power of the demagogue-dictator has worked itself out to a grim sequel not in America, where mob rule had been most anticipated and feared, but in Germany, Italy, Russia, China, and the "People's democracies" of eastern Europe.

What was wrong with the calculations of the fearers and predictors? Partly they failed to reckon with the strength of the constitutional tradition, but mainly they failed to take into account the pluralist character of power in America—its many loci, its widespread diffusion in one form or another, the heterogeneous quality of American society, and the talent for equilibrium it has shown.

The tyranny of the mob is a very real tyranny. It shows itself notably in America in periods after wars, when tensions have come to the breaking point, and on the brink of war, when the cult of the nation-state gives an opportunity to the loyalty hunters and the professional accusers. Yet it would be hard to point to any period in American history and say, "Here is where the majority ran riot in America and trampled upon freedom."* A close student of American power is more apt to study not the majority but the minorities—the lobbies, the pressure groups, the sectional interests, the corporate and trade-union leaders, the heads of the Congressional investigations. Even in the case of the loyalty hunts and the search for "subversives," the effective stimulus has not been majority hysteria but a cold campaign by pressure groups in the hunt for some particular quarry. A new feature on the landscape of American power is the "veto group," which pretends to act in the name of the majority but actually terrorizes it.

To understand the American pressure groups, one must understand that to move a huge and unwieldy mass, such as the American leviathan, you have to push very hard. The strength and variety of these pressure groups, the brazenness of their lobbyists, the vast sums they have spent on propaganda, their use of techniques as diverse as the corruption of government officials on the one hand and large-scale direct mailing on the other hand: these have often been described. The number of registered lobbyists in Washington, not taking account of those who operate under cover, exceeds the number of Congressmen. They are paid more than the President and the Supreme Court justices, and they have the big money at their disposal. There is little doubt that they influence legislation, in many cases help draft the laws; they are especially active in a war economy where big contracts are at stake; they

* For further discussion of this theme, see Sec. 10 of this chapter, "The Struggle for Civil Liberties"; also Ch. IX, Sec. 4, "Varieties of American Character."

often succeed in reaching and sometimes even supplying strategic members of the government.

The political theorists of the early twentieth century, including some Americans, used to write a good deal about guilds and hanker for a society in which a network of them would hold the power and perform the functions of government. In a sense there is a network of American pressure groups—from the farm bloc, the trade-unions, the churches militant, the ethnic groups and the patriotic societies down to protective associations for birds and historic shrines—that form a kind of *guildism* in American life. Sometimes they are merely a nuisance with which Congressmen and bureaucrats have learned to deal, sometimes they represent permanent group interests which they do not allow the legislators and administrators to forget. Always they express the individual's sense that he is powerless alone in so huge a society and must therefore band with others to exert pressure; they also express the principle of the right of free association gone berserk. Alongside this guildism there is also what has been called a *clientelism* that has developed in America, meaning that when a man has some particular interest at stake and wants to exert his power to protect or advance it, he turns as a client to a professional influence technician who knows—for a fee or a percentage—how to get what, where, when, and from whom.

I doubt whether any of these—interest groups, pressure groups or veto groups, guildism or clientelism, lobbyists or per-centers—will undermine the American Republic. Just as the tyranny of the majority in American life has been overrated, so also more recently has the destructiveness of minorities. Both have been facets of the effort to balance the principle of popular sovereignty with the fact of a richly diverse and pluralistic society. America's enemies nourished the hope of a nation so fragmented that it would succumb to a concerted attack, whether by arms or propaganda. The hope has proved wrong. So have the fears of those who felt that it was ripe for tyranny.

One can read in American history, with all its travail, an impressive capacity for the balancing and accommodation of interests. This has worked out best in the problem of the powers of the nation and the states. The authors of *The Federalist,* who first grappled with the problem systematically, saw beyond the abstract question of the distribution of authority-in-the-members as against authority-at-the-center. For them, as for most of the delegates at the Constitutional Convention, the term "federalism" had the accent on the central power, whereas today it has the accent on the power of the members. For them it was not so much a problem of judicious balancing as it was one of political survival itself.

They had to settle first the question of whether there would be a unified nation, and then the practical political question of whether they dared dispense with the states. The answer to the first was that a nation was a necessity, to the second that the states had to be retained. From that point on it was a question of the means of working out a dual system. It must be said for the framers of the Constitution that they contrived intricate but effective means. It was in the same pragmatic spirit that the great names in the history of federalist thinking worked —Justices Marshall, Taney, and Waite, Presidents Lincoln and Franklin Roosevelt.

For the moving force behind the increasing centralism of power in America one must, of course, look to the expanding technology. In 1787, while the Constitutional Convention was in session in Philadelphia, its members are said to have watched a demonstration of John Fitch's steamboat on the Delaware. The symbolism seems ironic, yet the constitutional framers had a strong enough feel for the realities of power to provide a framework even for the steamboat and its latter-day tribe of children. The same forces that led to welfare-state controls, and to the gigantism both of business and labor, led by the same logic to a steady growth in governmental centralism—"federalism" in the sense in which Hamilton and Madison used it. There is a peculiar futility in inveighing against only one of the leviathans of American life—that of government—without recognizing that it has come into being to balance the other leviathans.

There is a curious tenacity in the fallacy which sees the states as the champions of individual liberties and the United States as their enemy. The States' Rights doctrine has had a number of diverse champions: the Jeffersonians, the Federalists at the time of the Hartford Convention, the Southern Democrats, the Republicans who feared national social legislation. It was used by both the White Supremacy and the corporate groups to maintain an area of immunity from Federal control and keep the political power in the hands of state and local units, which are more amenable to pressures. This was the tactic employed in the struggle over the offshore submerged ("tidelands") oil deposits, which the Supreme Court held to be the property of the Federal government but which Congress by special legislation handed over to the states in 1953. Sometimes a "No Man's Land," in Franklin Roosevelt's phrase, has been created in between the unexercised state power and the forbidden Federal power. In general the appeal to States' Rights has been made whenever it was to the advantage of any party, section, or group to make it, with little regard for doctrinal consistency.

There is, I grant, a strong argument in favor of power on the rim and against power at the center. It is one to which the modern generations, with their sense of loss and alienation from the soil, are particularly open. There are many evidences of the grass-roots virility which is celebrated in American political oratory and editorials. Yet a student of American thought must learn to be wary of a fetishism of the grass roots. Aside from the greater safety from gigantism that decentralized decision offers, there is no inner healing power within the local governmental units that is denied to the central ones. In fact, the local governments which impressed De Tocqueville had become by James Bryce's time so corrupt that he called them "the one conspicuous failure of the United States," while Andrew D. White wrote that "with very few exceptions, the city governments of the United States are the worst in Christendom—the most expensive, the most inefficient, and the most corrupt."

These comments on American city government were made before the turn of the century. Since then there have been successive waves of municipal reform, the crucial improvement coming through the application of the technical managerial approach to city government. Perhaps because the larger unit draws on better talent and gets greater public attention, it still remains true, however, that the quality of government is better on the national than on the state level, and better on the state than on the city and county level. Nor should it be forgotten that the local unit is more vulnerable to the nonpolitical forms of power which may seek to dominate it. Thus there are some American cities which are "owned" by an interlocking directorate of business interests —perhaps the railroad company, the insurance company, the banks, the newspapers, the radio station, the local mill or factory.*

But these are marginal and somewhat moralistic considerations. Since the Civil War the steady movement toward power at the center has come as a result of felt needs rather than reasoned preferences or logical doctrines. Lincoln found it necessary to assert the Federal government's power not only as against the seceded states but also as against the governors of the loyal ones, who tried to fight the war as the heads of autonomous little empires. With the growth of an industrial network cutting across state lines, Justice Waite asserted the power of Congress under the "commerce clause," which was an important instrument for effective control of interstate business. With the Great Depression the breakdown of local finances led to a system of direct Federal aid to local units which transformed the whole power gridiron. Finally, in both the world wars, the needs of military power and of the war economy played hob with the traditional lines between governmental units.

* For an earlier discussion of city government, see Ch. III, Sec. 9, "City Lights and Shadows."

The building of a new defense plant at Willow Run in World War II, for example, gave rise to a new community which cut across the various township and county authorities who could not cope with the new housing, health, schooling, and policing problems except under central direction.

Yet it is characteristic of the American temper that after each extension of the Federal power, a new equilibrium is struck at the higher level. Hence the "new federalism" of the present generation, which runs toward the return of power to the local units. On questions like flood control, the co-operation of states with Federal agencies has been hard to get. A number of states have entered into interstate compacts on the allocation of common water resources. The Supreme Court has asserted the power of Federal control over trade wars between states but has interpreted state powers broadly in most other cases, including restrictive "right to work" laws and loyalty tests. Competition between Federal, state, and local governments for the tax dollar has grown sharper every year. On the other hand, there has been a working agreement for co-operation between Federal and state agencies regulating corporate securities, power companies, and communication utilities. Even where the Federal power is complete, as in the case of wartime rationing and the military draft, care is taken to put the administrative tasks in the hands of local groups who know their neighbors. And in the case of the Tennessee Valley Authority the seminal principle has been developed of decentralizing administration even where power has had to be centralized.

The spirit of the new Federal-state equilibrium can perhaps be best expressed by paraphrasing Lincoln's classic theme: Does it follow that a governmental system centralized enough to escape fragmentation must be so centralized as to destroy the spirit of local initiative? The American answer has been No. Nor should one conclude from the trend toward centralized power in America that it has carried everything before it in its triumphant career. America is still a highly complex and unwieldy system of crisscrossing governmental lines, a little as if there were forty-eight nations carved out on the state level, along with twenty or thirty small ones within each state on the city level. In fact, F. J. Turner's comment on the operation of sectionalism—that it converted American internal history into a struggle between nations—is still largely true, but it goes beyond sectionalism to the whole distribution of power.

The debate on the question of power at the center as against power at the rim continues with considerable vigor among American observers mainly because there is still some leeway in the allocation of power, and in many legislative and administrative instances the choices are still open. Hence the appeal to history and to the logic of American government. In assessing this appeal there can be little question that there are built-in controls in the Constitution itself which favor state and local power and close the issue in many cases. For example, the role of the states in selecting the President, through the Electoral College or (if there is no majority) through the House voting in state units, cannot be ignored. Neither can the Senate's great role in legislation and foreign policy, which is also based on the equal representation of the states; nor the fact that states decide the qualifications of voters (hence the effective disfranchisement of Negroes in the South for generations) and also control Congressional districting within broad limits set by Congress (hence the overrepresentation of the rural areas). How strong is this drive of the political mechanism toward state power is shown by another fact: much of the function of judicial review has been to be vigilant about the constant intrusions of state action into the realm of the national government. In a number of areas, as in the management of land and water resources, the crisscrossing of a double Federal system of jurisdictions and agencies has led to a jungle of decisions which only the expert can penetrate.

There are obvious weaknesses in any system which places too much power either directly at the center or on the extreme rim. The American system has escaped the weakness of a highly centralized prefecture setup, as in France, but it has not wholly escaped the weakening influence of extreme local power. Wherever these local units have tried to take on important functions on their own, there has been an evident lack of skill, financial means, and local initiative, which has been one of the principal factors in the expansion of Federal power. At the municipality level the immense number of units (there are some 120,000 in the United States), their lack of an effective tax base, and their failure to get home rule in many instances have underscored the weakness of local initiative.

What has been developing instead is an intermediate layer of government, through which the states, bolstered by Federal funds, have assumed many local and even national functions. The national government, through technical aid, through financial grants and tax offsets made conditional upon the states' living up to certain standards, has in effect pushed the states into adopting welfare programs, school-building programs, employee merit systems, inheritance taxes, and road-construction projects. The result has been that the states have become vehicles of what conservatives might call "creeping Socialism" if it were not state action rather than Federal action that was involved. For example, in the mid-1950s they spent nearly $4 billion on health and welfare activities, which was almost twice as much as the expenditure of the national government.

In an era of world struggle the American federative principle has taken on a deeper meaning than ever in its history. I do not refer here to the easy parallelism between the situation that faced the Constitutional Fathers and the one that now faces the world leaders. I mean, rather, that each of the Great Powers recently on the world scene has had to grapple with its own Federal problem. The Germans did it badly at home, which may partly account for their failure in terms of empire. The British did it well in their empire since the Durham Report but did not apply the principle in time to their Asian and Middle East dependencies. Both the Russians and the Americans, today locked in mortal stuggle, have served an apprenticeship in the Federal principle—the Russians, under Lenin, in seeking to hold the Czarist power together after the Revolution, and the Americans as I have described above.

The capacity for Federal relationships may decide how successfully each of the two rival empires will be able to hold its forces together and associate new ones to them. After a successful use of the principle of national autonomy under Lenin, largely under the stress of compulsion in consolidating the Revolution and minimizing civil conflict, the Russians too easily allowed themselves to attempt a resolution of the Federal problem by the overrigid use of Communist party discipline as a tying device between the supposedly autonomous but actually satellite units. America has not made the same mistake at home. The reason may be that, except for the final power of decision in the Supreme Court between the conflicting claims of Federal and local governments, American federalism has few tying mechanisms. A number of tying devices have, however, been developed through the guild professionalism of the technicians who operate in the welfare areas. Thus health officials, engineers, social workers, agricultural workers, the forestry service, and others have cut across the various strata of governmental jurisdiction in attacking particular problems. The deepest strength of federalism lies thus in the habits of mind developed in the course of settling the practical problems of the distribution of authority.

Thus the pluralist, pragmatist, and federalist character of American politics has compelled it to develop the arts of compromise and to achieve an equilibrium of conflicting powers in motion. Yet the fact is that Americans did not always succeed in settling their conflicts of authority or escape disaster. At one point the frame of both federalism and the party system could not contain the tensions, and the result was a Civil War. To be sure, America was not alone in its tensions, and the quarter century between 1840 and 1865, which saw the gathering forces and the explosion in America, witnessed in Europe also a series of bitter class conflicts and revolutions. The contemporary writings of Marx and Engels on the American Civil War interpret it as part of this world revolutionary surge toward freedom. Yet Lincoln saw it more realistically as a challenge to national unity—that is, to the traditional Federal balance. At the time of the Gettysburg Address he was using the Federal power to ride herd on the state governors who challenged it. "Government, of, by, and for the people" under American conditions could not dispense with an adequate degree of unity at the center.

The doctrinal struggle involved in the Civil War was Calhoun's doctrine of the "concurrent majorities"—actually a doctrine of minority power through veto—as arrayed against Lincoln's doctrine of national unity. Lincoln won, and by that fact the sovereignty of the minority was squeezed out of the American system: since the Federal system allows for autonomy enough in the constituent parts and at the rim, along with enough effective power at the center, it was unnecessary to make a fetish of the minority's veto power. It is this knack for framing their crucial problems in terms of equilibrium ("both/and") rather than of doctrinal struggle to the death ("either/or") which has helped Americans give continuity and survival to their history.

This is illustrated by the relative absence of class struggle in America. Actually the power of the contending classes, both of business and of labor, has been greater than in most European countries which have shown more class conflict. But Americans have perforce learned the arts of balancing their classes in the equilibrium as they have learned to balance their sections. This is true not only of the economy but of the society as a whole. The gigantism that has afflicted American life could long ago have destroyed it had not some sort of balance been achieved between the contending forms of bigness. Thus America developed not only Big Government but also Big Business, Big Labor, Big Distribution, the Big Press, the Big Church, and the Big Army. No one of these is monolithic: each of them in turn is a tangle of conflicting forces, and each in turn has had to achieve an equilibrium within itself. Thus the American system of power has become like a system of nebulae held together by reciprocal tensions in inter-galactic space.

But, unlike the nebulae of the physical universe, the dangers of disrupting the equilibrium are a constant concern. It is not only the traditional fear that one of the Bigs may overshadow and finally annex the others, and with them the principle of freedom, or that a combination of them might become imperialist and destroy the equilibrium. There is also the danger of a fetishism of the equilibrium principle itself, which could give each of the new forces the veto power that Calhoun once sought for each of the sections. Because of the problem of reaching a consensus among the giant structures that dominate American society, a number of "veto groups" have emerged—minorities with a strategic position, whose psychic intensity takes advantage of the equilibrium and draws a confining line around the diversity of American life. The problem of reaching a consensus has always been hard in America, yet it has always had to be solved. Otherwise government would be deadlocked and society stagnant, and the carving out of a line of direction for American growth would be frustrated.

6. The Governmental Managers

WHEN A CONSENSUS is reached, who converts it into a policy and carries it out? The formal and logical answer would be the President. Yet obviously one man, even with the help of his Cabinet and his closest advisers, cannot run a government and a nation in a technical age. Increasingly in the last century a bureaucracy has emerged, operating under the President and Cabinet but with a wide margin of responsibility for the day-to-day conduct of affairs. This has meant a transfer of the locus of power which has been little short of a revolution in governmental technology.

The men who run this governmental machine are, in effect, the managers of government. They are not the rulers of America in the sense of making the strategic over-all policy decisions, which are made, rather, by the President, his advisers, the leaders of both parties in Congress, and the leaders of industry and labor. It is these men on top who are there to make the policy decisions, and not their subordinates in the bureaucracies. Americans recognize this, in the newspapers or political debates or in ordinary speech, when they speak of "the Administration," by which they mean the immediate managers, the President, his Cabinet, and the Congressional leaders of his party. By using the term they put their finger on the essential fact. If the substance of power is located at the point where the big gaps in decision-making are filled in by day-to-day administration, then it is true that the administrators are the new men of power.

This is not a truth restricted to America or its government. Balzac saw the danger when he called the French bureaucracy a "great power wielded by pygmies." It applies equally to the corporations, trade-unions, armed forces, and even the churches and universities. We have seen in earlier chapters how far the bureaucratization of industry has been carried. It has been carried just as far in the government. In fact, there is a peculiar irony in the attacks made on government bureaucrats by the men who speak for "industry" but who are themselves simply another group of bureaucrats. The irony lies in the fact that American business enterprise has had an enormous impact on the forms and shape of American government enterprise. What first made a government bureaucracy necessary was the spate of scientific inventions which in turn created a vast industrial organization that needed regulation from without as well as order from within.

The government has also taken over from business enterprise its key ideas of scientific management, of classification of jobs, of the continuity of staff regardless of the changes of policy on top, of the distribution of function, of a hierarchy of prestige and power, of a set of fiscal controls, and of the idea of planning itself. It has taken from business also its standards of operation: what the American demands of a government bureau above all else is that its operations should be "businesslike." Finally, the newly emerging "government corporations" (like the TVA), which represent the probable form of any future quasi-collectivism in America, are simply business corporations run by a governmental bureaucracy, although the fact that they are being run for the general welfare rather than for private profit sets a different tone to their operation.*

Thus American government has grown a "fourth branch" to add to the three branches expressly provided for in the Constitution. There is a prevailing fear in the American mind that the fourth branch will grow so fast that it will shut off the light and nourishment from the other three. But it must not be forgotten that this fourth branch also has deep roots in American history, as shown by Leonard White's series of volumes viewing American governmental history in terms of the administrative process and seeing the men of the Revolution and of the Jefferson-Madison and Jackson periods primarily as administrators. In the early decades of American industrialism there was a heavy growth of regulatory laws in the state and local governments, so that the idea of *laissez faire* did not become dominant until later, after the triumph of the Northern business group in the Civil War. Even in the 1870s and 1880s a new base came to be laid for government regulation of railroad rates, of business practices, and of banking. But it was the two world wars and the New Deal which did most to insure the triumph of the new men of administrative power. The American Federal bureaucracy is the child of crisis and has fed and grown on crisis.

Despite the prevailing American opinion, bureaucracy is not linked

* For an earlier formulation of this theme, from the viewpoint of economics rather than administration, see Ch. V, Sec. 10, "The Emerging Amalgam."

with any radical idea of governmental function or of social policy. The British and Continental experience has shown that bureaucracies are needed under any philosophy of government; and, in fact, that even conservative governments cannot dispense with the regulatory state. Only in America has the term "welfare state" as a term of invective come to imply a form of Socialism imposed on the people by "left-wingers." The growth of a Federal bureaucracy can be charted through both Republican and Democratic administrations, but its great spurts of growth have come in Democratic administrations from Woodrow Wilson on. The efforts to grapple with the problems raised by the Great Depression, the two world wars, and the cold war, came largely under Democratic administrations; and there can be little question that they fitted in with the Jeffersonian purposes (although not with the Jeffersonian means) of the Democratic tradition.

Yet if we take Herbert Croly's definition of a welfare state as one which reaches for Jeffersonian ends through Hamiltonian means, and remember that the centralization of Federal power was closer to the Republican tradition while the doctrine of States' Rights was closer to the Democratic, it becomes clear that the technology of the new state power is politically neutral. For better or worse, every administration will have to use it. Each party can seek to maximize or minimize it and use it for one or another set of social purposes. But a bureaucracy knows no party lines. Its inherent nature is to professionalize the process of government, to achieve continuity of administration through all the changes in party power, to bring expertness to the technical problems of government, and to effect a fusion of legislative, executive, and judicial powers wherever necessary despite the formal separation of those powers.

It was an insight of Brooks Adams that all revolutions have followed on the breakdown of bureaucracies and have in turn depended for the consolidation of their power on the creation of new bureaucracies. But one must add that administrative breakdown and reconstruction are in turn the consequences of forces at deeper levels within the culture. This was true in the case of the Nazi revolution under Hitler after the breakdown of the Weimar bureaucracy, as it was also true of the Communist revolution under Lenin after the breakdown of the Czarist bureaucracy. In both cases the revolutionaries were quick to forge a new "steel frame of power" under a system of gauleiter and commissars.

This lights up the crucial difference between a democratic and a totalitarian bureaucracy. In the totalitarian case the bureaucracy is the servant of the party and its leaders, is built on the party cadres, and is responsible only to the party leaders who are also the state rulers. In the democratic case the bureaucracy is largely recruited by civil service, except for the top policy-making posts in which party patronage enters strongly, but the succession from one party to another is accomplished without violence. The bureaucracy has a continuity regardless of party changes and is accountable to the Constitution and the people under the "rule of law."

Every bureaucracy reflects thus the basic social organization and power structure of the society whose governmental business it administers. It is in itself neither ogre nor Messiah, neither a road to serfdom nor a way of salvation, but it can be used both destructively and creatively, depending on the inner social impulses and on the direction given them by the policy-makers at the top. That it can be an instrument of tyranny has been abundantly shown. But in a free society it can be kept free, as shown by both the experience of the Labor and semi-Socialist governments of western Europe and the less developed welfare state of America.

What was most creative about the New Deal period was less its economic or social philosophies, which were fuzzy, than the administrative strategies developed to meet specific emergencies. Their obvious result was the multiplication both of *ad hoc* bureaucratic agencies and a heavy new burden of taxation. Yet the withering barrage of criticism directed against the tax-fed bureaucrats stressed only the obvious negative aspects—the red tape, the routineering, the stuffiness and self-importance of men with power attaching to their office, the frequent cases of sheer incapacity for the job.

There has been a too animistic quality in the attacks, as if some whim of power or some demonic malevolence had brought the bureaucrats into being. What is missed is the fact that the welfare state, with its bureaucratic base, came in America as a response to the felt urgencies of modern industrial society. There was the need of setting a floor under economic insecurity; there were clashes of interest groups, which required the intervention of the government as umpire and as equalizer of unequal bargaining conditions. There were new industrial practices which had to be regulated if chaos was to be prevented; there were concentrations of economic power which had to be kept in check, lest they lead to the growth of a state within a state; and there were actual failures of functioning in various segments of the economy which brought the government in as entrepreneur and investor. Added to all these were the war economy and war services which could be run only through the state.*

The failure to meet these needs would have led to democratic disintegration. In this sense the "wonderland of bureaucracy" and the

* For an earlier discussion of the welfare state, see Ch. V, Sec. 10, "The Emerging Amalgam."

much derided "alphabetical agencies" and "Brain Trusts" of the New Deal were contrivances that kept the democratic idea vital in the face of overriding crisis. The new administrative corps was given the power to do what Congress and the Judiciary by themselves—and even the Executive by itself—could not do. Much of the appeal which America has for nontotalitarian peoples elsewhere comes not only from a going business system but even more from a going democracy, and the fact that both have been bureaucratized does not diminish the power of the appeal.

This does not exclude the real dangers presented by the new men of power if they are not checked. Every form of power can become cancerous and eat up the other forms. This has not happened in the American experience mainly because the bureaucracy is the servant of the whole state rather than being linked with a single-party system, and also because of the strong tradition of judicial review. The courts, it is true, have hesitated to set aside any administrative finding if it has some factual basis. They have, that is to say, refused to supplant the administrative agencies as fact-finders. But they have on the whole guarded against the invasion of the freedom and privacy of the individual by arbitrary administrative action, glimpsing the shadow of a police state in such arbitrariness. And they have insisted that where legislative power has been "delegated" by Congress to an agency, the delegation must be something other than what Justice Cardozo called a "vagrant roving commission." I suspect that the widespread American distrust of administrative agencies comes not so much from what they have done to the liberties of the people but from what they might do—that is to say, not from the American historical record but from a deep impulse in American political thinking. This impulse in turn has been bolstered by the experience of totalitarian systems and by the fear on the part of the possessing classes that a strong and independent bureaucracy might prove a leverage for social change and might prevent them from staffing the administration's key posts with their own people when they came to power.

The popular feeling about government bureaucrats combines mistrust, dislike, and contempt with a degree of fear. It may be found both in Congress and in the popular mind. The reasons for it are many, but they converge on the same deep current of feeling. To start with, Americans are suspicious of any kind of elite, and the bureaucrats come closer to looking and behaving like an elite than do the professional politicians in Congress or in other government posts. Ever since the Jacksonian doctrine that any man is equipped to learn and perform the tasks of government, Americans have clung to the notion that a trained corps of government servants is somehow a challenge to Americanism. There is also the strong feeling that bureaucrats are in a protected position when they are under civil service or have stayed in a government job so long as to pre-empt it. Behind this is the belief that every American should be compelled to prove himself from time to time in some market place: hence the classic charge that the bureaucrat has never had "to meet a pay roll or deliver a precinct." The run-of-the-mill American, who has to struggle in the labor or business market, feels that the men at the Washington desks have latched on to an easy thing and won't let go. Moreover, they are seen as people who spend the taxpayers' money but don't have to pay for it themselves. It is felt that somehow they are responsible for the burden of high taxes on the ordinary citizen, and that they spend it mainly for such un-American purposes as governmental planning. Much of the propaganda against bureaucracies exploits and bolsters these hostilities.

The fears involved in them have thus far proved baseless. But there are other dangers with much more substance. These are the dangers not so much of tyranny as of lack of creativeness, not so much from the leviathan of power as from the slough of stagnation. The haphazard gathering of a "Brain Trust" under the New Deal was at the start an emergency device and had to be institutionalized. The hewers of wood under the top bureaucrats inevitably became almost immovable parts of a civil-service system whose gods are not ardor and creativeness but seniority and stagnation.

The crucial problem of an administrative group is that of the recruiting of talent from the best brains and energies of the culture. This talent cannot be restricted to any single class or political outlook. Each party in power finds that it must take men, even in the policy-shaping posts, who are not wholly sympathetic with its basic aims. The problem of educating them is almost insoluble, since narrow technical capacity without a broad education can throttle the imagination, while education without technical competence and experience can lead to costly and largely academic forays. Moreover, even when they are trained, the administrative officials do not remain long in the government service. They are lured away by higher salaries and by offers from corporate groups or from private professional firms for which their government experience has made them valuable. It is the mediocre who tend to remain, and this trend—exactly the opposite of Vilfredo Pareto's "circulation of the elites"—is reinforced in American life by the fact that the best brains and energies are usually drawn off into business or are frightened away from government by the "security checks" and the "loyalty" investigations. There is a marginal difference of efficiency between the run of the government bureaus and the run of corporate enterprise which is largely due to the differences in the kind of talent available to each.

This is, however, not an inevitable affliction of government, as was shown in many New Deal agencies, which caught the imagination of young men. What the New Deal was able to do was to attract a new type of government servant who was an amalgam of the lawyer, the economist, the engineer, and the administrator. He had to fight the tradition of spoils and patronage, he had to learn how to get along with Congress, and often his relations with the corporate bureaucrats became intolerable. Yet he added something to the flavor of democratic government. As the original impulse weakened, the quality of the administrative groups also weakened. With the cold war came the deadly ideological ("security") purges of the government services, necessary only in a few cases where men of doubtful loyalty held sensitive posts, and resulting in the other cases in a destructive effect on the quality of the whole governmental process. Where the Grand Inquisitors entered, the margin of freedom necessary for creative thinking was squeezed out.* There has been therefore a steady diminution of the quality of American administration, both at home and in the far-flung foreign services, which forms a serious problem of effectiveness and prestige.

Obviously there are considerable dangers in allowing the civil service to be kept in a constant state of political anxiety, since it places a premium on the survival only of the conformist. Yet I do not wholly share the distress of C. Wright Mills at the American failure to make bureaucracy more rigid, or at the large number of "outsiders" in the upper ranks of the bureaucracy, among the 1,500 "keymen" who hold the policy-making posts. One cannot take the German bureaucracy of Max Weber's day and impose it as a model upon the American situation of today. German society was one of authority, hierarchy, strict order, with an educated class that was still limited. American society is fluid, with widespread education, with a passionate bent against hierarchy, with a high sense of the personal rather than impersonal values. Quite naturally Americans share the belief that each new President has the right to bring in his own "outsiders" (Roosevelt and Eisenhower both did it) in order to carry out the principles of his regime. The Germans felt that the task of government was to transform extraordinary problems into routine tasks and tie them together with neat co-ordination. The Americans do this in industry and do it well; but they regard human relations as quite another sphere, and government as part of human relations. Peter Blau has pointed out that the German ideal of

* For the "security" cases, see Sec. 10 of this chapter, "The Struggle for Civil Liberties."

an official who, in Weber's words, meets the public "in a spirit of formalistic impersonality, *'sine ira et studio,'* without hatred or passion, and hence without affection or enthusiasm," simply does not apply in the welfare agencies that form a growing segment of American state and Federal services, where contacts with clients are a major part of the satisfaction of the job.

It is also characteristic of Americans that a bureaucracy, once established, seems to them constantly in need of renewal and reorganization: hence the periodic plans of redrawing the blueprints of government, including that of the Committee on Administrative Management set up in 1936 under the New Deal and, more recently, the Hoover Commission. But the interesting fact about the voluminous reports of the latter was their stress on two highly American themes: first, the cutting away of waste, duplication, and surplus expenditures and man power; second, the plea for giving the President a clearer line of command and more control of his own establishment. Even in coming a long way from the Jacksonian doctrines of rotation in office and party spoils, Americans still clung to the notion of flexibility and change in administration. What Jackson was driving at, in his own rather primitive way, was a continuing method of reorganizing the government services and giving the new policies a group of devoted executives. Whatever Americans may feel about property in the economic realm, they have never come to feel that there are property rights in government jobs.

Herbert Luethy, writing about French parliamentary institutions and bureaucracy, has said that "France is not ruled but administered, and it is her apparent political instability which guarantees the stability and permanence of her administration." Almost the opposite is true of America. It is administered, to be sure, but primarily it is governed within a frame of major political decisions. Its impressive degree of political stability gives it the luxury at times of playing hob with its bureaucracy. Americans will, of course, have to settle down and become more sober and mature about their administrative tasks. They do not lack money, yet in their money economy the lower ranks of the bureaucrats are shabbily paid, reflecting the low esteem in which they are held in the culture. They are lopsided in their distribution: out of two and a half million civilian Federal employees, half of them are in the defense establishment and most of the others in the Post Office, the Veterans Administration, the Treasury, and Agriculture; the number of welfare employees is growing but is still only a small fraction of the whole. The professional career services are still in an early state of development: in the areas where they were strong during the security and patronage raids of the 1950s, the resistance proved most effective.

Most of all, they need to get away from the idea that a government servant cannot also be a person in his own right. There is a distinction to be drawn between political neutrality, without which a bureaucracy becomes chaotic, and the nullification of personality. A man can be politically detached yet also be excited by the professional idea he is seeking to fulfill, and have a sense of meaningful teamwork in an important task. Without that sense the whole work languishes, including even the formalized parts of it. Yet it will be difficult to achieve and maintain such a work spirit as long as the popular distrust and contempt for the bureaucrats continues. To overcome it will require considerably more political leadership on the part of the President, the parties, and the press than is likely to be forthcoming soon.

7. Tribunes of the People

THERE ARE TWO main agencies of the American government which have been entrusted by history and tradition with the safeguarding of individual rights and interests, whether against the governmental managers or any other force. They are the Supreme Court and Congress—one because it is the carrier of legal due process, the other because it is the representative assembly. In theory the whole of America is representative government, and each branch of it in one way or another represents the people in the sense of being government of and for the people. Yet traditionally there is one branch, Congress, which is considered to represent them most clearly and directly. Its members are chosen by state or locality and feel themselves to be part of "the folks back home." They are thus the American version of the Roman "tribunes of the people."

The idea of a separate representative tribunal is a master idea of Western parliamentary history, which Americans have inherited and to which they have given their own slant. It fits in with the American's distrust of government: one might say too glibly that a Congressman is sent to Washington not so much to *do anything* but to see that his constituents are not *done in* by "the Government." It fits in also with American localism: he is not sent to represent the national interest but only a geographical and local segment. Congress reflects many of the sectional, political, economic, religious, and ethnic antagonisms within the vast body of American life—which does not mean, however, that it is a true mirror of America.

Actually the representative idea has not worked out exactly as anticipated. The President, elected not by a single locality but by all the people and able to take a commanding view of their moods, emotions, and interests, has come to represent them as "the President of all the people." But the power structure in Congress is set up to reward those who come from "safe" districts (for the Democrats, the rural South; for the Republicans, the rural Midwest and New England) and to give disproportionate representation, especially in the Senate, to such economic interests as wool, silver, oil, natural gas, as well as the corn, hog, and dairy farmers.

Congress has become a problem child of the American governmental family. It is noisy, volatile, vulnerable to pressure groups and lobbies, often parochial in its outlook, jealous of its prerogatives, insecure about its position, implacable in its vendettas, bewildered by its mounting tasks. It has lost its reputation for great debate, has become intractable to party leadership and discipline and incapable of disciplining itself, and in recent generations it has developed fewer examples of the great leadership it once possessed. It seems less capable than ever of forming a steady majority which can carry through a planned and reasoned program of legislation. Only in the closing weeks of the session, under the hard driving of administration managers working with the majority and sometimes the minority leaders, does a legislative program get pushed through, with far too much carelessness and haste.

This has not prevented the persistence of a kind of folklore of Congress which gives it deep roots in the public mind. The people think of it at once as supreme legislator and supreme watchdog. In his legislative role the Congressman dresses himself up as the lawgiver, a seer who lays claim to his oracular role because he feels closer to the people at the "grass roots" than anyone else in "the Government." But he has also hewn out the image of himself as the eternally vigilant guardian of the people's interests as against the tyranny of the "Administration" —or, as he used to be called, "the palladium of the people's liberties." He sees himself as the sole watchdog of those liberties, and it is scarcely conceivable to him that the President or a Cabinet member or the head of an administrative agency might have an equal solicitude for freedom and an equal competence in judging how it is to be preserved.

Congress did not dream up these two roles. Its model was the British Parliament. The framers of the American Constitution followed the thinking of Montesquieu and Voltaire, who bungled the description of the actual role of the British Parliament in the eighteenth century and evolved the idea of three separated powers of government. The striking fact about the British system is that it fuses the legislative and executive powers in a single body, which is the Cabinet acting as part of the Parliament, and enables a majority to carry through a majority program. But in the American scheme Congress has clung to the idea of its sole guardianship of the legislative power and its monopoly of the watchdog function. Its model in British experience has been that of the Tudor and Stuart periods, when Parliament carried on a continuing battle with a series of absolute monarchs for the very life of the representative system. Once that battle was decided the British Parliament moved on to its present form, but the Tudor and Stuart image remained imbedded in the folklore of the American people and the glory image which the American Congressman has of himself.

It is not an unqualified image and has its paradoxes. The same American who cheers Congress because it is "agin" the Administration may find it hard to recall his own Congressman's name. The same American people who regard Congress as their watchdog are likely to breathe more freely when Congress has adjourned and the watchdog has gone home. All of which points to a gap between the folklore of Congress and the realities of the world in which Congress must function.

Actually there has been a sharp decline in the prestige and stature of Congress, corresponding to a decline in its policy-making functions. The operation of Congress in the technical age of physics and chemistry and electronics puts an enormous burden on an average man—which most Congressmen are. When you add to the burdens of modern technology the burdens of a world of competing imperial powers and clashing idea systems, it is no wonder that a Congressman's days become for him days of wrath, and his tenure a time of troubles which he must think of renewing before he is well launched on it. He feels himself (in Housman's phrase) "a stranger and afraid in a world he never made." As a result he tends to seek security in a redoubled militancy against the "Administration" or sometimes the "Interests," and in the solacing role of a Grand Inquisitor.

In the early decades of the new age of technology Congress shifted its emphasis from that of a debating body to a network of committees. The number of committees multiplied alarmingly, and periodically Congress sought to reorganize itself and cut away the unnecessary committee tissue. Yet here it ran into another difficulty—the system of seniority which gives the powerful committee chairmanships to those Congressmen who have outsat their colleagues, either because they are safe and silent men or, more likely, because they come from one-party constituencies like the Democratic South or the Republican Midwest, the safely Democratic "down state" big cities or the safely Republican "upstate" districts. The committee chairmen are therefore in many instances arrogant and reactionary old men, elected without much opposition and often from states (as in the South) where only a small segment of the people exercises the franchise. To match the dead hand of the seniority rule in committee, there is the paralyzing hand of the filibuster and unlimited debate on the floor of the Senate. Finally there is a lack of co-operative action between the two Congressional bodies and a lack of party discipline and coherence in both, which make Congress a battlefield of shifting blocs and coalitions inside the party structure, but manage nevertheless to create a working coalition hostile to the incumbent Administration.

The result is often government by deadlock. One may argue whether the deadlock comes because of governmental mechanisms or because the people, in their distrust of all government, want it that way—but the fact is there. Every President, after a brief honeymoon period, has had the experience of losing control over his own Congressional majority—if he had it to start with. The burden of linking the Executive with Congress falls on the operation of the party system, but that in turn is raked by a crossfire of sectional, doctrinal, economic, and personal disputes. The achievement of Franklin Roosevelt in keeping a tolerable degree of party unity within Congress during most of his first term on a program of drastic New Deal reform is almost unexampled, and was possible only because of the combination of deep crisis and skillful leadership. Something of the same sort happens also in wartime when external danger unifies Congress along with the nation. But the normal relation of Congress and the Executive is, as with many modern marriages, that of an exasperated cold war punctuated by periods of intermittent agreement.

To some extent the Presidents have themselves been responsible for this hostility. The burdens of the Presidency in a technical age are greater even than the burdens of Congress, and the vast administrative machinery by which the Executive must act is often cumbersome, arrogant, and in the worst sense bureaucratic. The Congressman who tries to get some action out of an administrative bureau is likely to feel like a rat imprisoned in a cage crisscrossed with red tape. He sees all around him waste and extravagance, and often the inexpertness of those who profess to be experts. His fury and contempt toward the "bureaucrats" may start as a commodity for home consumption by his constituents, but it runs the danger in the end of becoming habitual. He finds them men who, he feels, could never get elected to any post but hold their offices by patronage or civil service; and men, moreover, whose ideas seem to him outrageously different from the ideas of the "folks back home." He feels called upon to attack, investigate, and expose them. They in turn live in continual fear of his power and in unremitting contempt of his ignorance.

One can, of course, overstate this mutual hostility. There is considerable day-to-day co-operation between the bureaucrats in "the agencies" and the people "on the Hill." There are innumerable friendly ties between the two branches of the government, and even considerable "back-scratching" whereby favors as well as amenities are exchanged. Much of the hostility is an outward show by the Congressman for the benefit of his constituents and by the bureaucrat for the benefit of his colleagues. Yet the underlying strain is there, mainly because the Congressional leaders and the Executive have come in recent years to represent antagonistic social forces. For the past twenty years, since 1938, there has been a continuing alliance of some firmness between rural Southern Democrats and rural Midwest and New England conservative Republicans. This alliance has cut across both parties and has operated with an indifference toward the shades of party liberalism represented by Roosevelt, Truman, and Eisenhower.

What makes it worse from the Congressman's standpoint is, as I have noted, that much of the legislative initiative has in recent decades shifted from Congress to the Executive. This is mainly because of the technical complexity of the legislation, with which the administrative agencies are better able to cope because they are more specialized in it, but partly also for two other reasons: the increasing use of the President's veto, which gives him a chance to exercise a restraining hand on legislation; and his press conferences, which give him a leverage for directing its course. In these areas the Congressional committees sit almost constantly to consider and scrutinize the legislative proposals that actually come from the President or his advisers or one of the administrative agencies. The fact that the big expenditures are mostly in the areas of Presidential initiative makes Congress the more skeptical of them. In the mid-1930s, before the Hitler crisis in Europe became intense, the total House report on foreign aid called for an appropriation of not more than $100,000; in the recent annual budgets this has run into the billions.

Congressmen understand this and are resigned to it, yet they resent the dominating role of the Executive in foreign policy and several times have rebelled against the lines of State Department direction. In 1948 Congress forced on the Executive the China Aid Act, which changed the whole emphasis of Far Eastern policy; in 1950 it replaced a Korean aid measure with a Formosan one. In the same year it forced a big loan to Spain, incorporating it in the ECA Act and changing the emphasis of American policy toward Spain. Much of the major domestic legislation which liberals have to some degree fought—the Taft-Hartley, McCarran Immigration, Internal Security, and Tidelands Oil acts, and the Natural Gas Amendment—came by Congressional rather than Executive initiative. The same was true of the much needed Legislative Reorganization Act of 1946. Congress has been far from inactive legislatively and has fought hard to resist the inevitable loss of its legislative function in many technical areas.

More recently Congress and the President have attempted to work out a going system of co-operation in legislative policy. This is especially important on budgetary appropriations, on atomic energy, and on foreign policy, all of which have required not only a high degree of technical competence which Congress cannot alone command but also a continuing measure of liaison between the two branches. The problems of atomic energy and of foreign policy involve issues of national life and death which can scarcely be left to the mercies of deadlock. In these areas the President takes Congressional leaders into his confidence, using them as a kind of Privy Council with whom he consults before making his major proposals. During the periods of war and cold-war crisis this was supplemented by a "bipartisan" foreign policy, latterly again abandoned, which was often more rhetorical than real, but set an important precedent for future periods of crisis.

From the Congressional standpoint the galling fact about Presidential power is that it keeps eating into every new area of decision-making functions, and that in the area of foreign policy the President is the "sole organ" of foreign relations. The great Holmes decision in *Holland v. Missouri* extended almost indefinitely the powers of the President to legislate, in effect, through treaty-making and through Executive agreements. Even more, the swift pace of necessary tactical movement in the diplomatic and economic struggle for the world has meant that the President and Secretary of State often present Congress and the country with a series of *faits accomplis,* leaving Congress bothered and bewildered if not bewitched. The surprising support for the "Bricker Amendment," which sought to cripple the Presidential power over treaties and Executive agreements to an archaic degree, was largely an expression of the frustration of Congress and its suspicion of the Administration's foreign policy.

While both the Budget Bureau and the Atomic Energy Commission retain important ties with Congress, there are other bodies with crucial decision-making functions which are more dissociated from it. One is the National Security Council, made up chiefly of the defense, foreign policy, and psychological-warfare leaders, sitting in solemn council with the President. The other is the Central Intelligence Agency, which has charge of espionage and counterespionage abroad. These two groups, acting with the Atomic Energy Commission, have more to do with the shaping of the life-and-death decisions for the nation than any combination of Congressional committees.

What has been happening to Congress, in the large perspective, is that while its legislative responsibilities have grown more complex than ever and its burdens more demanding, the axis of policy-making initiative—even on legislative matters—has increasingly shifted to the Administration leaders and the bureaucracy. Congress has not lost its legislative function, but in comparison with the rate of increase of Executive power and involvements, it has been difficult for Congressional members not to feel that they are being passed by. Add this to the bipartisan conservative alliance that I have mentioned, largely rural, and one can understand the dogged resistance Congress has shown to new measures of a welfare democracy (except for farm legislation), to new legislative action meant to bolster Negro rights, to "internationalism" in the sense of foreign aid and diplomatic involvement, and to the maintenance of the liberties of the mind. Ralph Waldo Emerson had the notion that Congress was a safety valve for letting off the national steam: "A Congress [he wrote] is a standing insurrection and escapes the violence of accumulated grievances." History has shown instead a persistent, almost built-in, combativeness in Congress which seems to accumulate grievances. The traditional mistrust of the Executive, which Congress has always shared, has been sharpened by the new assertions of Presidential power—especially in foreign policy—which have come with the growth of the Presidential office.

Partly as compensation for its sense of loss and chagrin, partly because of the era of wars and cold wars, Congress has expanded its supervisory activities and shifted its attention to its role of a watchdog. The dramatic Congressional committees have now become the investigating committees. It is still true that the positions of power and prestige are those on the Rules Committee, the Foreign Relations Committee, the Appropriations Committee, or the Military Affairs Committee, and the able and experienced men aim at those. Yet the recognition of long and devoted service in these crucial posts may not be what paves the way to political advancement. Much of the drama of Congress is now centered in Congressional investigations, where a talented or demagogic Congressman can play the inquisitorial role, get the newspaper headlines, reach the people through radio and television, and become a household name. The committees serve not only as approaches to the spotlight but also as ways of resolving the terrible frustrations of a Congressman's life in giving him a sense of effectiveness and fulfillment.

The history of Congressional investigations in America* goes back a long way, and even further back there is a body of law and tradition in English history meant to protect the rights of the person in the inquisitorial process, some of which was taken over by the American Bill of Rights. The recent rash of Congressional investigations was thus in no sense new, although their pace and scope were transformed. It would not be hard to make out a strong case for the Congressional investigating power as a whole. The Federal bureaucracy has taken on vast and new powers, yet the bureaucratic wheels grind with terrible slowness, whether it be a passport application that is involved or a claim urged upon the Veterans Administration, or an application for a housing loan, or a labor contract. This not only adds to the Congressional load of private legislation and to the errand duties of a Congressman, but it also prods him into a sharper scrutiny of the bureaucratic maze. When he makes it, he finds how difficult it is to place responsibility for bureaucratic action, to find out where the blunders were made, where the buck was passed, where the corruption took place, and where—and here is where the anxieties of the cold war entered—the subversion may have taken place. Congress may thus feel that if it is to exercise its proper surveillance of the bureaucrats, gain access to their secrets, and fix responsibility, its members must turn themselves more than ever into glorified public personifications of the "private eye."

But the fact is that thus far the recent investigations raised many more problems than they solved. To the evils of government by deadlock they added the evils of government by inquisition. They often filled an important function in digging up necessary information that would otherwise have remained obscure or hidden, as in the case of the crusades by Norris and La Follette, or the railroad investigations under Senator Wheeler, or the investigation of defense contracts which placed a Senator called Harry Truman on the path to the Presidency. But the Congressional committee is not ideally suited to the task of detection of wrongdoing or the digging up of hidden items, as for example are the Moreland commissioners of New York State, or the Royal commissions of inquiry in the British system. Much depends on the kind of committee counsel and investigating staff that is chosen and the spirit that animates them, much also on the restraint and judgment of the leading members of the committee. During the 1945-55 decade the inquiries became decreasingly a pursuit of the facts and increasingly crusading inquiries or politically inspired; too often the committee chairman or counsel was out to "get" someone or prove a predetermined thesis, and too often a single committee member sat with the counsel

* For a further discussion, see Sec. 10, "The Struggle for Civil Liberties."

and questioned witnesses, while his colleagues were busy elsewhere. Similarly, while the British commissions cannot argue their case in the press until they have submitted their reports, the Congressional committee aimed for the headlines just as soon as it had a lead, thus making the press an integral part of the Congressional investigative process. Men and ideas found themselves condemned in the headlines long before the public had a chance to learn the facts.

This danger of prejudgment was greatest in the committee hearings themselves. Although in theory the investigations preceded any resort to the courts, the fact is that they became in effect prosecutions before tribunals which not only brought the charges but also sat in judgment on them. They had the power to summon witnesses, to compel attendance, to cite for contempt or for perjury. They have not developed procedural safeguards to protect the individual in the face of this punitive power, as the American courts have done. The record of the House Committee on Un-American Activities, and of the Senate (McCarran and Eastland) Subcommittee on Internal Security, was one that deeply troubled many Congressmen who did not believe in the Divine right of the Congressional inquisitors. These latter years were doubtless the years of growing pains for this new Congressional function, and a number of suggestions were made for a code of safeguards of individual rights. In the meantime a number of Congressmen were able to throw their weight around and organize what came close to being a reign of terror over the State Department, the other administrative officials, and men outside the government in professions like the movies, the theater, and the radio whose livelihood depended on their not becoming "controversial" figures.

Thus, if the Congressman had in the past tended to think of himself as a watchdog, his new role was that of the hound of heaven, divinely appointed to track down the sinners and execute the Lord's vengeance on them. This is the most crucial transformation that has taken place recently in both the power and the function of Congress. It turned that body into what Lippmann described as "a band of orators, investigators, prosecuting attorneys, and objectors." It afflicted Congress with a kind of broadcasting neurosis, in which it felt fulfilled only when it was exhorting the people to rise in wrath against the desecrators of the Temple. Thus this tribunal which was intended to represent and mirror public opinion set itself the primary task of arousing public opinion. It goes without saying that this consumes energy, time, and attention and has not done much to help the legislative process itself. That is still as clogged as ever, with hundreds of bills thrown into the Congressional hopper on the first day that Congress convenes, and thousands more piling up as the session goes on. As a result, the Congress that has normally operated by deadlock and obstruction now operates also by inflammation.

What I have said here applies to the mechanism itself and to some of the more volatile or more embittered figures who set the tone by which it functions. Their grievances against the Administration, or some agency or member of it, are likely to make them the more complacent to suggestions from interest groups which share their hostility and can play upon their injured self-esteem and rankling sense of inferiority. Despite the instances of efforts at outright corruption, scattered through the annals of Congress, bribery is marginal. The men who become spokesmen for the farm, labor, or veterans' blocs, or for the real estate or oil or natural gas or aviation lobbies, do not need to be bribed: they succumb more easily to flattery, calculation of electoral advantage, and a sense of identification with the interests of those groups.

Most Congressmen are neither heroes nor villains but well-meaning men caught in an almost impossible job. Half the Congressman's time is spent on trivial inquiries for his constituents, the other half in a desperate effort to keep up with the heavy volume of mail, with committee assignments which are multiple and far too burdensome, and in an anxious absorption with personal political tactic and fence-mending. The Congressman thus becomes in part a glorified errand boy, in part a vest-pocket Talleyrand.

He is subject to harrowing pressures from every side to shape his conduct to the parallelogram of forces brought to bear upon him. Since there is little of a cohesive and disciplined party system to take the responsibility for the decisions of the individual member as in England, the Congressman must carry almost the whole responsibility himself and is left to be buffeted by all the forces loose in his world. Given so exposed a position, he tends to follow the line that the press takes, which is generally the line taken also by the corporate groups, the veterans' groups, and perhaps the labor and church groups in his community: this means that he follows the stereotypes of his culture. When this involves a clash with his moral values, the result is either a corrosion of those values or exposure to political defeat. When it involves a clash with the majority of his constituency, he is likely to escape their vengeance by falling deeper into the embrace of powerful individuals in the community who can protect him.

But the chances are not strong that the Congressman will feel any anguish of mind or conflict of conscience. "The French deputy," writes Herbert Luethy, "is . . . able to have his heart on the left and his wallet on the right without their coming into conflict." The American Congressman is likely to wear both of them somewhere Right of Center. He will probably have his roots in the mentality of the small town and of the lower middle class in it. He may be a lawyer of moderate income, or engaged in a small business, or an editor, or a cog in one of the new corporate bureaucracies. His thinking is likely to be that of the interest groups with which he has spent his life. He will prefer the steady support of those groups to the unreliable and sporadic enthusiasm or wrath of the lower income groups. In short, he would rather have a steady job as Congressman than be a Spartacus. Some have charged Congress with being either delinquent or defective, and others have felt that it could do no wrong. But the fact is that Congress is neither an assembly of gods nor a pack of rascals but a fairly accurate mirror of the strengths, weaknesses, and tensions of American middle-class life, and the average Congressman is only an ordinary man under extraordinary pressures.

What makes the situation tragic is that Congress does get good human material. There is a creative minority in Congress, as elsewhere in American life, and there is a steady stream of men who come to Washington with a sense of freshness and even of mission. But Congress has ceased to be the main channel through which the political energies of America flow. It is no longer the arena of great debate, except in times of sharp crisis, and even then the Presidential role is the decisive one. The steady stream of demands for the "reform" of Congress has led to several Reorganization Acts, notably one in 1946. These have tried to limit the errand-boy functions of the Congressman, help him with expert consultants, diminish the number of committees, give him a chance for some reflection and creative thinking without which no man can grow in stature. But they have had only limited effectiveness, largely for the reasons I have set down in this section.

The procedural reforms can help the Congressman but they cannot resolve the basic dilemma of Congress. It is the dilemma of a body which still has, at least in theory, the control both over the purse and over the sword, both over appropriations and over the declaration of war; but which in effect finds that the decision over great events in a complex industrial society and a world in turmoil has passed to the President and to his experts, to the bureaucrats and generals and technicians. Caught in this dilemma, Congress has been groping for some new place in American life. The investigating committee has seemed a natural handle to grasp, but in its frustration Congress has used it like a group of violent men wreaking their sense of powerlessness on the nation. It remains to be seen whether Congress will be able to use it with greater restraint and combine the legitimate watchdog function with that steady and critical sifting of the great issues of the time, for which it was originally intended, instead of the trivia and details, which too often occupy its attention.

8. Law and Justice

American law had its roots in the method and body of the common law which the American colonists brought over with them from England. There was still a chance in the seventeenth century that the new settlements, especially since they resented the British judges, might develop their own system of law. But in the eighteenth century the English common law, which had served as a weapon in Parliament's struggle against the absolute monarchy, began to be taken over as a colonial weapon in the struggle for freedom. The great argument against the Writs of Assistance, delivered in 1761 before English judges in a Massachusetts court by James Otis, was an argument for freedom taken directly out of the common law tradition and the Parliamentary struggles. Once the political recourse to the English common law was fixed, it fixed also the dominance of the common law in the American legal system. Those who went to British legal thinkers to find arguments for freedom remained to absorb their approach to law.

The process was by no means inevitable, and there was always a chance that America would make a fresh start in law as in other areas: as late as the 1830s, writes Roscoe Pound, "it was still not wholly settled that we should receive the common law." The fact that this finally happened was due mainly to the influence of the great American judges and treatise writers of the pre-Civil War generation, like Kent, Story, Shaw, and Gibson. With the rise of a business economy the new American business class was glad to have an instrument like the common law, fashioned out of the experience of British life, ready at hand for dealing with the problems of commercial litigation and justice. The lines of conflict in the struggle that raged around the common law through the first half of the nineteenth century were drawn between a largely conservative group who were attracted by the spirit of the English property institutions which the common law embodied and a liberal opposition which feared a judge-made, piecemeal law and felt that Americans could organize a better and more rational system, closer to their own experience.

The common law, however, was the victor. The result has been an American legal system which has a continuity with the English much like the continuity of the American language with the English. There are local variants in usage, but the frame and tradition are the same. A legal system has emerged embodying a number of master ideas interwoven with those of politics, economics, society, and the American mind.

The first is that of experience as a guide to legal growth and therefore to justice. "The life of the law," said a young lawyer called Oliver Wendell Holmes, Jr., in the opening chapter of his book *The Common Law,* "has not been in logic. It has been in experience." He went on to talk of the "felt needs of the time," as the later Holmes—then a Supreme Court Justice—was to talk of the "hydraulic pressures" exerted on a decision by the practices, beliefs, and attitudes of the community. In recent years Holmes has been sharply criticized, especially by a moralist and natural-law school which feels that he exposed American law too nakedly to the animal appetites of society and the empiricism of the chance atom. But he best represented the tradition of American legal thinking, just as his friend William James best represented the spirit of American philosophy and social theory. Reading the famous Holmes-Pollock letters, one sees both the common ground and the differences between the British and American legal attitudes.

The idea of the primacy of experience carried with it the idea of the pluralism and the diversity of that experience. America embraced the common-law tradition largely because it offered room at the joints. Just as the cult of experience is a recoil from the rigidity of the Continental concepts of reason, so the cult of the case method in law is a recoil from the rigidity of Continental concepts of codified law derived from a fount of revealed wisdom. The idea of each case as a new bundle of experience, to be measured against other cases, fits into the American's conviction of the uniqueness of his own experience. It fits in also with a culture of diverse jurisdictions, of state and local governments, of regions and subregions, of plural religious sects and ethnic groups. The common law appealed to the English at the time of Edward IV largely because it brought unity into the diversity of feudal life. It appealed to Americans because it kept American growth from being cramped within rigid codes and fixed principles. Every body of law contains both a core of stability and a line of change: but if the English stress the element of precedent, which is that of tradition, the Americans stress the dynamism by which the lawyer and judge are able to fashion new law out of new social experience.

The battle of legal doctrines in America was fought out in the conflict between natural-law and common-law ideas. At first the two worked together: in the spirit of the common law the early American lawyers appealed to the "inalienable rights of Englishmen," as Jefferson was to base the American claim for independent nationality on "the laws of Nature and of Nature's God."* But later the natural-law doctrines, linked with an appeal to a "higher law" than statutes and other man-made laws, came to be used in a different way and for quite other ends. They were used to entrench statutes that sought to bolster the rights of the possessing groups, or to invalidate those that might undercut those rights. Thus natural law, like the common law itself, played at once a revolutionary and a conservative role in American legal thinking. To achieve continued growth, American law had to break away from the mechanical conceptions which had grown up around it, having their origin in the natural-law and "higher-law" doctrines but taking the form of rigid notions of legal principle. In the hands of unimaginative men this mechanical jurisprudence became a "slot-machine" theory of the law, by which a case was measured against a legal principle much as a nickel might be dropped into a slot, and the judgment was held to come tumbling out ready-made.

In contrast to this, the "revolt against formalism" (as Morton White has called it) reasserted the original spirit and intent of the common-law tradition. Professors Ames and Langdell expressed this revolt in the case method of legal study, through which several generations of lawyers were trained by studying not the "law-in-books" but the "law-in-action" in concrete situations. Justice Holmes was skeptical of all absolutisms: "There is in all men," he wrote, "a demand for the superlative, so much so that the poor devil who has no other way of reaching it attains it by getting drunk." He expressed this skepticism by a gentlemanly Darwinism, in which legal rules and decisions merely summed up the balance of conflicting interests, desires, and power forces at any time, with the judge standing by as umpire, discounting his own preferences. Justice Brandeis, more of a legal and social activist, expressed the revolt in a characteristic type of decision (originally the "Brandeis brief") which sought to keep the law abreast of social progress and found in history, economics, and statistics the envelope of social reality within which the meaning of a case was contained. Pound gave it the name of "sociological jurisprudence" and showed eruditely how it fitted into the history and spirit of the Anglo-American common law, which he made almost into a cult. Justice Cardozo viewed the "nature of the judicial process" from inside the judge's mind, describing how at best a judge must weigh considerations of precedent and change, history and contemporary pressures, private rights and public policy. Jerome Frank and Thurman Arnold called for a philosophy of "legal realism" which described judges, lawyers, and litigants as quite fallible human beings,

* For a further discussion of natural law and other themes considered in this section, see Ch. X, Sec. 2, "American Thought: the Angle of Vision."

and took account of how law impinged on American life not at the lofty levels of constitutional law and philosophy, but at the everyday level of business maneuvers and human entanglements.

In an interesting chapter on the legal profession, in his *American Democracy,* Harold Laski attacked the case method, accusing it of fragmentizing the American legal mind and of leading to the evasion of the social logic of the American class structure. Certainly, by dispensing with general propositions, it has offered a way of avoiding embarrassing political or economic commitments on the part of teachers and judges. Nor has it always escaped formalism, which has found its way into American law by an intricate network of jurisdictional and procedural rules. The mind of the typical lawyer tends to be atomistic and procedural, concerned with the proper forms and safeguards and with keeping his client out of trouble, and resourceful mainly in the legal means for accomplishing the limited objectives set for him. This is what has made the American lawyer so crucial a technician in the scope and growth of corporate power. But it has also led to his partial replacement by the "public-relations" expert, who stresses the irrationals of human conduct rather than the formalisms of legal action. A growing number of businessmen, tired of the expensive delays and intricacies of litigation, have had to include in their contracts a clause for the arbitration of differences. Yet the case-method approach, used along with social and documentary material, has helped keep American law from the paralyzing abstractions that plagued the more logical legal systems.

Three great foreign observers—Burke, De Tocqueville, and Bryce—noted successively how legal-minded the Americans were. Largely they have remained so. Their early interest in the law may have been due to its usefulness in providing intellectual weapons for the revolutionary struggle and the early days of nationhood, just as Gandhi went to London to study law and young Asians and Africans in our own time have turned to Marxist theory to fortify their national liberation movements. Later the law was crucial because it served as one of the two main elements of continuity, along with religion, in holding together a society-in-the-making. Among such a people the relation of law to the lines of social force was bound to continue as a meaningful one.

To start with, American law has been strongly individualist in its emphasis, which has sometimes been explained as the expression of Puritanism and the frontier spirit. Yet in many ways the Puritans cared less about the freedom of the individual than about his control by society; and as for the frontier spirit, its influence was great but only as part of a larger complex. In speaking of legal individualism, we must remember that the protection of the individual's freedom did not end the matter: just as important, perhaps even more so in an acquisitive society, was the protection of his right to improve his lot and enrich himself as a man of property, and the security of that property once it had been amassed. Hence the crucial areas of private law in America were contract (with labor law as merely a subheading of contract law), torts (with emphasis upon the intrusions upon a man's possessions), and equity (with emphasis upon the adaptation of the law to changing economic conditions, and the creation of new property rights not recognized in the formal and established law).

The realm of contract is of particular interest because of the role it has played in bridging the gap between private and constitutional law in America. It was only a step from the use of law in making private bargains and acquisitions secure to its use in fending off interference in the relations between a corporation and its employees. When, for example, New York passed an act at the turn of the century providing for a ten-hour day and sixty-hour week in bakeries in order to protect the health of the workers, the Supreme Court, in the famous case of *Lochner v. New York* (1905), struck it down on the ground that it violated the sanctity of contract. This was the occasion for the notable phrase that Justice Holmes used in his dissent: "The Fourteenth Amendment does not enact Mr. Herbert Spencer's *Social Statics*." The doctrine of liberty of contract was similarly used to invalidate statutes that tried to regulate collective bargaining between employers and employees, just as the common-law doctrine of "master and servant" and the rule of "contributory negligence" were used to leave the worker helpless in industrial accidents until the state compensation laws were finally accepted after a long struggle.

I have been speaking here of contract and related themes in the realm of public as well as private law: but the whole point is that the boundary between the two in America has been not nearly as sharp as is sometimes assumed; one of the master devices used by the lawyers and judges has been to take over the doctrines of private law, which developed in an English society of agriculture, small enterprise, and petty trade, and apply it to the area of public law, where giant business units were seeking to fashion a system of order according to their own interests and their own likes.

Something of the same sort happened in the field of equity. Originally it was intended in England as a way by which the new mercantile class sought to evade the burdens and loosen the rigidities of the still largely feudal phases of the common law. It developed as a "court of conscience" under a separate system of judges (chancellors), and with its own set of doctrines (such as the trust) and its own writs and injunctions. The American tendency has been, except in a few states, to use the same set of courts for both law and equity, but the doctrines and procedures of equity have had a far-reaching effect in the area of business, labor, and property. The management of inheritance and estates, through probate courts, has lent itself to the pressures and corruption of those who have large interests at stake in the inheritance of considerable fortunes. The "trust," once intended in England in order to make land law more flexible, became in America a device for the crushing of competition, the concentration of industrial power, and the pyramiding of corporate control in the hands of a small percentage of the ownership. The injunction, once meant as a way of giving relief through equity before an intolerable situation could become a *fait accompli,* came to be used in America by pliant judges as a way of paralyzing trade-union strike action. The device of equity receivership has been used in the case of looted or badly run railroads and other enterprises as a mode of effecting corporate reorganizations, and some of the most ingenious of American legal dodges have developed in this field, to the profit if not the glory of the American legal profession.

Thus it is that law in a business society develops in the direction required by the power of the dominant business groups. This is as true of American private law, as I have suggested in exploring only two or three areas of it, as it is in public law.* It is within this context that the individualism of American law takes on meaning by accomplishing two ends—that of treating the corporation as an individual personality and that of isolating the ordinary individual from the group action by which he seeks to protect himself in an age of mastodons. Some of the exacting studies of particular judges, like Carl Swisher on Taney, Charles Fairman on Miller, and Leonard Levy on Shaw, portray the harsh and rigorous individualism that pervaded virtually every area of law, private and public alike, during the era of economic *laissez faire.* The hero of American law, as Levy suggests, was the property-owning, liberty-loving, self-reliant, "reasonable" man, and if the giant corporation was recast by the law in the image of this man, it had its reasons for doing so. One should add that he was also the hero of American society, whether celebrated by Jefferson as the freehold farmer, by Hamilton as the town merchant, by Jackson and Frémont as the frontiersman, or by a string of people from Carnegie and McKinley to the current business writers as the independent businessman. There is a remarkable likeness between the American image of the ordinary man and the com-

* For a discussion of the relation of public and constitutional law to American society, see Sec. 9, "Keepers of the Covenant."

mon law's accepted ideal of the American, intended to be used as a standard on which to base legal judgment.

Despite this glamorized ideal, however, the attitudes of Americans toward their legal system are likely to vary from one class to another. For the top income groups the law is an instrument for security and a technology placed at the service of money and power. For the middle class the object is a law-and-order stability, and the law is valued by how effectively it copes with crime, corruption, and class disputes, particularly strike violence. For the trade-unions the law seems very close to a class monopoly, especially in the use of the court injunction to break strikes, and the strength of the state militias when thrown on the side of the corporate employers. For the lowest classes the law is trouble, and its officials are trouble whenever they are encountered. The legal technologies developed largely to meet the needs of the business groups, especially in corporate and tax law and procedure; but the dynamism of legal change has responded to the grievances and protests of the lower-income groups, and new law has emerged when the "sense of injustice" (in Cahn's phrase) has been sharpest.

If there were an American Montesquieu, seeking the "spirit of the laws" in American life, what salient themes and features would he pick? He would, I think, find American law cluttered and individualistic, a "wilderness of single instances"; in the main, uncodified; embodying many of the moralisms and taboos of the American mind in the past, yet changing slowly with changing needs; based on precedent, yet allowing for considerable leeway; for that reason, relatively unpredictable, especially in the "borderline cases" that form the delight of the lawyer; secular, being based on no divinely inspired and revealed source, nor on the original wisdom of some great "lawgiver"; careful of property rights and skillful in using old precedents of individual liberty for the purpose of consolidating new structures of corporate power; matter-of-fact, neither demanding nor receiving reverence, since it is meant for and administered by ordinary men.

The decisions most discussed in the law journals are those in the higher reaches of the legal system—in constitutional and administrative law, in the problems of Federal procedure and jurisdiction, and in the cases involving the rights of the person. Yet the impact of law upon ordinary Americans is most marked in the large areas of private law, like contracts and torts, and in the lower reaches of "courthouse law," both criminal and civil, where the American has his minor brushes and major encounters with the law. Here he forms the image of it that he carries around with him.

While power in America is widely diffused, as I have noted in an earlier section, legal force is the monopoly of the government alone: there are no nongovernmental tribunals (except for the defense services, which are an arm of the government) with the power to punish through the deprivations of freedom. The dramatic expression of the government monopoly of force is the criminal law. From the most sordid and banal cases of routine pickpocketing and prostitution in the police courts to the most sensational murder cases, the criminal law gives to the lives of bored and lonely Americans some fillip of distraction.

The administration of American criminal justice has been often scored as inefficient, corrupt, and archaic, and all three charges are probably true, but again probably no truer than of past eras and other societies. The supervision of criminal justice is mainly in the hands of the local authorities; the Federal courts handle crimes under Federal jurisdiction but try to minimize the appeals from local and state jurisdictions. A lawbreaker is tracked down by local police, prosecuted by a local district attorney and defended by a local lawyer, tried in a local courthouse in a trial reported prominently in the local press, convicted or cleared by a local jury, sentenced by a local judge, and shut up in a local or state prison. At every point there is a good deal of bungling, prejudice, poor judgment, or corruption. Yet on the whole there is a widespread feeling that the results are tolerably good and that the frailties of the whole process are a reflection of the frailties of the society in which it takes place.

The four symbols of "the law" for Americans are the policeman, the district attorney, the judge and jury, and the lawyer.

The encounters with the "cop" are part of American folklore, especially in the traffic violations which are the everyday concern of a motor civilization. The American is not overly impressed by police authority, considering the police officer as a badly paid job holder, not above being "fixed" by a bribe. The police, in turn, are assigned to dangerous and brutalizing tasks, especially in big cities where they must cope with lawless hoodlums spreading "terror in the streets"; and they are exposed to the temptations of petty bribery and the Big Money. An "honest cop," accordingly is considered by the cynics much rarer than he actually is. The fact is that police administration has its pathology, but that American cities from California to New York have been learning to use the new technologies of police science, as used for example by August Vollmer, the police chief of Berkeley, California, with motorized squads, a system of signal calls and radio communication, technically competent crime detection and identification, and a community-wide approach to juvenile delinquency and crime prevention.

The rise of a modern police system came very late in American cities: even with over 300,000 people, New York had only a "citizens' watch"; many cities had bloody riots that the ward constables and watch were helpless to handle, and not until 1844 was the first permanent police department set up in New York. In more than a century since then the connection of the police with vice and racketeering graft has been often spread on the record, from the Lexow Investigation of the 1890s to the Kefauver Committee a half century later. Steffens wrote his *Shame of the Cities* about corruption at the turn of the century, yet when Albert Deutsch made the rounds of much the same cities in the 1950s after the pivotal work of exposure by the Kefauver Committee hearings, while he still found corruption he also found skill and professional standards, and he concluded that few communities would tolerate for a moment the depths of police degradation that Steffens described.

Even more important than the problem of police honesty is that of equal justice under the law at the police and prosecutor level. It is hard, for example, to be a Negro in the South—in Birmingham or Biloxi—and expect human or just treatment at the hands of the local police. But it is almost equally hard for a Negro in Harlem, Chicago, or Detroit, or a labor organizer in almost any Southern or Midwest town, or a recent immigrant speaking with a telltale accent, to get equal treatment with others. Instances of police use of "third-degree" methods are common enough to have received recognition by the appeals courts. The inherent violence of modern life finds outlet both in the lawlessness of lawbreakers and the counter-lawlessness of some of the guardians of the law, especially when used against obscure and illiterate men. The Wickersham Report in the 1930s documented the use by police of the "third-degree" methods of secret pretrial examination to extort confessions, and the studies of crime reporters indicate that the practice persists.

Moving several layers up from the cops, the system of electing judges, district attorneys, county prosecutors, and the surrogates who administer estates and supervise bankruptcy proceedings, makes the administration of justice part of the machinery of political influence and power. Often these are regarded as plums in the cake of political patronage; and the theme of the crooked D.A., or one who is outwitted by the defense attorney, is a constant one in the movies and the crime stories. But so also is the D.A. who sets out to "clean up" the lawlessness of powerful criminals and politicians, and as a heroic figure is sought out for mayor, governor, or even President.

The prosecutor is the dominant figure of criminal law. If he has a flair for publicity he can leave ruined lives and reputations behind him on the road to political preferment. But he has also a vast discretionary power which allows him to decide what indictments to present to the Grand Jury, what lesser pleas to accept, what cases to bring to trial. The impact of the market on American law is shown in the bargaining process by which most of the business of a district attorney in the big cities is transacted: only one case out of fifteen in a city like New York is ever brought to trial, the rest being settled in pretrial negotiations through the D.A.'s office. This is a "marketing orientation" with a vengeance. As for the trial itself, the theory behind it is that of truth-by-combat. American justice has experimented with new psychological devices like the "lie detector," but it still clings chiefly to the adversary method of getting at the truth—one well suited to the popular American conditioning to games. Unlike the Continental system, the judge sits as referee instead of as inquisitor until the verdict is reached, when he becomes the vessel of punishment; the witnesses are the immediate targets; the real players are the battery of counsel; and the jury of one's peers weighs the evidence to reach its decision.

The jury system has latterly been under attack, mainly on the grounds that most jurymen are irritated with the burden of jury duty, that they are bored with the cases and incompetent to see through the tactics of lawyer and prosecutor or resist their blandishments, that in a press-dominated trial they are easily prejudiced and become the dupes of emotional manipulation. Descriptively this is not far of the mark. But the American as juror is part of the same equalitarian experiment that includes the American as husband or father, wife or mother, the American as voter, the American as consumer. The jury system is one of the remaining survivals of the Jacksonian idea that there is nothing over the head of the common man for which he cannot use his native intelligence. The purpose of the jury system is to elicit the common experience of men and bring it to bear on the problem of guilt and innocence. However well or badly it achieves this, it also performs the function of training the juror—and along with him the large body of newspaper readers—in the weighing of the human heart. Americans commit more misdemeanors than felonies, more crimes of fraud than of force, more offenses against property than against the person: but in every case there must be a scrutiny of motive.

To say that the juror usually does it badly is beside the point. He is probably no more easily duped as juror than the same man is in politics or love or family relations or the wilderness of commodities. If an open society is to survive, he must learn to find his way in each of these areas. To play God with a man's life or his freedom in the deliberations of a jury room may be more dramatic than to shape the destiny of a child in the nursery or of a whole nation in the polling booth, but it is no more important. In each case it is a God-playing role which cannot be delegated to an elite that claims to know best what is good for the rabble.

This may be related to the fact that Americans have become a nation of amateur sleuths. The "whodunit" is likely to thrive under democratic systems, as in both England and America, where legal judgments are not delivered by authoritarian tribunals but where the rules of evidence are rigorously applied. With the modern American press the evidence is sifted not only by the jury but (in notorious cases) by the whole locality or even the nation. From being a nation of jurymen it is only a step to being a nation of detectives. The "private eye," who shows up the complacency or stupidity of police officials and D.A.s, becomes a vicarious symbol of the revenge that every reader takes for his brushes with the law. The improbability of the murderer's identity in the whodunits (he is rarely the person to whom the evidence points) is a reflection of the premises of the law of evidence in a democracy. A basic assumption of American law is that a man is held innocent until he is shown to be guilty. It shocks an American to discover that an innocent man has spent years in jail before the evidence turns up that proves the mistake or the "frame." The jury system brings to bear on the evidence the non-expert flexibility of everyday experience; courtroom procedure brings to bear the accumulated wisdom of centuries spent in the guarding of a person's rights; but the whodunit brings to bear on the evidence the combined reader role of being at once detective and rebel. Since in a democracy "everyman is his own historian," everyman is also his own sleuth and his own judge and jury, and his triumph is that of showing up the authoritarian fable. American legal attitudes are to their marrow antiauthoritarian. That America is a government "of laws and not of men" is even more strikingly proved in the wish fulfillments of the whodunits than in the formal vindications of judicial review.

It need scarcely be added that the American attitude toward the courts is not always one of reverence. The exception is the higher courts, especially the Supreme Court. The lower ones, from the local magistrates and police courts up, command little respect. Unlike the Continent, there is no specialized training for the judicial profession as such. The judges come up from the ranks of lawyers and go back to legal practice when their terms are up or when they find a judge's salary inadequate. This preserves a circulation of talents and prevents the judges from being cut off from the realities of legal practice and procedure. But it is hard to respect "the dignity of the Court" when it is presided over by a man whom you knew only yesterday as your legal competitor and perhaps even inferior, since it is not always the lawyers of ability and integrity who achieve the judicial robes. The "contempt of court" procedures in America are less rigorously invoked than in the English courts, and the newspapers are given greater latitude in comment on a case before or during trial, especially in the more sensational criminal cases on which their circulation often depends. It is only recently that emphasis has been placed on the role of both prosecutor and defense attorney as officers of the Court, thus giving the judge greater control over court behavior. In his social position in the community, the judge has, however, the advantage even over the rich and successful lawyers; and in the South especially, the early tradition that arms and the law were the two professions of gentlemen, and that the able lawyer who became a judge was also the repository of learning and influence, has carried over to the present day.

De Tocqueville's famous chapter on the place of the lawyers in American society may seem an anachronism now, but it is not hard to see why they played so great a role in American history. In a new country, with claims and rights in flux and the distribution of authority still to be shaped, lawyers were needed to set lines of division and organize the local will. Since the feudal baron and the manorial lord no longer existed, and the clergyman and schoolteacher did not have the required prestige and worldliness, the lawyer emerged as the ideal amalgam of learning and practicality. He took his seat in the state assemblies and the national Congress, and with his knowledge of the drafting and interpretation of laws he became indispensable. As the country grew, the mounting needs of business enterprise and especially of corporate organization and reorganization gave further importance to the lawyers, who were now needed to tell the new ruling group what they could or could not do legally.

The role of the lawyer began to change. Whatever his failings, the early lawyer had a secular mental discipline that was almost the only one available in public affairs and had learned law as part of the arts of statecraft. The frontier lawyer and the circuit-riding judge had the vigor revealed in the later careers of men as divergent in social views as Justices Field and Miller of the Supreme Court. But when, after the Civil War, the big corporate interests began to move into the seats of power, disintegration set in. The lawyer became a hired man—the "Great Mouthpiece" for the corporations or for the marginal local bosses and racketeers.

With the turn of the century, men like Holmes, Brandeis, and Hughes made efforts to bring lawyers to a consciousness of the public responsibility of their profession. Holmes especially spoke of the chance that lawyers had to "study the law greatly" and to "wreak themselves" upon their subject by seeing "the relation between their fact and the frame of the universe." Brandeis spent his great talents on reform causes and became known as "the People's Attorney." The law schools and law journals subjected legal decisions to an intense scrutiny, setting standards for judicial decisions. The legal historians began to emphasize the brilliant names in the history of the American legal profession, from Marshall and Story to Stimson, Hughes, and Stone. The constitutional scholars became aware of the extent to which the lawyers, in their briefs and arguments, shaped the course of the law—sometimes even more creatively than the judges because they gave the judges their cues.

Yet one had to remain skeptical of whether a profession so tied to the holders of power could free itself and become autonomous. The big Wall Street legal firms tended to become "law factories," organized much like the big industrial corporations which they represented. In the struggles between labor and the corporations, the trade-unions proved powerful enough to develop their own competent legal staffs as well as their own research organizations. But the real test of law as a public service profession came after World War II, when the challenge to civil liberties found few members of the bar with the courage to risk their economic prospects by defending unpopular causes and hated men. The lawyers had moved a long way since the time when John Adams defended the British commander charged with the massacre of American patriots on Boston Common. The American attitudes toward the lawyer are hard to define. His social position varies with his success and wealth, but is likely to be a good deal higher than on the European Continent, and similar to that of a businessman or corporate executive. Yet the distrust of him persists.

Thurman Arnold pointed up the paradox of Americans' calling for law enforcement at the same time that they multiply the laws beyond the point of enforceability and violate them from day to day. This may be less an American trait than the very human one of wanting, in the sphere of the law as elsewhere, both to eat one's cake and have it. In all societies, formal codes are set up which go largely unheeded because their rigid enforcement would cripple the practical needs of social life and violate the insistent impulses of man's nature.

The Americans have sought to solve the problem by alternations of neglect and enforcement, as shown by their traffic regulations, their disastrous Prohibition experiment, their gambling and betting laws, their vice and narcotics laws. They have moved between the twin beats of complacency and conscience, cynicism and Puritanism, silence and crackdown. There will be long periods of "patterned evasion" of the legal norms through corruption and the "Big Fix." Then there will be a "crime wave" or some other index of alarm, followed by the inevitable crackdown on racketeers, "vice kings," fee-splitters, "ambulance-chasers," narcotics peddlers and addicts, gamblers, bookies, prostitutes, gang warriors, traffic violators, or just vagrants and bums. In this crackdown the police, prosecutors, judges, press, clergy, and politicians tumble over one another in an hysteria of legal enforcement, feeling at once virtuous and inwardly silly. Then a vast apathy will blanket the community, and the silence will be as before.

If this were not similar to other polarities in American life, one would be tempted to speak of it—with its alternating fits of elation and gloomy quiescence—as a sign of a manic-depressive personality. But it is more sensible to trace this pattern back to the Puritan attitudes, with their combination of moralism and practicality; or to cite the experience of frontier law, as shown in the California Gold Rush days, when the new communities had long spells of complacent laxity of law and in morals, followed by a reckless vigilantism. Behind the law-and-order crackdown there remains even in the modern period more than a trace of lawlessness and vigilantism. Judge Learned Hand, speaking of a roundup of vagrants and petty criminals listed on the police blotters by Grover Whalen when he was Police Commissioner, and the general approval of press and citizenry, pointed out that any of these men would bridle at the thought that someone should be punished at official whim without evidence of guilt: "they are loyal to our institutions in the abstract, but they do not mean to take them too seriously in application." One suspects that the law-and-order obsession of the American is fed by a sense of guilt about his own circumventions of the law, and by his increasing insecurity in a world in which the old codes no longer seem adequate. The enforcement crackdowns are thus related to the psychic and emotional sources from which come also the periodic raids on civil liberties.

There are other forms of patterned evasion. There is the deliberate circumvention of the law in tax evasion, or in the sabotaging of safety inspection codes. There are the cases where, as in divorce law, the legal norms take too rigorous a view of social needs, as by the paradoxical "rule of collusion" that no divorce will be granted where both husband and wife are anxious to have it. Here the American practice is the tacit legal violation of the law through uncontested divorce actions in fictitious jurisdictions. Finally there are the areas of legal distortion through archaism, as in the law governing sex offenses, where the punishment of "statutory rape" or of "sodomy" takes an approach to human behavior based on the Hebraic-Puritan theological tradition, without taking into account the insights of psychology.

While American law is a loosely fitting coat, draping the figure of American life too haphazardly at some points while pinching too tightly at others, the Americans find it a fair approximation and have learned to live with it. They might even feel uncomfortable with too snug a fit. They take their system of law a little as the French or Italians take their system of Catholicism—observing most of its rituals, living up to few of its precepts, but clinging to it nonetheless with a tenacious if genial infidelity.

I have spoken of the particularism, the pragmatism, and the matter-of-factness of the American legal system, of the relation of the great areas of private law to American property and class attitudes, of the spirit and temper of American criminal law, of the policeman, prosecutor, judge, and lawyer as symbols of the administration of justice, of the somewhat schizoid attitude Americans take toward law enforcement, and of the loose but operative fit between the law and the social realities.

Another instance of the affinity of the spirit of American law and of American life is in the unpredictability of both. One of the major aims of all legal systems is to achieve the maximum security and stability through predictability. Where the law is codified and handed down by authoritarian tribunals as part of a centralized system of justice, the predictability of judgments is great but there is likely to be little dynamism in the society. In America the opposite is true. Justice Holmes once defined law as quite simply "the prediction of what the courts will do in a given case." Or, as he put it, the law is "the hypostasis of a prophecy"—which is to say that it is a gamble. The "bad man" gambles on what he can get away with; the law is the croupier playing for the house against him.

This element of risk in law, which might prove too costly in a less dynamic society, fitted the mood of the Americans as long as the element of risk was strong in their society as well. The large number of state jurisdictions, each with its own line of precedents on disputed points of law, added to the confusion and the unpredictability. One reason perhaps why the litigiousness of Americans is not as great as in some other social systems, despite a "litigation neurosis" to be found in certain personality types, has been that litigation is expensive and risky, and the delays long. What American society has always wanted—and American law as well—is to get the disagreements settled and to move on.

Yet not without at least a backward glance at the moral base of the legal decisions and solutions. American law, like English, focuses not on abstract right and wrong but on specific acts within a frame of traditional moral codes. But these codes are not always clear enough to resolve the question of whether the moral claims as between plaintiff and defendant should be translated into legal penalty and award. In a perceptive classification and review of the typical problems of the "moral decision" in the context of American law and society, Edmond Cahn notes the cases of injury to trespassing children at play, of sexual relationships, of the conduct of husband and wife in family disintegration, of honesty or deceit in business, of spite offenses against property, of tax cheating, of the impulse to rescue the unfortunate, of suicide and death.

Lecky pointed out that in an industrial civilization like England the needs of commerce and business put a premium upon honesty and truth-telling which did not apply in the preindustrial labor cultures. He called this "industrial veracity." This is even truer of American life, where the fabric of business would crumble if fraud were permitted to grow rampant and the law did not enforce at least a minimum of compliance with honesty. Given the fluid character of American family life and sexual mores, the same applies in those areas. To be sure, at no time in American life has there been a greater impulse to rethink questions of moral behavior than in the past quarter century, and at no time has there been a sharper challenge to the traditional codes, especially from psychology and psychiatry. It is in the American law journals and psychiatric publications that the question of the moral responsibility for crime on the part of a mentally unbalanced person was being most hotly debated: an effort was made to displace McNaghten's Rule—whether the accused knew that what he was doing was wrong—with one which (as in the decision in the Durham case) allows for the newly revealed subtleties of mental disturbance. Yet one may doubt whether this effort will wholly succeed.

With all the turbulence of shifting moral standards, American thinking is too deeply rooted in the idea of the individual's rights ever to become very relaxed about his obligations which form the other side of the shield. It is too concerned with the fullness of human personality ever to move away from the idea of individual responsibility. The forces that shaped American law in a frontier society, and then in a capitalist society, will continue to shape and reshape it in a society of abundance and welfare, where the collisions that occur have their greatest meaning in the quest for personal expression.

9. *Keepers of the Covenant*

At the apex of the American legal system stands the Supreme Court as interpreter of the Constitution. Walter Bagehot said that every government must contain something of the "dignified" or "majestic" principle, rooted in men's emotions and in what we should today call the irrational mind. Its purpose is to give government a cohesive force outlasting the temporary political changes. This element is enshrined in the Constitution, and amidst all the turbulences of history the Constitution as eidolon has remained a fixture in the American mind.

The fact that the Constitution is a written charter, lending itself thus to idolization; that it grew out of the War for Independence, has lasted since the beginning of the nation's history, and survived even a bloody Civil War; that within its framework America has risen to wealth and world power; that it has not been shattered by the tensions of the major depressions and wars; that under it American freedoms have not been extinguished, although they have at times been severely limited; that it has been the object of imitation by other peoples: these are some of the facts that have fed the Constitution cult. But beyond all these there is the human need for roots, which finds expression by clinging to some strong symbol of allegiance.

The symbol of the Constitution has fulfilled this need. It has been invoked by the Americans of earlier immigrant origins—the "native" Americans—and equally by the newer Americans who have worshiped it the more eagerly because they found in it the symbol of what makes Americans equal before the law. Amidst the change and decay of human circumstance the Constitution—presumably framed in wisdom, maintained by courage, and proved by time—must have seemed to almost all Americans the great fact which changeth not and therefore abideth.

Nevertheless, if one analyzes the imagery of belief it has embodied, this unvarying symbol has had a changing content. The Constitution started as a *compact*—whether of the states or of the people is still disputed. Later the Civil War burned it into the consciousness of Americans as a *symbol of indestructible union.* Later still, when the Supreme Court interpreted some of the constitutional doctrines in a way to invalidate legislation, the Constitution became in the popular mind mainly *a set of limitations* on the power of government. Only after the Supreme Court crisis under the New Deal did it clearly emerge as an *instrument of government,* capable of being used in the people's interests, flexible enough to be a living Constitution in a living society. Recently, under the tensions that have beset civil liberties everywhere, the Constitution has come to be stressed as *a code of freedom:* a set of guarantees of human freedom and a symbol of vigilance against the arbitrary use of man's power over man.

Since the Constitution is America's covenant, its guardians are the keepers of the covenant and therefore touched with its divinity. As the tenders of the sacred flame, the justices of the Supreme Court cannot help playing the role of a sacerdotal group. By reason of its technical function every priesthood exercises a political power: since they alone are privy to the mysteries on which the destiny of the tribe depends, the priests must be consulted on what is permissible and what is taboo in tribal policy—a veto power which filters every major political decision and is thus a form of decision-making even when the Court deliberately refrains from exercising its power.

The American Constitution started without a specific grant to its judicial priesthood of this taboo power ("judicial review"), although the explicit grant was debated at the Constitutional Convention and the evidence is that it was at least implicitly intended. But early in the Supreme Court's history Chief Justice John Marshall boldly asserted the power of the Court to decide the constitutionality of an act of Congress: the claim lay dormant for some time but was resumed in the mid-nineteenth century after it had been applied in many cases to the acts of state legislatures. While there was a bitter challenge to this power by the Jeffersonians and their constitutional theorist, John Taylor, and debate flared up anew with the Dred Scott decision, the income-tax cases, and other crises in constitutional history, the Court's assertion of judicial review was never effectively resisted.

The reasons are clear enough. It fitted well with the needs of a Federal system: the strongest argument for judicial review is the chaos that would flow from unresolved clashes between states and national government. It fitted with the fears the big corporations later felt in the face of rising movements for social legislation. Finally it fitted with the psychic hunger of Americans for a symbol of ultimate guardianship of their rights under the law. Holmes said of John Marshall that his greatness lay in the place he held in "the campaign of history"—the "fact that he was *there*." The role he served was as a crucial link between nationalism, constitutionalism, and a rising commercial system. In its exercise of the power of judicial review the Supreme Court has been one of the chief elements in the planetary struggle for power within the economy and the social structure.

One may stretch the term (as I have suggested earlier) and say that there are two Constitutions in America—one the formal Constitution as interpreted by the Federal judiciary, the second the structure of power within American society. With the triumph of the business system after the Civil War, the chief energies of the Court—especially in the period from 1885 to the Depression of 1929—were directed toward making the legal Constitution fit with the structure of economic power, thus bringing the two Constitutions into line. The purpose was to exempt the business groups from hampering legislative and administrative controls by both state and Federal governments. "There are certain fundamental social and economic laws," said Justice Sutherland two years before he was appointed to the Court, "beyond the right of official control." He was clearly a fit person to effect the legal encrustation of *laissez faire*. It showed again that public law in a capitalist state, perhaps even more than private law, tends to take the shape demanded by the protection of the dominant property interests.

But the business groups had to pay a costly price for this temporary victory. To gain the victory the Court had to distort traditional and established constitutional doctrine; to take the Fourteenth Amendment, framed to protect Negroes against discrimination by Southern states after the Civil War, and use it to ward off regulatory legislation from business corporations; to stretch the meaning of "person," as I have mentioned, to include the corporation; and to stretch the meaning of "due process" from the guarantee of normal judicial procedures to the tabooing of reformist legislation.

Once this was done, however, the door was opened wide to the use of the Constitution as a living instrument for the needs of a living society. The game of adapting constitutional doctrines could be played by a Miller, a Brandeis, a Black, and a Douglas as well as by a Field and a Sutherland. If there could be a constitutional theology of profits and property there could be a counter-theology as well. The Devil could learn to quote this particular Scripture. The pressure of labor and the farmers and of reform movements could become more clamorous, if less well financed, than the pressure of corporate interests. Whenever a conservative Court showed an inclination to stand pat against legislation that seemed to meet the felt needs of the day, the liberal groups had the ready answer of pointing to the free-and-easy handling of judicial concepts by conservative majorities when it suited their interests. A Constitution whose amending process is notable for its brass-bound rigidity showed surprising qualities of flexibility without formal amendment. As "Mr. Dooley" put it, with a certain sophistication about the implications of judicial review: "Whether or not trade follows the flag, one thing is clear: the Supreme Court follows the election returns." The seeming detachment of the Court from political struggles was illusory. The Supreme Court bench was the quiet spot in the center of a tornado.

The great crisis of the Supreme Court's role in American society came with the New Deal's challenge to the conservative Court majority. For almost three quarters of a century the Court had operated as a bottleneck of social policy; but the Great Depression of the thirties, bringing the need for a program adequate to meet it, broke the bottleneck. Thus the economic crisis brought along a constitutional crisis. Its first phase was the refusal of the Court majority to admit that a social program with which they disagreed could be constitutional, its second phase the effort of President Roosevelt's "court-packing plan" to secularize the judicial priesthood. The Roosevelt plan was beaten, but not until the third phase, when the priesthood had clearly shown it was ready to withdraw the taboo it had invoked.

Out of this came the present equilibrium of the Supreme Court as a power institution. The power of judicial review remains, and along with it much of the sanctity of the keepers of the Covenant. The "dignified" principle that encases the Constitution has happily not been broken. On the other hand, the Court's power to frustrate future movements which may seek to organize the national will in meeting an emergency, as the New Deal did, is no longer likely to go unchallenged.

"I may not know much about law," wrote Theodore Roosevelt in 1912, "but I do know how one can put the fear of God into judges." He was talking of the movement for the popular recall of judges. But such movements have lost their appeal, mainly because judges and lawyers and much of lay opinion have come to understand that judicial interpretation is flexible enough to make the crude device of recall unnecessary. Americans have learned some of the facts of life about the workings of the judicial process. They no longer believe so readily that judicial decisions are babies brought by constitutional storks. They know something of the pain and wrack of the whole adventure of social organization, with its deep-rooted problems and its difficult solutions, out of which new constitutional interpretations emerge and old ones are modified.

It need no longer be argued vehemently that there is a political cast to many Supreme Court appointments, but the argument is often greatly oversimplified. Certainly the Supreme Court has never been "democratic" in the sense that appointments are meant to represent a cross section of the nation. Nor is the Court democratic in the mechanically responsive sense of changing with the shifting waves of popular opinion: one of the reasons for giving the judges life tenure and putting them beyond the reach of political and popular vindictiveness was to fashion a judicial independence without which any effort to interpret the basic frame of constitutional principle as principle would be a sham. There can be too much flexibility in judicial interpretation, as well as too little, especially if the flexibility is dictated by opportunism and is a surrender to the passions of the moment.

The great appointments have been those of farsighted men who could grow on the bench into judicial statesmanship. Sometimes, as in the appointment of Holmes by President Theodore Roosevelt, these choices were made on the mistaken assumption that the judge would go along with the political policy of the President (after the Holmes dissent in the Northern Securities case, T. R. is reported to have cried, "I could carve out of a banana a man with more backbone."). In other instances the political purpose of the appointment is well known and is carried out, as when Jackson appointed Taney or when Truman appointed Vinson. Sometimes a judge has started his judicial career inauspiciously, as with Hugo Black's admission of early membership in the Ku Klux Klan, and grown to judicial greatness. Sometimes a series of remarkably able appointees have been followed by a series of mediocrities, as with the general level of President Truman's appointments (Burton, Vinson, Clark, and Minton) when compared with the general level of the Roosevelt appointments (Black, Reed, Frankfurter, Murphy, Douglas, Jackson, and Rutledge). Sometimes, as with Stone and Cardozo, the unmistakable sentiment of the whole legal profession has made the choice of a particular man inevitable.

Yet on the whole it has been true of membership on the Supreme Court, as of the Presidential office, that the garments of office have expanded or shrunk with the dimensions of the wearer. Some of the great judges, like Marshall appointed by Adams, Harlan appointed by Hayes, Stone appointed by Coolidge, Hughes appointed by Taft and reappointed by Hoover, and Warren appointed by Eisenhower, might well have made greater Presidents than the Presidents who appointed them. It is true that no member of the Court has ever been elected to the Presidency, although Hughes came close and Taft reversed the process. On the whole, however, it has been a healthy tradition that the Court should not be considered a pathway to Presidential office. The very fact that the Court does have decision-making power of vast political consequence makes it even more important for the justices to be invulnerable to the charge of playing for political advantage. It takes great courage to fill the role of final constitutional arbiter with an eye to the enduring lines of national growth and greatness, rather than of any particular group, pressure, or power.

It is not necessary for biographers wholly to unclothe the judges in order to disrobe them and show the street clothes under their traditional vestments of office. A Supreme Court judge is a human being, which means that he is a thinking and valuing animal, with emotions about his fellow human beings and often very decided convictions about the processes of government. Their earlier careers—as corporate and utility lawyers, as governors and Senators, as attorney generals or heads of administrative agencies, as law school teachers, as crusading reformers—are usually a pretty good indication of the kind of judges they will make. To take an instance almost at random, of a mediocre judge who was nevertheless as Chief Justice an efficient presider over the Court: Melville W. Fuller was a Northern Democrat who had been a prosperous business lawyer; he had opposed both Abolition and Secession, had disapproved of the Fourteenth Amendment, and had been a vehement champion of the doctrine of "hard money." It was not too hard to foretell that he would vote to hold the Federal Income Tax of 1894 unconstitutional.

Or to take a more eminent instance: after the experience of the nation with Taft as President it was not hard to project his career into the Supreme Court and predict that he would make a highly political judge. Taft later boasted that during one term as President he had been lucky to have six Supreme Court appointments to make, while his successor Woodrow Wilson could make only three in two terms. One of those three, McReynolds, who had shown social fervor as attorney general, turned the tables on the guessers and became a conservative (although still unpredictable) justice. But Taft regarded the other two, Brandeis and Clarke, as "of socialistic tendency"—and it might be added that the leaders of the legal profession and the holders of economic power agreed with him about Brandeis, as witness the massive effort to kill his nomination, first in the Senate Judiciary Committee and then in the vote on the floor. Taft saw shrewdly that one of the high stakes of the 1920 election was the fact that four of the justices had passed the retiring age and would probably have to be replaced. "There is no greater domestic issue," he said about the 1920 campaign, "than the maintenance of the Supreme Court as the bulwark to enforce the guarantee that no man shall be deprived of his property without due process of law." Harding's election underscored the political realism of Taft's view, for in three years there were four new appointments, including Taft himself, Sutherland, Butler, and Sanford; these four joined three other conservatives to form a bloc of seven who consistently outvoted and isolated Holmes and Brandeis. When Taft met his colleagues as Chief Justice he told them in conference, "I have been appointed to reverse a few decisions," and (he wrote later), "I looked right at old man Holmes when I said it." Even after Coolidge had appointed Stone, who seemed at first relatively "safe" but developed into a fearlessly independent member of the Court, there was still a minority of only three at best on crucial cases. When Hoover appointed Cardozo the potential minority became four, but his appointment of Roberts and Hughes kept the majority safe. It was this political approach to Court appointments which evoked the drastic and equally political counterapproach of the Franklin Roosevelt court-packing proposal, and later his deliberately political appointments of New Dealers to the Court.

I have given some detailed scrutiny here to the appointments in one period of the Court's history, but the same would be true of the earlier periods to a much higher degree. During the whole stretch of Republican Presidential power from 1860 to 1912 (except for Cleveland's terms) the proportion of property-minded, business-minded, and corporate-minded judges who reached the Court was, needless to say, very high. The striking fact is that great judges do manage to emerge from this process—men like Marshall, Taney, Miller, Harlan, Holmes, Hughes, Brandeis, Stone, Cardozo, Black, Frankfurter, Douglas, Warren. (There were also judges like Van Devanter, who was a brilliant craftsman although a reactionary one and unable to write.) It would be hard to find a governing group in any society to match these men in talent, character, vision, and statesmanship. They have proved a fit corollary to the gallery of great Presidents.

The task of the Chief Justice is especially difficult, since he must keep the Court as cohesive as possible, iron out differences that need not be aired, avoid too-public splits, assign the writing of the majority opinion (here he can exercise a subtle influence of great importance), and set the whole intellectual tone of the Court. Marshall, Hughes, Stone, perhaps Vinson, and certainly Warren lived up notably to the dimensions of this great office. The case of Stone, which can be read in meticulous detail in Mason's biography, is especially interesting. He was appointed Attorney General to sweeten the stench left by Harding's Daugherty; he campaigned for Coolidge with speeches that were stilted and stuffed-shirtish; he performed his job as Attorney General with distinction, yet when he was appointed to the Court a few liberal Senators, like Norris, who were distrustful of his having had the Morgan bank as a client, opposed his confirmation. "I have always been sorry," said Stone later, "that I didn't have the Morgan House for my clients more than I did." And Norris, in 1941, voted to confirm him as Chief Justice: Stone had shown that capacity to rise above his earlier conditioning which is the saving quality of greatness in a judge.

One of the problems of the Court has been the overwhelming pressure of judicial business. In 1925 Congress reorganized the Court's work, and later changes were made in the same direction so that the Court would not have to remedy the wrongs of every litigant on appeal, but could choose the cases involving important principles of constitutional interpretation. The real question has always been what approach the Court would adopt to these principles.

The traditional "great split" between the liberal and conservative views of the Court's function, which Franklin Roosevelt phrased in popular terms as a split between those who cared about "property rights" and those who cared about "human rights," still retains a good deal of its meaning. But the livelier controversy in recent years, which split the liberal camp itself, was the conflict between the school of social "activism" or "dynamism" and that of "judicial self-limitation" or "self-restraint." Both schools of judges went beyond the earlier pretense that there is something fixed and known, which is called "the law" and which judges make known to the people. They recognized what Charles E. Hughes meant when he said that "we live under a Constitution, but the Constitution is what the Supreme Court says it is." He gave the simplest possible definition of what has come to be called "judicial supremacy." The two schools differed, however, in the method by which they could best live up to their task of interpreting constitutional powers, rights, and immunities.

The "self-limitation" school, deriving largely from Justice Holmes and notably championed by Justices Frankfurter and Jackson, rested on Holmes's insistence that the judges should minimize their role, stay out of the social struggles as far as possible, accept state and Federal legislation unless clearly outside the powers of the legislatures, and decide cases on technical and procedural grounds where possible in order to avoid committing the Constitution to principles that may later prove mischievous. The philosophy of the school was well expressed by Justice Stone in the agricultural controls case, when he warned his colleagues that "the only restraint we have is our self-restraint." Ultimately it is based on the premise that judicial supremacy can become a form of tyranny, that judges are frail and ought to discipline their sentiments, that all of government and human life is a fragile process, and that a Court is wisest when it raises as few broad controversial issues of principle as possible.

One difficulty here of course is that even the decision to use self-restraint is an exercise of judicial power, and even a judge like Robert H. Jackson, who carried this principle far in most of his judicial opinions, broke it on something like the case of the religious liberties of the Jehovah's Witnesses. Another difficulty is that the principle of staying away from principles, and of narrowing every constitutional issue to the minimum one compatible with the immediate facts, can become a bleak function for the judicial process. The danger of the doctrine of judicial restraint is that it becomes judicial abdication. Still another danger, as I note below, is that when it is applied to the problems of legislative or administrative interference with civil liberties, it leaves the field of action open to arrogant or frightened and sometimes hysterical legislative majorities, acting often under the pressure of intense minorities in the population.

The "activist" school, championed by Justices Black and Douglas, was derived largely from Justice Brandeis and held that the Supreme Court has a positive role to play not only in guarding civil liberties but in setting a legal frame for the quest of a greater measure of economic and social democracy. This approach was strengthened by the philosophy of the New Deal and the appointments that Franklin Roosevelt made to the Court. At base it represents an instrumental approach to the judicial process. It candidly makes a distinction between the protection of individual freedom and the progress of economic and social advance. In the latter case it is willing to go along with legislative majorities and administrative action on the theory that these broad issues have been hammered out under long public debate and represent the response to the needs of the time. But in the case of civil liberties, where freedoms of long standing may be threatened by emotional new doctrines expressed through hasty majorities, it holds that the role of the Court is that of acting to protect the old freedoms against the new dangers. The field of administrative law is especially important because of its rapid recent growth: in this field the school of judicial restraint is unlikely to go beyond the findings of facts by administrative agencies and restricts itself to questions of law; the activist school, on the other hand, will review findings of fact if it suspects that they conceal an instance of arbitrary power by the agency. Just as the weakness of judicial self-restraint is that it may become a form of abdication, so the weakness of judicial activism is that it may become a form of arbitrary intervention by the Court itself into the other areas of government and into state action.

The period of the "cold war" during the decade after 1945 presented the Court with one of its great testing periods. The Court at first faltered. The classic distinction between belief and action was blurred, and the Court accepted the dubious notion that if a number of people "conspired" or "organized" to "advocate" subversion, Congress should legislate for their punishment. Once the gate was thus opened, some very dangerous freightage managed to get through. But it should be added that at the end of the 1945-1955 period the Court grew firmer. In 1957 came the climactic decision in the case of the California Communists under the Smith Act. Speaking through Justice Harlan, the Court defined "organize" strictly to mean the creation (not continuance) of an organization, and in defining "advocacy" it made incitement to action—rather than mere belief—the test for the juries to pass on. In the Watkins Case, Chief Justice Warren cut down the cancerous growth of the Congressional investigating power, held that a Congressional inquiry must be "in furtherance of a legitimate task of Congress" (adding "Who can define the meaning of 'un-American'?"), and reminded the Congressional committees that "there is no Congressional power to expose for the sake of exposure." It was clear that the Supreme Court had finally ridden out the cold-war crisis and had put into broad legal terms the calmer judgment of the majority of the American people.

There has been considerable recent discussion of whether the Supreme Court is a democratic or an undemocratic instrument of government.

The stronger view would seem that it is democratic in its response to the larger fluctuations of public opinion, and its accessibility to changing Presidential regimes. One should add, however, that for long stretches, especially from the 1880s to the 1930s, it lagged behind the best legal and judicial opinion. In essence what this means is that the Court is part of the changes and chances of its time, and also part of the power structure in the society as a whole. It was this quality, of being part of the power structure, that made the social thinkers of the 1930s and 1940s attack it as "undemocratic." On balance one may say that the Court is part of American democracy, but that it serves as a tempering influence both upon social and economic advance and also upon attacks on the freedom of the person.

The best type of judge is one who maintains the kind of skepticism of ideas which Holmes had, and has the saving impulse to restrain his own power that Stone had, but believes that even within this frame of skepticism and restraint the Court has both the duty and opportunity to make judicial action square with a social humanism of the kind Brandeis strove for. This means that there can be no single formula for the judicial process, and that the judge cannot escape the infinitely difficult task of weighing his intellectual caution and skepticism against his social boldness and his moral faith in human possibility.

One of the best instances of how a great Court acted in some such spirit, under a great Chief Justice, was the unanimous decision in the school segregation cases, written by Chief Justice Warren. It represented a break from the turn-of-the-century segregation decisions, and it broke with them sharply and boldly, without any apparatus of protective citation and without the hypocrisy of trying to "distinguish" so that an actual judicial change would seem to be no change at all. In this sense it was a political decision, yet not in the narrow spirit of being a partisan one. North and South alike, Republicans and Democrats on the Court, joined in it because it aimed to sum up the conscience and progress of the nation in the area of civil rights, and because it boldly completed a long line of decisions that had been moving in the same direction. It went outside traditional legal categories by taking notice of studies by psychologists and sociologists which showed that separate and segregated schools could not be "equal" because the fact of their separateness was the fact that left a scar on the minds of the schoolchildren, Negro and white alike. Yet it was a decision reached not in haste but only after long deliberation; and it directed that the states and the local school districts carry it out "with all deliberate speed."

In this sense the Court has an important role as a national educator, trying to set standards of social control taken from the best levels of thought and asking the nation as a whole to measure itself by those standards. It cannot ever place itself in the vanguard of social thought, since its job is to distill what has already been thought and done and translate it into legal norms. But neither does it have to wait forever, until the bold has been frustrated and destroyed or until the novel has become archaic. Its task is a creative one in the sense that it must recognize when the action and thinking of popular majorities is valid for the long term, and when it is dangerous, must seize upon the thinking of the creative minority to hold it up as a standard for the majority to follow. No Court that could do this in a sustained way has yet been put together in Supreme Court history, but it is a not impossible ideal.

10. The Struggle for Civil Liberties

THE AREA IN WHICH the Federal courts have performed their most crucial work of guarding the polity is that of civil liberties, and the shield of freedom has been the Bill of Rights. Watching from Paris while the battle over the Constitution was being waged at home, Jefferson wrote that the necessary guarantees were "freedom of religion, freedom of the press, freedom from monopolies, freedom from unlawful imprisonment, freedom from a permanent military, and a trial by jury." And again, "A Bill of Rights is what the people are entitled to against every government on earth." They got one, in the form of the first ten amendments to the Constitution. Along with other constitutional provisions, including the Fourteenth Amendment, they represent both substance and symbol of American freedom—although the commitment to them by majorities and minorities has often been notably weak in practice.

The most elusive word in the political vocabulary, "freedom" is also one of the most important in the American consciousness. It is the first image the American invokes when he counts the blessings of his state. The inheritor of the English and French revolutions, as well as of his own, he has gazed so long into the pool of freedom that he has fallen half in love with his own reflection in it. He may be at the base of the income pyramid or a segregated Negro in the South, yet whatever his place in the social system, he sets store by freedom: it gives him a yardstick to measure his deprivation and a hope that he can remedy it. The historical record shows that the denials of freedom are part of the scar tissue of American culture and not its principle of growth and being.

In the triad of American "liberal capitalist democracy," the "liberal" component has generally meant the freedom to make your own decisions in your political and personal life. There are many constraints that the American does not regard as the denial of freedom. The conditions of his job, the rules of his union, the rigors of business fluctuations, the tyrannies of the community, and the prejudices of his fellow men may in fact represent harsh constraints on him. Yet he does not consider them violations of his freedom because they come as the fabric of his everyday life, and not as encroachment by anyone in authority. He is prepared to accept the informal but not the formal constraints, those from within the culture but not those from political authority.

To be cramped by someone who has power or superior position in a graded official hierarchy—that is counted the real denial of freedom. For example, the Great Depression of the 1930s wiped out billions in property values and income, reduced many to pauperism, saddled others with burdens it took a lifetime to discharge: yet it was not held to have diminished American freedom. The real threat was held to be the structure of bureaucracy built to cope with the periodic economic breakdowns. The spirit of this thinking shows up in the story of the Negro, living in squalor and precariousness, who was asked what he had gained by exchanging the security of slavery for poverty in freedom, and who answered, "There's something about the *looseness* of this here freedom that I like."

The obvious defect of this conception is its negativism. It stresses freedom *from* the powers and principalities of organized government, but not freedom *for* the creative phases of living. It derives from the whole freedom constellation of the eighteenth century, which saw a simple and natural plan of self-regulating human life, complete with an economic and political theory, a psychology and a metaphysics, and which asked only that the government keep its hands off and leave it alone. It underscored *let live* but forgot that in the jungle of the industrial culture *let live* without *help live* can be morally empty.

Yet there are few civilizations in history in which freedom has flourished as it has in America. What explains it?

There have been three principal explanations—the environmental, the political, the economic. The environmentalists say that the isolation of America, cut off by oceans for centuries from the wars and embroilments of Europe and Asia, kept it from standing armies and internal crises, and therefore free. They say also that the continuing availability of frontier land gave an outlet to energies that might otherwise have clashed in civil conflicts. The economic explanation holds that the core of American freedom is the free-enterprise economy, on the theory that free markets make free men, that political and social freedoms could not have been preserved without freedom of investment and the job. The political explanation stresses the separation of powers, the limited state, and the *laissez-faire* tradition.

The environmental theories, with their core of truth, fail to note that geography is only part of a larger social environment, that the span of distance America had from the European centers was less important than the spaciousness of American institutions and their distance from European feudalism. Similarly, the economic approach must be seen as part of the economic expansionism of American life. During one phase of American history *laissez faire* played an important and releasing role; but later experience showed that a mixed economy was a better base for freedom, since one of the great threats to it is economic breakdown.

Finally there is the political argument from the separation of powers. But there are other forms of it more crucial than the traditional splitting of the three political areas of power: the separation of economic from political power, the separation of church from state power, the separation of military from civilian power, and the separation of majority passions from the power of the law. This seems the more productive approach.

American freedom has been largely interstitial, located in the crevices between necessary power systems. It is protected by the fact that the men who run the economy do not always run the country—and also the other way around. It is also protected by the fact that the men of religion, who shape and organize the supernatural beliefs of Americans, cannot use the power of the government to make their creed exclusive—and also the other way around, in the fact that the government cannot interfere with freedom of worship. Further, it is protected by the fact that those who can send men to death in war are themselves held to account by civilian authority—and again (the other way around) in the fact that the political leaders cannot make themselves military heroes and go off on adventures of glory. It is strengthened by the fact that there is an independent judiciary which need not, although it sometimes does, respond to temporary waves of popular hatred against particular groups—and (the other way around) by the tradition of judicial nonparticipation in the tensions of political life.

Thus freedom may be seen partly as a function of the way power is distributed, separated, and diffused in a society. Americans tend to think of the government as the prime enemy of freedom, and see the history of freedom in America as the story of a Manichaean struggle between the angels of (individualist) light and the hosts of (governmental) darkness. But governmental power is only one form of social power. Wherever power is concentrated, whether in a government bureaucracy, a corporate combine, a big trade-union, a military staff, a powerful opinion empire, or a church organization disciplined to action, those who care about freedom must find ways of isolating that power, keeping it from combining with other power clusters, and holding it to account and responsibility.

But this effort to hold power accountable, which may sometimes involve attempts to break it up in its concentrated form, may itself endanger freedom by rousing latent social hostilities. With its lusty energies American life has always had a considerable violence potential which has flared into actual violence when a challenge has been offered to the continuance of some power structure. For concentrated power, whatever its form, is never so dangerous as when it feels itself in danger. A number of the movements chipping away at the civil-liberties tradition have come from power groups that felt their status to be in jeopardy. This was true of the Federalists who passed the Alien and Sedition Acts; of the White Supremacy movement in the postwar South, using night riders to terrorize and disfranchise Negroes; of the Oriental Exclusion Acts, supported both by the landowners and the trade-unionists of the West Coast; of the vigilantist violence used against labor organizers in communities where the police are tied in with the holders of economic power, and where even the churches sanction the fusion.

The history of a people is, from one angle, the story of the seesawing acquisition and relinquishment of power by a number of competing and intermeshed groups. But to relinquish power is never pleasant. Sometimes it may lead to an almost paranoid fear of encirclement. Franklin Roosevelt expressed a double-edged truth when he listed "freedom from fear" as one of the Four Freedoms. It is a truth because freedom from fear, rightly understood, can assure all the other freedoms. It is double-edged because the effort to achieve freedom from fear of the threats and challenges of foreign powers, and of subversion within, involves a military posture for the entire nation which itself breeds further fears and therefore dangers to freedom. One of the great difficulties is to distinguish between the fears which have a basis in reality and those which are anxieties and hallucinations.

Every great crisis in civil liberties contains a mixture of fears of both sorts. After World War I there was a wave of raids and deportations; it arose from the uneasy feeling that the Russian Revolution had caused a shift in the world balance of power and spawned a fanatic faith threatening American survival. After World War II there was another wave of assaults on civil liberties. It had a number of interrelated phases: the Smith Act prosecution of Communist leaders, the security purges of government officials, the Congressional investigations of "Reds" and "subversives" in government agencies and in colleges and universities, the sharp restrictions on foreign travel, the security surveillance of scientists, the scrutiny of the associates and even the families of men in the armed services, the widespread use of wiretapping in the effort to get evidence on political suspects, the heaping up of dossiers which were often filled with trivial and hearsay material, the setting up (under the McCarran Act of 1950) of emergency detention camps for political suspects, the grant of unprecedented power to put together an "Attorney General's list" of subversive organizations which in effect served as a measuring stick for loyalty, the deportation of aliens as political undesirables, the blacklisting of movie, radio, and TV performers, the use of anonymous evidence against "security" suspects who had no chance to confront their accusers, the dismissal of political unreliables from presumably sensitive posts in private industry, and group pressures within small communities against suspected books and individuals in a movement that came to be called "cultural vigilantism."

There was a stronger base for fear of external danger in this later period than after World War I, since the challenge of Kremlin expansionism was real and the conspiratorial nature of Communism had been made amply clear. Most Americans learned enough about the techniques of Communist penetration, espionage, and propaganda to know the reality of the designs against them. Yet along with the recognition of real threats, there was also a mixture of neurotic fears and fantasies. Inevitably the vast power struggle and arms race awakened popular passions, and the crisis was all the sharper because the old fears of a welfare state were merged with the new fears of Communist penetration.

A "security syndrome" brought into active eruption many of the hatreds smoldering below the surface. The accusations against "subversives" sometimes had a factual base but were often a loose and enveloping cover for racist, religious, xenophobian, political, and economic hostilities. Despite its prosperity, American life generated enough frustrations to clamor for expression in the often unconsciously disguised catchwords of "loyalty," "security," and "Americanism." A segment of the American population which had always been potentially strong now found a target for its sense of grievance and its malaise. Seymour Lipset's concept of "status politics" came into use to express the extreme political positions taken by those who were fearful of the security of their status in American life, and a new "Radical Right" emerged to challenge the Left with an equal fervor and with an inverted form of some of the old Leftist dogmas.

In a searching analysis of the history of American civil liberties John Roche has concluded that the idea of a Golden Age of freedom in the past and of a later expulsion from Eden is an illusory one, and that the record has actually been one of advance. To test this the two periods of postwar crises are worth comparing. The actual dangers from the outside—from Communist world power and its conspiratorial organization —were greater in the later than in the earlier periods, and the Communist organization within the United States was more substantial and tight-knit, although Communist strength within America could easily be overestimated. The turnover of membership within the party was high, the residue of indoctrination slight, and the anti-Communist bitterness of former members considerable. In the early 1930s the Communists had made some headway among intellectuals, artists, and students, comparable to their hold on these groups in some continental countries, but by the 1950s this hold had vanished, and Communist leadership was reduced to an intellectually ragged group without distinction or prestige. Moreover, the fear of internal unrest which had plagued the American mind in 1919, especially with respect to the labor movement, had all but vanished in the prosperity and stability of the 1950s.

Yet there were three sharp differences between the periods that made the later one more dangerous. The first was that the methods used in the suppression of civil liberties were less blatant: the 1919 method was one of arrests, criminal trials, and deportations; the later methods included Congressional investigations, destructive publicity, purges, blacklists, and indirect pressures. Second, the resistance to them was more fragmented than it had been in the earlier period, partly because the fears were more complex and widespread, partly because there were greater divisions and disunity among liberals. These divisions in turn were the result of a thirty-year history of Communist treachery and ruthlessness within the United States as well as the shock of liberal disillusionment with the nature and methods of Kremlin power. Third, the popular unrest in the earlier period was considerable, fed by the fact that the new Communist creed coming out of Russia still seemed an idealistic one and made an appeal to a union movement still feeling its way and a group of intellectuals stirred by the great events of the time. This was not true in the later period. The fact that there was so little base in popular unrest for the structure of repressive measures was itself one of the dangerous facts about it, since it underscored its synthetic quality.

The one new factor in the American situation, missing in the earlier period, was the fact of atomic weapons at a time when America and Russia were locked in a struggle for world power. This was the major premise of the Great Fear, underlying each of the minor premises of the particular case involved. Many Americans, battered by a swift succession of bewildering events and by the repeated accusations against "disloyal" government servants, came to feel a sullen, brooding sense of secret dangers lying in wait for them in an era of incalculable death. While only a few of the accusations were against scientists who could deliver atomic secrets to Russia, the cases of the Rosenbergs, Sobell, and Gross were enough to precipitate the fears, and every new accusation—no matter how trivial, far-fetched, or baseless—took on a sinister meaning in the context of the possible betrayal of the new secrets. To add to this "torment of secrecy," as Edward Shils aptly called it, the new situation gave many people a chance to express a delayed reaction of hostility to the New Deal and its works. The two trials of Alger Hiss, linked in the minds of most people with the "bright young men" of the New Deal, seemed a symbol of a generation of betrayal.

In the minds of many, as Eric Goldman spelled it out in detail in a survey of the 1945-55 decade, this was the "Great Conspiracy." It mattered not that the secrets which counted were secrets of Nature that could not be guarded, to which every community of scientists had access; nor did it matter that not a single one of the thousands of "security cases" in Washington involved any charge of sedition, or that the whole notorious Fort Monmouth investigation failed to uncover a spy or even a Communist. What counted was not the facts but the fears, not the actual dangers of the betrayal of secrets but the trumped-up dangers shouted through the microphones. It was the publicity-conscious politicians who were most obsessed with secrecy. Shils noted that the British, less anxious about their security problem, had more concern for the privacy of the person, while the secrecy-conscious Americans reveled in a Roman holiday of publicity.

This was the American mood in the inquisitional years of the early 1950s that came to be called the era of "McCarthyism" after its principal symbol, and caused a good deal of apprehension abroad. One may overemphasize what Justice Douglas called the "black curtain of fear": there was much double-think by liberals who assumed that none of the accusations could be true and that the accusers were always self-interested and hysterical. There was also considerable double-think by ex-Communists and ex-fellow-travelers who (as Mary McCarthy put it) "carried with them into the democratic camp the emergency mentality of totalitarianism," viewing "the mass of ordinary people . . . as so much plasticine to be molded into a harder form through constant indoctrination."

In time the American political and intellectual leaders, groping between these destructive alternatives, found the way of sanity. Without flinching from the Medusa head of Communist reality, they refused to be panicked into surrendering hard-won American freedoms as their response. One of the striking developments was the emergence eventually of an articulate resistance, made up of men of diverse political viewpoints—a liberal Senator like Lehman, a conservative Senator like Flanders, commentators like Edward R. Murrow and Elmer Davis, a newspaper editor like James Wechsler, a New England Republican lawyer like Joseph Welch—around whom a demoralized public consensus could re-form its ranks and regain a sense of perspective. The Army-

McCarthy hearings were the turning point in this process because they confronted the highly emotional symbol of anti-Communism with the older and more deeply rooted symbol of national defense, and stripped away from McCarthy the outward show of nationalism to reveal underneath an anarchic thrust toward power which would have wrecked the civil-liberties tradition.

The judiciary played a role in this process. After a period of hesitation while the Federal courts agonized over finding some standard by which to delimit the area of permitted speech, the Supreme Court had to grapple openly with the problem in the *Dennis* case. Writing the decision on the Circuit Court level, Judge Learned Hand said the courts would have to decide "whether the gravity of the evil, discounted by its improbability, justifies such invasion of free speech as is necessary to avoid the danger." Despite the involved phrasing of this formula, what it said was clear enough: that the more serious the internal danger, the more justifiable is the governmental action to suppress freedom of speech.

What it did, in effect, was to change the Holmesian formula of "clear and present danger" into "clear and *probable* danger." Chief Justice Vinson adopted this approach in his opinion for the Court, but he spoke for only four of the justices in the 6-2 split. But in 1957 a reconstituted Court, headed by Chief Justice Warren, narrowed the application of the Smith Act by holding that the "abstract doctrine" of believing in the violent overthrow of existing institutions was not enough to convict a man. The essential distinction, wrote Justice Harlan, was between belief and incitement to action. This still left a blurred margin between the two, within which a judge and jury bent on sending political trouble-makers to jail could find ample means for their intent. There remained, moreover, the old question of how dangerous the incitement had to be to the Republic before it could eat away the First Amendment's protection of a man's political beliefs. On this question of the immediacy of the danger and the time element involved, Justice Brandeis' formula in *Whitney v. California* still seemed the best approach, although the Supreme Court has never adopted it. The test that Brandeis used was whether there was still any time left to carry on the process of public education in counteracting the error and evil of the propaganda that the government was seeking to suppress. This was a later version of Jefferson's belief that a democracy need not fear "to tolerate error so long as reason is free to combat it."

From this angle the hunt for dangerous thoughts made little sense in an America which continued both through war and postwar years in a strong and stable condition. Such an America could afford to dispense with the trappings of loyalty oaths for teachers, the widespread use of professional informers, and the harrying of political opponents, however misguided. It could afford the luxury of allowing freedom of expression even for those who would themselves deny freedom if they were in power, and even to a disciplined and subservient Communist party whose leaders were undoubtedly involved in a network of conspiratorial action. The crucial distinction between action and doctrine, including "conspiracy to teach" the doctrine, was one that Americans persisted in making, although it was beclouded by the tensions of the early 1950s. When the McCarran Senate Subcommittee and the Justice Department sought to press a perjury indictment against a writer and scholar, in the Lattimore case, because he had helped shape a viewpoint toward Asian policy which was widely repudiated later, Judge Luther Youngdahl sharply reasserted in a memorable opinion an American's right to be wrong.

Of the problems of legal and political theory with which Americans struggled in their civil-liberties crisis, one of the most perplexing concerned the problem of self-incrimination in testimony before Congressional investigating committees. The protection of the right to remain silent, which is part of the guarantee against self-incrimination in the Fifth Amendment, came out of a long history of struggle both in England and America. Interestingly enough this guarantee was first established in English law to protect persons accused of (and often guilty of) the religious and political crimes of heresy, schism, and sedition. Once the precedent had been set for them it was extended to common felons as well, in the area of criminal law. The religious and political cases, mainly involving Puritan dissenters in England and in America as well, were the trail blazers; the others followed. If Tudor and Stuart England had recognized freedom of religion, speech, assembly, and press, no explicit right against self-incrimination would have developed because none would have been needed.

Similarly, when the political climate in postwar America became harsh, whether for "heretics" or "conspirators," and when Congress and the courts narrowed the area of freedom of expression, they sought refuge in the Fifth Amendment ("stood on the Fifth"). It became clear that many Communists availed themselves of the constitutional protection as a way of evading damaging disclosures, along with non-Communists who used it because they found it distasteful to name names. The temptation was strong to brush aside the irritating obstacle presented by this guarantee, in the urgent drive to smash the Communist movement and its strength. The resort to the Fifth soon took on a public stigma, and while the government could do little except to pass "immunity statutes," private colleges and private industry usually rid themselves of anyone who took this stand. Yet on the whole the saner course—that of clinging to the constitutional safeguard, even at the cost of giving a tactical advantage to the enemies of democracy—was likely to prevail.

A balance sheet of civil liberties in the mid-1950s would stand somewhat as follows. Freedom of worship for all was established beyond any danger of being dislodged. The right of private parochial instruction was also established, but the doctrine of the separation of church and state was being challenged by the movement for religious instruction in the public schools. The area of freedom of speech was still in flux, and that of the freedom to stay silent was becoming clarified. The right of political association was shaky so far as the Communist party was concerned. The "right to knowledge and the free use thereof," involving freedom of teaching and research as well as of press, movies, and publication, was threatened less by the government than by organized citizen boycotts which extended to bookstores, libraries, theaters, and movie houses giving hospitality to a suspected writer or artist. The ban against wiretapping in Federal court cases still held firm. The rights of aliens in immigration and deportation cases did not get much recognition from the courts, but the safeguards of administrative procedural fairness were being strengthened there as well as in the passport cases involving the right of a citizen to travel. The struggle for the right of franchise for Negroes received a setback because of Southern bitterness over the school integration cases, but it was bound to be won; the same applied to the right of equal opportunity in education, travel, housing, and other areas, where it was the Supreme Court rather than Congress which represented the great line of advance.*

Despite many confusions on the question of freedom and security, there was a persistent belief that freedom is an unbroken web whose strands are interdependent, and that if it is arbitrarily broken at any point it becomes more breakable at all the others. Benjamin Franklin summed it up with his usual pungency: "those who would give up essential liberty to purchase a little temporary safety, deserve neither liberty nor safety." The real aim of the hunters of dangerous thoughts was less to protect national safety than to secure general conformity. In pursuit of that aim they were willing to endanger public freedom and veto the individual life. But the stakes of the civil-liberties crisis did not end in minority rights. Even more important was the process of genuine majority rule. The basis of the whole theory of the democratic will is that the people will have alternative courses of action between which they can make a choice. This is what Holmes meant in his famous dissent in the Abrams case in 1919 when he spoke of "the power of the

* For a further discussion of the struggle for Negro rights, see Ch. VII, Sec. 6, "The Negro in America."

thought to get itself accepted in the competition of the market." Unless alternative policies can be freely presented, the majority will becomes truncated and ultimately meaningless. Again we return to the Brandeis conception of democracy as a prolonged conversation among the people in which various groups seek to carry on a process of competitive education and persuasion.

There was one element in the American civil-liberties situation in the 1950s, that of its world impact, which had not applied to the same degree earlier. America was engaged in a competitive struggle for survival, waged against a totalitarian movement of world scope which could exploit every instance of American hypocrisy about democratic freedoms. A glaring instance of suppression of freedom, a case of lynching, or a "legal" jury murder of a Negro in a Southern state which the Federal government felt powerless to punish, was immediately telegraphed around the world and used to undermine American prestige. The most powerful weapon that America had in the struggle of ideas was the image of a free society. Whenever the enemies of civil liberties inside America tarnished that image they weakened American power and safety far more than could the shabby and pathetic cadres of Communist propaganda inside the nation.

The great force that has thus far broken the shock of the periodic assaults on freedom from within American life has been the civil-liberties tradition—the historical commitment of Americans to the public protection of the freedom of the individual person. Its roots go deep into the history of American thought and attitudes.

We may start with the Puritan (and generally Protestant) emphasis on the importance of the individual conscience. Beyond that there was the teaching, from the religious tradition, of the intensity of sacrifice for individual conscience and for the ideal of justice and equality. Broadening out still further, there was the emphasis on the individual personality and its sanctity, resting on the tradition of natural rights, the religious belief that each person has a soul, and the premise of potential individual creativeness. Add to this the property complex which has put a premium on the value of individual effort and its relation to reward, and the success complex which has linked freedom with the sense of competitive worth and the impulse for self-improvement.

Round it off with the two basic American attitudes toward freedom as an ingredient in the social process. One is the pragmatic attitude expressed in Holmes's phrase about the competition of ideas, which is a more astringent way of putting Milton's ". . . who ever knew Truth put to the worse, in a free and open encounter?" It says in effect that the idea which survives may not be necessarily the truth, but what better way does a society have for choosing the ideas it will live by? The second is the belief that the individual personality is more productive if it functions in freedom than if it must obey someone else's authoritarian behest. Put all these together, and in the convergence of intellectual, emotional, and institutional factors you get the strength of the American freedom constellation.

It is not the possession of any single group in American life, nor can it be left to the sole guardianship of any group—not even of the Supreme Court. The labor groups care about freedom of collective bargaining and freedom from strike-breaking violence, yet they may themselves be scornful of the civil rights of Negro workers whom some unions still exclude. The business managers are concerned about their freedom from government controls, yet American history is filled with the denials of freedom by employers to workers who sought to organize. Liberals claim the civil-liberties tradition as their own, yet some of the staunchest defenders of civil liberties have been conservatives, from John Adams through men like Charles E. Hughes and Henry L. Stimson. Some who have called themselves conservatives have forgotten that the civil-liberties tradition is the most precious heritage to conserve; some who have called themselves "liberals" have been known to run from the defense of freedom as soon as the firing became hot; while, in a different grain of "liberalism," there have been some so bemused by the "world revolution" of Communism that they did not face with realism the nature of the Communist threat to freedom.

In all the instances of faltering, the weakness that breaches the defense of the civil-liberties tradition is the lack of genuine commitment to freedom. This is sometimes the result of a poverty of moral generosity, sometimes the failure of imaginative insight into the plight of others and its meaning for the civilization as a whole. In the end it reduces itself to a contempt for the sovereignty of another's personality. Freedom is an inherent part of the development of personality. Wherever freedom is diminished for anyone, the personality—however noble or ignoble, intelligent or doltish—is thereby diminished. The diminution affects not only the personality deprived of freedom but others as well. For freedom is indivisible. What is disturbing to the student of contemporary America is not only the number of infringements of freedom but the fact that so few Americans who were not themselves targets rallied early or spontaneously to the support of the victims. Equally disturbing is the fact that many of the continuing threats to freedom come not from government action but from private boycotts.

For a clue we must go back again to the nature of freedom as the American conceives it. He sees it as the right of an individual against hostile forces outside—usually the government. But the individual is helpless to defend himself against the attacks on him, especially in an age of publicity when accusations made before a Congressional committee or by a speech on the floor of Congress or a resolution of a veterans' group gain wide circulation. He can be secure only if the group—committed by the social duty of defending his rights even as against itself—protects him against assaults until he is proved guilty of overt action or covert conspiracy involving sedition or treason. The test, of course, must be the law itself, operating through judicial procedures and not through some extrajudicial procedures or emergency measure.

Some of the critics of America abroad have cited these recent invasions of civil liberties as proof that the whole American concern for freedom is hypocritical. The charges do not sit well with cultures where the power of party and state spells the moral annihilation of the individual, and where the total fusion of diverse powers crushes the liberties of the person. Many Americans have not understood, however, that the reality of the totalitarian threat furnishes no adequate reason for betraying the whole career of freedom in America. The measures which seem to be dictated by the urgency of danger are in fact as badly calculated to meet the real threats to security within the nation as they are to advance the democratic cause in the rivalry for world position outside. The conditions of living in a contemporary industrial society are likely to produce, as Erich Fromm has pointed out, a fear of freedom and an impulse to escape from its burdens. But they are the burdens of self-government and of moral decision, and they cannot be escaped. Those who sell Americans short on the capacity to survive as a free people ignore the perilous but great career of American freedom that disproves their calculation.*

* For a discussion of related phases of the problem of freedom, see Ch. IV, Sec. 2, "Science in an Open Society"; Ch. VII, Sec. 5, "The Minority Situation," and Sec. 6, "The Negro in America"; Ch. IX, Sec. 4, "Varieties of American Character"; Ch. X, Sec. 2, "American Thought: the Angle of Vision"; Ch. XII, Sec. 4, "Landscape with Soldiers."

Acknowledgments

OVER THE SPAN during which this book was written I owe acknowledgments to my secretaries and assistants who labored faithfully along with me: to Frances Herridge, Carol Simon, Susan Steiner Satz, Gloria Howe, Alice Lide, and especially Ruth Korzenik, to whom fell much of the burden of helping prepare the book for press; to Donald McCormick for working with me during an entire summer at Southampton while a new draft came into being; to Jules Bernstein and Martin Peretz, my students at Brandeis University, who somehow survived a stormy and protracted siege during which we prepared the "Notes for Further Reading" together. I want to add my thanks to M. Lincoln Schuster, Henry W. Simon, Justin Kaplan, and Joseph Barnes of the staff of Simon and Schuster, who went far beyond their duty as publishers in order to help lick the book into shape.

Successive drafts of the book were mimeographed and used, year after year, as basic reading for my class in American Civilization at Brandeis University. I cannot overstate how much I owe to my colleagues and my students in that course, who put it to the test of using it as a tool for understanding the complex thing we call American Civilization, and gave it their best critical and creative efforts. I want to mention especially my colleagues in the course over a number of years—Henry Steele Commager, formerly at Columbia University and now at Amherst College, Merrill Peterson, now at Princeton University, Richard Akst, Bernard Rosenberg, Jerome Himelhoch, Arno J. Mayer, John Van Doren, and (most of all) Leonard Levy and Lawrence H. Fuchs. It is their book almost as much as it is mine. I want also to express my obligation to President A. L. Sachar of Brandeis University, who supported me enthusiastically in a drastically experimental venture in teaching American Civilization by cutting across all the established boundaries between the established disciplines.

Finally, and most of all, I want to thank my colleagues in the university world, and in the professions, business, labor, and the arts, who gave generously of their time and knowledge in a task which was obviously beyond my own powers. In a work of this scope no man's scholarship, even were he to spend a lifetime on it, could adequately cover every area treated in this book. Their generosity is all the greater because of the fact that, while many of them were friends of mine, others were willing to answer a stranger's call for help in the understanding of American Civilization. I do not dare to hope that together we have eliminated all errors, both of fact and interpretation. But I was determined, so far as humanly possible, to keep them to a minimum, and I was bold enough to ask some of the best people in every field to help me to that end. Each of them read a chapter or several chapters, or sometimes portions of a chapter, that were closest to his interests, and sent me both general criticisms and detailed—sometimes line by line—corrections and suggestions. In many cases I not only accepted their ideas but even adopted some of their phrasing because I could not hope to improve on it. To a great degree this book is thus a collaborative work, and belongs not to me but to the collective of American scholarship. I hasten to add that some of my colleagues may fail to recognize or to be willing to acknowledge the book as in any way their product, and I want to make it clear that none of them is to be held responsible for my views or for my sins of omission and commission.

I want to thank especially Louis Hartz of Harvard University for reading and criticising the larger portion of the book, although I am certain that it still falls far short of his exacting standards. The others to whom I want to express my obligation and thanks are: Adam Abruzzi, Stevens Institute of Technology; Walter Adams, Michigan State University; Arthur Altmeyer, U.S. Department of Health, Education, and Welfare; Wayne Andrews, N.Y. Historical Society; Conrad Arensberg, Columbia University; Stephen Bailey, Woodrow Wilson School of Public and International Affairs, Princeton University; Read Bain, Miami University in Oxford, Ohio; Carlos Baker, Princeton University; Jacques Barzun, Columbia University; Catherine Worster Bauer, University of California in Berkeley; Daniel Bell, *Fortune;* Francis Bello, *Fortune;* Bernard Berelson, Ford Foundation; Adolf A. Berle, Jr., Columbia University; Herbert Bloch, Brooklyn College; Herbert Blumer, University of California in Berkeley; Daniel J. Boorstin, University of Chicago; Kenneth Boulding, University of Michigan; Carl Bridenbaugh, University of California in Berkeley; Robert R. R. Brooks, Williams College; Harrison Brown, California Institute of Technology; Stuart Gerry Brown, Syracuse University; Lyman Bryson, Columbia University; Gilbert Burck, *Fortune;* Roger Burlingame, New York City; and James MacGregor Burns, Williams College.

Also Richard Centers, University of California in Los Angeles; Eliot D. Chapple, E. D. Chapple Co.; Thomas I. Cook, Johns Hopkins University; Lewis Coser, Brandeis University; Avery Craven, University of Chicago; Maurice Davie, Yale University; Joseph S. Davis, Food Research Institute, Stanford University; J. Frederick Dewhurst, Twentieth Century Fund; Stanley Diamond, Brandeis University; John Dollard, Yale University; David Donald, Columbia University; Elisha P. Douglass, Princeton University; Peter F. Drucker, Montclair, N.J.; Joseph W. Eaton, Western Reserve University; Albert Ellis, New York City; Leonard W. Feather, *Down Beat;* Robert H. Ferguson, Cornell University; Donald Fleming, Brown University; Lawrence K. Frank, Belmont, Mass.; Charles Frankel, Columbia University; Lawrence Fuchs, Brandeis University; Lewis Galantiere, Free Europe Committee; Maxwell Geismar, *The Nation;* Siegfried Giedion, Harvard University; Nathan Glazer, University of California; Eric F. Goldman, Princeton University; William J. Goode, Columbia University; George W. Gray, Rockefeller Foundation; William Haber, University of Michigan; Oscar Handlin, Harvard University; Robert J. Havighurst, University of Chicago; Robert L. Heilbroner, New York City; Melville J. Herskovits, Northwestern University; Richard Hofstadter, Columbia University; Arthur N. Holcombe, Harvard University; Alfred J. Hotz, Western Reserve University; Irving Howe, Brandeis University; Cuthbert C. Hurd, International Business Machines; Stanley Hyman, Bennington College; and Howard Mumford Jones, Harvard University.

Also George Kennan, Princeton Institute for Advanced Studies; James Klee, Brandeis University; Otto Klineberg, Columbia University; Clyde Kluckhohn, Harvard University; Philip M. Klutznick, Park Forest, Illinois; Marshall Knappen, University of Michigan; Mirra Komarovsky, Barnard College; John A. Kouwenhoven, Barnard College; Oliver Larkin, Smith College; Eric Larrabee, *Harper's;* Harold D. Lasswell, Yale University; Leonard Levy, Brandeis University; Charles E. Lindblom, Yale University; Donald J. Lloyd, Wayne University; Nelson Lowry, University of Minnesota; Samuel Lubell, New York City; Robert D. Lynd, Columbia University; Fritz Machlup, Johns Hopkins University; Archibald MacLeish, Harvard University; Herbert F. Marcuse, Brandeis University; A. H. Maslow, Brandeis University; Alpheus T. Mason, Princeton University; Margaret Mead, American Museum of Natural History; Ida C. Merriam, U.S. Department of Health, Education, and Welfare; C. Wright Mills, Columbia University; B. F. Ashley Montagu, Rutgers University; Hans J. Morgenthau, University of Chicago; Samuel Eliot Morison, Harvard University; Lewis Mumford, Amenia, N.Y.; and Henry A. Murray, Harvard University.

Also Ernest Nagel, Columbia University; Theodore Newcomb, University of Michigan; James R. Newman, Washington, D.C.; Reinhold Niebuhr, Union Theological Seminary; Saul K. Padover, New School for Social Research; Talcott Parsons, Harvard University; Merrill Peterson, Princeton University; Gerard Piel, *Scientific American;* David M. Potter, Yale University; Phillip Rieff, Brandeis University; David Riesman, University of Chicago; John P. Roche, Brandeis University; Clinton Rossiter, Cornell University; George de Santillana, Massachusetts Institute of Technology; Edward N. Saveth, New York City; Meyer Schapiro, Columbia University; Arthur M. Schlesinger, Harvard University; Arthur M. Schlesinger, Jr., Harvard University; Frederick L. Schuman, Williams College; Gilbert Seldes, New York City; Jose-Luis Sert, Harvard University; Harold Shapero, Brandeis University; Edward A. Shils, University of Chicago; Edward W. Sinnott, Yale University; Henry Nash Smith, University of California in Berkeley; Herman Somers, Haverford College; Pitirim Sorokin, Harvard University; George Soule, Bennington College; Ralph Spielman, University of Kentucky; Mark Starr, International Ladies Garment Workers Union; Marshall Stearns, Institute of Jazz Studies; George Stewart, University of California in Berkeley; Cushing Strout, Yale University; Adolph Sturmthal, Roosevelt University; and G. E. Swanson, University of Michigan.

Also George Terborgh, Machinery and Allied Products Institute; Lionel Trilling, Columbia University; Christopher Tunnard, Yale University; Harry R. Warfel, University of Florida; W. Lloyd Warner, University of Chicago; Walter Prescott Webb, University of Texas; Rush Welter, Bennington College; William Wheaton, University of Pennsylvania; Leslie A. White, University of Michigan; William Foote Whyte, Cornell University; William H. Whyte, Jr., *Fortune;* Mitchell Wilson, New York City; Carl Wittke, Western Reserve University; C. Vann Woodward, Johns Hopkins University; and Dennis Wrong, University of Toronto.

Finally, I want to say how much I owe to my wife, Edna Albers Lerner, who retained her belief in what must have seemed at times a monstrously unreal venture and discussed with me every major phase of it and every draft.

June 1957 MAX LERNER
New York City

Notes for Further Reading

(These notes are arranged so as to accompany each chapter and section of the text. They give the books and articles from which I have drawn and are meant as a guide to the interested reader who may wish to pursue some particular theme further. To avoid cluttering footnotes I have also indicated here the sources of particular references in the text. The date and place of publication of each book or article referred to are given only with the first reference in the notes for each chapter. Later references give author and title only.)

Chapter I: Heritage

SEC. 1—*The Sense of the Past:* The evocation of the American past draws on many sources, most of them in the standard American histories. I have a special debt to Henry Beston, *American Memory* (New York, 1937).

SEC. 2—*Sources of the Heritage:* For the ethnic origins of America, in addition to the chapter cited in the text from De Tocqueville, see Oscar Handlin, *Race and Nationality in American Life* (Boston, 1957). For the estimate of the antiquity of Indian life in America, see recent symposia held under the Wenner-Gren Foundation; also Kenneth MacGowan, *Early Man in the New World* (New York, 1950), and Frank C. Hibben, *Treasure in the Dust* (New York, 1950). For the Indian culture as a whole, see John Collier, *The Indians of the Americas* (New York, 1948), and D'Arcy McNickle, *They Came Here First* (Philadelphia, 1949); for a history of the Hopi, see *Culture in Crisis* by Laura Thompson (New York, 1950). Of the numerous valuable volumes by Paul Radin, see particularly *The Story of the American Indian* (New York, 1927), *The Road of Life and Death, A Ritual Drama of the American Indians* (New York, 1945), and *The World of Primitive Man* (New York, 1953), which draws heavily on the American Indian experience. For the intellectual history of the image of the Indian in the American mind, see Roy H. Pearce, *The Savages of America: A Study of the Indian and the Idea of Civilization* (Baltimore, 1953), and the anthology by Richard M. Dorson, *America Begins* (New York, 1950). For the painters of Indian life, see Bernard De Voto, *Across the Wide Missouri* (Boston, 1947); Lloyd Haberly, *Pursuit of the Horizon* (New York, 1948), on George Catlin; and *The West of Alfred Jacob Miller,* edited by Marvin C. Ross (Norman, Oklahoma, 1952). Parkman's *Oregon Trail,* a classic of American history, will be found in several editions; even more valuable are *The Journals of Francis Parkman,* ed., Mason Wade, 2 vols. (New York, 1947), from which the Parkman quotation in my text is taken. See also Harvey C. Wish, *Society and Thought in America,* 2 vols. (New York, 1950-52), Vol. I, Ch. 12, "The West of Jackson and Francis Parkman." The quote from Daniel Webster will be found in *American Heritage* (VII, No. 3), April 1957, p. 3—an issue that contains also a magnificent set of reproductions from George Catlin.

For the Negroes in the American heritage, see J. Saunders Redding, *They Came in Chains: Americans from Africa* (Philadelphia, 1950); Frank Tannenbaum, *Slave and Citizen: The Negro in America* (New York, 1947); E. Franklin Frazier, *The Negro in the U.S.* (rev. ed., New York, 1957), the most comprehensive study; Eric Williams, *Capitalism and Slavery* (Chapel Hill, 1944), and John Howard Lawson, *The Hidden Heritage* (New York, 1950), both of them written from a Marxist standpoint. For slavery, see Kenneth M. Stampp, *The Peculiar Institution* (New York, 1956), and for the history of the Negro, see John Hope Franklin, *From Slavery to Freedom* (New York, 1947). For the roots of the Civil War, see Avery Craven, *The Coming of the Civil War* (2nd ed., Chicago, 1957), and for its aftermath C. Vann Woodward's researches, especially *Reunion and Reaction* (Boston, 1951; new ed., New York, 1956); *Origins of the New South* (Baton Rouge, 1951);

and *The Strange Career of Jim Crow* (New York, 1955; new ed., New York, 1957). For studies in the Negro cultural tradition, see Margaret J. Butcher, *The Negro in American Culture* (New York, 1956), based on the work of Alain Locke. For the Negro religious experience in America, there is a suggestive passage in Arnold Toynbee, *A Study of History* (London, 1934), Vol. II, pp. 218-220. For the Negro tradition in music, see Marshall Stearns, *The Story of Jazz* (New York, 1956), especially Part 3. For other reading on the Negro in American society, see below the references to Ch. VII, Sec. 6 (on the Negro's place in American society), Ch. X, Sec. 1 (on his role in the churches), and Ch. XI, Sec. 7 (on his contribution to American jazz).

For the British influence, see Gerald W. Johnson, *Our English Heritage* (New York, 1949). For the Puritans and their impact on the tradition, see Perry Miller and Thomas H. Johnson, *The Puritans* (New York, 1938) for its excellent "General Introduction"; also Miller's *Orthodoxy in Massachusetts* (Cambridge, 1933); his *New England Mind: The Seventeenth Century* (New York, 1939), and *New England Mind: From Colony to Province* (Cambridge, 1953), and his *Jonathan Edwards* (New York, 1949). See also T. J. Wertenbaker, *The Puritan Oligarchy* (New York, 1947).

For the polyglot heritage, see Oscar Handlin, *Race and Nationality in American Life*. For other references, see Ch. III, Sec. 2, below, on the immigrant experience, and Ch. VII, Sec. 5 on the minority situation.

SEC. 3—*The Slaying of the European Father:* For the American attitudes toward the Old World, see Geoffrey Gorer, *The American People* (New York, 1948), Ch. 1, "Europe and the Rejected Father." The quotation from Emerson is from the closing paragraph of *English Traits* (rev. ed., Boston, 1881), p. 236. The comment on the Declaration by Julian Boyd will be found in his book *The Declaration of Independence* (Princeton, 1945). For the references to Frazer, see *The Golden Bough: A Study in Magic and Religion* (1-vol. ed., New York, 1922), especially Ch. 24, "The Killing of the Divine King." The quotation from Santayana is from his *Character and Opinion in the United States* (Anchor Books ed., 1956). On the American expatriates in Europe, I have found several books suggestive: Malcolm Cowley's *Exile's Return* (new ed., New York, 1954); Matthew Josephson, *Portrait of the Artist As an American* (New York, 1930); and Frederick J. Hoffman, *The Twenties: American Writing in the Postwar Decade* (New York, 1955), especially Chs. 1-3 and 5.

SEC. 4—*Why Was America a Success?* On the attitude of Americans toward their own role in history I have drawn upon Edward Saveth's excellent anthology, *Understanding the American Past* (Boston, 1954); Michael Kraus, *A History of American History* (New York, 1937); and Charles and Mary Beard, *The American Spirit: A Study of the Idea of Civilization in the United States* (New York, 1942). There are some good insights into the historians of the Middle Period in A. M. Schlesinger, Jr., *The Age of Jackson* (Boston, 1945). The quote from DeWitt Clinton will be found in Beard, *op. cit.*, p. 214. On the "American mission," see Clinton Rossiter's article with that title in *American Scholar* (Jan. 1951) as well as "The Shaping of the American Tradition," *William and Mary Quarterly* (Oct. 1954). The quotation from Rush Welter is from correspondence with the author; see also Rush Welter, "The Idea of Progress in America," *Journal of the History of Ideas* (June 1955). For the cult of the American Constitution, see Schechter, "The Early History of the Tradition of the Constitution," *American Political Science Review* (1915), Vol. IX, p. 707; Thurman Arnold, *The Symbols of Government* (New Haven, 1935); Ralph H. Gabriel, *The Course of American Democratic Thought* (rev. ed., New York, 1956); E. S. Corwin, "The Constitution As Instrument and As Symbol," *American Political Science Review* (Dec. 1936); and my *Ideas for the Ice Age* (New York, 1941), Part 4, Sec. 2, "Constitution and Court as Symbols," pp. 232-264. For capitalism as an explanation of American greatness, see Louis M. Hacker, *The Triumph of American Capitalism* (New York, 1940), and also Hacker's essay, "The Anti-Capitalist Bias of American Historians," in *Capitalism and the Historians*, ed., F. A. Hayek (Chicago, 1954). For a different viewpoint, see Charles and Mary Beard, *The Rise of American Civilization*, 2 vols. (New York, 1927), and *America in Mid-Passage* (New York, 1939). For criticism of Beard's historical views, see the essays by Richard Hofstadter, Howard K. Beale, Merle Curti and myself in the collective volume *Charles A. Beard: An Appraisal* (Lexington, Ky., 1954), and two essays of mine on his historical theory: "Charles Beard's Stormy Voyage," *New Republic* (Oct. 25, 1948), and "Beard: Civilization and the Devils," *ibid.* (Nov. 1, 1948). For Veblen on American capitalism, see his *Theory of Business Enterprise*

(New York, 1904) and *Absentee Ownership and Business Enterprise in Recent Times* (New York, 1923); also Joseph Dorfman, "The Satire of Thorstein Veblen's *Theory of the Leisure Class*," *Political Science Quarterly* (1932), Vol. XLVII, pp. 363-409, and my essays on Veblen in *Ideas Are Weapons* (New York, 1939), pp. 117-141. See also Thurman Arnold, *The Folklore of Capitalism* (New Haven, 1937), and on Arnold, see my essay in *Ideas Are Weapons*, "The Shadow World of Thurman Arnold," pp. 198-217, and Richard Hofstadter, *The Age of Reform* (New York, 1955), "The New Opportunism," pp. 314-326. For the critique of capitalism in the whole era of Populism and social reform, see Eric F. Goldman, *Rendezvous with Destiny* (New York, 1952), and Hofstadter, *The Age of Reform*. The references in the text to Parrington are to his *Main Currents in American Thought* (3 vols:, new ed., New York, 1956). The reference to Matthew Josephson is to his *Robber Barons* (New York, 1934). For Charles Beard's comments on Sumner and Turner, see his *The American Spirit*, p. 364. His quote on the theory of economic determinism is from his *Economic Interpretations of the Constitution* (New York, 1913; new ed., 1935); for criticism of this, see my *Ideas Are Weapons*, pp. 152-169; also the study by Robert E. Brown, *Charles Beard and the Constitution* (Princeton, 1956).

SEC. 5—*American History As Extended Genesis:* On Frederick Jackson Turner and the frontier theory, the classic essay is "The Significance of the Frontier in American History," written by Turner for the American Historical Association in 1893, and republished in his volume of essays, *The Frontier in American History* (New York, 1920). For a collection of critical essays on Turner's thesis, see the Amherst pamphlet series, *The Turner Thesis Concerning the Role of the Frontier in American History* (Amherst, 1949), including essays by Avery Craven, Louis M. Hacker, Carlton J. H. Hayes, George W. Pierson, Fred A. Shannon, and Benjamin F. Wright, Jr.

A key work on the whole problem, and in itself a major extension of the theory, is Walter Prescott Webb, *The Great Frontier* (Boston, 1952). Another fresh approach will be found in Henry Nash Smith, *Virgin Land: The American West As Symbol and Myth* (Cambridge, 1950). For the history of the westward movements, see Ray Allen Billington, *Westward Expansion* (New York, 1949), Bernard De Voto, *Across the Wide Missouri* and *The Year of Decision* (Boston, 1943). For the role of Jacksonian democracy in relation to the extended American genesis, see Arthur M. Schlesinger, Jr., *The Age of Jackson*, and for what I have called the "moving democratic idea," see Parrington, *Main Currents in American Thought*, especially Vol. II, and also F. O. Matthiessen, *The American Renaissance* (New York, 1941). The reference in the text to Potter is to David M. Potter, *People of Plenty* (Chicago, 1954).

SEC. 6—*Tradition and the Frame of Power*, and SEC. 7—*American Dynamism:* On the American tradition, see Richard Hofstadter, *The American Political Tradition* (New York, 1948), and Louis Hartz, *The Liberal Tradition in America* (New York, 1955), the first emphasizing the conservative aspects and the second the "liberal" aspects (using the term in its classical Lockean sense) of the main American tradition. The comment on George Fitzhugh in the text is from Hartz's discussion (Ch. 6). See also Russell Kirk, *The Conservative Mind: From Burke to Santayana* (Chicago, 1955), which includes a discussion of the early American Federalists, the Southern conservatives, the Adamses, Irving Babbitt, Paul Elmer More, and Santayana; and see his book of essays, *A Program for Conservatives* (Chicago, 1954). A delightful little book—half commentary, half documents—is Peter Viereck, *Conservatism: From John Adams to Churchill* (Princeton, 1956), which should be read along with the same author's *Conservatism Revisited* (New York, 1949) and *The Unadjusted Man* (Boston, 1956). Clinton Rossiter's work in this vein will be found in his *Seedtime of the Republic* (New York, 1953) and his *Conservatism in America* (New York, 1955). In a somewhat similar vein, see also Daniel Boorstin, *The Genius of American Politics* (Chicago, 1953). See also Richard N. Current, *Daniel Webster and the Rise of American Conservatism* (Boston, 1955). For a critique of the extreme Right, see the valuable collection of essays, *The New American Right*, ed., Daniel Bell (New York, 1955), including essays by Bell, Hofstadter, Riesman, Glazer, Viereck, Parsons and Lipset. The quote from Morison in Sec. 6 is from his Presidential Address in 1950 to the American Historical Association. The quote from Walt Whitman in Sec. 7 will be found in the anthology edited by Louis Untermeyer, *Walt Whitman: Poetry and Prose* (New York, 1949), and is also reprinted as part of the exchange with Emerson in Edmund Wilson, ed., *The Shock of Recognition* (New York, 1943). The reference to Niebuhr's work in Sec. 7 is to Reinhold Niebuhr, *The*

Nature and Destiny of Man (1-vol. ed., New York, 1953) and to his book of essays on contemporary themes, *Christian Realism and Political Problems* (New York, 1953). The reference to Lippmann is to his *Essays in the Public Philosophy* (Boston, 1955). The quote in Sec. 7 from F. Scott Fitzgerald will be found in his novel, *The Great Gatsby* (New York, 1925).

Chapter II: The Idea of American Civilization

SEC. 1—*Figure in the Carpet,* and SEC. 2—*Is America a Civilization?* I have drawn heavily here on Beard, *The American Spirit* (New York, 1942), where the quote from Mark Twain will be found, pp. 50-51. For the American civilization pattern as De Tocqueville saw it more than a century ago, see his *Democracy in America* (2 vols., new ed., by Phillips Bradley, New York, 1954). For the culture concept as developed by the anthropologists, see E. B. Tylor, *Primitive Culture* (London, 1881) Ch. 1 from which the quote in the text is taken. See also Ruth Benedict, *Patterns of Culture* (New York, 1934); Alexander Goldenweiser, *Anthropology: An Introduction to Primitive Culture* (New York, 1937); Ralph Linton, *The Tree of Culture* (New York, 1955), with a valuable selection of essays on "Theoretical Approaches" in Part 1, pp. 29-94; see also the most recent formulation of Margaret Mead's theoretical approach to the changing nature of culture in her *New Lives for Old: Cultural Transformation—Manus, 1928-1953* (New York, 1956); see also Leslie A. White, *The Science of Culture* (New York, 1949), especially Ch. 5. The quote in Sec. 2 from Kluckhohn and Kelly is from their dialogue on "The Concept of Culture" in *The Science of Man* (New York, 1950), edited by Ralph Linton.

SEC. 3—*Archetypal Man of the West:* The quote from Robert Payne is from his *Report on America* (New York, 1949), p. 42. The quote from Wyndham Lewis is from his *America and Cosmic Man* (London, 1948).

SEC. 4—*American Exceptionalism:* For the context of American life, see Louis M. Hacker, *The Shaping of the American Tradition* (New York, 1947) and Louis Hartz, *The Liberal Tradition in America* (New York, 1955); also Ralph Barton Perry, *Characteristically American* (Boston, 1949).

My list of outstanding books on various unique aspects of the American experience refers to the following: De Tocqueville, *Democracy in America* (2 vols., New York, 1954); Charles Dickens, *American Notes* (London, 1842)—for its setting in Dickens' life and thought, see Edgar Johnson, *Charles Dickens: His Tragedy and Triumph* (2 vols., New York, 1952), Vol. I, pp. 357-448; Lord James Bryce, *The American Commonwealth* (New York, 1888; rev. ed., 1891); see also Bryce's *"American Commonwealth": 50th Anniversary,* edited by Robert C. Brooks (New York, 1939); Walt Whitman, *Democratic Vistas* (New York, 1871) reprinted in Untermeyer, *Walt Whitman: Poetry and Prose* (New York, 1949); Henry and Brooks Adams, *The Degradation of the Democratic Dogma* (New York, 1919); see also Daniel Aaron, *Men of Good Hope* (New York, 1951), Ch. 1; Thorstein Veblen, *Absentee Ownership and Business Enterprise in Recent Times* (New York, 1923); Herbert Croly, *The Promise of American Life* (New York, 1909); see Eric Goldman, *Rendezvous with Destiny* (New York, 1952), Ch. 9, pp. 188-207; Waldo Frank, *The Rediscovery of America* (New York, 1929); D. H. Lawrence, *Studies in Classical American Literature* (New York, 1923); H. L. Mencken, *The American Language* (4th rev. ed., New York, 1955); André Siegfried, *America Comes of Age* (New York, 1927)—see also his more recent formulation, *America at Mid-Century* (New York, 1955); Robert and Helen Lynd, *Middletown: A Study in Contemporary Culture* (New York, 1929) and *Middletown in Transition: A Study in Cultural Conflicts* (New York, 1937); Margaret Mead, *And Keep Your Powder Dry: An Anthropologist Looks at America* (New York, 1942), and *Male and Female: A Study of the Sexes in a Changing World* (New York, 1949), especially Part 4, "The Two Sexes in Contemporary America"; D. W. Brogan, *The American Character* (New York, 1944) and *Politics in America* (New York, 1954); Geoffrey Gorer, *The American People* (New York, 1948); Wyndham Lewis, *America and Cosmic Man;* David Riesman, *The Lonely Crowd: A Study of the Changing American Character* (New Haven, 1950; rev. ed., New York, 1953), also his *Faces in the Crowd: Individual Studies in Character and Politics* (New Haven, 1951), and his *Individualism Reconsidered* (Glencoe, 1954); David M. Potter, *People of Plenty* (Chicago, 1954); Daniel J. Boorstin, *The Genius of American Politics* (Chicago, 1953); Louis Hartz, *The Liberal Tradition in America.*

SEC. 5—*National Character and the Civilization Pattern,* and SEC. 6—*Single Key—Or Polar Pattern?* On the pattern of American civilization and national character, in addition to the books listed in the footnote to Sec. 5, see Riesman, *The Lonely Crowd;* Potter, *People of Plenty;* Lee Coleman, "What Is American: A Study of Alleged American Traits," *Social Forces* (May 1941), Vol. XIX, pp. 492-9; and H. S. Commager, *The American Mind* (New Haven, 1950). For the new approach to national character by anthropologists and psychiatrists, see as an example Ruth Benedict's on Japan, *The Chrysanthemum and the Sword* (New York, 1946). For the philosophical approach, in addition to the books by Northrop and Morris cited in the text, see Walter A. Kaufmann's study, *Nietzsche* (Princeton, 1950).

Chapter III: People and Place

SEC. 1—*Is There an American Stock?* The definition which I give to "stock" is my own, but for the discussion as a whole I have been greatly helped by Otto Klineberg, *Race Differences* (New York, 1935), although I do not make him in any sense responsible for my views. Every student of the ethnic composition of America is indebted to the pioneer book by Boas cited in the text, as also to Boas' other works, of which I have found his *Anthropology of Modern Life* (New York, 1928) most useful; see also Ch. 2, "Man the Biological Organism," in Melville J. Herskovits, *Franz Boas* (New York, 1953) and Ruth Benedict, *Race: Science and Politics* (New York, 1943) and Oscar Handlin, *Race and Nationality in American Life* (Boston, 1957), especially Ch. 8, "What Happened to Race?" I have also profited from William C. Boyd, *Genetics and the Races of Man* (Boston, 1951) and Ashley Montagu, *Statement on Race* (New York, 1951) giving the results of the UNESCO conferences on race; also Arthur M. Schlesinger's essay, "The Role of the Immigrant" in his *Paths to the Present* (New York, 1949) as well as the anthology *This Is Race,* edited by Earl W. Count, (New York, 1950). The quotation from Earnest Hooton is from a newspaper interview shortly before his death.

SEC. 2—*The Immigrant Experience:* For the immigrant experience, Handlin's *The Uprooted* (Boston, 1951) has made a permanent niche for itself in the history of American immigration, alongside Marcus Lee Hansen's *The Immigrant in American History* (Cambridge, 1940) and *The Atlantic Migration, 1860-1907* (Cambridge, 1940).

Hansen's essay on "The Third Generation in America," first delivered as a paper to The Augustana Historical Society in 1938, is reprinted in Edward N. Saveth, *Understanding the American Past* (Boston, 1954) and in *Commentary* (Nov. 1952) pp. 492-500. The quotes from De Crèvecoeur are from *Letters of an American Farmer* (London, 1782); the quote from Bryce is from *The American Commonwealth* (New York, 1888). For the reception of Israel Zangwill's book, *The Melting Pot* (New York, 1923), see Eric Goldman, *Rendezvous with Destiny* (New York, 1952), pp. 78-79. Goldman's whole Ch. 4, "A Least Common Denominator," is good on the intellectual history of the immigrant integration controversy. On the same theme, see Handlin, *Race and Nationality in American Life,* especially Chs. 4-6; Barbara M. Solomon, *Ancestors and Immigrants* (Cambridge, 1956), and John Higham, *Strangers in the Land* (New Brunswick, 1955). For several good essays and bibliographies on the immigrant and his experience in America, see *Foreign Influences in American Life,* edited by David F. Bowers (Princeton, 1944). For the idea of "integration" as opposed to the "assimilation" of American foreign-born, the seminal studies are Horace M. Kallen, *Culture and Democracy in the U.S.* (New York, 1924) and Randolph Bourne's essay "Transnational America" in *A History of a Literary Radical and Other Essays* (New York, 1920); see also Nathan Glazer, "The Integration of American Immigrants," in *Law and Contemporary Problems* (Spring, 1956), pp. 256-269.

SEC. 3—*People in Motion:* On American mobility and the sense of place, Ch. 3, "We Are All Third Generation," in Margaret Mead, *And Keep Your Powder Dry* (New York, 1942), is suggestive. The reference to Stephen Benét is to his unfinished long poem, *Western Star* (New York, 1943). The reference to De Tocqueville's chapter is to *Democracy in America* (2 vols., Vintage ed.), Vol. II, Ch. 13, "Why the Americans Are So Restless in the Midst of Their Prosperity," pp. 44-147. On the migration to the western frontier, see the readings cited in the Notes to Ch. I, Sec. 5, especially Ray Allen Billington, *Westward Expansion* (New York, 1949); also Stewart H. Holbrook, *The Yankee Exodus: An Account of the Migration from New England* (New York, 1950). For the Ladies' Clubs and Literary Societies that formed in the wake of the westward migrations, see Chs. 5 and 6 of Louis B. Wright, *Culture on the Moving Frontier* (Bloomington, 1955); for the earlier westward movements that led to the finding and settling of the American continent, see Bernard De Voto, *The Course of Em-*

pire (Boston, 1952), along with his books covering the later period, *Across the Wide Missouri* (Boston, 1947), and *The Year of Decision* (Boston, 1943); see also the rousing history by an American ex-President, Theodore Roosevelt, *The Winning of the West* (3 vols., New York, 1894-1896). For the California gold rush, see the books by Oscar Lewis, especially *Silver Kings* (New York, 1947) and *Sea Routes to the Goldfields* (New York, 1949), and also *Gold Rush Album,* edited by Joseph Henry Jackson (New York, 1949). Salty volumes on the settlement of the West are J. Frank Dobie, *The Voice of the Coyote* (New York, 1949), and *The Mustangs* (Boston, 1952). For the American road system, see a series of volumes called *The American Trail Series,* published by Bobbs-Merrill & Co. (Indianapolis), especially Philip D. Jordon, *The National Road* (Indianapolis, 1948), and George R. Stewart, *U.S. 40* (Boston, 1953), a skillful synthesis of the geology, sociology, history, and literature connected with the origins of a single highway. On the automobile revolution, see David L. Cohn, *Combustion on Wheels: An Informal History of the Automobile Age* (Boston, 1944) and Frederick Lewis Allen, *The Big Change: America Transforms Itself 1900-1950* (New York, 1952), Ch. 8, "The Automobile Revolution." For opportunity migrations, see Carter Goodrich, ed., *Migration and Economic Opportunity* (Philadelphia, 1936).

SEC. 4—*Natural Resources: The American Earth:* For the American natural environment, the classic description of the look of the continent when the white settlers first came will be found in De Tocqueville, *Democracy in America,* Vol. I, Ch. 1, "Exterior Form of North America." In my own portrait of the continent I have drawn heavily on Henry Beston, *American Memory* (New York, 1937), John Bakeless, *The Eyes of Discovery* (Philadelphia, 1950), Walter Prescott Webb, *The Great Plains* (Boston, 1931), and Henry Nash Smith, *Virgin Land* (Cambridge, 1950). For the study of the relations of environmental and human patterns, see C. W. Thornthwaite in Carter Goodrich, ed., *Migration and Economic Opportunity,* pp. 202-250, and "The Living Landscape," a chapter in Paul B. Sears, *Charles Darwin* (New York, 1950); also James C. Malin, *The Grassland of North America* (Lawrence, Kansas, 1947), and Russell Lord, *Forever the Land* (New York, 1950). For waterways, see the *Rivers of America* series of volumes, published by Rinehart, with an essay by Constance Lindsay Skinner on "Rivers and American Folk," and especially Paul Horgan, *The Rio Grande* (New York, 1956). My reference in the text to recent studies of the Russian character emphasizing the landscape is to Sir John Maynard, *The Russian Peasant and Other Studies* (London, 1942), and Edward Crankshaw, *Russia and the Russians* (New York, 1948); for the British, see Jacquetta Hawkes, *The Land* (London, 1951); for a similar emphasis on landscape and climate in a study of American national character, see Graham Hutton, *Midwest at Noon* (Chicago, 1946). For a philosophical approach, see Alfred North Whitehead, *The Concept of Nature* (Cambridge, 1920). For American national resources in the setting of world resources, see Harrison Brown, *The Challenge of Man's Future* (New York, 1954), and Harrison Brown, James Bonner, and John Weir, *The Next Hundred Years* (New York, 1957). I have also found useful Bruce Bliven, *Preview for Tomorrow* (New York, 1953). The quote in the text from Ritchie Calder is from the *N.Y. Times Magazine* (July 9, 1950), pp. 15-17, 34-35. On erosion the best book is Paul B. Sears, *Deserts on the March* (Norman, Oklahoma, 1935). On the cattle-grazing lands in the public domain, see Wallace Stegner, "One-Fourth of a Nation—Public Lands and Itching Fingers," *Reporter* (May 12, 1953), pp. 25-29. On America's water resources, see Bernard Frank and Antony Netboy, *Water, Land, and People* (New York, 1950), and Albert N. Williams, *The Water and the Power* (New York, 1951); and on the politics of water resources, Remy Nadeau, *The Water Seekers* (New York, 1950). On hydro-electric development, the best source material is the massive *Report of the Water Resources Policy Commission,* 3 vols., (Washington, 1950-51), whose guiding spirit was Morris Llewellyn Cooke. On American forests, see Donald Culross Peattie, *A Natural History of Trees* (New York, 1950); Richard G. Lillard, *The Great Forest* (New York, 1947), and Rutherford Platt, *American Trees: A Book of Discovery* (New York, 1952); and on forest policy, see Luther H. Gulick, *American Forest Policy* (New York, 1951). For an over-all view of trends in the use of American resources and their exhaustion, see *Resources for Freedom,* the Report of the Paley Commission (the President's Materials Policy Commission, 5 vols., Washington, 1952), also the Proceedings of the *Mid-Century Conference on Resources for the Future,* Dec. 2-4, 1954 (Washington, 1954). An always valuable survey is made by the Twentieth Century Fund—*America's Needs and Re-*

sources, by J. Frederick Dewhurst and Associates (most recent ed., New York, 1956). In *Our Plundered Planet* (Boston, 1948) Fairfield Osborn gives a drastic picture of the destruction of soil and resources around the world, putting the American story in this larger setting. For a symposium on recent trends in American natural resources, see *National Policy for Economic Welfare at Home and Abroad,* edited by Robert Lekachman (New York, 1955). For regional planning as an approach to the problem of the rational use of resources, see David E. Lilienthal, *TVA: Democracy on the March* (New York, 1944; rev. ed. New York, 1953), and *Iowa Law Review* (Jan. 1947) Vol. XXXII, No. 2, devoted to river valley planning, especially the foreword by M. S. McDougal; and Alvin H. Hansen and Harvey S. Perloff, *Regional Resource Development,* No. 16 of the "Planning Pamphlets" (Oct. 1942) of the National Planning Association. For the Great Estate of the American natural environment, and an attitude of reverence for it, see Aldo Leopold, *A Sand County Almanac* (New York, 1949); also the files of *The Land,* edited by Russell Lord.

SEC. 5—*Human Resources: Population Profile:* On the American population and its trends, there is a good over-all survey, Paul H. Landis and Paul K. Hatt, *Population Problems* (New York, 1954). I have profited from a small handbook by Dennis H. Wrong, *Population* (New York, 1956); Chs. 20-21 in Kingsley Davis, *Human Society* (New York, 1949), and A. H. Hawley, *Human Ecology* (New York, 1950), pp. 104-174. The quote from De Tocqueville is from Vol. I, Ch. 18 of his *Democracy in America,* pp. 451-452. For an interesting projection of population trends into the future, see Morris L. Ernst, *Utopia, 1976* (New York, 1955), Ch. 4, "Our Population." For the doctrinal differences about American population trends, see the striking critique of the population theorists in articles by Joseph S. Davis, "Fifty Million More Americans," *Foreign Affairs* (April 1950), Vol. XXVIII, pp. 412-26; "Our Changed Population Outlook and Its Economic Significance," *American Economic Review* (1952), Vol. XLII, pp. 304-25; "The Population Upsurge and the American Economy, 1945-1980," *Journal of Political Economy* (1953), Vol. LXI, pp. 369-388, and "Economic Potentials of the U.S.," a paper read at the Columbia Bicentennial, in *National Policy for Economic Welfare at Home and Abroad,* with discussion, pp. 104-174; see also William Petersen, "The Scientific Basis of Our Immigration Policy," in *Commentary* (July 1955), pp. 77-86; for an opposing view questioning whether the current population trends are as basic as often assumed, see the technical monograph by Warren S. Thompson, "Problems of Population," in Bruce Bliven, *Twentieth Century Unlimited* (Philadelphia, 1950); also Kingsley Davis, "Ideal Size for Our Population," in *N. Y. Times Magazine* (May 1, 1955), pp. 12, 32-37. For an analysis of the human resources of America, see *Scientific American* (Sept. 1951), for a full issue devoted to that theme, especially the article on "Population" by Frank W. Notestein. See also Robert C. Cook, *Human Fertility: The Modern Dilemma* (New York, 1951). French commentators are always interested in demography; it is therefore interesting to compare the chapters on population in André Siegfried's two studies of America, separated by over a quarter-century: *America Comes of Age* (New York, 1927), and *America at Mid-Century* (New York, 1955). For a brief popular summary of changes in the American population profile, see F. L. Allen, *The Big Change,* Ch. 14, "More Americans, Living Longer." For a more somber view of these trends, see Harrison Brown, *The Challenge of Man's Future* and Paul K. Hatt, ed., *World Population and Future Resources* (New York, 1952). For an interesting theoretical approach, see Talcott Parsons, "Age and Sex in the Social Structure of the U.S.," *American Sociology Review* (1942), Vol. VII, pp. 604-616.

SEC. 6—*The Sinews of Welfare: Health, Food, Dwelling, Security:* On the criteria of American welfare, see the over-all survey in the Columbia Bicentennial volume, *National Policies for Education, Health, and Social Services,* ed. James E. Russell (New York, 1955). For the relation of diseases to a particular social structure and national character, see Henry E. Sigerist, *Civilization and Disease* (Ithaca, 1943), and for the same theme in American history, Richard H. Shryock, *Development of Modern Medicine* (rev. ed., New York, 1947), Chs. 5 and 12. Shryock also has an excellent essay exploring these relations in the case of a single disease: "The Yellow Fever Epidemics, 1793-1905," in Daniel Aaron, ed. *America in Crisis* (New York, 1952), pp. 50-70. See also John Powell, *Bring Out Your Dead* (Philadelphia, 1950). The quote from Sir William Osler will be found in Donald Fleming, *William H. Welch and the Rise of Modern Medicine* (Boston, 1954), a first-rate biographical study in the intellectual history of American medicine and public health. See also the American chapters in Paul de Kruif, *The Microbe Hunters* (New York, 1926). The quote from Laurence J. Henderson will be found in the article on "Doctors" by Alan Gregg which forms part of the number devoted to American human resources in the *Scientific American* (Sept. 1951), pp. 79-84. My figures on American diseases are mainly drawn from "Facts on the Major Killing and Crippling Diseases in the U.S. Today" compiled by the National Health Education Committee (New York, 1955); also from the Columbia Bicentennial volume; and from the 1955 *Annual Report* of Dean Willard C. Rappleye of the Columbia University College of Physicians and Surgeons, and from "Something Can Be Done About Chronic Illness," Public Affairs Pamphlet No. 176 (New York, 1951). On the Salk vaccine experience, see Len Root, "The Polio Gamble," *Reporter* (July 14, 1955), pp. 20-28, and Robert Crichton, "How Canada Handled the Salk Vaccine," *ibid,* pp. 28-32. For the new drugs currently being used in psychotherapy, see William Sargant, *Battle for the Mind* (New York, 1957), Ch. 3. For some perceptive insights into the intellectual history of medical science, see Alfred Cohn, *Minerva's Progress* (New York, 1946). For a competent layman's view of medical trends, see Bruce Bliven, *Preview for Tomorrow,* Ch. 5, "Longer and Healthier Lives." An interesting projection into the future of current trends in medicine and public health will be found in Morris L. Ernst, *Utopia, 1976,* Ch. 9, "The Healthy Body of 1976."

On social security, see the Columbia Bicentennial volume for current trends; see also the annual Proceedings of the National Conference of Social Work, published by the Columbia University Press, especially the 1955 and 1956 volumes. For the intellectual history of the social legislation which led to the Social Security Act and the welfare state, the indispensable book is Robert H. Bremner, *From the Depths: The Discovery of Poverty in the U.S.* (New York, 1956), giving the history of the rise of social work, the investigations into the condition of the poor at the turn of the century, the impact of the discovery of poverty on the literary conscience of America, the struggle for social legislation, and the role of social workers. See also Eric Goldman, *Rendezvous with Destiny,* especially Chs. 7, 10, 14, 15, and 18, and the same author's *The Crucial Decade: America 1945-1955* (New York, 1956); Ralph H. Gabriel, *The Course of American Democratic Thought* (2d ed., New York, 1956), especially Ch. 16, "The Religion of Humanity At Work" and Ch. 17, "The Evolution of the Philosophy of the General Welfare State," and H. S. Commager, *The American Mind* (New Haven, 1950), especially Ch. 10, "Lester Ward and the Science of Society." The quote from Emerson will be found in his essay "Self-Reliance" in *The Complete Essays and Other Writings* (New York, 1940), p. 149.

For American housing and the housing revolution, I owe much to the writings of Lewis Mumford: see especially his *Culture of Cities* (New York, 1938), *Sticks and Stones* (New York, 1924), *The Human Prospect* (Boston, 1955), and especially the collection of his "Sky Line" articles from *The New Yorker, From the Ground Up* (New York, 1956); I have also profited from James Marston Fitch, *American Building* (New York, 1948) and Christopher Tunnard and Henry Hope Reed, *American Skyline* (Boston, 1955). For the cultural history of housing, see the remarkable Ch. 8, "Shelter," in George R. Stewart, *American Ways of Life* (New York, 1954). For the history of tenement house reform, see Robert H. Bremner, *From the Depths,* pp. 204-212. For portraits of slum living in Chicago, see Theodore Dreiser, *The Color of a Great City* (New York, 1923); Edith Abbott, *The Tenements of Chicago, 1908-1935* (Chicago, 1936), and Nelson Algren, *The Man with the Golden Arm* (New York, 1949). For the impact of American slums on a recent foreign observer, see Simone de Beauvoir, *America Day by Day* (New York, 1956). For Negro housing, see St. Clair Drake and Horace Cayton, *Black Metropolis* (New York, 1955), and Robert Weaver, *The Negro Ghetto* (New York, 1948). For the problem of continued discrimination and segregation, see Charles Abrams, *Forbidden Neighbors* (New York, 1955).

On American food habits the best discussion is in Margaret Mead, "Manual for the Study of Food Habits," Bulletin 111, National Research Council (Washington, 1955), a pioneer exploration of the history, psychology and pathology of food habits and the emotional interactions which they involve. I have also learned much from George Stewart, *American Ways of Life,* Chs. 4 and 5 on food, and Ch. 6 on drink. See also A. M. Schlesinger, *Paths to the Present,* Ch. 12.

SEC. 7—*The Way of the Farmer:* On American farming there is good historical material in Charles and Mary Beard, *The Rise of American Civilization* (1-vol. ed., New York, 1930), especially Chs. 8,

11, and 12, and Charles A. Beard, *Economic Origins of Jeffersonian Democracy* (New York, 1927), especially Ch. 12; also Harry J. Carman and Harold C. Syrett, *History of the American People* (New York, 1952), Vol. I, Chs. 15 and 16, Vol. II, Chs. 2 and 6; and F. A. Shannon, *The Farmer's Last Frontier* (New York, 1945). For the figures on the changing farm population, see Gilbert Burck, "Magnificent Decline of United States Farming," *Fortune* (June 1955), and C. Wright Mills, *White Collar* (New York, 1951), "The Rural Debacle," pp. 15-20, which discusses the farmer as a member of the "old middle classes." For the changes in farming since 1940, see also Lowry Nelson, *American Farm Life* (Cambridge, 1954), and Ronald L. Mighell, *American Agriculture* (New York, 1955). For the farmer's effort to reorient himself to an industrial economy, see Carl C. Taylor, *The Farmers' Movement, 1620-1820* (New York, 1953). For the farmer's political role, see Arthur Holcombe, *The Middle Classes in American Politics* (Cambridge, 1940), especially pp. 158-193, which is the classic discussion of the influence of middle-class agrarianism on the American political system; also Samuel Lubell, *The Future of American Politics* (New York, 1952), Ch. 8, "Battle for the Farm Vote," and his *Revolt of the Moderates* (New York, 1956), Ch. 7, "Divided We Plow"; on price supports, see Gilbert C. Fite, *George W. Peek and the Fight for Farm Parity* (Norman, Okla., 1954); on the relation of the farm economy to the economy as a whole, and Big Farming as a "countervailing power," see J. K. Galbraith, *American Capitalism* (Boston, 1952), Ch. 11, "The Case of Agriculture." For the "rural mind," see Lowry Nelson, "The American Rural Heritage," *American Quarterly* (Fall, 1949); also Thorstein Veblen, *Theory of Business Enterprise* (New York, 1904), Ch. 9, "The Discipline of the Machine," reprinted in Max Lerner, ed., *The Portable Veblen* (New York, 1948), pp. 335-348; and *Absentee Ownership* (New York, 1923), Ch. 7, Sec. 2, "The Independent Farmer," pp. 129-141, reprinted in *The Portable Veblen*, pp. 395-406. For a popular discussion of the scientists who struggled with some of the technical problems of farm crops, see Paul de Kruif, *The Hunger Fighters* (New York, 1928). For the idealization of the farmer in American history, see Henry Nash Smith, *Virgin Land*.

SEC. 8—*The Decline of the Small Town:* On the small town, the references to De Tocqueville are to the Vintage ed., Vol. I, Ch. 5, pp. 61-101. The quote about Shannon Center is from *Time* (July 3, 1950), p. 10. Veblen's essay on "The Country Town" is from *Absentee Ownership*, Ch. 7, Sec. 3, pp. 142-165, reprinted in *The Portable Veblen*, pp. 407-430. For the movement to revive the small town, see Baker Brownell, *The Human Community* (New York, 1950), and Richard W. Poston, *Small-Town Renaissance* (New York, 1950). The references in the text to the Ladies' Clubs refer to the researches of Louis B. Wright, *Culture on the Moving Frontier*. Carol Kennicott will be found in Sinclair Lewis' novel, *Main Street* (New York, 1920). See also an article on Sauk Center today in *Life* (June 23, 1947), p. 100. The reference to T. S. Eliot is to *Notes Towards a Definition of Culture* (London, 1949); for another discussion of the face-to-face community, see Robert A. Nisbet, *The Quest for Community* (New York, 1953); *Sironia, Texas* is by Madison Cooper, 2 vols. (Boston, 1952); the reference to Maxwell Geismar is to his *Last of the Provincials* (Boston, 1947), which is one in a multi-volume history of the American novel. The reference to Homans is to George C. Homans, *The Human Group* (New York, 1950), Ch. 13, "Social Disintegration: Hilltown." In addition to the community studies of small towns mentioned in the text, see also James West, *Plainville, U.S.A.* (New York, 1945), which is about an anonymous town; Elin C. Anderson, *We Americans* (Cambridge, 1937), about Burlington, Vermont; and Townsend Scudder, *Concord: American Town* (Boston, 1947); see also Harriet L. Herring, *Passing of the Mill Village* (Chapel Hill, 1949).

SEC. 9—*City Lights and Shadows:* On the city, see Lewis Mumford, *The Culture of Cities*, sharply criticized by Meyer Schapiro in the *Partisan Reader* (New York, 1946), as well as William T. Ogburn, *Social Characteristics of Cities* (Chicago, 1937); see also Mumford's *City Development* (New York, 1945). For historical material, see Carl Bridenbaugh, *Cities in the Wilderness: The First Century of Urban Life in America 1625-1744* (New York, 1938), and also his *Cities in Revolt* (New York, 1955); also Adna F. Weber, *The Growth of Cities in the Nineteenth Century* (New York, 1899); Arthur M. Schlesinger, *The Rise of the City, 1878-1898* (New York, 1933), and the same author's *Paths to the Present*, pp. 210-223, "The City in American Civilization"; also Marshall B. Davidson, *Life in America* (2 vols., Boston, 1951), Vol. I, Ch. 7, "The Urban World," pp. 99-193—an excellent pictorial history; also John A. Kouwenhoven, *Columbia Historical Portrait of New York* (New York, 1953); also Lewis Mumford, *Sticks and Stones.* For books on particular American cities, see George Sessions Perry, *Cities of America* (New York, 1947), ranging from Portland, Maine, to Los Angeles; the June 7, 1949, issue of the *Reporter* contains articles on Gloucester, Mass., Decatur, Ill., Elmira, N.Y., Kansas City, and Los Angeles, and the issue of Dec. 20, 1940, contains several on city streets; for New York, see Lloyd Morris, *Incredible New York: High Life and Low Life in the Past 100 Years* (New York, 1951), also John Kouwenhoven, *Columbia Historical Portrait of New York,* and the special number of *Holiday* devoted to New York (April 1949), including a remarkable article by E. B. White which was reprinted in book form as *Here Is New York* (New York, 1949); also Alexander Klein, ed., *The Empire City: A Treasury of New York* (New York, 1955), and a special issue of the *N.Y. Times Magazine,* "New York City 1653-1953" (Feb. 1, 1953); for Chicago, see the special number of *Holiday* (Oct. 1951) devoted to Chicago, including an article by Nelson Algren reprinted as *Chicago, City on the Make* (New York, 1951); also A. J. Liebling, *Chicago, the Second City* (New York, 1952); Simone de Beauvoir, *America Day by Day;* Theodore Dreiser, *The Color of a Great City.* For symposia on cities, see W. A. Robson, ed., *Great Cities of the World* (New York, 1955), which includes New York, Chicago, and Los Angeles, with emphasis on government and planning; Robert S. Allen, *Our Fair City* (New York, 1947), emphasizing the darker side of urban politics in seventeen American cities; Ray B. West, ed., *Rocky Mountain Cities* (New York, 1949).

For a broad approach to the study of cities, the best book is Paul Hatt and Albert J. Reiss, *Reader in Urban Sociology* (Glencoe, Ill., 1951); see also the classic study by Robert E. Park and Ernest W. Burgess, *The City* (Chicago, 1925); another useful book of readings is T. Lynn Smith and C. H. McMahon, *The Sociology of Urban Life* (New York, 1951); see also Sven Riemer, *The Modern City* (New York, 1952). For particular phases of city life, see Harvey Zorbaugh, *The Gold Coast and the Slum* (Chicago, 1929); Robert Faris and H. W. Dunham, *Mental Disorders in Urban Areas* (Chicago, 1939); Lewis Wirth's consideration of the effects of *The Ghetto* (Chicago, 1929) on the Jewish mind; Clifford Shaw and Henry McKay, *Juvenile Delinquency in Urban Areas* (Chicago, 1942); on Italian slums, W. F. Whyte, *Street Corner Society* (Chicago, 1943); Caroline Ware, *Greenwich Village* (Boston, 1935). For city politics, see the "muckraking" classic by Lincoln Steffens, *The Shame of the Cities* (New York, 1904), and Charles E. Merriam, *Chicago: A More Intimate View of Urban Politics* (New York, 1929); and for the role of the city vote in national politics, see Samuel Lubell, *The Future of American Politics,* Ch. 3, "Revolt of the City," Ch. 4, "The Frontier Reappears," and Ch. 5, "Civil Rights Melting Pot." On the location of American cities, see Edward C. Kirkland, *Men, Cities, and Transportation: A Study in New England History 1820-1900* (2 vols., Cambridge, 1948). On city planning, see Robert A. Walker, *The Planning Function in Urban Government* (Chicago, 1950); Christopher Tunnard, *City of Man* (New York, 1953), and Christopher Tunnard and Henry Hope Reed, *American Skyline;* also Clarence Stein, *Toward New Towns for America* (Liverpool, 1951), on the garden cities. For city renewal, see J. L. Sert, *Can Our Cities Survive?* (Cambridge, 1942). For recent problems of city administration due to decentralization and flight to the suburbs, see A. A. Berle, "How Long Will New York Wait?" in the *Reporter* of Sept. 8, 1955, pp. 14-23, and an article on Los Angeles, "A City 200 Miles Long?" in *U.S. News and World Report* (Sept. 16, 1955). On the question of the degree to which urban life still appeals to various groups, see Arthur Kornhauser, *Attitudes of Detroit People Toward Detroit: Summary of a Detailed Report* (Detroit, 1952). For an interesting view of American cities by a foreigner, see Rupert Brooke, *Letters from America* (New York, 1916), Chs. 1-4, and H. W. Nevinson, *Farewell to America* (New York, 1922)—two of many descriptions by foreign travelers. For others, see Henry S. Commager, ed., *America in Perspective* (New York, 1948), and Allan Nevins, ed., *America Through British Eyes* (New York, 1948). For the quote in the text from E. B. White, see his book, *This Is New York.* The quote from Edith Wharton on the Manhattan street plan is taken from *A Backward Glance* (New York, 1934), p. 23; I have borrowed it from Tunnard and Reed, *American Skyline.* The quote from William Wheaton is from a letter to the author. The theories of urban development cited in the text are taken from selections in Hatt and Reiss, *Reader in Urban Sociology.* The migrations that went to form Brooklyn, to which the text refers, will be found discussed in

Ralph Foster Weld, *Brooklyn Is America* (New York, 1950). The phrase from William Bolitho is from his *Cancer of Empire* (London, 1924). The quote from Alfred Roth about the St. Louis slums will be found in *Time* (March 13, 1950). The quote from Patrick Geddes is from Lewis Mumford, *From the Ground Up*.

SEC. 10—*The Suburban Revolution:* On the suburbs, see W. H. Whyte, Jr., *The Organization Man* (New York, 1956), Part 7, "The New Suburbia: Organization Man at Home"—the best discussion because it puts the suburbs in their economic and cultural setting. Some of this material first appeared in *Fortune* (June, Aug. and Nov. 1953), under the general title of "The Transients"; these articles are still worth reading. See also A. C. Spectorsky, *The Exurbanites* (Philadelphia, 1955); *The Changing American Market,* by the editors of *Fortune* (New York, 1955), including a chapter by W. H. Whyte, Jr., "The Lush Suburban Market"—interesting because it sees the whole suburban revolution in terms of a revolution in markets; Lewis Mumford, *From the Ground Up,* also Clarence Stein, *Toward New Towns for America;* see also Frederick L. Allen, "The Big Change in Suburbia" and "Crisis in the Suburbs," *Harpers Magazine* (June and July 1954); also Harry Henderson, "The Mass-Produced Suburbs," *ibid,* (Nov. and Dec. 1953); Maurice Stein, "Suburbia, A Walk on the Mild Side," *Dissent* (Summer, 1957), and Russell Lynes, *The Tastemakers* (New York, 1954), Ch. 14, "Suburbia in Excelsis." For problems of planning presented by the suburban revolution, see Walter M. Blucher, "What Are the Main Problems Which Decentralization Is Creating in Metropolitan Ideas?" in *Proceedings of First University of California Conference on City and Regional Planning* (Berkeley, 1954). For a severe criticism of American suburban life, see Erich Fromm, *The Sane Society* (New York, 1955). John R. Seeley, R. A. Sim, and E. W. Loosley, *Crestwood Heights* (New York, 1956) is a Canadian study of much relevance to the American suburban experience. The quote from Trevelyan is from G. M. Trevelyan, *Illustrated English Social History* (London, 1951), Vol. III, p. 109. The reference to "subtopia" is from *Outrage* (London, June, 1955) by I. N. Nairn and other editors of *Architectural Review.* I have been puzzled by the problem of terminology in trying to describe the new sprawling city that is emerging on the American landscape. I have had to reject Mumford's term "regional city" as carrying connotations of a regional culture that do not go to the heart of the new developments; the term "metropolitan area" seems to evade the problem of defining the new city by calling it an "area." I have suggested "cluster city" because it emphasizes the cluster of suburbs around the nuclear city, and includes both. The term "nuclear city" can be used to refer more strictly to the area from which the suburbs have radiated.

SEC. 11—*Regions: the Fusion of People and Place:* On regionalism there are lively and informed surveys of each of the great American regions in turn in John Gunther, *Inside U.S.A* (2 vols., New York, 1947; Bantam ed., 1951). There are numberless descriptions by travelers: a convenient recent anthology is *A Collection of Travel in America by Various Hands,* edited by George Bradshaw (New York, 1948); a good book by a recent traveler is James Morris, *As I Saw the U.S.A.* (New York, 1956). The *American Folkways* series, ed., Erskine Caldwell (Duell, Sloan), is uneven in quality but contains some first-rate books on sub-regions. A theoretical approach will be found in Howard W. Odum, "The American Blend: Regional Diversity and National Unity," in *The Saturday Review* (Aug. 6, 1949), pp. 92-96, 169-172. The 3-volume *Report of the Water Resources Policy Commission* ed., Morris L. Cooke, contains rich material on each of the river valley regions, and a good initial statement in Vol. I, pp. 19-36. There is abundant literature on the TVA, and some of it deals with the cultural setting: see especially Robert L. Duffus, *The Valley and Its People: A Portrait of TVA* (New York, 1944) and Gordon R. Clapp, *The TVA* (Chicago, 1955), along with the original conception of river valley development by David E. Lilienthal, *TVA: Democracy on the March.* V. O. Key, Jr.'s article, "The Erosion of Sectionalism," in *Virginia Quarterly Review* (Spring, 1955), raises questions of the erosion of the whole regional concept that go beyond the South itself. On the economic problems of the older regions, see Seymour Harris, "Old-Age Security for Our Economic Areas," *N.Y. Times Magazine* (July 29, 1951), p. 17 ff.

On New England as a region, see George W. Pierson, "Obstinate Concept of New England," *New England Quarterly* (March 1955); see two books by Perry Miller, *The New England Mind: The Seventeenth Century* (New York, 1939), and *The New England Mind:*

From Colony to Province (Cambridge, 1953); also S. E. Morison, *The Puritan Pronaos* (2nd ed., New York, 1956). See also Ferris Greenslet, *The Lowells and Their Seven Worlds* (Boston, 1946); F. O. Matthiessen, *The James Family* (New York, 1947); Catherine Drinker Bowen, *Yankee from Olympus: Justice Holmes and His Family* (Boston, 1944), and the same author's *John Adams and the American Revolution* (Boston, 1950). The quote in the text from Henry Adams is from *The Education of Henry Adams* (Modern Library ed., New York, 1931), p. 7. The volume first appeared in Boston in 1918. There are a number of anthologies on Boston and other parts of New England: I have found great pleasure in June Barrows Mussey, ed., *We Were New England: Yankee Life By Those Who Lived It* (New York, 1937); Henry Beston, ed., *White Pine and Blue Water: A State of Maine Reader* (New York, 1950); Cleveland Amory, *The Proper Bostonians* (New York, 1947); and Robert N. Linscott, ed., *State of Mind: A Boston Reader* (New York, 1948).

On the Midwest the best single book, and a model of what foreign travelers do best on America, is Graham Hutton, *Midwest at Noon* (Chicago, 1946); see also the best of the Midwest anthologies, John T. Flanagan, ed., *America Is West* (Minneapolis, 1945); and for a good study of a state, John Bartlow Martin, *Indiana: An Interpretation* (New York, 1947).

On the South the best studies, unlikely to be surpassed for some time, are W. J. Cash, *The Mind of the South* (New York, 1941; Anchor reprint, 1954), and Benjamin B. Kendrick and Alex M. Arnett, *The South Looks at Its Past* (Chapel Hill, 1935). The best anthologies are Willard Thorpe, *A Southern Reader* (New York, 1955), bringing together historical, economic, political, and literary material, and the literary reader, Robert Jacobs and Louis Rubin, Jr., eds., *Southern Renascence* (Baltimore, 1953). For regional history, see a recent collection of volumes, *A History of the South,* edited by Wendell H. Stephenson and E. Merton Coulter, 6 vols. (Baton Rouge, 1947-53), including books by Coulter and C. Vann Woodward. The completed series will include ten volumes. For a 1-volume history, see Francis B. Simkins, *The South, Old and New: A History, 1820-1947* (New York, 1947). For a broad approach to Southern regionalism, see Howard W. Odum, *Southern Regions of the U.S.* (Chapel Hill, 1936), and his *The Way of the South: Toward the Regional Balance of America* (New York, 1947), which is a looser and more discursive book. On the Southern agrarians, who emerged briefly in the 1920s with an attitude and program for a revival of Southern energies see their symposium *I'll Take My Stand, By Twelve Southerners* (New York, 1930) and their later manifesto, *Who Owns America?* (Boston, 1936), ed. by Herbert Agar and Allen Tate; see also Donald Davidson, *The Attack on Leviathan* (Chapel Hill, 1938). On the economics of the South, see Calvin B. Hoover and B. U. Ratchford, *Economic Resources and Policies of the South* (New York, 1951), and also one of the studies of the National Planning Association, *Why Industry Moves South* (Washington, 1949). For Southern politics, V. O. Key, Jr., *Southern Politics in State and Nation* (New York, 1949) is at once massive in its factual base and full of insights; see also Alexander Heard, *A Two-Party South* (Chapel Hill, 1952). For self-criticism by Southerners, the classic book is George W. Cable, *The Silent South* (New York, 1889); see also Virginius Dabney, *Liberalism in the South* (Chapel Hill, 1932); Hodding Carter, *Southern Legacy* (Baton Rouge, 1950), and *Virginia Quarterly Review*, Vol. XXXI, No. 2 (Spring, 1955), a whole issue of the magazine devoted to the New South, and including two first-rate articles, "The Erosion of Sectionalism" by V. O. Key, Jr., and "An Epitaph for Dixie" by Harry S. Ashmore. For studies of particular Southern states, Thomas Jefferson set a standard in his *Notes on the State of Virginia* (new ed., Chapel Hill, 1955), which has been hard to match since originally published; but see John Gould Fletcher, *Arkansas* (Chapel Hill, 1947), a remarkable blend of history and poetic insight; and, for Mississippi, see David L. Cohn, *Where I Was Born and Raised* (Boston, 1948), and William A. Percy, *Lanterns on the Levee* (New York, 1941). For the Negro experience in the South, see Reading Notes for Ch. I, Sec. 2, and Ch. VII, Sec. 6. But I want to mention here the series of remarkable autobiographies about Negro life in the South, including Booker T. Washington, *Up from Slavery* (New York, 1903); Richard Wright, *Black Boy* (New York, 1945), and J. Saunders Redding, *No Day of Triumph* (New York, 1942). To this should be added B. A. Botkin, *Lay My Burden Down: A Folk History of Slavery* (Chicago, 1945) and—on the life of the sharecropper, whether Negro or white—an evocative book by James Agee *Let Us Now Praise Famous Men* (Boston, 1941).

On the Southwest there is nothing

comparable to the commentary on the South. But see J. B. Priestley, *Midnight on the Desert* (London, 1937), and J. B. Priestley and Jacquetta Hawkes, *Journey Down a Rainbow* (New York, 1955), the latter covering the whole region from Texas to California—both books go well beyond travel impressions; see also a number of recent books by Joseph Wood Krutch, writing mainly as a naturalist but with overtones that reach to an understanding of the regional life as a whole, especially *The Desert Year* (New York, 1952); also Edmund Wilson, *Red, Black, Blond, and Olive* (New York, 1956), Part 1, "Zuni," pp. 3-68, dealing mainly with the meaning of the ritual dances. On the same subject, see Erna Fergusson, *Dancing Gods* (New York, 1931); and see her *Our Southwest* (New York, 1940), and *New Mexico: A Pageant of Free Peoples* (New York, 1951), dealing with the Indians, the Spanish, and the "gringo" elements in the culture of the Southwest. For Texas there are still only fragmentary discussions, but see a series of articles on the Texas oil millionaires by Theodore White in the *Reporter* (May 25, June 8, 1954).

On the West, there is a good survey by Morris E. Garnsey, *America's New Frontier* (New York, 1950), and Ray B. West, ed., *Rocky Mountain Cities;* see also a good collection of readings, ed., Stuart H. Holbrook, *Promised Land* (New York, 1945). For California, see Robert G. Cleland, *From Wilderness to Empire* (New York, 1944), and *California in Our Time, 1900-1940* (New York, 1947). For other readings on the West, see my Notes for Further Reading, Ch. III, Sec. 3, "People in Motion," where I discuss the literature of the "Yankee exodus" and the gold rush.

Chapter IV: The Culture of Science and the Machine

SEC. 1—*The Enormous Laboratory: Science and Power:* On the history of American science and the power built upon it, the best single volume is Mitchell Wilson, *American Science and Invention* (New York, 1954), a popularized survey which has both sweep and detail; also see James P. Baxter, *Scientists Against Time* (Boston, 1946), and Bernard Jaffe, *Men of Science in America* (New York, 1944). For particular scientists and periods, see Donald Fleming, *J. W. Draper and the Religion of Science* (Philadelphia, 1950); Dirk J. Struik, *Yankee Science in the Making* (Boston, 1949); Thomas Coulson, *Joseph Henry, His Life and Work* (Princeton, 1950); I. Bernard Cohen, *Benjamin Franklin: His Contribution to the American Tradition* (New York, 1953), and *Benjamin Franklin's Experiments*, ed., I. Bernard Cohen (Cambridge, 1941), with a long historical introduction on Franklin's work in science and electricity. The material in my text about Franklin leans heavily upon this Introduction; also, on America's greatest theoretical scientist, see Lynde P. Wheeler, *Josiah Willard Gibbs: The History of a Great Mind* (rev. ed., New Haven, 1952), and Muriel Rukeyser, *Willard Gibbs* (Garden City, 1942), an impressionistic and poetic book which will not be wholly replaced by more balanced ones. For contemporary American science, the Sept. 1950 issue of *Scientific American* is devoted to "The Age of Science, 1900-1950," and the Sept. 1952 issue deals with the principle of automatic control and the feedback, and includes an excellent essay by Ernest Nagel; see also the *Scientific American Reader* (New York, 1953) for a number of articles from the files of the magazine, written with great expository force and vividness; there is also a series of small volumes on various aspects of science, edited by the editors of the magazine, including *The Physics and Chemistry of Life, The New Astronomy,* and *Atomic Power* (published by Simon and Schuster). For studies of the meaning of science, see James B. Conant, *On Understanding Science* (London, 1947), and his *Science and Common Sense* (New Haven, 1951); also an anthology edited by James R. Newman, *What Is Science?* (New York, 1955); F. S. C. Northrop, *The Logic of the Sciences and the Humanities* (New York, 1949), and Lyman Bryson, *The Science of Freedom* (New York, 1947). A brief study which is a model of exposition is Lincoln Barnett, *The Universe and Dr. Einstein* (New York, 1948). The quote in the text from Spengler refers to his *Decline of the West* (New York, 1927-28). In the discussion of natural rights and John Locke, the reference to Walton Hamilton is to his essay, "Property—According to Locke," *Yale Law Journal* (1931-32); the reference to Merle Curti is to "The Great Mr. Locke, America's Philosopher, 1783-1861" in *Probing Our Past* (New York, 1955).

SEC. 2—*Science in an Open Society:* For further readings on the relation of science to freedom and control, see Edward Shils, *The Torment of Secrecy: The Background and Consequences of American Security Policies* (Glencoe, 1956), a forthright book which has a sense of the psychological complexities of the subject and its social implications, but is uncompromising about the values both of science and of freedom; see also Walter Gellhorn, *Security, Loyalty, and Science* (Ithaca, 1950); Charles P. Curtis gives a summary of the Oppenheimer security hearings, along with a commentary, in *The Oppenheimer Case: The Trial of a Security System* (New York, 1955); the hearings themselves have been published: "In the Matter of J. Robert Oppenheimer, Transcript of Hearing Before Personnel Security Board," U.S. Atomic Energy Commission Publications (Washington, 1954); for a perceptive commentary on the trial, see Philip Rieff, "The Case of Dr. Oppenheimer," *The Twentieth Century* (Aug.-Sept. 1954), pp. 113-24, 218-32. Oppenheimer's own Reith Lectures for the British Broadcasting Corporation have been republished as *Science and the Common Understanding* (New York, 1956). The *Fortune* study by Francis Bello, referred to in the text, will be found in the June 1954 issue of the magazine. For Russian science, see *Bulletin of Atomic Scientists,* Vol. VIII, Nos. 2 and 3, Feb. and March 1952, "The State of Russian Science Today, A Symposium"; also *Soviet Science,* a collection of essays under the auspices of the American Association for the Advancement of Science (Washington, 1952), and Barrington Moore, Jr., *Terror and Progress—USSR* (Cambridge, 1954). The quote from Jefferson in the text will be found in an Appendix to Oppenheimer, *Science and the Common Understanding.*

SEC. 3—*Big Technology and Neutral Technicians,* and SEC. 6—*The Culture of Machine Living:* On technology, a basic book is Siegfried Giedion, *Mechanization Takes Command* (New York, 1948); see also a series of books by Roger Burlingame: *The March of the Iron Men* (New York, 1938), *Engines of Democracy* (New York, 1940), and *Backgrounds of Power: The Human Story of Mass Production* (New York, 1949). I owe thanks to Ray Ginger for his comment on my Sec. 3 ("Big Technology and Neutral Technicians") when it first appeared as an article in the *American Quarterly,* Vol. IV (Summer, 1952), p. 100. Ginger's criticism was "On American Technology, 1810-1860," *ibid.,* Vol. V, (Winter, 1953), p. 357. I am also grateful to the editors of *Perspectives* for including in their French edition two articles commenting on mine, by Jean Fourastie and Jacques Ellul, *Profiles,* No. 14 (Winter, 1956), pp. 3-32. For the technological and social consequences of automation, I have used Norbert Weiner, *The Human Use of Human Beings* (New York, 1950; rev. ed., 1954) and George Soule, *Time for Living* (New York, 1955). Peter F. Drucker, *The New Society: The Anatomy of Industrial Order* (New York, 1950) is his best book in an American setting, and I have learned from it even where I have disagreed; see also his book of collected magazine pieces, *America's Next Twenty Years* (New York, 1957), especially Chs. 1 and 2. At times in my text I carry on a friendly argument with Thorstein Veblen: the relevant book of his here is *The Instinct of Workmanship and the State of the Industrial Arts* (New York, 1914). Several excerpts from it will be found in *The Portable Veblen,* ed., Max Lerner (New York, 1948), pp. 306-34; his *Imperial Germany and the Industrial Revolution* (New York, 1915), written around the idea of the "merits of borrowing" industrial technology, is also worth reading, and a selection from it will be found in *The Portable Veblen,* pp. 349-63. On engineering, see James K. Finch, *Engineering and Western Civilization* (New York, 1951), and John Mills, *The Engineer in Society* (New York, 1946); also Richard Shelton Kirby *et al., Engineering in History* (New York, 1956). On the problems of patents and technology, see Walton Hamilton, *Patents and Free Enterprise* (Washington, 1941). The consequences of technology for the American outlook are traced with subtlety and fullness in David Potter, *People of Plenty* (Chicago, 1954). Searching questions about the future of the impact of American technology on modern man are raised by Erich Kahler, *Man the Measure* (New York, 1943); Friedrich C. Junger, *The Failure of Technology* (Chicago, 1949), and Robert Jungk, *Tomorrow Is Already Here* (New York, 1955)—the last two being portraits in almost Orwellian terms. The reference in the text to Wilbur and Orville Wright is taken from Fred C. Kelly, *The Wright Brothers* (New York, 1943); see also *Miracle at Kitty Hawk,* ed., Fred C. Kelly (New York, 1941), a selection of Wright letters, and *The Papers of Wilbur and Orville Wright,* ed., Marvin W. McFarland, 2 vols. (New York, 1953). I give these citations in some detail because the case of the Wright Brothers and the airplane is a good starting point for any study of the conditions of invention in America and the nature of technological change. The reference in the text to the "Soviet of engineers" is to Veblen's book, *The Engineers and the Price System* (New York, 1921); several excerpts from it will be found in *The Portable Veblen,* pp. 431-65. The reference in the text to the "managerial revolution" is to James A. Burnham, *The Managerial Revolution* (New York, 1941). The reference to Isis and Osiris is to a book with that title by Lawrence Hyde (London, 1947). The reference to Meier's study of the political attitudes of scientists is to Richard Z. Meier, in the *Bulletin of Atomic Scientists* (July-9, 1951).

SEC. 4—*Work and the Automatic Factory:* On the factory as a social system and the attitudes of workers toward management and toward their work, the best single book is Reinhard Bendix, *Work and Authority in Industry* (New York, 1956). For the seminal contributions of Frederick W. Taylor, see his *Scientific Management* (New York, 1947), and especially his testimony before the House Committee to Investigate the Taylor and Other Systems of Shop Management, taken in 1912 and reprinted in this book. Another pioneering study was Frank B. Gilbreth, *Motion Study* (New York, 1911). A very different approach was taken by Elton Mayo, in his *The Human Problems of an Industrial Civilization* (New York, 1933), and *The Social Problems of an Industrial Civilization* (Cambridge, 1945); Mayo's studies were the foundation of an entire new school of personnel management and "human relations." The work of other members of this school will be found in R. J. Roethlisberger and W. J. Dickson, *Management and the Worker* (Cambridge, 1940), and R. J. Roethlisberger, *Management and Morale* (Cambridge, 1941). Bendix' book, *Work and Authority in Industry,* which comprises studies of the "ideologies of management" in four cultures, contains a chapter on "the American experience" (Ch. 5) which includes suggestive criticisms of both Taylor and Mayo. See also Gordon R. Taylor, *Are Workers Human?* (Boston, 1952); Peter F. Drucker, *The New Society,* and Wilbert E. Moore, *Industrialization and Labor: Social Aspects of Economic Development* (Ithaca, 1951). For the work concept, I have leaned heavily on an all-too-brief book by Daniel Bell, *Work and Its Discontents* (Boston, 1956), and on the brilliant insights of Adam Abruzzi, *Work, Workers, and Work Measurement* (New York, 1956), especially Part 3. Mayo's pathbreaking work in the Hawthorne Experiment has led to a massive body of commentaries, some of which will be found in George C. Homans, *The Human Group* (New York, 1950), Chs. 14 and 16; in Bendix, *op. cit.;* in Abruzzi, *op. cit.;* in Bell, *op. cit.;* and in Delbert C. Miller and W. H. Form, *Industrial Sociology* (New York, 1951); a more popular version will be found in Stuart Chase, *Men At Work* (New York, 1945), and his *Roads to Agreement* (New York, 1951). For a labor viewpoint, see William Gomberg, *A Trade Union Analysis of Time Study* (New York, 1955); see also W. Lloyd Warner and J. O. Lowe, *The Social System of the Modern Factory. The Strike: A Social Analysis* (New Haven, 1947). For the history of the doctrine of work, see Andriano Tilgher, *Work: What It Has Meant to Men Through the Ages* (New York, 1932), on which C. Wright Mills has partly based his Ch. 10, "Work," in *White Collar* (New York, 1951); see also Rexford Hersey, *Zest for Work* (New York, 1955). For De Tocqueville's view of the American gospel of work, see *Democracy in America,* Vol. II, Ch. 18. For early American factory experience, especially in the Lowell mills, see Hannah Josephson, *The Golden Threads* (New York, 1949), and the novel by Samuel Hopkins Adams, *Sunrise to Sunset* (New York, 1950). The quote in the text from Mitchell Wilson is from correspondence with the author. For the era of the sweatshops, of child labor, and of the seventy-two-hour week, see Robert H. Bremner, *From the Depths* (New York, 1956), especially Part 3. For the period of the assembly line, see Charles R. Walker and Robert H. Guest, *The Man on the Assembly Line* (Cambridge, 1952). The reference in the text to the Roper survey is to his reports in *Fortune* for May and June 1947. The reference to the almost completely automatic chemical factory will be found in "The Factory of the Future," in the April 1952 number of *Factory Management and Maintenance,* pp. 78-80.

SEC. 5—*The Wilderness of Commodities:* On the consumer and his living standard, the key work is David Potter, *People of Plenty,* and there is a good popular treatment in Frederick L. Allen, *The Big Change* (New York, 1952), Ch. 15, "The All-American Standard," pp. 209-33. See also J. S. Davis, "Standards and Content of Living," *American Economic Review* (March 1945), pp. 1-15, and the same author's paper in the Columbia Bicentennial volume, *National Policy for Economic Welfare at Home and Abroad* (New York, 1955), pp. 128-132. The concepts of "conspicuous consumption" and "conspicuous waste," which have become part of the American vocabulary of self-criticism, come from Thorstein Veblen. *Theory of the Leisure Class* (New York, 1899), especially Ch. 4,

"Conspicuous Consumption," and Ch. 5, "Pecuniary Standard of Living," reprinted in *The Portable Veblen,* pp. 111-151. Also see Paul and Percival Goodman, *Communities* (Chicago, 1947). The reference in the text to Riesman's "nylon war" is to an essay which will be found reprinted in his *Individualism Reconsidered* (Glencoe, 1954), pp. 426-34. The reference to Waldo Frank is to his *Rediscovery of America* (New York, 1929). The reference to Giedion is to his *Mechanization Takes Command.* Erich Fromm's concept of the "marketing orientation" of the personality is in his *Man for Himself* (New York, 1947), pp. 67-82—a book from which I have learned much and which seems to me the most productive of Fromm's writing. The reference to Riesman's categories of "inner-directed" and "other-directed" personalities is to his *The Lonely Crowd* (New Haven, 1950; rev. ed., New York, 1953). For the Great Market, see *The Changing American Market,* by the editors of *Fortune* (New York, 1955); also Julius Hirsch, ed., *New Horizons in Business* (New York, 1956), especially Chs. 2 and 3. The reference in the text to Motivational Research, as a bolstering to the Great Market, is to the work of Dr. Ernest Dichter of the Institute of Motivational Research, and has been analyzed by Vance Packard in *The Hidden Persuaders* (New York, 1957), Part 1, especially Ch. 16. The figures in the text from Frederick C. Mills are cited in George Soule, *Time for Living.*

For machine culture, see the Notes for Further Reading for Sec. 3.

Chapter V: Capitalist Economy and Business Civilization

SEC. 1—*American Capitalism: Trial Balance,* and SEC. 10—*The Emerging Amalgam:* For an over-all view, there is a first-rate symposium *An Examination of the American Economic System* in the "American Round Table Series," sponsored by the Advertising Council (1st part, June 23, 1952; 2nd part, Oct. 2, 1952, New York), with Lewis Galantiere as the Reporter and Henry M. Wriston as the Moderator. The give and take between businessmen, union economists, management consultants, and academic men (among them Galantiere, Elliot V. Bell, Jacob Viner, Peter Drucker, Henry S. Commager, Clinton S. Golden, Boris B. Shishkin, Allan Nevins, and Robert E. Wilson) tells more about the complexities of the economy than most textbooks. For an excellent over-all sociological view, see Robin Williams, Jr., *American Society* (New York, 1951), Ch. 6, "American Economic Institutions." For a brilliant general theory of capitalism to serve as a frame for American capitalism, see Joseph Schumpeter, *Capitalism, Socialism, and Democracy* (New York, 1950). For the theory of the Welfare State and the planned economy, see Abba P. Lerner, *The Economics of Control* (New York, 1944), and W. Arthur Lewis, *Principles of Economic Planning* (London, 1949); J. K. Galbraith, *American Capitalism: The Concept of Countervailing Power* (Boston, 1952); Adolf A. Berle, Jr., *The 20th Century Capitalist Revolution* (New York, 1954), and C. H. Hession, S. M. Miller, and C. Stoddard, *The Dynamics of the American Economy* (New York, 1956). See also Thomas C. Cochran and William Miller, *The Age of Enterprise: A Social History of Industrial America* (New York, 1942); for the emergence of the contemporary economy, and for specific periods see George Soule, *Prosperity Decade: From War to Depression 1917-1929* (New York, 1947), and Broadus Mitchell, *Depression Decade: From New Era Through New Deal 1929-1941* (New York, 1947); *Making Capitalism Work,* by Dexter Keezer and Associates (New York, 1950), is an anthology of vigorous affirmation. For a Keynesian view, see *The New Economics,* ed., Seymour Harris (New York, 1948), containing comments by a number of writers on the basic text of J. M. Keynes, *The General Theory of Employment, Interest, and Money* (New York, 1936).

For a statement of traditional theory, powerfully revised to meet the onslaught of the Keynesian school, see Henry C. Simon, *A Positive Program for Laissez-Faire* (Chicago, 1934), which should be balanced with Alvin Hansen, *Fiscal Policy and Business Cycles* (New York, 1941). A series of studies by the National Resources Planning Board have been of historic importance, especially *The Structure of the American Economy* (Washington, 1940); similarly the *TNEC Reports,* mentioned in the text, will still be found useful. For a history and critique of the TNEC inquiry, and a survey of the evidence presented to it, see David Lynch, *The Concentration of Economic Power* (New York, 1946); K. William Kapp, *The Social Costs of Private Enterprise* (Cambridge, 1950) sets forth the wasteful and irrational elements of the American economic system. The sharpest indictment of the system is Thorstein Veblen's: his most important books are *The Theory of Business Enterprise* (New York, 1904), and *Absentee Ownership and Business Enterprise in Recent Times: The Case of America* (New York, 1923). A satiric work on capitalist attitudes is Veblen's *The Theory of the Leisure Class* (New York,

1899), and it was followed by Thurman Arnold's *Folklore of Capitalism* (New York, 1935). For a contemporary Marxist critique of capitalism, particularly with an eye to the case of America, see Paul M. Sweezy, *The Theory of Capitalist Development* (new ed., New York, 1956), and *The Present As History* (New York, 1953); also Paul A. Baran, *The Political Economy of Growth* (New York, 1957), especially Chs. 3 and 4, "Standstill and Movement Under Monopoly Capitalism." For a very different analysis, see *The Triumph of American Capitalism* by Louis M. Hacker (New York, 1940); also an article addressed mainly to meet European criticisms of the American economy—Lewis Galantiere, "America Today," in *Foreign Affairs* (July 1950). For some recent trends in the thinking of American economists about capitalism, see John McDonald, "The Economists," *Fortune* (Dec. 1950), pp. 109-38; Daniel Bell, "The Prospects of American Capitalism," *Commentary* (Dec. 1952), pp. 603-12.

SEC. 2—*The Rise and Decline of the Titan:* On the businessman, see Hession, Miller, and Stoddard, *The Dynamics of the American Economy*, Ch. 5, "Age of the Moguls," and Ch. 6, "Age of the Managers," and C. Wright Mills, *The Power Elite* (New York, 1956), Ch. 6, "The Chief Executives." The phrase in the text, "The Tycoon is Dead," is taken from a *Fortune* advertisement in *Time* for Aug. 20, 1951. For a history of the Titans, see Stuart Holbrook, *The Age of the Moguls* (New York, 1950); for highly critical accounts of them and their methods, see Gustavus Myers, *History of Great American Fortunes*, 3 vols. (Chicago, 1909-10; Mod. Lib. ed., New York, 1936), and Matthew Josephson, *The Robber Barons: The Great American Capitalists 1861-1901* (New York, 1934); see also Charles and Mary Beard, *The Rise of American Civilization* (1-vol. ed., New York, 1930), Chs. 14-16, and *America in Mid-Passage* (New York, 1939), especially Chs. 1 and 2; see also Frederick Lewis Allen, *The Lords of Creation* (New York, 1935). For the dark days in the Great Depression, see Arthur M. Schlesinger, Jr., *The Crisis of the Old Order* (Boston, 1957), and the sharp and suggestive essay by Walton Hamilton, "When the Banks Closed," in Daniel Aaron, ed., *America in Crisis* (New York, 1952). The De Tocqueville passage in the text will be found in his *Democracy in America* (Vintage ed.), Vol. II, Ch. 2, p. 171; the reference to Dickens is to his *American Notes* (London, 1842). The Cowperwood Trilogy by Dreiser includes *The Financier* (New York, 1912), *The Titan* (New York, 1914), and *The Stoic* (New York, 1947). For biographies of American businessmen, see Frederick Lewis Allen, *The Great Pierpont Morgan* (New York, 1949), Allan Nevins, *Ford: The Times, The Man, The Company* (New York, 1954), and Nevins and Frank E. Hills, *Ford: Expansion and Challenge 1915-1933* (New York, 1957) as examples of a revisionist trend. A critical but balanced view will be found in Robert L. Heilbroner's *The Quest for Wealth* (New York, 1956), especially Chs. 8-10. There is an interesting interchange between Allan Nevins and Matthew Josephson, "Should American History Be Rewritten?"—A Debate, *The Saturday Review* (Feb. 6, 1954); the paper by Nevins calling for a rethinking of the role of the Titans in the industrialization of America will be found in Edward Saveth, ed., *Understanding the American Past* (Boston, 1954). The reference in the text to John Chamberlain is to his article in *Fortune*, "The Businessman in Fiction," (Nov. 1948). For the current trends in the study of the businessman, see "The Businessman and the Social Scientist," *Clearing House Bulletin*, Vol. III, No. 3 (1955), pp. 22-24.

SEC. 3—*The Corporate Empire:* On the corporation, the best over-all view, sympathetic without being uncritical, is A. A. Berle, Jr., *20th Century Capitalist Revolution:* it ends on the hopeful note of an appeal for a "City of God" which will serve as a frame for corporate capitalism. The decisive book for the study of the corporation has been A. A. Berle and Gardiner C. Means, *The Modern Corporation and Private Property* (New York, 1933); while its figures are out of date, and Berle in his subsequent writings has come to temper the harshness of its criticism, it is still worth study for its basic analysis. It in turn followed two earlier books—Veblen's *Absentee Ownership and Business Enterprise*, and W. Z. Ripley, *Main Street and Wall Street* (Boston, 1927). A good recent study is Peter F. Drucker, *The Concept of the Corporation* (New York, 1946). The best estimate of the present degree of corporate concentration of power is M. A. Adelman, "The Measurement of Industrial Concentration," *Review of Economics and Statistics* (Nov. 1951), Vol. XXXII, No. 4. This work is the source of the statistics on business concentration used in this section, as they are quoted in Berle, *The 20th Century Capitalist Revolution*, pp. 25-26. For a theoretical approach to monopoly, see Edward Chamberlin, *The Theory of Monopolistic Competition* (Cambridge, 1933), and Arthur R. Burns, *The Decline of Competition* (New York, 1936); for the situation a generation ago, see Clair Wilcox, *Competition and Monopoly in American Industry*, Tenn. Monograph No. 21 (Washington, 1940); for the situation at mid-century, see George W. Stocking and Myron W. Watkins, *Monopoly and Free Enterprise* (New York, 1951); also Corwin D. Edwards, *Maintaining Competition* (New York, 1949); Fritz Machlup, *Political Economy of Monopoly* (Baltimore, 1952); A. D. H. Kaplan, *Big Enterprise in a Competitive System* (Washington, 1954); David E. Lilienthal, *Big Business—A New Era* (New York, 1952); T. K. Quinn, *Giant Corporations: Challenge to Freedom* (New York, 1955); Marshall E. Dimock, *Free Enterprise and the Administrative State* (University of Alabama, 1951); and Joel B. Dirlam and Alfred E. Kahn, *Fair Competition, the Law and Economics of Anti-Trust Policy* (Ithaca, 1954). On a new development in the growth of monopoly, see Walter Adams and Horace M. Gray, *Monopoly in America: The Government As Promoter* (New York, 1955), emphasizing the extent to which government action and policies, including the regulation of public utilities, the tax write-offs, defense procurement, surplus property disposal, and the atomic arms race, carry monopoly in their wake. See also, for a critique of the Galbraith thesis as applied to the problem of monopoly, Walter Adams, "Competition, Monopoly, and Countervailing Power," *Quarterly Journal of Economics* (Nov. 1953), Vol. LXVII, No. 4, pp. 469-92.

For the ethical aspects of corporate power, see Berle, *The 20th Century Capitalist Revolution*, Kenneth Boulding, *The Organizational Revolution* (New York, 1953), stressing the relation between economics and religion, and Marquis W. Childs and Douglass Cater, *Ethics in a Business Society* (New York, 1954). An excellent recent analysis is O. W. Knauth, *Business Practices, Trade Position, and Competition* (New York, 1956). A more acid view will be found in C. Wright Mills, *The Power Elite* (New York, 1956), Ch. 15, "The Higher Immorality"; also Walton Hamilton, *The Politics of Industry* (New York, 1957), especially the discussion of "Conscience and the Corporation" in Ch. 5. The whole of Hamilton's book is "institutional economics" in its best sense, bringing together history, economics, administration, law and politics, and deflating some of the more tenacious myths about the corporation and the government.

SEC. 4—*The Property Revolution:* On the concept and realities of property, there is a suggestive essay by Walton Hamilton, "Property—According to Locke," *Yale Law Journal* (1931-2). See also a special number of the *Journal of Legal and Political Sociology* devoted to the theme of "Property and Social Structure," Vol. I, Nos. 3 and 4 (April 1943); as well as my essay, "The Supreme Court and American Capitalism" in *Ideas Are Weapons* (New York, 1939); see also, for a study of the interrelations of business power, social theory, and legal action, Robert G. McCloskey, *American Conservatism in the Age of Enterprise: A Study of William Graham Sumner, Stephen J. Field, and Andrew Carnegie* (Cambridge, 1951).

SEC. 5—*Business and Its Satellites:* On the sweep of business power and influence, see Harold J. Laski, *The American Democracy* (New York, 1948), Ch. 5, and C. Wright Mills, *The Power Elite*, especially Ch. 13, "The Mass Society," and Ch. 14, "The Conservative Mood." For the stock market and its control, see W. O. Douglas, *Democracy and Finance* (New Haven, 1940); for an earlier period, see Louis D. Brandeis, *Other People's Money* (New York, 1913) on the financial intrigues uncovered by the Pujo Investigation. An account of the stock market boom and crash will be found in Frederick Lewis Allen, *Only Yesterday* (New York, 1931); see also Walton Hamilton, "When the Banks Closed," in Daniel Aaron, ed., *America in Crisis*. A basic book on stock investment is Benjamin Graham, *The Intelligent Investor* (New York, 1954), making the distinction between "security analysis" (for the "intrinsic values" of securities) and "market analysis" (for the market fluctuations); see also John B. Williams, *The Theory of Investment Value* (Cambridge, 1937). For a good exposition of the stock market, see Paul A. Samuelson, *Economics: An Introductory Analysis* (New York, 1948). See also John McDonald, "Notes on Stock Speculation," *Fortune* (June 1951), pp. 110-11, 134-42. The quote in the text from Frederick Macauley, will be found in this work. On salesmanship, see C. Wright Mills, *White Collar* (New York, 1951), Ch. 8, "The Great Salesroom"; also David Riesman, *The Lonely Crowd* (New Haven, 1950).

On advertising, see David M. Potter, *People of Plenty* (Chicago, 1954), Ch. 8, "The Institution of Abundance: Advertising"; see also Ralph M. Hower, *The History of an Advertising Agency: N. W. Ayer and Son at Work, 1869-1949* (Cambridge, 1949); Vance Packard, *The Hidden Persuaders* (New York, 1957), and Marshall McLuhen, "American Advertising," pp. 435-42 in Bernard Rosenberg and David M. White, eds., *Mass Culture: The Popular Arts in America* (Glencoe,

1957). American novelists have been attracted to the theme of the salesman's and advertiser's arts, from Herman Melville's *The Confidence Man,* edited with introduction by Elizabeth Foster (New York, 1954), and Mark Twain's *Gilded Age* (Hartford, 1873) and his *Adventures of Huckleberry Finn* (New York, 1891); to Frederic Wakeman's *The Hucksters* (New York, 1946), Al Morgan, *The Great Man* (New York, 1955), and Budd Schulberg, *A Face in the Crowd* (New York, 1957). On public relations there are books by two of the founders of the profession: Edward L. Bernays, *Propaganda* (New York, 1928), and *The Engineering of Consent* (Norman, Oklahoma, 1955), and Ivy L. Lee, *Publicity* (New York, 1925); unfortunately such brilliant current practitioners of the arts of public relations as Benjamin Sonnenberg and Carl Byoir have not as yet put on record accounts of their techniques and approaches. A good historical summary will be found in Eric F. Goldman, *Two Way Street: The Emergence of the Public Relations Counsel* (Boston, 1948); see also Norton E. Long, "Public Relations of the Bell System," *Public Opinion Quarterly* (1937), and E. S. Turner, *The Shocking History of Advertising* (New York, 1933). The best study of the public relations counsel and his impact on political life is Stanley Kelly, Jr., *Professional Public Relations and Political Power* (Baltimore, 1956). The implications of "motivational analysis" for politics are also discussed by Vance Packard in *The Hidden Persuaders,* Chs. 17-21. For an amusing but sharp view of what both advertising and publicity consciousness have done to the language and mentality of American business, see W. H. Whyte, Jr., *Is Anybody Listening?* (New York, 1952), especially Ch. 10, "The Social Engineers," and Ch. 11, "Groupthinkers."

On the corporate executive, see Chester L. Barnard, *The Functions of the Executive* (Cambridge, 1938); *The Executive Life* by the editors of *Fortune* (New York, 1956); C. Wright Mills, *The Power Elite,* Ch. 6, "The Chief Executives"; W. H. Whyte, Jr., *The Organization Man* (New York, 1956); Reinhard Bendix, *Work and Authority in Industry* (New York, 1956), especially "Managerial Conceptions of the 'Manager,'" pp. 297-308, and Warner and Abegglen, *Occupational Mobility in American Business and Industry, 1928-1952* (Minneapolis, 1955). The quote in the text from Barnard is from an article by Robert Sheehan on "Organization and Management" in *Fortune* (June 1948), pp. 188-92.

SEC. 6—*The Reach of the Business Spirit:* On the relation between business and other areas of American life, see Blaire Bolles, *How to Get Rich in Washington* (New York, 1952); Paul Douglas, *Ethics in Government* (Cambridge, 1954); H. H. Wilson, *Congress: Corruption and Compromise* (New York, 1951), and C. Wright Mills, *The Power Elite.*

SEC. 7—*Revolution in the Trade Union,* and SEC. 8—*Labor and American Society:* On labor and trade unions, the historical works of John R. Commons and associates in *The History of Labor in the U.S.* (New York, 1926-35), and of Selig Perlman, *A Theory of the Labor Movement* (New York, 1928, rev. ed., 1949) are crucial. A considerable body of commentary has developed around it. I have found especially useful two articles by Philip Taft—"A Rereading of Selig Perlman's 'Theory of the Labor Movement,'" *Industrial and Labor Relations Review* (Oct. 1950), Vol. IV, No. 1, pp. 74-77, and "Commons-Perlman Theory: A Summary," in the *Proceedings* of the Third Annual Meeting of the Industrial Relations Research Association, pp. 1-6; and an article by Adolph Sturmthal, "Comments on Selig Perlman's Theory," *Industrial and Labor Relations Review* (July 1951), Vol. IV, No. 4, pp. 483-96; the chapter on "American Labor" in H. J. Laski, *The American Democracy* is in effect a running controversy with Perlman's theory. Out of the vast number of volumes on American labor history I have found Foster Rhea Dulles, *Labor in America* (New York, 1949), useful, and also Harold U. Faulkner and Mark Starr, *Labor in America* (New York, 1944) is a compact and lucidly written survey. For the crucial leadership of Gompers, see the recent solid and balanced study by Philip Taft, *The AFL in the Time of Gompers* (New York, 1957). No comparable work has been done on the history of the CIO, but whoever does it will be indebted to Matthew Josephson, *Sidney Hillman: Statesman of American Labor* (New York, 1952); Irving Howe and B. J. Widick, *The UAW and Walter Reuther* (New York, 1949); Saul Alinsky, *John L. Lewis* (New York, 1949), and James A. Wechsler, *Labor Baron: A Portrait of John L. Lewis* (New York, 1942). For the more violent phases of American labor history, see Louis Adamic, *Dynamite: The Story of Class Violence in America* (New York, 1934). For the place of the American labor movement in the national economy, see Charles E. Lindblom, *Unions and Capitalism* (New Haven, 1949), a work of sharp reasoning from which I have learned, even while differing with it in my text; see also Frank Tannenbaum, *The Labor Movement* (New York, 1921); an uneven but provocative critique of American labor, written from the viewpoint of the anti-Communist Left, is Sidney Lens, *Left, Right, and Center: Conflicting Forces in American Labor* (Hinsdale, Illinois, 1949); also see Sumner H. Slichter, *The American Economy* (New York, 1948), analyzing it as a "laboristic economy." Much of the attention of recent scholarly work has turned to the internal structure of the trade union and its functioning as a democracy: see especially Jack Barbash, *The Practice of Unionism* (New York, 1956); Philip Taft, *The Structure and Government of Labor Unions* (Cambridge, 1955); and Lloyd Ulman, *The Rise of the National Trade Union* (Cambridge, 1955), which deals in great detail with the period from 1850 to 1900 and concentrates on the internal structure and practices of the unions during their formative era. On recent trends in the labor movement, see Daniel Bell, "The Language of Labor," and "Labor's Coming of Middle Age" in *Fortune* (Sept. and Oct. 1951). For the relation of the worker to the American class system, see Notes for Further Reading on Ch. VII, Sec. 4.

SEC. 9—*Poverty and Wealth:* On American income distribution, the history of American wealth and the contemporary situation of the "top rich" is discussed in Richard Heilbroner, *The Quest for Wealth* (New York, 1956), and in C. Wright Mills, *The Power Elite;* for an earlier book on the rich, see Gustavus Myers, *History of Great American Fortunes,* 3 vols. For the history of American poverty and its impact on the American conscience, see Robert H. Bremner, *From the Depths: The Discovery of Poverty in the U.S.* (New York, 1956). For the distribution of income, see Paul A. Samuelson, *Economics, An Introductory Analysis,* Chs. 4 and 5. For a skeptical approach to the current belief that a "people's capitalism" has drastically changed the distribution of income, see Gabriel Kolko, "America's Income Revolution," *Dissent* (Winter, 1957), pp. 35-55. See also Sumner Slichter, "The High Cost of Low Incomes" in *N.Y. Times* (March 5, 1956).

Chapter VI: The Political System

The discussion of the American political system draws particularly on two British volumes—Harold Laski, *The American Democracy* (New York, 1948), and D. W. Brogan, *Politics in America* (New York, 1954), following the pattern of Lord James Bryce, *The American Commonwealth* (New York, 1888, 1891; new ed., New York, 1950).

SEC. 1—*The Style and Genius of American Politics,* and SEC. 2—*The Democratic Idea:* For the theoretical formulations, see De Tocqueville, *Democracy in America,* Vol. I. Ralph Barton Perry, *Puritanism and Democracy* (New York, 1944) draws the line between the secular and religious facets of the democratic spirit. Carl Becker, *The Declaration of Independence* (New York, 1922, rev. ed., 1942) is an invaluable study in the history of ideas. *The Federalist* illuminates the development of the structure of the government. The Edward M. Earle edition (Washington, 1938) of these papers is by far the best available. See also Clinton Rossiter, *Seedtime of the Republic* (New York, 1952). *The Age of Jackson* (Boston, 1945) by Arthur M. Schlesinger, Jr., is a study of the growth of democracy in the Jacksonian period. R. H. Gabriel, *The Course of American Democratic Thought* (rev. ed., New York, 1956) and Henry Steele Commager, *The American Mind* (New Haven, 1950) are first-rate studies of the development of the democratic idea, particularly in the later period. One of the rare works of fresh interpretation in American intellectual history is Louis Hartz, *The Liberal Tradition in America* (New York, 1955). Also see Walter Lippmann, *Essays in the Public Philosophy* (Boston, 1955). Edward Mims, Jr., *The Majority of the People* (New York, 1941) is an unjustly neglected book, full of theoretical insights. See also my own *Ideas for the Ice Age* (New York, 1941) and Robert A. Dahl, *A Preface to Democratic Theory* (Chicago, 1956). Vernon L. Parrington's *Main Currents in American Thought,* especially the first two volumes (New York, 1927-1930; new ed., New York, 1956), is still a basic source. Substantial studies of American critics of democracy can be found in David E. Spitz, *Patterns of Anti-Democratic Thought* (New York, 1949). For the works of some of the writers from this perspective, see Irving Babbitt, *Democracy and Leadership* (Boston, 1924); Paul Elmer More, *The Shelburne Essays,* 2 vols. (Boston, 1904-21); George Santayana, *Character and Opinion in the United States* (New York, 1920); and the brilliantly satirical *Notes on Democracy* by H. L. Mencken (New York, 1926). See also Russell Kirk, *The Conservative Mind* (Chicago, 1953).

SEC. 3—*Presidency and Demos:* Several recent volumes have aided me in my thinking on the American President. They are Clinton Rossiter, *The American Presidency* (New York, 1956), and Sidney Hyman, *The American President* (New York, 1954). Two books by E. S. Corwin are helpful: *The President: Office and Powers* (rev. ed., New York, 1948), and *The Presidency Today* (New York, 1956), written with Louis W. Koenig. Harold Laski, *The American Presidency* (London, 1940), written during the New Deal, follows in the path of D. W. Brogan, *The American Political System* (London, 1933) in stressing the strengthening of the Presidency. Stefan Lorant's *The Presidency* (New York, 1951) is a popularly written, informal, illustrated history; see also Eugene M. Roseboom, *A History of Presidential Elections* (New York, 1957). I have also used Wilfred E. Binkley, *The Powers of the President* (New York, 1937); E. Pendleton Herring, *Presidential Leadership* (New York, 1940); and George F. Milton, *The Use of Presidential Power, 1780-1943* (New York, 1944). Richard Hofstadter, *The American Political Tradition* (New York, 1948) includes several incisive chapters on the underlying thinking of American presidents. Douglas Southall Freeman, *George Washington,* 6 vols. (New York, 1948-54) is the standard biography of the first President; among the best biographical material on other chief executives is Dumas Malone, *Thomas Jefferson and His Time,* of which three volumes have thus far appeared (Boston, 1948-56); also Irving Brant, *James Madison,* 5 vols. (New York, 1941-50); Arthur M. Schlesinger, Jr., *The Age of Jackson;* Benjamin P. Thomas, *Abraham Lincoln: A Biography* (New York, 1952); Carl Sandburg, *Abraham Lincoln—The Prairie Years,* 2 vols. (New York, 1926) and *Abraham Lincoln—The War Years,* 4 vols. (New York, 1934); the essays in David Donald, *Lincoln Reconsidered* (New York, 1956); Allan Nevins, *Grover Cleveland: A Study in Courage* (New York, 1932); H. F. Pringle, *Theodore Roosevelt* (New York, 1931), and *The Politics of Woodrow Wilson* (New York, 1956), ed., by August Heckscher. See the two studies by John M. Blum, *The Republican Roosevelt* (Cambridge, 1954) and *Woodrow Wilson and the Politics of Morality* (Boston, 1956). On Franklin D. Roosevelt much has been written, and Frank Freidel's multi-volume biography, *Franklin D. Roosevelt,* of which three volumes have been published (New York, 1952-1956), is bound to become the standard one. Meanwhile, the one-volume study of FDR's leadership, *Roosevelt: The Lion and the Fox* (New York, 1956) by James MacGregor Burns, is a brilliant political biography. Projected on a more ambitious scale, *The Age of Roosevelt* by Arthur M. Schlesinger, Jr., will be a multi-volume work; its first volume, *The Crisis of the Old Order* (Boston, 1957), presents the prelude to the New Deal with literary skill and a feel for the drama of ideas. See also "Roosevelt and History" in my *Ideas Are Weapons* (New York, 1939) and "The Presidential Office" and "Two Presidents in War Time" in my *Ideas for the Ice Age.* The reference to the rating of Presidents in the text is from pp. 95-97 of *Paths to the Present* (New York, 1949) by Arthur M. Schlesinger. For the vice-presidency and the problems of the succession, see Irving G. Williams, *The Rise of the Vice Presidency* (New York, 1956), and his pamphlet, *The American Vice-Presidency: New Look* (New York, 1954), along with *Seven by Chance* (New York, 1948) by Peter Levin; and E. W. Waugh, *Second Consul* (Indianapolis, 1956). See also Corwin, *The President: Office and Powers* and Corwin and Koenig, *The Presidency Today.*

SEC. 4—*The Party System and the Voter:* On American parties and elections, James Madison, Essay No. 10 in *The Federalist,* gives an essential key to understanding the American pattern of political parties. I have leaned heavily on Samuel Lubell's *The Future of American Politics* (New York, 1952), and his *Revolt of the Moderates* (New York, 1956). Wilfred Binkley, *American Political Parties* (New York, 1943), is a competent historical text, as is Claude Bowers, *Party Battles of the Jackson Period* (New York, 1922). Other sources are E. E. Schattschneider, *Party Government* (New York, 1942); Pendleton Herring, *The Politics of Democracy* (New York, 1940); D. W. Brogan, *Government of the People* (New York, 1933), and James M. Burns, *Congress on Trial* (New York, 1949), particularly Chs. 3 and 11. Matthew Josephson, *The Politicos* (New York, 1938), and *The President Makers* (New York, 1940), have received less attention than his *The Robber Barons,* but are likely to prove more enduring. See also Willmoore Kendall and Austin Ranney, *Democracy and the American Party System* (New York, 1956), which attempts to synthesize in one volume the opinions of a member of the radical right and those of a liberal. Sigmund Neumann, ed., *Modern Political Parties* (Chicago, 1956) is a very useful collection of essays. M. Ostrogorski, *Democracy and the Organization of Political Parties,* 2 vols. (New York, 1908) is an excellent comparative study of America and England. A brief history of dissident political groups in America is W. B. Hesseltine, *The Rise and Decline of Small Parties* (Washington, 1948), and see Herbert Agar, *The Price of Union* (Boston, 1950) for a discussion of the need for loose party discipline. John Gunther provides much information on regional politics in *Inside USA* (rev. ed., New York, 1951). An excellent and highly factual account of politics in the South is *Southern Politics in State and Nation* (New York, 1949) by V. O. Key, Jr., whose *Politics, Parties, and Pressure Groups* (New York, 1948) is equally useful, along with Dayton McKean, *Party and Pressure Politics* (Boston, 1949). Several volumes on voting behavior have appeared, particularly Paul Lazarsfeld, and associates, *The People's Choice* (New York, 1944), and Bernard Berelson, Paul F. Lazarsfeld, and William N. McPhee, *Voting* (Chicago, 1954). A. N. Holcombe, *The Middle Classes in American Politics* (Cambridge, 1940), Lawrence H. Fuchs, *The Political Behavior of American Jews* (Glencoe, 1956) and Nathan Glazer, "Immigrant Groups and Politics," in *Commentary* (July 1952) have provided information on the voting behavior of various groups within the population. Paul T. David, Malcolm Moos, and Ralph M. Goldman, ed., *The National Story* (Baltimore, 1954) is the major book in the five-volume series on *Presidential Nominating Politics in 1952*. Dean Acheson, *A Democrat Looks at His Party* (New York, 1956); Arthur Larson, *A Republican Looks at His Party* (New York, 1956), and Malcolm Moos, *The Republicans* (New York, 1956) shed much light on contemporary partisan politics. See Bernard Berelson and Morris Janowitz, eds., *Reader in Public Opinion and Communication* (Glencoe, 1950) for readings that range over the entire field of public opinion. For theoretical works, Graham Wallas, *Human Nature in Politics* (London, 1908) and Walter Lippmann, *Public Opinion* (New York, 1922) are still both readable and valuable. See also "Freedom in the Opinion Industries" in my *Ideas Are Weapons*. Gerald W. Johnson's characterization of political manipulators as "The Founding Uncles" is in one of a number of articles under that title in *The Reporter* (Jan. 17, 1950).

SEC. 5—*Power and Equilibrium:* On the power system in American life, for contemporary approaches to the nature of power, see Harold Laski, *The State in Theory and Practice* (New York, 1935) and *A Grammar of Politics* (rev. ed., New York, 1937); George Santayana, *Dominations and Powers* (New York, 1951); Bertrand de Jouvenal, *On Power: Its Nature and the History of Its Growth* (Geneva, 1945; New York, 1948), and Bertrand Russell, *Power: A New Social Analysis* (London, 1938). For power on the local scene, see Floyd Hunter, *Community Power Structure* (Chapel Hill, 1955). See also "Machiavelli and Machiavellism" in my *Ideas for the Ice Age*, and "Power Is What You Make It" in my *It Is Later Than You Think* (rev. ed., New York, 1943). *The Federalist* lays the theoretical framework for the development of the concept of federalism in American life, which is further discussed in De Tocqueville, *Democracy in America*. See also John Calhoun's classic *Disquisition on Government*, excerpted in H. S. Commager, ed., *Living Ideas in America* (New York, 1951). For a lucid exposition of the political process, see James M. Burns and Jack W. Peltason, *Government by the People* (New York, 1952), particularly Chs. 6 and 11; and the Columbia Bicentennial volume, ed., Arthur W. MacMahon, *Federalism, Mature and Emergent* (New York, 1955), which includes valuable essays by Herbert Wechsler, Franz Neumann, Adolph A. Berle, David B. Truman, and Paul A. Freund. Of interest also is Harold Laski, "The Obsolescence of Federalism," *New Republic* (May 30, 1939). See also David Lilienthal, "Political Centralization and Administrative Decentralization" in Bishop and Hendel, eds., *Basic Issues of American Democracy* (New York, 1951). C. Wright Mills, *The Power Elite* (New York, 1956) is the sharpest recent attack on the theory of equilibrium in contemporary America; see also Arthur Kornhauser, ed., *Problems of Power in American Democracy* (Detroit, 1957), especially the essay by Robert S. Lynd, "Power in American Society As Resource and Problem." A well-documented volume on pressure groups is Karl Schriftgiesser, *The Lobbyists* (Boston, 1951), as well as V. O. Key, Jr., *Politics, Parties and Pressure Groups*. See also Ch. 10 of S. K. Bailey and H. D. Samuel, *Congress at Work* (New York, 1952). John Gunther, *Inside USA*, describes regional pressure groups and interests.

SEC. 6—*The Governmental Managers:* For the "fourth branch" of the government, see Robert K. Merton *et al.*, ed., *A Reader in Bureaucracy* (Glencoe, 1952); James M. Landis, *The Administrative Process* (New Haven, 1938), and, for contemporary changes in the power and functions of the manager, James A. Burnham, *The Managerial Revolution* (New York, 1941). See also Leonard D. White, *Introduction to the Study of Public Administration* (New York, 1938), and the same author's *The Federalists* (New York, 1948), *The Jeffersonians* (New York, 1951), and *The Jacksonians* (New York, 1954). See also John P. Roche and Murray S. Stedman, Jr., *The Dynamics of Democratic Government* (New York, 1954), Chs. 8 and 9; James M. Burns and Jack W. Peltason, *Government by the People*

Chs. 17 and 22-25; Harry K. Girvetz, *From Wealth to Welfare* (Stanford, 1950), especially Part 1, as well as John Millett, *Management in the Public Service* (New York, 1954). My essay on the government managers, "The Administrative Revolution in America," is reprinted in my *Ideas for the Ice Age;* see also a symposium, "The Limits of the Welfare State" by Louis Hacker, Charles E. Lindblom, and myself, *American Scholar* (Fall, 1950), and Robert A. Dahl and Charles Lindblom, *Politics, Economics, and Welfare* (New York, 1953). For a recent sociological approach to bureaucracy, see Peter Blau, *Bureaucracy in Modern Society* (New York, 1956), and his *Dynamics of Bureaucracy* (Chicago, 1955); also see Ordway Tead, *The Art of Administration* (New York, 1951), and Philip Selznick, "An Approach to a Theory of Bureaucracy," *American Sociological Review* (Feb. 1942), Vol. VIII, pp. 49-54. For the reference in the text to Brooks Adams, see his *Law of Civilization and Decay* (reprint, New York, 1943), with introduction by Charles A. Beard. The quote from Herbert Luethy is from his *France Against Herself* (New York, 1955), p. 40.

SEC. 7—*Tribunes of the People:* On the American Congress, the classic discussion is in Woodrow Wilson, *Congressional Government* (Baltimore, 1884; reprint, 1956, with introduction by Walter Lippmann). The legislative process is explained in Stephen K. Bailey, *Congress Makes a Law* (New York, 1949) and his *Congress at Work,* written with Howard D. Samuel. For contemporary general studies, see James M. Burns, *Congress on Trial;* Bertram M. Gross, *The Legislative Struggle* (New York, 1953), and George B. Galloway, *The Legislative Process in Congress* (New York, 1953). E. E. Schattschneider is sharply critical of the committee system in "Congress in Conflict," *Yale Review* (1951), Vol. XLI. Ernest S. Griffith, *Congress: Its Contemporary Role* (New York, 1951) is a defense of the legislature in the face of much criticism. For a comparative frame of reference, see John P. Roche and Murray S. Stedman, Jr., *Dynamics of Democratic Government,* Chs. 6 and 7. For detailed discussions, see Roland Young, *This Is Congress* (New York, 1943), and his *Congressional Politics in the Second World War* (New York, 1956); H. H. Wilson, *Congress: Corruption and Compromise* (New York, 1951) is a sharp, if now somewhat dated, discussion of corrupt pressures on the legislators. Dean Acheson, *A Citizen Looks at Congress* (New York, 1956) is excellent for the relation of Congress to the other branches of government. An important study of the legislative role in international relations is Robert A. Dahl, *Congress and Foreign Policy* (New York, 1950). For further reading on Congressional investigations, see Sec. 10 below, on "The Struggle for Civil Liberties."

SEC. 8—*Law and Justice:* My understanding of the reception of British law draws heavily on the work of Dean Roscoe Pound, particularly *The Spirit of the Common Law* (Boston, 1921), *Interpretations of Legal History* (New York, 1923), *Law and Morals* (Chapel Hill, 1923), and his monumental *The Formative Era of American Law* (Boston, 1939). Helpful volumes dealing mainly with the history of American legal thought are Benjamin F. Wright, *American Interpretations of Natural Law* (Boston, 1942); Richard B. Morris, *Studies in the History of American Law* (New York, 1930); James Willard Hurst, *The Growth of American Law: The Lawmakers* (Boston, 1950) and *Law and the Conditions of Freedom* (Madison, 1956); William W. Crosskey, *Politics and the Constitution in the History of the United States,* 2 vols. (Chicago, 1953), and Mark A. De Wolfe Howe, *Readings in American Legal History* (Cambridge, 1949). On the growth of state law, see Leonard Levy, *The Law of the Commonwealth and Chief Justice Shaw* (Cambridge, 1957). Two of the leading Justices of the Supreme Court have contributed major theoretical works: Oliver Wendell Holmes, *The Common Law* (Boston, 1881), and Benjamin Cardozo, *The Growth of the Law* (New Haven, 1924) and *The Nature of the Judicial Process* (New Haven, 1921). I must, of course, also refer to Jerome Frank, *Law and the Modern Mind* (New York, 1930), and his *Courts on Trial* (Princeton, 1949), as well as Edmond Cahn, "Jerome Frank's Fact Skepticism and Our Future," *Yale Law Review* (May 1957) and Cahn's books, *The Sense of Injustice* (New York, 1951) and *The Moral Decision* (Bloomington, 1955). See also Morris R. Cohen, *Law and the Social Order* (New York, 1933), and Robert McCloskey, ed., *Essays in Constitutional Law* (New York, 1957). One of the best sections in Harold Laski, *The American Democracy,* is his discussion of the legal profession on pp. 571-82. The development of American jurisprudence is seen within the more general framework of our intellectual history in H. S. Commager, *The American Mind* and Morton G. White, *Social Thought in America* (New York, 1949). See also Thurman Arnold, *Symbols of Government* (New Haven, 1935) and *The Folklore of Capitalism* (New Haven, 1943). An essay on the latter work, "The Shadow World of Thurman Arnold," and a more general article, "The Jungle of Legal Thought," are found in my *Ideas Are Weapons.* The reference to Justice Holmes's comment on the Fourteenth Amendment and Spencer's *Social Statics* is found in his opinion in "Lochner vs. New York" in my *The Mind and Faith of Justice Holmes* (Boston, 1943). Many useful references are included in the Notes for Further Reading for the next section.

SEC. 9—*Keepers of the Covenant:* Several volumes on the historical development of the Supreme Court are particularly useful: Charles Warren, *The Supreme Court in United States History* (Boston, 1922); C. G. Haines, *The American Doctrine of Judicial Supremacy* (rev. ed., Berkeley, 1932); Bernard Schwartz, *The Supreme Court* (New York, 1957), and Lewis B. Boudin, *Government by Judiciary* (New York, 1932). See also E. S. Corwin, *Twilight of the Supreme Court* (New Haven, 1934); Charles Evans Hughes, *The Supreme Court of the United States* (New York, 1927); Edmond Cahn, ed., *Supreme Court and Supreme Law* (Bloomington, 1954), and Fred Rodell, *Nine Men* (New York, 1955).

Among works dealing with particular themes in Supreme Court history are Robert Jackson, *Struggle for Judicial Supremacy* (New York, 1947), and C. Herman Pritchett, *The Roosevelt Court* (New York, 1943), and his *Civil Liberties and the Vinson Court* (New York, 1954). Paul Freund, *On Understanding the Supreme Court* (Boston, 1949) and Clinton Rossiter, *The Supreme Court and the Commander in Chief* (Ithaca, 1951) are most helpful in understanding the nature of the powers of the Court. H. S. Commager, *Majority Rule and Minority Rights* (New York, 1943) is sharply critical of judicial review.

Much of the biographical material on individual Justices sheds light on the functioning of the Court itself, particularly Albert J. Beveridge, *Life of John Marshall,* 4 vols. (Boston 1916-19); C. B. Swisher, *Roger B. Taney* (New York, 1935); Charles Fairman, *Mr. Justice Miller and the Supreme Court* (Cambridge, 1938); Merlo J. Pusey, *Charles Evans Hughes,* 2 vols. (New York, 1951), and R. G. McCloskey, *American Conservatism in an Age of Enterprise* (Cambridge, 1951), which includes a discussion of Stephen J. Field.

I may cite more extensively the works on recent members of the Court: Felix Frankfurter, *Mr. Justice Holmes and the Supreme Court* (Cambridge, 1938); Felix Frankfurter, ed., *Mr. Justice Holmes* (New York, 1931), including essays by Benjamin Cardozo, Morris R. Cohen, John Dewey and Harold Laski; Felix Frankfurter, ed., *Mr. Justice Brandeis* (New Haven, 1932), including articles by Charles Evans Hughes, Oliver Wendell Holmes, and myself; Samuel J. Konefsky, *The Legacy of Holmes and Brandeis* (New York, 1956), and Alpheus Thomas Mason, *Brandeis: A Free Man's Life* (New York, 1946). The work of Mark A. De Wolfe Howe is relevant here both as editor of the revealing *Holmes-Pollock Letters,* 2 vols. (Cambridge, 1941) and the *Holmes-Laski Letters,* 2 vols. (Cambridge, 1953), and as the author of *Justice Holmes: The Shaping Years* (Cambridge, 1957), part of a projected multi-volume work. For a further understanding of recent Court trends, see Alpheus T. Mason, *Harlan Fiske Stone* (New York, 1956); John Frank, *Mr. Justice Black: The Man and His Opinions* (New York, 1948); Samuel J. Konefsky, ed., *The Constitutional World of Mr. Justice Frankfurter* (New York, 1949); John P. Roche, "The Utopian Pilgrimage of Mr. Justice Murphy," *Vanderbilt Law Review* (Spring, 1957), and John P. Frank, "Justice Murphy: The Goals Attempted," *Yale Law Journal* (Dec. 1949).

My own *Ideas Are Weapons* contains essays on John Marshall, Roger Taney, Oliver Wendell Holmes, Jr., Louis D. Brandeis, Hugo Black, "The Supreme Court and American Capitalism," and "Minority Rule and the Constitutional Tradition." "Constitution and Court as Symbols," "Notes on the Supreme Court Crisis," and "Constitutional Crisis and the Crisis State" are found in my *Ideas for the Ice Age.* See also my *The Mind and Faith of Justice Holmes* and "The Supreme Court," *Holiday* (Feb. 1950). Relevant material for this section will also be found in the Notes for Reading for Secs. 8 and 10 of this chapter. The reference to "Mr. Dooley" is from Elmer Ellis, ed., *Mr. Dooley at His Best* (New York, 1938), p. 77.

SEC. 10—*The Struggle for Civil Liberties:* The number of volumes available on the subject of civil liberties is legion and has increased with the recent assaults on individual rights. Among the most basic volumes are Zechariah Chafee, Jr., ed., *Documents on Fundamental Human Rights,* 3 vols. (Cambridge, 1951-52; *Free Speech in the United States* (Cambridge, 1941), and *Blessings of Liberty* (Philadelphia, 1956); Merle Curti, *Roots of American Loyalty* (New York, 1946); Thomas I. Emerson and David M. Haber, eds., *Political and Civil Rights in the United States* (New York, 1952), and Alan Barth, *The Loyalty of Free Men* (New York,

1951). See also H. S. Commager, *Freedom, Loyalty, and Dissent* (New York, 1954); Leo Pfeffer, *The Liberties of an American* (Boston, 1956), and Learned Hand, *The Spirit of Liberty* (New York, 1953).

Specialized studies of value are Robert K. Carr, *Federal Protection of Civil Rights: The Quest for a Sword* (Ithaca, 1947); Milton Konvitz, *The Constitution and Civil Rights* (New York, 1947), and Osmond K. Fraenkel, *The Supreme Court and Civil Liberties* (rev. ed., New York, 1955). The major works on freedom of religion in America are Leo Pfeffer, *Church, State and Freedom* (Boston, 1953); Paul Blanshard's highly controversial *American Freedom and Catholic Power* (Boston, 1949), and Joseph L. Blau, *Cornerstones of Religious Freedom in America* (Boston, 1949).

Problems of academic freedom are considered in Robert M. MacIver, *Academic Freedom in Our Time* (New York, 1955); Richard McKeon, Robert K. Merton and Walter Gellhorn, *The Freedom to Read* (New York, 1957), and Russell Kirk, *Academic Freedom* (Chicago, 1955), which conveys the position of the radical Right. The national security program is the subject of highly competent studies by Eleanor Bontecou, *The Federal Loyalty-Security Program* (Ithaca, 1953); Edward A. Shils, *The Torment of Secrecy* (Glencoe, 1956); Alan Barth, *Government by Investigation* (New York, 1955), and Harold Lasswell's earlier but most useful *National Security and Individual Freedom* (New York, 1950). See also Morton Grodzins, *Americans Betrayed* (Chicago, 1949) and *The Loyal and the Disloyal* (Chicago, 1956).

For books presenting critical reactions to the McCarthy era, see Telford Taylor, *Grand Inquest* (New York, 1955); James Wechsler, *The Age of Suspicion* (New York, 1953); Elmer Davis, *But We Were Born Free* (Indianapolis, 1953), and Norman Thomas, *The Test of Freedom* (New York, 1954). Protection from self-incrimination is considered in two strongly contrasting books: Erwin Griswold, *The Fifth Amendment Today* (Cambridge, 1955), and Sidney Hook, *Common Sense and the Fifth Amendment* (New York, 1957)—the latter's *Heresy, Yes—Conspiracy, No* (New York, 1953) was sharply reasoned and exerted considerable influence. Robert K. Carr, *The House Committee on Un-American Activities, 1945-50* (Ithaca, 1952) and Samuel A. Stouffer, *Communism, Conformity, and Civil Liberties* (New York, 1955) shed much light on recent developments. A Cornell University study includes three especially enlightening reports on civil liberties in the individual states: Edward L. Barrett, Jr., *The Tenney Committee* (Ithaca, 1951); Vern Countryman, *Un-American Activities in the State of Washington* (Ithaca, 1951), and Walter Gellhorn, *The State and Subversion* (Ithaca, 1952).

Some of the features of the national hysteria are discussed in Daniel Bell, ed., *The New American Right* (New York, 1955). The most significant books on the Alger Hiss case are Whittaker Chambers, *Witness* (New York, 1952); Alger Hiss, *In the Court of Public Opinion* (New York, 1957), and Alistair Cooke, *A Generation on Trial* (New York, 1950). Material dealing with the J. Robert Oppenheimer hearings and the relationship of science to the security program is included in the Notes for Further Reading for Ch. IV, Sec. 2. Other books on civil liberties are mentioned in the bibliographies for Secs. 1, 2, 3, 8 and 9 of this chapter.

Index

ITALICIZED PAGE NUMBERS INDICATE PRINCIPAL TREATMENT.

Text pages 1 through 464 are in Volume One.
Text pages 465 through 950 are in Volume Two.

A

B

C

D

G

K

L

M

N

O

P

S

U

V

Y

Z

About the Author

Max Lerner, author, teacher, and columnist, received his B.A. at Yale in 1923, his M.A. at Washington University in 1925 and his Ph.D. at the Robert Brookings Graduate School of Economics and Government in 1927. He has been a member of the Social Science Faculties of Sarah Lawrence College, Harvard University, and Williams College. At present he is Professor of American Civilization at Brandeis University and a regular columnist for the New York *Post*. He has been Managing Editor of the Encyclopedia of the Social Sciences, editor of the *Nation*, contributing editor for *The New Republic*, on the editorial board of the *American Scholar*, and editorial director of the newspapers *PM* and the *Star*, and he is widely known as a lecturer and radio commentator. He is married, the father of six children, and he makes his home in New York City.

His previous books have included: *It Is Later Than You Think* (1938; rev. ed. 1943), *Ideas Are Weapons* (1939), *Ideas for the Ice Age* (1941), *The Mind and Faith of Justice Holmes* (1943), *Public Journal* (1945), *Actions and Passions* (1949), *The Unfinished Country* (1959), *Education and a Radical Humanism* (1962), and *The Age of Overkill* (1962). He has published editions of Machiavelli's *The Prince and the Discourses*, Adam Smith's *The Wealth of Nations*, the *Portable Veblen* and Jack London's *Iron Heel*.